WASHINGTON ON VIEW

THE NATION'S CAPITAL

SINCE 1790

VIEW OF WASHINGTON CITY.

WASHINGTON ON VIEW

THE NATION'S CAPITAL SINCE 1790

J O H N   W.   R E P S

THE UNIVERSITY OF NORTH CAROLINA PRESS   *Chapel Hill and London*

© 1991 The University of North Carolina Press

The paper in this book meets the guidelines for permanence and
durability of the Committee on Production Guidelines for Book
Longevity of the Council on Library Resources.

95 94 93 92 91   5 4 3 2 1

Publication of this work was made possible in part through a grant from the
Division of Research Programs of the National Endowment for the Humanities,
an independent federal agency whose mission is to award grants to support
education, scholarship, media programming, libraries, and museums, in order
to bring the results of cultural activities to a broad, general public.

Publication of this book was also supported by the Wachovia Fund for
Excellence and a grant to the author from the Kiplinger Foundation of
Washington, D.C.

Printed in Singapore

Library of Congress Cataloging-in-Publication Data

Reps, John William.
   Washington on view : the nation's capital since 1790 / by John W. Reps.
      p.   cm.
   Includes bibliographical references and index.
   ISBN 0-8078-1948-4 (alk. paper)
   1. Washington (D.C.)—Description—Views.   2. Washington
(D.C.)—Description.   3. Washington (D.C.)—History—Pictorial
works.   4. Prints—19th century—Washington (D.C.)   5. Prints,
American—Washington (D.C.)   6. Washington (D.C.) in art.
I. Title.

F195.R34   1991
917.53'0022'2—dc20   90-46782
                                                           CIP

To

my friends

and colleagues

in Beijing

and Moscow,

Hou Renzhi and

Sergey Ozhegov

Contents

Introduction

THIS book traces the process of growth and change in the city of Washington from its founding in 1791 to the early years of the present century. It uses artists' views, written descriptions, and narrative and explanatory essays to do so. It thus combines the history of this city's urban development with an examination of its printed images and its topographical literature.

The reader will find most of the significant printed views showing the national capital and its principal public buildings reproduced at generous size, each accompanied by descriptions and impressions of Washington recorded by those who saw the city during the period when the view was published. A narrative caption explains the significance of each illustration, lists the method of printing, identifies those responsible for its creation, states the size of the original, and names the collection in which the image can be found.

The book thus presents the city as artists, surveyors, visitors, and residents of the time captured its likeness in pictures and words while it grew from a tiny settlement to a major urban center. Explanatory and interpretative chapters supplement each group of these contemporary records and summarize the major events that shaped Washington, introduce the authors and artists who witnessed them, and identify the significant changes taking place in the physical fabric of the city.

Most of the views and maps reproduced in this book show the entire city or large portions of it rather than illustrate only individual streets or buildings. The exceptions are such major structures as the Capitol, the White House, the Treasury, the Patent Office, and the Smithsonian Institution, which provided centers around which much of the city's life and business developed. The focus, therefore, is on the city as a whole and how it appeared and was perceived throughout its formative years.

With only a few exceptions that include several early images of Washington existing only in manuscript form, printed illustrations have been used. These had the greatest impact in shaping the popular conception of the capital city's appearance and character, since individual drawings and paintings could have been seen by only a small number of people. Publishers of engravings, aquatints, or lithographs, however, issued them in multiple copies that provided information about Washington to countless individuals, however far away they might be from the city itself.

Similarly, except for some manuscript documents in the first few years of the city's existence, most of the descriptive passages also appeared in printed form, the majority in books, but others in newspapers, magazines, reports, guides, broadsides, and other published works. These, too, obviously reached far more eyes than unprinted letters, reports, memoranda, or diary entries intended to be read only by the recipient and known otherwise only to the author.

Whether in pictorial or text form, however, these printed materials provided the sources from which most persons at home or abroad learned about the American capital city and the features of it that struck visitors and residents as significant, uncommon, typical, or remarkable. Taken together, verbal and graphic pictures of the capital city supplement and compliment one another and create vivid impressions of Washington as it grew and changed.

Such views and descriptions surely affected how even residents perceived and felt about their city by introducing them to or concentrating their attention on features of Washington they may have overlooked or neglected. This was particularly true of the many bird's-eye perspectives that displayed the entire city in a manner that no one could have seen in fact. Such high-level views must have revealed aspects of the community's physical structure or its setting that surprised or enlightened even longtime inhabitants or frequent visitors.

It is no wonder that writers and artists produced so many verbal and graphic images of this city. The circumstances of its founding, its highly unusual design, its enormous size, and the difficulties it faced during its early years all attracted observers and commentators. As the capital of an expanding, prosperous, and ever more populous nation, Washington naturally attracted an abundance of observers even before the Civil War altered its character so swiftly.

That conflict focused the attention of the nation and the world on Washington. The expansion of the federal bureaucracy during the war and the mass migration of freed slaves to the city immediately afterward changed its character dramatically. Journalists and illustrators came to record Washington's transformation from a dusty Southern town to a true city.

The last thirty years of the nineteenth century witnessed equally striking changes and even more rapid growth and expansion. These years saw modern utilities installed, thoroughfares graded and paved, many additional public buildings constructed and others enlarged, the tidal flats of the Potomac reclaimed, and a series of civic beautification projects carried out or proposed. During this same period, however, several decisions created conditions that threatened to destroy the unique character established by the original plan. The permission granted by Congress to erect a railroad station and its yards and train shed on the Mall was only one of a series of serious and nearly fatal blunders.

At the turn of the century, then, with Washington celebrating its centennial as the national capital, the city faced a crisis in its physical development. Fortunately, the creation of the Senate Park Commission in 1901 resulted in a long-range plan for the central portion of the federal capital centered on the Mall. It is that plan, largely carried out over the next three-quarters of a century, that shaped the character and appearance of the monumental heart of the modern metropolis.

This volume concentrates on such form-shaping events in the history of Washington and how writers, artists, illustrators, and mapmakers recorded the results. Public decisions concerning city planning and building development determined the original distinctive form of the city and continued to influence the constantly changing urban pattern throughout the nineteenth century. By that time, photographs had largely replaced lithographs and engravings as the principal means of illustrating the appearance of cities. With the drastic decline in hand-drawn, printed urban images, an era in graphic communication that had begun in Renaissance Europe came to an end.

But what an era it was! Views of Washington can be found in a wide variety of forms: single-sheet prints intended as wall hangings, bookplates, illustrations in newspapers or magazines, decorative lettersheets and billheads, panels in souvenir view booklets, and maps and pictures in guidebooks, reports, brochures, and other publications. Some show only the city's skyline as seen from across the Potomac, others look across the rooftops from atop one of the public structures, and several display the city as if viewed from a point high in the air.

Printmakers used several techniques in reproducing multiple images of artists' sketches, drawings, or paintings of Washington. Engravings on copper, steel, or wood use printed lines to define the shape of objects and make use of hatching or cross-hatching to simulate tonal characteristics. Mezzotints, by contrast, show a rich variation in tonal quality from velvety blacks to brilliant highlights.

Aquatints and lithographs frequently combine linear with tonal features, depending on the effect intended by the artist and the skill of the printmaker. By the beginning of the present century, halftone illustrations offered printers and publishers still another method for reproducing images of the city. Brief explanations of these techniques will be found in Appendix B, and occasional text references to certain features will help readers unfamiliar with the subject.

Few of the many printed images of Washington came from artists and printmakers who resided in the city, and although several Washington publishers issued views drawn by others, the city never became a center for this specialized branch of the graphic arts. Baltimore, Philadelphia, and New York all exceeded Washington in age and size, and their well-developed printing and publishing industries offered far superior facilities and an established group of experienced artists capable of producing anything that could be sold in the Washington market.

Washington was fortunate in that an accomplished artist and skilled lithographic printer from nearby Baltimore seems to have adopted the capital city in addition to his own as a place to be recorded frequently and from a variety of viewpoints. It is thus to Edward Sachse that we owe some of the most compelling images of Washington from 1852 to 1871, views drawn by him or a staff artist and skillfully printed by him in color at his Baltimore press. Sachse published some of these views himself or joined in doing so with Casimir Bohn of Washington.

Whether in color or black and white, skillfully executed or carelessly drawn and printed, large or small, low-level or bird's-eye perspective, these views by Sachse and many other artists add to our knowledge of how the city appeared at several stages of development in its early period and in almost any year one chooses in the second half of the nineteenth century. In addition—and no less important—the views appeal to both our aesthetic and antiquarian tastes and offer insights into the skills and techniques used by printmakers of another era.

The printed descriptions are no less valuable, functioning—for our purposes—as extended commentaries on what the artists saw. They also provide valuable word pictures of Washington's appearance during those times in the city's early life when no artists produced graphic images of the city. Together, views and words allow us to reconstruct reliable impressions of Washington as it once existed and enable us to experience vicariously what it was like to live in or visit the national capital during its formative years.

As Washington begins its third century of existence, it seems appropriate to look back in this way at the first half of its life as a city and national capital. During this period when it grew from youth to a vigorous middle age, it acquired the basic framework on which it would continue to develop to our own day. This volume also serves to commemorate the golden era of printed city views, a form of American popular art and commercial illustration that has not yet been adequately appreciated and of which those of the city of Washington provide particularly fine and representative examples.

The reader will first encounter an introductory chapter describing the origins of the city, how its planner designed it, and the ways others modified his initial design. A selection of graphic and written documents of this period follows. These are grouped in what I refer to as *folios*—passages of text from sources contemporary with one or more images of the period.

These first folios include reproductions of maps of the region in which Washington was located and of the site that was selected for it, a proposed plan for the city by Thomas Jefferson, and the design prepared by Pierre Charles L'Enfant that is responsible for the city's distinctive form and pattern. These are accompanied by extracts from laws, diary entries, letters, newspaper accounts, and other contemporary written sources that describe the Washington of this era.

The remainder of the book is similarly divided, each chapter corresponding to a significant period of the city's development. These chapters draw on a variety of sources to summarize the major events, civic development, and building activity of the period. A selection of impressions and descriptions of Washington written at the time is then juxtaposed with reproductions of the printed views published during the same period.

For early periods of the city's history, descriptions and related documents far outnumber the small number of views. Indeed, for the first years of Washington's existence there are no printed views whatsoever. A few maps of Washington are the only surviving graphic records of this period of urban development, and it is through them and written passages only that one learns about how the city appeared.

Elsewhere, maps are used mainly to show the extent of building coverage at various stages of the city's growth in order to make it easier to understand what the scenes of the period reveal or what passages of text describe. In subsequent sections, the division between graphic and written records comes more into balance as Washington sat for its portrait for an increasing number of urban viewmakers.

Biographical information on these artists as well as some of the authors of written accounts can be found in the chapter text or footnotes and in the narrative and analytical captions for the illustrations in each folio. Those captions end with bibliographic entries of each illustration for the use of those having special interests, or who may be building collections or carrying out curatorial duties.

To residents of Washington, to those elsewhere who have a special fondness for the city, and to all others who may open this book for a variety of reasons, the author can only wish as much pleasure in reading and looking at it as he had in assembling and organizing its contents.

WASHINGTON ON VIEW

THE NATION'S CAPITAL

SINCE 1790

1 Washington, D.C., 1790–1791: The Father of His Country Selects a Virgin Site for the Birth of a City

EARLY in 1791 a Georgetown newspaper announced the arrival of two visitors to this Maryland community. Both were to play important roles in a series of events that changed the character of the little town and its surroundings beyond all recognition. The writer identified the first of these newcomers as "Maj. Andrew Ellicott, a gentleman of superior astronomical abilities. He was appointed by the president of the United States to lay off a tract of land ten miles square on the Potomac for the use of Congress. He is now engaged in this business and hopes soon to accomplish the object of his mission."

A more recent visitor, one whose influence would be even more profound and lasting, reached Georgetown the previous "Wednesday evening." The newspaper identified this personage in its version of phonetic French as "Major Longfont, a French gentleman employed by the president of the United States to survey the lands contiguous to Georgetown where the federal city is to be built. His skill in matters of this kind is justly extolled by all disposed to give merit its proper tribute of praise. He is earnest in the business and hopes to be able to lay a plat of that parcel of land before the president upon his arrival in this town."[1]

Andrew Ellicott and Pierre Charles L'Enfant both came at the request of George Washington, who late in January issued a presidential proclamation designating this location in Maryland and Virginia as a federal district of 100 square miles. There the capital of the infant United States was to be planned. Washington selected the site under the terms of an act of Congress he had approved the previous July, legislation authorized by a provision in the Constitution.

Both constitutional provision and legislative enactment came only after prolonged debate, vigorous disagreement, and eventual political compromise. Northerners wanted the seat of government in the North—either in an existing city or some new location—while Southerners just as eagerly sought the capital for their region. In the end the South won the capital location in exchange for an agreement to support the funding of the debts of the former colonies by the federal government.[2]

Thomas Jefferson recorded his role in bringing about the political compromise that settled this issue. One day in the spring of 1790 as he was about to enter the president's residence in New York he met Alexander Hamilton, secretary of the Treasury. According to Jefferson, Hamilton "walked me backwards & forwards before the president's door for half an hour" while he told Jefferson that several states might secede if the issue over the national debt could not be peaceably resolved.

Jefferson suggested that Hamilton dine with him the following day and that he "would invite another friend or two; bring them into conference together, and . . . form a compromise which was to save the Union." At the dinner Jefferson took no part in the discussion, but his Southern friends agreed to support a bill to fund the debt if "some concomitant measure should be adopted to sweeten it a little to them."

The "sweetening" was an agreement by Northern advocates of the funding measure to "fix the seat of government . . . at Philadelphia . . . for ten years, and to Georgetown permanently afterwards." Jefferson recalled that "two of the Potomac members (White & Lee, but White with a revulsion of stomach almost convulsive) agreed to change their votes & Hamilton undertook to carry the other point."[3]

The legislation Congress subsequently passed in July 1790 authorized the location of the seat of government somewhere along an eighty-mile stretch of the Potomac River between the mouth of the Anacostia (or Eastern Branch, as it was often referred to) and that of the Connogocheague River, some eighty miles to the north. Three commissioners appointed by the president and under his direction were to "define and limit a district of territory" not more than ten miles square.

1. Georgetown *Weekly Ledger*, 12 March 1791.

2. Writings on the seat of government location issue and how it was resolved are numerous, the most recent being Bowling, *Creating the Federal City*.

See also the editorial notes by Julian P. Boyd, editor of *The Papers of Thomas Jefferson*, 17:163–208, 452–72. Boyd also prepared another equally complete note on the selection of the exact site for the capital in 19:3–58. In these three notes Boyd cites pertinent literature, including works that reach conclusions different from his. Other works include Bowling, "'A Place to Which Tribute is Brought,'" and Formwalt, "Conversation between Two Rivers." For a treatment of this subject in the nineteenth century, see Swayne, "Site of the National Capital."

3. Jefferson, *The Anas*, 176–77. Both Congressmen mentioned by Jefferson in this passage represented Virginia. They were Alexander White and Richard Bland Lee. A Maryland member of the House of Representatives, Daniel Carroll, also changed his vote in the House when the assumption bill passed. Jefferson wrote several letters about this matter to his friends. See, for example, the long summary of the issue in his letter to James Monroe sent from New York on 20 June 1790, in Jefferson, *Papers*, 16:536–38.

The act authorized the commissioners to purchase or accept by gift such land on the eastern (Maryland) side of the Potomac as the president deemed proper for federal use. The commissioners were to "provide suitable buildings for the accommodation of Congress and of the president, and for the public offices" by the first Monday in December 1800. On that date the seat of government was to move from Philadelphia, where it was to be located for the preceding decade after being transferred from New York.[4]

Folio 1 contains the relevant portions of the constitutional provisions relating to a seat of government as well as extracts from the statute that made it effective, a law usually referred to as the Residence Act. The folio also includes the essential parts of a proclamation referred to shortly. That document, issued by President Washington, designated the boundaries of what became the District of Columbia. The illustration in folio 1 from a map published in 1755 shows the regional setting for the future capital whose exact boundaries these official measures determined.

Strangely, the Residence Act made no provision for municipal government, specifying only that until December 1800 the laws of Maryland and Virginia would continue in force in the respective portions of the federal district. Nor did the legislation say anything about a town or city, but Thomas Jefferson surely expressed the general understanding of members of Congress and other officials when he wrote the president that "I have no doubt it is the wish, & perhaps expectation [that the site should] be laid out in lots & streets."[5]

The evidence is clear that Washington had already decided to locate the new city in the vicinity of Georgetown, but he nevertheless began a token tour of inspection in October 1790 to visit other possible sites on the Potomac. At each place he listened to arguments in its favor from residents of towns and villages in the vicinity. On 22 January 1791 he appointed the three commissioners called for by the Residence Act, and two days later he issued a proclamation designating the site extending from Georgetown to the mouth of the Anacostia.[6]

Sometime prior to 29 January 1791 President Washington requested L'Enfant's assistance. Jefferson wrote to the commissioners of the federal district to inform them of this event: "The president, having thought Major L'Enfant peculiarly qualified to make such a Draught of the Ground as will enable himself to fix on the Spot for the public Buildings; he has been written to for that purpose."[7]

In taking this step Washington turned to a veteran of the Revolution—a Frenchman trained as an artist, who volunteered to fight against the British on the American side. L'Enfant came to this country with a group of fellow Frenchmen in 1777 at the age of twenty-three. Serving first at his own expense as a volunteer, he eventually received a commission as a captain in the Corps of Engineers, and in 1783 was promoted to major.[8]

Probably L'Enfant first met Washington when General Lafayette arranged for him to paint the portrait of the commander-in-chief at Valley Forge. After the war, L'Enfant designed the insignia for the Society of the Cincinnati, an organization of officer-veterans of which Washington served as president-general. On a visit to France in 1783–84 L'Enfant, at Washington's request, conferred membership on a number of Frenchmen after making arrangements for the medal of the order to be struck in Paris.

When he returned to America, L'Enfant began to practice architecture in New York. There, in 1788, he designed a temporary building for a Federalist pageant promoting the ratification of the Constitution. In 1788–89 he planned the remodeling of New York's city hall to serve as the first United States capitol and the site of President Washington's inauguration. It was therefore not as a stranger nor in an act of presumption that in September 1789 L'Enfant wrote the president asking to be appointed planner for a new capital city:

> The late determination of Congress to lay the Foundation of a city which is to become the Capital of this vast Empire, offer so great an occasion of acquiring reputation, to whoever may be appointed to conduct the execution of the business, that Your Excellency will not be surprised that my Ambition and the desire I have of becoming a usefull citizen should lead me to wish a share in the undertaking.[9]

The two may have discussed this matter, or there may have been further correspondence that has not survived. In one way or another, L'Enfant doubtless learned that nothing could be done until Congress passed a statute implementing the constitutional provision. However, the record is silent on this matter and begins only with Jefferson's letter to the commissioners at the end of January and his first communication with L'Enfant on 2 March 1790, describing the latter's

---

4. The text of the "Act for Establishing the Temporary and Permanent Seat of the Government of the United States" appears in Tindall, *History of Washington*, 33–34.

5. Note by Jefferson, "Proceedings to be had under the Residence act," 29 November 1790, in Padover, *Jefferson*, 31. Jefferson's note continued with many suggestions about the amount of land needed, how the town should be planned, sites re-

quired for public buildings, dimensions of lots and the layout of blocks, methods of acquiring land by inducing proprietors to donate much of it, and a host of other details indicating his intense interest in the subject.

6. Thomas Johnson, Daniel Carroll, and David Stuart were the three commissioners.

7. Jefferson, *Papers*, 19:68.

8. There are two biographies of L'Enfant: the

Introduction by J. J. Jusserand to Kite's *L'Enfant and Washington*, and Caemmerer, *Life of L'Enfant*.

9. L'Enfant to Washington, New York, 11 September 1789, as quoted in Caemmerer, *Life of L'Enfant*, 172–79. L'Enfant's letter continued: "No nation perhaps had ever before the opportunity offerd them of deliberately deciding on the spot where their Capital city should be fixed, or of combining every necessary consideration in the choice of situation—and altho' the means now within the power of the country are not such as to

pursue the design to any great extant it will be obvious that the plan should be drawn on such a scale as to leave room for that aggrandisement & embellishment which the increase of the wealth of the Nation will permit it to pursue at any period however remote—viewing the matter in this light I am fully sensible of the extant of the undertaking and under the hope of the continuation of the indulgence you have hitherto honored me with I now presume to sollicit the favor of being Employed in this Business."

assignment in these words: "You are desired to proceed to George town where you will find Mr. Ellicot employed in making a survey and map of the federal territory. The special object of asking your aid is to have drawings of the particular grounds most likely to be approved for the site of the federal town and buildings."[10]

Jefferson wrote from Philadelphia. Presumably L'Enfant was in New York. Yet we know from his first letter to Jefferson sent from Georgetown on 11 March that he had arrived there two days earlier. No evidence exists, but circumstances suggest strongly that L'Enfant knew that the president and the secretary of state would ask for his help, and he had held himself in readiness to journey to Georgetown as soon as the request arrived.

More than a month earlier the president wrote a confidential letter to friends in Georgetown asking them to begin negotiations to buy land between Georgetown and a stream called Goose Creek (later the Tiber) that entered the Potomac a short distance downstream from Rock Creek, the eastern boundary of Georgetown. Washington cautioned them to pretend to act as private individuals and to conceal their quasi-official capacity as his agents. Folio 2 shows the site where the city was to be located and the boundary lines dividing the land into several large plantations.

Washington and Jefferson at first favored a spot along the north bank of the Anacostia near its mouth, where the water was deep enough for oceangoing ships. Here in 1770 Daniel Carroll, the owner of 160 acres on the Anacostia, laid out a town that he named Carrollsburg. The president and his secretary of state then turned their attention to the land between Georgetown and the Tiber. A substantial part of this site had also been platted as a town, a place that its proprietor, Jacob Funk, called Hamburg (or Hamburgh) when he subdivided his 130-acre tract in 1771. Land ownership patterns at both places threatened to create problems.[11]

Although few persons had built houses at Carrollsburg or Hamburg, many more owned vacant lots that would need to be acquired. Fortunately, although Congress had not authorized the use of eminent domain for the purpose of creating a capital city, the state of Maryland obligingly did so. However, that legislation limited the aggregate area that could be acquired in this manner to 130 acres, the exact size of the Hamburg town plan.

In another confidential letter to his Georgetown agents, Washington explained how he hoped to proceed:

> The Maryland Assembly has authorized a certain number of acres to be taken without the consent of the owners. . . . This will be principally useful as to the old lots of Hamburg. However, by purchasing up lots . . .

we shall be free to take, on the terms of the act . . . other lands in our way . . . whose proprietors refuse all arrangment. . . . Take measures immediately for buying up all the lots you can in Hamburg, on the lowest terms you can, not exceeding the rate of twenty-five pounds the acre. . . .

> Dispatch a private agent for this purpose . . . or do it by any other means which . . . may not excite suspicions of their being on behalf of the public.[12]

Washington and Jefferson adopted another strategy to reduce land acquisition costs for the site they now favored. They directed L'Enfant to begin his site analysis along the Anacostia, hoping that his appearance there would make the proprietors of land along the Tiber fear that the new town would be located south of their location unless they reduced the price of their land.[13]

These letters and actions all suggest that Washington and Jefferson believed that a site of only modest size would be sufficient for their needs. This conclusion receives strong support from two further items to be discussed shortly: a sketch plan for the Hamburg site that Jefferson gave the president late in March, and a significant provision in a draft proclamation concerning land for the public buildings that the president planned to issue but deleted at the last moment for reasons that will be explained below.

Probably their views would have prevailed except for L'Enfant's presence and his powers of persuasion. It is wholly reasonable to believe that L'Enfant played a major role in persuading Washington to think of a city plan many times more extensive that he had hitherto considered. The events and circumstances leading to this can be summarized briefly.

Although, as instructed, L'Enfant began his surveys along the Anacostia, his expansive nature and imagination soon led him to conceive of a city embracing both locations as well as land adjoining the borders of the combined sites. In a letter to Jefferson on 11 March 1791 giving his first impressions of the region, he wrote of the opportunities he saw "to run streets and prolong them on grand and far distant point[s] of view."[14]

10. Jefferson, *Papers*, 19:355–56
11. Brief histories and reproductions of manuscript plats of both of these paper towns can be found in Reps, *Tidewater Towns*, 247–51.

12. Washington to William Deakins, Jr., and Benjamin Stoddert, 17 February 1791, in Washington, "Writings," 10–11.
13. On 2 March, Washington wrote again to his Georgetown friends: "Majr. L'enfant . . . is directed to begin at the lower end and work upwards, *and nothing further* is communicated to him. . . . I expect that your progress . . . will be facilitated by the presumption which will arise on seeing this operation begun at the Eastern branch, and that the proprietors nearer Georgetown who have hitherto refused to accommodate, will let themselves down to reasonable terms" (Washington to Deakins and Stoddert, 2 March 1791, in "Writings," 11).

14. L'Enfant was unwise enough to reveal his opinions in Georgetown and thus to stimulate the hopes of proprietors around Hamburg that their lands would be required for the new city. Both Washington and Jefferson privately deplored L'Enfant's apparent failure to understand the need to proceed on such matters with more discretion, and Jefferson wrote him their desire "that the public mind should be in equilibrio" between the Carrollsburg and the Hamburg sites and that "we shall be obliged to you to endeavor to poise their expectations" (Jefferson to L'Enfant, 17 March 1791, in *Papers*, 20:80).

Second, L'Enfant obviously did not take literally his assignment, admittedly ambiguous as penned by Jefferson, to make "a survey and map" of the "grounds most likely to be approved for the site of the federal town and buildings." Jefferson asked him in doing so to draw the "hills, vallies, morasses, and waters" and to give "some idea of the height of the hills above the base on which they stand."

Instead, when Washington came to Georgetown on 28 March 1791 to meet with the commissioners, Ellicott, and L'Enfant and to deal with the proprietors, he found L'Enfant well prepared to argue the case for incorporating the entire triangle formed by the Anacostia and the Potomac into a city plan on a scale never approached in North America and at few, if any, places elsewhere in the world. It seems almost certain that L'Enfant had some sketches to illustrate these ideas.

Is there evidence to support this thesis? An important item is a long undated note written by L'Enfant obviously directed to President Washington. In it L'Enfant refers to the possibilities of a "grand City . . . lying between the Eastern Branch and Georgetown." This communication analyzes widely separated sites for public buildings, and, throughout, it conveys the concept of a huge urban community.[15]

Given L'Enfant's tenacity and his propensity to write at length to explain and justify his actions, one can be certain that he expressed his ideas fully and persuasively to his president and former commander-in-chief. He doubtless argued that the character and scale of the city he now envisaged would require the use of the entire region under consideration, not just one or the other of the two sites Washington and Jefferson had considered.

L'Enfant himself refers to this in a letter written to Jefferson a few days after the Georgetown meeting. On 4 April he informed the secretary of state that the president had ordered "the survey to be continued and the deliniation [sic] of a grand plan for the . . . City to be done on principle[s] conformable to the ideas which I took the liberty to hold before him as . . . proper."[16]

A few days later L'Enfant wrote a much longer letter to Alexander Hamilton giving a full account of his activities concerning the proposed city. He told his patron that two factions of landowners, "one next to George town & the other contiguous to the Eastern Branch," threatened the success of the project. In his uncertain English and his erratic spelling L'Enfant told Hamilton that "I . . . gave imagination . . . full Scope . . . on a . . . more extansive location . . . and . . . vantured some remarks thereon the which I submitted to the president on his arrival at this place and was fortunate enough to see meet with his approbation."[17]

Washington may have welcomed L'Enfant's vision of a city vastly larger than hitherto considered as a way to resolve two vexing problems. To plan a city required not only land for the government buildings but the power to establish an appropriate pattern on private property of streets, blocks, lots, and sites for civic and municipal uses. Neither the president nor the commissioners possessed such power under the Residence Act.

Further, the president faced two bitterly opposed factions of property owners in the region. Both the Carrollsburg and the Hamburg-Georgetown interests were then contending hotly for the prize of having the capital located on or adjacent to their property. The decision to choose one would result in strong opposition from the other. Ensuing delays were dangerous, for the president knew that nearly everyone in Philadelphia was united in the wish to retain the capital in that city and would take every political advantage of signs of dissension or delay on the banks of the Potomac.

Folio 3 contains extracts from Washington's diary entry for 19 March 1791 and his letter to Jefferson two days later. These record how he resolved both issues by adopting L'Enfant's concept of an enormous city occupying the entire triangle formed by the two rivers. Calling the two groups together, he told them that neither site would suffice but that both were needed. He warned that the entire project might be defeated if there were further contention and delays.

Washington's arguments, reputation, character, and prestige proved persuasive, and the following day the proprietors offered to cede their land in trust to the president, gave him full powers to decide on and adopt a city plan, authorized the federal government to take title to all of the land in streets and to half of the city lots, and required payment only for sites reserved for the public buildings at a modest £25 per acre. The remaining city lots would be distributed to the proprietors in proportion to their original holdings.

Under these circumstances, when the president issued his proclamation on 30 March designating the exact boundaries of the federal district, he omitted a section from the document that Jefferson had drafted and the president had approved earlier. This specified that the Capitol would be located on the "highest summit of lands in the town heretofore called Hamburg" and that other public buildings would be located nearby between Georgetown and the Tiber. Washington explained to Jefferson that this matter could and should wait until L'Enfant had prepared the city plan.

15. Whether presented to the president late in March at that critically important meeting in Georgetown with the proprietors or drafted afterward (but not later than 15 April), this document reflects the state of L'Enfant's thinking when he talked to the president in Georgetown. See "Note relative to the ground lying on the eastern branch of the river Potomac" in Kite, *L'Enfant and Washington*, 43–48. It was printed earlier in the Columbia Historical Society, *Records* 2 (1899): 26–48.

16. Jefferson, *Papers*, 20:83–84.

17. L'Enfant to Hamilton, Georgetown, 8 April 1791, in *Papers of Alexander Hamilton*, 8:253–56. L'Enfant continues in his sometimes almost incomprehensible brand of English: "In pursuence of this new plan none of the [two] offers made could be acceptable; nay more, the extant of the territory of the [two] *taken together* appeared too contracted and the President resolving rather to delay than to part from the determination which he now had taken of securing what ever extant of territory may be wanting[,] every one soon yielded to termes in fact, both just & equally advantageous to Individuals and the best calculated to secure to the publick a sufficiency of means to push on with vigour and succes the rasing of the Intended city."

Jefferson must have learned of Washington's decision with mixed feelings. Certainly he applauded the president's ability to obtain full control over the entire city site. Moreover, the agreement Washington reached with the proprietors resembled one of the two methods of land acquisition that Jefferson had suggested in a meeting with the president the previous September. Further, since he shared the deep concern Washington had over delays in beginning the city, Jefferson surely welcomed the news that the attitude of the proprietors apparently would no longer be a problem.[18]

However, Jefferson probably felt some disappointment that his own preferences for the appropriate site had been overruled. Even stronger must have been his regret that a sketch plan he had prepared for that site, and which he had probably given to the president on the eve of his departure for Georgetown, would not be refined and elaborated and ultimately carried out. That plan is illustrated in folio 4, which also presents Jefferson's ideas of how an American city should be laid out.

Because Jefferson did not explain his city plan other than by a few notes on the drawing, some comment on its features seems appropriate. He proposed an orthogonal city composed of straight streets intersecting at right angles every 600 feet and thus creating square blocks. The blocks to be sold first bordered or stood near the two large sites for the Capitol and the president's house. The grounds of these buildings extended to the banks of the Tiber and were connected by what Jefferson labeled "public walks."

Beyond this initial nucleus the drawing shows scores of dots. These mark the intersections of streets that might eventually be needed if the city grew. Jefferson's drawing identifies this portion of his plan with the note "to be laid off in future." The drawing includes several other elements: soundings in the river and some notes about navigation, the banks of Rock Creek and the Georgetown boundaries, and—superimposed on the blocks around the square for the president—the outlines of the Hamburg town plat.[19]

A few days after the eventful meeting in Georgetown, the president sent Jefferson's drawing to L'Enfant. In doing so he explained that the secretary of state had prepared this design when it appeared that the capital would need to be restricted to a site of limited size in the vicinity of Hamburg. Evidently it was this drawing with its undeviating commitment to the gridiron system Jefferson favored so strongly that provoked L'Enfant's impassioned condemnation of this approach to urban design, a portion of which is also quoted in folio 4.

None of this artistic hostility appeared in a letter that L'Enfant wrote to Jefferson on 4 April 1791. Its text appears in folio 5, which also contains part of Jefferson's response and the portion of a communication from Jefferson to the president relating to this matter. L'Enfant's letter asked for guidance concerning the "number and nature" of the public buildings that would be needed in the city and also requested several European city maps that he thought would be helpful—not to imitate, he was careful to state, but to "strengthen the Judgment" about design decisions.

Jefferson promptly sent him the maps, including those of the four cities illustrated in folio 5, asking for care in their treatment and their eventual return. Strangely, he seems not to have said a word to L'Enfant about the public building requirements. This seems particularly odd, since it was Jefferson who originated the idea that an American capital city should provide distinct sites for buildings, each to accommodate one of the three branches of government, house the chief executive, or provide space for a public market.[20]

He made this proposal and saw it enacted into law in the expansion of Richmond, Virginia, when it replaced Williamsburg as the capital in 1779. Moreover, it was Jefferson who planned the addition to the city a year later. His revision of the initial design—also in 1780—set aside the separate sites he had advocated. Only later, during his absence in France, were the three adjacent locations for the executive, legislative, and judicial branches consolidated into a single Capitol Square.[21]

If Jefferson had complied with L'Enfant's request for guidance on the "number and nature" of the public buildings, the plan for the city of Washington might have differed significantly from the adopted design. L'Enfant did not designate a site for the Supreme Court, although in a report to the president on 19 August he mentioned a square "intended for the Judiciary Court."[22]

L'Enfant, a Frenchman who grew up under a monarchy and with artistic rather than political interests, probably had little understanding of the role of the courts in American society. Indeed, at that time few, if any, could have predicted

18. In September 1790, Jefferson suggested two methods by which land might be acquired for the capital city. The first was to buy or take by eminent domain whatever was needed, paying double the value it "would have been had there been no thought of bringing the federal seat" to the location. The second was to persuade each proprietor to "cede half his lands to the public,; to be sold to raise money" ("Jefferson's Report to Washington on Meeting Held at Georgetown," 14 September 1790, in *Papers*, 17:462).

19. If Jefferson had gone with Washington to Georgetown, his ideas for a town on the Hamburg site might have prevailed over arguments advanced by L'Enfant for using both of the contending sites and much of the adjoining land as well. Apparently Washington's initial intention was to have Jefferson present at the Georgetown meeting. Jefferson refers to this in a letter to Thomas Mann Randolph, Jr., written 24 February 1791 in which Jefferson states that the president "has intimated to me a wish that I would accompany him as far as George town to assist in fixing the site of the public buildings, plan of the town, &c." (*Papers*, 19:328–31).

20. Hening, *The Statutes at Large*, 10:86. In contemplation of a new capital for Virginia, Jefferson introduced a bill with these features in 1776. It was modified in committee, and the final version was passed in 1779. For the background and history of this legislation, see the editorial note by Julian P. Boyd in Jefferson, *Papers*, 2:271–72.

21. This, Jefferson's first involvement with a city planning project, is summarized in Reps, *Tidewater Towns*, 269–75.

22. The full text of L'Enfant's 19 August memoir to the president is in Columbia Historical Society, *Records* 2 (1899): 38–48. An abridged version can be found in Kite, *L'Enfant and Washington*, 67–72.

how important the Supreme Court would become in the federal system. This explains, perhaps, why L'Enfant's plan for the city of Washington failed to provide a site for the Court of equal importance and having equivalent access and visibility to and from the Capitol and the White House.

However, Jefferson, with his training in the law, his passion and concern for the separation of powers, and his experience in planning one capital city with equivalent sites for each branch of government, probably could have changed this if he had intervened or merely responded to L'Enfant with more than maps and polite good wishes. Perhaps the secretary of state felt upstaged by this former comrade-in-arms of Washington whose powers of persuasion at Georgetown diverted the president from the course the two statesmen had previously agreed to so recently in Philadelphia.[23]

Whatever his attitude toward L'Enfant and the direction events had taken, Jefferson, for the moment at least, ceased to play an active part in the planning of the city. The stage now belonged to L'Enfant, and he lost no time in assuming the dominant role. Working with great speed, the planner submitted to the president on 22 June a long memorandum describing his preliminary proposals. The text refers to a drawing that no longer exists, but it formed the basis for the one reproduced in folio 6, a facsimile of the final plan to come from L'Enfant's hand.

L'Enfant combined a utilitarian grid with a system of great diagonal avenues. He told the president that he first selected the important sites and planned rectilinear streets to fit, making the "distribution regular with every street at right angles." He next laid out streets "in different directions, as avenues to and from every principal place," explaining to the president that by doing so he could introduce variety, provide direct connections between important places, create axial vistas, and give the impression of a more compact city.

It was in this report that he made a strong argument for placing the Capitol on Jenkins Hill, the most prominent elevation of the entire site within reasonable distance from the rivers. He described his proposal to divert the waters of Tiber Creek through the lower level of the Capitol and direct them down the western slope of the hill in a great cascade. The water would then flow into a canal that L'Enfant proposed to connect the Potomac and the Anacostia, following at its western end the lower portion of the Tiber.[24]

A few days after L'Enfant presented his ideas and his plan to the president, Washington visited Georgetown and on 30 June accepted the conveyances of land from the proprietors as they had agreed to in March. A Philadelphia newspaper reported that then the president "submitted to the inspection of the proprietors, and a large number of gentlemen attending, a plan of the city, which had for several weeks occupied the time and talents of Col. L'Enfant, assisted by the Baron de Graff, and which, with some small alterations, he had determined to adopt."

The newspaper described the decision to place "the buildings for the Legislature . . . on Jenkins's Hill" and to locate the president's house and executive offices "on the rising ground adjoining Hamburg within one mile of George-Town, and about one and a quarter from the houses of legislation." This was, claimed the dispatch, a decision that caused "the most general approbation" and one that satisfied "each interested individual" as well as giving "due attention to public conveniences and the public interest."[25]

Not everyone looked favorably on the long distance separating the legislative and executive branches of government. Writing at length in a rival Philadelphia newspaper, "AMICUS" castigated this decision as an undoubted "manifest impropriety" that resulted from a compromise to satisfy the two groups of landowners. This writer—the first recorded critic of the Washington plan—pointed out that the frequent communication required between legislators and administrators would be impaired by this feature of the city plan.

He described conditions that would prevail in the last few days of a session of Congress "when a great deal of business is expedited, and bills, resolutions and messages are sent hot and hot to the president as fast as they can be cooked up, and the president sends them back as fast as he can sign and answer, what glorious confusion there will be in the great street which is to connect the two extremes of the town!"

The anonymous author suggested it would then be "absolutely necessary to employ post-horses, and establish relays" unless "a number of running footmen are imported from Europe for the occasion." He visualized "committee-men, secretaries, and public officers, full gallop, whip and spur, jostling each other" as they kicked "up a dust to the great merriment of the honest citizens of Goosecreek."

He found one consolation in that only two groups of proprietors had been active in contending for the sites of public buildings, for "had there been three parties, and three hills . . . it is not improbable that to give a douceur to the third

23. There is some indication that Jefferson had not fully grasped the implications of the Georgetown meeting. In writing L'Enfant on 10 April 1791, sending him European city maps and wishing him well, he appears to think that all the public buildings would still be located in close proximity and placed in the vicinity of the Hamburg townsite. Note this passage: "Considering that the grounds to be reserved for the public are to be paid for by the acre, I think very liberal reservations should be made for them, and if this be about the Tyber and on the back of the town it will be of no injury to the commerce of the place, which will undoubtedly establish itself on the deep waters towards the Eastern branch and mouth of Rock creek; the water about the mouth of the Tyber not being of any depth. Those connected with the government will prefer fixing themselves near the public grounds in the center, which will also be convenient to be resorted to as walks from the lower and upper town" (*Papers*, 20:86). The phrase "lower and upper town" doubtless reflects Jefferson's belief that the city would occupy land along the Tiber but also extend to the slightly higher elevations immediately to the north.

24. L'Enfant to Washington, 22 June 1791, Columbia Historical Society, *Records* 2 (1899): 32–37.   25. Philadelphia *Federal Gazette*, 5 July 1791, p. 3.

party, the Senate would have been perched up on the third hill, at the distance of a mile or two from the Representatives."[26]

By the end of August 1791, only six months after he began work, L'Enfant presented to the president a far more detailed plan for the city. Its legend and descriptive text provided important details about his design, and further information comes from a report L'Enfant submitted to the president at the same time. The original drawing is now so badly faded as to be almost illegible, but a facsimile prepared in 1887 allows us to understand and appreciate its features.[27]

The entire plan appears in folio 6 in the facsimile version published in 1887. This includes notes added by those responsible for copying the manuscript. A detail of the central portion of the facsimile is reproduced in folio 7, together with transcriptions of most of the notes and descriptive legend that L'Enfant lettered on his drawing. This complex plan is easier to understand if one feature is studied at a time. We can then examine how each of these elements combines with other parts of the design.[28]

L'Enfant chose the locations for major buildings early in the planning process. For the Capitol—the meeting place of the legislature—he selected Jenkins Hill as the most prominent spot near the center of the city. It was a place he described in his June letter to the president as "a pedestal waiting for a superstructure," adding "I am confident were all the ground cleared of wood, no other situation could bear a competition with this."

For the presidential residence (later to become known as the White House, the title that will hereafter be used) L'Enfant found another favorable place where the land sloped upward from the Potomac River. Located more than a mile west and north of Capitol Hill, this site enjoyed a fine view down the Potomac River. Offices of the executive branch of the government were to be placed nearby.

On another elevation about one-third of the distance from the Capitol to the White House is the large square L'Enfant may have intended for the Supreme Court. Although his drawing does not specifically designate the spot for this purpose, it seems likely that this is the site L'Enfant intended when, in his report to the president on 19 August, he listed "the Judiciary Court" as one of the possibilities for one of the city's squares.[29]

Despite an unequivocal provision in the Constitution calling for the separation of church and state, L'Enfant nevertheless identified a site for what he described as a "church . . . intended for national purposes such as public prayer, Thanksgivings, funeral orations, &c." It was to occupy one square a short distance northwest of Judiciary Square. Three other sites for churches appeared on his drawing. He probably intended to show others, or he may have done so, and the color he used for this purpose may have disappeared.

Three blocks south of the National Church there is a large square. Adjoining it one can see a kind of harbor where a canal widens and projects into the north bank. Probably this is the market and exchange that, at his meeting with the proprietors in Georgetown at the end of June, President Washington promised would be placed between the Capitol and the White House. It was at that meeting that Washington displayed L'Enfant's preliminary plan but specified that changes would be made in it.[30]

In the southeastern quarter of the city, two short canals lead inland from the Anacostia River. Since L'Enfant labeled each "canal to the market," he doubtless intended to place other markets for this part of the city at the end of these water connections to the Anacostia. Halfway between this second market district and the Capitol, L'Enfant designed a large, elongated space reached by several radial avenues and many grid streets. Although there is no evidence to support such a conclusion, this may be where L'Enfant intended to place the City Hall and other offices of local government.

Directly east of this site is a large square located on the bank of the Anacostia. Two diagonal avenues converge on it, and several grid streets provide additional access. L'Enfant may have had this place in mind for the hospital, the use to which it was put early in the nineteenth century.

Finally, L'Enfant's plan shows a number of buildings regularly arranged on the point of land at the mouth of the Anacostia River, a peninsula known for many years as Greenleaf's Point. Fortified with a one-gun battery as early as 1794, what is now Fort Leslie J. McNair has remained a military precinct since the beginning of the city and was the site of the Washington arsenal, a U.S. penitenti-

26. Philadelphia *General Advertiser*, 12 July 1791, pp. 2, 3. Seven years later Washington explained his reasons for wishing the buildings for the two branches of government to be so widely separated: "The daily intercourse which the Secretaries of the Departments must have with the President, would render a distant situation extremely inconvenient to them; and not much less so would one be close to the Capitol; for it was the universal complaint of them all, that while the Legislature was in Session, they cou'd do little or no business;—so much they were interrupted by the individual visits of members (in office hours) and by calls for papers.—Many of them have declared to me that they have been obliged often to go home and deny themselves in order to transact the current business" (Washington to Alexander White, Mount Vernon, 25 March 1798, in "Writings," 200).

27. The report is dated 19 August 1791. Its text can be found in Columbia Historical Society, *Records* 2 (1899): 38–48. An edited version appears in Kite, *L'Enfant and Washington*, 67–72. The L'Enfant manuscript is described and analyzed in Stephenson, "Delineation of a Grand Plan."

28. With a grant from the National Geographic Society, the Division of Geography and Maps of the Library of Congress has commissioned experts in filtered, infrared, and ultraviolet photography and computer enhancement to reconstruct the original image as drawn by L'Enfant. The results will be reported in a volume cataloging, describing, and reproducing the maps of Washington that is scheduled for publication in 1991 under the editorship of Richard Stephenson.

29. From very early days this large reservation that eventually became the site of the Washington City Hall was commonly referred to as Judiciary Square.

30. Washington's diary for 19 June 1791, records that he told the proprietors "that a Town house, or exchange wd be placed on some convenient ground between the spots designed for" the Capitol and White House ("Writings," 28).

ary, and now the National War College. L'Enfant doubtless intended this for military purposes although no notation to this effect appears on his drawing.

In his statement of 19 August, L'Enfant mentioned a few other institutions that would be provided for: a "national bank," a theater, and "Colleges and Academies." We do not know where he proposed to put them, but doubtless he would have selected spots in or facing some of the many civic spaces that he planned throughout the city. As his map shows, these varied in size and shape, and their locations on the axes of both radial and grid streets offered highly visible and attractive sites for such purposes.

L'Enfant specified the use of twenty-one of these places. Both the legend and the drawing identify with the letter *E* what L'Enfant described as "Five grand fountains intended with a constant spout of water." Each fountain occupied at least a portion of a square, one being at or near what may have been the exchange and another at or near the possible site for the City Hall.

Three major monuments received special attention. At the intersection of the Capitol and White House axes, L'Enfant proposed to place the statue of President Washington that Congress had recently authorized. On the bank of the Potomac to the south he provided for a column dedicated to the navy. One mile east of the Capitol he planned a square for an Itinerary Column from which all distances would be measured.

L'Enfant designated by numbers fifteen other squares for which each of the fifteen states would have special responsibilities for development. He suggested that each state embellish its square with "Statues, Columns, Obelisks, or . . . other ornament." He believed that such public investment would attract private building along the streets and avenues connecting the squares and would thus promote rapid growth of the city.

This was part of a strategy for urban growth that he explained to the president in his June report accompanying the preliminary plan. L'Enfant recommended that development

> should be begun at various points equi-distant as possible from the center; not merely because settlements of this sort are likely to diffuse an equality of advantages over the whole territory allotted, and consequently to reflect benefit from an increase of the value of property, but because each of these settlements by a natural jealousy will most tend to stimulate establishments on each of the opposed extremes.[31]

In addition to the fifteen squares set aside for the states, the plan includes more than two dozen additional open spaces in the form of squares, circles, triangles, and other shapes. Nearly all of these can be found at the multiple intersec-

tions of radial and grid streets. Here L'Enfant cut back the acute angles to create building sites that would be more convenient and attractive.

To connect and provide access to these public buildings, monuments, fountains, markets, civic open spaces, and state squares, L'Enfant designed a combined radial and grid street system. He planned each major avenue 160 feet wide with double rows of trees planted in strips 60 feet wide on each side of an 80-foot roadway. Other streets "leading to public buildings or markets" were to be 130 feet in width, with all others 110 feet wide.

L'Enfant planned more streets on the grid pattern. His drawing does not make clear which of these were to be the most important. The pattern that emerges after identifying those that appear to be the widest suggests no obvious system; however, L'Enfant may not have drawn all the streets to scale. An examination of the grid streets that lead on axis to public building sites or civic squares is more helpful. This reveals a general policy of relatively even distribution of such streets throughout the city.

The spacing of these grid streets varies throughout the city. Closely spaced streets in one direction create narrow, elongated city blocks. Closely spaced streets in both directions result in small, square blocks. These predominate in the eastern half of the city, but it is not clear why this is so. Possibly L'Enfant thought that it was here that families of lower income would be living.

Other combinations of closely and widely spaced streets produce blocks of different sizes and shapes. The dimensions and locations of squares and civic sites are closely related to street spacing, but it is impossible to determine from the plan which of these features determined the other.

L'Enfant singled out three thoroughfares of special importance. In a memorandum to the president he referred to what is now Pennsylvania Avenue as the one connecting the Capitol and the White House and described it as "most magnificent and most convenient." In an earlier letter he mentioned this as a link between Georgetown and a bridge across the Anacostia River. L'Enfant also pointed out that streets between the Capitol and the White House leading to the avenue would be "proper for shops."

The legend on the drawing emphasizes the importance of a second street. This leads from the Capitol eastward to the proposed Itinerary Column and on to the Anacostia bridge. In the modern city this is East Capitol Street. L'Enfant proposed to locate the principal shopping district along this thoroughfare, where sidewalks on either side would "pass under an Arched way under whose cover Shops will be most conveniently and agreeable situated." These arcaded shops were also to line the sides of Capitol Square at the western terminus of the street.

On the west side of the Capitol, L'Enfant planned a third major thoroughfare that he called the "Grand Avenue" and which was to be 400 feet wide. This was to provide the major axis of the city and was to begin at the base of Capitol Hill and extend about one mile to the west. There it would intersect the south axis of the

31. L'Enfant to Washington, 19 August 1791, in Kite, *L'Enfant and Washington*, 54–55.

White House at the monument to George Washington that the Congress had recently authorized.

L'Enfant planned his Grand Avenue to be "bordered with gardens, ending in a slope from the houses on each side." He colored these sites red on his drawing, and he described them in the legend as "the best calculated for spacious houses and gardens, such as may accommodate foreign Ministers, &c." In modern Washington these locations on the north and south of what is now the Mall are occupied by the city's great public museums.

The plan focuses strongly on this part of the city, and the number of radial and axial grid streets providing access to the Capitol and the White House emphasizes the importance of these two buildings. Pennsylvania Avenue joins them by a direct line. The intersection of the west axis of the Capitol and the south axis of the White House provides a different kind of link. Together these form a triangle connecting the buildings of the two branches of American government that are in constant interaction.[32]

Here also L'Enfant brought together several landscape elements to create an extended belt of green and open space in the very center of the most formal and ceremonial part of the city. He planned what he called the "Congress Gardens" to occupy the western half of Capitol Square. The lawns on either side of Grand Avenue continued this westward as a wide shaft of open space.

L'Enfant connected this at its western end with what he called a "well improved field" occupying a large expanse of land south of the canal and along the banks of the Potomac River. North of the canal the "President's park . . . of about 1800 feet in breadth and ¾ of a mile in length" completed this generous expanse of open space.

L'Enfant thus brought elements of the natural landscape into the heart of the city. In doing so he combined garden and urban design in a civic composition of enormous scale, great complexity, and almost bewildering variety. Although not without its faults, it surely ranks among the greatest of city plans in world history.

L'Enfant's achievement is all the more remarkable because of the speed with which he worked. He first visited the site of the proposed city in March. In August, only six months later, he submitted his plan to the president. Surely no planner has ever prepared a design of this magnitude in such a brief period while working without previous surveys or topographic information.

This may explain some of the shortcomings in his plan that critics have noted. One of the most serious is the enormous distance from the Capitol to the White House, a separation so great that their reciprocal relationship is nearly lost. There are also the countless awkward street intersections where the grid and radial systems come together at sharp angles.

L'Enfant attempted to overcome this latter problem in part by creating plazas at these points of multiple intersections. Even so, however, the places left for buildings are often too small or of unsuitable shape to achieve the kind of definition and enclosure he probably intended for these civic spaces. Given time, he probably could have overcome or reduced in importance some of these problems, although the commissioners began to sell lots in the new city as early as 17 October 1791 and, presumably, after that time no further changes could have been made—at least not any modifications affecting lots that had passed out of the hands of the commissioners.

Moreover, for reasons that the next section will discuss, L'Enfant was removed from his assignment by order of the president. When offered a small sum and a lot in the city as compensation, he refused and spent much of his remaining years haunting the halls of Congress seeking suitable recognition for his services. He died in poverty after being taken in by the daughter and son-in-law of a man whose house he had demolished for intruding on one of the planned avenues of the city. Soon, all but his name was forgotten.[33]

Nearly a century later his services to the nation were finally recognized. In 1909 his body was brought from its burial place on a nearby plantation to Washington where it lay in state in the rotunda of the Capitol. At a ceremony commemorating L'Enfant's role in planning the capital city, the vice-president of the United States, the chief commissioner of the District of Columbia, and the French ambassador praised his accomplishments. Then his body was taken to Arlington Cemetery and buried with full military honors in a tomb high on a hill overlooking the city he had helped to create.

A brief inscription on the slab of marble marking his grave contains the usual birth and death dates as well as the date of his reburial. The most appropriate and moving feature, however, is a replica carved in stone of the plan he devised for the city in 1791.

The tomb stands near the top of the hill occupied by the Lee-Custis Mansion. From it one looks eastward to the great monuments of the city he planned. In a larger sense, Washington itself serves as L'Enfant's best memorial, for it is to this versatile, talented, but temperamental French designer that America owes its most elaborate, monumental, and successful of its city plans.[34]

32. In "L'Enfant's Washington," Jackson argues that L'Enfant intended the central focus of the city to include the area between Pennsylvania Avenue and its mirror image on the south of the Mall, Maryland Avenue.

33. For the text of two memorials submitted by L'Enfant to Congress in 1800, see "L'Enfant Memorials."

34. Many questions about L'Enfant's plan have gone unanswered during the two centuries that have passed since he prepared the design for Washington. Light might have been cast on at least some of the puzzling elements in his plan if his other drawings had survived. As I note in the next chapter, L'Enfant claimed that many of these existed but were stolen from his quarters. Although unlikely, it is not impossible that some of the missing L'Enfant papers exist and may yet become available.

The Constitution of 1787 gives Congress an important power.

To exercise exclusive legislation in all cases whatsoever over such district (not exceeding ten miles square) as may, by cession of particular States and the acceptance of Congress, become the seat of Government of the United States, and to exercise like authority over all places purchased by the consent of the legislature of the State in which the same shall be, for the erection of forts, magazines, arsenals, dockyards, and other needful buildings. (United States Constitution, article I, section 8)

Congress authorizes a site for the permanent seat of government on the Potomac River.

Sec. 1. Be it enacted . . . That a district of territory, not exceeding ten miles square . . . be located . . . on the river Potomac, at some place between the mouths of the Eastern Branch and Connogocheague . . . and the same is hereby accepted for the permanent seat of the government of the United States. . . .

Sec. 2. And be it further enacted, That the president . . . be authorized to appoint . . . three commissioners, who . . . shall, under the direction of the president, survey, and . . . define and limit . . . a district of territory under the limitations above mentioned. . . .

Sec. 3. And be it (further) enacted, That the said commissioners . . . shall have power to purchase or accept such quantity of land on the eastern side of the said river, within the said district, as the president shall deem proper for the use of the United States . . . and shall, prior to the first Monday in December . . . [1800] provide suitable buildings for the accommodation of Congress, and of the president, and for the Public offices of the government of the United States. . . .

Sec. 5. And be it (further) enacted, That . . . all offices attached to the . . . United States, shall be removed to, and until the said first Monday in December, in the year one thousand eight hundred, shall remain at the city of Philadelphia. ("An Act for Establishing the Temporary and Permanent Seat of the Government of the United States")

President Washington proclaims boundaries of the federal district on 24 January 1791.

I do hereby declare and make known that the location of . . . the . . . district of ten miles square shall be found by running four lines of experiment . . . beginning the first of the said four lines . . . at the point on Hunting Creek [southwest half a mile from the Alexandria court-house and then due southeast to the Creek].

Then beginning the first . . . line due northwest ten miles; thence the second into Maryland, due northeast ten miles; thence the third line due southeast ten miles; and thence the fourth line due southwest ten miles, to the beginning on Hunting Creek.

And the said four lines . . . being so run, I do hereby declare . . . that all that part within the said four lines . . . is now fixed upon, and directed to be surveyed, defined, limited, and located . . . for the permanent seat of the Government of the United States. (Washington, "Writings," 4–6)

A Maryland newspaper applauds the location of the future national capital.

The City of Washington, in the district of *Columbia* . . . stands at the junction of the rivers Patowmac [*sic*] and the Eastern-Branch, extending nearly four miles up each, including a tract of territory, exceeded in point of convenience, salubrity, and beauty, by none in America, if any in the world—For, although the land is apparently level, yet, by gentle and gradual swellings, a variety of elegant prospects are produced; while there is sufficient descent to convey off the water occasioned by rain. . . .

The Eastern-Branch is one of the safest and most commodious harbors in America . . . and is abundantly capacious.

The writer sees a bright future for the new city.

This metropolis, being situated upon the great post-road, exactly equidistant from the northern and southern extremities of the Union, and nearly so from the Atlantic to Fort-Pitt, upon the best navigation, and in the midst of the richest commercial territory in America, commanding the most extensive internal resources, is by far the most eligible situation for the residence of Congress; and . . . it will grow up with a degree of rapidity hitherto unparalleled in the annals of cities, and will soon become the admiration and delight of the world. (The Baltimore *Maryland Journal*, 30 September 1791, reprinted in the *Philadelphia Gazette*, 8 October 1791; *The New-York Magazine; or Literary Repository*; and, in London, in *The Universal Magazine of Knowledge and Pleasure*, July 1793, p. 41)

Joshua Fry and Peter Jefferson Draw a Map Showing the Setting of the Capital

After the governor of Virginia received instructions from England to prepare an accurate map of his colony, he turned to Joshua Fry and Peter Jefferson. Fry taught mathematics in Williamsburg at the College of William and Mary, while Jefferson, the father of the future president, had a good deal of practical experience in surveying. In 1746 and 1749 the two surveyed important boundary lines within and on the borders of the colony.

They finished their new assignment in 1751 and presented the results in March 1752. The first printed version on four sheets appeared in England in late 1753 or early 1754. The original map was reissued many times in England, each with slight modifications. Two French maps also used the Fry-Jefferson delineation: a single-sheet engraving of 1757 and one printed on two folio-size sheets in 1777. A portion of the first French version is reproduced here.

The selected detail focuses on the area that was to become the national capital. Near the center of this part of the map is Alexandria, first called Belhaven, as the map indicates. This little Virginia city at the mouth of Hunting Creek was later to mark the southern corner of the District of Columbia. A few miles up the Potomac on the eastern bank a traveler would have come to the mouth of the Eastern Branch, or Anacostia. Further upstream, Goose Creek and Rock Creek entered the Potomac. Rock Creek marked the southern boundary of Georgetown, founded in 1751 while Fry and Jefferson were conducting their survey and thus too late to be included.

The map also locates major plantations. The name *Washington* on the right bank of the Potomac below Alexandria identifies the site of Mount Vernon. Its proximity to the site selected for the capital city may suggest why the president regarded the location with such favor.

Carte de la Virginie et du Maryland. Dressée sur la Grande Carte Angloise de Mrs. Josué Fry et Pierre Jefferson. Drawn by Robert de Vaugondy, Géographe ordinaire du Roi. Engraved by E. Haussard in 1755. [Paris, 1757?]. Engraving, 18⅞ × 25³/₁₆ in. (48 × 64 cm.). John W. Reps.

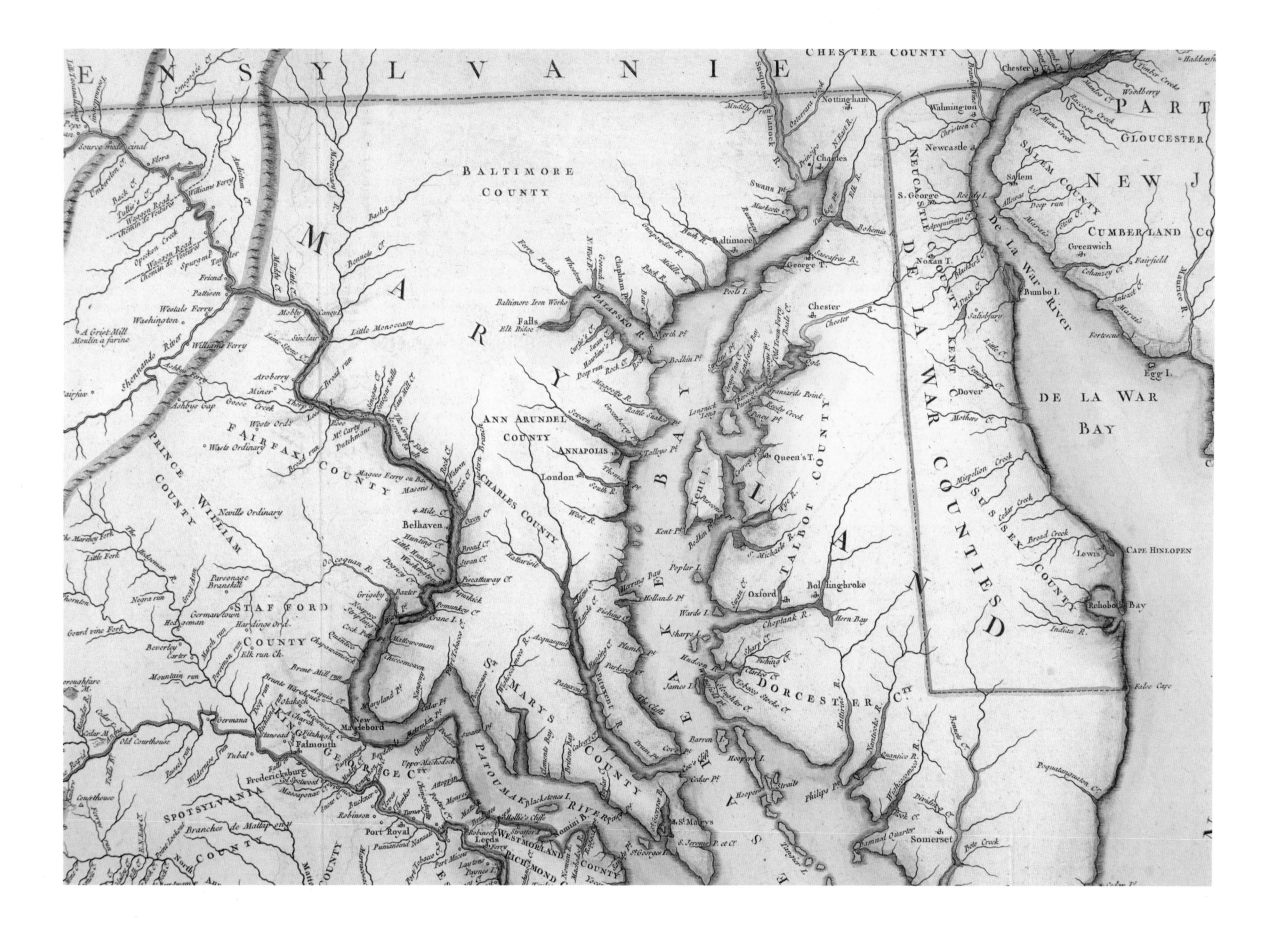

Folio 2. Washington Seeks Help in Acquiring Land near Georgetown and Receives a Planner's Analysis Advocating a Larger Site

*The president secretly commissions friends to
buy land for the government.*

Gentlemen: In asking your aid . . . permit me at the same
time to ask the most perfect secrecy.

The federal territory being located, the competition for the
location of the town now rests between the mouth of the Eastern branch, and the lands on the river, below and adjacent to
Georgetown. In favor of the former, Nature has furnished powerful advantages. In favour of the latter is it's vicinity to Georgetown. . . . These advantages have been so poised in my mind
as to give it different tendencies at different times. There are
lands which stand yet in the way of the latter location and
which, if they could be obtained . . . would remove a considerable obstacle to it, and go near indeed to decide what has been
so long on the balance with me. . . .

These are . . . the lands on the S West side of a line to be run
from where the Road crosses Goose creek (in going from Georgetown to the Eastern branch). . . .

The object of this letter is to ask you to endeavor to purchase
these grounds of the owners for the public . . . but as if for
yourselves, and to conduct your propositions so as to excite no
suspicion that they are on behalf of the public. . . .

I . . . add that all the dispatch is requisite which can consist
with the success of your operations, and that I shall be glad to
hear by post of your progress. (Letter, 3 February 1791, in Washington, "Writings," 9)

*On 11 March 1791, Pierre Charles L'Enfant reports his
impressions of the site to Thomas Jefferson.*

I . . . [rode] from the Eastern branch towards Georgetown
up the hights and down along side of the bank of the main river
and along side of Goose and Rock creeks as far up as their
springs.

As far as I was able to judge through a thick fog, I passed on
many spots which appeared to me really beautiful and which
seem to dispute with each other . . . [which] commands the
most extensive prospect on the water. The gradual rising of the
ground from Carrollsburg towards the ferry road, the level and
extensive ground from thence to the bank of the Potomac as far
as Goose Creek—present a situation most advantageous to
run streets and prolong them on grand and far-distant points
of view.

*He finds the area between Rock Creek and
Tiber Creek less desirable.*

The remainder part of that ground towards Georgetown is
more broken. It may afford pleasant seats, but, although the
bank of the river between the two creeks can command as
grand a prospect as any of the other spots, it seems to be less
commendable . . . not only because the level surface it presents
is but small, but because the hights from beyond Georgetown
absolutely command the whole. (L'Enfant to Jefferson, in Padover, *Jefferson*, 45–47)

*At the end of March 1791 L'Enfant analyzes the possibilities of
a site far larger than President Washington had considered.*

After coming . . . from the Eastern branch ferry, the country is level and on a space of about two miles each way presents
a most eligible position for the first settlement of a grand City,
and one . . . the more advantageous in . . . lying between the
Eastern Branch and Georgetown. . . .

On that part terminating in a ridge to Jenkin's Hill and
running . . . parallel with and . . . half a mile off from the
river Potomac . . . [are] . . . many of the most desirable positions . . . for . . . the Public Edifices. . . .

Considering how in . . . time a city so happily situated will
extend over a large surface of ground, much deliberation is
necessary . . . to determine . . . a system . . . to render the
place commodious and agreeable to the first settler, [while]
. . . capable of [being] enlarged by progressive improvement.
(L'Enfant, "Note," 27–31)

L'Enfant conducts a visitor around the site in April 1791.

As soon as I arrived at Georgetown, I rode with Major L'Enfant . . . over the greatest part of the ground; the Major pointed
out to me all the eminences, plains, commanding spots, projects of canals by means of Rock creek, Eastern Branch, and
. . . Goose creek, which intersects the plan of the city along the
Eastern Branch, quays, bridges, etc., magnificent public walks,
and other projects.

The ground pleased me much; the Major is enraptured with
it; "nothing," he says, "can be more admirably adapted for the
purpose; nature has done much for it, and with the aid of art
it will become the wonder of the world." (William Loughton
Smith, *Journal*, 61–62)

Many Persons Own Land on the Site for the Capital City

Between Georgetown and the Anacostia River lay
two townsites that had been surveyed but not developed. Carrollsburg, at the mouth of the Anacostia,
had the advantage of deep water, and Jefferson at first
thought that the capital should be located here. He and
Washington then turned their attention to the land occupied by and in the vicinity of Hamburgh, another
platted town with only a few occupants. It lay near the
mouth of Goose Creek, soon to be called by the grander
name of the Tiber.

Although this map does not show the road referred
to by Washington in his letter to his Georgetown confi-
dants, it must have followed generally the line of what
became Pennsylvania Avenue. All of Hamburgh lay to
the southwest, with much of the land outside that town
belonging to David Burnes. It was here that Washington and Jefferson thought the new city should be
located, and it was for this limited site that Jefferson
prepared a sketch plan reproduced in folio 4.

L'Enfant persuaded Washington to consider a much
larger area, and when the landowners between Rock
Creek and the Anacostia agreed to make their land
available, the president directed him to prepare a plan
for the entire area shown on the map.

E. F. M. Faehtz and F. W. Pratt, assisted by S. R.
Seibert, a civil engineer, compiled this map from research information provided by Dr. Joseph M. Toner.
Although doubtless containing some errors, it provides
the best available record of the land ownership pattern
immediately prior to the events that led to the creation
here of an entirely new and enormous city.

*Sketch of Washington in Embryo, viz, Previous to Its Survey by
Major L'Enfant.* Compiled by E. F. M. Faehtz & F. W.
Pratt, based on research by Dr. Joseph M. Toner, with
help by S. R. Seibert, C.E., Washington, 1874. Lithograph, 15½ × 20¼ in. (39.4 × 51.6 cm.). Geography
and Maps, Library of Congress.

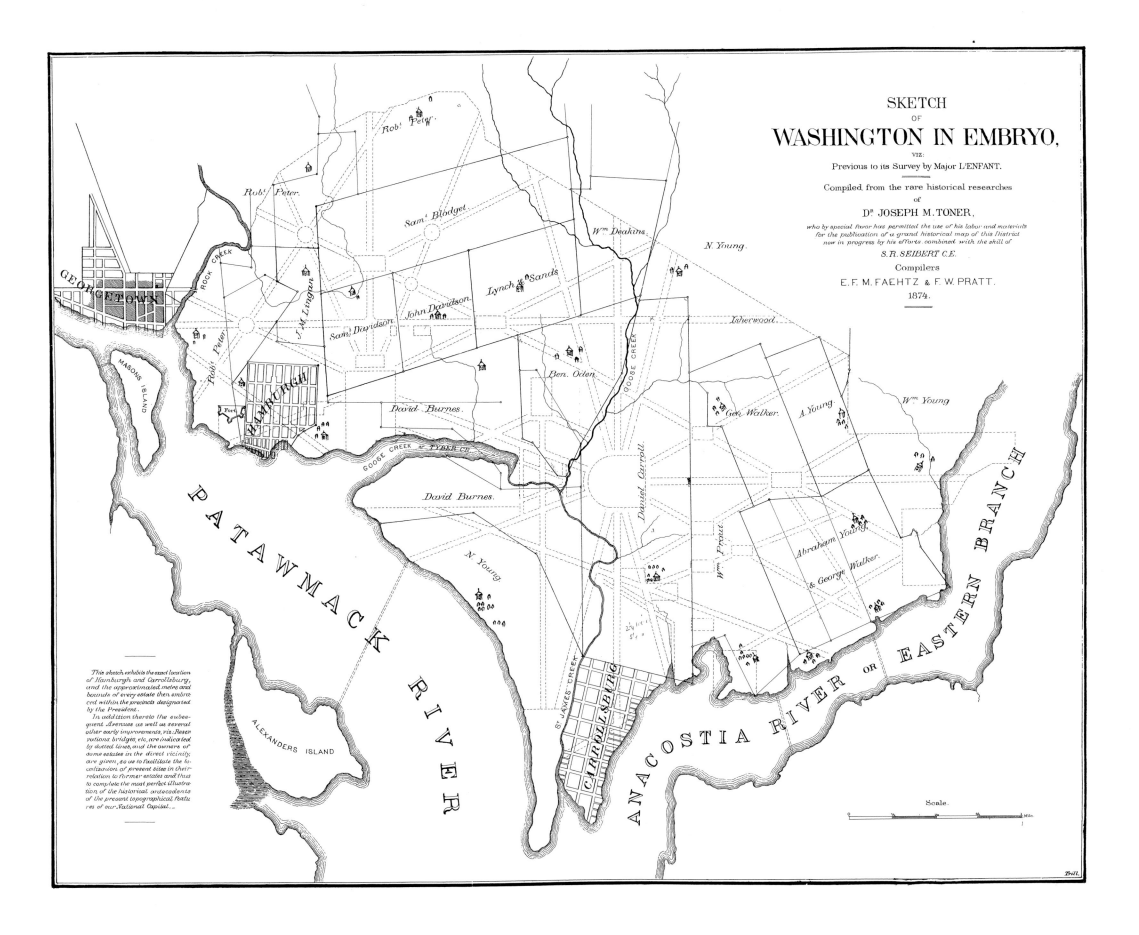

SKETCH
OF
WASHINGTON IN EMBRYO,
VIZ:
Previous to its Survey by Major L'ENFANT.

Compiled from the rare historical researches
of
Dr. JOSEPH M. TONER,
who by special favor has permitted the use of his labor and materials
for the publication of a grand historical map of this District
now in progress by his efforts combined with the skill of
S. R. SEIBERT C.E.
Compilers
E. F. M. FAEHTZ & F. W. PRATT.
1874.

GEORGETOWN

ROCK CREEK

Robt Peter

Robt Peter

Robt Peter

Rob. Peter

Saml Blodget

Wm Deakins

N. Young

J. M. Lingan

Saml Davidson

John Davidson

Lynch & Sands

Isherwood

Ben. Oden

GOOSE CREEK

Geo. Walker

A. Young

Wm Young

MASONS ISLAND

Fort

HAMBURGH

David Burnes.

Daniel Carroll

Wm Prout

Abraham Young
& George Walker.

GOOSE CREEK or TYBER CR.

David Burnes.

N. Young

PATAWMACK RIVER

ALEXANDERS ISLAND

ST JAMES CREEK

CARROLLSBURG

ANACOSTIA RIVER OR EASTERN BRANCH

This sketch exhibits the exact location
of Hamburgh and Carrollsburg,
and the approximated metes and
bounds of every estate then embraced within the precincts designated
by the President.
In addition thereto the subsequent Avenues as well as several
other early improvements, viz: Reservations, bridges, etc. are indicated
by dotted lines, and the owners of
some estates in the direct vicinity,
are given, so as to facilitate the lo-
calization of present sites in their
relation to former estates and thus
to complete the most perfect illustration of the historical antecedents
of the present topographical features of our National Capital.

Scale.
Mile.

13

Folio 3. The President and the Proprietors Agree on Favorable Terms for a Site Extending from Georgetown to the Anacostia

Washington's diary records meeting Ellicott and L'Enfant in Georgetown on March 28.

I examined the Surveys of Mr. Ellicot who had been sent to lay out the district of ten miles square for the federal seat; and also works of Majr. L'Enfant who had been engaged to examine & make a draught of the grds. in the vicinity of George Town and Carrollsburg on the Eastern branch.

The president reveals how the next day he told the proprietors to cooperate.

I represented that the contention in which they seemed to be engaged, did not . . . comport either with the public interest or that of their own; that while each party was aiming to obtain the public buildings, they might by placing the matter on a contracted scale, defeat the measure altogether . . . that neither the offer from George-Town or Carrollsburgh separately, was adequate to the end of insuring the object. That both together did not comprehend more ground nor would afford greater means than was required for the Federal City; and that, instead of contending which of the two should have it they had better, by combining more offers make a common cause of it. (Washington, "Writings," 16)

The proprietors offer land to the federal government on generous terms.

We . . . do hereby agree . . . to convey, in trust, to the president . . . the whole of our respective lands which he may think proper to include within the lines of the Federal city . . . on the conditions following:
The president shall have the sole power of directing the Federal city to be laid off in what manner he pleases.
He may retain any number of squares he may think proper for . . . public uses; and the lots only which shall be laid off shall be a joint property between the trustees on behalf of the public and each present proprietor, and the same shall be fairly and equally divided between the public and the individuals. . . .
For the streets the proprietors shall receive no compensation; but for the . . . lands . . . taken for public buildings . . . or uses, the proprietors whose lands shall be taken shall receive at the rate of 25 pounds per acre. (Agreement signed in Georgetown, 31 March 1791, in Columbia Historical Society, *Records* 35-36 [1935]: 44-46)

Washington sends Jefferson the good news.

The terms . . . are That all the land from Rock-creek along the river to the eastern-branch and . . . to or above the ferry including a breadth of about a mile and a half, the whole containing from three to five thousand acres, is ceded to the public, on condition that, when the whole shall be . . . laid off as a city, (which Major L'Enfant is now directed to do) the present Proprietors shall retain every other lot, and for . . . land . . . taken for public use . . . they shall be allowed . . . Twenty five pounds per acre. . . . No compensation is to be made for the ground . . . occupied as streets or alleys.

Washington deletes part of a proclamation drafted by Jefferson that would have located the public buildings near the Tiber.

I do hereby . . . declare . . . that *(the highest summit of lands in the town heretofore called Hamburg . . . with a convenient extent of grounds circumjacent, shall be appropriated for a Capitol for the accommodation of Congress, & such other lands between Georgetown & the stream heretofore called the Tyber, as shall on due examination be found convenient & sufficient, shall be appropriated for the accommodation of the president of the U.S. for the time being, & for the public offices of the government of the U.S.).
*the part within ( ) being conjectural, will be . . . rendered conformable to the ground when more accurately examined. (Padover, *Jefferson*, 53)

The president explains why he modified his proclamation.

The enlarged plan of this agreement having done away the necessity and indeed postponed the propriety, of designating the particular spot, on which the public buildings should be placed, until an accurate survey and sub-division of the whole ground is made, I have left out that paragraph of the proclamation. (Washington, "Writings," 19-20)

A Philadelphia newspaper informs its readers of the event.

On Monday last the president of the United States . . . arrived in this town, and . . . had the pleasure . . . to reconcile the various views and interests of the proprietors of lands . . . in obtaining a tract . . . upwards of four thousand acres, in the very centre of the Federal Territory. (Philadelphia *General Advertiser*, 9 April 1791)

Andrew Ellicott Surveys the Federal District

This map of the District of Columbia drawn by Andrew Ellicott clearly shows the relationship between the generously large site for the city that L'Enfant planned in 1791 and the ten-mile square district around it. Ellicott prepared this map as part of his initial task to survey the district boundaries. He began at a point designated by the president, himself a fully qualified and experienced surveyor. Although the congressional act specified that the southern limit of the territory was to be the Anacostia River, the president obtained an amendment permitting him to fix Jones Point at the mouth of Hunting Creek in Alexandria as the southern corner of the district.

In January 1793 Jefferson wrote Ellicott stating that the president wanted "the outlines at least of the city, and perhaps of George town" to be shown. Jefferson asked Ellicott to consider adding the words *or Annakostia* after the name of the Eastern Branch. Both these changes appear on the printed version published in 1794, the approximate time being established by Ellicott's letter to the commissioners on 9 December 1793 informing them that "the map . . . has been some months in the hands of the engraver and will be finished early in the spring."

It shows the locations of the milestones that Ellicott placed as permanent surveying marks along the four sides of the district. He also drew the lines of the principal streets and public sites of the city as he had fixed them on his drawing used for the engraved versions of the city plan published in 1792. Ellicott used hatching to indicate the hills and valleys within the district as well as land lying within a half-mile of its boundaries. Unfortunately, he did not show the topography within the city itself, perhaps because its delineation had been a responsibility of L'Enfant's. We are thus left without a conclusive record of the configuration of the city's site by the person best equipped to provide that information.

Territory of Columbia. Drawn by Andw. Ellicott. Printed by Joseph T. Scott. [Philadelphia?, 1794]. Engraving, 22 × 22 in. (55.8 × 55.8 cm.). Geography and Maps, Library of Congress.

Thomas Jefferson records some thoughts about the capital city.

[Sites should be reserved] for the federal Capitol, the offices, The president's house & gardens, the town house, Market house, publick walks, hospital. For the president's house, offices & gardens, I should think 2. squares [i.e., blocks] should be consolidated. For the Capitol and offices one square. For the Market one square. For the Public walks 9. squares consolidated.

The expression [in the Residence Act] 'such quantity of land as the president shall deem *proper for the U.S.*' is vague. It may therefore be extended to the acceptance or purchase of land enough for the town: and I have no doubt it is the wish, and perhaps expectation. In that case it will be to be laid out in lots and streets. I should propose these to be at right angles as in Philadelphia, and that no street be narrower than 100. feet, with foot-ways of 15. feet. Where a street is long & level, it might be 120. feet wide. I should prefer squares of at least 200. yards every way, which will be of about 8. acres each. . . .

The lots to be sold out in breadth of 50 feet: their depths to extend to the diagonal of the square.

I doubt much whether the obligation to build the houses at a given distance from the street, contributes to its beauty. It produces a disgusting monotony. All persons make this complaint against Philadelphia, the contrary practice varies the appearance, & is much more convenient to the inhabitants.

In Paris it is forbidden to build a house beyond a given height, & it is admitted to be a good restriction. It keeps down the price of ground, keeps the houses low and convenient, and the streets light and airy. Fires are much more managable where houses are low. This however is an object of Legislation. . . .

1500 Acres would be required in the whole, to wit, about 300 acres for public buldings, walks &c and 1200 Acres to be divided into quarter acre lots, which, due allowance being made for streets, would make about 2000 lots. (Notes, 29 August and 14 September 1790, in Jefferson, *Papers*, 17:460–62)

Washington sends L'Enfant a sketch plan by Jefferson for the Hamburg site and a second unidentified city plan.

Although I do not conceive that you will derive any material advantage from an examination of the enclosed papers, yet, as they have been drawn by different persons, and under different circumstances, they may be compared with your own ideas of a proper plan for the Federal City (under the prospect which now presents itself to us.) For this purpose I commit them to your *private* inspection until my return from the tour I am abt. to make. The rough sketch by Mr. Jefferson was done under an idea that *no* offer worthy of consideration, would come from the Land holders in the vicinity of Carrollsburg (from the backwardness which appeared in them); and therefore, was accommodated to the grounds about George Town. The *other*, is taken up upon a larger scale, without reference to any described spot. (Washington, "Writings," 22–23)

L'Enfant tells the president that a "grand plan" is needed for the city.

In viewing the intended establishment in the light and considering how in process of time a city so happily situated will extend over a large surface of ground, much deliberation is necessary . . . to determine on a plan . . . that . . . [will] render the place commodious and agreeable to the first settler, [while] it may be capable of . . . [being] enlarged by progressive improvement . . . which should be foreseen in the first delineation in a grand plan of the whole city combined with the various grounds it will cover and with the particular circumstance of the country all around.

L'Enfant vigorously condemns grid plans.

It is not the regular assemblage of houses laid out in squares and forming streets all parallel and uniform that . . . is so necessary, for such a plan could only do on a level plain and where no surrounding object being interesting it becomes indifferent which way the opening of streets may be directed.

But on any other ground a plan of this sort must be defective, and it never would answer for any of the spots proposed for the Federal City, and on that held here as the most eligible it would absolutely annihilate every [one] of the advantages enumerated and . . . alone injure the success of the undertaking.

Such regular plans indeed, however answerable they may appear upon paper or seducing as they may be on the first aspect to the eyes of some people must even when applyed upon the ground the best calculated to admit of it become at last tiresome and insipid and it never could be in its origin but a mean continuance of some cool imagination wanting a sense of the real grand and truly beautiful only to be met with where nature contributes with art and diversifies the objects. (L'Enfant, "Note," 31)

Jefferson Sketches a Plan in March 1791 for a Capital City on Tiber Creek

This drawing by Thomas Jefferson incorporates many of the ideas he listed in his notes on town planning prepared in late August and mid-September 1790. He probably gave it to Washington four months later near the end of March, shortly before the president left for Georgetown to meet with the proprietors, Ellicott, L'Enfant, and the commissioners. Washington took with him a draft proclamation prepared by Jefferson designating the site along the north bank of the Tiber as the city's location. At that time both men thought that obtaining even this much land would be difficult, and neither conceived of a site the size of the one that Washington was able to acquire through the agreement he reached with the proprietors.

Jefferson's city plan called for blocks 600 feet square arranged in a grid extending eleven blocks east and west by three blocks deep. Two large sites two blocks apart were to be connected by "public walks," a mall-like strip of open space along the north bank of the Tiber. One was to be used for the Capitol and the other for the presidential residence. Notes on the drawing tell us that lots in and around these public reservations were "to be sold in the first instance." Regularly spaced dots beyond this initial urban nucleus identify the intersections of future grid streets bounding many additional city blocks that could be "laid off in [the] future." Jefferson thus conceived of a compact original settlement that could be expanded in an orderly fashion as the population increased.

It was doubtless this plan that provoked L'Enfant's vigorous attack on gridiron street systems. Jefferson may never have seen these comments that L'Enfant sent to Washington, but he soon realized that his ideas on the layout of cities and those of the French planner differed at many points.

Untitled and undated map drawn by Thomas Jefferson, probably in March 1791. Manuscript, 15½ × 9⅞ in. (39.3 × 25.1 cm.). Manuscripts, Library of Congress.

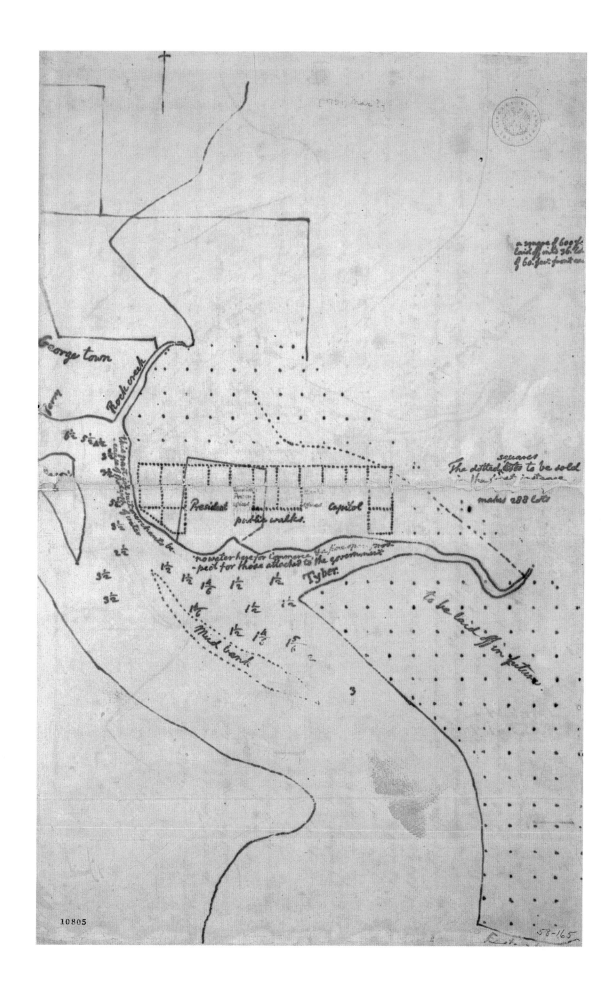

a square of 600 f[eet]
laid off into 36 lot[s]
of 60 feet front ea[ch]

George town

Rock creek

St. state

squares

The dotted lots to be sold
in the first instance

makes 288 lots

President

public walks.

Capitol

no water here for Commerce, the sion opens, not
-pect for those attached to the government

Tyber.

Mud branch

to be laid off in future

10805

58-165

Folio 5. L'Enfant Tells Jefferson of His New Assignment and Borrows Some European City Plans from Him

L'Enfant tells Jefferson that the president has directed him to plan the city.

Great as were my Endeavor . . . at the moment of the president['s] arrival at this place . . . I could present him no more but a rough drawing in pincel of the several Surveys which I had been able to run—Nevertheless . . . I had the satisfaction to see the little I had done agreeable to his wish, and the Confidence with which he has been pleased since to Honor me in ordering the survey to be continued and the delineation of a grand plan . . . of the City to be done on principle[s] conformable to the ideas which I took the liberty to hold before him. (L'Enfant to Jefferson, 4 April 1791, in Jefferson, *Papers*, 20:83)

He also informs Alexander Hamilton of his new assignment.

The president has been pleased . . . in directing I should delin[e]ate a grand and general plan for the . . . city the which I have engaged to have got ready by the time when he return[s] from his southern tour . . . about the 20 of jun next. (L'Enfant to Hamilton, 8 April 1791, in Hamilton, *Papers*, 8:255)

L'Enfant asks Jefferson about public building requirements and requests maps of European cities.

The number and nature of the publick building[s] with the necessary appendix I should be glad to have a Statement of as speedily as possible. And I would be very much obliged to you . . . if you could procure for me what Ever may fall within your reach—of any [maps] of the differents grand city now existing such as for Example—as London—madry [i.e., Madrid]—paris—Amsterdam—naples—venice—genoa—florence together with particular maps of any such sea ports or dock yards and arsenals as you may know to be the most compleat in their Improvement.

He declares his intention to design a unique plan.

I would reprobate the Idea of Imitating and that contrary of Having this Intention it is my wish and shall be my Endeavour to delinate on a new and original way the plan the contrivance of which the president has left to me without an restriction so Ever. Yet the contemplation of what exist[s] of well improved situation[s], iven . . . deffactive ones, may serve to suggest a variety of new Ideas and is necessary to refine and Strengthen

the Jugement particularly in the present instance when having to unite the usfull with the Commodious and agreable viewing these will by offering means for comparing Enable me the better to determine with a certainty the propriety of a local[e] which offer an Extansive field for combinations. (L'Enfant to Jefferson, 4 April 1791, in Jefferson, *Papers*, 20:83–84)

Jefferson sends several of his city maps to L'Enfant.

I am favored with your letter of the 4 inst., and in compliance with your request I have examined my papers and found the plans of Frankfort on the Mayne, Carlsruhe, Amsterdam, Strasburg, Paris, Orleans, Bordeaux, Lyons, Montpelier, Marseilles, Turin, and Milan, which I send in a roll by this Post. They are on large and accurate scales, having been procured by me while in those respective cities myself. As they are connected with the notes I made in my travels, and often necessary to explain them to myself, I will beg your care of them and to return them when no longer useful to you, leaving you absolutely free to keep them as long as useful. I am happy that the president has left the planning of the Town in such good hands, and have no doubt it will be done to general satisfaction. . . . Having communicated to the president, before he went away, such general ideas on the subject of the Town, as occurred to me, I make no doubt that, in explaining himself to you on the subject, he has interwoven with his own ideas, such of mine as he approved: for fear of repeating therefore, what he did not approve, and having more confidence in the unbiassed state of his mind than in my own, I avoid interfering with what he may have expressed to you. (Jefferson to L'Enfant, 10 April 1791, in Jefferson, *Papers*, 20:86)

Jefferson informs the president what he has done and offers some further support for the grid plan.

I received last night from Majr. L'Enfant a request to furnish him any plans of towns I could, for his examination. I accordingly send him by this post, plans of Frankfort on the Mayne, Carlsruhe, Amsterdam, Strasburg, Paris, Orleans, Bordeaux, Lyons, Montpelier, Marseilles, Turin and Milan, on large & accurate scales. . . . They are none of them however comparable to the old Babylon, revived in Philadelphia, & exemplified. (Jefferson to Washington, 10 April 1791, in Jefferson, *Papers*, 20:88)

Jefferson Lends L'Enfant Some European City Plans

In his *Notes on Virginia*, Jefferson wrote of city location and growth with a scholar's insights. Although in several brief passages elsewhere in his writings he criticized the influence of cities, in Europe he enjoyed their architectural and intellectual resources. His library included many atlases and volumes with engraved city plans and views, and he collected maps of European cities during his travels there. The specific town plans he sent L'Enfant cannot be identified, but those reproduced here show four places whose designs may have influenced L'Enfant.

Karlsruhe, that most excessively (almost obsessively) radial of all city plans, may have caught L'Enfant's attention. Turin, with its single long radial and what was intended as another terminating at the same point, possibly suggested how radial and grid systems could be combined with each other. L'Enfant knew Paris from his days there as an art student and had returned for a visit in 1783–84. Its radial boulevards, royal parks, and civic squares offered a host of prototypes for him to study. Amsterdam, too, with its ring canals may have given L'Enfant ideas about the need to organize urban space in whatever patterns best fit the landscape.

Hoch Fürstlich Baaden Durlachischer Residenz Schloss und Stadt Karls-Ruhe. Drawn by Christian Thran, engraved by G. Pfaunz, published by Andreas Jac. Malchenbauer, Karlsruhe. Undated. Engraving, 15½ × 13¼ in. (39.3 × 33.6 cm.): facsimile, detail. John W. Reps.

Avgvsta Tavrinorvm. From Jan Blaeu, *Theatrum Saubaudiae*, Amsterdam, 1682. Drawn by Joannes Thomas Borgonius. Engraving, 20⁵/₁₆ × 29½ in. (51.5 × 75.1 cm.), detail. John W. Reps.

A Plan of Paris &c. Published by John Rocque, London, ca. 1754. Engraving, 16⁷/₈ × 25⁵/₈ in. (42.9 × 65.1 cm.), detail. John W. Reps.

Plan de la Grande & Fameuse Ville Marchande d'Amsterdam. Published by the widow of Nicolas Visscher, [Amsterdam], ca. 1710. Engraving, 17⅛ × 29³/₁₆ in. (43.5 × 74.1 cm.), detail. John W. Reps.

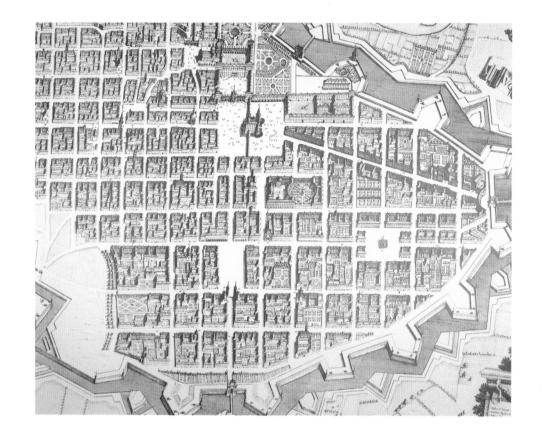

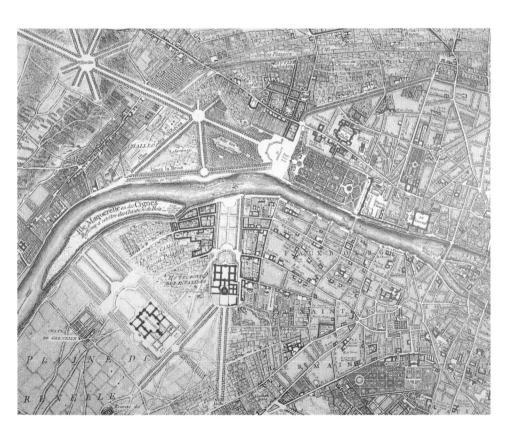

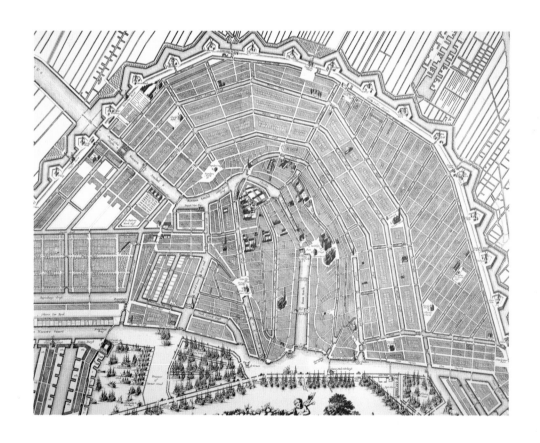

L'Enfant refers to a drawing showing his plan.

In delineating the plan for the intended city here annexed, I regretted very much being hindered by the shortness of time from making any particular drawing of the several buildings, squares, and other improvements which the smallness of the scale of the general map, together with the hurry with which it had been drawn could not admit of having lain them down, as correct. . . . My whole attention was directed . . . in submitting . . . to you a first drawing, correct only as it respects the situation and distance of objects.

He explains the reasons for his system of streets.

Having determined some principal points to which I wished to make the others subordinate, I made the distribution regular with every street at right angles, North and South, east and west, and afterwards opened some in different directions, as avenues to and from every principal place, wishing thereby not merely to [contrast] with the general regularity, nor to afford a greater variety of [sites] with pleasant prospects, which will be obtained from the advantageous ground over which these avenues are chiefly directed, but principally to connect each part of the city . . . by making the real distance less from place to place, by giving to them reciprocity of sight and by making them thus seemingly connected, promote a rapid settlement over the whole extent. . . . Some of these avenues were also necessary to effect the junction of several roads to a central point in the city, by making these roads shorter. . . .

These avenues I made broad, so as to admit of their being planted with trees leaving 80 feet for a carriage way, 30 feet on each side for a walk under a double row of trees, and allowing ten feet between the trees and the houses.

L'Enfant proposes sites for the Capitol and the president's house.

I could not discover [a site] in all respects so advantageious [sic] . . . for erecting the Federal House [as] the western end of Jenkin's Heights [which] stands really as a pedestal waiting for a super-structure. . . .

The spot I assigned [for the presidential palace] I chose somewhat more in the wood, and off the creek than when you stood in the partition line [in order to] lessen the distance to the Federal House, and . . . to obtain a more extensive view down the Potomac, with a prospect of the whole harbor and town of Alexandria; also to connect with more harmony the public walks

and avenue of the Congress House with the garden park and other improvements round the palace.

L'Enfant justifies the great distance between the two buildings.

The distance from the Congressional house will not be too great . . . as . . . no message to nor from the president is to be made without a sort of decorum which will doubtless point out the propriety of [a] Committee waiting on him in [a] carriage should his palace be even contiguous to Congress.

To make however the distance less to other officers I placed the three grand Departments of State contiguous to the principal palace; and on the way leading to the Congressional house, the gardens of the one together with the park and other improvements . . . are connected with the public walk and avenue to the Congress house in a manner as must form a whole as grand as it will be agreeable and convenient to the whole city . . . and all along side of which may be placed play houses, rooms of assembly, academies and all such sort of places as may be attractive to the learned and afford diversion to the idle.

He describes his proposal for a great cascade.

I propose . . . letting the Tiber . . . [issue] from under the base of the Congress building . . . [to] form a cascade of forty feet high, or more than one hundred wide, which would produce the most happy effect in rolling down to fill up the canal and discharge itself in the Potomac, of which it would then appear the main spring when seen through that grand and majestic avenue intersecting with the prospect from the palace, at a point . . . designated . . . for . . . a grand equestrian statue. (L'Enfant to Washington, 22 June 1791, in Kite, *L'Enfant and Washington*, 52–58)

L'Enfant claims he has produced a city plan that the world will envy.

I wished to promot[e] in the delination of a plan wholly new and which combined on a grand scale will require exertions above what is the idea of many but . . . not . . . beyond your power to procur. . . . I remain assured you will conceive it essential to pursue with dignity the operation of an undertaking of a magnitude so worthy of the concern of a grand empire in the compleat achievement . . . over whose progress the eyes of every other nation enveying the opportunity denied them will stand judge. (L'Enfant to Washington, 19 August 1791, in Columbia Historical Society, *Records* 2 [1899]: 48)

L'Enfant Designs a City for the Ages in Only a Few Months

L'Enfant prepared at least four drawings showing features of his plan. The written material accompanying them supports the conclusion that he had fixed on the major features of his design by 22 June, when he showed Washington the first version. On 19 August 1791 L'Enfant referred to a second drawing as a "map of dotted lines." On this he probably delineated the center lines of major streets and the boundaries of the proposed public reservations. Neither has survived. L'Enfant also referred to a larger city plan, evidently a working copy used in running the lines of the streets and avenues. L'Enfant submitted his plan to the president in August. That manuscript is now faded and difficult to read. A facsimile prepared in 1887 recorded all of its important features, although not with complete accuracy.

L'Enfant's plan was to be engraved, but after many delays and his dismissal from his assignment, a version prepared by Andrew Ellicott and Thomas Jefferson was substituted. His design included all of the land that the proprietors had made available a few months earlier. Each landowner thus had reason to believe that some part of the federal city would be developed on his property and that he could expect to benefit financially from the project.

L'Enfant's drawing is an important document in the history of city planning—not only in the United States but in the entire world. No other essay in urban design rivaled it in its combination of enormous scale, integration of radial and grid street patterns, and number and variety of public building sites and civic spaces. What is more remarkable is the speed with which the planner worked. He determined the main elements within his first five months at the task and further refined the design by the end of the summer.

Plan of the City Intended for the Permanent Seat of the Government of t[he] United States. Facsimile of a manuscript by Peter Charles L'Enfant in the Library of Congress. Published in Washington by the U.S. Coast and Geodetic Survey, 1887. Lithograph, 27½ × 46½ in. (69.8 × 118 cm.). Olin Library, Cornell University.

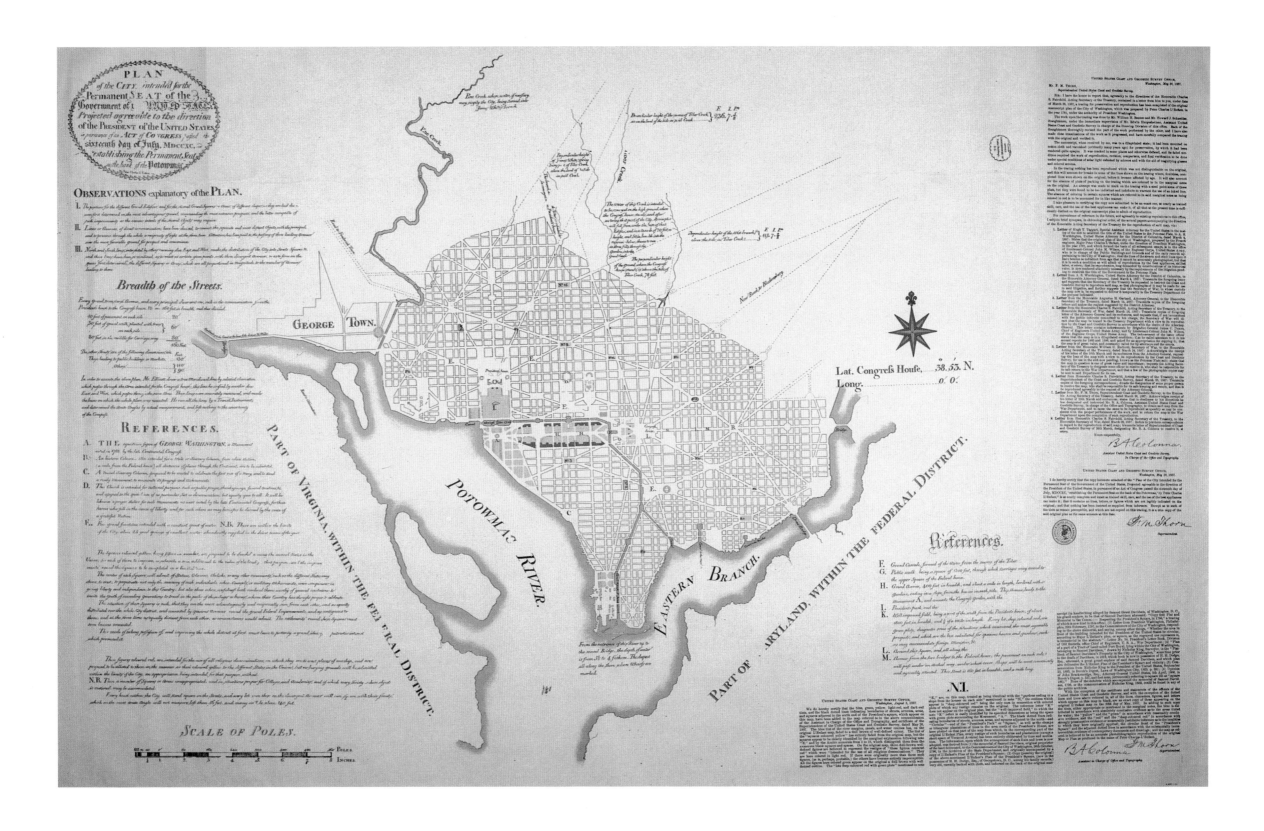

2 I

Folio 7. L'Enfant Lists the Major Features of His Plan for the New Capital

Notes on L'Enfant's drawing explain the basis for the design.

I. The positions for the different Grand Edifices, and for the several Grand Squares . . . were first determined on the most advantageous ground. . . .

II. Lines or Avenues of direct communication . . . connect the separate and most distant objects with the principal, and . . . preserve . . . a reciprocity of sight at the same time.

III. North and South lines, intersected by others running due East and West, make the distribution of the city into streets, squares, etc., and those lines have been so combined as to meet at certain given points with those divergent avenues, so as to form . . . different Squares or Areas which are all proportional in magnitude to the number of avenues leading to them.

The legend identifies major buildings, squares, monuments, and open spaces.

A. The equestrian figure of George Washington, a Monument voted in 1783 by the late Continental Congress.

B. An historic Column—also intended for a Mile or itinerary Column, from whose station (a mile from the Federal house) all distances of places throughout the Continent to be calculated.

C. A Naval itinerary Column, proposed to be erected to celebrate the . . . Navy and to stand a ready Monument to consecreate its progress and achievements.

D. This Church is intended for national purposes, such as public prayer, thanksgiving, funeral orations etc. and assigned to the special use of no particular Sect or denomination, but equally open to all. It will be likewise a proper shelter for such monuments as were voted by the late Continental Congress for those heroes who fell in the cause of liberty and for such others as may hereafter be decreed by the voice of a grateful Nation

E. Five grand fountains intended with a constant spout of water.

F. Grand Cascade, formed of water from the sources of the Tiber.

G. Public walk, being a square of 1200 feet, through which carriages may ascend to the upper Square of the Federal House.

H. Grand Avenue, 400 feet in breadth, and about a mile in length, bordered with gardens, ending in a slope from the houses on each side. This Avenue leads to Monument A. and connects the Congress Garden with the

I. President's park and the

K. well-improved field, being a part of the walk from the president's house of about 1800 feet in breadth, and ¾ of a mile in length. Every lot, deep-colored red with green plots, designates some of the situations which command the most agreeable prospects, and which are the best calculated for spacious houses and gardens, such as may accomodate foreign Ministers etc.

L. Around this Square and all along the

M. Avenue from the two bridges to the Federal House, the pavement on each side will pass under an Arched way under whose cover Shops will be most conveniently and agreeably situated. This street is 160 feet in breadth and a mile in length.

L'Enfant summarizes his proposal for promoting rapid growth by creating nodes of development under state sponsorship.

The Squares colored yellow, being fifteen in number, are proposed to be divided among the several States of the Union, for each of them to improve, or subscribe a sum additional to the value of the land. . . .

The center of each square will admit of Statues, Columns, Oblisks, or any other ornaments such as the different States may chose to erect; to perpetuate not only the memory of such individuals whose Counsels or military achievements were conspicuous in giving liberty and independence to this Country; but also those whose usefulness hath rendered them worthy of general imitations. . . .

The situation of these Squares is such, that they are the most advantageously and recipricolly seen from each other, and as equally distributed over the whole City district, and connected by spacious avenues round the grand Federal Improvements, and as contiguous to them, and at the same time as equally distant from each other, as circumstances would admit. The settlements round those Squares must soon become connected.

N.B. There are a number of squares or areas unappropriated, and in situations appropriate for Colleges and Academies and of which every Society whose object is national can be accomodated. . . .

Every house within the City, will stand square on the Streets, and every lot even those on the divergent avenues will run square with their fronts, which on the most acute angle will not measure less than 56 feet, and many will be above 140 feet. ("Observations Explanatory of the Plan" and "References," on a manuscript drawing by Peter Charles L'Enfant, *Plan of the City, Intended for the Permanent Seat of Government of the United States*. The text of the references first appeared in print in the *Gazette of the United States*, 4 January 1792, pp. 286–87)

A Closer Look at the L'Enfant Plan Reveals Important Features

L'Enfant placed the Capitol on the highest point of land, leading to it eight diagonal boulevards and three major grid streets from the north, east, and south. On the western axis of the Capitol he projected his 400-foot-wide Grand Avenue leading to a statue of General Washington located on the south axis of the presidential residence. Around that building L'Enfant proposed to group the major executive departments. Another web of radial and grid thoroughfares provided access from all directions. L'Enfant linked this center of executive authority and the Capitol by one of his great diagonal avenues, soon thereafter named for the commonwealth of Pennsylvania.

His plan identified many other public building sites, locations for monuments, and civic squares. He placed these at multiple intersections of radial and grid streets for best access and greatest visibility down the long axial lines of the composition. He identified fifteen of these for special treatment. Each was to be embellished and developed by one of the fifteen states then existing. He expected that citizens from each state would build houses in the vicinity of their square. In this way L'Enfant hoped to promote rapid growth in all directions from these fifteen urban nodes and thus achieve speedy development of the entire city.

It is the area shown on this detail that one sees in most of the printed city views published throughout the nineteenth century. Although Ellicott and Jefferson altered this plan in many respects and other changes occurred in later years, L'Enfant's basic concept remained intact. The distinctive street pattern, with its avenues radiating from the Capitol, what became known as the White House, and other public sites, helps to orient one in interpreting what these views show.

Plan of the City Intended for the Permanent Seat of the Government of t[he] United States. Detail of facsimile of a manuscript by Peter Charles L'Enfant in the Library of Congress. Published in Washington by the U.S. Coast and Geodetic Survey, 1887. Lithograph, 27½ × 46½ in. (69.8 × 118 cm.). John W. Reps.

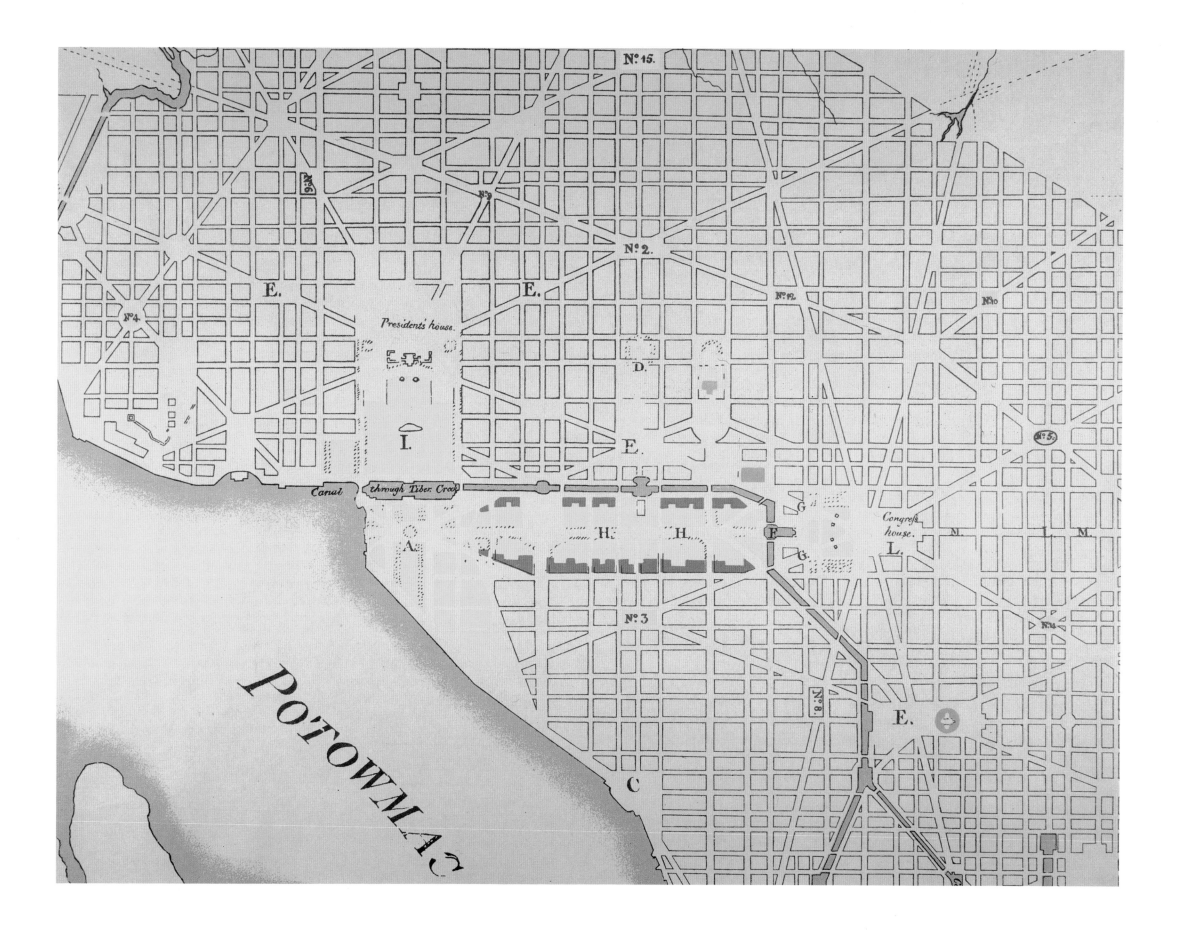

No. 15.

No. 9

No. 9

No. 2.

No. 12.

No. 10

E.

E.

No. 4

President's house.

D.

E.

No. 5.

I.

Canal   through Tiber. Creek

G

A.   Congress house.

H.   H.   F.   L   M   L   M

G.   L.

No. 3

No. 14

No. 8   E.

POTOWMAC

C

23

2 The Infant Instant City: Revising the Plan and Beginning to Build the New Seat of Government

AT the end of August 1791 President Washington had every reason to believe that whatever other difficulties might remain in the development of the new capital, its planning lay in capable hands. He had approved L'Enfant's preliminary plan the last week in June at a meeting in Georgetown where he went to accept the deeds of the proprietors. Afterward he identified the locations for the Capitol and the president's house and showed L'Enfant's preliminary city plan to the proprietors. Washington's diary records the event:

> A Plan was also laid before them of the City in order to convey to them general ideas of the City—but they were told that some deviations from it would take place—particularly in the diagonal Streets or avenues, which would not be so numerous; and in the removal of the presidents house more westerly for the advantage of higher ground—they were also told that a Town house, or exchange wd. be placed on some convenient ground between the spots designed for the public buildgs. before mentioned,—and it was with much pleasure that a general approbation of the measure seemed to pervade the whole.[1]

Three weeks later he wrote of these events to his former aide-de-camp and private secretary, David Humphreys, then serving as minister to Portugal. Washington reported "that all matters between the proprietors . . . and the public are settled to the mutual satisfaction of the parties" and added "that the business of laying out the city, the grounds for public buildings, walks, &c. is progressing under the inspection of Major L'Enfant with pleasing prospects."[2]

The president must also have been encouraged when L'Enfant brought with him to Philadelphia in August a revised and more detailed plan incorporating the changes he had promised the proprietors. In a long memorandum prepared in Georgetown and dated 19 August explaining his thoughts to Washington, L'Enfant described his vision of the new city in words calculated to impress and hearten the president:

> The grand avenue connecting the palace and the Federal House will be magnificent, with the water of the cascade [falling] to the canal which will extend to the Potomac; as also the several squares which are intended for the Judiciary Courts, the National Bank, the grand Church, the play house, markets and exchange, offering a variety of situations unparalleled for beauty, suitable for every purpose, and in every point convenient.

However, L'Enfant then turned to a matter that must have wrinkled the presidential brow. Although L'Enfant felt certain that lots in the city would "command the highest price at a sale," he proceeded to argue at length against selling any land in the city that year. Instead, he advocated that the government first embark on a program of public improvements, including construction of the canal, development of the public grounds between the Capitol and the president's house, "bringing the various squares to their intended shape" and "leveling every grand avenue and principal street."

Only then, L'Enfant asserted, should land be put up for sale, for not until public improvements had been completed or were well under way could the government expect to realize substantial prices. He was convinced that premature auctions would "be confined to a few individual speculators who will not be interested to improve the lots." He thus elaborated on a point he had raised in a memoir he had prepared in June to accompany his preliminary plan. At that time he recommended that improvements

> should be begun at various points equi-distant as possible from the center; not merely because settlements of this sort are likely to diffuse an equality of advantages over the whole territory allotted, and consequently to reflect benefit from an increase of the value of property, but because each of these settlements by a natural jealousy will most tend to stimulate establishments on each of the opposed extremes.[3]

1. George Washington diary entry for Wednesday, 29 June 1791, in "Writings," 27–28. Following the March meeting in Georgetown when Washington and the proprietors reached general agreement on the transfer of the site in trust to him, problems had arisen over the exact form the conveyances should take and the boundaries of the area that would be acquired. These matters caused the president considerable anxiety. News of these difficulties reached him during his trip to the South and are reflected in his letters from Richmond to the commissioners on 13 April 1791 and from Charleston on 7 May 1791. See "Writings," 23–26.

2. George Washington to David Humphreys, 20 July 1791, in Washington, "Writings," 28.

3. For the entire document, see Kite, *L'Enfant and Washington*, 52–58, and for the portion quoted, 54–55.

L'Enfant recognized the urgent need for funds to erect the public buildings and complete other improvements necessary by December 1800 when the city was scheduled to assume its role as the seat of government. He proposed to the president that money could be obtained by "borrowing a sum on the credit of the property itself," estimating that the government would become the owner of "15,000 lots . . . as half of the property left for improvement after deduction is made for streets and . . . public uses."[4]

L'Enfant's proposal and other matters that needed to be resolved caused the president to meet with Jefferson, James Madison, and perhaps others at the end of August. It is conceivable that L'Enfant was there as well. In a note to his secretary of state listing thirteen items that he wished to discuss, Washington began with a question clearly prompted by his planner's proposal: "Will circumstances render a postponement of the Sale of Lots in the Federal City advisable?" He also raised the issue of the necessity and wisdom of borrowing money to finance public improvements.[5]

Political, financial, and legal imperatives caused Washington to overrule L'Enfant. The president and his advisers decided to proceed with lot sales as already advertised by the commissioners for mid-October, and they concluded that borrowing funds was unwise and perhaps illegal. Jefferson and Madison left for Georgetown almost immediately to meet with the commissioners, to review what needed to be done to promote development, and to discuss other matters relating to the federal city.

At that meeting on 8 September Andrew Ellicott proposed a policy to govern land sales. He advocated selling lots only between Georgetown and Hamburg and along the Anacostia, believing that eventual public improvements would not change their value materially. Lots in the vicinity of the two major public buildings, the streets connecting them, and fronting the public gardens should be reserved for later sales when improvements had increased their value.[6]

The following day the commissioners wrote to L'Enfant to provide some details for the map of the city he was arranging to have printed in Philadelphia. They told him to title it "A Map of the City of Washington in the Territory of Columbia" and to number the north-south streets and designate the east-west streets by letters of the alphabet, both systems to begin at the Capitol. They asked him to have "10,000 of the maps struck on the best terms, and as soon as possible," doubtless expecting that at least some copies would be available for display or distribution at the forthcoming sale.[7]

Almost immediately things began to go wrong. L'Enfant chose a recently arrived Frenchman named Pigalle to engrave the map, probably late in August. More than a month later the president's private secretary, Tobias Lear, asked Pigalle about the progress of the work. On 6 October Lear wrote to L'Enfant that Pigalle told him he had been unable to obtain a suitable copper plate until two days before. Pigalle also informed Lear that the map he had to work from was unsatisfactory and that he needed "the large draft" that L'Enfant had taken with him to Georgetown.[8]

At the first sale of lots on 17 October, therefore, the commissioners could not display printed maps to potential purchasers who were thus unable to determine the locations of the lots for which they were expected to bid. Further, as he wrote Lear after the sale, L'Enfant refused to make available for this purpose any of his drawings showing "the general plan" of the city. He claimed that the absence of any such map made it possible for the commissioners to get an "advantageous price . . . for a number of lots" located in parts of the city of no special importance.[9]

When the president learned of this astonishing event, he wrote a long letter to one of the commissioners, expressing "a degree of surprize and concern" over "such perverseness in Major L'Enfant as his late conduct exhibited." He assured the commissioner that "through a direct channel, though not an official one," he had informed L'Enfant that "he must, in future, look to the commissioners for directions." Washington also promised that "when I see Major L'Enfant . . . I shall endeavr. to bring him to some explanation of the terms on which he will serve the public."

4. The skillful manner in which L'Enfant states his case suggests, as Julian Boyd noted, that he received help from an outside source. Boyd believes this may have been Francis Cabot, a recent arrival in Georgetown from Massachusetts. See Boyd's editorial note in Jefferson, *Papers* 20:36 n. 93.

5. According to Boyd in Jefferson, *Papers*, 20:37, this is the only document "Washington is known to have drawn up on matters relating to the capital instead of having Jefferson perform the task." Padover, *Jefferson*, 67–68, provides the complete text. It is fascinating to find the president of the United States concerned with such matters as the desirability of permitting wooden houses in the city, the height to which houses should be built "especially on the principal Streets or Avenues," and whether or not "Stoups, and projections of every sort and kind into the Streets" should "be prohibited *absolutely*."

6. See Jefferson, "Notes on Commissioners' Meeting," in Padover, *Jefferson*, 70–74. The commissioners, Jefferson, and Attorney General Madison also agreed, as Jefferson's notes record, that on the map of the city, "the public squares [are] to be left blank except that for the Capitol and the other for the executive Departments, which are to be considered as appropriated at present, all other particular appropriations of squares to remain till they are respectively wanted."

7. Commissioners to L'Enfant, 9 September 1791, in Padover, *Jefferson*, 74–75.

8. In a letter to Lear from Mount Vernon on 2 October, the president clearly expresses his expectations that the engraved map would be finished shortly thereafter: "How does the engraving of the Federal City advance? Send me some of the first that are struck off and let the others be disposed of as was agreed on" (Washington to Lear, 2 October 1791, in *Writings of George Washington*, 31:381–82). A portion of Lear's letter to L'Enfant is in Kite, *L'Enfant and Washington*, 74–75. On this matter, see also Boyd, "Fixing the Seat of Government," 40–42.

9. L'Enfant's explanation for his behavior is written in his usual convoluted brand of English: "The advantageous price obtained for a number of lots, the less advantage in their local being wholly owing to the care I took to prevent the exhibition of the general plan at the spot where the sale is made must convince that enabling individuals to then compare the situation offered for sale with many others apparently more advantageous would have depreciated the value of those lots that sold the most high" (L'Enfant to Lear, 19 October 1791, in Kite, *L'Enfant and Washington*, 75–78).

Washington also referred to the problem of obtaining an engraved map of the city and the excuses offered by Pigalle for not having one ready in time for the sale:

There has been something very unaccountable in the conduct of the Engraver, yet I cannot be of the opinion the delays were occasioned by L'Enfant. As soon, however, as a correct draught of the City is prepared, the same, or some other person shall be pressed to the execution. I say a *correct* draught, because . . . Mr. Ellicott has given it as his opinion it was lucky that Engravings did not come out from the first plan inasmuch as they would not have been so perfectly exact as to have justified a sale by them.[10]

These incidents—the first recorded acts of his procrastination and intransigence—began a pattern of behavior by L'Enfant that deeply troubled the president, Jefferson, and the commissioners, and which within a few months resulted in his dismissal. It would be needlessly tedious to follow in detail the entire series of events, as they can be reconstructed from surviving documents, the complaints against the commissioners lodged by L'Enfant, their replies and defense, and the appeals to Washington from all parties of this conflict. The documents presented in folio 8 and a brief summary here will suffice.[11]

On 20 November 1791, workmen acting under orders from an absent L'Enfant began demolishing the house of Daniel Carroll of Duddington, a nephew of one of the commissioners. Carroll had started construction of his residence before the site of the city had even been determined, but L'Enfant warned him that because the structure intruded six feet into one of the planned streets it must be removed. Carroll sought a court order to prevent the demolition, but L'Enfant proceeded to pull down the house before a judge had time to act.

That precipitous and imprudent act set off a flurry of protests, threatened court action, charges and countercharges, and letters of explanation, justification, and admonishment. The statements of the president at this time reveal a chief executive almost obsessively reluctant to dispense with the services of a person whose skills he admired and valued but gradually coming to realize that in L'Enfant he dealt with a proud, vain, ambitious, and temperamental artist who could not be made to understand that the commissioners were his superiors.

Nor could L'Enfant seem to understand that the severe budget difficulties facing the commissioners made impractical the policy he insisted on of creating many centers of development simultaneously. Only the proprietors favored such a course of action. Eager to benefit financially from the very beginning, they all wanted capital improvements made on or near their land immediately instead of waiting until the city grew outward from the immediate vicinity of the two major buildings with which the president and the commissioners were most concerned.[12]

Further acts of insubordination followed, each justified by L'Enfant as being taken for the good of the future city but seen by the commissioners as steps that were either unwarranted or unwise. Equally distressing to the president and Jefferson were repeated failures by L'Enfant to make any progress whatsoever in arranging for a printed map of the city. They also expected him to prepare designs for some of the public buildings, but in this, too, they experienced nothing but disappointments.

Relations between L'Enfant and the commissioners worsened. The president realized that more than good personal relations were at stake. Many persons in New York, Philadelphia, and elsewhere in the East strongly opposed locating the capital on the Potomac. News about difficulties and controversies over how best to plan and develop the new city would support their attempts to overturn the decision that placed the seat of government in the South.[13]

Conciliatory—almost pleading letters—to Carroll, the commissioners, and

10. Washington to David Stuart, 20 November 1791, in Washington, "Writings," 32–33. This statement clearly indicates that L'Enfant had prepared at least two versions of his revised plan. The manuscript that has survived may not have been the most recent.

11. The works previously cited by Boyd, Kite, and Padover provide the text of relevant documents. Boyd finds little to admire in L'Enfant's conduct, although he concedes that Washington did not make it clear to L'Enfant at the beginning of his assignment that he was to be subordinate to the commissioners. Kite champions L'Enfant and casts the commissioners and Jefferson in the roles of villains. Washington is seen by Boyd as too reluctant to fix the blame on L'Enfant for his actions and too ready to excuse his conduct. Kite describes Washington as understanding of and sympathetic toward L'Enfant but finally persuaded by Jefferson to dismiss him.

12. It was probably L'Enfant's policy of simultaneous development at many locations rather than the design features of his plan that earned him the support of the proprietors. After L'Enfant had been fired, the proprietors attempted to get him reinstated. On 9 March, thirteen of the fifteen landowners in the site sent L'Enfant a letter of tribute stating that they hoped "some mode of accommodation may be devised, to admit of your return." That letter accompanied a petition asking for him to be continued as city planner. George Walker, one of the proprietors, presented it to the president after writing Jefferson a letter stating that "This dismission of Major L'Enfant has given great alarm to the Proprietors . . . and am afraid the affairs of the City will come into public investigation if means cannot be adopted by which Major L'Enfant may be yet continued." See the text of these and later communications and Washington's and Jefferson's explanations to the proprietors about this matter in Kite, *L'Enfant and Washington*, 167–81.

13. Opposition in the North and East to the Potomac location for the capital was widespread. One early criticism appeared in a Hartford, Connecticut, newspaper in a letter advancing arguments against the site that many others repeated: "Extract of a letter from a gentleman to his friend in this town, dated March 27, 1791. Before you receive this, you will see an account that Mr. Elicott and Maj. L'Enfant are laying out the federal town and a plan of the public buildings on the Potowmac. To a man acquainted, as you are, with the world, there cannot be a more laughable truth, than a serious intention of building a Federal Town as it is called; that is, a town for the residence of Congress. . . . But if Congress are in session but a small part of the year, their expences will not support this great town. Will trade or manufactures support this huge town? If they will not, agriculture certainly will not. The very growth and being then of this town will depend on commerce or manufactures; for I deny that any other human means will make and maintain a large town. . . . But otherwise neither grants of money, nor acts of congress will have the least effect. We may expend ten millions of money in erecting accommodations for people, but if the place is not naturally designed for business, people will not live there" (*Hartford Courant*, 11 April 1791, p. 3).

L'Enfant having failed, Washington made a final effort to persuade L'Enfant to accept the primacy of the commissioners. He sent Tobias Lear to see L'Enfant, but the planner turned him away brusquely, stating that he had heard enough of the subject.

The president, having endured much already, regarded this as a personal insult and resolved to end the matter. The mezzotint portrait by Edward Savage reproduced in folio 8 suggests both how important Washington regarded the city plan and his determination to assert his authority even if it meant taking the drastic step of discharging its designer.[14]

On 27 February 1792 Jefferson wrote to L'Enfant, stating that he was doing so as instructed by the president and informing him that "notwithstanding the desire he has entertained to preserve your agency in the business, the condition upon which it is to be done is inadmissible & your services must be at an end." Thus, after not quite a year from his appearance on the site, L'Enfant found himself removed from all further responsibilities for the planning and development of the city he had designed.

More than two months earlier, on 13 December 1791, Washington had sent a copy of the L'Enfant plan to Congress, stating that he was placing before the members of the House and Senate "the plan of a City that has been laid out within the District of ten miles square which was fixed upon for the permanent seat of the Government of the United States." Since no printed version of the city plan yet existed, the president used for this purpose the drawing that L'Enfant presented to the president in August or another and possibly somewhat altered later version.

Efforts to obtain a printed map continued, but these encountered many frustrations and delays. Those most concerned with the project knew how valuable printed copies would be in advertising the city at home and abroad, providing evidence to skeptics that real progress was being made in developing the new capital, and, of course, for display and distribution at future land sales. The documents in folio 9 provide some of the details, and the accompanying illustration shows the first separately issued version (i.e., not a book or journal plate) to be published.

This plan of the city, engraved in Boston by Samuel Hill and printed in Philadelphia by Robert Scott, became available by the time the commissioners held the second sale of lots in Washington on 8 October 1792. A little more than a month later two Philadelphia engravers, James Thackara and John Vallance, delivered the first copies of a substantially larger and much more striking plan of the city. It is this Thackara and Vallance version that came to be regarded as the authoritative record of the government's intentions for the capital city.[15]

Folio 10 contains an illustration of this engraving and a series of documents relating to changes made in the earliest as well as in the revised plans prepared by L'Enfant. Andrew Ellicott made some of these changes—perhaps most of them. Ellicott succeeded L'Enfant, and his surveys of street lines and boundaries of squares and other public reservations had to be reconciled with the more generalized and less precise locations of features in the city as L'Enfant designed and sketched them.

Jefferson, too, evidently altered certain features. On the L'Enfant manuscript the identification in pencil of the "President's House" is in his hand. Probably his notation replaced the word *palace* that L'Enfant invariably used in referring to this building. Presumably the president approved or acquiesced in most of the changes, although for reasons that remain unknown Ellicott and Jefferson ignored his suggestion that L'Enfant's name be added to the map.

Because the Thackara and Vallance engraving contains only Ellicott's name, it is usually referred to as the Ellicott plan. Further, since it was Ellicott who appears to have been in closest contact with the engravers, it will be consistent to discuss the changes as if he alone were responsible. Nevertheless, it is just as likely that Jefferson played an equally influential role in making these modifications, and it seems highly unlikely that Ellicott would have modified L'Enfant's plan in any substantial manner without Jefferson's knowledge.

Ellicott changed L'Enfant's design in many ways, the most obvious being the alignment of Massachusetts Avenue. Ellicott straightened this very long thoroughfare at its eastern end and had it terminate at a much larger reservation on the Anacostia somewhat north of the equivalent open space shown on L'Enfant's manuscript. He also eliminated five short radial avenues that appear on the L'Enfant plan, while adding two short radials southeast and southwest of Capitol Hill.

In a more important change, Ellicott removed twelve of L'Enfant's proposed

14. The role of Edward Savage (1761–1817) in creating the image and the print in folio 8 is described in the caption to that illustration. Further information about his career can be found in Naeve, "'The Best likeness'"; in "Edward Savage"; and in the notes to entry 202 in Fowble, *Two Centuries of Prints*.

15. James Thackara (1767–1848) and John Vallance (1770–1823), who engraved and printed the Ellicott plan of Washington, began their partnership in 1790 in Philadelphia, where Thackara served an apprenticeship under Robert Scott, an English engraver and watchmaker, and James Trenchard, the editor-publisher of the *Columbian Magazine*. Thackara and Vallance, a native of Glasgow who came to America in 1771, each produced their first engravings for that journal in 1786. As partners, they and other engravers began preparing the hundreds of plates used in the encyclopedia of twenty-one volumes published by Thomas Dobson, a project not completed until 1803. The pressure of this work may explain why they took so long to finish the Washington engraving. They may also have delayed the project in order to prepare the much smaller version of the plan that the *Columbian Magazine* published in March 1792. Both men joined with other artists in founding the Association of Artists in America in 1794. Although short-lived, this organization later led to the creation of the Pennsylvania Academy of the Fine Arts, of which Thackara served as curator from 1816 to 1828 and whose treasurer in 1816 was Vallance. Thackara also operated a Philadelphia bookshop, was assistant clerk and later clerk of the Pennsylvania House of Representatives, and was commissioner for the building of the Eastern State Penitentiary from 1821 to 1833. See Crompton, "Thackara."

civic squares. Ellicott added only one space of this type, a small circle east of the Capitol corresponding to one he eliminated farther east on this same street. Many alterations in the size and shape of squares and public building sites can also be noted. It would be tiresome and unnecessary to examine all of these, but, to take only one example, a comparison of the site for the Capitol shows that Ellicott enlarged the north-south dimension and introduced a curved eastern boundary, among other changes in its outline.[16]

L'Enfant provided a detailed legend that identified specific uses for many squares and public building sites. Ellicott showed the location only for the Capitol and the president's house. Indeed, it was not until 2 March 1797—only two days before the end of his administration—that George Washington issued a proclamation designating the exact boundaries of the seventeen sites reserved for the federal government under the provisions of the trust created when in the summer of 1791 the proprietors conveyed their land so that the new city could be planned.[17]

L'Enfant claimed that his design had been completely ruined by the many changes that Ellicott made. One can understand his anger without necessarily agreeing with him. Certainly the elimination of so many of his squares constituted a major modification, but the large number still remaining provided the city with an ample supply of locations for public buildings, statues, fountains, gardens, and other attractive features.

Perhaps L'Enfant referred to a more fundamental matter. One scholarly study suggests that L'Enfant did not design the radial avenues to run precisely straight for great distances but instead offset them slightly at each civic square along their course. Projections of the center lines of some avenues on his manuscript do show slight but perceptible changes in direction at intervening open squares, a discrepancy previously attributed to hasty or careless drafting.[18]

According to this study, however, L'Enfant understood that a visual axis such as that from the Capitol to the White House is far too long to be fully effective. The much shorter distances from square to square would have been more in keeping with such axial relationships found in many European cities. Moreover, filtered photographs of the manuscript show that L'Enfant may have intended that squares be entered via gates cut through buildings whose upper stories would connect with those lining the sides of each square to form a completely enclosed space. This theory is supported by a curious provision of the original building regulations:

> The way into the squares being designed in a special manner for the common use and convenience of the occupiers of the respective squares . . . the proprietors of the Lots adjoining the entrance into the squares, on arching over the entrance, and fixing gates in the manner the Commissioners shall approve, shall be intitled [sic] to divide the space over the arching and build it up with the range of that line of the square.[19]

Whatever the truth of this matter, it was the Ellicott plan that governed the development of the city in its initial years. Surveyed street lines and the boundaries of public building sites and civic squares generally followed the outlines of this engraving. On this two-dimensional base the new city gradually took form as lot owners began to erect buildings. The two most important federal structures provided accommodations for the Congress and the president. Around them clustered many of the first private structures of the city.

The president, his secretary of state, and the commissioners all expected that L'Enfant would design the Capitol and the president's house. When Jefferson, as requested by L'Enfant, sent several European city plans from his collection, he ended his letter with this passage:

> Whenever it is proposed to prepare plans for the Capitol, I should prefer the adoption of some one of the models of antiquity, which have had the approbation of thousands of years, and for the president's House I should prefer the celebrated fronts of modern buildings, which have already received the approbation of all good judges. Such are the Galerie du Louvre, the Gardes meubles, and two fronts of the Hotel de Salm. But of this it is yet time enough to consider.[20]

Washington undoubtedly spoke to L'Enfant about this matter and apparently assured him that in addition to planning the city, he would also serve as the architect for the two chief buildings. In writing to L'Enfant the day after Jefferson discharged him, the president first taxed him for the delays he had caused in failing to arrange for an engraving of the city plan and then blamed him for his similar delinquency in carrying out his architectural assignments: "In like man-

16. This change, like some others, precipitated a legal battle with Samuel Davidson, the owner of some of the land adjoining the square. See Tindall, *History of Washington*, 217.

17. The text of the proclamation can be found in Washington, "Writings," 190–95. Possibly the president waited until the eve of his departure to issue this to postpone payment to the landowners for the 541 acres that the trustees then conveyed to the federal government. The proclamation refers to an attached map, a survey recently completed by James R. Dermott. For some reason the map did not accompany the proclamation, and more than a year later President Adams needed to re-issue the proclamation with the map attached. Since this was prepared specifically to govern the conveyance of land, the proprietors naturally looked carefully at the shape and size of all public reservations as well as at the other open spaces at many intersections of grid and radial thoroughfares. Controversy arose when the proprietors contended the commissioners had cut back on the angles at these intersections, thus—in effect—creating several new, smaller squares, for which, under the terms of the original land agreement, the government was not required to make payment, while reducing the abutting lots.

18. For complete details of this theory of the origins and intentions of the L'Enfant plan, see Jennings, "Artistry as Design."

19. "Terms and Conditions declared by the President of the United States, this seventeenth day of October, seventeen hundred and ninety-one, for regulating the Materials and Manner of the Buildings and Improvements on the Lots in the City of Washington," paragraph 6 in the text of the broadside quoted in Phillips, *Beginnings of Washington*, 33–37.

20. Jefferson to L'Enfant, 10 April 1791, in Padover, *Jefferson*, 59.

ner five months have elapsed and are lost, by the compliment which was intended to be paid you in depending *alone* upon your plans for the public buildings instead of advertising a premium to the person who should present the best."[21]

On 1 March, Jefferson wrote informally to Commissioner Daniel Carroll to tell him that L'Enfant had been discharged and that the commissioners would now need "to advertise for plans of the buildings." Five days later Jefferson sent a formal communication from Philadelphia to the commissioners, enclosing the text of advertisements announcing a competition for designs of the Capitol and the president's house. "Both of them," he added, "are subject to your pleasure" and when returned will "be advertised here and elsewhere."[22]

At a meeting on 14 March 1792 the commissioners resolved to place advertisements in newspapers of "the principal towns in the United States," announcing a competition for the design of the president's house. The winner, at his choice, would receive $500 "or a medal of that value." Designs were to be received by 14 July and were to consist of "ground plats, elevations of each front and sections through the building in such directions as may be necessary to explain the internal structure."

Conscious of the need for economy, the commissioners included a statement favoring a design that could be implemented in stages. "It will be a recommendation of any plan," they wrote, "if the Central part of it may be detached and erected for the present with the appearance of a complete whole and be capable of admitting the additional parts in future if they shall be wanting."[23]

The commissioners also used essentially the same procedure for selecting a design for the Capitol. They recognized the greater complexity of this assignment by announcing that the award to the winning entry, in addition to $500 or a medal of like value, would include a lot in the new city "designated by impartial judges." The advertisement repeated preference for a building that could be built in stages and imposed the same requirements for the drawings that competitors were to submit. As to the special requirements of the building itself, the advertisement was brief but specific:

> The building to be of brick, and to contain the following apartments to wit: a conference-room and a room for the Representatives, sufficient to accommodate three hundred persons each; a lobby or ante-room to the latter; a Senate room of twelve hundred square feet area; an ante-chamber; twelve rooms of six hundred square feet each for Committee rooms and clerks' offices.[24]

The commissioners received a number of submissions for the president's house, including one by Jefferson himself signed only "A.Z." It closely resembled one of the "modern" buildings that Jefferson so admired: the handsome sixteenth-century Villa Capra (usually referred to as the Villa Rotonda) by Andrea Palladio. It was, however, another Palladian design that the commissioners ultimately selected, the work of Irish-trained James Hoban, then practicing architecture in Charleston.[25]

Before submitting his design, Hoban journeyed north to inspect the site, arriving in the city of Washington with a letter of introduction from the president himself. Washington explained that several Charlestonians had recommended Hoban to him during his Southern trip the previous spring. The president carefully explained that he had no personal "knowledge of the man or his talents, further than the information which I received from the Gentlemen in Carolina."[26]

Nevertheless, such an introduction could scarcely fail to help the thirty-year-old Hoban. Whether presidential influence aided his cause or not, the commissioners declared Hoban's design the winner and retained the young architect to refine his plans and supervise the construction of the building. It was a competently designed structure that closely resembled Leinster House in Dublin, although Hoban may have used for his model an engraving in James Gibbs's *Book of Architecture*, one of the many eighteenth-century volumes illustrating executed or proposed buildings.[27]

The first of the two illustrations in folio II shows this building from the north,

21. Washington to L'Enfant, 28 February 1792, in Washington, "Writings," 46. On 1 March, Jefferson wrote about L'Enfant's dismissal to George Walker, one of the principal proprietors, stating that "measures will be taken to procure plans for the public buildings, in which business five months have been lost in a dependance on Majr. Lenfant, who has made no preparations of that kind" (Padover, *Jefferson*, 101). However, if L'Enfant is to be believed, he had at least prepared preliminary drawings of these structures. In a memorial to Congress on 7 December 1800, L'Enfant referred to "Sketches . . . of the Intended Edifices and . . . for the *aqueducs*, the *bridges*, the grand *dock* and *Canal &c.*" as among those taken without his permission when someone removed a trunk and other materials from his quarters ("L'Enfant Memorials," 102). An affidavit in February 1803 places the theft at the end of December 1791 when persons employed by the commissioners seized L'Enfant's "papers, drawings, manuscripts, directions, everything relative to the projected work of the city at the time in the hands of the surveyors." This material included "a trunk and several boxes containing books . . . ,

other plans of this deponent's own drawings for the Capitol and the President['s] houses, these and all matters which he had in reserve such as preparatory designs for the city canal, for bridges, market-houses, the great walk and gardens and number of other sketches of projects for enterprise." See Exhibit T 1, pp. 139–41, in James Dudley Morgan, "Maj. Pierre Charles L'Enfant."

22. Jefferson to Daniel Carroll, 1 March 1792; Jefferson to Messrs. Johnson, Carroll, and Stewart, 6 March 1792, in Padover, *Jefferson*, 102–4. The second letter indicates that the advertisement had been considered earlier, since Jefferson mentions that the "sketch of an advertisement for the plan of a Capitol" had been sent to the president by Commissioner Thomas Johnson and was being "returned with some alterations." Jefferson's drafts of the advertisements can be found in Padover, *Jefferson*, 106, 119–20.

23. There is a reproduction of the page of the manuscript record book of the commissioners containing this resolution opposite p. 3 of Jensen, *The White House*.

24. As quoted in Hazelton, *National Capitol*, 14.
25. The designs submitted in the competition are reproduced, with biographical sketches of their authors and much other useful information, in Butler, *Competition 1792*.

26. Washington to Commissioners, 8 June 1792, in Washington, "Writings," 55–56.
27. An engraving of Leinster House and the Gibbs plate are both reproduced in Jensen, *The White House*, 8.

half a dozen years after President and Mrs. Adams took up residence there in December 1800. It was far from complete at that time. Abigail Adams complained that "not one room or chamber is finished of the whole." There was no drying yard, and the First Lady hung the presidential laundry in one of the reception rooms. Many early visitors to the city were also disappointed or shocked by the appearance of the building and its grounds, feelings represented by those quoted in folio II.[28]

The second engraving by William Strickland from a drawing by George Munger depicts the remains of the building following its destruction after British troops set it on fire in 1814. Its fire-blackened walls remained, but the roof and the interior were gutted. Reconstruction required nearly three years, but most of the work was finished when President James Monroe arrived in March 1817.[29]

The white paint used to conceal the smoke stains on its walls led most people to refer to the building as the White House. However, a Baltimore newspaper first applied this title to the light-colored stone building in 1810 to distinguish it from the majority of buildings of Washington that were built of brick.[30]

Selecting a design for the Capitol proved more troublesome. Both the president and the secretary of state anxiously awaited submissions, but when, on 9 July 1792, the president wrote to Commissioner David Stuart about his forthcoming trip to Georgetown, a disappointed Washington expressed his concern about the designs he had seen: "I shall bring with me, or send on if I am likely to be delayed, the plans for the public buildings which were sent, I believe by the commissioners, to Mr. Jefferson; but if none more elegant than these should appear on or before the 10th, instant, the exhibition of architecture will be a very dull one indeed."[31]

Evidently Washington's forebodings were justified, for none of the sixteen designs submitted for the Capitol met his approval, and Jefferson and the commissioners were likewise disappointed with what they saw. Nevertheless, they encouraged one of the competitors, Etienne Sulpice Hallette, to continue work on a modification of his design. Stephen Hallet (as he Americanized his name) had come to Philadelphia from France just before the French Revolution. He seems to

have been no more than a competent draftsman, and his design for the Capitol—although apparently the best of a bad lot—excited no one.[32]

William Thornton, a Scottish-born physician who had received his training at Edinburgh University and who was then residing in Philadelphia, asked permission to submit a design even though the deadline had expired. He had read with interest about the competition but, having no theoretical or practical experience in architecture, needed time to study the subject. After some months consulting books in the Philadelphia library, he began work on a design that he brought to the attention of Washington and Jefferson.[33]

On the last day of January 1793 the president sent an enthusiastic letter about Thornton's design to the commissioners: "The grandeur, simplicity, and beauty of the exterior; the propriety with which the apartments are distributed, and economy in the whole mass of the structure, will I doubt not give it a preference in your eyes, as it has done in mine and those of several others whom I have consulted, and who are deemed men of skill in architecture."[34]

Thornton's plan for a central rotunda modeled after the pantheon in Rome and flanked by wings for the two legislative bodies also met with the approval of the president's more architecturally sophisticated and knowledgeable secretary of state, and Jefferson's added endorsement was thus joined with Washington's strong approval. It is hardly surprising to learn that the commissioners unanimously endorsed Thornton's design.[35]

However, both they and the president felt that they had incurred some obligation to Hallet. Their solution produced an awkward, and in the end unworkable, arrangement. Since Thornton knew little about practical building, the commissioners directed James Hoban to supervise the project although he had little time from his duties at the White House. They also assigned Hallet to estimate the costs of construction and to serve as both draftsman and assistant supervisor.

Hallet, piqued at what he regarded as an injustice in substituting Thornton's

28. This view of the north facade of the White House may have been sketched by Charles Janson, the author of the book on whose title page this aquatint appeared. However, the other illustrations in Janson's book were appropriated without attribution from the larger engraved views of Philadelphia drawn, engraved, and published in 1800 by William Birch. It is quite likely, therefore, that Janson took his image of the White House from some as yet unidentified source.

29. The artist of this White House view, George Munger (1781–1825), was a native of Connecticut who in his later life practiced as an artist in New Haven. Although William Strickland

(1788–1854) is far better known for such architectural designs as the Second Bank of the United States in Philadelphia and the Tennessee state capitol in Nashville, in his earlier years he made a living as a painter and engraver after spending a two-year apprenticeship to Benjamin H. Latrobe beginning in 1803. Strickland's life and work are the subject of Gilchrist, *Strickland*.

30. The definitive history of the White House is the two-volume work by William Seale, *The President's House*. See also Jensen, *The White House*.

31. Washington to David Stuart, 9 July 1792, in Washington, "Writings," 57.

32. Reproductions of Hallet's design and those

of some others can be found in Junior League of Washington, *City of Washington*, 66–68. See also the plates following p. 156 in Padover, *Jefferson*. The most detailed study of the building is Brown, *History of the United States Capitol*. This includes reproductions of dozens of architectural plans, elevations, and sections that trace its original construction and subsequent changes through the end of the nineteenth century.

33. Thornton recalled on 12 October 1802, nearly a decade after he provided the accepted design, "The president and secretary of state published a premium of a gold medal or $500 and a lot for a house in the city of Washington for the best plan and elevation of a capitol of the United States. I lamented not having studied architecture, and resolved to attempt the grand undertaking and study at the same time. I studied some

months and worked almost night and day, but I found I was opposed by regular architects from France and various other countries." Statement by Thornton quoted in Clark, "Doctor and Mrs. William Thornton," 176.

34. Washington to Commissioners, 31 January 1793. The following day he wrote privately to Commissioner David Stuart and repeated his assessment of Thornton's plan for the Capitol: "Doctor Thornton's plan for the Capitol is so much superior to any I have seen, that I have no hesitation in giving it a decided preferrence [sic]" (Washington, "Writings," 70, 72).

35. Jefferson wrote Commissioner Daniel Carroll that he found Thornton's "plan of a capitol" to be "simple, noble, beautiful, excellently distributed, and moderate in size" (Padover, *Jefferson*, 171).

design for his and in a position to further his own ends, immediately began to change Thornton's plans. Some of these modifications merely reflected Hallet's different taste, while others addressed more fundamental issues of how Thornton's impractical interior floor plan could be modified without destroying the attractive facade.

This muddle of lines of authority inevitably led to confusion and conflicts, but a conference in Philadelphia of all parties helped to resolve the immediate issues and made it possible to begin work on the foundations of the Capitol. On 18 September 1793, in a Masonic ceremony, President Washington laid the cornerstone for the building, after which the party of participants and spectators "retired to an extensive booth, where an ox of 500 lbs. was barbacued [sic], of which the company generally partook."[36]

Nevertheless, quarrels between the architects, lack of adequate funds, and a shortage of skilled members of the construction trades hindered progress. Given the difficulties facing the commissioners and their subordinates, it seems remarkable that anything got built. What the members of Congress found when they arrived to take up their legislative duties in December 1800 was a more or less complete Senate wing on the north, some foundations and walls begun for the House wing, and very little in between.

The first illustration in folio 12 depicts the next stage of the Capitol with the southern or House wing completed. William Russell Birch drew and engraved this image for the title page of a book Birch published in 1808. When President Jefferson appointed Benjamin Henry Latrobe as architectural supervisor for the federal city, work began on a wooden link between the two stone wings. It was this building of two stone wings connected by a wooden arcade that British troops burned in 1814, leaving the structure as shown in the second illustration of the folio, an engraving by William Strickland from a drawing by George Munger.[37]

The documents excerpted in folios 11 and 12 provide another way of seeing the White House and the Capitol through the eyes of early residents and visitors. As today, these two buildings then attracted the curious and the admiring. At this earlier time, the critical and the skeptical also came to view and judge their appearance. Whatever their conclusions, everyone felt compelled to write about their impressions and reactions. Their words enrich the engraved images of the period and give them added meaning, just as the illustrations help us today to recapture the initial excitement of the first-time spectator on a visit to the American capital.

Others looked at Washington as a splendid opportunity for speculation in land, and it was not long after the publication of the Hill and Ellicott engravings that the commissioners began to receive inquiries about lot purchases in wholesale quantities. Several of these came by way of contacts made through the president or the secretary of state. On 20 August 1793, for example, the president wrote to the commissioners a letter of introduction to the bearer, James Greenleaf. Washington explained his interest:

> This Gentlemen . . . has it in contemplation to make certain proposals to you for building a number of houses . . . provided he can have lots upon such terms & conditions as may correspond with his interest in the undertaking while it tends, at the same time, to promote the great object of the City.—I am pursuaded, Gentlemen, that you will listen with attention and weigh with candour any proposals that may promise to promote the growth of the City.[38]

Washington and the commissioners, of course, shared a common concern about problems in raising funds for constructing the buildings, making streets, building bridges, and completing all the other public improvements needed to assure the success of the city by having everything in readiness for the transfer of the seat of government at the end of 1800. The first individual sales of lots having failed to produce any significant amount of revenue, they were receptive to proposals for transfers of land in much larger quantities.

Thirty-year-old James Kent, later the chief justice of the New York Supreme Court and chancellor of New York, recorded some of the details of the most important of these speculative transactions:

> In September 1793 the wealthy and enterprising James Greenleaf purchased 3000 lots of ground at [£]25 Maryland currency and this gave a sudden and amazing spring to the importance of the city. In Dec. 1793 Mr. Greenleaf associated Robert Morris and John Nicholson of Philadelphia both men of large capital and fertile minds with him in his speculations and purchased for Mr. Morris 3000 lots in the city at [£]34 M.C. a lot. The purchasers are bound to erect yearly a small number of houses on each 3rd lot for 7 years. Here then are 6000 lots owned by this powerful company & great and immediate improvements are in contemplation.[39]

36. From a report in the Boston *Columbian Centinel* for 5 October 1793, as quoted in Hazelton, *National Capitol*, 22–24. Although the account lists "James Hoban and Stephen Hallette, architects" as among the dignitaries in the procession, Thornton apparently was absent.

37. William Birch (1755–1834) came to America from England in 1794 at the age of thirty-nine. In Philadelphia he executed many miniature enamel paintings before publishing an elaborate twenty-eight-plate set of engraved views of Philadelphia in 1800. The much smaller view of the Capitol appeared on the title page of a far more modest publication that Birch issued in 1808 from his home near Bristol, Pennsylvania. See Snyder, "William Birch."

38. Washington to Commissioners, 20 August 1793, in Washington, "Writings," 87.

39. Statement by James Kent in 1793, as quoted from an unidentified source in Junior League of Washington, *City of Washington*, 70. The terms of the agreement between Greenleaf and the commissioners required payment for the lots in seven annual installments and the construction of ten houses each year during that period. The commissioners were to obtain loans of $2,200 each month until they had finished the public buildings.

A year and a half later the president seemed to have changed his mind about the wisdom of such transactions. He wrote to Daniel Carroll that although he had "yielded my assent to Mr. Greenleaf's first proposition," he had been opposed to a later transaction that doubled the number of lots purchased on credit. Now, he pointed out, "the persons to whom you have sold are reselling to others [at] an immense profit." Why, the president asked, "are not the commissioners as competent to make bargains" selling lots directly?[40]

By mid-1795, after Greenleaf had disposed of his interest to Robert Morris and John Nicholson, an increasingly worried Washington directed Edmund Randolph, then secretary of state, to "call upon Messrs. Morris & Nicholson . . . and in earnest & strong terms represent to them, the serious consequences which must inevitably result to the public buildings in the federal City, if the deficiency, or part thereof, due on their contract is not paid."[41]

A year later, the president recorded his feelings on the continued failure of the speculators to make good on their debt. Writing from Mount Vernon to the commissioners, Washington complained that "the continual disappointments of Messrs. Morris & Nicholson are really painful." Then, referring to repeatedly broken promises by the speculators, he added mournfully: "One would hope that their assurances were not calculated for delay and yet they seem to admit of hardly any other interpretation."[42]

Although some houses and other buildings resulted from the venture begun by Greenleaf, by 1797 Morris and Nicholson declared their enterprise bankrupt. Some buildings begun by them stood only half built, and the failure of this syndicate that had controlled one-third of the available lots discouraged others from investing in Washington real estate. As a result, the enormous city contained very few buildings.[43]

The commissioners reported that on 15 May 1800 the city consisted of 109 brick houses and 263 of wood. By mid-November of the following year 84 brick and 151 wooden houses had been added to the total, with another 79 brick houses and 35 wooden houses under construction. In 1800 the population of the new city was only 3,210. Georgetown's population then stood at 2,993, while Alexandria could boast of 4,971 residents. Another 1,941 lived elsewhere in the district but outside the boundaries of the three cities.[44]

While the commissioners were engaged in their transaction with Greenleaf, one of the most energetic of the proprietors, George Walker, temporarily shifted his efforts to promote the city to England, where in the spring of 1793 he issued the broadside reproduced in folio 13. In composing its text he borrowed without attribution paragraph after paragraph of a description of the city plan that a Baltimore newspaper had published a year and a half earlier. Walker added only a few passages of his own to this highly laudatory account of the new city.

At the same time the president's private secretary, Tobias Lear, writing anonymously, issued a little book, *Observations on the River Potomack*, portions of which are quoted in folio 13. Undoubtedly this publication had Washington's blessing, and he may well have instigated this project in the belief that it would help to stimulate interest in the capital. The commissioners could thus expect to benefit through increased land sales and at higher prices, and the notion that the city was not only new but permanent would become more firmly fixed in the American mind.

Washington himself knew a thing or two about land development and sales from his early years as a surveyor and in helping to manage the great domain of Lord Fairfax that occupied an enormous area of colonial Virginia. Now as president he tried to use that knowledge in promoting the city that bore his name—not out of any thought of personal gain, but in the conviction that this new and extravagantly designed city must succeed as a symbol of the national unity that he had done so much to achieve.

An earnest desire to create a city, however, did not necessarily guarantee success—or even more than minimum progress toward that goal in the early years of the nascent capital. Virtually all of the visitors to the site in the first decade of development commented on how little evidence of substantial city growth they had encountered. The accounts excerpted in folios 14 and 15 are, in this respect, typical of many other reactions by visitors or new residents.

In quite a different manner than L'Enfant advocated, the concept of a city growing outward from several points of initial development was being realized. However, instead of each node being created by a planned program of public works and improvements that would stimulate private development in the vicinity, the government concentrated its limited resources only on two widely separated sites: the Capitol and the White House; and around them, private builders erected some of the city's first dwellings, lodging houses, and shops.

Elsewhere, however, unguided by any systematic program of public investment, speculative landowners put up buildings anywhere purchasers might wish to buy or rent. The result was what Isaac Weld noted in 1796: houses so scattered that "a spectator can scarcely perceive any thing like a town." It was a pattern that was to persist for many decades, and echoes of Weld's comment reverberate down the corridors of time during the first half of the nineteenth century.

The two illustrations in folios 14 and 15 reinforce the impressions one gets from reading the accounts of the period. Both come from the pen of an English-trained artist of considerable ability, George Isham Parkyns. Born in Nottingham about

40. Washington to Daniel Carroll, 7 January 1795, in Washington, "Writings," 113–14.

41. Washington to Edmund Randolph, 22 July 1795, in Washington, "Writings," 137.

42. Washington to the Commissioners, 1 July 1796, in Washington, "Writings," 162.

43. For an extended account of this early speculative enterprise, see Clark, *Greenleaf and Law*.

44. Commissioners' report cited in Hazelton, *National Capitol*, 25; U.S. Census population reports for the Second Census.

1850, Parkyns began exhibiting landscape engravings and paintings as early as 1772 and began work on the plates for *Monastic Remains and Ancient Castles in Great Britain*, a publication he completed in 1820 long after he returned to England in 1800. About 1793 he came to the United States, later traveling to Canada where he produced four views of Halifax.[45]

Shortly after his arrival in this country he and his associate, a New York publisher named James Harrison, announced their intention to publish a series of twenty-four folio-size prints of American landscape scenes. They planned to execute each print in aquatint, a process that, when skillfully done and hand colored, could produce superb results. Harrison and Parkyns promised prospective subscribers that the views would be "selected from some of the most striking and interesting prospects in the United States," and each view was to be "accompanied with a descriptive account of its Local, Historical, and other incidental Peculiarities."

The artist and the publisher specified the conditions under which this series would appear:

I. That the work shall be published by Subscription: and that each Subscriber shall engage to take the whole set of Views, and pay for each engraving, if black or brown, 3 dollars; and if coloured, 5 dollars.

II. That the dimensions of each engraving shall be 24 by 17 inches . . . and published upon paper of a superior quality. The publication to commence immediately and one engraving to be delivered to the Subscribers, on the first Monday of each succeeding month. . . .

III. That with the last View of the series, shall be delivered an engraved Title Page; an elegant characteristic Vignette; a Map of the Route, connected with the prospects exhibited in the course of the work; and an Alphabetical List of the Subscribers.[46]

Although Harrison and Parkyns exhibited some of the drawings for this projected series in New York and evidently made other efforts to attract subscribers, they apparently failed to secure enough subscribers to undertake such an ambitious publishing venture. In addition to the view of Washington reproduced in folio 14, the only other prints from this projected series show Annapolis and Mount Vernon.[47]

To draw the scene depicted in the large print dated 1795, Parkyns stood just beyond a fork in the road leading northwest to the heights above Georgetown. From that vantage point the artist could look toward the Potomac River and see Analostan (now Roosevelt) Island and beyond to the mouth of the Anacostia. Although Parkyns appears to have exaggerated the heights of the wooded hills in his view, he did not show any nonexistent buildings.

Indeed, only if one looks very carefully can one find a suggestion that this attractive landscape contains any structures whatsoever. They appear just to the left of center on the far bank of the Potomac, and the artist probably intended them to represent the waterfront of Georgetown. This scene reminds us that in 1795 little visible evidence existed of the elaborate city that would soon begin to take form as the period of preparation and planning gave way to construction of the first public buildings.

Parkyns also drew Washington in 1800, a view used in one of the volumes of John Marshall's *Life of George Washington*, published in 1804. Reproduced in folio 15 with several accounts of the city's appearance as recorded by visitors of the period, this view also documents how few buildings could be seen and how sylvan the site remained as the first decade of the capital city's existence came to a close.

The impressions of the city in folio 15 left by three visiting Englishmen— Thomas Twining, Isaac Weld, and Francis Baily—all emphasize the slow pace of city building that so many observers noted during the early years of Washington's development. All three were struck by the wooded condition of the site and the few structures that existed. This characteristic of Washington was slow to change, as demonstrated by the maps, views, and descriptions of the city presented in the two chapters to follow.

45. Aside from brief entries in biographical dictionaries of artists and engravers, little seems to have been written about Parkyns. See Mc-Peck, "George Isham Parkyns," and Fergusson, "George Isham Parkyns." Reproductions of two of his Halifax views and brief notes about them can be found in McCord Museum of McGill University, *Everyman's Canada*, exhibit items 14–17.

46. New York *American Minerva*, 10 March 1795, as quoted in Stokes and Haskell, *American Historical Prints*, 39–40.

47. McPeck in "George Isham Parkyns" states that Parkyns produced two views of Washington in 1795, "one from the Virginia shore, the other from Georgetown." The second view is an aquatint with the title "View of the Suburbs of the City of Washington." It is a waterfront scene, probably of Georgetown. Most of this limited view is reproduced on the cover of the *Quarterly Journal of the Library of Congress* 30 (July 1973).

Folio 8. L'Enfant Demolishes a House, Receives a Warning from Jefferson, Clashes with the Commissioners, and Is Fired by the President

The commissioners inform Washington of a disturbing event.

We are sorry to be under the disagreeable necessity of mentioning to you an Occurance which must wound your feelings. On our meeting here today, we were to our great astonishment informed that, Majr. L'Enfant, without any Authority from us, & without even having submitted to our consideration, has proceeded to demolish, Mr. Carroll's house. (Padover, *Jefferson*, 78)

The president expresses his concern to Jefferson.

Mr. L'Enfant's letter of the 19th. of October to Mr. Lear— Mr. Lear's answer of the 6th. instant . . . in which I engrafted sentiments of admonition . . . His reply of the 10th. to that letter, together with the papers I put into your hands when here, will give you a full view of the . . . Major's conduct; and will enable you to judge from the complexion of things how far he may be spoken to in decisive terms without losing his services; which in my opinion, would be a serious misfortune.— At the same time *he must know*, there is a line beyond which he will not be suffered to go.—Whether it is zeal,—and impetuous temper, or other motives that lead him into such blameable conduct, I will not take upon me to decide—but be it what it will, it must be checked; or we shall have no Commissioners. (Washington to Jefferson, 30 November 1791, in Jefferson, *Papers*, 22:358)

The president admonishes L'Enfant on 2 December.

In future I must strictly enjoin you to touch no man's property, without his consent, or the previous order of the Commissioners. I wished you to be employed in the arrangements of the federal city. I still wish it: but only on condition that you can conduct yourself in subordination to the authority of the Commissioners, to the laws of the land, & to the rights of it's citizens. (Washington to L'Enfant, 2 December 1791, in Jefferson, *Papers*, 22:368)

The president turns to Jefferson for advice.

The conduct of Majr. L'Enfant and those employed under him astonished me beyond measure! and something more than even appears, must be meant by them! When you are at leisure I should be glad to have a further conversation with you on this subject. (Washington to Jefferson, 18 January 1792, in Padover, *Jefferson*, 88)

Jefferson warns L'Enfant that he must take orders from the commissioners.

I am charged by the president to say that your continuance would be desirable to him; & at the same time to add that the law requires it should be in subordination to the Commissioners. . . . I must beg the favor of your answer whether you will continue your services on the footing expressed in this letter. (Jefferson to L'Enfant, 22 February 1792, in Padover, *Jefferson*, 93)

L'Enfant defends his actions.

My desire to conform to the judgment and wishes of the president have really been ardent. and I trust my actions always have manifested those desires . . . ; nor am I conscious in a single instance to have had any other motive than an implicit conformity to his will. . . .

[The commissioners] . . . though apparently acknowledging themselves obliged to me for affording necessary information, on receiving it have uniformly acted in opposition thereto . . . and appear rather to have endeavored to obtain that knowledge from me the more effectually to defeat my intentions. . . . The inquietude I feel must continue to the end to impede the business, which will oblige me to renounce the pursuit of that fame, which the success of the undertaking must procure, rather than to engage to conduct it under a system which would . . . not only crush its growth but make me appear the principal cause of the destruction of it. . . .

If therefore the law absolutely requires without an equivocation that my continuance shall depend upon an appointment from the Commissioners—I cannot nor would I upon any consideration submit myself to it. (L'Enfant to Jefferson, 26 February 1792, in Padover, *Jefferson*, 95–99)

L'Enfant is dismissed.

From your letter received yesterday . . . and your declarations in conversation . . . it is understood you absolutely decline acting under the authority of the present Commissioners, if this understanding of your meaning be right, I am instructed by the president to inform you that notwithstanding the desire he has entertained to preserve your agency in the business, the condition upon which it is to be done is inadmissible & your services must be at an end. (Jefferson to L'Enfant, 27 February 1792, in Padover, *Jefferson*, 100)

Edward Savage Portrays President Washington Holding the City Plan

In 1789 Harvard University commissioned a young Boston artist named Edward Savage to paint George Washington's portrait. Two years later at the age of thirty, Savage went to England seeking more training, experience, and exposure to art than could be found in America. In London Savage portrayed the president in two prints. He first produced a bust-length portrait executed in stipple engraving in 1792. The next year he published the more elaborate print reproduced here showing the seated president dressed in an elegant velvet suit. Savage here employed the difficult art of mezzotint engraving. It is unlikely that he had mastered this technique himself, and he probably arranged for a competent craftsman to put his drawings on copper for him.

This portrait shows the president holding one of the engraved plans used to advertise the city's existence. Savage doubtless saw one of the engravings and realized that it could be used to add interest to the print and make the likeness seem to have been done only recently. Its appearance in the same year as a promotional tract written by the president's private secretary and a broadside issued in London by one of the proprietors must have helped to direct English attention to and arouse curiosity about the planned capital of a former colony.

It also reflected Washington's deep concern for the success of the city, concern that sometimes exceeded his prudence. In the same year that Savage published his portrait, the president wrote to the commissioners introducing and commending to them Mr. James Greenleaf, who wished to buy city lots in wholesale quantities. This speculative transaction soon proved a financial disaster for all concerned. Nevertheless, Washington never seemed to doubt that the city to which he gave his name would ultimately prove a success.

George Washington Esq. President of the United States of America. From the Original Portrait Painted at the request of the Corporation of the University of Cambridge in Massachusetts. Drawn, engraved, and published by E. Savage, No. 54, Newman Street [London]. Mezzotint, 18⅜ × 13⅞ in. (46.8 × 35.2 cm.). John W. Reps.

The president's private secretary tells L'Enfant of a delay in printing the city map.

To my great surprise and mortification M. Pigalle . . . informed me that he had not been able to get the plate of copper for the engraving . . . till two days ago, and that in consequence it would not be possible for him to have a single plate struck off before the end of the month. (Tobias Lear to L'Enfant, 6 October 1791, in Kite, *L'Enfant and Washington*, 74)

Ellicott informs the commissioners on 23 February 1792 of L'Enfant's refusal to release his drawings.

On my arrival [in Philadelphia] I found that no preparation was made for an engraving. . . . Upon this representation being made to the president and Secretary of State, I was directed to furnish one for an engraver, which with the aid of my Brother was compleated last monday and handed to the president. In this business we met with difficulties of a very serious nature. Major L'Enfant refused us the use of the Original. What his motives were God knows—The plan which we have furnished, I believe will be found to answer the ground better than the large one in the Major's hands—I have engaged two good artists (both Americans) to execute the engraving, and who will begin the work as soon as the president comes to a determination respecting some small alterations. (Ellicott letter, 23 February 1792, in Phillips, *Beginnings of Washington*, 29–30)

Washington suggests seeking an additional engraver in Boston.

The Engravers say *eight weeks* is the *shortest* time in which the Plan can be engraved: (probably they may keep it eight months). Is not this misteriously strange! . . . The current in *this* City sets so strongly against the Federal City, that I believe nothing that *can* be avoided will ever be accomplished in it.

Are there any good Engravers in Boston? If so, would it not be well to obtain a copy (under some other pretext) and send it there, or even to London with out anyone (even Ellicot's) being apris'd of it.? (Washington to Jefferson, 4 March 1792, in Padover, *Jefferson*, 103)

The president tells the commissioners on 6 March 1792 of his efforts to have the plan printed.

It is impossible to say with any certainty when the plan of the City will be engraved. Upon Major L'Enfant's arrival in this place in the latter part of December, I pressed him in the most earnest manner to get the plan ready for engraving as soon as possible. Finding there was no prospect of obtaining it through him (at least in any definite time) the matter was put into Mr. Ellicott's hands to prepare about 3 weeks ago. He has prepared it; but the engravers who have undertaken to execute it, say it can not certainly be done in less than 2, perhaps not under 3 months. (Washington, "Writings," 48)

Samuel Blodget engages a Boston engraver to print the plan.

By last nights post I have recd information that Mr. Hill contracted to engrave the Plan of the City of Washington for 150 Dollars, he has promised to touch nothing in the line of his proffesion [*sic*] till this work is compleated . . . in all June at furthest.

Blodget reports the shipment of the plan to Philadelphia.

The Bearer of this will deliver you four first impressions of the City of Washington, from the plate executed by your order, for Mr. Hill, who wishes to make some slight additions before he sends it forward to you. (Blodget to Jefferson, Boston, 3 May and 25 June 1792, in Padover, *Jefferson*, 139–40, 146)

Jefferson sends the Hill plan to the commissioners on 11 July 1792.

I now send a proof sheet of the plan of the Town engraving at Boston. I observe the Soundings of the Creek and River are not in it. It would be well to know of Mr. Ellicott whether they were in the original sent to Boston.

Jefferson sends the commissioners the plan printed in Philadelphia.

You will receive by tomorrows Stage, 500 Copies of the City of Washington with the Soundings—It has been proposed here to sell them at 3/4 of a Dollar, and the Boston plans at 3/8. on this you will be pleased to decide. (Jefferson to commissioners, 11 July and 13 November 1792, in Padover, *Jefferson*, 153, 157–58)

Samuel Hill Engraves the First Separate Map of the New City

President Washington, irritated and frustrated by the repeated delays of engravers in Philadelphia, asked Jefferson to have a printed version of the plan prepared in Boston, or even London. His letter indicates that he believed Philadelphia printers were delaying their work in order to undermine the project of creating the new capital. He also hints at some distrust of Ellicott in this matter. Jefferson turned for help to a well-to-do former Bostonian, Samuel Blodget, Jr., who had only recently moved to Philadelphia. It was Blodget who made the necessary arrangement with Samuel Hill, a well-known Boston engraver.

Proofs of Hill's engraving did not reach Jefferson until the end of June 1792. President Washington wanted river soundings added, and Jefferson wrote to the commissioners requesting Ellicott to furnish that information to Hill if he had not already done so. Evidently that message did not reach Hill in time since no soundings appear. Hill shipped the engraved plate from Boston to Philadelphia on the sloop *Juno*. It arrived 20 July 1792, but it did not reach a Philadelphia printer named Scott until sometime after mid-August. Scott printed 4,000 copies of the plan at the rate of 100 a day and had some ready for display at the second sale of Washington city lots on 8 October. It thus seems to be the first "official" plan of the city to be printed.

Three smaller and far less detailed versions appeared earlier: in *The Universal Asylum, and Columbian Magazine* for March 1792, engraved by Thackara and Vallance; in the May 1792 issue of *The Massachusetts Magazine*, engraved by Hill; and the third engraved by Tiebout in *The New-York Magazine* for June 1792. All reflect the changes in L'Enfant's design mentioned in the documents and caption for the next illustration.

Plan of the City of Washington in the Territory of Columbia, ceded by the States of Virginia and Maryland to the United States of America and by them established as the Seat of their Government, after the Year MDCCC. Engraved by Samuel Hill, Boston, [1792]. Engraving, 17 × 22 in. (43.1 × 55.8 cm.). Geography and Maps, Library of Congress.

PLAN
*of the City of Washington
in the Territory of Columbia.
ceded by the States of*
VIRGINIA *and* **MARYLAND**
to the **United States** *of* **America**,
and by them established as the
SEAT *of their* **GOVERNMENT**,
after the Year
MDCCC.

Engraved by Sam.l Hill, Boston.

GEORGE TOWN.

Road leading from the Canal at the Lower Falls, distant 3½ miles.

Lat. Capitol.......... 38.53. N.
Long. .... 0 , 0.

President's House

Capitol.

POTOMAK RIVER.

PART OF VIRGINIA WITHIN THE TERRITORY OF COLUMBIA.

EASTERN BRANCH.

PART OF MARYLAND WITHIN THE TERRITORY OF COLUMBIA.

Observations
explanatory of the Plan.

I. THE positions for the different Edifices, and for the several Squares or Areas of different shapes, as they are laid down, were first determined on the most advantageous ground, commanding the most extensive prospects, and the better susceptible of such improvements as either use or ornament may hereafter call for.

II. LINES or Avenues of direct communication have been devised, to connect the separate and most distant objects with the principal, and to preserve through the whole a reciprocity of sight at the same time. Attention has been paid to the passing of those leading Avenues over the most favorable ground for prospect and convenience.

III. NORTH and South lines, intersected by others running due East and West, make the distribution of the City into Streets, Squares, &c. and those lines have been so combined as to meet at certain given points with those divergent Avenues, so as to form on the spaces first determined, the different Squares or Areas.

SCALE OF POLES.

Breadth of the Streets.

THE grand Avenues, and such Streets as lead immediately to public places, are from 130 to 160 feet wide, and may be conveniently divided into foot ways, walks of trees, and a carriage way. The other Streets are from 90 to 110 feet wide.

IN order to execute this plan, Mr. ELLICOTT drew a true Meridional line by celestial Observation, which passes through the Area intended for the Capitol; this line he crossed by another due East and West, which passes through the same Area. These lines were accurately measured, and made the bases on which the whole plan was executed. He ran all the lines by a Transit Instrument, and determined the acute Angles by actual measurement, and left nothing to the uncertainty of the Compass.

37

The president promises the proprietors in June 1791 that an early version of the plan will be changed.

A Plan was also laid before them of the City in order to convey to them general ideas of the City—but they were told that some deviations from it would take place—particularly in the diagonal Streets or avenues, which would not be so numerous; and in the removal of the presidents house more westerly for the advantage of higher ground—they were also told that a Town house, or exchange wd. be placed on some convenient ground between the spots designed for the public buildgs. (Washington, "Writings," 27–28)

L'Enfant recalls in 1800 altering his plan.

Q. 15 . . . Were there not several lines of avenues suppressed from the original design; and did not this suppression cause a derangement in the lines also of some of the right angled streets?

A. There were some such alterations but these were made by myself at the recommendation of the president & . . . Mr. Jefferson, as early as august 1791 before I prepared the map for engraving, and at the request of the original proprietors of one particular section of the city. ("L'Enfant Memorials," 99–100)

On 15 February 1792 the president asks Jefferson to discuss with him proposed changes in the city plan.

Before I give any decided opinion upon the letter you have written to Majr. L'Enfant or on the alterations proposed for the engraved plan, I wish to converse with you on several matters which relates to this business. This may be, if nothing on your part renders it inconvenient, immediately after 8 o'clock to-morrow—at which hour I breakfast, and at which, if agreeable to you, I should like to see you. (Kite, *L'Enfant and Washington,* 139)

Washington tells the commissioners in 1796 about changes made by Jefferson.

This plan you shall receive by the first safe hand who may be going to the Federal City.—By it you may discover (tho' almost obliterated) the directions given to the Engraver by Mr. Jefferson, with a pencil, what parts to omit. (Washington, "Writings," 175–76)

In a letter to Tobias Lear on 17 February 1792 L'Enfant vigorously criticizes Ellicott's version of his plan.

Mr. Young informing me that his engraver would soon be engaged for Mr. Ellicott on the plate for the city, induced me to go to his house and see how far the draft was advanced—This draft to my great surprise I found in the state in which it now is, most unmercifully spoiled and altered from the original plan to a degree indeed evidently tending to disgrace me and ridicule the very undertaking. . . . [In pencil:] All the lineaments of the ground from which the whole direction of avenues can alone be perceived having been suppressed.

A month later L'Enfant tells the proprietors of changes made without his consent.

I cannot disguise to you that much has already been attempted by the contrivance of an erroneous map of the city about to be published, which partly copied from the original has afterwards been mangled and altered in a shameful manner in its most essential parts. (Kite, *L'Enfant and Washington,* 142, 166)

Washington in 1797 summarizes the circumstances leading to changes in the plan.

That many alterations have been made from L'Enfant's plan by Major Ellicott, with the approbation of the Executive, is not denied; that some were deemed essential is avowed; and, had it not been for the materials which he [Ellicott] happened to possess, it is probable that no engraving from Mr. L'Enfant's draught ever would have been exhibited to the public. . . . [It] is mistaken [to] suppose . . . that the transmission of Mr. L'Enfant's plan of the city to Congress was the completion thereof.—So far from it, it will appear by the message which accompanied the same that it was given as matter of information only, to show what state the business was in, & the return of it requested—That neither house of Congress passed any act consequent thereupon.—That it remained as before, under the controul [sic] of the Executive.—That afterwards several errors were discovered and corrected, many alterations made, and the appropriations (except as to the Capitol & Presidents house) struck out under that authority, before it was sent to the Engraver; intending *that* his work, & the promulgation thereof, were to give it the final, & regulating stamp. (Washington, "Writings," 187)

Thackara and Vallance Finally Print the Official City Plan

James Thackara and John Vallance—the two young Philadelphia engravers engaged by Ellicott to print the plan of Washington—did not deliver their large and handsome engraving until 13 November 1792. In taking almost a year they infuriated everyone involved with developing the new city, for Washington, Jefferson, and the commissioners knew that it would be almost impossible to sell lots if would-be purchasers did not know the location of building sites on which they were asked to bid. The time taken by the two engravers now seems fully justified considering the stunning results they achieved. The bold lines of the engraving bring out the striking geometric patterns of the street system that L'Enfant devised. No more attractive example of urban cartography can be found. At the upper right the elegant calligraphy of the title block summarizes the circumstances of the city's creation. The legends at lower left and lower right are much-simplified versions of those on L'Enfant's manuscript.

However, the engraving omits L'Enfant's name. Only Ellicott's appears, as the person who determined the city's precise meridian and who surveyed all the lines. L'Enfant was justifiably incensed over such an obviously intentional slight. He also objected to the design changes made without his approval, including the straightening of Massachusetts Avenue, the elimination of twelve civic squares and five radial avenues, and many alterations in the shapes of public building sites and open spaces. To L'Enfant, all such changes seemed disastrous. To us two centuries later they appear far less important. What remained virtually intact was L'Enfant's underlying concept of a formal and monumental urban design based on multiple axial connections between major buildings, conceived on an enormous scale, and fitted to the site with skill and imagination.

Plan of the City of Washington in the Territory of Columbia, ceded by the States of Virginia and Maryland to the United States of America, and by them established as the Seat of their Government, after the Year MDCCC. Line engraving by Thackara and Vallance, Philadelphia, 1792. 21 × 29 in. (53.3 × 73.6 cm.), restrike. John W. Reps.

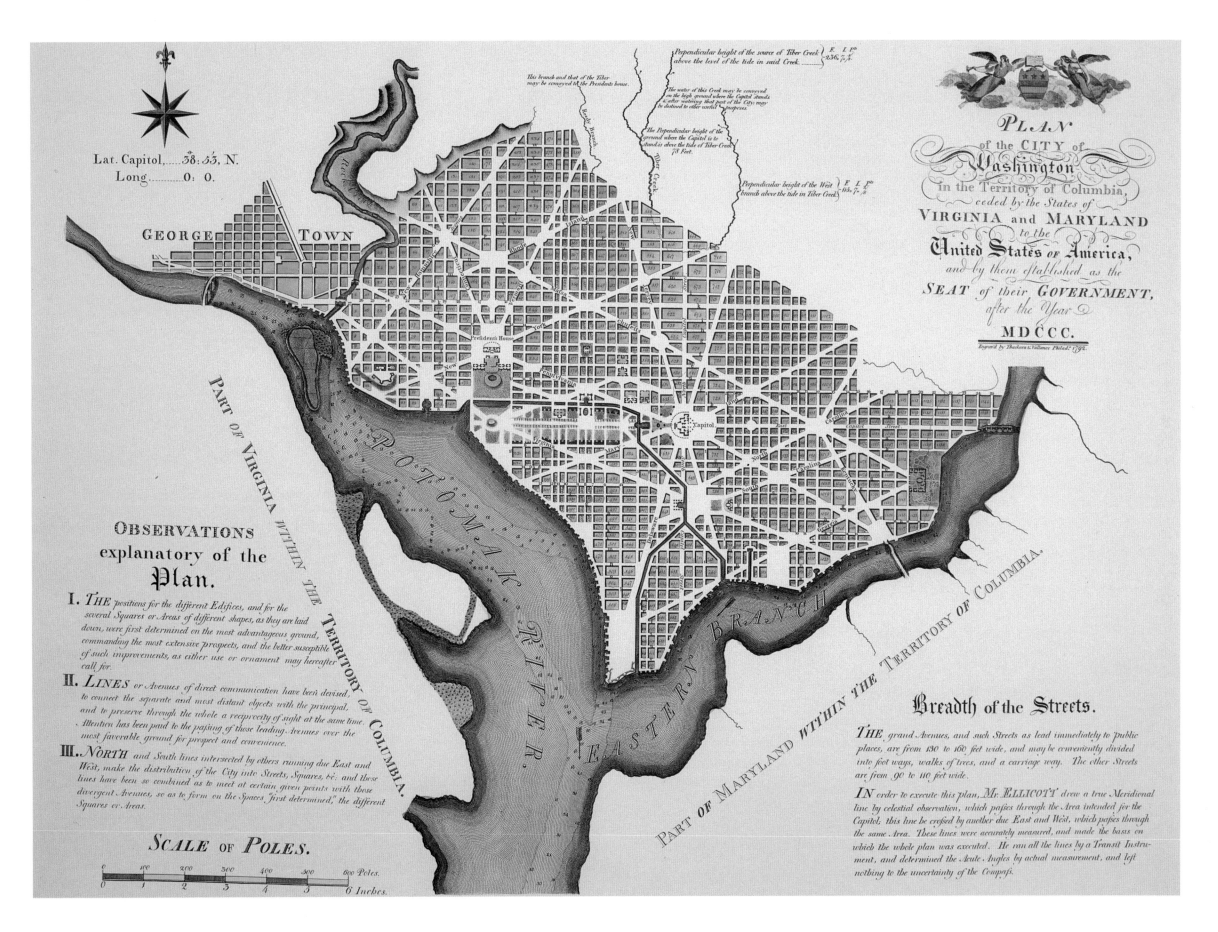

*President Washington tells one of the commissioners
of his preferences for the building.*

For the presidents House, I would design a building which should also look forward, but execute no more of it at present than might suit the circumstances of this Country when it shall be first wanted. A plan comprehending more may be executed at a future period when the wealth, population, and importance of it shall stand upon much higher ground than they do at present. (Washington to David Stuart, 8 March 1792, in Washington, "Writings," 51)

Francis Baily sees the building in 1796.

Our first walk was to the president's House, which is a building of stone about the size of Whitehall. It is nearly completed; and when fitted up will be a handsome edifice. It commands a fine view of the harbour, and also of the Capitol, *to which* there is a broad street intended to be built. (Baily, *Journal*, 126–27)

*A Boston newspaper provides the dimensions of the
building and praises its appearance.*

The president's House in Washington, built of white free stone, is in length 175 feet 7 inches, and breadth 83 feet 5 inches—rooms 26½ feet long—19 feet high—walls outside, 2 feet 9 inches, and inside 2 feet. The beautiful imagery appears pleasing to the fancy, and captivating to the eye, there were two stories of this delightful edifice, compleated in May 1796, and since the guarantee of the new loan, they go on rapid in building. (*Boston Gazette*, 5 February 1798)

*The secretary of the Treasury has mixed feelings about
the building in 1800.*

The president's house, or *palace*, is about as large as the wing of the capitol . . . except that it is not so high. It is highly decorated, and makes a good appearance, but is in a very unfinished state. I cannot but consider our Presidents as very unfortunate men, if they must live in this dwelling. It must be cold and damp in winter, and cannot be kept in tolerable order without a regiment of servants. It was built to be looked at by visitors and strangers, and will render its occupants an object of ridicule with some, and of pity with others. (George Gibbs, *Memoirs of Oliver Wolcott*, 2:377)

*A visiting Englishman pokes fun at the display
of executive laundry in 1803.*

The Palace is . . . without any fence but a few broken rails upon which hang his excellencys stockings and shirts to dry and his maids blue petticoat—acting almost as wings to this stone building are two immense brick piles which contain the public offices such as Secretary of State[,] Treasury and post office. (Letter by an unidentified English visitor in 1803, in Junior League of Washington, *City of Washington*, 85)

*Benjamin Latrobe writes to Philip Mazzei in May 1806 and
blames George Washington for some of the city's deficiencies.*

General Washington knew how to give liberty to his country but was wholly ignorant of art. It is therefore not to be wondered, that the design of a physician, who was very ignorant of architecture was adopted for the Capitol and of a carpenter for the president's house. The latter is not even original, but a mutilated copy of a badly designed building near Dublin. (Latrobe, "Construction of the Public Buildings in Washington," 223)

*Charles Janson sees the president's house in 1806
and describes it in his book.*

The president's house is certainly [*sic*] a neat but plain piece of architecture, built of hewn stone, said to be of a better quality than Portland stone, as it will cut like marble, and resist the change of the seasons in a superior degree. Only part of it is furnished; the whole salary of the president would be inadequate to the expence of completing it in a style of suitable elegance.

*Janson notes the disgraceful condition of the grounds
around the president's house.*

The ground around it, instead of being laid out in a suitable style, remains in its ancient rude state, so that, in a dark night, instead of finding your way to the house, you may, perchance, fall into a pit, stumble over a heap of rubbish. The fence round the house is of the meanest sort; a common post and rail enclosure. This parsimony destroys every sentiment of pleasure that arises in the mind, in viewing the residence of the president of a nation, and is a disgrace to the country. (Janson, *The Stranger in America*, 206)

James Hoban Designs the Presidential Mansion

In the spring of 1792 the commissioners advertised in many newspapers that they were offering a prize of $500 or a gold medal of equal value for the design of the presidential residence. An Irish-born and -trained architect named James Hoban, then practicing his profession in Charleston, won the competition over several competitors. Hoban designed a simple but impressive facade, using elements that had been thoroughly explored and tested in eighteenth-century manor houses in England and Ireland. On either side of the entrance, with its four Ionic columns, two identical wings extended to the east and west. On the lower floor windows, segmented and triangular pediments alternate, while the windows of the second floor are smaller and rectangular in outline.

Construction proceeded slowly, but by the spring of 1799 the exterior walls of white sandstone and the roof had been completed. When President and Mrs. John Adams arrived to occupy the house at the end of 1800, they found it far from complete, only partly furnished, and with little to commend it except the splendid view down the Potomac from the south windows. By 1807, when Charles Janson used an engraved image of the building on the title page of his informative book on America, Thomas Jefferson—with the help of the talented Benjamin Latrobe—had made the place somewhat more comfortable. In the summer of 1814 the British set fire to the building, as they did to the nearby offices for the executive branch of government. William Strickland's engraving depicts the appearance of the building: a gutted shell with only the smoke-blackened walls still in place.

Front View of the President's House in the City of Washington. Unsigned title page vignette from Charles William Janson, *The Stranger in America.* London, 1807. Aquatint, view only, 3½ × 6 in. (8.8 × 15.2 cm.). Machen Collection, Historical Society of Washington, D.C.

A View of the Presidents House in the City of Washington after the Conflagration of the 24th August 1814. Drawn by George Munger and engraved by W[illiam] Strickland. Engraving, 11½ × 17 in. (29.2 × 43.2 cm.). Prints and Photographs, Library of Congress.

A VIEW of the PRESIDENTS HOUSE in the CITY of WASHINGTON

after the Conflagration of the 24th August 1814.

Francis Baily admires the Capitol in 1796.

The Capitol stands upon the highest ground in the city, and commands a still better view of the harbour, as the prospect extends a considerable way down the river. The Capitol, which is also of stone, was in a great state of forwardness; and it was expected to be finished before the time appointed for the removal of Congress, January, 1800. It is impossible to say what kind of an appearance it will make when it is finished; but, if I may judge from what was already done, I think I may pronounce it to be a building worthy the taste and enterprise of a free and flourishing people. (Baily, *Journal*, 127)

Another Englishman describes the appearance
of buildings on and near Capitol Hill in 1803.

The first notice you have of this embryo London (or to be more in tone with the American modesty this embryo Rome) is a small stone between two stumps of trees upon which is inscribed "The boundary of the City." This is proper enough for you have got about two miles to go before you fall in with a single inhabitant to tell you so. Immediately upon leaving this stone you rise a hill and come upon a large plain . . . and then first see the Capitol, a ponderous unfinished mass of brick and stone . . . one or two brick buildings with corresponding sheds, half a dozen stragling [*sic*] houses or fragments of houses fill up the view till you get there which now being the highest ground gives you a complete command of the Potomack with both its branches, together with George Town—I can compare the cite [*sic*] upon which the Capitol stands and about a mile in circumference to the top of a Quakers hat and the rest of this imperial city comprised on its brim.

He tells of other buildings nearby.

Directly opposite . . . and distant about two hundred yards is half a dozen handsome brick houses . . . fitted up for boarding lodgers and an hotel—a few irregular paltry single houses and hovels make up the rest of this side. On the South between the crown and the brim to follow my old metaphor, Mr. Law has built half a row of houses from eight to ten much like the other ones mentioned before and somebody else has been goose enough to follow his example and fill up the same space on the

opposite side of the street—this is about a quarter of a mile from the Capitol and the only spot till you get to George Town (three miles,) which can be called anything like a street. There now only remain the N and W sides. The first will soon be finished as there are not above ten buildings over the whole space and those a moderate walk from one another on the West. (Letter in 1803 from an unidentified English visitor, in Junior League of Washington, *City of Washington*, 84)

John Melish is impressed by the Capitol and the view
from Capitol Hill in 1806.

On walking out to the Capitol Hill, I had a fine view of the whole scite [*sic*] of the city, which is very large, extending a mile and a half in each direction north and south of the Capitol; to the east two miles; and to the west nearly two miles and a half. The buildings, though numerous, being scattered over this large space, give it more the appearance of a thickly-settled country than a city; and, very few of them extending in the direction we came, we had travelled a good way into the city before I saw it.

The view from the Capitol is really superb. The whole country round is handsomely settled, with elegant houses; and the view is terminated to the west, south-west, and north-west, with highlands. To the south, is the river Potomac, with Alexandria pleasantly situated on its banks . . . ; and to the west is the president's house, a stately edifice, about a mile distant; beyond which, handsomely situated on the brow of the hill, is Georgetown. . . .

The Capitol . . . is an elegant building of hewn stone, and consists of two wings and a portico in the middle. The north wing was quite complete, and the whole legislative business was transacted in it for the time. (Melish, *Travels*, 1:193–95)

In 1816 Henry Knight notes the ruined condition
of the Capitol burned during the War of 1812.

The Capitol, of Corinthian order, its vast central rotundo and dome being yet unbuilt between the wings, is an enormous double-block of massive free-stone, scathed and smutched by the late war-fire, and scowling like desolation. The conflagration of the library was a specimen of Vandalism. (Knight, *Letters*, 37)

The Capitol Is Built and Burned

William Thornton, a physician, won the competition held by the commissioners for the design of the Capitol on which work began in September 1793. Thornton, an amateur, needed the help of James Hoban, designer of the presidential residence, to prepare working drawings and supervise construction. By December 1800 the north wing had been more or less completed in time for Congress to meet there when it moved from Philadelphia. In 1807 the House of Representatives was able to occupy the south wing, and it is the building as it then stood that the English-trained artist and engraver William Birch depicted with an eagle bearing the shield of the United States hovering overhead. By that time Benjamin H. Latrobe had taken over the task of director of works. He designed a wooden arcade, to connect the two wings facing each other, over the otherwise empty space intended for the domed rotunda that Thornton had designed.

In 1814 British troops occupying the city set fire to the building. The blaze destroyed the roof and the interior of the south wing and heavily damaged the older north or Senate wing. The results appear in the second illustration of the Capitol. It was not until 1819 that Latrobe could complete the restoration of the building and Congress could resume its deliberations within its walls. Both illustrations show the eastern front that Thornton had intended as the building's principal entrance. However, the parts of the city on the western side of the Capitol grew more rapidly, and that side became the favored entryway for those with business in the halls of Congress.

The Capitol at Washington. Title page illustration for William [Russell] Birch, *The Country Seats of the United States of North America.* Springland near Bristol [Pa.], 1808. Engraving, view only, ca. 3 × 5 in. (7.6 × 12.7 cm.). Rare Books, Library of Congress.

A View of the Capitol of the United States after the Conflagration of the 24th August 1814. Drawn by George Munger and engraved by W[illiam] Strickland. Engraving, 11½ × 17 in. (29.2 × 43.1 cm.). Prints and Photographs, Library of Congress.

The Capitol at Washington.

Designed and Published by W. Birch Enamel Painter Springland near Bristol, Pennsyla. 1808.

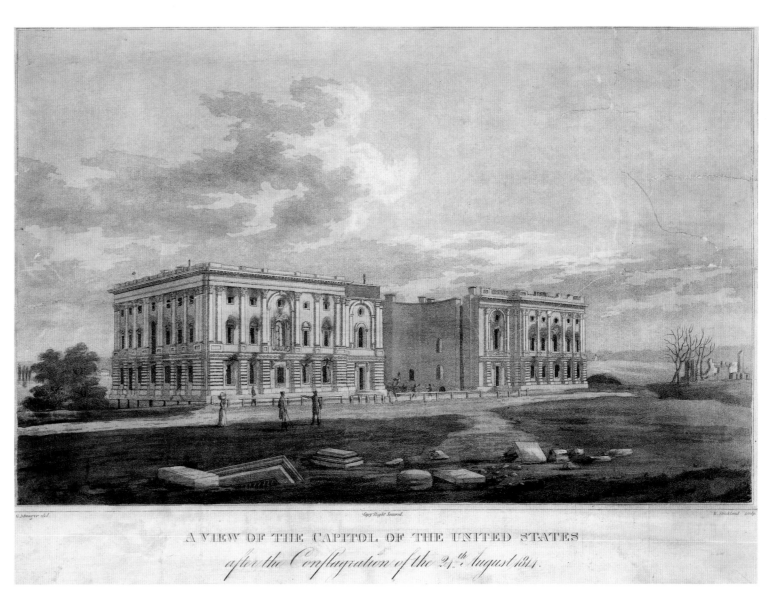

G. Munger del.   Copy Right Secured.   W. Strickland sculp.

A VIEW OF THE CAPITOL OF THE UNITED STATES

after the Conflagration of the 24th August 1814.

*Washington's private secretary boosts the city
in a book published in 1793.*

The public buildings . . . are begun and progress with much spirit. They are on a scale equal to the magnitude of the objects for which they are preparing; and will . . . be executed in a stile [*sic*] of architecture, chaste, magnificent and beautiful. They will be built with beautiful white stone; which is pronounced certainly equal, if not superior, to the best Portland stone. . . .

Besides the buildings for the accommodation of the government . . . a very superb Hotel is erecting, the expence of which is defrayed by a lottery, the Hotel being the highest prize.

He describes the beneficial effect of land sales.

The price of lots has lately risen very much, and a great increase of price is still expected, as the object comes to be more investigated, and better understood.

After furnishing very ample funds for the accomplishment of every object in the city . . . a large surplus of lots will remain the property of the city, which hereafter may, and undoubtedly will be so applied, as to defray the annual expences incident to the city; and the citizens, and their property will be forever free from a heavy tax, which is unavoidable in other large cities.

He extols the advantages of a planned city.

Among the many advantages which will be derived to this city over almost all other large cities, from the circumstance of its being originally designed for the capital of a great nation, may be ranked as the foremost; the width of the streets, (none of which are less than ninety feet, and from that to one hundred and sixty,) and the attention which will be paid to levelling or regulating the streets . . . in such a manner as to avoid any future inconvenience to such buildings as may be erected in the early establishment of the city, and to give that declivity to them . . . which will readily and effectually carry off all filth in the common sewers. ([Lear], *Observations*, 131–33)

A distinguished French visitor comments on speculation.

Mr. Morris was among the first to perceive the probability of immense gain in speculations . . . and in conjunction with Messrs. Nicholson and Greenleaf . . . purchased every lot he could lay hold on. . . . Of the commissioners he bought six thousand lots. . . . The conditions of his bargain . . . concluded in 1793, were, that fifteen hundred of the lots should be chosen by him in the north-east quarter of the city, and the remaining . . . wherever Mr. Morris and his partners chose to select them; that he should erect an hundred and twenty houses of brick . . . within the space of seven years; that he should not sell any lot before the first of January 1796, nor without the like condition of the building; and finally, that the payment . . . should be completed within seven years, to commence on the first of May 1794 . . . that is to say, about sixty-eight thousand dollars yearly, the purchase money for the whole being four hundred and eighty thousand dollars.

The lots purchased by Mr. Morris from individuals amounted to nearly the same number. (La Rochefoucauld-Liancourt, *Travels*, 3:622–23)

*The secretary of the Treasury describes speculative
madness to his wife in 1800.*

There appears to be a confident expectation that this place will soon exceed any city in the world. Mr. Thornton, one of the commissioners, spoke of a population of 160,000 people, as a matter of course, in a few years. No stranger can be here a day and converse with the proprietors, without conceiving himself in the company of crazy people. Their ignorance of the rest of the world, and their delusions with respect to their own prospects, are without parallel. Immense sums have been squandered in buildings which are but partly finished, in situations which are not, and never will be the scenes of business. (Oliver Wolcott to Mrs. Wolcott, in George Gibbs, *Memoirs of Oliver Wolcott*, 2:378)

Charles Janson records the results of land speculation.

Speculation, the life of the American, embraced the design of the new city. Several companies of speculators purchased lots, and began to build handsome streets, with an ardor that soon promised a large and populous city. Before they arrived at the attic story, the failure was manifest; and in that state at the moment are the walls of many scores of houses begun on a plan of elegance. (Janson, *The Stranger in America*, 203)

George Walker Promotes the
New Capital City in London

Although in 1796 he fought with the commissioners over rights to triangular pieces of land at intersections of radial and rectangular streets, George Walker was perhaps the most energetic promoter of the city of Washington. He issued this broadside in London in March 1793.

Walker borrowed freely and extensively from a long and detailed description of the city and its plan published in the *Maryland Journal* in the fall of 1791. He added this account of progress up to the end of January 1793: "Most of the streets were run, and the squares divided into lots.—the canal was partly dug, and the greatest part of the materials provided for the public buildings. . . . Last summer several private houses were erected and a great many proprietors of lots were preparing to build this ensuing summer."

As one of the proprietors, Walker hoped to profit from the location of the national capital. Like the other owners of land on the site, he looked forward to being reimbursed for any of the land within the boundaries of his estate that the plan proposed for public buildings.

More important, Walker and his fellows were to have half of the lots left after the street and avenues were surveyed. All of them expected—wrongly, as it turned out—that demand would be high and that values would rise.

Walker evidently believed that English investors would be eager to buy land in the new metropolis. While his broadside advertised and promoted the city generally, surely he hoped to interest potential buyers in lots within his own portion of the site east of the Capitol.

A description of the situation and plan of the city of Washington, now building, for the Metropolis of America and established as the permanent residence of Congress after the year 1800. Broadside, published by George Walker, London, York Hotel, Bridge Street, Blackfriars, 12 March 1793. Geography and Maps, Library of Congress.

A DESCRIPTION OF THE SITUATION AND PLAN

OF THE

CITY OF WASHINGTON,

NOW BUILDING FOR

THE METROPOLIS OF AMERICA,

AND ESTABLISHED AS THE PERMANENT RESIDENCE OF CONGRESS AFTER THE YEAR 1800.

THE CITY of WASHINGTON, in the diſtrict of COLUMBIA, now building for the permanent ſeat of the Government of the United States, ſtands at the junction of the rivers Potomac and the Eaſtern Branch, extending about four miles up each, including a tract of territory, exceeded in point of convenience, ſalubrity, and beauty, by none in America, if any in the world:—For, although the land is apparently level, yet, by gentle and gradual ſwellings, a variety of elegant proſpects are produced, while there is a ſufficient deſcent to convey off the water occaſioned by rain.

Within the limits of the city are twenty-five never-failing ſprings of excellent water; and, by digging wells, water of the beſt quality is readily had; beſides, the never-failing ſtreams that now run through that territory, are alſo to be collected for the uſe of the city.

The EASTERN BRANCH is one of the ſafeſt and moſt commodious harbours in America, being ſufficiently deep for the largeſt ſhips, for about four miles above its mouth; while the channel lies cloſe along the edge of the city, and is abundantly capacious.

The City, being ſituated upon the great poſt road, exactly equidiſtant from the northern and ſouthern extremities of the union, and nearly ſo from the Atlantic Ocean to the Ohio river, upon the beſt navigation, and in the midſt of the richeſt commercial territory in America, commanding the moſt extenſive internal reſources, is by far the moſt eligible ſituation for the reſidence of Congreſs; and as it is now preſſing forward, by the public ſpirited enterpriſe of the people of the United States, and by foreigners, it will grow up with a degree of rapidity, hitherto unparalleled in the annals of cities, and will ſoon become the admiration and delight of the world.

The inland navigation of the Potomac is ſo far advanced, that craft loaded with produce now come down that river and its ſeveral branches, from upwards of one hundred and eighty miles to the great falls, which are within fourteen miles of the New City. The canals at the great and little falls are nearly completed, and the locks in ſuch forwardneſs, that, in the courſe of the enſuing ſummer, the navigation will be entirely opened between tide water and the head branches of the Potomac, which will produce a communication by water between the City of Waſhington, and the interior parts of Virginia and Maryland, by means of the Potomac, the Shannandoah, the South Branch, Opecan, Cape Capon, Patterſon's Creek, Conoochegue, and Monocaſy, for upwards of two hundred miles, through one of the moſt healthy, pleaſant, and fertile regions in America, producing, in vaſt abundance, tobacco of ſuperior quality, hemp, Indian corn, wheat and other ſmall grain, with fruit and vegetables peculiar to America, in vaſt abundance, and equal in quality to any in the United States.

The lands upon the Potomac above the City of Waſhington, all around it, and for ſixty miles below, are high and dry, abounding with innumerable ſprings of excellent water, and are well covered with large timber of various kinds. A few miles below the City, upon the banks of the Potomac, are inexhauſtible mountains of excellent freeſtone, of the white and red Portland kinds, of which the public edifices in the city are now building. Above the City, alſo upon the banks of the river, are immenſe quantities of excellent coal, limeſtone, and marble, with blue ſlate of the beſt quality.

The founding of this City, in ſuch an eligible ſituation, upon ſuch a liberal and elegant plan, will by future generations be conſidered as a high proof of the judgement and wiſdom of the preſent Preſident of the United States, while its name will keep freſh in mind, to the end of time, the many virtues and amiable qualites of that great man.

The plan of this City, agreeably to the directions of the Preſident of the United States, was deſigned and drawn by the celebrated Major L'ENFANT, and is an inconceivable improvement upon all other cities, combining not only convenience, regularity, elegance of proſpect, and a free circulation of air, but every thing grand and beautiful that can poſſibly be introduced into a city.

Two haſty impreſſions of this plan were uſhered to the public laſt ſpring, one done at Philadelphia upon a ſmall ſcale, and another done at Boſton upon a larger;—theſe did not exhibit the ſoundings of the harbours, and were defective with regard to the limits of the City upon the Eaſtern Branch.

The laſt and beſt impreſſion of the plan is that lately publiſhed at Philadelphia upon the large ſcale, although it contains ſeveral miſtakes in the ſoundings of the Eaſtern Branch; for, where there is thirty-five feet water, it only ſhews twelve and eighteen. This river has, however, been ſounded by authority, and is found to contain thirty and thirty-five feet to near the upper end of the city, where it is eighteen and twenty feet deep.

The City is divided into ſquares or grand diviſions, by the ſtreets running due North and South, and Eaſt and Weſt, which form the ground-work of the plan. However, from the Capitol, the Preſident's Houſe, and ſome of the important areas in the City, run tranſverſe avenues or diagonal ſtreets, from one material object to another, which not only produce a variety of charming proſpects, but remove that inſipid ſameneſs that renders ſome other great cities unpleaſing. Theſe great leading ſtreets are all one hundred and ſixty feet wide, including a pavement of ten feet, and a gravel walk of thirty feet planted with trees on each ſide, which will leave eighty feet of paved ſtreet for carriages. The reſt of the ſtreets are in general one hundred and ten feet wide, with a few only ninety feet, except North, South, and Eaſt Capitol Streets, which are one hundred and ſixty feet. The diagonal ſtreets are named after the reſpective ſtates compoſing the Union, while thoſe running North and South are, from the Capitol Eaſtward, named, EAST FIRST STREET, EAST SECOND STREET, &c. and thoſe Weſt of it are in the ſame manner called WEST FIRST STREET, WEST SECOND STREET, &c. thoſe running Eaſt and Weſt are from the Capitol Northward named, NORTH A STREET, NORTH B STREET, &c. and thoſe South of it are called SOUTH A STREET, SOUH B STREET, &c.

The ſquares, or diviſions of the City, have their numbers inſerted in the plan, and amount to eleven hundred and fifty.—The rectangular ſquares generally contain from three to ſix acres, and are divided into lots of from forty to eighty feet front, and their depth, from about one hundred and ten to three hundred feet, according to the ſize of the ſquare.

The irregular diviſions produced by the diagonal ſtreets are ſome of them ſmall, but are generally in valuable ſituations.—Their acute points are all to be cut off at forty feet, ſo that no houſe in the City will have an acute corner.—The lots in theſe irregular ſquares will all turn at a right angle with the reſpective ſtreets, although the backs of the houſes upon them will not ſtand parallel to one another, which is a matter of no conſequence.

By the rules declared and publiſhed by the Preſident of the United States, for regulating the buildings within the City, all houſes muſt be of ſtone or brick—their walls muſt be parallel to the ſtreets, and either placed immediately upon them, or withdrawn therefrom at pleaſure. The walls of all houſes upon ſtreets one hundred and ſixty feet wide muſt be at leaſt thirty feet high; but there is no obligation impoſed to build or improve in any limited time.

The area for the CAPITOL (or houſe for the Legiſlative Bodies) is ſituated upon the moſt beautiful eminence in the City, about a mile from the Eaſtern Branch, and not much more from the Potomac, commanding a full and complete view of every part of the City, as well as a conſiderable extent of the country around.—The PRESIDENT'S HOUSE will ſtand upon a riſing ground, not far from the Banks of the Potomac, poſſeſſing a delightful water proſpect, together with a commanding view of the CAPITOL, and ſome other mat[illegible] parts of the City.

Due ſouth from [illegible]e Preſident's houſe, and due weſt from the Capitol, run two great pleaſure parks or malls, which interſect and terminate upon the Banks of the Potomac, and are to be ornamented at the ſides by a variety of elegant buildings, and houſes for foreign Miniſters, &c.

Interſperſed through the City, where the moſt material ſtreets croſs one another, are a variety of open Areas, formed in various regular figures, which in great cities are extremely uſeful and ornamental.

Fifteen of the beſt of theſe Areas are to be appropriated to the different States compoſing the Union; not only to bear their reſpective names, but as proper places for them to erect ſtatues, obeliſks, or columns, to the memory of their favourite eminent men.—Upon the ſmall eminence, where a line due weſt from the Capitol, and due ſouth from the Preſident's houſe would interſect, is to be erected an equeſtrian ſtatue of GENERAL WASHINGTON, now PRESIDENT of the UNITED STATES.—The build ing where Maſſachuſſetts and Georgia ſtreets meet, is intended for a *Marine Hoſpital*, with its gardens.

The AREA at the ſouth end of Eaſt Eight Street is for the GENERAL EXCHANGE, and its public walks, &c.—The broad black line, which runs along part of NORTH B STREET, and, ſeparating joins the Eaſtern Branch at two places, is a CANAL, which is to be eighty feet wide, and eight feet deep —The AREA, where SOUTH G STREET croſſes the canal, is intended to contain a CITY HALL, and a baſon of water; there being now a very large ſpring in the middle of it.

The AREA, at the junction of the rivers, is for a FORT, MAGAZINES, and ARSENALS.

At the eaſt end of EAST CAPITOL STREET is to be a BRIDGE, and the preſent Ferry is at the lower end of KENTUCKY STREET, where the great road now croſſes the Eaſtern Branch.—The Tyber, which is the principal ſtream that paſſes through the City, is to be collected in a grand Reſervoir beſide the Capitol, from whence it will be carried in pipes to different parts of the City; while its ſurplus will fall down in beautiful caſcades, through the public gardens weſt of the Capitol, into the canal.—In various parts of the City places are allotted for MARKET HOUSES, CHURCHES, COLLEGES, THEATRES, &c.

The PRESIDENT of the UNITED STATES, in locating the ſeat of the City, prevailed upon the proprietors of the ſoil to cede a certain portion of the lots in every ſituation, to be ſold by his direction, and the proceeds to be ſolely applied to the public buildings, and other works of public utility within the City. This grant will produce about fifteen thouſand lots, and will be ſufficient, not only to erect the public buildings, but to dig the canal, conduct water through the City, and to pave and light the ſtreets, which will ſave a heavy tax that ariſes in other cities, and conſequently render the lots conſiderably more valuable.

The grants of money made by *Virginia* and *Maryland*, being hitherto ſufficient, few of the public lots have yet been ſold; but a ſale is advertiſed to commence on the 17th day of September next, when it is expected the demand will be conſiderable, as the monied men in America have now turned their attention to that great national object.

When the writer of this left Waſhington, on the end of January laſt, moſt of the ſtreets were run, and the ſquares divided into lots:—The canal was partly dug, and the greateſt part of the materials provided for the public buildings, which are to be entirely of freeſtone poliſhed, and are now carrying on with all poſſible expedition.—Laſt ſummer ſeveral private houſes were erected, and a great many proprietors of lots were preparing to build this enſuing ſummer.

In conſequence of the eſtabliſhment of NATIONAL FAITH, ORDER, and GOOD GOVERNMENT, by the NEW CONSTITUTION, immenſe fortunes have been amaſſed in America within theſe three years paſt, by the National Debt and Bank Stock appreciating to their full value, as well as by the rapid riſe in the value of back lands.—The public lots in the City of Waſhington open the next field for ſpeculation in America, and there is every probability of their being run up to an enormous price, as ſoon as the public buildings are conſiderably advanced; for although lands in America, from their quantity, are leſs valuable than thoſe in Britain, yet lots in cities generally ſell as high.

Having every opportunity to be thoroughly acquainted with the ſubject, the preceding conciſe account of the progreſs of that grand and novel undertaking is reſpectfully offered to the public, by

Their obedient Servant,

GEORGE WALKER.

LONDON, *York Hotel*, *Bridge-ſtreet*, *Black-friars*,
March 12, 1793.

Folio 14. Some Early Visitors Record Varied Impressions of the New City

An Englishman describes Washington in 1794.

The whole area of the city consists of upwards of four thousand acres. . . . Many houses are already built, and a very handsome hotel, which cost in the erection more than thirty thousand dollars. . . . [The city] is now apportioned into one thousand two hundred and thirty-six lots. . . . The deepest lots are two hundred and seventy feet, by seventy. . . . [A block] has from twenty to thirty lots in it. The value of each lot is from forty pounds to two hundred pounds sterling.

He learns of many proposed buildings but questions the scale of the undertaking.

There is to be a national University erected there, as well as the Mint, Pay Office, Treasury, supreme Courts of Justice, Residences for the Ambassadors; in short, all the Public Offices. The city is to be built . . . of a fine white stone found in the neighborhood. . . . Each house is to be forty feet from the ground to the roof, in all the principal streets, which are to be from seventy to one hundred feet wide. . . . One of the streets . . . is marked out to be four miles long. The question still with me is, whether the scheme is not too magnificent for the present state of things. (Wansey, *Journal*, 219–26)

Isaac Weld provides some details about early building regulations.

The ground in general, within the limits of the city, is agreeably undulated; but none of the risings are so great as to become objects of inconvenience in a town. . . .

By the regulations published, it was settled that all the houses should be built of brick or stone, the walls to be thirty feet high, and to be built parallel to the line of the street, but either upon it or withdrawn from it, as suited the taste of the builder. However, numbers of wooden habitations have been built; but the different owners have all been cautioned against considering them as permanent. They are to be allowed for a certain time only, and then destroyed.

Weld observes the slow progress of construction.

The only public buildings carrying on as yet, are the president's house, the capitol, and a large hotel. . . . The hotel is a large building of brick, ornamented with stone; it stands between the president's house and the capitol. In the beginning of the year 1796, when I last saw it, it was roofed in, and every exertion making to have it finished with the utmost expedition. It is anything but beautiful. The capitol, at the same period, was raised only a very little way above the foundation. The private houses are all plain buildings; most of them have been built on speculation and still remain empty. The greatest number, at any one place, is at Green Leafs Point . . . just above the entrance of the eastern branch. (Weld, *Travels*, 72–89)

Francis Baily admires the plan for the city during his visit in 1796.

I presume you know upon what principle the new city is laid out: the president's House and the Capitol are situated upon two eminences; and other different rising grounds in the site are fixed on, with an intention of erecting obelisks, statues, &c. to eminent men. These eminences communicate with each other by means of streets proceeding from one to the other, like radii from a centre. . . . This is the groundwork of the plan; and by this method those natural risings will be made subservient to the elegance and beauty of the city; and that general mode of laying out a town by means of streets crossing each other at right angles and at certain distances, without any regard to the position of the ground, will be avoided.

Baily describes what he saw during his visit.

From the Capitol we walked down to the Point, where there is a place marked out for a battery. The view from here is extremely delightful:—On each side, a fine river, flowing with a gentle current along the base of a hilly and romantic country . . . with the distant view of Alexandria and its towering steeples, about six miles below, projecting apparently into the middle of the river. In the rear is the still nearer view of Georgetown, and of the president's House and the Capitol. All tend to render it one of the most delightful and pleasant sites for a town I have ever remarked in the whole of the United States.

He notes that much work remains to be done.

The canal and the gardens, as well as the bridges, which you see marked down in plan, are not yet begun; they are still in the same state of nature that they were before the city was marked out. (Baily, *Journal*, 126–28)

An English Artist Draws the Washington Landscape

On 1 September 1795 George Isham Parkyns in London and James Harrison in New York issued this aquatint view of Washington. In March of that year, Parkyns and Harrison announced an ambitious plan to produce twenty-four views of American landscapes. As a notice of this series in the *American Minerva* stated, "among these are a view of Mount Vernon, City of Washington, Philadelphia, & New York." A later account mentioned that descriptive text would accompany each 17-by-24-inch view and that these would appear on the first Monday of succeeding months. Each print was to cost $3 each, or—if colored—$5. The publishers promised that the aquatints would be printed "upon paper of a superior quality."

Parkyns and Harrison evidently did not obtain enough subscribers, for only the views of Washington, Annapolis, and Mount Vernon can be found. A second but much smaller view of Washington by Parkyns (illustrated in folio 15) does not belong to this series but appeared as a book illustration. Although Parkyns's Washington view is a highly attractive landscape, it tells us far more about the site than it does about the city. A few buildings can just be seen on the shore to the left of the island in the Potomac. Parkyns romanticized the topography, making the mountain rising beyond and to the left of the wagon road plunging downhill almost Alpine in its dimensions.

From his distant position above Georgetown, Parkyns could hardly have seen much of the site except the heavily wooded hills that he depicted so skillfully. In truth, however, there was very little in the way of urban development to be seen at this early date, as the travel accounts of Isaac Weld and Francis Baily quoted in the text of this folio attest.

Washington. Drawn by G[eorge] I[sham] Parkyns. Published by I [i.e., James] Harrison at the Apollo [New York] Sepr. 1st, 1795, and according to act of Parliament by G. E. Parkyns, Esqr. London. Aquatint, 17⅛ × 23⅞ in. (43.5 × 60.6 cm.). Prints and Photographs, Library of Congress.

Thomas Twining records his impressions after seeing Washington on 17 April 1796.

I entered a large wood through which a very imperfect road had been made, principally by removing the trees, or rather the upper parts of them. . . . After some time this indistinct way assumed more the appearance of a regular avenue, the trees here having been cut down in a straight line. Although no habitation of any kind was visible, I had no doubt but I was now riding along one of the streets of the metropolitan city. I continued in this spacious avenue for half a mile, and then came out upon a large spot, cleared of wood, in the centre of which I saw two buildings on an extensive scale, and some men at work on one of them. . . . Advancing and speaking to these workmen, they informed me that I was now in the centre of the city, and that the building before me was the Capitol, and the other destined to be a tavern. As the greatest cities have a similar beginning, there was really nothing surprising here, nor out of the usual order of things; but still the scene which surrounded me—the metropolis of a great nation in its first stage from a sylvan state—was strikingly singular. I thought it the more so, as the accounts which I had received of Washington while at Philadelphia, and the plan which I had seen . . . had prepared me for something rather more advanced. Looking from where I now stood I saw on every side a thick wood pierced with avenues in a more or less perfect state. These denoted the lines of the intended streets, which already appeared in the engraved plan with their future names. (Twining, *Travels in America*, 100–101)

Isaac Weld also saw Washington in 1796 and confirms Twining's description of a sylvan city.

Were the houses that have been built situated in one place all together, they would make a very respectable appearance, but scattered about as they are, a spectator can scarcely perceive any thing like a town. Excepting the streets and avenues, and a small part of the ground adjoining the public buildings, the whole place is covered with trees. To be under the necessity of going through a deep wood for one or two miles, perhaps, in order to see a next door neighbour, and in the same city, is a curious, and I believe, a novel circumstance. The number of inhabitants in the city, in the spring of 1796, amounted to about five thousand, including artificers, who formed by far the largest part of that number. (Weld, *Travels*, 1:86)

Francis Baily visits Washington in 1796 and concurs in this judgment.

The private buildings go on but slowly. There are about twenty or thirty houses built near the Point, as well as a few in South Capitol Street and about a hundred others scattered over in other places: in all I suppose about two hundred: and these constitute the great city of Washington. The truth is, that not much more than one-half the city is *cleared*:—the rest is *in woods*; and most of the streets which are laid out are cut through these woods, and have a much more pleasing effect now than I think they will have when they shall be built; for *now* they appear like broad avenues in a park, bounded on each side by thick woods; and there being so many of them, and proceeding in so many various directions, they have a certain wild, yet uniform and regular appearance, which they will lose when confined on each side by brick walls.

The canal and the gardens, as well as the bridges, which you see marked down in the plan, are not yet begun; they are still in the same state of nature that they were before the city was marked out. In fact, were it not for the president's House and the Capitol, you would be ignorant that you were near the spot intended for the metropolis of the United States. (Baily, *Journal*, 39)

Ten years later another English visitor found conditions little changed.

So very thinly is the city peopled, and so little is it frequented, that quails and other birds are constantly shot within a hundred yards of the Capitol, and even during the sitting of the houses of Congress. (Janson, *The Stranger in America*, 205)

In 1816 Henry Knight writes of sheep grazing and plans for a vineyard near the Capitol.

Around the Capitol, instead of parks of deer . . . you may see, up the summer hills, a few straggling flocks; not rivalling the sheep of Aleppo . . . but, small scraggy animals. . . . There has been a proposition, by a foreign citizen, to enclose, and plant an extensive vineyard near the Capitol, for the purpose of expressing wines. (Knight, *Letters*, 38)

George Isham Parkyns Produces
a Misleading View of Washington

If visitors to the site of Washington in the latter years of the eighteenth century ever saw this view of the city in 1800, they would surely have marveled at the seemingly rapid progress in the construction of the Capitol. This building appears at the right-hand side of the illustration, just to the left of the two boat masts. Its small but distinct silhouette clearly is meant to convey a building of two wings surmounted by a central dome.

In depicting the Capitol in this state, the artist, George Isham Parkyns, anticipated events by nearly three decades, since the dome was not completed until 1827. This bit of anticipatory detail makes one look with some suspicion at the buildings shown along the waterfront to the right of what must represent the arched bridge over Rock Creek leading to Georgetown. It seems unlikely that structures of that number and size actually existed. Nor was the relief of the site quite so pronounced and dramatic as the artist made it appear; Jenkins Hill, the location of the Capitol and the highest point in the city, rose only about eighty feet above the Potomac.

Parkyns drew this to illustrate a book on George Washington, and he may have wished to portray in the most favorable light the capital that the first president had done so much to create. Or, as occasionally happened, the engraver—possibly at the publisher's direction—may have added buildings or exaggerated the topography to give the illustration greater appeal. At least in one respect the view is quite accurate: in 1800 the overwhelming proportion of the land within the embryonic city lay completely vacant and undeveloped.

The City of Washington in 1800. Drawn by [George Isham] Parkyns, engraved by Heath. Published Nov. 19, 1804 by Richard Phillips, 71 St. Paul's Church Yd. [, London]. From John Marshall, *The Life of George Washington* (London: R. Phillips, 1805), vol. 3. Kiplinger Collection.

49

3 Washington in the Early Nineteenth Century

IN 1800 the city of Washington finally became the capital of the United States, an event that many persons in the East and North hoped would never occur, despite the provisions of the Residence Act of 1790. The city seemed far from ready to assume its new responsibilities as the permanent seat of government, and few officials appeared eager to leave the comforts of Philadelphia for the raw, new, sprawling, and amorphous community that had been pushed into existence on the Potomac.

Shipments of records and equipment arrived late in May at the Georgetown wharf. From there wagons hauled the records and equipment for the 131 employees of the government's civil establishment to such offices as were then available. President John Adams began a ten-day visit on 3 June with a stop at Georgetown that evening. The next day he inspected the still incomplete White House and the nearby building to the east designated for the Treasury Department. A reception at the Capitol organized by residents of the city followed on 5 June.[1]

Because Adams's term expired in March 1801, he did not play a significant part in the development of Washington, but earlier in his administration he found himself in a bitter controversy over a proposed major change in the city plan. This occurred in 1798 when Adams expressed to Alexander White, one of the commissioners, his belief that buildings for the executive departments should be located near the Capitol. Adams felt that it would be more efficient to have all government officials close together, thus making frequent communication easier and more likely to occur.

When they heard Adams's position, landowners with holdings in the vicinity of the White House vigorously protested that this violated the understanding reached between Washington and the proprietors at the crucial meeting in Georgetown in the spring of 1791. In a pointed letter to the commissioners, two of the proprietors who owned land near the White House and Georgetown recalled this event:

> We hope it will not be forgotten that the late President, at a meeting between himself and the proprietors . . . produced the plan of the city

. . . placing the offices for the Treasury and other Departments near the president's House. . . . At the same time the president explained his reasons for fixing these buildings convenient to the president's House. . . . Nor can you have forgotten . . . that President Washington fixed on the actual spots for these buildings when on his way to Congress in October, 1796.[2]

Caught in the middle of this argument, the commissioners appealed to the former president for his opinion. Washington, writing from Mount Vernon in March 1798, noted his opposition to President Adams on this matter and stated his position forcefully and bluntly:

> Where or how the houses for the president and other public officers may be fixed is to me as an *individual* a matter of moonshine; but the reverse of the president's reason for placing the latter near the Capitol was my motive for fixing them by the former. The daily intercourse which the Secretaries of the Departments must have with the president, would render a distant situation extremely inconvenient to them; for it was the universal complaint of them all, that while the Legislature was in Session, they cou'd do little or no business;—so much they were interrupted by the individual visits of members (in office hours) and by calls for papers.[3]

---

2. Robert Peter and Samuel Davidson to the Commissioners, 15 March 1798, as quoted in Wilhelmus Bogart Bryan, "Central City," 140. Daniel Carroll of Duddington, whose house L'Enfant demolished, owned land near the Capitol and, many years later, remembered the events differently. In a statement to the House of Representatives Committee on Public Buildings on 17 March 1818, Carroll stated: "I had always understood that [the buildings for executive offices] were to be placed near the capitol; and about 1791 or 92 when the plan of the city was laid before the proprietors by Gen. Washington no site was fixed on except for the Capitol and the President's House" (Bryan, "Central City," 141).

3. George Washington to Alexander White, 25 March 1798, in Washington, "Writings," 199–

200. Earlier in this letter Washington seems to admit that the reason he changed his mind about planning a city of smaller size on the Hamburg site was to secure land on favorable terms by pitting one group of proprietors against the other. He wrote to White that "the principal which operated for fixing the site for the two principal buildings, were understood and found necessary at the time to obtain the *primary* [emphasis his] object, i.e., the ground and means for either purpose." This comes after an earlier assertion that "it has always been my opinion, and so I have expressed it, that the proprietors of the City of Washington (with some exceptions) are by their jealousies and the modes they pursue to promote their local Interests, amongst its worst enemies."

1. For the early years of Washington as the seat of government, the indispensable work is Green, *Washington: Village and Capital.* Also helpful, although more specialized, is Young, *Washington Community.*

Adams withdrew his objections to locating executive departments near the White House, and on 23 June 1798 the commissioners signed a $39,511 contract for the construction of a building to house the Treasury. It was this brick office building designed by George Hadfield for a location to the east of the White House that Adams came to inspect on his trip from Philadelphia in the summer of 1800. Ten months earlier the commissioners contracted for an almost identical structure to be erected on the west side of the White House for the use of other executive departments.[4]

When the day arrived for the first meeting of Congress in the Capitol, only the north or Senate wing had been completed, and the expected session on 17 November had to be postponed four days for lack of a quorum. Then, when a heavy snowfall the day before blanketed the city, a procession the citizens had scheduled to mark the occasion was canceled. It was just as well, because local residents could not agree on who should preside over the ceremonies.

Congress had a surprise and a shock for the residents of the new city when its members assumed political control over the district: there was to be no local self-government except for those who lived in Alexandria or Georgetown, whose existing municipal status continued unchanged. Congress decreed that Maryland and Virginia laws would remain in force in the two portions of the federal territory but that residents of the district could not vote for national offices.

It was not until May, 1802 that Washingtonians obtained a municipal charter. This provided for a mayor appointed by the president and an elected council divided into two chambers. An amendment in 1804 and a new charter in 1812 expanded somewhat the powers of the municipality, provided for direct election of the city council, and gave its members the authority to choose the mayor. The division of responsibility between federal and local governments in Washington for carrying out and paying for public improvements began with this action and has remained troublesome ever since.[5]

The anticipated building boom that the arrival of Congress was supposed to generate proved to be short lived, and a leisurely pace of construction charac-terized Washington during its first two decades as the national capital. The map reproduced in folio 16 shows the locations of buildings constructed up to 1802, the year the map was published in Philadelphia by Mathew Carey.[6]

This first printed map to show the location of building development is obviously inaccurate in some details: its failure to show the White House, its portrayal of the Mall as being planted in regular rows of trees, and its depiction of the canal as if built. Nevertheless, the manner in which it shows the private buildings of the city stretched along only a few streets or avenues and concentrated in only a few places is supported by descriptions of visitors and residents and by the commissioners' census of buildings.[7]

The young Irish poet Thomas Moore stopped for a time in Washington in 1804 during Jefferson's presidency. In a description and criticism of the city in verse, he emphasized its undeveloped condition, referred to President Jefferson, and mocked the comparisons made by Americans between the new capital and ancient Rome:

In fancy now beneath the
    twilight gloom
Come, let me lead thee o'er
    this second Rome,
Where tribunes rule, where
    dusky Davi bow,
And what was Goose Creek once
    is Tiber now.
This fam'd metropolis, where
    fancy sees

Squares in morasses, obelisks
    in trees;
Which second sighted seers
    e'en now adorn
With shrines unbuilt and heroes
    yet unborn,
Though now but woods and J——
    they see.
Where streets should run and sages
    ought to be.[8]

Folio 16 also presents descriptions of the city as seen by a new legislator (later to become secretary of the Treasury), a skilled designer, and two English visitors at the dawn of the nineteenth century. All testify to the raw and unfinished appearance that characterized the city at this time. Benjamin Henry Latrobe, an architect, attributed this to the difficulties of achieving concentration of develop-

4. Tindall, *History of Washington*, 213–14. Daniel D. Reiff, in his *Washington Architecture*, p. 23, states that "in 1797, George Hadfield designed a structure for the Treasury Department, which was to be located east of the President's House, about parallel to its south facade. This same design was duplicated and used by the Commissioners for the Executive and War Department building which was to be built on a corresponding spot to the west of the President's House." In his "Architectural Career of George Hadfield," p. 53, George Hunsberger erroneously states that Hadfield's Treasury building plans "were approved by Washington late in 1797," since by that time John Adams was president.

5. Green, *Washington: Village and Capital*, 31; Tindall, *History of Washington*, 225. Green describes the duties of the council under the charter of 1812: "The council was to provide for support of the poor, see to repair of the streets, build bridges, safeguard health and abate nuisances, regulate licenses, establish fire wards and night patrols, levy a real estate tax, and, after 1804, it might open public schools. Local property assessment fell to presidentially-appointed justices of the peace, and a superintendent, also chosen by the President, replaced the commissioners who had charge of the sale of public lots in the city."

6. The commissioners' enumeration of houses built and being built on each block of the city near the end of 1801 can be found in Padover, *Jefferson*, 245–52.

7. The publisher of the map, Mathew Carey, an Irishman, settled in Philadelphia in 1784, beginning a printing and publishing business within a year. He became well known for his atlases, including *The American Atlas* (1795), the first atlas of the United States. He retired in 1822, and his firm was carried on by Henry C. Carey, his son, and Isaac Lea, his son-in-law. As Carey and Lea, the business continued to produce atlases as well as other publications. See Ristow, *American Maps and Mapmakers*, 151–53. A more accurate map showing the location of houses completed through 1800 can be found in Young, *Washington Community*, 67 fig. 2. Young compiled this from a survey made in 1801 that reported by city blocks the houses completed by May 1800 or completed or under construction by November 1801. The pattern of his map resembles the engraving in folio 16, although indicating somewhat broader bands of development than the narrow ribbons shown on Carey's map.

8. "To Thomas Hume, Esq., M.D. from the City of Washington," in Thomas Moore, *Poetical Works*.

ment in a plan with its "distribution of the public buildings over a space five miles in length and three in breadth."

Latrobe also blamed the feuding proprietors, land speculators, and the competition from Baltimore, Alexandria, and Georgetown for retarding the city's growth. He pointed out that most of the commerce of Washington passed through the hands of merchants in Alexandria and Georgetown, towns that had "accordingly prospered and increased, and may be compared to a pair of fat twins who are suckled by a consumptive mother."

The fattest of the twins—Alexandria—not only enjoyed the prestige of being part of the national capital, but it occupied by far the best site in the vicinity for waterborne transportation and commerce. Although Georgetown stood at the head of navigation on the Potomac, its harbor suffered from silting and required extra time and effort to reach it by sailing craft. In Washington itself, the Anacostia offered reasonably adequate anchorages, but shoreline facilities lagged behind those of either of its older and better-established port rivals.

To many persons Alexandria seemed far more attractive than the capital. Folio 17 contains portions of several early descriptions of the town, all but Charles Janson's in 1806 testifying not only to its commercial prosperity but to its handsome appearance and fine buildings. Probably most visitors—and certainly nearly all of the residents—would have agreed with the duc de La Rochefoucauld-Liancourt, who praised Alexandria as "beyond all comparison, the handsomest town in Virginia, and indeed . . . among the finest of the United States."

The engraving reproduced in folio 17 displays Alexandria's street system in 1798, the year after this French duke stepped ashore from the boat from Washington. He found a city that public officials had enlarged twice since Fairfax County Surveyor John West surveyed the plan in 1749 with the help of a seventeen-year-old George Washington. In 1785 a new act of expansion for the first time authorized private landowners to lay out new streets, and this map, surveyed by Colonel George Gilpin, records the further growth of Alexandria's grid street pattern that took place.[9]

The precise Cartesian rectangles of Alexandria's city blocks give no hint of the many handsome and dignified houses erected near the waterfront nor of the smaller but still attractive dwellings built elsewhere. Moreover, Alexandria exhibited little of the sprawling, disjointed pattern to be seen in Washington. Instead, two- and three-story townhouses with party walls formed unbroken street facades that would not have been out of place in the fashionable residential squares of London.

Certainly it was this kind of urbane feeling that L'Enfant had hoped and expected for Washington. Surely Benjamin Henry Latrobe, the English-born engineer and architect whom Jefferson appointed surveyor of public buildings in March 1803, would also have liked to see Washington become something more than an elaborate two-dimensional street plan. Latrobe came to this country in 1796 and shortly thereafter met President Washington, whose efforts to create the capital city Latrobe regarded as inadequate.

Writing to an Italian friend in 1806, he observed sarcastically that the idea of establishing a new capital had been "one of the off-springs of that revolutionary enthusiasm which elevated the American mind far above the aera [sic] in the life of our nation." In a reference to the president's cautious and rather grudging investment in building two houses in the city to encourage development there, Latrobe continued: "After the law had established that there should be a city, General Washington seems to have thought that everything had been done towards making it. He himself built two indifferent houses in it. Everything else was badly planned and conducted."[10]

With Jefferson's support, Latrobe completed the south or House of Representatives wing of the Capitol, linking it to the Senate wing with a wooden arcade. In 1804 he prepared plans for the locks needed for the canal to connect the Potomac with the Anacostia, but this project did not get under way until 1810 and required five more years to complete. Latrobe and Jefferson also planned several changes in the White House, including terraces on either side that concealed various outbuildings. Latrobe drew the plans for the portico that was later added to the north facade and for the semicircular extension made to the south front of the building.[11]

9. This act of the Virginia assembly ordered that new extensions of Washington Street—the main east-west thoroughfare—be surveyed 100 feet wide. That legislation also permitted the city to widen existing portions of that street to the new width by taking the needed land through eminent domain proceedings. A levy on all property in the city was authorized to pay the costs of land acquisition. See Hening, *The Statutes at Large*, 12:205–6. Col. George Gilpin, who drew this map, was among the business and civil leaders of Alexandria. For many years he was active in the Potowmack Company, headed by George Washington. This enterprise began the canal along the Potomac River that was intended to provide a connection with the Ohio River and thus promote trade and commerce at Georgetown, Washington, and Alexandria. Gilpin himself at times functioned as an engineer, supervising construction of some of the canal works. Among other activities in his busy life, Gilpin also served as a director of the Bank of Alexandria and as a justice of the peace. The name of the map's engraver, Thomas Clarke, first appears in 1797 on a series of plates for the *American Universal Magazine*, published in Philadelphia. Apparently he moved to New York City that year, where he worked until 1800. Perhaps Clarke learned his trade in the shop of Thackara and Vallance, for the clean, bold lines of his Alexandria map of 1798 echo the style of the much better

known Ellicott map of Washington that Thackara and Vallance executed in Philadelphia in 1792.

10. B. H. Latrobe to Signor Mazzei, 29 May 1806, as quoted in Latrobe, "Construction of the Public Buildings in Washington," 222. This passage immediately precedes the statement excerpted in folio 16 beginning "L'Enfant's plan has in its contrivance everything that could prevent the growth of the city." President Washington bought two lots in Washington. One was located between First and Second streets southeast on the south side of Pennsylvania Avenue. The other, on

which he built two houses, was between B and C streets on the west side of North Capitol Street. For the letters the president wrote from Mount Vernon concerning the two buildings, see "Writings," 203–5, 208–14, and 217–32. The best treatment of Latrobe's work in Washington is Carter, "Benjamin Henry Latrobe."

11. For one of Latrobe's meticulously prepared statements of work accomplished and further improvements needed in the public buildings, see his "Report of the Surveyor of the Public Buildings of the United States at Washington, March

Despite these and other public projects and some private building as well, Washington remained an undistinguished place. Charles Janson, a careful and perceptive English visitor to the city in 1806, best captures conditions in the city and its appearance at that time. Folio 18 contains several excerpts from his book, *The Stranger in America*. The folio also contains a reproduction of the rare aquatint view by George Beck published in London in 1801 although probably based on a painting by this English artist that was executed a few years earlier.[12]

Unlike the earlier view by Parkyns only a few years before, Beck's delightfully composed landscape provides a revealing look at the federal city as it began to take form. From it one can appreciate the surprise and shock felt by so many early visitors expecting to see a great city and encountering only the small and isolated clumps of buildings separated by broad expanses of open fields or wooded hills. What Janson called the "curious patch-work appearance" of the place is nowhere better conveyed than by an examination of Beck's splendid aquatint.

Beck's view appeared too early to show an important feature of the city completed in 1809. In order to improve transportation to and from Alexandria, civic leaders of that town secured approval from Congress to construct a bridge from a point below Arlington Heights to the spot where Maryland Avenue terminated at the bank of the Potomac. For many years this remained the only such structure across the river.

The map in folio 19 shows the location of the bridge. This large engraving also contains inset views of the south front of the White House and the east front of the Capitol, the facade that Thornton expected would face toward the most populous part of the city. Robert King, who drew this map, was an experienced surveyor who knew Washington thoroughly, and the map that he published in 1818 thus accurately reflected the streets, blocks, and public reservations as fixed on the ground. King also included an indication of the hills and ridges in the city, using a system of hachures like that employed by Ellicott in his map of the District of Columbia.[13]

This map seems to be the first printed depiction of Washington that was both drawn and engraved in the city, for until this time Washington apparently had no craftsmen with the skills required to produce such a print. Instead, publishers sent the work of artists or cartographers to be engraved in Boston, Philadelphia, or London. Indeed, throughout the nineteenth century, Washington was never able to overcome its late start as a city, and most of the artists and printmakers of Washington views lived and worked elsewhere. Conrad Schwarz, who engraved King's map, soon sought employment with the government rather than attempt to make a living as an independent engraver.[14]

When King published this engraving in 1818, both the White House and the Capitol were still being restored following their burning by British troops during the War of 1812. That occurred on 24 and 25 August 1814 when the invaders torched both buildings, the War and Treasury offices flanking the White House, and the federal arsenal near the mouth of the Anacostia. Capt. Thomas Tingey, the Navy Yard commandant, destroyed his own installation along with several ships to prevent them from falling to the enemy. Only the Patent Office and Post Office, both then quartered in a structure built to house a hotel, survived among the public buildings.[15]

Latrobe wrote to Jefferson that at the Capitol, while portions of the Senate wing escaped with only partial damage,

> in the House of Representatives the devastation has been dreadful. There was here no want of materials for conflagration. . . . The whole was soon in a blaze, and so intense was the flame, that the glass . . . was melted. . . . The stone is . . . unable to resist the force of flame. . . . The exterior of the columns and entablature, therefore, expanded far beyond the dimensions of the interior, scaled off, and not a vestige of fluting or sculpture remained around. The appearance of the ruin was awfully grand when I first saw it, and . . . threatened immediately to fall.[16]

It was in working on the reconstruction of the Capitol that Latrobe designed his famous capitals for the sixteen columns supporting the rotunda, composed, as

23, 1808," in Padover, *Jefferson*, 399–413. Two of the watercolor renderings Latrobe made to show proposed changes in the White House are reproduced in Jensen, *The White House*, 12.

12. The painting, owned privately, is reproduced in Junior League of Washington, *City of Washington*, 36. Of Beck's career we have only fragmentary information. He established himself as an artist in England, where he exhibited at both the Royal Academy of Arts and the Society of Artists of Great Britain. In 1796 and 1797 he lived in Baltimore and then moved to Philadelphia, where he remained until 1804. He painted Niagara Falls that year and Pittsburgh in 1806. Eventually he settled in Lexington, Kentucky, and in the year of his death he exhibited, at the Pennsylvania Academy of the Fine Arts, some landscapes and a

painting of the estate of William Hamilton of Philadelphia. Several beautifully executed aquatints bearing his name were engraved in London by T. Cartwright and published by Atkins & Nightingale of London and Philadelphia, the view of Georgetown and Washington among them. Other scenes in this series issued in 1801 show Philadelphia, Baltimore, the Great Falls of the Potomac, and views of Niagara Falls published by George Nightingale in 1805 and Wright's Ferry on the Susquehanna River in 1809. All of these works are in the Stokes Collection at the New York Public Library and are listed in Deák's *Picturing America*. Her notes on Beck and his views are entries 220–22 and 229.

13. With his father, Robert Sr., and brother, Nicholas, Robert King had prepared the official

plats and maps of the city from 1796 to 1817. The Washington surveys by the three Kings, all of them English, are described in Ralph E. Ehrenberg, "Mapping the Nation's Capital."

14. Conrad Schwarz (1790–?) was born in Germany and received his training as a stipple engraver in Amsterdam and Baltimore. Several portraits by Schwarz in this medium were published in Baltimore in 1814 by Fielding Lucas, Jr. Schwarz probably moved to Washington by 1817, since the map was being advertised for sale in the *National Intelligencer* by music and book seller William Cooper at the end of February 1818. Schwarz filed his naturalization papers in Washington three months later with Cooper as one of his witnesses.

Schwarz may have worked for Cooper, but in 1821 he became a draftsman with the Navy Department, where he worked until 1846.

15. It was Dr. William Thornton, designer of the Capitol and later a commissioner of the district, who saved these two offices. As superintendent of patents, he "convinced the British Major that the patent models were private property and to destroy them would be a crime against civilization" (Green, *Washington: Village and Capital*, 62). A tornado on the second day of the burning of Washington completed the devastation.

16. Latrobe to Jefferson, undated, in Padover, *Jefferson*, 473–76.

Latrobe wrote Jefferson with an enclosed sketch, "of leaves and flowers of the tobacco plant." These later elicited both criticism and praise from visitors, depending on their attitudes toward the value of tradition or innovation in architecture.

Other critics objected to the use of Italian marble in rebuilding the Capitol. Morris Birkbeck, an Englishman, made this point forcefully in one of the documents in folio 19, stating this action showed "how un-American is the whole plan." He must have overlooked Latrobe's tobacco-leaf capitals when he added that he "would have preferred native decoration for the seat of the legislature."

By the time Birkbeck visited Washington in 1817, much of the task of rebuilding the ruined city had been completed. After some initial soul-searching about the possibility of moving the seat of government elsewhere, Congress proved reasonably generous in making funds available for the needed repairs of public buildings. After Latrobe supervised the extensive reconstruction of the Capitol and improved it structurally in the process, Congress reoccupied the building in December 1819. Since the fire, its members met in a brick hall hastily erected on the east side of Capitol Square, where the Supreme Court is now located. Several wealthy citizens financed this "Brick Capitol" to forestall a possible move of the government to another city.

During this period the city at last began to attract many new residents, and for several years Washington enjoyed a modest building boom. The Washington Canal finally opened late in 1815 amidst predictions this would stimulate the industrial development so many persons in the district had looked forward to for so long. The canal—too shallow for heavy barges and, before long, rank with stagnant water and refuse—proved to be a liability to Washington rather than an asset and eventually had to be filled, a subject that will be dealt with in a later chapter.

The end of the decade found the nation in a depression brought on by speculation in land and the issuance of paper money by the unregulated banks of the period. Early in 1819 Washington real estate values collapsed, many businesses declared bankruptcy, the government could not sell any of the lots it still owned, banks failed, and unemployment soared. Nevertheless, the census of 1820 listed 13,247 residents, up from 8,208 the decade before and only 3,210 in 1800. In 1820 the black population numbered 3,641, or about one-quarter of the total. Of the blacks, nearly half—1,696—were free, while slaves numbered 1,945.[17]

Although its population had multiplied several times in the three decades since its founding, Washington still presented an unfinished and incomplete appearance that continued to surprise and disappoint visitors—particularly those from foreign countries. Lt. Francis Hall noted in 1816 that "the city in its present state, being commenced from the extremities instead of the centre, has a dis-

jointed and naked appearance," an observation repeated—as was to be true many times later—by the anonymous English visitor whose descriptions and criticisms appear in folio 20 along with those by Isaac Candler.

Many visitors, anxious to see the planned city, arrived with high expectations. Maps of Washington like that reproduced in folio 20 may have been partly responsible for their attitudes. This map appeared in an important early atlas of America published in Philadelphia in 1822 by Henry C. Carey and Isaac Lea. It is a close copy of one printed in 1819 in Edinburgh or a somewhat different version published a year later in France. In turn, both of these possible prototypes owed their origins to the topographical map of the district prepared by Andrew Ellicott more than twenty years earlier.[18]

All three accentuate the city blocks with fine hatched lines, a method of depiction that makes the streets, public building sites, and civic squares stand out. However, hatching was also often used on city maps to indicate those portions occupied by buildings. To someone in a far-off location and unfamiliar with Washington through either firsthand experience or from reading, such a map might well suggest that every block in the city had been developed and every street had been improved.

It is not surprising, therefore, that many visitors expressed disappointment at what they saw. John Duncan, a Scottish observer at this time, bluntly told his readers about his feelings on the matter:

> To lay out the plan of a city . . . is one thing, and to build it is another; of all the regularity and system which the engraved plan exhibits, scarcely a trace is discernible upon the ground. Instead of beginning this gigantic undertaking in a central spot, and gradually extending the buildings from a common focus, they appear to have commenced at once in twenty or thirty different places, without the slightest regard to concentration or the comforts of good neighborhood.[19]

17. For the major events of the period between the War of 1812 and 1820, see Green, *Washington: Village and Capital*, 64–118. She provides population information in table 3, p. 183.

18. Carey and Lea were son and son-in-law of Mathew Carey. Both of the engravers also worked in Philadelphia. James H. Young followed that craft from 1817 to at least 1866, the latter half of that period as chief engraver for S. Augustus Mitchell, the most prolific publisher of atlases at that time. In 1822 and 1823 Young formed a partnership with George Delleker, who was active in Philadelphia during 1817–24. Among other work, Delleker had produced several engraved portraits of naval heroes of the War of 1812 as well as some miniature painted portraits. Young and Delleker engraved more than a dozen of the fifty-three plates in the atlas that Carey and Lea published. It must have required all the efforts of the two engravers for many months and doubtless was regarded by them as a major contract. The reduced prototype of the Ellicott district survey that served as their model was first engraved by W. & D. Lizars in 1819 for the three-volume work by D. B. Warden, *Statistical, Political, and Historical Account of the United States* (Edinburgh, 1819). The French edition of this book in 1820 contains a version of the map engraved by Tardieu.

19. Duncan claimed that "a stranger looking round him for Washington, sees two houses here, and six there, and a dozen yonder." He found these "scattered in straggling groups over the greater part of three or four square miles." Although he pointed out that the "city does not contain above fourteen thousand inhabitants," they were located "in so many different places, that the public crier . . . is obliged to make the circuit on horseback" (John M. Duncan, *Travels*, 254).

However, not all visitors were wholly displeased with what they saw in the new capital. Most persons admired the Capitol, and the complex of buildings made up of the White House and the offices of the executive departments also drew favorable comments from many observers, both foreign and domestic. The wife of the French minister in Washington, the Baroness Hyde de Neuville, left us the best record of how these buildings appeared during this period when in 1820 she sketched the five structures as she saw them looking south from Lafayette Square.[20]

The first illustration in folio 21 reproduces this primitive but charming scene. The two buildings on the left housed the State and Treasury departments, while those on the right provided accommodations for the departments of Navy and War. As befitted their more prominent positions fronting on Lafayette Square, the State and War departments had their northern entrances marked by colonnades supporting pediments.

The second illustration provides a more detailed look at the State Department building about ten years after the baroness completed her watercolor sketch. It was the ensemble created by the five buildings occupying the White House square that drew admiring comments from Anne Royall, in 1826, and the even more well traveled Englishman James Silk Buckingham in 1838 when he journeyed through America and wrote extensively about its towns, landscape, manners, and politics. Folio 21 contains portions of these and other descriptions of the White House and its neighboring buildings.[21]

The White House continued to attract visitors. The view of the White House at the upper left of folio 22 was printed about 1832 by the Philadelphia firm of Cephas Childs and Henry Inman and shows the presidential residence from the southeast with the semicircular portico that Jefferson and Latrobe had planned many years earlier. Put on stone by George Lehman, this lithograph may have been copied from an engraved version of the same image that appeared at about the same time.[22]

The next two illustrations of folio 22 show the building as it appeared from Lafayette Square in the 1840s. By that time John Quincy Adams had had the grounds landscaped and fenced, and not long after Andrew Jackson's inauguration in 1829 he added the north portico that Latrobe had designed in Jefferson's administration. These lithographs by the Kellog firm in Hartford and, slightly later, by Augustus Köllner and his Paris publisher show what awaited visitors brought there by their guides from about 1830 onward.[23]

Equally rare—although not so attractive—is the final view at lower right. This is unsigned and its date is unknown, although it was doubtless published in Germany and probably copied from a well-known engraving. The title is printed in mirror image, indicating that it was intended to be viewed through an instrument having a reflecting mechanism allowing the viewer to read the title correctly. Such prints became popular during the eighteenth century and continued to be produced thereafter, although apparently in fewer number.[24]

The accounts of reactions to the White House transcribed in folio 22 provide a representative selection of those written during the period between the end of the War of 1812 and the outbreak of the Civil War. Although most visitors found the building impressive in size and appearance and admired the view down the Potomac, many called attention to its unhealthy location. The tidal flats of the river and the stagnant waters of the canal gave the surroundings a ripe odor and guaranteed a plentiful supply of mosquitoes, a problem that every inhabitant of the White House regarded as highly objectionable.

By the end of the 1820s the Capitol, too, had finally been completed. Several architects had modified Thornton's original design in several details, as did Charles Bulfinch, the famous Boston designer who assumed direction over its completion in 1818 after Latrobe had carried out the initial phases of reconstruction. By 1829 the gleaming stone structure topped by its restrained low dome dominated the Washington skyline.

The four illustrations in folio 23 show the two quite different faces the building

20. For the artist of this important watercolor, see the caption to the illustrations in folio 21 as well as Andrews, "The Baroness Was Never Bored," and the note to entry 254, pp. 168–69, in Deák, *Picturing America*.

21. Charles Burton (1807?–?) drew the State Department view. Like so many other artists of this period, he, too, was English. He also was an engraver. Burton drew several etched and engraved views of New York City that George Melksham Bourne, a dealer in prints, stationery, music, and artists' supplies, published in 1831. These are listed in Deák, *Picturing America*, entry 392.

22. George Lehman (?–1870) worked during 1830–32 for the Philadelphia firm formed in 1830 by Cephas Grier Childs (1793–1871) and Henry Inman (1801–1846). Lehman replaced Inman in 1833 as Childs's partner. For this period in Philadelphia lithography and the place of Childs and Inman in American printmaking, see Wainwright, *Philadelphia in the Romantic Age of Lithography*, 6–29. The engraving that Lehman may have copied is among the plates found in Hinton, *History and Topography of the United States*. The priority of publication has not been established.

23. Daniel Wright Kellogg (1807–1874) established his lithographic firm of D. W. Kellogg & Company in Hartford in 1830. After 1836 most of the direction of the firm came from his two brothers, Edmund Burk Kellogg (1809–1872) and Elijah Chapman Kellogg (1811–1881), and in 1842 the company became known as E. B. & E. C. Kellogg. The Kellogg view reproduced here was published sometime before that date. For their work, see Steinway, "The Kelloggs of Hartford"; Knittle, "The Kelloggs"; "S. St. J. Morgan Collection"; and Phipps, "Connecticut's Printmakers." Augustus Köllner (1812–1906) began his artistic career as an engraver in Stuttgart at the age of sixteen. He later moved to Paris where he worked as an engraver and etcher, leaving for America in 1839. He worked first for the Washington lithographic firm of Philip Haas, but by the fall of 1840 he had established himself in Philadelphia, where he did lithographs for many of the city's lithographers. Beginning in 1848 he began an ambitious series of views that were printed in Paris. His lithographs of Washington belong to this group. See Wain-

wright, "Augustus Kollner"; Mann, "Augustus Kollner"; and Kelly, *The South on Paper*, 47–48.

24. William Bartlett, whose work is to be discussed shortly, drew what is almost surely the prototype of this German print in the late 1830s. The viewing device referred to in the text was known as an optical pillar or a diagonal mirror. The instrument consisted of a pedestal topped by a hinged mirror mounted behind a magnifying glass. The print was placed flat on the table behind the device, and its enlarged and reversed image (with the title then readable) could be seen through the glass as reflected by the mirror. More elaborate versions were also made. The Winterthur Museum has one enclosed in a cabinet whose large magnifying glass looks much like an early television screen.

turned to the world. The first, drawn by Charles Bulfinch, the architect, and engraved in aquatint by Henry and J. Stone, is notable for its beauty, rarity, and as one of the earliest separately issued views of Washington or its buildings to be printed in the city. Although Stone obviously was a skilled printmaker and Washington's pioneer lithographer, his few recorded prints testify to the difficulties he encountered trying to market his products in a city with few cultural interests and a transient population that came and went with the convening and adjournment of Congress.[25]

The Bulfinch-Stone aquatint depicts the Capitol's east front, the side nearly everyone expected would face toward the most populous part of the city and that had been designed as the principal entrance. Beyond the landscaped grounds a forecourt led to the great stairway and the massive but graceful portico sheltering the entryway. Another view of this facade is at the upper right, a scene from the northeast put on stone no later than 1832 by George Lehman of Philadelphia and published in Washington by Thompson & Homans.

The third view shows the western facade. The most prolific topographic artist of the time, the Englishman William H. Bartlett, drew the engraving reproduced at lower left. Bartlett first visited America in 1836, and soon thereafter he passed through Washington to sketch both the Capitol and the White House. Engraved versions of these appeared with many others by him showing American cities, buildings, major works of civil engineering, and landscapes in the two-volume *American Scenery*.[26]

Nathaniel Parker Willis wrote the text for this work, which first appeared in installments in 1839, each part consisting of eight text pages and four of Bartlett's drawings engraved on steel by several engravers in London employed by the publisher, George Virtue. One of the accounts in folio 23 is from the passage Willis composed to describe the Capitol as the artist shows it here from a point on Pennsylvania Avenue a few blocks to the northwest of Capitol Hill. The last view in the folio is the work of Augustus Köllner, who drew the Capitol at the same time he did his lithograph of the White House illustrated in the previous folio.

Folio 23 also contains an excerpt from the long account of her visit to Washington written by Frances Trollope, the mother of the novelist Anthony Trollope. Her book, *Domestic Manners of the Americans*, contained highly critical comments about and sometimes savage attacks on Americans and the American way of life. Its publication aroused vigorous protests and defiant rebuttals by citizens of this country, but no one seemed to object to her observations about the city of Washington, which she praised with the same extravagance she used in complaining about many other aspects of the country in which she lived for several years.

Two other extracts from Frances Trollope's book can be found in folio 24, beginning with her first glimpse of the city in daylight as she began her observations with an early morning visit to the Capitol in 1830. The second must have pleased Washingtonians because it praises the city and condemns earlier criticisms by so many visitors. She stated emphatically that although only "a very small part of [the plan] has been as yet executed," she saw "nothing in the least degree ridiculous about it."

Five years later an equally independent and remarkable Englishwoman entered an opposing brief into the record. Harriet Martineau, an accomplished writer on political economy, came to America in 1834 at the age of thirty-two. She published her impressions of the country in two books, *Society in America* (1837) and *Retrospect of Western Travel* (1838), and it is an extract from the latter that folio 24 also includes.

Martineau disagreed sharply with Frances Trollope's optimistic view of the city and its future, indicating her belief that the seat of government would soon be moved to the West, probably Cincinnati. Although she managed two words of admiration for the Capitol, calling it a "splendid building," she professed to be "taken by surprise" on seeing it only because "so sordid are the enclosures and houses on its very verge."

The view reproduced in this folio would seem to justify her appraisal. Thomas Doughty sketched this scene for a rare lithograph published in 1832 by Childs & Inman, whose views of the White House and Capitol were reproduced in previous folios. This illustration of a large segment of Washington is among the earliest American city views executed in lithography during the first decade that method of printing was used commercially in America. This technique for creating multiple images came to dominate the field of city views and was employed for most of the largest and most attractive portraits of Washington.[27]

---

25. Henry Stone was active in Washington as an engraver, portrait painter, and lithographer from 1822 to 1846. It was in the former year that he introduced lithography to Washington, making him among the very first to use that medium in the United States. A brief notice on 15 November 1822 and an advertisement five days later in the *Washington Gazette* announced the arrival of this new method of printing to Washingtonians. John Thomas Carey provides the text of these two passages and much additional information about Stone and his work in his "The American Lithograph," 63–66. From 1837 Stone worked in the Patent Office, first as a draftsman and later as an assistant patent examiner. J. Stone was his brother, James. See Wright and McDevitt, "Henry Stone, Lithographer."

26. For Bartlett and his work, see Cowdrey, "William Henry Bartlett," and Alexander M. Ross, *William Henry Bartlett*.

27. Thomas Doughty (1793–1856) left the leather business in Philadelphia at the age of twenty-seven to devote himself to art. Almost immediately he became a successful landscape painter and, with Thomas Cole and Asher B. Durand, is regarded as one of the founders of the Hudson River school of painters. His paintings number over 400 and are highly regarded. During his early years as an artist he traveled between Philadelphia, New York, and Boston, exhibiting frequently, and either in these places or—more likely—in the Philadelphia establishment of Cephas Childs, he learned about lithography. In 1830–32 he drew and put on stone twenty-seven lithographs, all but four being plates for *The Cabinet of Natural History and American Rural Sports* that he and his brother, John, produced. Included among the four lithographs by him executed in 1832 not connected with the *Cabinet* is the view of Washington reproduced here. His printmaking career is the subject of Looney, "Thomas Doughty, Printmaker."

Doughty looked from the City Hall, a building then far from complete and one to be described and illustrated in the chapter to follow. It stood on a portion of Judiciary Square, one of the major public reservations four blocks north and west of the Capitol. Between Judiciary Square and Capitol Hill stretched an expanse of broken terrain with only a few scattered buildings in between. Many visitors commented about this aspect of the city, including Capt. Basil Hall who pointed out to his readers the peculiar appearance of a city that consisted only of widely scattered clusters of buildings:

> This singular capital . . . is so much scattered that scarcely any of the ordinary appearances of a city strike the eye. Here and there ranges of buildings are starting up, but by far the greater number of the houses are detached from one another. The streets, where streets there are, have been made so unusually wide, that the connexion is quite loose; and the whole affair, to use the quaint simile of a friend at Washington, looks as if some giant had scattered a box of his child's toys at random on the ground.[28]

Seven years later Tyrone Power, the popular Irish comedian, found Washington unchanged in this respect. He referred to "thinly-furnished streets" that "extended in dotted lines," and "the meagre supply of buildings" that created such an "irregular and detached appearance" that "all design becomes confounded." Power echoed Hall's conclusion: "It seemed to me as though some frolicsome fairy architect, whilst taking a flight with a sieveful of pretty houses, had suddenly betaken her to tipping them over this attractive site as she circled over the valley in her airy car."[29]

Thus, although Washington's population had increased during the 1820s by almost 50 percent, reaching 13,117 in 1830, the area of the city was so vast and the small concentrations of buildings were so widely spaced that it almost totally lacked any urban character. Both Alexandria and Georgetown, each with more than 8,000 inhabitants, occupied far less space, and their streets, lined by unbroken rows of brick dwellings, provided a sharp contrast to those of the capital city.

Doughty's view in folio 24 also suggests the primitive condition of the streets serving this portion of Washington. Even a decade later, as James Berrett, a former mayor, recalled, "there was not a paved street in the city." Instead, "the streets were all mud" with gutters "formed of cobble-stones rendered necessary to carry off the drainage, which at that time was entirely upon the surface." Mayor Berrett also remembered the difficulties in crossing these muddy thoroughfares on foot: "The sidewalks were very imperfect. The crossings from one side of the street to the other were formed by flagstones of about a foot in dimension, so that the citizens desiring to pass from one side of the street to the other had to find the corner of the street before they had reached this passage-way."

This city lacked basic utility services as well, since, as Berrett described the prevailing situation even in the 1840s, "there was no gaslight and no water except what was taken from the pumps." The few street lamps burned oil and were "sparsely distributed," so that "on dark nights the population had to grope their way about the town as best they could."[30]

No better evidence exists of the singular character of Washington in the 1830s than the map of the city by Henry Tanner reproduced in folio 25. Although published in his *New Universal Atlas* of 1836, the map shows conditions about three years earlier. It was then that a fire destroyed the Treasury, which Tanner shows as one of the four nearly identical buildings flanking the White House. Tanner identifies this and other buildings in a detailed legend at the lower left.[31]

Although this legend is quite useful in locating the principal features of the capital city, it is Tanner's depiction of the built-up portions of the city that is of special interest. Note how each of these neighborhoods forms a kind of urban island, a pattern whose beginnings were recorded on the map of 1802 reproduced in folio 16. The city of the mid-1830s thus existed as a kind of archipelago of neighborhoods separated from one another almost as if divided by water instead of expanses of undeveloped land.[32]

One such island of buildings adjoined the Navy Yard on the Anacostia; a second encircled the Capitol; a third bordered the Patent Office; and yet another surrounded the White House and the executive offices. The much older settlement of Georgetown formed a fifth island of development. Here and there, smaller groups of buildings floated in a sea of vacant blocks and empty streets. Not until after the Civil War would these intervening spaces be filled and a more conventional urban development pattern at last emerge.

In the opinion of Theodore Dwight, whose comments appear first in folio 25,

---

30. Berrett, "Address." In 1897 Berrett's memory of conditions in Washington may not have been entirely accurate. In 1832 Congress appropriated $115,000 "for macadamizing Pennsylvania Avenue and grading the President's square and . . . $23,000 . . . for piping water into the Capitol" (Green, *Washington: Village and Capital*, 127).

31. Henry Schenck Tanner (1786–1858) began his career as an engraver in Philadelphia working with his brother, Benjamin. Although he displayed his skills as an engraver for many of the maps drawn and published by John Melish, he established his reputation as a geographer with the publication in 1818–23 of his *New American Atlas*. The map of Washington illustrated here comes from one of his many later atlases, *A New Universal Atlas* published by Tanner in Philadelphia. For his ca-

reer, see chap. 13, "Henry S. Tanner," pp. 191–206, in Ristow, *American Maps and Mapmakers*.

32. Tanner may have based his delineation of the built-up portion of Washington on personal observation. His reputation as an accurate cartographer suggests that his depiction of the city can be relied on. Later editions of his atlas published in 1844 and 1846 by S. Augustus Mitchell of Philadelphia included the Washington map with no changes. By this time, of course, many more buildings existed, and the map was badly out of date. It may be of interest to note that these later states of the map were printed by lithography, doubtless through the transfer process by which impressions from the copper plates of the original were put on stone.

---

28. Basil Hall, *Travels in North America*, 2:1.

29. Power, *Impression of America*, 1:213.

President Washington and his colleagues simply miscalculated in believing that the city would become important enough to attract any significant number of residents. Joseph Varnum, Jr., also criticized the plan as "in many respect an exceedingly impracticable one," stating flatly that L'Enfant provided "twice as many streets as are required" and that the numerous radial avenues also "cut up" the blocks in such a way as to "leave everywhere awkward space" for building. Varnum added his own ideas about how the city could have been laid out to avoid these problems but still retaining the great avenues that he regarded as "a grand feature, worthy of the nation."

Just two years before Tanner's map appeared, Lewis P. Clover of New York published the superb aquatint etching and engraving reproduced in folio 26. The artist was George Cooke, a grocery and chinaware salesman who at the age of twenty-six decided to turn his amateur talents as an artist into a professional career. Prior to 1825 he produced 130 portraits in a period of only twenty-eight months. During the years 1826–31 he studied in Italy and France and then returned to America where he specialized in landscape painting.[33]

William J. Bennett, a highly skilled English master of aquatint, used this medium of printmaking to reproduce Cooke's attractive composition. Bennett used Cooke's images for four other prints that Clover also published as part of an extensive series of views of American port cities. Their quality is unsurpassed. As a recent study of his work states, "as prints, Bennett's aquatints are equal in finish and elegance of style to the finest of English colored aquatints."[34]

The Cooke-Bennett print of 1834 showing Washington is the most attractive view of the American capital city published up to that time, and it provides by far the best glimpse of one of Washington's earliest and most important neighborhoods. This comprised the buildings of the Navy Yard on the Anacostia and the private structures erected to the east, west, and north—the latter extending part way up the gradual ascent to Capitol Hill.[35]

Benjamin Henry Latrobe designed the Navy Yard barracks, docks, sail lofts, and other structures. After its defenders in the War of 1812 burned them to prevent equipment from falling to the British, the yard was rebuilt with improved facilities and shops. Visitors admired the ingenious machinery that pulled ships' hulls out of the water and into a huge building for repairs and refitting. This structure is one of the two that appear most prominently in the foreground of the view. One of the accounts in folio 26 provides a detailed explanation of how ships could be drawn through its arched opening so that work could be done in sheltered surroundings.[36]

Cooke probably drew or painted this scene in 1832 or 1833, for it must have taken some time for Bennett to prepare his beautiful aquatint version. Cooke looked toward the Capitol from the south bank of the Anacostia, a viewpoint nearly opposite the axis of sight presented in the illustration reproduced in folio 24. Although the Cooke-Bennett view depicts a city that seems to be more developed than that slightly earlier lithograph, huge expanses of open or sparsely built land are clearly evident.

Only a single line of buildings faces Pennsylvania Avenue between the Capitol and the White House, although on the other side of that thoroughfare the city appears to be solidly built up for three or four blocks to the north. In this section the most prominent building is the City Hall, a structure drawn here somewhat out of proportion and shown in a more complete state than it was in fact.

To the left—west of the Capitol—the Mall stretches formlessly toward the Potomac. South of this unimproved expanse of land one can see only scattered buildings, with a little cluster of them located at the point where the Long Bridge crossed the Potomac and ended at the termination of Maryland Avenue extending southwest from the Capitol. Washington at this time was indeed a city of distances—some of them magnificent, perhaps, but most of them merely dreary, drab, and boring.

One other view of this time and type clearly documents the peculiarly dispersed character of Washington in the 1830s. This lithograph, drawn and published by the Norwegian artist Peder Anderson, put on stone by Fitz Hugh Lane, and printed in Boston by Thomas Moore, is reproduced in folio 27. Accompanying it are several accounts by contemporary travelers who criticized the city's widely scattered buildings.[37]

33. Cooke (1793–1849) exhibited his work at such places as the Boston Athenaeum, the National Academy, the Pennsylvania Academy, and the American Academy. His painting of Athens, Georgia, is in the collection of the University of Georgia. See Rudolph, "George Cooke and His Paintings."

34. Roylance and Finlay, *Pride of Place*, x. This work reproduces several of his aquatints. Bennett's aquatints are also reproduced in Mayor, "Aquatint Views." For notes on and reproductions in color of the views of Richmond, Virginia, New York as seen from Brooklyn Heights, and Detroit, see Deák, *American Views*, 62–65, 70–73. Of the Bennett views, Roylance and Finlay have this to say: "All have a quality of happy inspiration that denies all suggestion of any city discomforts of poverty, dirt, congestion or turmoil. Serenity reigns supreme with mirror-smooth harbors, decoratively becalmed sailing ships, and sunlit city horizons. Any storms will quickly pass in these halcyon visions. Could this gently wind-tossed English harbor scene really be Staten Island, this American Athens Baltimore, this marble Acropolis Richmond, or this Virgilian prospect Detroit? Perhaps. In the first half of the nineteenth century these cities were still young and full of the ardent optimism of a new Republic."

35. The Navy Yard occupied one of the seventeen federal reservations in Washington—those areas officially designated for public buildings or purposes and whose original owners received compensation at the agreed-on rate of £25 per acre. As surveyed, Reservation Seventeen—originally named Exchange Square—consisted of thirty-seven acres, some of which extended into the Anacostia River. Benjamin Stoddert, the first secretary of the navy, selected this site as one of six navy yards planned during the administration of John Adams when the country feared war with France, adding three additional acres in 1800.

36. In 1805 and 1806 the yard launched two large vessels, the brig *Hornet* and the ship *Wasp*, both of which fought in the War of 1812. The yard also provided repair facilities for much larger warships built elsewhere, including the *Constitution*, the *President*, and the *Essex*. Plans of the Navy Yard in 1799, 1814, 1828, 1866, 1872, 1889, 1898, 1903, 1911, and 1917, along with a brief history of the yard's development, can be found in U.S. Naval Facilities Engineering Command, *Washington Navy Yard Master Plan*, 15–24.

37. For notes on Anderson, see the annotations to entries 475 and 488 in Deák, *Picturing America*, 1:320, 330, and Haugen, "Story of Peder Anderson." For Lane, now recognized as one of Amer-

Frederick Marryat and James Silk Buckingham both visited Washington in 1838, the year Anderson published his view. Marryat compared the Capitol to "a general without an army, only surrounded and followed by a parcel of ragged little dirty boys." Buckingham likened it to "a town rising into existence, but gradually arrested in its progress, and now stationary in its condition." Another Englishman, George Combe, asserted that "the town looks like a large straggling village reared in a drained swamp."

However, to Tyrone Power, who joined his fellow Britons in noting and criticizing the city's scattered pattern when examined at close quarters, Washington seemed a different and better place when seen from a distance. In a book written after his first performance tour of the United States in 1836, he tells his readers that after crossing "the interminable-looking bridge" spanning the Potomac, he "often halted and turned my horses's head" to gaze at the "extensive and varied views of the Potomac, together with George-town and the Capitol." Power described his feelings when looking at Washington from this vantage point on the Virginia shore—one similar to that chosen by Anderson when he sketched the city for his lithograph:

> Nothing, in fact, can be more panoramic than the aspect of [Washington and Georgetown], lying in one of the best-defined and most beautiful of natural amphitheatres, and flanked by the grandest of rivers. At the distance of five or six miles all the meannesses of the city are lost sight of, and the extreme ends, so widely apart and so worthily bounded, by the Capitol on the north and the president's mansion, with the surrounding offices belonging to the state department, on the south, combined with the dock-yard and a few other large public buildings in the middle distance, give to the metropolis of America an aspect no way unworthy of its high destiny.[38]

Looking at Anderson's view makes one believe that it must have been Irish good cheer and charity that produced such comments. For even at this distance the city looks raw and unfinished. The Mall was then a bleak expanse of turf, weeds, and muddy soil lapped by the often stagnant waters of the Potomac. The White House grounds, although more elevated, appear no more inviting. And, from Georgetown on the left to the penitentiary and the arsenal at Greenleaf's Point on the right, the city stretches interminably in a thin and irregular ribbon of buildings of which no more than half a dozen seem to be of impressive size or character.[39]

Many foreign diplomats commented unfavorably on these conditions. Most of them seemed to regard their appointment for service in Washington as a banishment from civilization. One of these, the immensely learned, wise, and witty Portuguese minister plenipotentiary to the United States from 1816 to 1820, the Abbé Correa da Serra, apparently coined that durable phrase, "The City of Magnificent Distances," used by so many after him to characterize Washington.[40]

Foreign writers, travelers, and diplomats might poke fun at the city as did an occasional visitor from Philadelphia, New York, or Boston, but most Americans—including, of course, nearly all local residents—looked forward to a more impressive community in the future. As Basil Hall recorded in his book in referring to the District of Columbia, "This space contains one hundred square miles; and many persons in that country believe the time will come when their capital shall cover the whole area of this great square."[41]

Such differences of opinion continued through the remainder of the century, as will be evident in documents presented in subsequent chapters. Many of these concern the several major public buildings begun after the mid-1830s or, in the case of the City Hall that was started in 1820, brought to a more finished state of completion in that later period. Some, like the City Hall and the later and larger Patent Office and Post Office, stimulated the erection of private dwellings in their vicinities and thus helped to fill up some of Washington's vast empty spaces.

The Smithsonian Institution, granted by Congress a site on the south side of the Mall, provided a model that could be used in locating other educational and cultural institutions. However, the decision to build the enormous Treasury so that its southern portico cut off the view of the White House from the approach along Pennsylvania Avenue from the Capitol represented a serious error by both Congress and President Jackson.

Whether beneficial or not, all of these buildings attracted artists to record their appearance for members of the American and foreign publics whose interest in Washington increased as did the nation's population, territory, and status among the governments of the world. Some artists depicted only the individual structures, while others provided new images of the entire city showing its changing skyline from a number of vantage points. In the process, they produced many of Washington's most attractive and compelling prints.

ica's most important artists in the first half of the nineteenth century, see Wilmerding, *Fitz-Hugh Lane, 1804–1865,* and Wilmerding, *Fitz Hugh Lane.* See also Tatham, "Pendleton-Moore Shop."

38. Power, *Impressions of America,* 1:247–48.

39. In noting the publication of Anderson's view, a writer in one Washington newspaper attested to its accuracy: "Mr. Anderson, a promising young artist, has just published a beautiful lithographic view of this city, after an original drawing from his own pencil. All the prominent objects in the city and vicinity are marked with great accuracy, and will enable all who have not seen the metropolis to form a pretty correct idea of its general appearance and the adjacent scenery" (*Niles' National Register,* 7 July 1838, p. 288).

40. Whether he originated that epithetical title or not, Correa was responsible for another observation about the capital and the president who saw to its founding: "Every man is born with a bag of folly which attends him through life. Washington was born with a small bag, which he kept to himself, and never imparted any of it to the world, until the metropolis of the nation was founded, when he emptied the whole of it in this city." For these words attributed to Correa, see Richard Beale Davis, *Abbé Correa in America,* 105, and sources cited by Davis in notes 21 and 22.

41. Basil Hall, *Travels in North America,* 2:2.

A congressman tells his wife about conditions in the capital.

Around the Capitol are seven or eight boarding houses, one tailor, one shoemaker, one printer, a washing-woman, a grocery shop, a pamplets and stationery shop, a small dry-goods shop, and an oyster house. This makes the whole of the Federal city as connected with the Capitol. At the distance of three-fourths of a mile, on or near the Eastern Branch, lie scattered the habitations of Mr. Law and of Mr. Carroll, the principal proprietaries of the ground, half a dozen houses, a very large but perfectly empty warehouse, and a wharf graced by not a single vessel.

*He notes the presence of some buildings
undertaken by early land speculators.*

And this makes the whole intended commercial part of the city, unless we include in it what is called the Twenty Building, being so many unfinished houses commenced by Morris and Nicholson, and perhaps as many undertaken by Greenleaf, both which groups lie, at the distance of half-mile from each other, near the mouth of the Eastern Branch and the Potowmack, and are divided by a large swamp from the Capitol Hill and the little village connected with it. (Albert Gallatin to Mrs. Gallatin, Washington, 15 January 1801, in Nicolay, *Our Capital on the Potomac*, 63)

*Benjamin Latrobe comments in 1806
on the capital's design and location.*

L'Enfant's plan has in its contrivance everything that could prevent the growth of the city. The distribution of the public buildings over a space five miles in length and three in breadth prevents the possibility to concentration. The proprietors of the soil, on which the town is to be spread, are rivals and enemies and each opposes every project which appears more advantageous to his neighbor than to himself. Speculators, of all degrees of honesty and of desperation, made a game of hazard of the scheme. The site itself is upon a river noble in its extent and depth of water below the city, but above it of difficult navigation and running through a country comparatively barren in the materials of commerce—agricultural produce. On the map the Potomac appears a mighty river, but in fact it is . . . the drain of a montainous and barren country. But the principal disadvantage under which the city labors is the preoccupation of its commerce by Baltimore and Alexandria and George-

town. The principal part of near a million of dollars disbursed in the Federal City passes through Alexandria and Georgetown to our large seaports. These two towns have accordingly prospered and increased, and may be compared to a pair of fat twins who are suckled by a consumptive mother. (Latrobe to Philip Mazzei, in Latrobe, "Construction of the Public Buildings in Washington," 222–23)

*Two English visitors in 1806 have similar impressions
of a widely scattered community.*

Being told that we were entering Washington city, I continued looking for the houses for some little time; but seeing none, I thought I had misunderstood the gentleman who made the remark, and turning round for an explanation, he told me, laughing, that we were almost in the very middle of it. (Melish, *Travels*, 1:193)

*The second traveler, Charles Janson,
confirms Melish's impressions.*

After enumerating the public buildings, the private dwellinghouses of the officers of government, the accommodations set apart for the members of the legislature, and the temporary tenements of those dependent on them, the remainder of this boasted city is a mere wilderness of wood and stunted shrubs, the occupants of barren land. Strangers after viewing the offices of state, are apt to enquire for the city, while they are in its very centre.

Janson refers to Isaac Weld's account of the city a decade earlier.

Ten years ago Mr. Weld, speaking of the president's house, tells us of its being then erected and of an hundred acres of land left for pleasure-ground, and a park or mall, to run in an easterly direction towards the Capitol—that the buildings on either side of this mall, were all to be elegant of their kind, and that among the number it was *proposed* to have houses built at the public expence for the accommodation of public ministers. This traveller then proceeds with informing us that other parts of this city are appointed for churches, theatres, colleges, &c. In nearly the same state as Mr. Weld saw the city so long ago, it still remains, except indeed that some of the few houses which were then building, are now falling to ruin, the unfortunate owner having been ruined before he could get them roofed. (Janson, *The Stranger in America*, 205)

A Philadelphia Publisher Issues the First Map of the City Showing the Extent of Development

In 1802 Mathew Carey published in Philadelphia an excellent travelers' guide for those taking the main road between Philadelphia and the new capital. It consisted of a series of strip maps showing the route and the roads and streets that intersected it. At the Washington end, Carey included the full-page map of Washington that is reproduced here.

It is one of the most valuable records available for documenting the location and extent of building development in the infant city. One can note the linear configuration of the built-up portions of Washington, extending from Georgetown at the left, along Pennsylvania Avenue to and beyond the White House to the Capitol, and then angling to the south toward the Anacostia River. Beyond these clusters of buildings lay only open land crossed by streets that had been surveyed but remained unbuilt.

This map is also the first to name the great expanse of land stretching west from Capitol Hill as the "Mall." The cartographer gave it an imaginary formal planting of trees, as he did to the grounds of the White House and its axial extension across the Tyber to the Potomac. Visitors relying on this map must have been surprised and dismayed to find there only the mud flats of the river. They would also have been misled by the lines of the canal—then still unbuilt and not even begun. The map also identifies a large space opening to the Potomac west of the White House grounds as "University." Here again, although George Washington and the commissioners discussed possible sites for such an institution, neither he nor Adams and Jefferson who followed him designated a site for this purpose.

Washington City. From S. S. Moore and T. W. Jones, *The Traveller's Directory . . . of the Main Road from Philadelphia to Washington.* Philadelphia: Mathew Carey, 1802. Engraving, 4⁵/₃₂ by 6³/₈ in. (10.6 × 16.2 cm.). Olin Library, Cornell University.

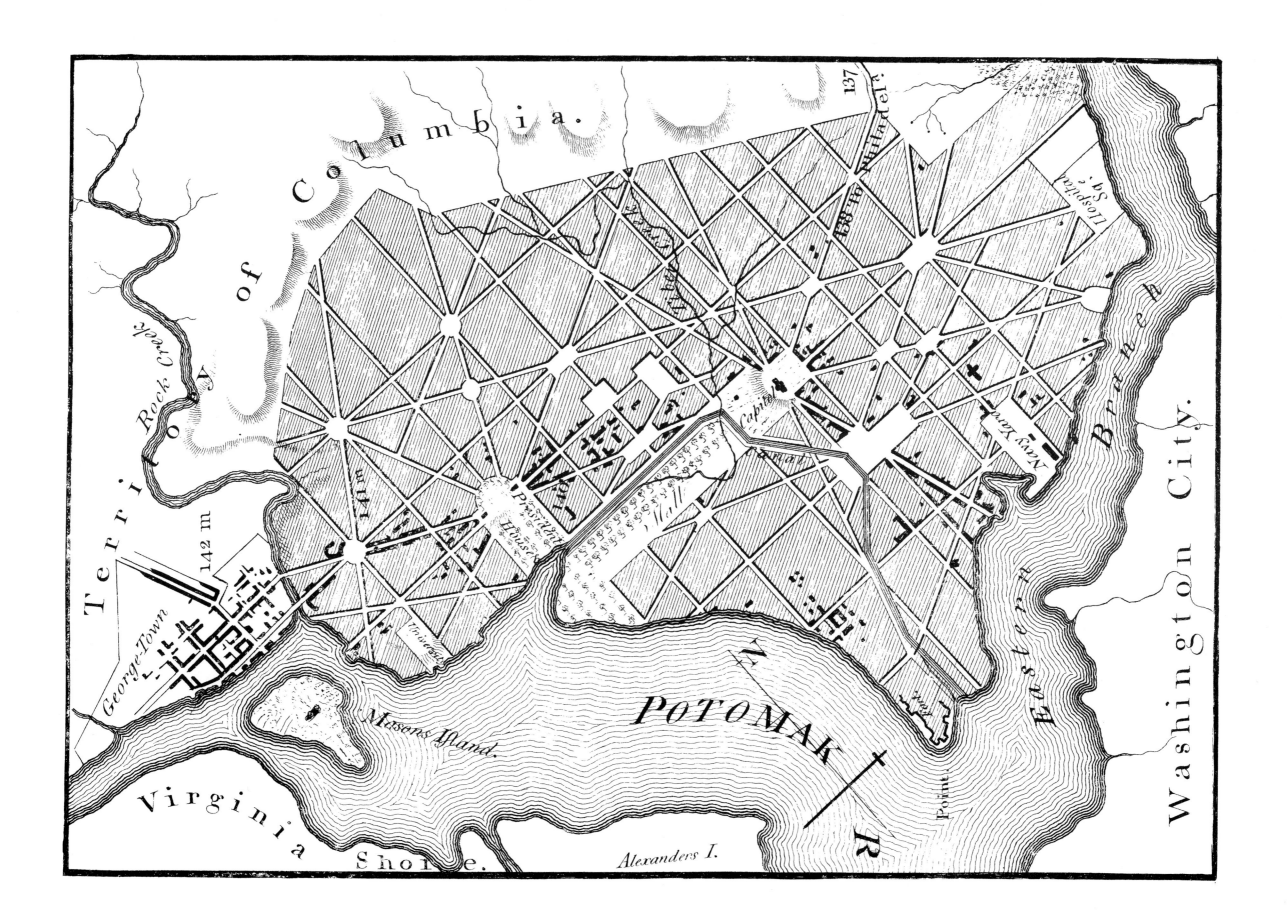

Territory of Columbia.

Rock Creek

142 m

Terr111ory

George-Town

Virginia Shore.

Masons Island.

Alexanders I.

POTOMAK R

Point.

N

President's House

University

Capitol

Canal

Mall

Tiber Creek

Rock Creek

137

Philadelphia St

Hospital Sq.

Navy Yard

Eastern Branch

Washington City.

In 1790 William Smith notes the town's prosperity.

Alexandria is a considerable place of trade . . . well situated on the river. . . . It . . . is now thriving rapidly; the situation of the Town, a capital one, a fine eminence, plain level, and bounded by a pretty range of hills, an excellent, safe, and commodious harbour, a fine back country to it, will soon make it a very important post; much business is done here; there are about 3,200 inhabitants; the houses principally of brick; the streets are not paved and being of clay after rain they are so slippery it is almost impossible to walk in them. I went to the top of Colonel Howe's house, a very lofty one, the prospect a magnificent one. The Town laid out at right angles, the harbour, river to great distance, with its windings, creeks, and island, the extensive plain contiguous to the city, all formed a fine scene. (William Loughton Smith, *Journal*, 62–63)

A royal visitor in 1797 praises Alexandria as the handsomest town in the state.

I went by water from Federal-City to Alexandria, which is a distance only of six miles. The Potowmack, the whole way from one place to the other, is two miles in breadth; and its banks are well cultivated, and covered with a considerable number of houses. The Maryland side being more elevated presents a finer aspect. . . .

Alexandria is, beyond all comparison, the handsomest town in Virginia, and indeed is among the finest of the United States. It stands on a small plain, elevated however a few feet above the river, and so as not to be incommoded by the water.

He describes the city plan.

This town, which was begun about thirty years since, is built on a regular plan. Streets sufficiently wide intersect each other at right angles; and spacious squares add to its beauty, convenience, and salubrity. Almost all the houses and warehouses are of brick. Although all the buildings have not an appearance of magnificence, all are convenient and neat; and the houses are of two stories. The quays are large and commodious, and extend along the river every way. (La Rochefoucauld-Liancourt, *Travels*, 3:665)

John Melish stops in Alexandria in October 1806 and records his observations.

Alexandria is situated on the west bank of the Potomac, in the south-east corner of the district of Columbia. It is laid out on the plan of Philadelphia, the streets crossing one another at right angles, and they are broad and airy. It contained, by the census of 1800, 4096 free inhabitants, and 875 slaves; the population has since greatly increased. The public buildings are a court-house and jail, a bank, and an episcopal church. I observed considerable shipping in the river, and learned that the inhabitants have a pretty extensive trade, principally in flour and tobacco. (Melish, *Travels*, 1:213)

In 1806 Charles Janson considers Alexandria attractive but finds it suffering the aftereffects of an epidemic of yellow fever.

Alexandria was about eight years ago a very flourishing place; but the great losses sustained from the capture of American vessels by the French in the West Indies, occasioned many failures. In the year 1803, the yellow fever, which broke out there for the first time, swept off a number of its inhabitants. These shocks have so deeply affected the mercantile interest, that the town has but two or three ships in the trade with Great Britain and there is little prospect of its ever attaining to its former prosperity.

Alexandria, first called Belhaven, is laid out upon the plan of Philadelphia; and being well built and paved, in point of uniformity and neatness it somewhat resembles that city on a small scale. Its situation is elevated, commanding a view of the river and the opposite shore of Maryland. (Janson, *The Stranger in America*, 213–14)

The publisher of the first printed plan of Alexandria loses the drawing and advertises for its return.

The subscriber some time since lent to one of his acquaintances a plan of the town of Alexandria, neatly drawn by Col. Gilpin—He cannot at present recollect who it was that borrowed it, but he begs that whoever has it in possession will be kind enough to return it. John V. Thomas. (*Alexandria Advertiser*, 21 September 1797)

John Thomas Publishes a Map of Alexandria in 1798

Although in 1797 the publisher of this street plan of Alexandria misplaced the drawing from which it was to be made, he recovered it in time for this engraving to be published the following year. His notice about his loss in the *Alexandria Advertiser* in September 1797 revealed, however, that Col. George Gilpin had prepared the survey. Probably Gilpin began where the two diagonal lines intersect at the mouth of Hunting Creek, the point designated by President Washington in 1791 as the starting point for the boundaries of the federal district.

Alexandria came into existence in 1749 after the Virginia assembly authorized its creation. Trustees acquired sixty acres of land for this purpose, and the Fairfax County surveyor, assisted by a young man named George Washington, platted it into a little grid of straight streets intersecting at right angles stretching seven blocks along the Potomac and extending inland two and a half blocks. The town prospered, and in 1762 and again five years later the trustees secured permission from the assembly to extend it. They simply added additional streets parallel and perpendicular to the first to create a much larger grid of blocks of identical size and shape, except for those along the waterfront. Only Washington and Franklin streets—both 100 feet wide—differed from all the 66-foot thoroughfares.

The style of the engraving resembles the 1792 plan of Washington printed by Thackara and Vallance. The title and legend are simple but elegant, the stream lines in the rivers are meticulously executed, and two sides of each block are rendered in bolder lines to give the city plan an almost three-dimensional feeling. The engraver, Thomas Clarke, worked in Philadelphia until 1797 and surely had seen the plan of the capital on which he probably modeled his own engraving of Alexandria.

Plan of the Town of Alexandria. in the District of Columbia 1798. [Drawn by Colonel George Gilpin in 1797], engraved by T[homas] Clarke, New York, and published in Alexandria, Virginia by I. [i.e., John] V. Thomas in 1798. Engraving, 23½ × 18½ in. (59.7 × 47 cm.). Geography and Maps, Library of Congress.

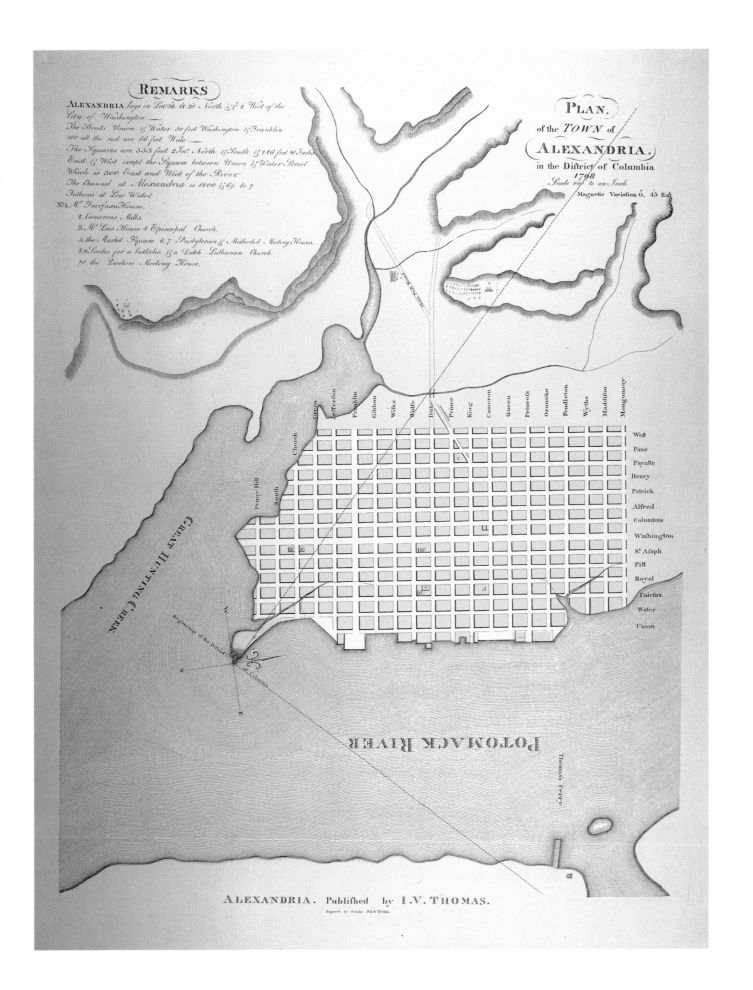

Charles Janson complains of the entrances to the city as dangerous for the traveler.

The description given [the city of Washington] by interested scriblers, may well serve to raise an Englishman's curiosity, and lead him to fancy the capital of Columbia a terrestrial paradise.

The entrance, or avenues, as they are pompously called, which lead to the American seat of government, are the worst roads I passed in the country; and I appeal to every citizen who has been unlucky enough to travel the stages north and south leading to the city, for the truth of the assertion. . . . In the winter . . . every turn of your wagon wheel . . . is for many miles attended with danger. The roads are never repaired; deep ruts, rocks, and stumps of trees, every minute impede your progress, and often threaten your limbs with dislocation.

He is unfavorably struck by what he sees on his arrival.

Arrived at the city, you are struck with its grotesque appearance. In one view from the capitol hill, the eye fixes upon a row of uniform houses of twelve in number, while it faintly discovers the adjacent tenements to be miserable wooden structures, consisting, when you approach them, of two or three rooms one above another. Again, you see the hotel, which was vauntingly promised, on laying the foundation, to rival the large inns in England. This, like every other private adventure, failed: the walls and the roof remain, but not a window! . . . Turning the eye, a well finished edifice presents itself, surrounded by lofty trees, which never felt the stroke of the axe. The president's house, the offices of state, and a little theatre . . . terminate the view of the Pennsylvania, or Grand Avenue.

Janson describes the appearance of the landscape.

In some parts, purchasers have cleared the wood from their grounds, and erected temporary wooden buildings: others have fenced in their lots, and attempted to cultivate them; but the sterility of the land laid out for the city is such, that this plan has also failed. The country adjoining consists of woods in a state of nature, and in some places of mere swamps, which give the scene a curious patch-work appearance. . . .

Some half-starved cattle browzing among the bushes, present a melancholy spectacle to a stranger, whose expectation has been wound up by the illusive description of speculative writers.

He points out the lack of recreational and cultural facilities.

Neither park, nor mall, neither churches, theatres, nor colleges, could I discover so lately as the summer of 1806. A small place has indeed been erected . . . called a theatre, in which . . . the Virginia company of comedians were nearly starved the only season it was occupied. . . . Public offices on each side of the president's house, uniformly built of brick, may also, perhaps, have been built subsequent to that period.

Janson summarizes the early building regulations.

That great man who planned the city, and after whom it is named, certainly entertained the hopes that it would at some future period equal ancient Rome in splendor and magnificence. Among the regulations for building were these—that the houses should be of brick or stone—the walls to be at least thirty feet high, and to be built parallel to the line of the street.

Janson states that the city's growth has been disappointing.

Though the permanent seat of government has been fixed at Washington, its progress has been proved to be less rapid than any other new settlement supported only by trade. The stimulus held out by the presence of congress has proved artificial and unnatural.

He describes the difficulties of navigation.

The navigation of the river is good from the bay of Chesapeak, till the near approach to the city, where bars of sand are formed, which every year encroach considerably on the channel. . . . This is another great disadvantage to the growth of the city. It never can become a place of commerce, while Baltimore lies on one side, and Alexandria on the other; even admitting the navigation to be equally good.

He finds the only thriving neighborhood near the Navy Yard.

The only part of this city which continues to encrease is the navy-yard, but this circumstance is entirely owing to the few ships of war which the Americans have in commission, being ordered there to be fitted out and paid off. Tippling shops, and houses of rendezvous for sailors and their doxies, with a number of the lowest order of traders, constitute which is called the navy-yard. (Janson, *The Stranger in America*, 202–8)

A Landscape Artist Captures the Image of the City of Washington at an Early Date

George Beck, an English landscape painter who came to America in 1795, is believed to have painted this scene shortly before the end of the eighteenth century although the printed version was not published until the summer of 1801. The viewpoint Beck selected seems to be almost identical to that used by Parkyns in 1795 (reproduced in folio 14), and Beck may have been guided to that spot after seeing Parkyns's print. The two views convey quite a different image of the nascent capital, this one suggesting that significant progress had been made in developing the site.

In the center of the print Beck shows in the distance a cluster of buildings on what is evidently intended to be Greenleaf Point at the mouth of the Anacostia. To the left and below that, the artist has depicted the arched bridge over Rock Creek, an improvement that was one of the early public works carried out by the commissioners to link the nearly vacant city site with the established community of Georgetown.

Unless Cartwright, the aquatint engraver (doubtless in London) contributed significantly to the composition of this splendid and quite rare print, one must conclude that Beck was an artist of substantial skill and experience. In this country he produced only a handful of works, so perhaps his sophisticated talents were not appreciated as they might have been elsewhere. His other aquatints include one of the Great Falls of the Potomac and a handsome view of Baltimore. Not much seems to be known about Beck except that he lived in Baltimore, Philadelphia, and—perhaps—Pittsburgh before moving to Lexington, Kentucky, where he made his home from 1808 until his death in 1812.

George Town and Federal City, or City of Washington. Drawn by G[eorge] Beck, engraved by T. Cartwright. Published June 1st. 1801 by Atkins & Nightingale, No. 143, Leadenhall Street, London. & No. 35 North Front Street, Philadelphia. Aquatint, 16⁷⁄₁₆ × 22¹³⁄₁₆ in. (41.7 × 57.9 cm.). Prints and Photographs, Library of Congress.

65

*David Baillie Warden describes the city
for a book published in 1819.*

The site of the city extends from north-west to south-east about four miles and a half, and from north-east to south-west about two miles and a half. The houses are thinly scattered over this space; the greatest number are in the Pennsylvania avenue between the capitol and the president's house, from the latter towards Georgetown, and near the barracks and navey-yard on the eastern branch. The public buildings occupy the most elevated and convenient situations. . . . The Pennsylvania street, or avenue, which stretches in a direct line from the president's house to the capitol, is a mile in length, and 160 feet in breadth; the breadth of the narrowest streets is from 90 to 100 feet.

Warden lists the major public buildings.

The most eligible places have been selected for public squares and public buildings. The capitol is situated on a rising ground, which is elevated about eighty feet above the tide-water of the Potomac. . . . This edifice will present a front of 650 feet, with a colonnade of 260 feet. . . . The centre, or great body of the building, is not yet commenced, but the two wings are nearly finished. . . .

The president's house consists of two stories, and is 170 feet in length and 85 in breadth. . . . The view from the windows fronting the river is extremely beautiful. . . .

The Public Offices, the Treasury, Department of State, and of war, are situated in a line with and at the distance of 450 feet from the president's House. These buildings, of two stories, have 120 in front, 60 in breadth, and 16 feet in height, and are ornamented with a white stone basement, which rises six or seven feet above the surface. . . .

The Patent Office, constructed according to the plan of J. Hoban Esq. (who gained the prize for that of the president's house,) consists of 3 stories, and is 120 feet long, and 60 feet wide. (Warden, *Account of the United States*, 3:194–99)

*Henry Cogswell Knight tells his brother about
the city plan in 1816.*

Washington-City is about three hundred miles from the sea, at the head of tide water, on the Maryland side of the Potomac, which flows by the city through the District. Its plan, by Pierre C. l'Enfant, is said to be improved upon that of every other city in the world. Its broad eccentric avenues, each called after a state; its transverse and conjugate intersections, alphabetically and numerically named; uniting the *utile dulce*; present a facility of communication, with extensive and beautiful prospects, and invite a healthful and unopposed circulation of air. Wide areas, of different dimensions and shapes, are left for public squares, and future promenades. But although the famous metropolis of our country, and notwithstanding its boasted elevated centre, and diverging radii of perspective avenues, the Federal-City is now in semblance not unlike a rough chariot-wheel, horizontal on the ground, with nothing but the nave, and three or four spokes, yet apparent. (Knight, *Letters*, 36)

Morris Birkbeck visits Washington in 1817.

The Federal City contains, including George Town, which is only separated from it by a creek, about 20,000 inhabitants, scattered over a vast space, like a number of petty hamlets in a populous country. The intended streets, radiating from the capital in right lines, are, for the most part, only distinguishable from the rugged waste by a slight trace, like that of a newly-formed road, or in some instances by rows of Lombardy poplars, affording neither ornament nor shade, but evincing the exotic taste of the designer.

He calls the design of the Capitol "un-American."

The Capitol and the president's house are under repair from the damage sustained in the war. Ninety marble capitals have been imported at vast cost from Italy to crown the columns of the Capitol, and shew how *un*-American is the whole plan. There is nothing in America to which I can liken this affectation of splendor, except the painted face and gaudy head-dress of a half-naked Indian.

This embryo metropolis, with its foreign decorations, should have set a better example to the young republic, by surrounding itself first with good roads and substantial bridges, in lieu of those inconvenient wooden structures and dangerous roads, over which the legislators must now pass to their duty. I think too, that good taste would have preferred native decoration for the seat of the legislature. (Birkbeck, *Notes*, 28–29)

Robert King Produces a Map of Washington

On 27 February 1818 the Washington *Daily National Intelligencer* carried a notice about a new and large engraved map of the city. It provides an appropriate caption for the illustration reproduced here.

"An authentic plan of the Metropolis of the United States has long been a desideratum. . . . [T]he plans hitherto published are not only on too small a scale, and too indistinct for easy reference, but are *notoriously incorrect*, and become obsolete from various alterations which have since been made.

"The one now offered to the public, it is confidently presumed, will fully supply these defects. Its accuracy cannot be questioned, having been made from actual survey on the ground, and adjusted conformably to the subsequent and final alterations authorized by the president of the United States.

"It is printed on a beautiful paper made expressly for the purpose—its size 33 inches by 26. The avenues, streets and squares are distinctly marked and numbered—the various springs and runs which intersect the ground are carefully laid down—the eminences designated so as to enable persons at a distance to form a correct idea of the surface of the city—and the engraving executed in a very superior style. It is embellished with a view of the south front of the president's house, and of the east front of the capitol, taken from the original draughts; the whole forming not only a safe guide in all transfers of property, but a very handsome ornament for the parlor or counting room.

"The price is 3 dollars in the sheet, or 5 dollars handsomely mounted on rollers, or done up in a book form for the convenience of travellers."

A Map of the City of Washington in the District of Columbia established as the permanent Seat of the Government of the United States of America taken from actual survey as laid out on the ground. Drawn by R[obert] King, Surveyor of the City of Washington. Engraved by C[onrad] Schwarz, Washn. Copyrighted by Rt. King, District of Columbia, [1818]. Engraving, 24 × 31 in. (61 × 78.7 cm.). Geography and Maps, Library of Congress.

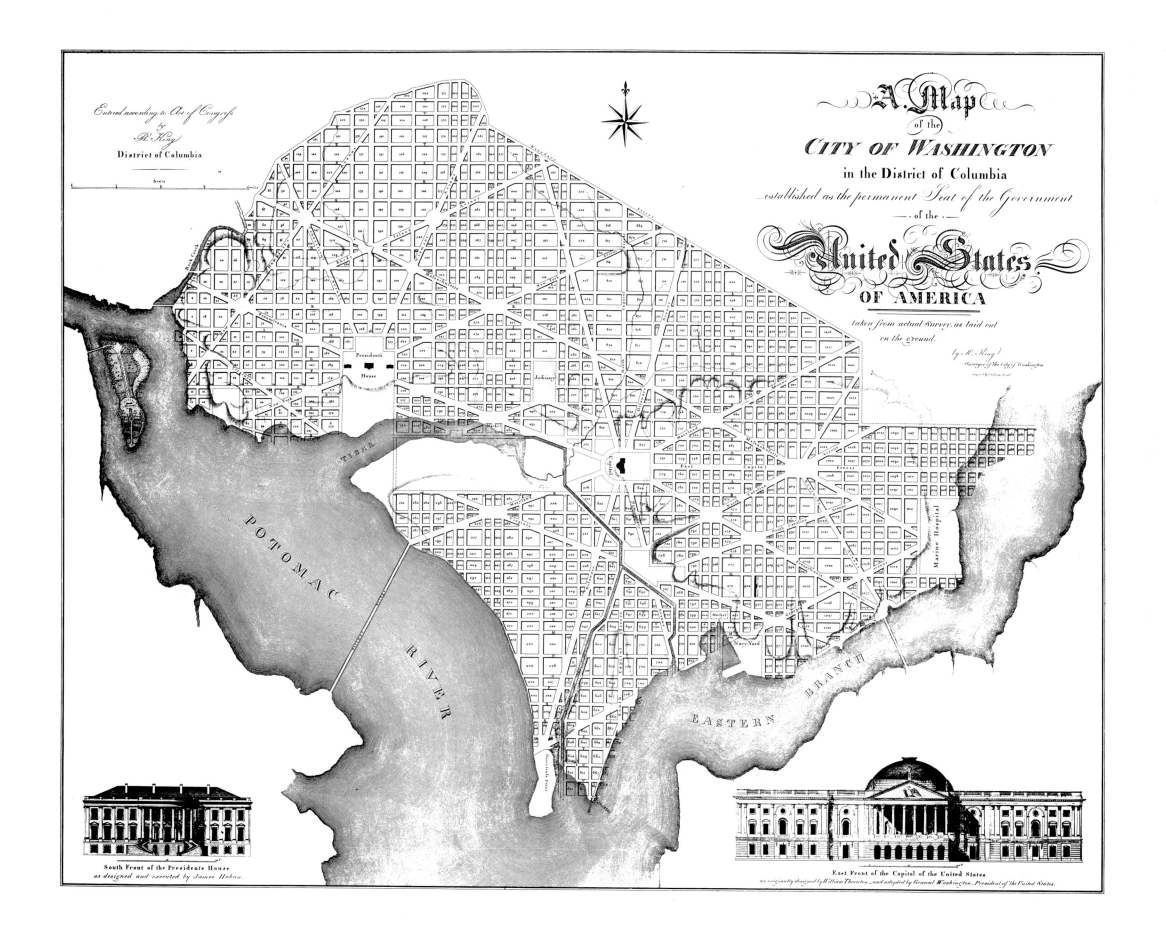

A Map of the
CITY OF WASHINGTON
in the District of Columbia
established as the permanent Seat of the Government
of the
United States
OF AMERICA

taken from actual Survey, as laid out
on the Ground.

by R. King
Surveyor of the City of Washington

South Front of the Presidents House
as designed and executed by James Hoban.

East Front of the Capitol of the United States
as originally designed by William Thornton and adopted by General Washington, President of the United States.

67

An anonymous English writer registers
his disappointment on first seeing the city.

I was much disappointed upon arriving at Washington. I had been told, indeed, that I should see a straggling city; but I had no idea that I should find the houses so very much scattered as they really are. . . .

The plan of the city is on a vast scale, and it will be many a long year before even one half of it will be completed. Instead of beginning from a centre or nucleus, from which it might gradually have expanded, the whole was laid out, and the lots sold, wherever individuals chose to select them. Owing to this, every one selected the spot, which he thought would be most desirable when the city should be finished; and consequently very few streets are as yet completed.

He criticizes Congress for the lack of development.

Instead of fostering the infant metropolis, and taking a pride in ornamenting, embellishing, and increasing it, as one would naturally have supposed; the Congress has, on the contrary, been but a cold-hearted protector, and has acted the part of a step-father rather than of a parent. In fact, it has done little more than provide for its own convenience; for as the Capitol, the president's house, and the public offices, were necessary buildings, the city owes the Congress no thanks for them.

The author records his opinions about the Capitol
and the view from Capitol Hill.

The Capitol is a large and splendid mass of buildings, but though handsomely ornamented and embellished, has, at present, rather a heavy appearance, probably occasioned by its being perfectly isolated. . . .

The eminence on which it stands, rises gradually from the Potowmac, which it completely overlooks. Indeed the view from the western portico is one of the finest I every saw. Immediately beneath is the most populous and best built part of the city. Pennsylvania Avenue, the principal street, commences at the Capitol, and terminates at another eminence, on which stands the large and handsome mansion of the president.

He concludes his remarks with praise
for the City Hall and the city's location.

The City Hall, when finished, will be the handsomest building in the United States. It fronts the Potowmac, and com-

mands a very advantageous view of the city. Few places could have been selected possessing greater natural beauties, and, at the same time, better adapted for the scite [*sic*] of a metropolis. I think, indeed, that Washington, in point of situation, ranks first among the American cities. (*An Excursion through the United States*, 38–45)

Isaac Candler views the city with ambivalent feelings.

The person who laid its plan was a Frenchman, who took care to have some diagonal streets to diversify it, as well as to afford opportunity for the display of the glories of architecture. If the outline be ever filled up, Washington will be a metropolis worthy of the country: at present, it is a straggling and not very captivating place, having in conjunction with Georgetown . . . a population of twelve thousand in a space three miles long and half a mile wide.

He tells his readers about the public buildings and city streets.

The president's House is substantial and plain, and not destitute of elegance. It would be considered in England a good second-rate country seat. The Capitol, with several considerable defects, is the largest and finest building in the United States. If placed beside the Houses of Parliament, it would cast them in the shade; for England . . . cannot boast of the structures where her legislators assemble. The street from the president's House to the Capitol is upwards of a mile long, very wide, having a double row of trees on each side, and with moderate sized brick houses. In some of the other streets, are rows of elegant private dwellings, though the best of them, even those occupied by foreign ministers, will not compare with the houses of the wealthy merchants of Baltimore and Boston.

He is disappointed by the view from the Capitol.

The view from the Capitol is very extensive, but neither beautiful nor grand. The Potowmac with its two branches, is to be sure an object on which the eye satisfactorily rests; but then the landscape is so brown, so bleak (almost every thing appearing stunted), and so destitute of villages, that it affords little gratification to the spectator. The embryo city appears meaner, than a walk through it would lead one to imagine. ([Candler], *A Summary View of America*, 34–35)

Carey and Lea Map the District of Columbia in 1822

Maps like this may have been one of the reasons so many visitors found Washington disappointing. The neatly done, fine hatching used to bring out the pattern of blocks and streets conveys the impression of a city that is fully built up. Only by reading the description of the city printed in fine type alongside the map would someone consulting the atlas learn that while "the ground embraced in the plan of the city is very extensive, . . . only a small portion of it is yet occupied with buildings."

Further, the outlines of many public buildings (in addition to those of the Capitol and the White House) suggest a handsome metropolis graced by large and attractive civic structures. The map also shows the Mall lined on both sides by orderly rows of buildings—the cartographer's duplication of a feature used on the Thackara and Vallance plan of 1792 interpreting L'Enfant's description of how he hoped this part of the city would develop. Carey and Lea showed as well the proposed 400-foot-wide Grand Avenue running down the Mall's center that L'Enfant planned as the main axis of the city. All this would cause visitors who had relied on the map to be disappointed by the reality of the raw and dispersed community that occupied the site.

Map publishers traditionally have borrowed heavily from earlier works. In this case, Carey and Lea closely modeled their map on an engraving dated 1815 by P. A. F. Tardieu for Warden's *A Chorographical and Statistical Description of the District of Columbia* published in Paris in 1816. Warden also used it in 1820 for a French edition of his *Statistical, Political, and Historical Account of the United States* and had a similar map engraved by W. & D. Lizars for the Edinburgh edition of 1819. Warden and Tardieu acknowledged their source as the Ellicott map of 1794, *Territory of Columbia*, reproduced in folio 3.

Geographical, Statistical, and Historical Map of the District of Columbia. Engraved by Young & Delleker. From *A Complete Historical, Chronological and Geographical American Atlas.* Philadelphia: H[enry] C. Carey & I[saac] Lea, 1822. Engraving, 10¾ × 10½ in. (27.3 × 26.6 cm.). John W. Reps.

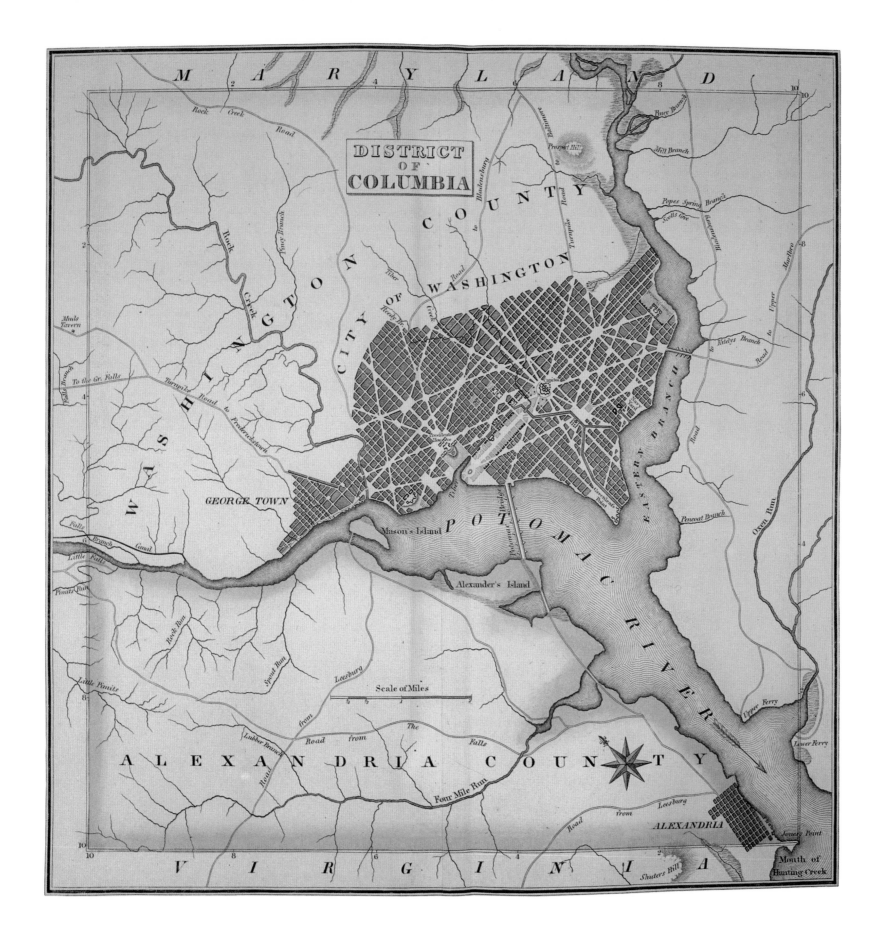

An early American atlas lists the city's
public buildings in 1822.

The principal public buildings and establishments are, 1, the Capitol, which is finely situated on an eminence, commanding a view of every part of the city, and a considerable portion of the adjacent country. According to the original plan, it is to be composed of a central edifice and two wings. . . . 2, the president's house, situated about a mile and a half west of the capitol, on the avenue leading to Georgetown. It is 170 feet by 85, and two stories high: 3, four spacious brick buildings, erected in the vicinity of the president's house, for the accommodation of the different departments of government: 4, a comfortable marine barrack, with a house for the residence of the commandant of the marine corps: 5, an extensive navy-yard, situated on the eastern branch, which forms a safe and commodious harbour. Here is an elegant marble monument, erected by American officers to the memory of their brethren who fell before Tripoli: 6, a small fort, which, from the extreme southern point of the land on which the city stands, commands the channel of the Potomac; and 7, the general post-office, a brick edifice, about a mile west-north-west of the capitol, where the patent office is also kept.

Besides the buildings and establishments above enumerated, Washington contains a city-hall, a theatre, a penitentiary, a circus, a masonic hall, four banks, . . . and 14 houses for public worship. ([Candler], *A Summary View of America*, unpaged text on map 21)

Anne Royall visits Washington in 1826 and
tells her readers about the principal buildings.

The president's house [is] on the left, while the capitol is on the right, as you advance in an eastern direction. . . . The capitol, however, which may aptly be called the eighth wonder of the world, eclipses the whole. This stupendous fabric, when seen at a distance, is remarkable for its magnitude, its vast dome rising out of the centre, and its exquisite whiteness. The president's house like the capitol, rivals the snow in whiteness. It is easily distinguished from the surrounding edifices, inasmuch as they are of brick. Their red walls and black, elevated roofs, form a striking contrast to the former, which is not only much larger, but perfectly white, and flat on the top. From the point just mentioned, it has the appearance of a quadrangle; it displays its gorgeous columns at all points looking down upon the neighboring buildings in silent and stately grandeur. The

War Office, Navy Office, the Treasury department, the Department of State, the General Post Office, and the City Hall are all enormous edifices.

She is captivated by what she sees.

These edifices; the elevated site of the city; its undulating surface, partially covered with very handsome buildings; the majestic Potomac, with its ponderous bridge, and gliding sails; the eastern branch with its lordly ships; swelling hills which surround the city; the spacious squares and streets, and avenues, adorned with rows of flourishing trees, and all this visible at once; it is not in the power of imagination to conceive a scene so replete with every species of beauty. ([Royall], *Sketches of History*, 130–31)

A book published in 1830 describes the
offices of the executive departments.

At the distance of about 200 yards, on the east of the president's house, are situated two buildings for the Department of State and of the Treasury; and at the same distance on the west are two others for the War and Navy Departments. These buildings are all of the same dimensions and construction; they are 160 feet long and 55 feet wide, of brick, two stories in height; they are divided in their length by a broad passage, with rooms on each side, and a spacious staircase in the center. The two most northerly buildings are ornamented with an Ionic portico of six columns and pediment. The grounds about these offices have been graduated and planted of late years, and the shrubbery begins to present a pleasing appearance. (Elliot, *Historical Sketches*, 164–65)

J. S. Buckingham sees the four executive department buildings
in 1838 before the new Treasury is built.

The public offices of the government are situated in the immediate neighbourhood of the president's dwelling. . . . These are all spacious, neat, and well-built edifices, suitably adapted to their respective purposes, but with nothing superfluous. As each occupies the centre of an open piece of ground, with lawn in front, railed off on all sides, they have a commanding appearance, from the ample space and air by which they are surrounded. (Buckingham, *America*, 1:311)

The Government Provides Office Space
for the Executive Departments

In 1820 the Baroness Hyde de Neuville, wife of the French minister to Washington, looked south from Lafayette Square and sketched the White House and its neighboring buildings. Two of these flanked the presidential residence on the east and the west. To the east, on the baroness' left, stood the offices of the departments of State and the Treasury. The two on the right housed the departments of War and the Navy.

The artist, born Anne-Marguérite-Henriette Rouillé de Marigny, came to America as a French exile in 1807 with her husband, Jean-Guillaume Hyde de Neuville, an unswerving supporter of the French monarchy who had somehow escaped the guillotine. After the fall of Napoleon, the baroness and her husband sailed to France in 1814, only to return to America two years later when the baron became envoy extraordinary and minister plenipotentiary to the United States. In Washington the baroness continued to sketch and paint, and it is thanks to her inquisitive eye that we have this informative view of the center of executive authority at such an early date.

The second illustration shows the State Department building as seen from the northwest. This structure, completed in 1816, was of brick, as were its three companions, one of which—the Treasury Building—appears at the far right. The State Department building and its counterpart for the Department of the Army on the west side of the White House and also facing Lafayette Square featured handsome porticoes that provided dignified entrances to these attractive offices.

Washington City 1821. Painting by Madam Hyde de Neuville from a sketch drawn in 1820. Watercolor, 5³/₈ × 9¹/₄ in. (13.6 × 23.5 cm.). Stokes Collection, New York Public Library.

The Department of State, Washington. Drawn by C[harles] Burton, N.Y., engraved & printed by Fenner Sears & Co., and published in London in 1831 by I. [i.e., John] T. Hinton and Simpkin & Marshall. From Hinton, *History and Topography of the United States.* Engraving, 4¹/₂ × 5¹³/₁₆ in. (11.5 × 14.7 cm.). John W. Reps.

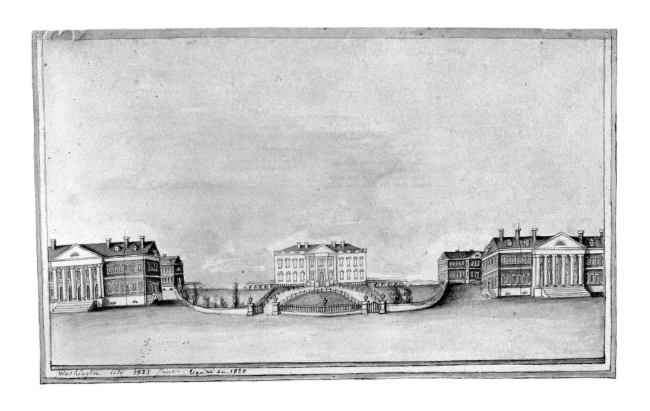

D. B. Warden saw the White House in 1816.

The president's house . . . resembles Leinster-house, in Dublin, and is much admired. Even the poet Moore styles it a "grand edifice," a "noble structure." (Warden, *Account of the United States*, 3:97–98)

An Englishman in 1838 called it "comfortable but unostentatious."

The president's house, which is next in importance to the Capitol among the public buildings of Washington, is situated at a distance of about a mile and a half from that edifice, at the western extremity of Pennsylvania avenue, of which these two buildings form the apparent termini at opposite points.

This residence is about the size and character of many of the country-seats of our middle-class gentry, baronets, esquires, and wealthy commoners, who live in a comfortable, but unostentatious style. It has 170 feet of front, and is 86 feet deep, with a good Ionic portico, a sweeping carriage-road up to the entrance, and a small lawn railed in before it; while behind is a semicircular projection and portico, which looks out on the river Potomac and the opposite shore of Virginia. (Buckingham, *America*, 1:310–11)

In 1846 a Scottish journalist and lawyer admired the grounds and described the neighboring buildings.

In the midst of a large open square, on a piece of high ground overlooking the Potomac, though about a quarter of a mile back from it, is the president's House, or the "White House," as it is more generally called. It is a spacious and elegant mansion, surrounded by soft sloping lawns, shaded by lofty trees, and dotted with shrubbery. Within this square, and forming, as it were, its four angles, are the four departments of State, those of the Treasury, of State, of War, and of the Navy, each of which is approached by the public from one of the four streets which encompass the Executive grounds. To each a private path also leads from the president's house, the chief magistrate sitting, as it were, like a spider, in the centre of his web, from which he constantly overlooks the occurrences at its ex-

tremities. With the exception of the Treasury, which is new, the departments are plain brick buildings, painted in singular taste, of a sort of diluted sky-blue colour. (Mackay, *The Western World*, 1:111–12)

Anthony Trollope in 1861 liked the appearance of the White House from Lafayette Square.

The president's house—or the White House as it is now called all the world over—is a handsome mansion fitted for the chief officer of a great Republic, and nothing more. I think I may say that we have private houses in London considerably larger. It is neat and pretty, and with all its immediate outside belongings calls down no adverse criticism. It faces on to a small garden, which seems to be always accessible to the public, and opens out upon that everlasting Pennsylvania Avenue, which has now made another turn. Here in front of the White House is President's Square, as it is generally called. The technical name is, I believe, La Fayette Square. The houses round it are few in number,—not exceeding three or four on each side, but they are among the best in Washington, and the whole place is neat and well kept. President's Square is certainly the most attractive part of the city. The garden of the square is always open, and does not seem to suffer from any public ill-usage.

But Trollope finds the location of the White House to be unhealthy.

The president's house is nice to look at, but it is built on marshy ground, not much above the level of the Potomac, and is very unhealthy. I was told that all who live there become subject to fever and ague, and that few who now live there have escaped it altogether. This comes of choosing the site of a new city, and decreeing that it shall be built on this or on that spot. Large cities, especially in these latter days, do not collect themselves in unhealthy places. Men desert such localities—or at least do not congregate at them when their character is once known. But the poor President cannot desert the White House. He must make the most of the residence which the nation has prepared for him. (Anthony Trollope, *North America*, 315–17)

The White House Is Changed and Enlarged

The four views in this folio record the appearance of the White House during 1832–48. Cephas Childs and Henry Inman printed the earliest in 1832 at their Philadelphia press, one of the pioneer lithographic establishments in the country. George Lehman drew the view from the southwest showing the semicircular south portico that was completed in 1824. On the upper right is another rare print from D. W. Kellogg's firm in Hartford. Published sometime between 1830 and 1840, it provides an early glimpse of the north portico that workmen finished in 1829 from plans prepared years before by Thomas Jefferson and Benjamin Henry Latrobe.

The illustration at lower left looks at the White House from nearly the same point and reveals the improved appearance of the White House grounds. Augustus Köllner, a German artist and engraver who worked in Paris before coming to America, drew this attractive print as one of several fine views of Washington buildings he published in 1848 after sending his drawings to Paris to be put on stone and printed. The last view is undated and has its title printed in mirror image. This German lithograph must have been designed to be looked at through a viewing device whose mirror reversed the title to make it readable.

Presidents House. On Stone by Geo[rge] Lehman From Childs & Inman's Press [Philadelphia, 1832?]. Lithograph, 7 × 9⅝ in. (17.8 × 24.4 cm.). Machen Collection, Historical Society of Washington, D.C.

View of the president's House. Washington, D.C. Lith of D. W. Kellogg & Co. 110 [Main] St. Hartford, Conn., [1832–40]. Lithograph, 10⅞ × 14¹⁵⁄₁₆ in. (27.6 × 37.9 cm.). Machen Collection, Historical Society of Washington, D.C.

Washington. President's House. Drawn by Aug[ustus] Köllner. Lithographed by Deroy and printed by Cattier, [Paris]. Copyright by Köllner, 1848. Published in New-York and Paris by Goupil, Vibert & Co. Lithograph, 7½ × 11 in. (19 × 27.9 cm.). Kiplinger Collection.

Das Weisse Haus Zu Washington. [Title in mirror image] Unsigned and undated lithograph, 5⅞ × 7³⁄₁₆ in. (14.9 × 18.2 cm.). Machen Collection, Historical Society of Washington, D.C.

*Frances Trollope first sees the Capitol
early on a spring morning in 1830.*

I am ill at describing buildings, but the beauty and majesty of the American capitol might defy an abler pen than mine to do it justice. It stands so finely too, high, and alone.

The magnificent western facade is approached from the city by terraces and steps of bolder proportions than I ever before saw. The elegant eastern front, to which many persons give the preference, is on a level with a newly-planted but exceedingly handsome enclosure, which, in a few years, will offer the shade of all the most splendid trees which flourish in the Union, to cool the brows and refresh the spirits of the members. The view from the capitol commands the city and many miles around, and it is itself an object of imposing beauty to the whole country adjoining. (Frances Trollope, *Domestic Manners of the Americans*, 2:3)

*Nathaniel Parker Willis gives his impressions
of the east facade of the Capitol in 1839.*

The Capitol presents a very noble appearance, as the spectator advances to it. . . . Its height, the ascending terraces, the monument and its fountain, the grand balustrade of freestone which protects the offices below, and the distinct object which it forms, standing alone on its lofty site, combine to make up the impression of grandeur, in which its architectural defects are lost or forgotten.

Willis mentions its striking appearance in winter.

There are many favourable points of view for this fine structure, standing, as it does, higher than the general level of the country. Besides those presented in the different drawings in this work there are views from the distant eminences, which are particularly fine, in which the broad bosom of the Potomac forms the background. The effect of the building is also remarkably imposing when the snow is on the ground, and the whole structure, rising from the field of snow, with its dazzling whiteness, looks like some admirable creation of the frost. (Willis, *American Scenery*, 2:65, and 1:36)

*Alexander Mackay describes the Capitol
on his visit to Washington in 1846.*

It is a thousand pities that its front is not turned upon Penn-sylvania-avenue. The city being intended to grow the other way, the front of the Capitol was turned to the east; but the town having taken the contrary direction, the legislative palace has the appearance of turning its back upon it. But notwithstanding this, it has a most imposing effect, rising, as it does, in classic elegance from its lofty site, over the greensward and rich embowering foliage of the low grounds at its base. As seen at one end of the Avenue, from the grounds of the president's house at the other, there are few buildings in the world that can look to better advantage. I have seen it when its milk-white walls were swathed in moonlight, and when, as viewed from amid the fountains and shrubbery which encircle it, it looked more like a creation of fairy-land than a substantial reality. Passing to the high ground, on its eastern side, we have its principal front, the chief feature of which is a deep Corinthian portico, approached by a double flight of steps, and from which seems to spring the lofty dome, which crowns the building, and gives solidity to the whole, by uniting it, as it were, in one compact mass. (Mackay, *The Western World*, 1:112)

*A Virginia guide published in 1845
lists some impressive dimensions.*

The building . . . covers an area of more than an acre and a half; the length of the front is 352 feet, including the wings; the depth of the wings is 121 feet. . . . A projection on the east or main front, including the steps, is 65 feet wide; and another on the west front, with the steps, is 83 feet wide. In the projection on the east front, there is a noble portico of 22 lofty Corinthian columns; and in the west front there is a portico of 10 Corinthian columns. The height of the building to the top of the dome is 120 feet. (Henry Howe, *Historical Collections of Virginia*, 535)

*An Argentine observer in 1847 sees the building
illuminated by gas and electricity.*

A reservoir of gas provides fuel for the six thousand jets which illuminate the spacious monument. At the time I was there they were close to completing the electric light apparatus which will be placed above the cupola on a mast sixteen rods high and should illuminate the city and almost the whole District of Columbia. (Sarmiento, *Travels in the United States*, 258)

Charles Bulfinch Completes the Capitol

Charles Bulfinch came to Washington from Boston in 1818 as the architect of the Capitol. Then fifty-five, his extensive experience, native talent, and cultivated taste made him America's preeminent architect. By 1829 Bulfinch completed the Capitol more or less as Thornton had conceived it nearly four decades earlier. Bulfinch built a low, copper-covered wooden dome to shelter the rotunda linking the Senate with the House and designed small domes for each of the legislative chambers.

The views in this folio depict the building at this stage of its development, beginning with the rare aquatint of 1826 by the early Washington printing firm of Henry Stone. It shows the east elevation of the Capitol from a drawing by Bulfinch. A few years later George Lehman drew the building from the northeast as a companion print to his lithograph of the White House. Two later prints, a steel engraving of 1837 from a drawing by William H. Bartlett, and Augustus Köllner's lithograph of 1848, record how the Capitol appeared from the west.

Capitol Washington, D.C. 1826. Drawn by C[harles] Bulfinch. Engraved by H[enry] & J[ames] Stone. Published by H & J. Stone. Aquatint, 8 × 16 in. (20.3 × 40.6 cm.). Machen Collection, Historical Society of Washington.

The Capitol. NE View. Drawn by G[eorge] Lehman. Printed by Childs & Inman [Philadelphia, ca. 1832]. Published by Thompson & Homans, Washington. Lithograph, 7⅜ × 9½ in. (18.7 × 24.1 cm.). Machen Collection, Historical Society of Washington, D.C.

View of the Capitol at Washington. Drawn by W[illiam] H[enry] Bartlett, engraved by C. J. Bentley. Published by Geo[rge] Virtue, 26, Ivy Lane, London, 1837. From Nathaniel Parker Willis, *American Scenery*. London: G. Virtue, 1840. Steel engraving, 5⁵⁄₁₆ × 7 in. (13.4 × 17.8 cm.). Kiplinger Collection.

Washington Capitol (West Side). Drawn from nature by Aug[ustus] Köllner. Lith by Deroy. Printed by Cattier. Published in New York and Paris by Goupil Vibert & Co. Copyright 1848 by Aug. Köllner. Lithograph, 9½ × 11⅝ in. (24.1 × 29.5 cm.). Kiplinger Collection.

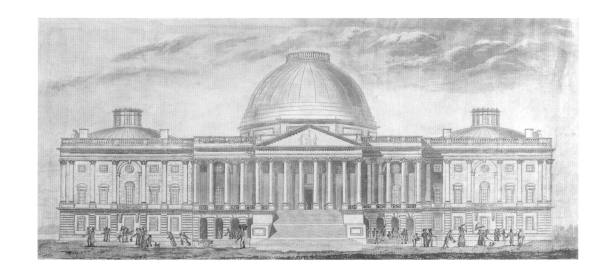

Frances Trollope praises the Capitol in 1830.

The mists of morning still hung around this magnificent building when first it broke upon our view, and I am not sure that the effect produced was not the greater for this circumstance. At all events, we were struck with admiration and surprise. None of us, I believe, expected to see so imposing a structure on that side the Atlantic.

This otherwise unrelenting critic of all things American is delighted by the city as well.

I was delighted with the whole aspect of Washington; light, cheerful, and airy, it reminded me of our fashionable watering-places. It has been laughed at by foreigners, and even by natives, because the original plan of the city was upon an enormous scale, and but a very small part of it has been as yet executed. But I confess I see nothing in the least degree ridiculous about it; the original design, which was as beautiful as it was extensive, has been in no way departed from, and all that has been done has been done well. From the base of the hill on which the capitol stands extends a street of most magnificent width, planted on each side with trees, and ornamented by many splendid shops. This street, which is called Pennsylvania Avenue, is above a mile in length, and at the end of it is the handsome mansion of the president; conveniently near to his residence are the various public offices, all handsome, simple, and commodious; ample areas are left round each, where grass and shrubs refresh the eye. In another of the principal streets is the general post office, and not far from it a very noble town hall. Towards the quarter of the president's house are several handsome dwellings, which are chiefly occupied by the foreign ministers. The houses in the other parts of the city are scattered, but without ever losing sight of the regularity of the original plan; and to a person who has been travelling much through the country, and marked the immense quantity of new manufactories, new canals, new railroad, new towns, and new cities, which are springing, as it were, from the earth in every part of it, the appearance of the metropolis rising gradually into life and splendour, is a spectacle of high historic interest.

Commerce had already produced large and handsome cities in America before she had attained to an individual political existence, and Washington may be scorned as a metropolis, where such cities as Philadelphia and New York exist; but I considered it as the growing metropolis of the growing population of the Union, and it already possesses features noble enough to sustain its dignity as such. (Frances Trollope, *Domestic Manners of the Americans*, 2:2–5)

On her visit five years later, Harriet Martineau came to the opposite conclusion.

The city itself is unlike any other that ever was seen, straggling out hither and thither, with a small house or two a quarter of a mile from any other; so that, in making calls "in the city," we had to cross ditches and stiles, and walk alternately on grass and pavements, and strike across a field to reach a street. . . .

The approach to the city is striking to all strangers from its oddness. I saw the dome of the Capitol from a considerable distance at the end of a straight road; but, though I was prepared by the descriptions of preceding travellers, I was taken by surprise on finding myself beneath the splendid building, so sordid are the enclosures and houses on its very verge.

The author recalls the views from the Capitol dome.

From the summit of the Capitol we saw plainly marked out the basin in which Washington stands, surrounded by hills except where the Potomac spreads its waters. The city was intended to occupy the whole of this basin, and its seven theoretical avenues may be traced; but all except Pennsylvania Avenue are bare and forlorn. A few mean houses dotted about, the sheds of a navy-yard on one bank of the Potomac, and three or four villas on the other, are all the objects that relieve the eye in this space intended to be so busy and magnificent.

She calls the city a mistake.

The city is a grand mistake. Its only attraction is its being the seat of government, and it is thought that it will not long continue to be so. The far western states begin to demand a more central seat for Congress, and the Cincinnati people are already speculating upon which of their hills or tablelands is to be the site of the new Capitol. Whenever this change takes place all will be over with Washington. (Martineau, *Retrospect of Western Travel*, 1:109, 121)

Childs and Inman Publish a View of the Capitol in 1832

Even Harriet Martineau confessed surprise at the "splendid building" she first saw from "a considerable distance" and then approached to admire under closer scrutiny. The Capitol dominated Washington from its location atop Jenkins Hill, and it provided a superb vantage point from which one could look out over the city and gaze on the surrounding landscape broken by the broad sweep of the Potomac.

Other than the Capitol and the White House, the only civic building of significance in the early part of the 1830s was the City Hall. This occupied a slight rise in ground north of Pennsylvania Avenue and was the intended location of what L'Enfant referred to as the "judiciary court," by which he doubtless meant the Supreme Court. This site stood between Fourth and Fifth streets, at the intersection of two short diagonal avenues, Louisiana and Indiana, and with the awkwardly named 4½ Street providing a long axis to the south. Although called Judiciary Square from a very early date, it became the site for the City Hall.

The accompanying view shows the large extent of undeveloped land between this location and the Capitol as T. Doughty sketched the scene for a lithograph that the Philadelphia firm of Childs & Inman published in 1832. This view and those by George Lehman of the Capitol and the White House for the same printers are apparently the earliest images of Washington executed in the medium of lithography, then still in its first decade of commercial use in the United States. It is the first and among the few views to show any portion of the city north of Pennsylvania Avenue as seen looking to the southeast. This part of the city then presented a forlorn appearance with only a few small and unimpressive structures visible on the rough and unkempt landscape.

The Capitol, Washington, D.C. West Front from the City Hall. Sketched and drawn by T[homas] Doughty. Printed and Published by Childs & Inman, Corner of 5th & Walnut Sts. Philadelphia, 1832. Lithograph, 5⅛ × 8 in. (13 × 20.3 cm.). Kiplinger Collection.

The Capitol, Washington, D.C.

West Front from the City Hall.

Sketched and Drawn by T. Doughty.

Philadelphia. Pub.d by Childs & Inman Corner of 5th & Walnut Streets 1832.

Theodore Dwight in 1834 calls the design a miscalculation.

I never visit Washington without being reminded of the miscalculations which were made by some of our wisest men, in relation to the growth of the city in population and importance. The magnificence of the plan is evident to every eye, and so is the total want of power to complete it. Broad avenues, named after the states, stretch indeed from the centre towards various points; but some of them are impassable, and others lead to nothing worth seeing. Unlike the great roads which met in the Roman forum in the days of Roman greatness, they are more like some of them at the present day, which conduct only to a deserted and steril [*sic*] region in the vicinity. ([Dwight], *Things As They Are*, 17)

Joseph Varnum, Jr., in 1848 criticizes the plan in a major American journal.

In Washington's correspondence, we find frequent allusions to . . . Major L'Enfant, a Frenchman of talents, but apparently obstinate, and unwilling to be advised by others. His plan, though attractive in the outline upon paper, was, in many respects an exceedingly impracticable one, and led to the sacrifice of one or two of the most beautiful eminences in the city.

He first laid down two sets of streets, distinguished by letters and numbers, and intersecting each other at right angles, as at Philadelphia. Had he stopped here, he would have consulted the interests of those who were to have erected private buildings; but there would have been nothing in it sufficiently distinctive of the national character of the city. It was desirable to bring the public buildings into view from the most distant quarters, that there might be direct communication with them all. Accordingly, immense avenues, varying from a hundred to a hundred and sixty feet in width, were made to radiate from particular points, such as the capitol and the president's house; the consequence is, that, in the first place, there are twice as many streets as are required, and, in the second place, the avenues, intersecting the rectangular streets, cut up the squares into triangles and oblongs, spoil the most prominent corner-lots, and leave everywhere awkward space.

Varnum tells how the plan could have been improved.

The design of these avenues was a grand feature, worthy of the nation; but the architect should either have laid them down first, to serve, as it were, for the great arteries of the city, and then, taking these as base lines, made such other streets to connect as necessity required; or, he should, in the first instance, have marked out a much smaller number of rectangular streets. Thus, the building-lots on the side streets would have been sufficiently large to admit of court-yards in front, with appropriate shrubbery, and made it in a short time, with a small population, a really attractive "*rus in urbe*," after the style in New Haven, Hartford, and the more retired parts of Richmond.

The eminence over which Louisiana Avenue is made to climb, and which will be more generally recognized as the site of the unfinished brick building called the city hall, should have been entirely reserved for some public purpose, instead of being traversed by three or four streets, so near each other as to make it impossible to erect other than small slender two-story houses.

He praises the site.

We speak thus particularly, relative to the defects in the plan, in order to show the changes which have been made in the appearance of the ground, and to shift the censure for any want of beauty that may present itself in the present aspect of the site, from those who made the selection, to those who abused its advantages by adopting such a design.

He supports placing the Capitol and the White House far apart.

The "magnificent distances," at which the executive are separate from the legislative departments, have been made a ground of complaint; but we think there was much judgment shown in the choice of these situations. A suitable and prominent position was assigned to each edifice, which could not have been the case had they all been congregated in one place, unless a structure as large as the palace of Versailles had been erected. . . . Again, it was thought that their immediate vicinity to the legislative halls, would offer a great temptation to the clerks to neglect their duties, in order to hear the debates, and that the constant intrusion of members of Congress would interrupt the public buildings. ([Varnum], "The Seat of Government of the United States," 147–48)

Henry Tanner Publishes a Map Showing the Buildings and Streets of Washington

Henry Tanner, the country's leading map publisher in the 1830s, included this informative plan of Washington in his *New Universal Atlas* of 1836. Although his sources of information about the built-up portions of the city (shown here by the closely hatched blocks) remain unknown and the accuracy of the information is impossible to verify, his map is probably a close representation of reality.

Clusters of houses and places of retail business could be found near the Navy Yard, around the Capitol, north of Pennsylvania Avenue between the Capitol and the White House, and surrounding that building and the executive offices. Smaller and equally discrete neighborhoods existed south of the Mall, between that location and the Anacostia, and to the east of Georgetown. That older community remained what was probably the most thickly settled portion of the region.

Tanner's fine map also provides ample evidence to support Joseph Varnum's criticism in *Hunt's Magazine* that the city had "twice as many streets as are required." What Varnum did not make clear is that this also provided scores of highly visible sites not only for the buildings of the federal government but for such structures as churches, schools, theatres, and banks—sites Tanner identifies in his detailed legend.

This is also a useful record of the status of the federal buildings in the mid-1830s before several major projects altered the urban landscape. For example, one can see that the four offices for the executive departments still flanked the White House and those on the east had not yet been displaced by the huge Treasury. Also, no structure occupied the large square seven blocks east of the White House where L'Enfant had proposed locating a National Church and where the Patent Office was soon to be started.

City of Washington. Drawn and published by H[enry] S. Tanner. From H. S. Tanner, *A New Universal Atlas* (Philadelphia: H. S. Tanner, 1836). Engraving, 11½ × 14½ in. (29.2 × 36.8 cm.). Geography and Maps, Library of Congress.

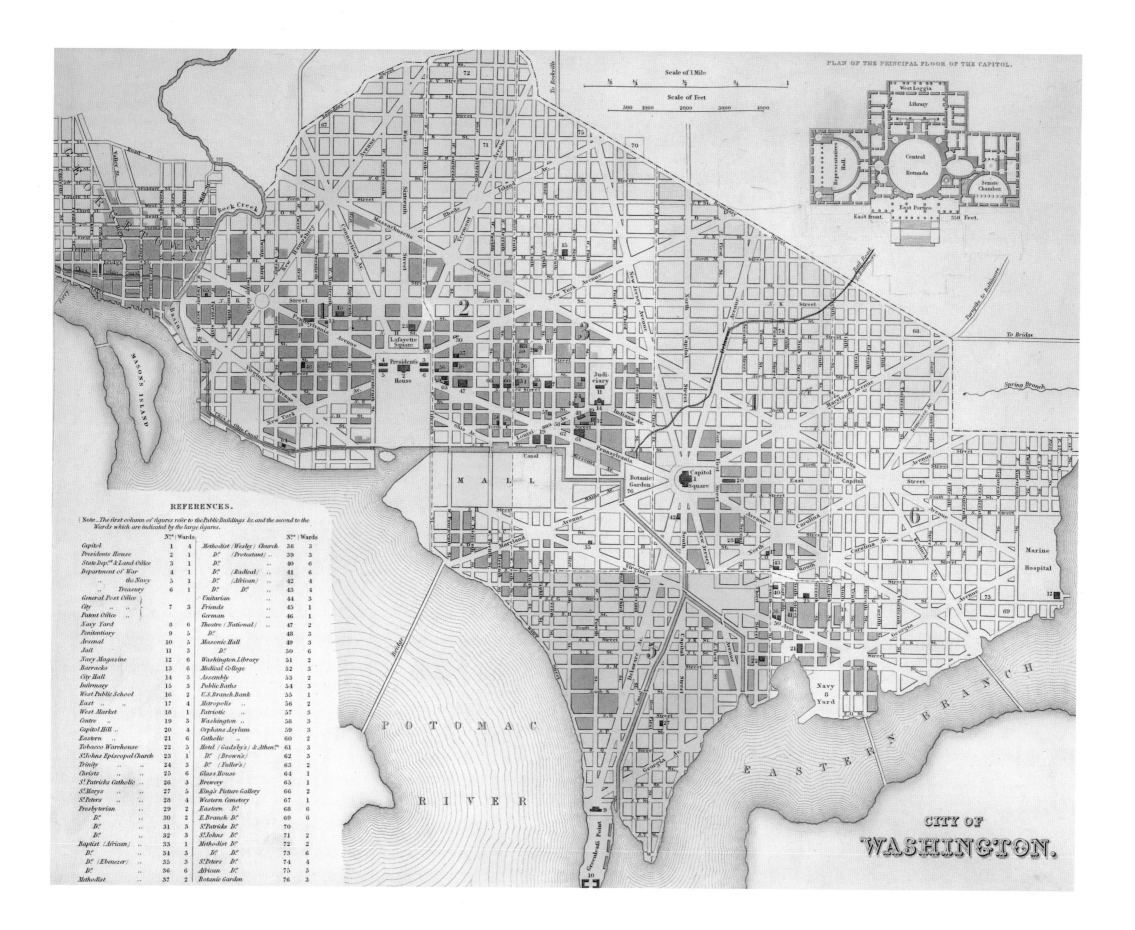

PLAN OF THE PRINCIPAL FLOOR OF THE CAPITOL.

West Loggia

Library

Representatives Hall

Central Rotunda

Senate Chamber

East Portico

East front.   350 Feet.

Scale of 1 Mile

⅛   ¼   ½   ¾   1

Scale of Feet

500   1000   2000   3000   4000

MASON'S ISLAND

ROCK CREEK

Lafayette Square

Presidents House

Judiciary

MALL

Botanic Garden

Capitol Square

Marine Hospital

Navy Yard

POTOMAC RIVER

EASTERN BRANCH

Greenleaf's Point

CITY OF
WASHINGTON.

REFERENCES.

(Note..The first column of figures refer to the Public Buildings &c. and the second to the Wards which are indicated by the large figures.

	Nos.	Wards
Capitol	1	4
Presidents House	2	1
State Dept. & Land Office	3	1
Department of War	4	1
the Navy	5	1
Treasury	6	1
General Post Office		
City	7	3
Patent Office		
Navy Yard	8	6
Penitentiary	9	5
Arsenal	10	5
Jail	11	3
Navy Magazine	12	6
Barracks	13	6
City Hall	14	3
Infirmary	15	3
West Public School	16	2
East	17	4
West Market	18	1
Centre	19	3
Capitol Hill	20	4
Eastern	21	6
Tobacco Warehouse	22	5
St Johns Episcopal Church	23	1
Trinity	24	3
Christs	25	6
St Patricks Catholic	26	3
St Marys	27	5
St Peters	28	6
Presbyterian	29	2
Do	30	1
Do	31	3
Do	32	3
Baptist (African)	33	1
Do	34	3
Do (Ebenezer)	35	6
Do	36	6
Methodist	37	2

	Nos.	Wards
Methodist (Wesley) Church	38	4
Do (Protestant)	39	3
Do (Radical)	40	6
Do (African)	41	6
Do Do	42	4
Unitarian	43	4
Friends	44	1
German	45	1
Theatre (National)	46	1
Do	47	2
Masonic Hall	48	3
Washington Library	49	3
Medical College	50	6
Assembly	51	2
Public Baths	52	3
U.S. Branch Bank	53	2
Metropolis	54	3
Patriotic	55	1
Washington	56	2
Orphans Asylum	57	3
Catholic	58	3
Hotel (Gadsby's) & Athenm	59	3
Do (Brown's)	60	2
Do (Fuller's)	61	3
Glass House	62	2
Brewery	63	2
King's Picture Gallery	64	1
Western Cemetery	65	1
Eastern Do	66	2
St Patricks Do	67	1
St Johns Do	68	6
Methodist Do	69	6
Do Do	70	
St Peters Do	71	2
African Do	72	6
Botanic Garden	73	6
	74	1
	75	3
	76	3

*Benjamin Latrobe describes the entrance
he designed for the Navy Yard in 1804.*

The design of the main gate . . . has been made with a view to the greatest economy compatible with permanence and appearance worthy of the situation. This gate will fall exactly into the range of the Georgia avenue as well as of the Eighth street east of the Capitol, one of the principal streets of this part of the city. (Hibben, *Navy-Yard, Washington*, 22–23)

David Warden lists the buildings at the Navy Yard about 1816.

The public buildings at the navy-yard are the barracks, a work-shop, and three large brick buildings for the reception of naval stores. The barracks, constructed of brick, are 600 feet in length, 50 in breadth, and 20 in height. At the head of the barrack-yard is the colonel's house, which is neat and commodious. The work-shop, planned by Latrobe, is 900 feet in length. (Warden, *Account of the United States*, 3:198)

*An English naval officer visits the yard in 1826
and records his impressions.*

The area is about forty acres in extent, a considerable portion of which is unoccupied, although the gun-wharf and ordnance stores are contained within its bounds. The commissioner, or captain, has a small house near the entrance. I could observe no other residences belonging to officers. . . . There were two frigates on the slips; one, in progress of building, was to be called the Susquehana. . . .

In this place, they have a foundry of iron-tanks, for the supply of vessels not under the rank of frigates. They have likewise a machine, containing a partial application of steam to the making of blocks. (De Roos, *Personal Narrative*, 16–18)

*Another English visitor admires the Navy Yard memorial and
marvels at the ingenious machinery for hauling ships.*

The entrance to the Navy-yard is through a very handsome, though simple, arched gateway of white stone. Immediately fronting this is a beautiful little rostrated column of white mar-

ble, surmounted by the American eagle. Round the column, and standing on a large and elevated pedestal of the same material, are some fine emblematical statues. This monument was erected by the officers of the American navy, to the memory of their comrades who fell at Tunis. It is one of the handsomest and most chaste little monuments that I have ever seen, and was made in Italy. . . .

The chief curiosity in the Navy-yard is the ingenious and beautiful machinery, contrived by Commodore Rodgers, for hauling up vessels of war out of the water; and thus obviating the necessity of dry docks, which, owing to the small rise and fall of the tide, could not be constructed without great difficulty. Large strong beams are run completely through the vessel, entering at the port-holes on one side and coming out at those on the opposite, while both the ends of the beams rest upon an inclined plane that slopes down to the water. Attached to each beam, just where it enters the porthole, are two very strong chains, which are fastened to a large block of wood, made to fit the keel. These chains are tightened by wedges and screws—and by this means, the ship is supported on its keel the same as when on the stocks. A large chain or two is put entirely round the vessel, from the bows to the stern, and to these a cable is attached, which is stretched forward to a windlass. The vessel is thus easily drawn up out of the water. Indeed, 150 men were able to draw up the Potowmac the largest frigate I ever saw. . . . Over the whole machine a very handsome roof has been built, which completely protects the vessel. (*An Excursion through the United States*, 46–47)

James Silk Buckingham visits the Navy Yard in 1838.

This yard occupies about thirty acres of area in space; it is walled-in toward the land, and is open towards the Anacosta river, or, as it is more generally called here, the Eastern branch. It was first projected by the president Jefferson, and during his administration was well sustained. It is fitted with every requisite for the building, rigging, and equipping of ships of war, of any size: the vessels already built here, are among the finest which the navy of the United States contains; besides several sloops of war, the frigates Essex, Potomac, Brandywine, and Columbia, each of forty-four guns, which was also built here, is one of the noblest vessels of her class. (Buckingham, *America*, 1:313)

William Bennett Creates an Aquatint Masterpiece from George Cooke's Painting of Washington

In 1834 William J. Bennett, a highly skilled English artist and aquatint engraver, completed one of his finest works. Using a painting by George Cooke, he produced a superb scene of Washington as seen from a distance looking across the Anacostia River from the southeast to the Navy Yard and the city's skyline beyond.

Cooke was an American who began to draw and paint while a grocery and chinaware salesman. In 1826 he went to Europe to study, returning to America five years later. In addition to his painting of Washington, Cooke's views of Richmond, Charleston, and West Point provided Bennett with images for other aquatints. They form part of the most accomplished series of city views ever created in this country, offering attractive scenes of places from New Orleans to Boston and even such Western settlements as Buffalo and Detroit.

The Cooke-Bennett view of Washington is the best early depiction of the extensive Navy Yard structures along the north side of the Anacostia River. Among other buildings, it shows the covered dry dock whose reflection in the unnaturally still waters of the river adds to the pictorial quality of the view. On the horizon the Capital dome dominates that portion of the scene. The image of the White House at the left end of the buildings lining Pennsylvania Avenue exaggerates the size of the building. Either Cooke or Bennett also rotated the White House so that its south front appears to be facing Pennsylvania Avenue, a bit of artistic license doubtless exercised in the interests of providing more information about the building's appearance than would have been possible with a more realistic representation.

City of Washington from Beyond the Navy Yard. Painted by G[eorge] Cooke. Engraved by W[illiam] Bennett. Published by Lewis P. Clover, 180 Fulton St., N.Y., 1834. Aquatint engraving, $17^{11}/_{16} \times 24^{5}/_{8}$ in. (44.9 × 62.5 cm.). Prints and Photographs, Library of Congress.

*A Hungarian in 1831 records some criticisms
of the city and its plan.*

The buildings for the most part are scattered and the land beyond the capital [*sic*] is empty, except for stakes to mark the future street. The haphazard construction gives a very strange appearance to the city, and many people are critical of the grandiose design. In particular, some object to the broad avenues, which, in addition to the tree-planted malls, leave a middle lane wide enough to accommodate three ordinary streets. All this spaciousness, some people hold, detracts from the community spirit. (Farkas, *Journey in North America*, 186)

*Charles Augustus Murray can find nothing good to say
about the city that he visited in 1834.*

In truth it is impossible to imagine a more comfortless situation for a town, or a town more foolishly and uncomfortably laid out. The houses are small, and their walls thin; the streets are so broad as to render the insignificant appearance of the buildings more remarkable; and the dust in dry weather is only to be equalled in annoyance by the filth and mud after rain. . . .

The inhabitants seem to have persisted, in defiance equally of experience and common sense, in believing that their city was one day to become the centre of wealth and commerce, as it is of legislature; and appeared disposed to overlook the trifling impediments that the soil of all the neighbouring country is wretchedly poor, that the channel of the Potomac is so shallow that neither merchant-ship nor frigate, nor any craft of five hundred tons burthen, can come up to their harbour of Georgetown; and that, moreover, they must compete with the neighbouring wealthy and flourishing town of Baltimore. (Murray, *Travels in North America*, 143–44)

A famous travel writer condemns the city in 1838.

Everybody knows that Washington has a Capitol; but the misfortune is that the Capitol wants a city. There it stands, reminding you of a general without an army, only surrounded and followed by a parcel of ragged little dirty boys; for such is the appearance of the dirty, straggling, ill-built houses which lie at the foot of it. (Marryat, *Diary in America*, 153)

Another visitor in 1838 tells why he disliked the city plan.

The plan is not so remarkable for its symmetry as those of many American cities; for though there are three great avenues running the whole length of Washington from east to west,—each therefore nearly five miles long, and 150 feet broad, and these again are crossed by four similar avenues at right angles running nearly north and south,—yet these are intersected by so many diagonal lines, and the smaller streets are made to run at angles so oblique to the general design, that amidst much that is straight and regular, there is also much that is crooked and confused.

The greatest defect of the city, however, is this, that very few portions of it are built up in continuity; the dwellings are so scattered over it in detached groups, fragments of streets, and isolated buildings, that it has all the appearance of a town rising into existence, but gradually arrested in its progress, and now stationary in its condition. The Capitol . . . was intended to be the centre of the city; and if measures had been taken, when this edifice was erected, to let off only those lots of land which were around the Capitol, so as to confine the buildings to its immediate vicinity before any others were erected beyond it, and thus progressively to have spread from the centre to the extremities, it would even now have been a handsome city. But, from the distant lots of land having been sold as freely as those near the centre, the purchasers have built up their mansions and planted their gardens around the extremities, so that Washington has been truly called "a city of magnificent distances;" and it might have been added, "with barren tracts and swampy morasses between them." (Buckingham, *America*, 1:293–94)

An English phrenologist dismisses Washington in a few words.

On approaching Washington, the first object that presents itself is the capitol, a large massive building painted white to resemble marble, with a dome not of very successful proportions. The town looks like a large straggling village reared in a drained swamp. (Combe, *Notes on the United States*, 1:264)

Peder Anderson and Fitz Hugh Lane Create the First Large Lithographic View of the City

The Peder Anderson who drew this view came to America from Norway in 1830 at the age of twenty. Views of Lowell and Worcester, Massachusetts, in 1835 and 1837 are the only earlier examples of his efforts to depict cities. In Washington he met George Washington Parke Custis who evidently invited Anderson to paint the city from the lawn of his home. Anderson thus found his way to a spot identified in a guidebook published in 1830 by Jonathan Elliot: "The best bird's eye view of the City is from an elevated ridge near the Potomac Bridge, where the eye surveys the lofty hills at a distance, forming the background on the Virginia side—the public buildings, and most of the houses of the city in front, and the river rolling in majesty on the left." The artist served as his own publisher, arranging to have his painting reproduced at Thomas Moore's lithographic establishment in Boston. Fitz Hugh Lane, then at the beginning of his own career as an artist, put Anderson's drawing on stone.

The view confirms the common complaint of both foreign and domestic critics that the city extended over such an immense area that the handful of major public buildings and the modest number of houses and commercial establishments could not properly fill its streets. To the right of center, the Capitol sits in almost lonesome splendor, connected to such minor concentrations of buildings as comprised the Navy Yard neighborhood and the vicinity of the White House by the slenderest threads of urban development. The vacant stretch of the Mall extends west from the Capitol, lined on its north edge by the Washington Canal whose dank, marshy mouth linked with the mud flats that festered just beyond the immediate grounds of the White House.

View of the City of Washington. The Metropolis of the United States of America. Taken from Arlington House the Residence of George Washington P. Custis Esq. Drawn and copyrighted by P[eder] Anderson, lithographed by F[itz] H[ugh] Lane, and printed in Boston by T[homas] Moore, 1838. Lithograph: 18⁷⁄₁₆ × 36³⁄₁₆ in. (46.9 × 92.1 cm.). The Mariners Museum, Newport News, Virginia.

On stone by F.H. Lane

Entered according to Act of Congress
in the year 1838 by P. Anderson, in the
Clerks Office of the District Court at
Washington D.C.

VIEW OF THE CITY  OF WASHINGTON.

THE METROPOLIS OF THE   ARLINGTON HOUSE   UNITED STATES OF AMERICA.

TAKEN FROM ARLINGTON HOUSE, THE RESIDENCE OF GEORGE WASHINGTON P. CUSTIS ESQ.

83

4 Washington in the 1830s and 1840s: Decades of Building, Change, and Growth

DURING the 1830s and 1840s the face of Washington changed substantially. The government constructed several major buildings, the newly appointed regents of the Smithsonian Institution completed the first part of their building on the Mall, and a private organization raised enough funds to begin the long-delayed Washington Monument. Residents regarded these improvements with pride and satisfaction, and because these structures occupied important sites, they strongly influenced the impressions visitors formed of the capital city.

One figure dominated architectural design in Washington at this time: Robert Mills, self-styled as the "first *native born American* to enter the study of architecture in the United States." Born in Charleston, Mills was forty years old at the beginning of the decade in which he rose to prominence as architect for several monumental structures that promised to give the city some of the character that L'Enfant had envisioned.[1]

After studying at the College of Charleston, Mills began his architectural career in 1800 by working briefly for James Hoban, the Irish-born designer of the White House who had practiced in Charleston, planned the South Carolina State House at Columbia, and was then supervising architect of the Capitol. On his way north to become Hoban's draftsman, Mills passed through Richmond and was captivated by the Virginia capitol that Jefferson had helped to design.

After Mills had absorbed much of what Hoban could teach, he accepted Jefferson's invitation to live for a time at Monticello, his home in Charlottesville. There he studied the extensive collection of architectural books in Jefferson's library. Jefferson also introduced Mills to Benjamin H. Latrobe, appointed by the president as surveyor of public buildings, and from 1803 to 1808 Mills served the versatile and talented Latrobe as clerk and draftsman.[2]

In 1808 Mills began an independent practice of architecture in Philadelphia,

where for Latrobe the previous year he had supervised construction of the Bank of Philadelphia. For the next nine years Mills designed a variety of buildings. In 1814 Mills won a competition for the design of a monument to President Washington that was begun the following year in Baltimore, where Mills moved in 1817. He designed this as a great Doric column rising 160 feet above the ground from a square base and topped with a portrait statute of a standing Washington seventeen feet tall. Completed by 1829, it was widely admired.[3]

In 1820 Mills became a member of the South Carolina Board of Public Works as well as state engineer and architect and civil and military engineer of the state. In this capacity, Mills supervised construction of highway and canal projects, a state hospital for the insane, and many state-financed buildings used by city and county governments, most of which he designed or revised. Four courthouses and as many jails were among these, as well as his better-known "Fireproof Building" in Charleston—a structure for the protection of public records.[4]

In 1830 Mills returned to Washington where he succeeded in securing commissions for the design of several federal customhouses in New England as well as a bridge over the Potomac River. By the mid-1830s, therefore, it could be argued that no one in America could equal Robert Mills in training and experience in large-scale, monumental building design. It was at this stage of his already nota-

---

1. Mills described himself in a footnote to his *Statistics of South Carolina*, according to Gallagher in *Robert Mills*, 3.

2. Fisk Kimball, the author of the biographical sketch of Mills in the *Dictionary of American Biography*, states that "from Latrobe, the father of the Greek revival in America, he [Mills] imbibed not only his knowledge of Greek forms, but his principles of professional practice and his scientific engineering skill." See "Mills, Robert," in *Dictionary of American Biography* (1957), 7:10.

3. In Philadelphia, in addition to many private mansions, his commissions included such important public structures as the Pennsylvania State House at Harrisburg, several churches in Philadelphia and Richmond, the Burlington County, New Jersey, prison, and remodeled wings for Independence Hall. In Baltimore for three years Mills continued an active career, designing two churches as well as serving as the chief engineer and president of the water works. Several of the architect's preliminary designs for the Baltimore monument to George Washington are reproduced in Gallagher, *Robert Mills*, opposite pp. 108 and 110.

4. During this period Mills also drew plans for three notable structures in Camden, South Carolina: the courthouse, the Presbyterian Church, and a monument to General DeKalb. It was at this time, too, that Mills submitted a design for the Bunker Hill Monument in Charlestown, Massachusetts. Of this latter design—a Doric column similar in spirit to his Washington Monument in Baltimore—Kimball tells us that Mills "states in sketches of his life that he proposed an obelisk form, doubtless as an alternative, and considered that his idea had been adopted in the executed work." See Kimball, "Mills," in *Dictionary of American Biography*, 7:12. The architect's work in his native state is the subject of Marsh, *Robert Mills*. More recent scholarship on Mills appears in the essays by several scholars in John M. Bryan, *Robert Mills*.

ble career that he was selected to design a new building for the Department of the Treasury.

The government needed the new building badly. From 1797 to 1833 the Treasury Department occupied the southernmost of two executive office structures flanking the White House on its east side. Its destruction by fire in 1833 offered the chance to provide adequate space for a branch of the government that had grown substantially and had overcrowded the old building. The president and Congress considered a number of possible sites, but no decision on this matter had been reached when William P. Elliot and Robert Mills were invited to submit designs for the building.[5]

Mills proposed a long T-shaped structure whose main facade faced east and had a short projection extending westward from the rear of the principal wing. Although this was approved, Congress could not agree on which site should be used. Finally, the legislators conferred the power to decide on President Jackson, who chose neither of the three previously discussed locations but instead directed that the building be built on the site of the old Treasury with its northern end connected to the State Department building that faced Lafayette Square.[6]

The building that Mills designed extended south along Fourteenth Street, with a long colonnade in the Ionic order providing a facade of a type and scale hitherto unknown in Washington, or, indeed, anywhere else in the country. Several congressmen had second thoughts about the wisdom of the building's location when they realized that a future southern entrance wing would block the view to the White House from Pennsylvania Avenue. Their objections did not halt construction, however, and in what for Washington was the remarkably short time of four years, the gleaming new Treasury stood completed as designed.

Massive as was this structure in 1840 with the completion of the Mills design, it represented only a portion of the much larger building it was to become after three additions. The first began in 1855 and required five years to finish. This provided the impressive south entrance, a design executed by Ammi B. Young who conformed to the style that Mills had established. As had been feared, this destroyed the visual link between the Capitol and the White House.

During the Civil War the government constructed a west wing that Isaiah Rogers designed, and in 1866 the old State Department building was demolished to make way for the north and final wing completed in 1869 from plans prepared by A. B. Mullett. It is this fully completed Treasury that Edward Sachse of Baltimore depicted sometime in the early or mid-1860s in the lithograph reproduced in folio 28. The artist stood across the intersection of Pennsylvania Avenue and Fourteenth Street and looked northwest to the south entrance and the great colonnade rising from the sidewalk along the street. Sachse anticipated the completion of the north wing, obligingly drawing that distant portion as if finished.[7]

While most visitors regarded the Treasury as perhaps the most majestic sight after the Capitol, others, such as Joseph Varnum, Jr., a resident and close observer of Washington affairs, strongly objected to its location. First in a series of articles published in *Hunt's Merchants' Magazine* in 1848, later that year in a book composed entirely of the magazine pieces, and in 1854 in a revised edition, Varnum lamented the decision to block the vistas to and from the White House along both Pennsylvania Avenue and F Street. Folio 28 includes an excerpt from this portion of Varnum's book.[8]

Mills was involved with another massive government building project that also began in 1836. This was the Patent Office, built on the site that L'Enfant designated for the National Church. It was a splendid and appropriately scaled structure for this commanding, elevated site that looked south along the axis of Eighth Street to the still unimproved Mall and beyond to the Potomac. Only the locations chosen for the Capitol, the White House, and the City Hall (to be discussed later) rivaled or excelled it in prominence.

On L'Enfant's plan the long axis of Eighth Street began at the northern edge of the city and passed through two of the fifteen important civic squares he proposed for the states of the union, before terminating at the northern side of the site. To the south, this Eighth Street axis extended through the center of a market on the north side of the canal, crossed the Mall and passed through yet another of the state squares, and ended at L'Enfant's proposed Naval Itinerary Column. On his engraving, Ellicott eliminated one of the state squares to the north but otherwise left unchanged the remaining civic spaces through which the Eighth Street axis passed.[9]

showed individual buildings while others provided images of the entire city. His contributions to the city's iconography will become more apparent in the next chapter, which discusses and presents his several large and elaborate lithographs of the entire city. For several years before his departure for the United States—probably in 1848—Sachse operated a small printing and publishing business in his native city of Görlitz in Silesia. In Baltimore Sachse worked for E. Weber & Co. before striking out on his own by 1850. He printed and probably drew views of Baltimore, Richmond, and Norfolk before issuing his first print showing Washington in 1852. He specialized in multi-stone color lithography, and his work in this medium nearly always exhibited a very high level of printing skills. Although most of his views used Eastern subjects, in the early and mid-1850s he produced several stunning color portraits of Mid-western cities. The close proximity of Baltimore to Washington, Sachse's renown as an artist and printer, and his vigorous exploitation of the market for scenes of Washington and its buildings doubtless discouraged any other urban viewmaker from settling in the city.

8. The extract in folio 28 concerning the Treasury is but one of the observations and insights by this perceptive critic that have been used in the present work.

9. Here and throughout I have used the modern street numbers. Those on the L'Enfant manuscript differ somewhat. The civic square on the Eighth Street axis north of the Patent Office came to be known as Mount Vernon Square. In the city plan this is clearly one of the most important locations in the city, placed as it is at the crossing of Massachusetts Avenue running northwest-southeast and New York Avenue on its southwest-north-

5. The sites examined included Lafayette Square, a location south of the White House, and the block bounded by F, G, and Seventh and Eighth streets—the eastern half of the site first proposed by L'Enfant for the National Church.

6. For this information and much other material about the buildings of Washington begun in the 1830s, I have relied on Reiff, *Washington Architecture*, 19–47.

7. Edward Sachse was an important Baltimore artist, printer, and publisher who depicted Washington in many fine lithographs. Some of these

Although William P. Elliot, Mills's competitor for the Treasury commission, drew the plans for the Patent Office, Mills supervised the construction of its south wing and designed some of the interior vaulting before builders finished the first phase of the structure in 1840. Mills later planned the foundations for the east and west wings, additions completed in 1852 and 1856, respectively. A north wing begun in 1856 took eleven years to finish because construction had to be suspended during the Civil War.[10]

The view in folio 29 is another of the fine lithographic portraits of important Washington buildings issued by Edward Sachse. Although Sachse did not date this print, he may have drawn and published it on the occasion of the final completion of this huge and imposing building in 1867. Sachse used most of his space to show us either the north or south facade (they are virtually identical) with a porticoed entrance reached by a stairway on the axis of Eighth Street.

The vista to and from the south was particularly impressive, although the successive market buildings that stopped the axis at the foot of the slope did little to enhance it. In the 1930s the National Archives provided a more effective termination, and with the completion in 1990 of the semicircular market square project that opens to Pennsylvania Avenue, this important feature of the original city plan has finally achieved some of its intended prominence.[11]

Unlike the Capitol, the White House, and the Treasury—each built of sandstone that ultimately had to be covered or replaced—the Patent Office contract for all but the south wing specified the use of marble. Many visitors took note of this, including the two correspondents for *Harper's Magazine* whose comments on the building also appear in folio 29. One of these writers declared that "on a clear moonlight night" there was no more beautiful sight than "this immense edifice of pure marble, glistening with the moonbeams."

Of course, not everyone found the building flawless, and early in the Civil

War when Anthony Trollope visited Washington he expressed his dislike for the number, size, and style of the windows that the architects had designed, and he found the entry stairs "more gratifying to the eye than to the legs." He also felt that "if the streets round it were finished [the building] would be more imposing." Nevertheless, he had to admit that the Patent Office had "fine" porticos and that the whole structure was "massive and grand."

Before builders could complete the first or south wing of the Patent Office, Congress authorized another important federal building on an adjoining block to the south. Here, since 1800, stood one of Washington's early landmarks—Blodgett's Hotel at Eighth and E streets—designed by James Hoban and purchased by the federal government in 1810. Both the Patent Office and the Post Office Department occupied this structure, but in December 1836 its destruction by fire moved Congress to approve a new building for the Post Office Department.[12]

Robert Mills obtained the commission to design this building on the block bounded by E, F, Seventh, and Eighth streets. It thus faced the southeast facade of the Patent Office as well as the Eighth Street approach to that building from the Mall. The site thus lacked the axial prominence that provided such visibility for the Patent Office. Mills seems to have recognized this in his design, as the slightly inaccurate view reproduced in folio 30 reveals. He chose not to emphasize the entrances in the middle of each facade except to make the pilasters there somewhat more prominent and to cap them with unobtrusive sloping parapets (not the low pediments shown in this view, another of the lithographs that Augustus Köllner drew).[13]

The southern portion with wings extending northward along Seventh and Eighth streets was finished by 1842, but the final section facing the Patent Office was not occupied until after the Civil War. In that addition, Thomas U. Walter followed the Mills design for the exterior. This elegant and restrained building flanking the strong axis of Eighth Street begged for an equally refined companion on the west side of that potentially strategic thoroughfare. If such a structure had ever been built, the three buildings would have formed an imposing focus of federal activity that the site both demanded and justified.

The other major public building illustrated in folio 30 is the City Hall, designed in 1820 by George Hadfield. Hadfield first came to Washington in 1795 to replace Stephen Hallet as superintendent of construction of the Capitol, a position he filled until the commissioners dismissed him three years later. Hadfield also drew the plans in 1797 for the Treasury Building east of the White House, a

east alignment. K Street also enters the square from the east and west. On L'Enfant's drawing, K Street seems slightly wider than most of the other grid streets. Ellicott drew it as wide as the avenues and matched in width by only a few others in the grid system. It was at this meeting of three very wide thoroughfares that the Washington Public Library was completed in 1902 on Mount Vernon Square after Andrew Carnegie contributed $375,000 for its construction. This handsome structure provides a suitably impressive termination for vistas along the two avenues, Eighth Street, and K Street. The construction of a new public library west of the Patent Office from a design by Mies van der Rohe made the old Carnegie building available for other uses. At an earlier time the North Liberties Market occupied the eastern half of Mount Vernon Square, a reservation that Eighth Street divided into two parts.

Alexander Shepherd—of whom, more later—had the building demolished in 1872.

10. Reiff, *Washington Architecture*, 38–39; Louise Hall, "The Design of the Old Patent Office." Thomas U. Walter succeeded Mills as the architect for the east and west wings, the latter being finished under the direction of Edward Clark. Walter began the north wing, and Clark again took over for the last two years that saw the building finally completed in the form we know it today.

11. Many observers will be able to master their enthusiasm for the semicircular colonnaded facade of the Market Place buildings facing the National Archives. If the postmodern era of American architecture can produce nothing better than this example of applied archaeology, it would be better to move swiftly on to whatever is the next fad of a profession that seems to have lost philosophy, direction, and standards.

12. For a reproduction of a drawing of Blodgett's Hotel in 1803 by Nicholas King, see Junior League of Washington, *City of Washington*, 86. The same drawing is also illustrated in Gutheim, *Worthy of the Nation*, 40, and Gutheim and Washburn, *The Federal City*, 9.

13. When I reproduced this view in my *Monumental Washington* (fig. 27), I erroneously followed the date then assigned by the staff to this undated lithograph in the collection of the Library of Congress. Daniel Reiff, in his *Washington Architecture*, 39 n. 77, has noted this error and has pointed out how Köllner misleadingly rendered the parapets and substantially reduced the size of the chimneys.

structure the commissioners duplicated on the other side of the presidential residence. On Jefferson's recommendation he also prepared the designs for the city jail and the arsenal at Greenleaf's Point.[14]

The City Hall occupied a commanding site bounded by Fourth and Fifth streets and extending from D Street north three blocks to G Street. Two short diagonal boulevards—Louisiana and Indiana avenues—led to its southern edge from the southwest and southeast. City officials had high hopes for this structure but not much money. The result was a building with an attractive and ambitious design but one that seemed to take forever to complete and that in the end had to be taken over by the federal government.

The difficulties encountered by the city in this project stemmed from the unsatisfactory arrangements made by Congress for financing municipal improvements and the related problems of administration of a city with such an unusual plan and pattern of development. The municipality possessed limited financial resources to carry out the many obligations imposed on it, for the federal government owned a very large proportion of the land that the city could not tax.

Moreover, L'Enfant's plan saddled the municipality with the upkeep of a street system that occupied a greater percentage of the land than any other city in the nation. Further, the dispersed nature of Washington caused by the decision to separate by such distance the major offices of the national government also made urban services far more costly than normal.

For decades the federal government declined to bear a reasonable share of the costs of local services and improvements borne by the municipality that it had called into existence. A very substantial fraction of municipal funds went for expenses required only because the place served as the seat of national government and administration. In his oration when the cornerstone was laid for the City Hall, John Law expressed the resentment local leaders felt toward Congress for refusing to acknowledge its obligation to shoulder at least part of the financial burden of providing urban services.[15]

It was no wonder that the municipality found itself unable to build more than

a portion of Hadfield's design. His plan called for a handsome entrance portico on a central wing 250 feet long that was to be crowned with an enormous, low dome. Two 50-foot-wide extensions on either end thrust southward to create a formal entrance courtyard that opened toward Pennsylvania Avenue. The view in folio 30 printed and published by Edward Sachse in the 1860s shows these features as the artist looked north from across D Street.[16]

Like the Patent Office site, this location, too, had been intended by L'Enfant for another purpose. From the very beginning of Washington, everyone referred to the public reservation it occupied as Judiciary Square, and it was probably here that L'Enfant intended to locate the Supreme Court—a use referred to by him in one of his rather confusing memoranda to President Washington as the "Judiciary Court." Strangely, he omitted any reference to this on the detailed legend of his only surviving plan for the city.[17]

In 1823 city fathers persuaded Congress to add $10,000 to the $80,000 the municipality had already spent to build the east wing. In return the government got the use of half of the expanded building for court purposes. In his Washington guide published in 1848, George Watterston told his readers that "the south front of this fine building only is completed," and that "the outside is not yet finished, it being intended to be stuccoed and to have porticoes in the centre and a colonnade at each end."[18]

The following year Congress provided an additional $30,000 to build the west wing, but only to secure additional space for the federal courts whose needs had

14. Hadfield's sister, Maria, was the wife of the artist Richard Cosway. Maria Cosway met Jefferson in Paris not long after his arrival as American minister in 1784. They saw one another frequently and may have been lovers. Whatever the truth of the matter, Jefferson retained fond memories of Maria Cosway, and his sponsorship of Hadfield may have been one way of expressing his feelings. Of course Jefferson also loved architecture and wished to further the tastes of Americans in this aspect of art. Hadfield had received excellent training in England and came to America in 1795 after winning a gold medal from the Royal Academy for a design for a national prison and being supported by the academy while he studied in

Rome. See Hunsberger, "Architectural Career of George Hadfield."

15. See *Ceremonies and Oration at Laying the Cornerstone of the City Hall of the City of Washington* (Washington, D.C.: Jacob Gideon, Jr., 1820). Law also complained that Congress had even failed to improve sites in the city under federal jurisdiction, noting that the Mall existed as an eyesore because "no attempt to improve [it] has been made; not a tree has been planted; not even a common fence encloses it." Daniel Reiff in his *Washington Architecture*, 28–33, summarizes the financial difficulties of the municipality as related to physical improvements. See also Green, *Washington: Village and Capital*, 89, for this example: "In more than

twenty years Congress had appropriated for the capital about $15,000 exclusively for work on Pennsylvania Avenue and roads about the President's house, whereas in 1821 alone the condition of the streets impelled the city to spend $43,000 on them."

16. The view in folio 30 is another of the invaluable (if occasionally inaccurate) depictions of major Washington buildings printed and published in Baltimore by Edward Sachse. In the case of the City Hall print, he added a dome to the building, although by the time the view appeared, that feature had been given up as too expensive. As we shall see in a subsequent chapter, in his large lithographs of the entire city, Sachse stubbornly persisted in portraying certain other buildings and monuments as originally designed rather than as they actually appeared at the time.

17. The prominence of the site argues strongly that L'Enfant chose this location for a building to house the third branch of federal government. His drawing shows a civic space and building extending three blocks north and south, a feature duplicated in a slightly different configuration by Ellicott. The site occupied an elevation exceeded in the central portion of the city only by Capitol

Hill, rising thirty feet above the level of Pennsylvania Avenue two blocks to the south down a gentle slope. The two short but wide diagonal avenues leading to and from the square—Louisiana, running to the southwest, and Indiana, extending southeast—seem to have little or no functional reason for existence and must have been planned by L'Enfant simply to open vistas and give more visual exposure to a building placed there. Further, the awkwardly named 4½ Street extending south from the square appears to have been introduced into the grid system solely to provide a strong axis terminating at the midpoint of the square's southern limit. On Ellicott's engraving, this street has a southern terminus as well, ending at the large public reservation on Greenleaf's Point.

18. Watterston, *New Guide to Washington*, 82–83, described how the building was divided: "The eastern half of the City Hall is occupied by the Circuit and Criminal Courts of the United States for the county, and their offices, for which Congress gave but $10,000. The Court room occupies half the centre of the building and the first floor of the eastern projection. . . . The second story is appropriated to the use of the . . . juries, and the

virtually superseded municipal activities. Eventually the entire building became a judicial center after the federal government took title to the City Hall in 1873, giving added meaning to the appellation Judiciary Square. Later construction on this large public reservation included the addition in 1881 of a north extension to Hadfield's design.

The Treasury, Patent Office, Post Office, and City Hall all reflected the taste for buildings designed after Roman or Greek models. Two structures begun in the 1840s that have both become Washington icons contrasted strongly with one another in this respect, as in others as well. Robert Mills, who designed the Washington Monument, plainly found his inspiration in classical civilization. James Renwick, on the other hand, looked to medieval Europe for the architectural elements he used in his Norman-style, red sandstone Smithsonian Institution.

Both of these important structures occupied sites on the Mall, until then—more than half a century after L'Enfant planned the city—only a dreary expanse of nearly vacant and unsightly territory that the federal government had almost entirely ignored. These first efforts to take advantage of the central feature of the city plan helped to determine the future development of the Mall in ways that their sponsors and designers could not have foreseen.

Both projects had their origins in events years before construction began, even, in the case of the Washington Monument, before the city was planned, when, on 7 August 1783, the Continental Congress resolved "that an equestrian statue of General Washington be erected at the place where the residence of Congress shall be established." It was with this in mind that L'Enfant provided a highly visible site for such a memorial located where the southern axis of the White House met the western axis of the Capitol.

Given George Washington's contributions to the new nation and the near-universal respect and admiration expressed by both his fellow citizens and foreign associates and observers, it seems inexplicable that it took so long for a suitable monument to be erected to him in the national capital. Efforts by his admirers began nine days after his death in 1799 and continued fruitlessly in 1816, 1819, 1824, 1825, and 1832, the latter year being the centennial of Washington's birth.[19]

Finally, in 1833 the librarian of Congress, George Watterston, took the lead in organizing the Washington National Monument Society with the purpose of raising funds and constructing a suitable monument. Led by respected public figures, the society in 1836 announced a competition for the design of a monument. There were many competitors and a variety of designs, but the society selected the entry submitted by Robert Mills as the one to be followed.[20]

This promising beginning aside, the history of the monument's construction is one of delays, changes, frustrations, and disappointments. The society hoped to raise $1,000,000 in a national campaign that it engaged agents to begin. Their efforts produced only $30,000. The government denied the society's request for a site, did so again in 1844, and only in 1848 did Congress finally authorize the monument's construction on public grounds "not otherwise occupied," leaving the exact location to officials of the society and the president of the United States acting jointly.

Perhaps Mills's design caused some of these difficulties. Although earlier he had designed the Bunker Hill Monument across the Charles River from Boston as a tall, simple stone shaft capped by a pointed top in the manner of ancient obelisks, for the monument in Washington he wrapped his bluntly pointed obelisk in an elaborate colonnaded base in which he proposed to house a national pantheon. The first illustration in folio 31, a lithograph by Charles Fenderich of Washington, shows what Mills proposed and what the association set out to build.[21]

Many persons must have looked on this design as excessively fussy and far too pretentious to honor a person who helped create and then led a nation celebrating democratic equality and who in the popular mind was thought to have been direct and unostentatious in his actions. For the more sophisticated, the combination of two quite different architectural forms could not have held much appeal. Moreover, the timing of the first plea for funds proved unfortunate, for by 1837 the nation had entered one of the periodic financial depressions that nearly every decade brought most capital spending to a halt.[22]

---

basement story is occupied by attorneys and others, who rent the room of the Corporation."

19. All of these attempts to provide a suitable monument to Washington are summarized with other information about the monument in U.S. Federal Writers' Project, *Washington*, 317–29.

20. Chief Justice John Marshall, who in 1799 on Washington's death proposed erecting a marble tomb for him in the capital city, served as the society's first president. Former U.S. president James Madison succeeded to that office on Marshall's death in 1835. For the designs submitted in the competition, see Freeman, "Design Proposals for the Washington National Monument." Reproductions of Mills's original drawing and an engraved version by William Bartlett are juxtaposed in an illustration opposite p. 116 in Gallagher, *Robert Mills*.

21. Charles Fenderich (1805–1887?) was a Swiss who served an apprenticeship under a lithographer in Zurich, subsequently worked in Mulhouse and Paris, and came to the United States in 1831. In Philadelphia the firm of Childs & Inman employed him for a time. He and a fellow Swiss, John Casper Wild, entered into a brief partnership, but in 1834 Fenderich established his own press. From 1837 to 1849 he lived in Washington where he had a shop on Pennsylvania Avenue between Tenth and Eleventh streets. While in Washington he published nearly 100 lithographic portraits of statesmen and other public figures.

In 1849 he joined a group going to California led by another artist and draftsman, Joseph Bruff, whose curious view of the Mall is reproduced in folio 34. Fenderich lived in several places in California, probably dying in San Francisco. For a reproduction of one of Fenderich's portraits, see fig. 21 in Cosentino and Glassie, *The Capital Image*. Fenderich's career is traced and his lithographs cataloged in Parker and Kaplan, *Charles Fenderich*. This publication contains microfiche images of more than 200 of his lithographs.

22. In its passage on the history of the monument, the U.S. federal Writers' Project guide, *Washington*, describes the Mills design as a "grand international hodgepodge," calling "for a decorated Egyptian shaft 700 feet high, mounted on a conic Babylonian base, the whole surrounded by a circular Greek temple, 100 feet high and 250 feet in diameter. . . . Above the east doorway there was to be a 30-foot figure of Washington, clad in a Roman toga, sitting in a Greek chariot drawn by Arabian steeds driven by an Etruscan winged Victory."

The accounts excerpted in folio 31 help to trace the construction history of the Washington Monument, including the period from 1854 to 1880 that Mark Twain refers to so hilariously in the passage quoted from *The Gilded Age*. It was during that span of twenty-six long years after the society's funds ran out that the monument stood as an embarrassingly incomplete stone stump rising 152 feet high above the rubble and mud around its base. It is the monument in this unhappy state just as the first phase of its construction was drawing to an end that Frank Leslie depicted in the second illustration in folio 31.[23]

Not everyone rejoiced when work eventually resumed in 1880, four years after Congress passed its first appropriation for this purpose. Shortly before that took place, a New York newspaper commented sourly on the latest effort to raise funds to complete the shaft. In doing so, the writer referred to rumors that the foundation was inadequate to support the weight that would be added by the new construction:

> The appeal for a Fourth of July contribution to the Washington Monument will not amount to much. Public judgment on that *abortion* has been made up. The country has failed in many ways to honor the memory of its first president, but the neglect to finish this monument is not among them. A wretched design, a wretched location, and an *insecure foundation* match well with its empty treasury. If the public will let the big furnace chimney on the Potomac flat alone and give its energy instead to cleaning out morally and physically the city, likewise named after the Father of his Country, it will better honor his memory.[24]

At last on 6 December 1884, workmen laid the capstone and set the cast aluminum pointed tip in place. A dedication ceremony took place on 21 February the following year, but it was not until 9 October 1888 that one could enter and climb 898 steps to the top of the 555-foot shaft or ride a steam-powered elevator requiring five minutes to make the ascent. At the top, small paired observation windows in each face provided views to the cardinal points of the compass. The tangible memorial to George Washington that more than a century earlier the Continental Congress resolved to build finally stood complete.

No one seeing this majestic obelisk for the first time can fail to be moved by the Washington Monument's simple beauty, its smooth, tapering faces bereft of any ornamentation and its immense scale fitting perfectly the grand spaces of the city plan. Happily differing substantially from Mills's overly ornate design as well as the earlier conventional concept of the hero's equestrian statue, the monument rises in the center of governmental Washington as a unique urban landmark as well as a symbol of national unity.

In one respect, however, the monument posed a serious problem for the realization of L'Enfant's vision of the Mall and how that central corridor of planned open space should be linked to the only slightly less important extension of the White House grounds southward to its meeting with the Mall. It was at this point that L'Enfant's plan called for the Washington Monument to be located, but when the time came at last to lay the foundation for this structure, soil conditions there and its elevation lower than a nearby rise in the ground dictated a different location.

While the chosen site fell only a negligible 123 feet south of the long Capitol axis, it lay 370 east of the much shorter axis of the White House. Unavoidable as this may have been, given the type and size of the monument the society selected, this constituted a major departure from the original city plan—one of far greater visual consequence than placing the Patent Office on the site for the National Church or devoting to municipal activities the location intended for the Supreme Court.[25]

One year after construction began on the Washington Monument, another building that had been long discussed finally got under way. This was the Smithsonian Institution, made possible by the strange and unexpected bequest in 1829 by an English scientist who had never been in America, James Smithson. His will made his nephew the chief beneficiary but provided that if he should die childless, his entire fortune was to pass "to the United States of America, to found at Washington, under the name of the Smithsonian Institution, an Establishment for the increase and diffusion of knowledge among men."

23. The wood engraving from the New York *Illustrated News* is signed "Leslie." This is Frank Leslie (1821–1880), born Henry Carter, the son of a well-to-do glove manufacturer in Ipswich, England. He preferred and had greater talent for drawing and wood engraving than for making and selling gloves and in 1841 began work for the *Illustrated London News*. This large and lavish publication pioneered in the English-speaking world the marriage of text and illustrations in a popular news and travel weekly. In 1848 Leslie came to New York and produced wood engravings for American illustrated publications, including *Gleason's Pictorial Drawing-Room Companion*, published in Boston, and the New York *Illustrated News*. He then founded several magazines and newspapers of his own, including *Frank Leslie's Illustrated Newspaper*, whose first issue appeared in December 1855. For three decades this large-folio, profusely illustrated weekly and its slightly older rival, *Harper's Illustrated*, competed vigorously for the best writers, artists, and engravers. Issues of these journals and those of *Gleason's* and *Every Saturday*, to name the most important, have become valuable sources of images for modern scholars and antiquarians. See Gambee, *Frank Leslie*, and Reinhardt, *Out West on the Overland Train*, 5–9.

24. *New York Tribune*, 1 July 1875, as quoted in Gallagher, *Robert Mills*, 119.

25. The substitute site selected for the monument did not prove entirely suitable either. Before construction resumed in 1880, government engineers had to rebuild the original base, pouring a concrete slab below the old stonework 13½ feet thick and 126½ feet square. This extends slightly more than 23 feet beyond the outer edge of the original base. In addition, the engineers constructed a continuous buttress extending from the shaft outward to the new base so as to distribute the great weight of the monument over a larger area. Since all of this work was located below grade, none of this elaborate construction can be seen. For a description of the work undertaken at that time, see Caemmerer, *Washington, the National Capital*, 291–92.

Following the unmarried nephew's death, the Court of Chancery in 1838 transferred to the federal government about $550,000, representing the principal plus accrued interest. That sum was promptly invested in state bonds until a decision could be reached about how to proceed. In good Washington fashion, that required eight years of discussion, debate, and controversy until Congress in 1846 passed legislation creating the Regents of the Smithsonian Institution, authorizing the erection of a building on the Mall, and limiting its cost to the nearly quarter of a million dollars that had accrued in interest during the long delay about how the funds should be used.[26]

The building committee of the regents visited several Eastern cities and Cincinnati to meet architects and invited them to submit plans. They chose a design prepared by James Renwick, Jr., of New York City. Two views in folio 32 show this remarkable building as seen from the northwest or Mall side and the southeast (their subtitles being incorrect). Both of these lithographs appeared in *Hints on Public Architecture*, a book published in 1849 when only the east wing had been completed.[27]

Its author held firm ideas about architecture, especially as applied to public buildings, believing strongly that the Norman or Lombard style offered great possibilities. Unlike most architectural theoreticians or critics, this person occupied a position that enabled him to see that his ideas were carried out. He was no less a figure than Senator Robert Dale Owen from Indiana, who had led the successful congressional campaign to establish the Smithsonian and who chaired the building committee of the board of regents.[28]

In his book Owen identified the style of Renwick's building as "that of the last half of the twelfth century; the latest variety of the rounded style" prior to the development of "early Gothic." Owen stated that the Smithsonian building would compare favorably with any actual examples of what he called "the Lombard, the Norman, the Romanesque and the Byzantine school." He summarized the general characteristics of the building:

The semicircular arch, stilted, is employed throughout, in doors, windows and other openings. The windows are without elaborately traceried heads. The buttresses are not a prominent feature, and have no surmounting pinnacles. The weather-mouldings consist of corbel-courses, with bold projection. The towers are of various shapes and sizes; and the main entrance from the north, sheltered by a carriage porch, is between two, of unequal height.[29]

This romantically picturesque structure of red sandstone departed markedly from anything heretofore erected in Washington. It reflected Owen's belief that the federal buildings designed on classical models were inappropriate. Although Owen in his book expressed the hope that the Norman or Lombard style used for the Smithsonian would be so accepted as to "deserve to be named as a National Style of Architecture for America," in this he would be disappointed.

Whether Washington and the nation needed more buildings in this style now seems questionable, but in at least one respect it is unfortunate that federal officials did not use this building as a model. Unlike many projects undertaken for normal federal purposes, construction of the Smithsonian proceeded at a reasonable pace from its beginning in 1847 until its completion in 1855.[30]

The Smithsonian's location on the south side of the Mall with its entrance on that side facing Tenth Street made it highly visible, all the more so because of the bleak, unplanted surroundings that stretched to the east and west. Owen doubtless regarded this as desirable, since he hoped it would serve as a national model of good taste. Doubtless for that reason Owen and his colleagues decided to place it well into the Mall rather than along its southern edge.

Possibly they knew of L'Enfant's proposal for what he called a "Grand Avenue 400 feet in breadth, and about a mile in length" running down the center of the Mall, for the distance from the north edge of the entrance porte cochère of the Smithsonian to the true axis of the Capitol is over 250 feet. There is even room for a 400-foot "Grand Avenue" whose center line would lie along a line drawn from the center of the Capitol to the Washington Monument, a line diverging slightly to the southwest because of the monument's asymmetrical location.[31]

The time had not yet come when the federal government was ready to undertake directly the development of the Mall, for through the 1840s the only significant structures occupying sites there had been constructed by quasi-public orga-

26. The history of the Smithsonian can be traced in the annual reports of the board of regents beginning in 1846. A late nineteenth-century collection of materials on this subject can be found in George Brown Goode, *The Smithsonian Institution*. The best summary I have found is in Reiff, *Washington Architecture*, 89–99. This includes a useful analysis of the building, discusses its place in the development of American architecture, and speculates on why its style had so little effect on subsequent buildings in Washington.

27. Using the architectural drawings by the Smithsonian's architect, James Renwick, Adam Weingärtner (?–?) drew the two elevations of the

building on stone. He and Louis Nagel (1817–?) operated a lithographic shop in New York from 1849 to 1856. The imprint tells us that Napoleon Sarony (1821–1896) did the figures for the two prints. Sarony and his partner, Henry B. Major (?–?), began their ten-year association in 1844. At the time of these two views, they occupied premises at 117 Fulton Street. Sarony specialized in portraiture, and his abilities in drawing figures doubtless led to his selection for this joint effort. In his *America on Stone*, Peters traces Sarony's career on pp. 350–56 and describes the work of Nagel and Weingärtner on pp. 291–94.

28. James Renwick doubtless materially helped

Owen in writing his book, a publication the regents authorized early in 1847 a few weeks after choosing Renwick's design for their building.

29. Owen, *Hints on Public Architecture*, 104–5.

30. The cornerstone ceremony was held in May 1847. Two years later the east wing had been finished, and by 1852 all the remaining exterior work

was done. In the spring of 1855 the building stood completed, lacking only some furnishings and equipment.

31. As Reiff points out in his *Washington Architecture*, 120 n. 126, I misleadingly stated in my *Monumental Washington*, 42, that the Smithsonian Institution "encroached" on the Mall.

nizations. The only federal expenditure for a building on the Mall had been for a greenhouse constituting the so-called Botanic Garden built in 1842. This occupied a small site at the base of Capitol Hill just south of the center line of the Mall.[32]

Nor had the federal government been responsible for many other improvements in Washington aside from the Capitol, the buildings for the executive departments, and the immediate surroundings of these structures. Jefferson's partly successful efforts to plant trees along Pennsylvania Avenue gave this thoroughfare some of the intended character that it lacked because of the undistinguished character of the few buildings along its path. Otherwise, the government refused to make any substantial street improvements, and the municipality could afford only modest sums for this purpose.

The comments quoted in folio 33 about the most important artery in the city—Pennsylvania Avenue—reflect this policy of neglect. Dusty when dry, the avenue turned into a quagmire when it rained, and the majority of travelers who shared their experiences in the city through the printed word were generous in expressing their dismay and disgust at encountering such conditions. Circumstances on other streets of lesser importance must have been equally bad and were probably even worse.

Artists saw this part of the urban world with a happier vision. Indeed, from a distance and on a pleasant day Pennsylvania Avenue must have seemed attractive to many other persons as well. The two views reproduced in folio 33 from books published in the 1830s present both ends of the Capitol–White House axis for our inspection under these conditions.

The earlier engraving appeared in 1834 as an illustration added to the American edition of a European world geography published in Boston. The artist, John Rubens Smith, looked from the Capitol to the White House, and from this vantage point was able to include most of the built-up portion of Washington lying west of Capitol Hill. Smith took some liberties in depicting the White House, enlarging its image substantially and rotating it counterclockwise to reveal more of its facade than would have been visible from where the artist sat to sketch this scene.[33]

Smith apparently intended the building he shows at the far right to represent the City Hall on Judiciary Square. Although, like the image of the White House,

this, too, provides only an approximation of the building's appearance, it does suggest the prominence of the site and argues for its suitability as the intended location of the Supreme Court. At our feet we see the Capitol end of Pennsylvania Avenue and can appreciate how effective the tree planting must have been to define the boundaries of that thoroughfare before enough buildings existed to assume that function.[34]

The second view in folio 33 offers a more dramatic scene. Here the artist, William H. Bartlett, drew the Washington townscape as he could see it atop the roof of the semicircular projection of the White House. The Capitol dominates this engraving as it did in reality. However, one should make allowances for Bartlett's usual practice—one he shared with other artists of the time—of exaggerating the height of hills and thus emphasizing any buildings located at their crests.

It would not be long after the publication of Bartlett's view that this vista from the executive mansion to the halls of Congress would be destroyed by the new Treasury, then under construction. Bartlett's engraving also shows another lost vista, that extending to and from the White House along F Street, the thoroughfare Bartlett included at the left of his view. Finally, we can see half-hidden in the foliage below us at the entry to the White House grounds a gate with a carriage entrance in the center and pedestrian entries on either side. This, too, vanished when the Treasury reached its full length with the completion of its south entrance.

A new generation of visitors to Washington in the 1840s followed their predecessors in expressing their frank impressions of the city. Folio 34 contains four excerpts from books written by English travelers and observers of this period. Three of the four wrote critically about what they saw. The most famous of these—no less a personage than Charles Dickens—seemingly found nothing in Washington that merited a word of praise or even acceptance. Instead, Dickens castigated every feature of the city: its plan, its climate, and its buildings. In the process, Dickens added a new derogatory epithet, "The City of Magnificent Intensions," to those already current.[35]

32. Nathaniel Willis in his *American Scenery*, 2:65, referred to a future botanical garden on this spot in a passage probably written about 1839: "The waste lands which lie at the foot of Capitol Hill might be marshes in the centre of a wilderness for any trace of cultivation about them; but they are appropriated for a botanical garden, which Congress shall find time to order its arrangement and cultivation."

33. The White House image is inaccurate in another respect. The facade Smith displays appears to have a pedimented colonnade projecting in front, not the semicircular extension of the real building. What we see more nearly resembles the north elevation of the White House, which of course would be completely invisible from the Capitol.

34. John Rubens Smith (1775–1849) was a distinguished Anglo-American artist who came to the United States at thirty-one after establishing a firm reputation in England as a portrait artist and teacher. He settled first in Boston in 1806, moved to New York ten years later, returned to Boston in 1827 for two years, and finally established his residence in Philadelphia until returning to New York in 1844, where he died five years later. In all these places he taught at his own academy and created scores of paintings, drawings, and prints. Several of his views along the Hudson River executed in 1818–28 were engraved by John

B. Nagle, the engraver of Smith's view of Washington's Pennsylvania Avenue. This small print used as a book illustration scarcely does credit to Smith's artistic skills. For his career in England and America, see Edward S. Smith, "John Rubens Smith."

35. On an earlier page in his book Dickens described some other impressions of Washington: "Take the worse parts of the City Road and Pentonville [in London], or the straggling outskirts of Paris, where the houses are smallest, preserving all their oddities, but especially the small shops and dwellings occupied in Pentonville (but not in

His contemporary, Colonel Maxwell, compared Washington to "a deserted village." A few years later their fellow Englishman Eliot Warburton referred to the city as "a rich architectural joke—a boasting, straggling, raw, uncomfortable failure, of infinite pretension in the plan" and "wretched and imperfect in the execution." Of those represented here, only Thomas Grattan admired Washington. Further, he expressed his annoyance at how the city's shortcomings had been "sarcastically specified by disappointed or splenetic visitors."

As one-time British consul in Massachusetts during 1839–46, Grattan knew far more about America and Americans than most of the authors of travel books like Dickens, Warburton, and Maxwell. He also possessed a sense of history, stating while in Washington he "could not help imagining that the place, in all its vastness, was filled with the spirit of its immortal founder," George Washington. Grattan regarded the city's "whole design" as "a monument to him" and believed that "the unfinished plan, slowly going on towards completion, bore the impress of his large and reflective intellect."[36]

Although a minority of Americans may have shared the opinions of Dickens and other critics, most citizens seem to have regarded the national capital with pride. The construction of the Treasury, the Patent Office, and the Post Office promised to provide some of the dignity and splendor appropriate for the seat of government of a nation that now extended to the Mississippi River and would shortly expand to full continental dimensions.

Nowhere is this better expressed than in the curiously distorted but thoroughly fascinating lithographic portrayal of the city illustrated in folio 34. This abstraction of Washington in the guise of a view looks toward the Capitol from a point on the Mall west of the Washington Monument. Joseph Goldsborough Bruff, a native Washingtonian who attended West Point in 1820–22, topographical draftsman, and amateur artist, fashioned this arresting image for a frontispiece illustration in a two-volume study of trade and taxation in the United States published in 1847.[37]

Bruff constructed this graphic celebration of Washington by relocating where necessary all the important buildings of the city so that each appeared to best advantage. In doing so, he took the kind of liberties with reality that he would not

have dared to do in work for the U.S. Bureau of Topographical Engineers, where he is known to have been stationed in 1849 before departing for the California gold fields to sketch and write extensively about his experiences.[38]

The artist also completed with his lithographic crayon the construction of both the Washington Monument and the Smithsonian Institution, structures prominently featured to the right of center. Bruff drew the White House at the far left, "moving" it into our field of vision and rotating it so that we look directly at its southern facade. The porticoed building immediately to the right of the White House is evidently intended to be the Treasury, and the two structures above and to the right of the Treasury must be the Patent Office and the Post Office.

A canal boat being towed along the north side of the Mall at the left, ships in the waters of the Potomac on the right, and a team of horses pulling a Conestoga wagon near the lower right depict the major means of available transportation. In the foreground and extending from left to right Bruff assembled a collection of agricultural implements, industrial components, symbols of scientific activities, allegorical figures symbolizing liberty and bounty, patriotic slogans, scrolls listing the nation's resources, and a portrait of the immortal Washington, among other emblems of progress and power. The title of the entire view, "Elements of National Thrift and Empire," would seem to be more appropriately applied to this captivating array of foreground objects.

The view in folio 35 provides an almost complete contrast to Bruff's architectural and topographical fantasy. Edward Weber, then Baltimore's most noted lithographer, printed this captivating view for Casimir Bohn of Washington, who first published it in 1849 and used it again in 1854 as a folded illustration for his *Handbook of Washington*. With its principal image showing the city as seen looking west from the terrace of the Capitol and a frame composed of twenty vignettes depicting individual buildings and locations in and around the city, it is one of the most attractive of all Washington prints.[39]

The imprint does not identify the artist, but it may well have been Edward Sachse, several of whose smaller lithographs of individual buildings appear in

Washington) by furniture brokers, keepers of poor eating-houses, and fanciers of birds. Burn the whole down; build it up again in wood and plaster; widen it a little; throw in part of St. John's Wood; put green blinds outside all the private houses, with a red curtain and a white one in every window; plough up all the roads; plant a great deal of coarse turf in every place where it ought *not* to be; erect three handsome buildings in stone and marble anywhere, but the more entirely out

of everybody's way the better; call one the Post Office, one the Patent Office, and one the Treasury; make it scorching hot in the morning, and freezing cold in the afternoon, with an occasional tornado of wind and dust; leave a brick-field, without the bricks, in all central places where a street may naturally be expected; and that's Washington" (*American Notes*, 115).

36. Grattan, *Civilized America*, 1:164–65.

37. Mayo, *Systems of the United States*.

38. According to Cobb, "The Washington Art Association," 132, Bruff, at the age of forty-five, organized "the Washington City and California Goldmining Association and spent the years 1849–51 in California, together with Charles Fenderich, early lithographer of the District of Columbia. He was active as an officer of the Washington Art Association and in his latter years he was employed in the Office of the Architect of the Treasury."

39. Information about Weber's prints can be found in several places in McCauley, *Maryland Historical Prints*. Little seems to be known about Bohn. The Washington city directories for 1843

and 1846 do not list him, but the 1850 and 1853 directories identify him as a bookseller located on the south side of East Capitol Street between First and Second streets. The address given in the 1855 directory is 3 East Capitol Street, evidently the same location. In 1858 he appears under the heading of "Map Publisher" at 418 First Street East at the corner of East Capitol, with his residence at the same address. By 1860 Bohn had moved his business to 568 Pennsylvania Avenue and is listed as a seller of "prints, books, &c," retaining his residence at "418 1st east." It is not clear if this was First Street NE or SE.

earlier folios. Sachse came from Germany where he drew, printed, and published several small, city views among many other lithographic prints. By 1848—perhaps before—Sachse was working for Weber and may have been assigned to draw or assist on the Washington view. This might explain Sachse's continuing fascination with Washington, for—as will be seen—he produced far more portraits of the city than any other artist.[40]

In the main view one can see on the right the City Hall, the Patent Office, and the Post Office. The artist also depicted the Treasury at the approximately correct size while exaggerating the height of the White House. The Washington Monument appears here as if completed according to the Mills design with the colonnaded base. To its left the Smithsonian Institution stands forlornly alone in the midst of the wasteland of the Mall. It too seems to be finished, although in 1849 only a portion of the building had been completed.

Near the left side in the distance one can just make out the Long Bridge across the Potomac, first built in 1809 but replaced or repaired often when swept away or damaged by floods or ice. The view also provides a revealing glimpse of the Washington Canal, generally following the course of the Tiber as it led from the Potomac, along the north side of the Mall, and then bent sharply at the foot of Capitol Hill toward its connection with the Anacostia four blocks west of the Navy Yard. A few rickety bridges provided pedestrian and vehicular crossings of the canal between the Mall and the more heavily built-up portion of the city along and north of Pennsylvania Avenue.

The vignettes offer more details about all of the important buildings and sites in the city. Those at the top portray both elevations of the Capitol, the White House, and the four major structures whose origins have been reviewed in this chapter. The top vignette in the vertical panel on the right is one of the few depictions of the War and Navy buildings located immediately west of the White House. The artist sketched these as he saw them looking southeast toward the portico entrance on the north side of the War Department.

Also in the right-hand panel the artist included among the vignettes the Naval Observatory completed in 1844 on an elevated site near the Potomac. The profile of its revolving dome housing the astronomical telescope appears in the main view roughly midway between the White House and the Washington Monument. The lower panel of vignettes includes possibly unique images, for the time, of the U.S. arsenal near Greenleaf's Point and Georgetown College, a Jesuit institution and the oldest such Catholic institution in the United States.

A fitting accompaniment to this splendid printed portrait of the capital are the descriptive and critical observations set down by Alexander Mackay, a particularly acute observer who visited Washington in 1846 and commented at length on what he saw. A Scot with legal training, Mackay became a minister, a journalist, and a geographer. One student of the literature calls his three-volume work published in 1849, *The Western World, or, Travels in the United States in 1846–47*, "the finest ante-bellum British travel work on America."[41]

Earlier folios included briefer excerpts from his book where he recorded his favorable opinions about the Capitol, the Post Office, the City Hall, and the White House with its surrounding buildings. He also called the Patent Office "an imposing pile" and regarded the Treasury as "a handsome building" with "one of the finest . . . colonnades in the world." On the other hand, he strongly criticized Pennsylvania Avenue for its excessive width, the unimpressive character of the buildings he found along it, and the miserable conditions of its surface.

Moreover, Mackay noted that although the city could claim several fine buildings, separated, as they are, at great distances from each other, their effect is entirely lost. He suggested that "it would have been much better had they all been placed together, so as to have formed a noble square." He noted that "as they are, Washington has no visible centre—no one point upon which converge the ideas of its inhabitants."[42]

Without ridiculing the city or questioning the motives of its founders and planners, Mackay nevertheless strongly criticized the location chosen for Washington, what he regarded as its excessively large and overly elaborate design, and its scattered pattern of development. Looking at the city from the dome of the Capitol, he saw only a collection of "incipient country villages, with here and there a few scattered houses of wood or brick . . . and ever and anon a street just begun and then stopped, as if it were afraid to proceed any further into the wilderness."

Washington had then reached a population of 40,000, more than double the figure two decades earlier and an impressive 70 percent higher than in 1840. Nevertheless, even with its several new and large public buildings, the city of Washington thus struck this open-minded and unbiased observer as little changed from the rustic scene described early in the century by the first generation of visitors to see the city and set down their reactions to it.[43]

The decision to place the centers of federal activity such great distances apart may have prevented any single neighborhood from achieving dominance over the

40. It might have been while in Washington working on the Weber-Bohn view of ca. 1849 that Sachse met Bohn. In 1850 Bohn published Sachse's own first city view—a large image of Baltimore—after the artist began his own business, and the two collaborated on two more views in 1851. A unique impression (presumably the first state) of Sachse's view of Washington in 1852 also bears Bohn's name as publisher, although all other impressions list E. Sachse & Co. as publisher.

41. Rapson, *Britons View America*, 241.
42. Mackay, *The Western World*, I:111–12.
43. Population of the city of Washington was 18,827 in 1830, 23,364 in 1840, and 40,001 in 1850. Of these, 5,448, 6,521, and 10,271 were African-Americans, about two-thirds of them being free and the others slave.

others, but through the first half of the nineteenth century it produced an urban structure that appealed to few on functional grounds and offered less to the eye than would have been possible under a more conventional policy of grouping all public buildings in one complex.

During the next twenty years, however, the pace of population growth accelerated, additional buildings altered the appearance of the city, the Civil War changed forever the character of the federal government and the city from which it was administered, and the stage was set for the next era of growth beginning in the early 1870s. Then, an unprecedented program of public works transformed Washington into a city with streets and municipal services as modern as any in the land and stimulated further urban change and expansion throughout the 1880s. The two chapters to follow will trace these developments and introduce the graphic and written impressions of the artists and writers who observed and recorded them.

Joseph Varnum, writing in Hunt's Merchants' Magazine *in 1848, notes how the needs of the government have changed.*

All the archives of the Treasury, War, State, Indian, and Pension Departments, were formerly kept in two buildings—now the Treasury, alone, occupies an edifice as large as six of those; it was important, then, that each department should have a building to itself, so constructed that it might, at any future time, be enlarged, without marring its appearance; and also, that there might be space enough, in the immediate neighborhood, for the residences of the officers employed therein.

He criticizes the location of the Treasury for blocking important views.

Before leaving this part of the subject, we must advert to a gross encroachment on the plan, which gives rise to comment on the part of every stranger visiting the city. The treasury building, when finished, will be a noble edifice, and will have probably cost $1,200,000; but it is so badly situated as to ruin its appearance, and entirely exclude from view the president's house, and to obstruct the distant and beautiful prospect from the East room of that edifice, through the line of F street. The building, although nearly four hundred feet in length, will scarcely be visible except from the street immediately before it; and the three finest porticoes will front upon the president's kitchen garden. The necessity is involved of taking down the State Department, which has cost upwards of $90,000, and, also, of erecting a building to correspond for the other department[s] on the West side of the executive mansion; a blunder entirely inexcusable when there were so many excellent sites at command. It is now past remedy. Before the basement was completed, an attempt was made in Congress by Mr. Lincoln, of Massachusetts, to suspend the progress of the work; in which, we believe, he would have succeeded had there been any interest felt in the subject, by individuals or associations professing to foster architecture and the fine arts in other parts of the country, who might, perhaps, have operated to some purpose through their representatives in Congress. We mention it here for the purpose of expressing the hope that the many works of this kind, hereafter to be erected in Washington, and the objects of the fine arts with which it is constantly proposed to embellish them, will not escape the notice of our academies of design, and men of taste in other cities. ([Varnum], "The Seat of Government of the United States," 151)

Mrs. Trollope's son comes to Washington three decades after his mother and inspects the still incomplete Treasury as it appeared in 1861.

The Treasury Chambers is as yet an unfinished building. The front to the south has been completed; but that to the north has not been built. Here at the north stands as yet the old Secretary of State's office. This is to come down, and the Secretary of State is to be located in the new building, which will be added to the Treasury.

Anthony Trollope pronounces the building the prettiest in the city.

This edifice will probably strike strangers more forcibly than any other in the town, both from its position and from its own character. It stands with its side to Pennsylvania Avenue, but the avenue here has turned round, and runs due north and south, having taken a twist, so as to make way for the Treasury and for the president's house, through both of which it must run had it been carried straight on throughout. These public offices stand with their side to the street, and the whole length is ornamented with an exterior row of Ionic columns raised high above the footway. This is perhaps the prettiest thing in the city, and when the front to the north has been completed, the effect will be still better.

He describes some of the details of the building.

The granite monoliths which have been used, and which are to be used, in this building are very massive. As one enters by the steps to the south there are two flat stones, one on each side of the ascent, the surface of each of which is about 20 feet by 18. The columns are, I think, all monoliths. Of those which are still to be erected, and which now lie about in the neighbouring streets, I measured one or two—one which was still in the rough I found to be 32 feet long by 5 feet broad, and 4½ deep. These granite blocks have been brought to Washington from the State of Maine. The finished front of this building, looking down to the Potomac, is very good; but to my eyes this also has been much injured by the rows of windows which look out from the building into the space of the portico. (Anthony Trollope, *North America*, 314-15)

The Treasury Gets a Huge, New, and Imposing Building

The Treasury first occupied one of the four buildings for executive departments erected on either side of the White House. George Hadfield designed its first home in 1797, a structure burned by the British in 1814. Rebuilt in 1817, this also went up in flames in 1833. Robert Mills designed a new building, but a controversy over its location had to be decided by President Andrew Jackson, who in 1836 selected the location along Fourteenth Street immediately east of the White House.

The building joined the old State Department on the north but did not extend south along Fourteenth Street beyond the northern side of Pennsylvania Avenue. However, the building's southern wing with its staircase and portico—constructed according to a design by Ammi B. Young in 1855-60 and shown prominently in this view—completely blocked the vista to the White House along the Pennsylvania Avenue axis from the Capitol.

Work began in 1862 on plans drawn by Isaiah Rogers for the west wing facing the White House and was completed in 1864. Finally, after the demolition of the State Department in 1866, the north wing facing Lafayette Square was finished in 1869 following a design by A. B. Mullett.

Edward Sachse's lithograph, probably published between 1861 and 1867, shows the building as a visitor or resident would have seen it coming from the Capitol along Pennsylvania Avenue and pausing to look northwest from the southeastern corner of the intersection of Pennsylvania Avenue and Fourteenth Street. It is little wonder that nearly everyone found impressive this sight of Mills's forest of Ionic columns extending along the west side of Fourteenth Street and forming a peristyle of truly imposing dimensions.

U.S. Treasury. Printed by E. Sachse & Co. Balto. Published by C. Bohn, Washington, [1861-67?]. Lithograph, 4⅝ × 7⅝ in. (11.7 × 19.3 cm.). Prints and Photographs, Library of Congress.

U. S. TREASURY.

In his book on Virginia of 1845, Henry Howe tells of the ambitious plans for the Patent Office.

The Patent-Office, in addition to other spacious apartments, has one room in the upper story 275 feet by 65 and when completed by wings, according to the original design, will be upwards of 400 feet in length. It is considered one of the most splendid rooms in America, and is devoted to the grand and increasing collections of the national institution. The portico of this building is of the same extent as that of the Parthenon, at Athens, consisting of 16 columns, in double rows, 50 feet high. In the war-office was formerly kept the fine collection of Indian portraits, painted from the original heads by King. These valuable pictures are now in the custody, and adorn the collections of the national institution, in the patent-office. (Henry Howe, *Historical Collections of Virginia*, 538)

A correspondent for Harper's New Monthly Magazine *in 1852 notes a change in the choice of building materials.*

Through a wholly mistaken economy, the Capitol and almost all the public edifices are built of a sandstone found in the vicinity, which is incapable of resisting the action of the atmosphere, and the cost of the paint required to preserve it equals that of erecting new walls every thirty years. The error has been at last perceived, and the wings to the Patent Office, and the additions to the Capitol now being erected, are of pure white marble.

She explains how the Patent Office serves as a public museum.

Here are deposited all the models for which patents have been granted, the original Declaration of Independence, the camp-chest and a part of the wardrobe of Washington, the gifts presented to our naval and civil officers by foreign powers, pictures, busts, Indian portraits, the collections of the National Institute, and all the treasures of the Exploring Expedition under Commodore Wilkes. (Lynch, "A Sketch of Washington City," 3, 8)

Seven years later the same journal describes the building which then lacked only its north wing.

On a clear moonlight night there is nothing more beautiful than this immense edifice of pure marble, glistening with the moonbeams, and almost speaking to the beholder of the vastness of his country's power and the worth of its Union. . . . There are porticoes on the south, east, and west sides—the south portico being copied from the Pantheon. The total height is 74 feet 11 inches; it is 275 wide by 406 feet 6 inches long. In the third story are saloons for the exhibition and preservation of models, although until recently the space was occupied by an immense collection of curiosities which is now more properly deposited in the Smithsonian Institution. ("Washington in 1859," 15)

Anthony Trollope informs his readers about the Patent Office in 1861.

Opposite to that which is, I presume, the back of the Post-office, stands the Patent-office. This also is a grand building, with a fine portico of Doric pillars at each of its three fronts. These are approached by flights of steps, more gratifying to the eye than to the legs. The whole structure is massive and grand, and, if the streets round it were finished, would be imposing. The utilitarian spirit of the nation has, however, done much toward marring the appearance of the building, by piercing it with windows altogether unsuited to it, both in number and size. The walls, even under the porticoes, have been so pierced, in order that the whole space might be utilized without loss of light; and the effect is very mean. The windows are small and without ornament,—something like a London window of the time of George III. The effect produced by a dozen such at the back of a noble Doric porch, looking down among the pillars, may be imagined.

Trollope describes the interior, part of which then served as a military hospital.

In the interior of the building the Minister of the Interior holds his court, and of course also the Commissioners of Patents. Here is, in accordance with the name of the building, a museum of models of all patents taken out. I wandered through it, gazing with listless eye, now upon this, and now upon that; but to me, in my ignorance, it was no better than a large toy-shop. . . . Wandering about through the Patent-office I also found a hospital for soldiers. A British officer was with me who pronounced it to be, in its kind, very good. At any rate it was sweet, airy, and large. In these days the soldiers had got hold of everything. (Anthony Trollope, *North America*, 314)

The Nation Provides an Archive of Its Inventive Genius

Work started in 1836 on the Patent Office occupying the site proposed by L'Enfant for the National Church. This square stood on what L'Enfant intended to be one of the most significant axes in the city. To the north it passes through two of the fifteen state squares. To the south it crosses one of the five squares L'Enfant hoped to embellish with a great fountain, another state square, and ends at the place on the Potomac bank he reserved for a Naval Itinerary Column. The central market and, after 1935, the National Archives destroyed this long south axis that the original planner of the city thought so important.

In a diverse and secular America a national church was out of the question. Instead, the country erected here an imposing Greek temple to enshrine the results of the inventive faculties of mankind. William P. Elliot designed the Patent Office's south wing, finished in 1840. Thomas U. Walter prepared plans for the east and west wings on foundations built under the direction of Robert Mills, who had supervised construction of the original wing. Walter completed the east and west wings in 1852 and 1856, respectively, and began the final part of the building on the north side in 1856. It was not until 1867 that this huge and majestic building finally stood completed as Elliot had first conceived it more than three decades before.

The view published by Edward Sachse is undated. This faithful Baltimore recorder of the changing face of Washington may have printed it as early as 1861 when he produced many other lithographs of the city and its buildings. Or it may have been published around 1867 to mark the completion of the structure. Sachse's artist stood at the southeast corner of the intersection of F and Seventh streets to sketch the building as he looked at the south and east wings.

Patent Office. Printed by E. Sachse & Co. Balto., [1861–67?]. Lithograph, 4⅝ × 7⅝ in. (11.8 × 19.3 cm.). Prints and Photographs, Library of Congress.

PATENT OFFICE.

*An Englishman admires the City Hall in 1822,
two years after construction began.*

The City Hall, when finished, will be the handsomest build-ing in the United States. It fronts the Potowmac, and com-mands a very advantageous view of the city. (*An Excursion through the United States*, 45)

*An 1848 guidebook records that a quarter of a century later
the building is still incomplete.*

The south front of this fine building only is completed. It was planned by an architect named George Hadfield, and com-menced in 1820, out of the proceeds of the sale of a lottery privilege granted to the Corporation by Congress; but from the failure of the lottery agent, it has been mainly built out of the funds of the Corporation. The outside is not yet finished, it being intended to be stuccoed, and to have porticoes in the centre and a colonnade at each end.

The City Hall is built on a reservation called Judiciary square, and which terminates Four-and-a-half street. Immedi-ately north of the City Hall, stands the *old Jail*, and on the northeast angle of the square has recently been erected a spa-cious brick edifice of the Gothic order, three stories high, stained to resemble granite, and neatly designed, which will hereafter be used as the Jail of the county.

*The guidebook also tells of the recent completion
of the General Post Office, designed seventeen years earlier.*

The new and splendid edifice just completed is cased with white marble, brought from the vicinity of New-York, and is the only marble building now in Washington; the material of the other public buildings being sand or freestone, granite, and brick. It occupies the southern portion of square four hundred and thirty, and fronts on E street north, between Seventh and Eighth streets west. Its principal front is two hundred and four feet, and the fronts on Seventh and Eighth streets one hundred and two feet, forming a hollow square in the rear of one hun-dred feet in width, built of granite. The order is a rich Corin-thian. The centre of each front is ornamented with four fluted columns, and the facades with pilasters of marble, surmounted by their entablature and blocking. (Watterston, *New Guide to Washington*, 64, 82)

*Alexander Mackay visits the City Hall
and Post Office in 1846.*

Turning from [Pennsylvania] Avenue to the right, we have at the top of the street, which we thus enter, a large unfinished brick building, with the holes occasioned by the scaffolding yet in the walls, and with a liberty pole rising to the very clouds in front of it. This is the City Hall, the funds for building which were raised by lottery; but some one decamping with a portion of them, the building, which was founded in chance, runs a chance of never being completed. Continuing almost in the same line to the westward, we come to the General Post Office, the choicest architectural *bijou* in Washington, being a neat classic structure built of white marble, and about the size of Trinity House. Its beauties are, however, almost lost from de-fect of site, the fate of so many of our own finest public edifices. (Mackay, *The Western World*, 2:111)

Harper's New Monthly Magazine *reports in 1859
on the recent extension of the Post Office.*

The General Post-Office has been enlarged by extending the building around the entire square, leaving a court-yard in the centre of 95 feet by 194 feet for light and air. The architec-tural style is palatial, and the order a modified Corinthian. . . . The Seventh Street front . . . is the grand entrance for the General Post-Office department, and harmonizes with the en-trance to the Patent-Office which is on the next block north in the same street. The entrance for the mail wagons on Eighth Street consists of a grand archway, the spandrils of which are ornamented with sculpture representing Steam on one side, and on the other Electricity, while a mask representing Fidelity forms the key-stone. . . . Mr. T. U. Walter, the architect of the capitol, who designed this extension of the Post-Office, has given the best evidence of his ability to discharge fitly his im-portant obligations to the people, in the excellent arrangements, he has here devised to combine simplicity, convenience, and beauty. We doubt if there is a building in the world more chaste and architecturally perfect than the General Post-Office as now completed. Without the imposing grandeur of its neighbor the Patent-Office, it is so symmetrical, and the details so faithfully executed, that it carries us back to the palmy days of Italian Art. ("Washington in 1859," 13)

Robert Mills and George Hadfield Design
Two of the City's Early Public Buildings

Progress on the building to house the services ad-ministered by the postmaster general began in 1836 on a design by Robert Mills. The site selected was a poor one, occupying a smaller than usual block bounded by E and F and Seventh and Eighth streets immediately south of the site intended by L'Enfant for the National Church. Unlike all other Washington public buildings, no long axial views to or from the structure were possi-ble. This was unfortunate, for the building itself was restrained and dignified and one that nearly all foreign visitors admired.

In 1820 work began on the Washington City Hall, a building designed by George Hadfield. It occupied what L'Enfant may have regarded as the third most important site in his plan—a location he probably in-tended for the Supreme Court. It stood on the axis of two short diagonal avenues and a street extending di-rectly south almost all the way to Greenleaf's Point. The large elongated square was called Judiciary Square from the very beginning of the city, also suggesting that the planners and founders of Washington expected it to be occupied by a building for the Supreme Court.

The structure erected here did indeed come to be used by circuit and criminal courts of the United States—first sharing and then overcrowding the municipal offices for which the building was intended. Hadfield's original design called for a very large dome. This was never constructed, and hopes for it were abandoned sometime during the thirty years it took to complete construction, a record for procrastination that seems remarkable even in a city where no public building was ever built for its estimated cost and where nearly all of them lagged well behind even the most pessimistic con-struction schedule.

General Post-Office. Drawn by Aug[ustus] Köllner. Litho-graphed by Deroy. Printed by Cattier. Published by Goupil Vibert & Co., New-York & Paris, 1848. Litho-graph, 9½ × 11⅝ in. (24.1 × 29.5 cm.). Kiplinger Col-lection.

Washington. City Hall. Printed by E. Sachse & Co., Bal-timore, [1861–67?]. Lithograph, 4½ × 7⁵⁄₁₆ in. (11.4 × 18.5 cm.). Machen Collection, Historical Society of Washington, D.C.

*Joseph Varnum in 1848 tells of efforts
to build a monument to George Washington.*

In the year 1783, Congress voted an equestrian statue to General Washington at the future seat of government; and in the plan of the city, the commissioners . . . selected as a site the lower part of the Mall, near the Potomac, but, for the want of appropriations, it was never carried into execution. . . . The National Monument Association collected, some years' [*sic*] since about $30,000 in subscriptions of one dollar, all over the country; this sum was well invested, and now amounts, with the interest, to about $63,000. A new subscription is now opened . . . and every encouragement has been received for believing that a large additional amount will be collected. (Varnum, *The Seat of Government*, 39)

A writer for Harper's New Monthly Magazine
reports on progress through 1852.

About midway between the Capitol and the president's house, stands the national monument erected to the memory of Washington. As yet it has only reached the elevation of about one hundred feet. . . . At present there are some fears expressed that the contributions will not be sufficient to carry on the work, and that to another generation will belong the glory of completing it. (Lynch, "A Sketch of Washington City," 12)

*A guidebook in 1862 describes the design and
the status of the project.*

The design of the Washington Monument contemplates a shaft 600 feet in height. The marble obelisk . . . is 55 feet square at the base. This foundation is 81 feet square and extends eight feet below the surface. The wall of the obelisk is 15 feet thick at the base, and gradually tapers on the outside. The inside of the wall is perpendicular, and the enclosed space is 25 feet square. The 15 foot wall will ascend until the gentle taper reduces it to two feet in thickness. . . .

The pantheon base, as represented in engravings, was a part of the plan originally selected, but it is now highly probable that it will be dispensed with, and that the plain square base, which is characteristic of the obelisk, will be substituted. This change in the plan, while it reduces the cost of the Monu-

ment to one-half the sum contemplated in connection with the pantheon, will, at the same time, conform it to the recognized rules of art. . . .

The Monument is now 170 feet high, and has cost thus far $230,000. The total cost of the obelisk has been estimated at $552,000. The pantheon was estimated to cost $570,000 alone; but a plain and appropriate base may be built for less than a tenth of that sum. (*Morrison's Stranger's Guide* [1862], 36–37)

Anthony Trollope visits the site in 1861.

I wandered down . . . one Sunday afternoon. The ground was frozen and I could walk dry-shod, but there was not a blade of grass. . . . There, on the brown, ugly, undrained field, within easy sight of the president's house, stood the useless, shapeless, gracious pile of stones. It was as though I were looking on the genius of the city. It was vast, pretentious, bold, boastful with a loud voice, already taller by many heads than other obelisks but nevertheless still in its infancy,—ugly, unpromising, and false. . . . It is still possible that both city and monument shall be completed; but at the present moment nobody seems to believe in the one or in the other. (Anthony Trollope, *North America*, 318)

*In 1874 Mark Twain pokes fun at the still incomplete
Washington Monument.*

The Monument to the Father of his Country towers out of the mud—sacred soil is the customary term. It has the aspect of a factory chimney with the top broken off. The skeleton of a decaying scaffolding lingers about its summit, and tradition says that the spirit of Washington often comes down and sits on those rafters to enjoy this tribute of respect which the nation has reared as the symbol of its unappeasable gratitude. The Monument is to be finished, some day, and at that time our Washington will have risen still higher in the nation's veneration, and will be known as the Great-Great-Grandfather of his Country. The memorial Chimney stands in a quiet pastoral locality that is full of reposeful expression. With a glass you can see the cow-sheds about its base, and the contented sheep nibbling pebbles in the desert solitudes that surround it, and the tired pigs dozing in the holy calm of its protecting shadow. (Twain and Warner, *The Gilded Age*, 221–22)

America Commemorates the Father
of His Country with a Shaft That Took
Fifty Years to Complete

Proposals to memorialize George Washington began early, continued over a very long period of time, and did not finally succeed until more than a century after the Continental Congress in 1783 authorized an equestrian statue of him. Further discussion of the matter in Congress and elsewhere produced no results. In 1833 the Washington National Monument Society first met and chose Chief Justice John Marshall president, but neither Marshall nor his equally prominent successors proved capable of raising sufficient funds to proceed.

In 1836 the society invited designs that would "harmoniously blend durability, simplicity, and grandeur" and selected one by Robert Mills. The lithograph on the left side of the page shows Mills's concept for an obelisk rising from an elaborate colonnaded base that was to house a national pantheon. Money came in slowly, and Congress waited until 1848 to authorize a site on the Mall. Because of poor soil conditions, the location at the intersection of the Capitol and White House axes could not be used, and construction began 370 feet to the east and 123 feet to the south of this spot on 4 July 1848.

Six years later, when funds ran out, construction stopped with the shaft at a height of 152 feet. Until 1880 when construction resumed, this ungainly stone stump stood forlornly much as the artist for the *Illustrated News* pictured it in 1853: an object of ridicule by visitors and shame on the part of residents. It was not until 1885 that the monument finally could be dedicated and a further three years until it would be opened to visitors.

Design of the Washington National Monument to be Erected in the City of Washington. Designed by Robert Mills. Printed and copyrighted by Charles Fenderich, Washington, 1846. Lithograph, 22 × 14¾ in. (55.8 × 37.4 cm.). Machen Collection, Historical Society of Washington, D.C.

Present State of the National Monument to Washington at the City of Washington. Engraved by [Frank] Leslie. From the New York *Illustrated News*, 8 January 1853. Wood engraving, 14 × 9½ in. (35.5 × 24.1 cm.). Kiplinger Collection.

Folio 32. Congress Finally Meets the Terms of James Smithson's Bequest and Provides a Site for the Smithsonian Institution on the Mall

A Washington guidebook of 1848 tells its readers about the founding of the Smithsonian Institution.

In the year 1826 [sic] Mr. James Smithson, a British subject . . . bequeathed under certain contingencies which have since been realized, the whole of his property amounting to $508,318.45 "to the United States of America, to found at Washington, under the name of the Smithsonian Institution, an establishment for the increase and diffusion of knowledge among men." One of those contingencies was, that in the event of the death of his nephew, Henry James Hungerford (who was in fact, his natural son) without issue, legitimate or illegitimate, the whole of his property was to go to the United States for the purpose above mentioned. Mr. Hungerford died without leaving any children in 1835, and in 1836 an act was passed by Congress authorizing an agent to be appointed to recover the funds. . . . This agent, Mr. Rush of Philadelphia, succeeded in obtaining the money, and in 1838 it was deposited in gold in the mint at Philadelphia. . . . After an interval of eight years, congress finally passed a hasty act in 1846 to carry into effect the benevolent intentions of the testator, which provides that the Institution shall be located in the city of Washington and bear the name of Smithson according to his desire. . . . The Board of Regents are to select a suitable site for buildings, and when the site shall be selected, a suitable building of plain and durable materials is to be erected by commissioners—a geological and mineralogical cabinet to be furnished—and also, a chemical laboratory, library, gallery of art, &c. The minerals, books, manuscripts and other property of Smithson now in the State Department to be deposited in the Institution. (Watterston, *New Guide to Washington*, 221)

Joseph Varnum in 1848 sees the construction of the Smithsonian Institution as an opportunity to improve the Mall.

There is now some prospect that what has been so long delayed by the indifference of Congress, will be, in part, accomplished indirectly by the liberality of an individual. The proposed Smithsonian Institute [sic] is to be placed on the side of the mall, and its agricultural and botanical grounds are to be laid out in front. The erection of this will lead to the improvement of Maryland Avenue, a noble street, equal in size to the Pennsylvania, and connecting one gate of the capitol with the Potomac bridge, as the last-named connects the other gate with the president's house and Georgetown. (Varnum, *The Seat of Government*, 25)

Harper's New Monthly Magazine in 1852 records the construction of the Smithsonian Institution.

By a law enacted in 1846, the president, cabinet, and some other officers of the government . . . constitute the Smithsonian Institute [sic], the immediate superintendence being given to a Secretary. By the authority of these officers . . . a picturesque and stately pile has been erected of red freestone, in the Norman or Romanesque style of architecture, comprising a library, lecture-room, museum, laboratories, and galleries of art. Its length is four hundred and fifty feet, and its breadth one hundred and forty. . . .

The importance of the Smithsonian Institution in the centre of our country, and the benefits it will confer, have not yet been truly estimated. Science, literature, and art will concentrate here; and in the enlightened encouragement they will receive, they will diffuse their radiance over the whole length and breadth of the land. (Lynch, "A Sketch of Washington City," 11–12)

A later correspondent for Harper's Monthly *mentions a monument to Andrew Jackson Downing in front of the Smithsonian.*

Midway of the Mall stands the Smithsonian Institution, which has undergone little change, except that the various objects of curiosity, including articles brought home by the Japan and other exploring expeditions, have been removed from the Patent-Office, and placed here. In front of the building is the monument erected to the memory of the lamented Downing. ("Washington in 1859," 9)

Anthony Trollope in 1862 wrestles with the building's style.

Its style was bastard Gothic; by this, I mean that its main attributes are Gothic, but that liberties have been taken with it, which, whether they may injure its beauty or no, certainly are subversive of architectural purity. It is built of red stone, and is not ugly in itself. There is a very nice Norman porch to it, and little bits of Lombard Gothic have been well copied from Cologne. But windows have been fitted in with stilted arches, of which the stilts seem to crack and bend, so narrow are they and so high. And then the towers with high pinnacled roofs are a mistake,—unless indeed they be needed to give to the whole structure that name of Romanesque which it has assumed. (Anthony Trollope, *North America*, 317)

James Renwick Designs the Smithsonian Institution in the Lombard Style

In 1846 a building committee appointed by the regents of the Smithsonian Institution began work. Its members visited five cities, consulted with major architects of the time, and considered plans submitted by Robert Mills and Dr. David Owen, brother of the committee's chairman, Senator Robert Dale Owen of Indiana. Early in 1847 the regents selected one of two designs prepared by James Renwick, Jr., of New York City.

A month later the regents approved the publication of Senator Owen's *Hints on Public Architecture*. This work, written with Renwick's assistance and containing the two illustrations presented here, appeared in 1849. That April workers finished the east wing of the building whose cornerstone had been laid 1 May 1847. Owen's scholarly book referred to Renwick's design as based on "what has been variously called the Lombard, the Norman, the Romanesque and the Byzantine school." Owen explained that the structure "consists of a main centre building two stories high, and two wings, of a single story, connected by intervening ranges; each of these latter having, on the north, or principal front, a cloister, with open stone screen.

"The main building has, in the centre of its north front, two towers, of which the higher reaches an elevation of 145 feet. On its south front it has a single massive tower, 37 feet square, including buttresses, and 91 feet high. On its northeast corner stands a double campanile, 17 feet square, and . . . at its southwest corner, an Octagonal Tower. . . . There are nine towers in all, including a small one at each wing."

Smithsonian Institution, from the North East [i.e., northwest].

Smithsonian Institution from the South West [i.e., southeast]. Both views drawn by J[ames] Renwick, Architect. [Buildings by (Adam) Weingärtner, landscape and figures by (Napoleon) Sarony]. Printed by Sarony & Major, 117 Fulton St., N.Y. From Robert Dale Owen, *Hints on Public Architecture*. Lithographs, each 7¾ × 10¹¹⁄₁₆ in. (19.7 × 27.1 cm.). John W. Reps.

*John Latrobe recalls the appearance
of Capitol Hill and Pennsylvania Avenue in 1812.*

From the foot of . . . [Capitol Hill, Pennsylvania] avenue stretched off towards the president's house. In the centre was a gravelled road, with a deep ditch on each side, separating it from gravelled footways which ran between rows of Lombardy poplars. . . . All this was in 1812. . . .

In summer the old avenue was fair travelling. In winter it was bad enough. In winter and summer, however, it was better than the present vast expanse of rubble stone pavement—for the dimensions of the carriage way were contracted, and the Lombardy poplars,—poor shade trees as they were,—afforded a relief to the glare of the broad, unbroken highway. (Latrobe, "Construction of the Public Buildings in Washington," 224–25)

*Lt. Francis Hall takes note of conditions along
Pennsylvania Avenue and decries the absence of trees.*

From the foot of the Capitol hill there runs a straight road, (intended to be a street,) planted with poplars for about two miles, to the president's house, a handsome stone mansion, forming a conspicuous object from the Capitol Hill: near it are the public offices and some streets nearly filled up: about half a mile further is a pleasant row of houses, in one of which the president at present resides: there are a few tolerable houses still further on the road to George Town, and this is nearly the sum total of the City for 1816. It used to be a joke against Washington, that next door neighbours must go through a wood to make their visits; but the jest and forest have vanished together; there is now scarcely a tree betwixt George Town and the Navy Yard, two miles beyond the Capitol, except the poplars I have mentioned, which may be considered as the *locum tenentes* of future houses. (Francis Hall, *Travels in Canada and the United States*, 327)

*A Swedish nobleman and naval officer objects
to conditions on Pennsylvania Avenue in 1819.*

The busiest street is Pennsylvania Avenue, but it is not paved, so that in dry and windy weather one chokes with dust raised by the many carriages traveling to and from the Capitol. In the rainy weather, too, the mud is intolerable and one sinks in mire up to the ankles. The sidewalks on both sides of the road are not entirely paved either. (Klinkowström, *America 1818–1820*, 31)

*Charles Murray claims to have been blinded and choked
by the avenue's dust.*

The only tolerable street is the Pennsylvania Avenue, which is above a mile long, and is the best piece of macadamized road in the United States; but they appear never to scrape off the dust; and I have been more nearly blinded and choked there, after three days of dry weather in March, than ever I have been in Rotten Row on a Sunday in June; though in the former case the dust was raised by one solitary hackney-coach, and the latter was the joint production of horses and carriages to be counted by thousands. (Murray, *Travels in North America*, 143–44)

*A Scottish lawyer and journalist turns urban design critic
in describing Pennsylvania Avenue after seeing it in 1846.*

The first feature about the avenue that strikes you, is its amazing width. The houses visible on the opposite side, are three hundred feet distant from you, enough to destroy all community of interest and feeling between them, if houses had either one or the other. There seems, in fact, to be little or no bond of union between them; and instead of looking like the two sides of one and the same street, they seem as if they were each a side of two different streets. The mistake of this prodigality of surface was discovered too late to be remedied. In the first place, it destroys the symmetry of the street; for, to be well-proportioned, the houses on either side should rise to a height of twenty stories at least, whereas they are, generally speaking, only three. In the next place, the cost of keeping it in order is ruinous; and as Pennsylvania-avenue is the Broadway of Washington, all the other streets are beggared for the sake of the pet. To pave it was like attempting to pave a field—a circumstance to which is attributable the fact, that the rest of the streets, with the exception of their broad ample brick footways, are left unpaved. In wet weather, to cross any of them, even Pennsylvania-avenue, is a hazardous matter. Nobody ever crosses them for pleasure. It requires serious business to drag you from one side to the other. (Mackay, *The Western World*, 2:110–11)

Pennsylvania Avenue Gradually Takes Form

In the early stages of planning the city, President Washington and Secretary of State Thomas Jefferson decided on building regulations that limited the height of buildings everywhere in the city to three stories but *required* buildings constructed along the principal avenues to be built to this height. They thus hoped to line L'Enfant's monumental thoroughfares with structures having a uniform cornice line that would strengthen such imposing vistas as that along Pennsylvania Avenue between the Capitol and the White House.

Alas, few persons came forward with the money or the will to build such buildings, and when Jefferson became president, he resolved that if bricks and mortar would not enclose the streets and define the lines of view, trees could be made to accomplish this goal. He intended to plant quick-growing Lombardy poplars first and later add or substitute oaks and elms, but it was not until 1815 that a city ordinance provided for 400 English elms to replace the poplars. Later, sycamore, linden, oak, and maple trees were added. The views reproduced here, published in 1834 and 1839, show the effect of these efforts.

The artist of the earlier engraving looked northwest along Pennsylvania Avenue from the Capitol to the White House, drawing the latter building much larger than it would have appeared in reality and turning it slightly to reveal its facade. Five years later the celebrated William Bartlett looked in the opposite direction toward the Capitol from atop the semicircular projection on the south facade of the White House.

Washington. Drawn by J[ohn] R[ubens] Smith, engraved by J. B. Neagle. From M. Malte-Brun, *A System of Universal Geography.* Engraving, 6¼ × 8⅛ in. (16 × 20.5 cm.). Olin Library, Cornell University.

Washington from the president's House. [Titles repeated in French and German]. Drawn by W[illiam] H. Bartlett. Engraved by H. Wallis. Published by Geo. Virtue, London, 1839. From Nathaniel Parker Willis, *American Scenery.* Steel engraving, 6½ × 7³⁄₁₆ in. (16.5 × 18.2 cm.). Kiplinger Collection.

Lt. Col. A. M. Maxwell disliked almost everything he saw during his visit in 1840.

Morally and physically, this place has little to recommend it. It impressed me with the idea of a deserted village in an unwholesome country; and the low, broad, slowly-moving Potomac, with its marshy banks, must make it unhealthy, particularly at this sultry season. Take the Capitol and government offices away from it, and it is the most forlorn and melancholy place, bearing the name of a capital, I ever was in. . . .

It is true that its streets and squares are marked out, and are to radiate from its splendid Capitol as from a common centre; but all this is a mere project, never likely to be realised. In the meantime you can have a day's shooting over its projected streets. (Maxwell, *A Run through the United States*, 177–79)

Charles Dickens levels his biggest verbal guns at the city, which he visited in 1842.

Take the worst parts of the City Road and Pentonville, or the straggling outskirts of Paris. . . . Burn the whole down, build it up again in wood and plaster; widen it a little . . . ; put green blinds outside all the private houses, with a red curtain and a white one in every window; plough up all the roads; plant a great deal of coarse turf in every place where it ought *not* to be; erect three handsome buildings in stone and marble, anywhere, but the more entirely out of everybody's way the better; call one the Post Office, one the Patent Office, and one the Treasury; make it scorching hot in the morning, and freezing cold in the afternoon, with an occasional tornado of wind and dust; leave a brick-field without the bricks in all central places where a street may naturally be expected; and that's Washington.

Dickens coins a new title for the city.

It is sometimes called the City of Magnificent Distances, but it might with greater propriety be termed the City of Magnificent Intentions. . . . Spacious avenues, that begin in nothing, and lead nowhere; streets, mile-long, that only want houses, roads, and inhabitants; public buildings that need but a public to be complete; and ornaments of great thoroughfares, which only lack great thoroughfares to ornament—are its leading features. . . . To the admirers of cities it is a . . . pleasant field for the imagination to rove in; a monument raised to a deceased project, with not even a legible inscription to record its departed greatness.

Such as it is, it is likely to remain. (Dickens, *American Notes*, 116–17)

George Warburton calls Washington an architectural joke.

Washington is so well described in the epithet of "The city of magnificent distances" that it is scarcely possible to add anything to convey a clearer idea of it. It is indeed a rich architectural joke—a boasting, straggling, raw, uncomfortable failure, of infinite pretension in the plan, wretched and imperfect in the execution. The situation is very fine, that is, the situation of the Capitol—the city is everywhere. Hotels, lodging-houses, the dwellings of the official people, the public offices, dockyard and arsenal—scattered about at the most ludicrously inconvenient distances, on muddy, back-settlement-looking roads, of enormous width—are the component parts of inflated absurdity. ([Warburton], *Hochelaga*, 2:91)

The former British consul in Massachusetts from 1839 to 1846 files a dissenting opinion.

First impressions of places are at once the most vivid and most true, before local influences or the force of habit deaden one's perceptions as to faults or merits. I am, therefore, ready and glad to state that the whole appearance of Washington struck me with pleased astonishment. I had read so much of its wild and lonesome aspect, of its unfinished streets, its morasses and "magnificent distances," sarcastically specified by disappointed or splenetic visitors, that my mind was quite prepared to realise their worst exaggerations. My admiration of its fine position, the vastness of its plan, and the progress of its filling up, was probably greater than it would have been, had I come there without any preconceived notions. To my view Washington was a grand conception, imperfectly carried out, but by no means the absurd abortion it is generally represented.

It was not a place of mushroom growth, run rapidly up, like the flimsy constructions which overspread the country, but a solid city, founded on a grand scheme, which it may require a century to carry out. (Grattan, *Civilized America*, 1:163–65)

An Artist in 1847 Creates an Image of Washington, Celebrating Its Public Buildings

Although most visiting Englishmen let no opportunities pass to criticize the city's plan, its widely separated and sparsely developed neighborhoods, and the design of its public buildings, most Americans proudly regarded the national capital as an example of democratic achievement and native creativity. Nowhere is this better exemplified than in the frontispiece illustration to an otherwise unremarkable book on the public economy of the United States published in 1847.

The artist, Joseph Bruff, produced a kind of Washington architectural collage that brings together in the field of view the major public buildings of the capital city, no matter where located. We seem to be looking directly east toward the Capitol on the hill in the distance. In the foreground an attenuated and prematurely completed Washington Monument thrusts its slender shaft toward the heavens from a decorated sculptural base. The artist completed on paper another structure that had only just been started—the Smithsonian Institution standing within its own fenced and landscaped grounds immediately to the right of the monument.

In order to include the White House, the old Treasury, the Patent Office, and Post Office in the scene, the artist simply moved them into the field of vision so he could add their images at the left. Similarly, he brought the Potomac River northward to show several buildings along its shore on the right-hand side of the print. Extending from the lower left to the water at the right is the canal, complete with canal boat being towed by two horses. Symbols of agricultural prosperity, liberty, science, and patriotism decorate the foreground of this extraordinary symbolic representation of the city of Washington near the middle of the nineteenth century.

Elements of National Thrift and Empire. Drawn by J[oseph] G. Bruff, printed by E. Weber & Co. Balto. [Published by J. & G. S. Gideon, Washington, 1847.] From Robert Mayo, *A Synopsis of the Commercial and Revenue Systems of the United States*. Lithograph, 6⅜ × 8¼ in. (16.2 × 20.9 cm.). Olin Library, Cornell University.

Alexander Mackay introduces the city to his readers.

To convey to the mind of the reader any thing like an adequate idea of Washington is no easy task. It so violates one's preconceived notions of a capital, and is, in its general features, so much at variance with the estimate which one forms of the metropolitan proprieties, that it is difficult, in dealing with it as a capital, to avoid caricaturing a respectable country town. It is as unique in its physical character as it is in its political position, answering all its purposes, yet at the same time falling far short of its expectations.

He believes in seeing the city from the top of the Capitol.

Washington presents itself in two distinct aspects, one comprising that which it is, and the other that which it was to be. The difference between the intention and the reality is great indeed, and can only be appreciated by viewing the city from some point, from which both design and execution can be estimated together. The point in every way most favourable in this respect, is the dome of the Capitol; and, with the reader's consent, we will ascend it together, and take a bird's-eye view of Washington.

The view from this elevated point is extensive, and in some respects pleasantly varied. The whole of the district of Columbia is within the range of your vision, with a considerable expanse of the circumjacent States of Maryland and Virginia. You have water, town, and field at your feet, with long stretches of forest beyond, and hazy wooded slopes in the distance.

Both the site and the plan of Washington are beneath you, as if delineated on a gigantic map. The ground upon which the city is laid out is on the north bank of the Potomac, at the head of tide-water, and about 120 miles from Chesapeake Bay. On the noble estuary of that river the southern side of the city rests, being flanked on the eastern side by a broad and deep creek, called the East Branch. In a northern or western direction, there are no particular marks to designate its limits.

Mackay criticizes the location chosen for the capital.

If the design of its founders was too grand for realization, it was because of its being incommensurate with the wants of the locality. In a commercial point of view it is a superfluity, and politically and socially speaking, it is not that powerful magnet which, like the centralizing capitals of the old world, can draw to itself the wealth and fashion of the country. In that on which

they chiefly relied for its future greatness, its projectors committed a capital blunder. There are too many social and political centres in the United States for the presence of the federal government to command at Washington a monopoly of the wealth, the talent, and the fashion of the country.

He explains the basis of the city plan.

The Capitol was very appropriately selected as the centre of the whole plan. From it was to radiate magnificent avenues, of indefinite length in some directions, and of an almost fabulous width in all. Having secured this great frame-work, it was easy to fill up the rest of the diagram. In these avenues all the side streets were to begin and terminate; the whole being conceived pretty much on the plan of an out-door spider's web. . . . Some of these avenues are laid out and can be traced, from a variety of marks, by the eye, others having, as yet, no definite existence but in the intellect of the surveyor. . . . From the direction of the East Branch to Georgetown, one avenue was laid out, extending for about three miles, broken only in two places by the grounds of the Capitol and those of the president's house. This is in the main line of the town, and nearly one-half of it is covered with grass.

The author summarizes what has been carried out.

The main body of the town lies to the west of the Capitol, on low ground, completely overlooked by the elevated plateau, on the slope of which that pile is built. The basis of the part of the town is Pennsylvania-avenue, running almost from your feet, a broad straight course for a full mile, until it terminates in the grounds of the president's house, built upon a similar though a less elevation than the Capitol. On the north this avenue is flanked by a low ridge, which the city completely covers. . . . In this direction, and in this only, has the city any thing like a town look about it. In every other direction, you have nothing but incipient country villages, with here and there a few scattered houses of wood or brick, as the case may be, and ever and anon a street just begun and then stopped, as if it were afraid to proceed any further into the wilderness. Taking a rapid glance at the whole, plan and execution considered, it reminds one of an unfinished piece of lady's needlework, with a patch here and there resting upon the canvass, the whole enabling one to form an idea, and no more, of the general design. (Mackay, *The Western World*, 2:108–10)

Edward Weber and Casimir Bohn Print and Publish a View of Washington from the Capitol

Casimir Bohn, a Washington publisher of views and guidebooks, issued this attractive and informative lithograph in 1849. Bohn sold the print separately and also used it in a guidebook to the city, folding the lithograph several times to fit inside the book's covers. The anonymous artist looked west from the portico of the Capitol to the Mall, the distant Potomac, and the White House and Treasury at the far end of Pennsylvania Avenue. This large print was the first separately issued image to depict the city as it could be seen from the Capitol, a perspective that—altered to show the Capitol in the foreground—became the favored viewpoint of many later artists and illustrators.

The view portrays the new Smithsonian Institution much as it would look when finished, although in 1849 its construction had only begun. The Robert Mills design for the Washington Monument also appears here as if finished and with the pantheon base that was never constructed. The artist provided more information about both structures in two of the twenty vignettes surrounding the principal view. These vignettes include images of St. Patrick's Church and Georgetown College as well as both the Navy Yard and the arsenal, the latter occupying a site at Greenleaf's Point where the Anacostia joins the Potomac. Another vignette shows the naval observatory that stood on a hill near the Potomac west and a little south of the White House. Its small dome provided another landmark on the Washington skyline.

Georgetown can be seen in the large vignette at bottom center. The bridge across the Potomac is an aqueduct, a crossing of the river by a branch of the Chesapeake and Ohio Canal, begun in 1828 and by 1850 extending as far inland as Cumberland, Maryland. The "water-trough bridge," as some referred to it, allowed canal barges to bypass Georgetown with its shallow harbor and proceed southward to Alexandria where deeper draft ships awaited canal boat cargo.

View of Washington City and Georgetown. Unsigned view, printed by E. Weber & Co., Baltimore. Published by Casimir Bohn, Washington, D.C., 1849. Lithograph, 19½ × 27 in. (49.7 × 68.7 cm.). Kiplinger Collection.

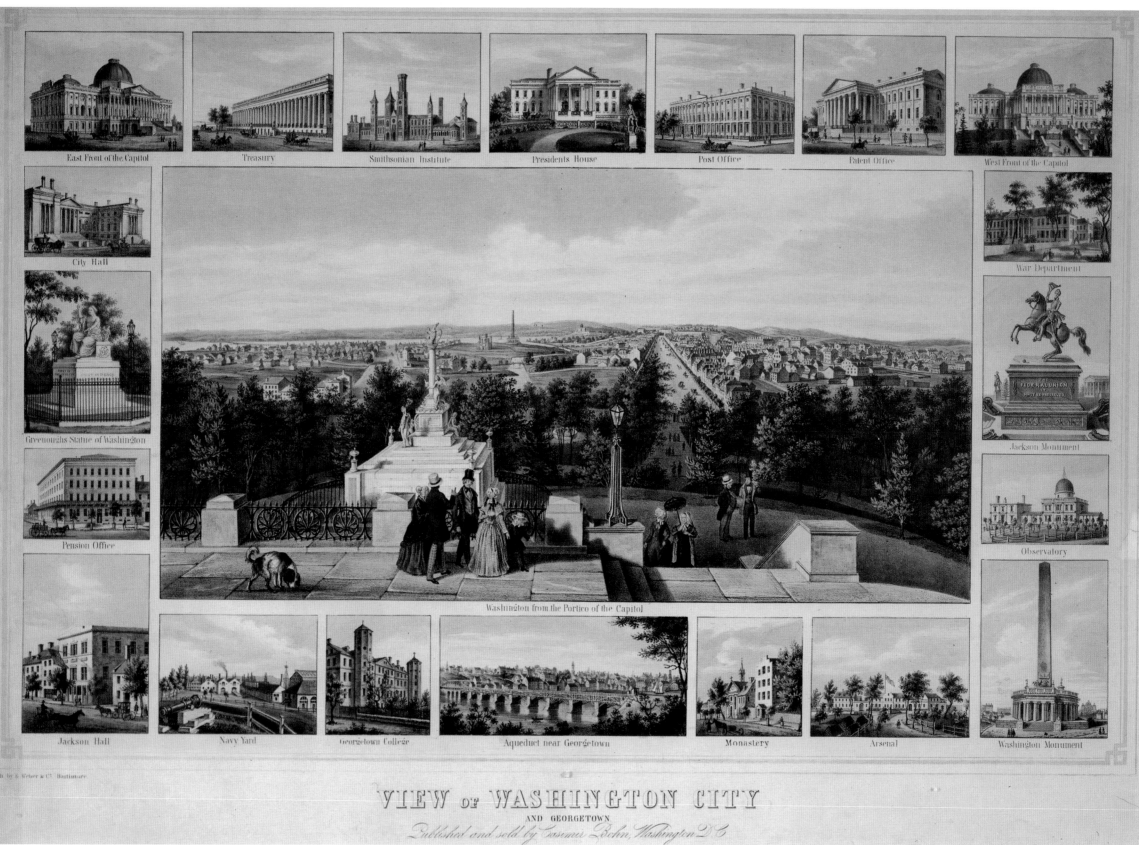

East Front of the Capitol

Treasury

Smithsonian Institute

Presidents House

Post Office

Patent Office

West Front of the Capitol

City Hall

War Department

Greenoughs Statue of Washington

Jackson Monument

Pension Office

Observatory

Washington from the Portico of the Capitol

Jackson Hall

Navy Yard

Georgetown College

Aqueduct near Georgetown

Monastery

Arsenal

Washington Monument

VIEW of WASHINGTON CITY
AND GEORGETOWN.
Published and sold by Casimir Bohn, Washington D.C.

5 Andrew Jackson Downing Plans the Mall, and the Capitol Acquires New Wings in the 1850s

THE major buildings begun or completed in the previous two decades substantially enhanced Washington's appearance and—except for the Smithsonian—further reinforced the style and scale of public architecture established earlier by the Capitol and the White House. Nevertheless, at mid-century much of the land south of Pennsylvania Avenue remained undeveloped, and the city still seemed to many observers an unattractive place with little real urban character.

Carl Schurz, an intelligent and sophisticated German political refugee who had arrived in the United States two years earlier, first saw Washington in 1854 and recalled his disappointment:

> My first impressions of the political capital of the great American Republic were rather dismal. Washington looked at that period like a big, sprawling village, consisting of scattered groups of houses which were overtopped by a few public buildings. . . . The departments of State, of War, and of the Navy were quartered in small, very insignificant-looking houses which might have been the dwellings of some well-to-do shopkeepers who did not care for show.

Like so many other visitors, Schurz noted the absence of even a single impressive thoroughfare, complaining that "there was not one solidly built-up street in the whole city—scarcely a block without gaps of dreary emptiness." He found it strange that no system of house numbering existed, but instead "they were designated by calling them 'the first of the five' or the 'fifth of the seven' on Pennsylvania Avenue, or on Seventh Street, as the case might be." He wrote amusingly of a hazard at the foot of Capitol Hill:

> Pennsylvania Avenue, not far from the Capitol, was crossed by a brook called Goosecreek, alias "the Tiber," which was spanned by a wooden bridge; and I was told—perhaps falsely—that congressmen in a fuddled state, going home in the dark after an animated night-session, would sometimes miss the bridge and fall into the water, to be fished out with difficulty by the sergeants-at-arms and their assistants.

Schurz stopped at the National, one of the capital's main hotels, but he found it "dingy beyond description." In exploring the residential part of Washington, he saw "hardly half a dozen residences, if as many . . . , that had the appearance of refined, elegant, and comfortable homes." Like other visitors of the time and earlier, he complained of streets that were "ill-paved, if paved at all" that were "constantly covered with mud or dust." Recalling the familiar and often-used phrase describing Washington as "the city of magnificent distances," Schurz observed:

> But there was nothing at the ends of those distances, and, excepting the few public buildings, very little that was in any way interesting or pleasing. In many of the streets, geese, chickens, pigs, and cows had still a scarcely disputed right of way. The city had throughout a slouchy, unenterprising, unprogressive appearance, giving extremely little promise of becoming the beautiful capital it now is.[1]

No better illustration exists of conditions in Washington at the beginning of the decade than the lithograph reproduced in folio 36. Robert P. Smith drew this scene and entered it for copyright in 1850. Nothing seems to be known of Smith, but he deserves to be remembered as the earliest to portray the city looking west from an elevated position with the Capitol in the foreground. His view clearly shows the forlorn condition of the nearly vacant Mall whose vast expanse of open and unimproved land contrasted strongly with the more densely built-up neighborhoods of the city at the right of the view extending north of Pennsylvania Avenue.[2]

As later folios will make clear, it was this same imaginary vantage point that Edward Sachse used again and again in the remarkable series of printed urban portraits of Washington that he issued over two decades beginning in 1852. Starting with Smith's view and using successive Sachse lithographs for comparison, one can follow the development of that part of the city lying west of the Capitol, where most of its residents lived and worked and where the government had built its major public buildings.

Sachse also followed Smith in another respect. Smith, like the artist of the Weber-Bohn lithograph of 1849 in folio 35, depicted the Washington Monument as if it had been completed according to Robert Mills's original design. The series

---

1. Schurz, *Reminiscences*, 1:19–21. Schurz's three-volume work was published in 1908.

2. Smith does not appear in the 1846, 1850, and 1853 Washington city directories.

of views Sachse issued from 1852 through 1871 showing the Capitol from the east were identical in this respect. Smith also elected to show the still unfinished Smithsonian Institution as it would eventually appear when the building opened to the public several years later.

As the illustrations reproduced in this and the following chapter will demonstrate, persons who visited Washington for the first time and who were familiar with one of the Smith or Sachse lithographs must have been puzzled and disappointed when they went to look at the Washington Monument. One should note, however, that indulging in what might be termed anticipatory detail was not confined to views of Washington, nor was it uniquely the practice of Smith and Sachse. Other artists of this city and other places as well not infrequently pushed ahead the hands of the clock in this manner.[3]

Joseph Varnum, Jr.'s, remarks about the unattractive conditions of the public grounds also appear in folio 36. They include his comments on how little attention the Congress had paid to the Mall and how few of its members had any knowledge of the purposes L'Enfant had in mind when he created this space in his city plan. Varnum noted that the Mall had "been left a mere cow-pasture; when a very small outlay in planting trees, and laying out walks and drives, would make it a second Champs-Elysees."

This resident of Washington and perceptive observer of its development complained again of congressional ignorance about the original city plan when he stated that "comparatively few, even of the members of Congress, are aware" that the Mall "belongs to the government, or what the design of the architect was." He called upon Congress "at once" to take "some action" to complete the Mall "as the only thing, at present, wanting to give a finish to the capitol grounds." Then, in a revealing phrase, he stated that an improved Mall was needed to "connect the villages forming the city."

An earlier chapter's comments on the map of Washington in 1836 in folio 25 noted the island-like configuration of Washington's neighborhoods—conditions that Varnum referred to in the passage just quoted. A similar map showing the developed portion of Washington in 1850 against the much vaster expanse of its planned extent is reproduced in folio 37. This indicates that while the "villages" north of Pennsylvania Avenue had become a single linear community, elsewhere one could find only sparsely built-on streets leading to the scattered settlements east of the Capitol, around the Navy Yard, and south of the Mall.[4]

The recollections of Byron Sunderland accompanying this illustration provide vivid descriptions of just how unfinished the city remained despite the grandeur of several public buildings and the elaborate character of the street plan. He states that Washington looked like "an overgrown, tattered village" and that only one-third of the city had been developed. These conditions would slowly change as efforts were made to improve the city. Not all met with success, however, including the first official effort to replan the Mall with presidential sponsorship.

This project began with every hope of having beneficial results when President Fillmore in 1850 retained America's most prominent landscape designer, Andrew Jackson Downing, to plan both the grounds of the White House and the Mall. Downing edited the leading journal in the field, the *Horticulturist*, and he was well known in addition to his writings for his romantic "naturalistic" designs for rural estates.[5]

Downing also had written compellingly about the need for public parks in American cities, pointing out how popular the several rural cemeteries had become since the opening in Cambridge, Massachusetts, of Mount Auburn Cemetery in the early 1830s. Its design, like that of Greenwood Cemetery in Brooklyn, New York, and Laurel Hill in Philadelphia, incorporated all the features of the English naturalistic or curvilinear style, described here in 1848 by an admiring visitor to Mount Auburn: "The avenues are winding in their course and exceedingly beautiful in their gentle circuits, adapted picturesquely to the inequalities of the surface of the ground, and producing charming landscape effects from this natural arrangement, such as could never be had from straightness or regularity."[6]

Other than occasional small squares, American cities lacked public parks, and many persons found rural cemeteries attractive places for an afternoon or weekend outing. Guidebooks with suggested travel routes offered visitors information about the monuments, while more elaborate publications with engraved illustrations provided more permanent reminders of the beauty of these attractively landscaped retreats from the city's noise and turmoil.

Mount Auburn evidently became so popular as a place for picnics and other activities regarded as inappropriate for a burial place that its management had to prohibit the introduction of refreshments into its precincts. Another regulation forbade the discharge of firearms, suggesting that hunting had also become one of the recreational activities carried on there. It is no wonder: with urban populations rapidly increasing and no public pleasure ground available, those who had

3. In a chapter on the accuracy of nineteenth-century American lithographic city views, I provide some additional examples of this practice by other artists elsewhere. See chap. 9, "Lithographic City Views: Reliable Records of the Urban Past," in Reps, *Views and Viewmakers*, 67–72.

4. Lloyd Van Derveer, who published this map, gives his address as Camden, New Jersey. In 1852 when he issued a map of Orleans County,

New York, his address was 15 Minor Street, Philadelphia. James Keily, identified as the surveyor of the map, also did work for the Philadelphia map publishing firm founded by Robert Pearsall Smith. These included maps of Dinwiddie and Henrico counties in Virginia and Salem and Gloucester counties in New Jersey. In partnership with J. W. Otley, Keily also produced maps of Mercer, Middlesex, and Somerset counties,

New Jersey. See Ristow, *American Maps and Mapmakers*, 350, 352, 386, 392. The Washington map contains an amusing error of nomenclature indicating Keily's unfamiliarity with the area. The mouth of the canal south of the White House is labeled Timber Creek.

5. According to Reiff, *Washington Architecture*, 114, "Downing was contacted in October 1850, by

a number of local gentlemen: Joseph Henry (Secretary of the Smithsonian), Walter Lenox (mayor of Washington), and Ignatius Mudd (Commissioners of Public Buildings) at the urging of W. W. Corcoran and with the approval of President Fillmore." Reiff provides an informed treatment of Downing's plan on pp. 113–22.

6. Cornelia W. Walter, *Mount Auburn*, 14.

the means of transportation resorted to rural cemeteries as the only available substitute for the open fields and woods of the natural landscape.[7]

The invitation to Downing to come to Washington must have seemed to him a marvelous opportunity to put his design theories into effect. Here he could create—not a cemetery that might do double-duty as a place of recreation nor a park located at the outskirts of a metropolis where access would be possible only for part of the population—but a huge recreation ground in the very heart of the city where everyone could find enjoyment.

Downing brought to Washington strong convictions bordering on dogma about "correct" design, and it is unlikely that he deliberated at any length about whether or not his revered naturalistic style was the most appropriate for the central open space of a city whose plan stemmed from an entirely different approach to organizing exterior space. Downing made his position clear in the first paragraph of his report to President Fillmore, where he declared that among his three objectives in his plan for the Mall was the provision of "an example of the natural style of Landscape Gardening which may have an influence on the general taste of the Country."

In his report and the drawing done to accompany it, Downing put forth his ideas of how his goals could be accomplished. Major sections of Downing's report to the president appear in folio 38. Also included is a copy of his plan of 1851 redrawn sixteen years later for use in the report of the chief of the U.S. Army Corps of Engineers. The drawing is rather confusing, with north at the bottom. On it one can see the White House at the lower right-hand corner. At lower left Downing drew only a portion of the western slope of Capitol Hill, with the Mall extending westward to the right.[8]

Briefly summarized, Downing's plan proposed a large, circular parade and field south of the White House, whose grounds were to be entered from Pennsylvania Avenue through a marble arch. He linked the White House grounds by a suspension bridge with what he called the Monument Park south of the canal. The vicinity of the monument would be planted "wholly with *American* trees, of large growth, disposed in open groups, so as to allow of fine vistas of the Potomac River."

Downing located Evergreen Garden east of Monument Park on a sixteen-acre portion of the Mall, designed with paths forming a series of concentric ellipses. East of this lay the Smithsonian Pleasure Grounds, which he designed as "an arrangement of choice trees in the natural style. The plots near the Institution would be thickly planted with the rarest trees and shrubs." In this way he hoped "to give greater seclusion and beauty to its immediate precincts."

Fountain Park occupied the next section to the east, centering on a pond and fountain. Beyond, where the botanical garden already existed, Downing proposed a new design using "hardy plants." A gate would provide egress from the Capitol grounds to this linked system of gardens and open spaces. Downing asserted that a visitor entering from here or Pennsylvania Avenue would be able to pass over "some of the most beautifully varied carriage-drives in the world. . . . The foot paths . . . would give additional interest by showing the grounds more in detail."

In his concluding remarks, Downing claimed that "the straight lines and broad Avenues" of L'Enfant's baroque city "would be pleasantly relieved and contrasted by the beauty of curved lines and natural groups of trees in the various parks." And he repeated and elaborated on the theme he sounded at the beginning of his report: that the Mall—replanned in this manner—would provide "a Public School of instruction in everything that relates to the tasteful arrangement of parks and grounds, and the growth and culture of trees."[9]

At least one journalist at the time held high expectations that Downing's plan for comprehensive development of the Mall might be carried out. Writing admiringly of the design, Anne Lynch told the readers of *Harper's New Monthly Magazine* for December 1852 that "the transformation of this marshy and desolate waste into a National Park has been already begun." She looked forward to the ultimate completion of the project within "four or five years."[10]

However, an editorial footnote in this article, excerpted in folio 39, announced the sad news of Downing's tragic death at the age of thirty-seven earlier that year. Without his presence, support for the project rapidly dwindled, and in the end only the Smithsonian grounds were planted to follow the spirit of his recommendations. Some paths and carriageways elsewhere on the Mall also reflect his influence, but as a later writer in *Harper's* noted in 1859, "little has been done toward beautifying" the Mall.[11]

What would Washington have looked like if Downing's naturalistic plan had been carried out and Robert Mills's design for the Washington Monument had been fully implemented? An artist who specialized in producing large and impressive lithographic views of American cities provided an answer. Reproduced in folio 39 is the striking, large-folio lithograph published in 1852 as drawn by Benjamin Franklin Smith, with some assistance on the monument's appearance from none other than Robert Mills himself.

7. See Dearborn, *Dearborn's Guide*. The proliferation of literature on rural cemeteries and their relation to the American park movement during the latter half of the nineteenth century has been remarkable. For my treatment of the subject in my study of American city planning history in 1965, *The Making of Urban America* (pp. 325–48), I found only a few helpful sources. The following more recent studies examine the subject: three articles by Barbara Rotundo, "The Rural Cemetery Movement," "Mount Auburn Cemetery," and "Mount Auburn"; Stanley French, "The Cemetery as Cultural Institution"; and Donald Simon, "Green-Wood Cemetery."

8. Reproductions of Downing's manuscript are also in Reps, *Monumental Washington*, 52 fig. 29, and Gutheim, *Worthy of The Nation*, 55. See also Reps, "Romantic Planning in a Baroque City," and Washburn, "Vision of Life for the Mall."

9. Downing, "Explanatory Notes."

10. Lynch, "A Sketch of Washington City," 5–6.

11. For Downing's death in the sinking of a Hudson River steamboat, see Proctor, "Tragic Death."

Smith was one of four brothers from Maine who, beginning in 1846 when George and Francis Smith began work as subscription agents for the itinerant viewmaker Edwin Whitefield, drew, sold, and published more than forty attractive views of American cities. Benjamin was the artist of the family—only twenty-two when he drew the Washington view. He joined George, Francis, and the fourth brother, David, in this business after beginning his career in Albany as an artist and lithographer in 1846 at the age of sixteen.[12]

Their Washington view appeared during a busy year for the group, for in 1852 the Smith Brothers produced two splendid views of New Orleans and one each of St. Louis and Cincinnati. In the previous two years they had issued scenes of Pittsburgh and New Haven and two handsome lithographs of Philadelphia in addition to other prints. Although Benjamin had collaborated with other artists on some of these views, he undertook the Washington scene as his sole responsibility.[13]

The Smiths, apparently unaware of Washington's reputation for delay or abandonment of public improvements, evidently felt little reluctance to prepare a view of the city showing how it would appear if Downing's proposals for the public grounds and the Mills design for the Washington Monument were completed. So little do we know about the circumstances of its preparation, however, that it is not entirely impossible that someone commissioned the Smiths to publish the view in the hope that its appearance would aid those who favored carrying out the Downing plan and the Mills design.[14]

Could this have been Robert Mills, anxious to couple his monument design with the more recent proposals for the Mall by Downing? Two letters to Mills from Benjamin Franklin Smith contain just the barest hint of such sponsorship. At the least they indicate Mills's interest in Smith's view and his willing cooperation in providing information that would show off his monument design to best advantage.

Smith first wrote Mills on 23 April 1852 and began with some points Smith needed clarified for a separate view of the monument that Mills had evidently engaged Smith to prepare. Smith then continued with the passage quoted in folio 39. Another sentence informed Mills that Smith intended to send his drawing "to Washington for a few days to a Mr. Thompson of the Treasury Dept. and will let you know so that you may be able to see it." The second letter a week later asked Mills to send on any suggestions for how the view might be improved.[15]

No record exists of any comments Mills may have made to Smith, but by far the most prominent object in the lithograph is the Washington Monument as Mills intended it to look. Indeed, this partially conceals one of the important features of Downing's plan: the suspension bridge across the canal that would provide an effective link between the Mall and the presidential grounds by way of a carriageway following a winding course from the bridge toward the White House and Treasury. South of the latter building one can just see the great arch that Downing proposed as the entrance to the White House grounds from Pennsylvania Avenue.

Smith included at the far right of his view a small portion of the Smithsonian Institution. Between that building and the monument, the artist sketched his interpretation of how the Mall would appear when the lawns and trees had been planted and the graceful curves of the paths and carriageways and been constructed. The Mall appears more convincing than do the tall-masted sailing vessels plying the canal at center right. Confined by two low bridges spanning this narrow channel, these ships could have voyaged no more than a few hundred feet.

This lithograph provided an image that Charles Magnus of New York promptly copied at smaller size, a practice he indulged in throughout most of his printing and publishing career. The folio shows two versions of the same image, illustrating how Magnus skillfully exploited various markets for images of cities. One is mounted on black paper and bordered with gold, evidently intended either for framing as an imitation of a glass-mounted, enamel matted print or as an image to be seen with the aid of an optical viewing device.[16]

12. The firm also commissioned several other, more experienced artists, like John William Hill, to sketch cities, either with Benjamin or as the sole artist for others. The business addresses of the Smith Brothers firm appearing in the imprints of their views almost always coincided with those of their various New York printers. The "firm" may therefore not have had a real office.

13. The Smiths pursued their viewmaking occupation for the eight-year period beginning in 1848 when they and Whitefield jointly published three of Whitefield's views. In 1849 they struck out on their own with prints of Pittsburgh and New Haven that Benjamin drew. Nearly everything I have been able to find concerning the Smith Brothers' career in this field can be found in my biographical note in Reps, *Views and Viewmakers*, 206–8. That work contains briefer notes

on Hill (pp. 183–84) and Whitefield (pp. 215–16). The later note is almost entirely based on Bettina Norton's full-length study of the artist, *Edwin Whitefield*. An analysis of the Hill-Smith view of St. Louis is in Reps, *Saint Louis Illustrated*, 80–85, where it is reproduced in color as fig. 5-1.

14. No other Smith Brothers view resembles the Washington prints in this respect, for in all their other lithographs the depiction is essentially accurate and reflects almost entirely the buildings that then existed in the city. I have no doubt that minute inspection of all of the Smith Brothers' views would reveal a few cases where the artist obligingly "completed" a structure or two not then finished. The Washington view—by contrast—includes so many features that were only proposed that it belongs in a different category.

15. I am grateful to Pamela Scott, architectural historian, of Washington, D.C., who found the letters among the papers of Robert Mills and provided me with copies. See Mills, *Papers*, 2978, 2980.

16. Very little has been published about Magnus. A study of some aspects of his activities is being carried out by Helena Zinkham, Division of Prints and Photographs, Library of Congress. She presented preliminary results of her findings in a still unpublished paper given at the New York Historical Society at the 1986 North American Print Conference. Charles Magnus was a prolific publisher of lithographs and engravings. His output included single-sheet views, illustrated letter-sheets, song sheets with illustrations, and decorative and patriotic envelopes, often using the same image in more than one way. For example, Magnus printed parts of the lithographs reproduced in folios 40 and 44 of Washington in 1862 and Alexandria, Virginia, in 1863 on envelopes sold during the Civil War. He obviously hoped that persons would purchase the complete set in order to be able to assemble the entire view. See Deák, *Picturing America*, 415, notes for entry 611. The six envelopes comprising the Washington view of 1862 are shown assembled in Grant, *Handbook*, 1–2; see

The second view by Magnus is the identical image printed to occupy the top half of the first page of a folded illustrated lettersheet. Lettersheets of this type were extremely popular in nineteenth-century America, particularly those containing city views. Magnus sold his products widely, and doubtless Washington stationery shops offered his Washington lettersheet for sale as an attractive item for both tourists and residents.

The folio also contains an extremely rare version of the Smith Brothers lithograph. For reasons that are impossible to explain, the firm issued this print in 1853, only a year after publication of the first version. Although of substantial size, it is smaller than the earlier Smith Brothers print of Washington. It is also quite different in character, with its precise lines resembling an engraving more than the lithograph of the previous year. What the Smiths had in mind in publishing this reduced image can only be a matter of conjecture.

Although the Mall never resembled what Downing proposed and the Smiths depicted, another major project undertaken at the same time altered substantially the largest and most visible structure in Washington. This was the enlargement of the Capitol, an undertaking that reflected the increasing need for additional space for Congress in a nation enjoying steady and rapid population growth and engaged in territorial expansion. The building that Thornton designed and that Latrobe and Bulfinch modified and completed could no longer house comfortably or even tolerably the members of Congress, who by the early 1840s numbered nearly 300.

As early as 1843 the House and the Senate recognized that the crowded conditions needed attention, and they passed a resolution calling for the secretary of war to prepare plans for the Capitol's enlargement. In response to this request, William Strickland, architect, and officers of the Topographical Bureau prepared a plan for a south wing to be added to the Capitol, an extension measuring over 100 by 150 feet. However, nothing came of this proposal, and it was not until almost a decade later that Congress took effective steps to provide for enlarging the building.[17]

In 1850 the Committee on Public Buildings recommended the approval of a Capitol expansion plan prepared at its request by Robert Mills. After this failed to gain acceptance, the Senate Committee on Public Buildings instead offered a prize of $500 "for the plan which may be adopted by the Committees on Public Buildings (acting jointly) of the two Houses of Congress, to be paid out of the contingent fund of the Senate."[18]

The committee selected four designs as having special merit, dividing the premium equally among their authors. Mills was then asked to prepare a plan combining the best features of all the competition submissions, but at this stage President Fillmore intervened. In his annual message of December 1851 he noted that Congress more than a year earlier had passed an act providing "for the extension of the Capitol according to such a plan as might be approved by the president." An appropriation of $100,000 was authorized to be spent under the president's direction "by such architect as he should appoint."[19]

On 11 June 1851 President Fillmore had selected for this purpose Thomas U. Walter, one of the four whose designs had shared the prize offered by the Senate. In his report to the secretary of the interior six months later, Walter described his design, one whose general features the president had approved shortly before appointing Walter to his new position:

> The extension of the Capitol consists of two wing buildings placed at the north and south ends of the present structure, at the distance of forty-four feet from it, with connecting corridors. Each building is one hundred and forty-two feet eight inches front, from north to south, by two hundred and thirty-eight feet ten inches deep, from east to west, exclusive of the porticoes and steps; the corridors consist of passages leading from the centre building to the wings, of twenty-one feet four inches in width, with outside colonnades, which make the entire width of each corridor fifty-six feet eight inches.[20]

Porticoes on three sides of each of the new wings would make the building even more imposing. Those on the east front towering above flights of thirty-nine steps were to have a center projection as well, "forming a double portico in the centre of the façade, similar in general design to that of the present eastern portico [of the original building]." Walter explained the pains he took in designing the addition to make the massive additions harmonize with the existing structure:

> The architecture of the exterior is designed to correspond in its principal features to that of the present building, and the disposition of the various parts is intended to present the appearance of one harmonious structure, and to impart dignity to the present building, rather than to interfere with its proportions, or detract from its grandeur and beauty.[21]

How well Walter succeeded can be seen clearly in the first view reproduced in folio 40, the first of the several Sachse lithographs of Washington drawn to include the east front of the Capitol and showing the city as the artist looked northwest from his imaginary elevated easel. In 1852 when Sachse issued this print the new wings had only been started, but using Walter's drawings as a guide, Sachse

also the individual sections and other illustrations Magnus used on envelopes on pp. 30, 31, and 32 of section 4, pp. 24, 25, 26, and 27 of section 5.

17. Hazelton, *The National Capitol*, 51–52.

18. Advertisement in the Washington *National Intelligencer* in issues appearing daily from 30 September to 21 October 1850, as quoted in Brown, *History of the United States Capitol*, 2:116.

19. As quoted in Brown, *History of the United States Capitol*, 2:119.

20. Thomas U. Walter, *Report*, 2.

21. Ibid., 3.

"finished" the Capitol on paper. At that time the new and much larger dome that now tops the building had not been considered.

Walter had enough experience with and knowledge of the leisurely pace of completion associated with most buildings in Washington. However, he had some reason to hope that the legislators would make sufficient funds available promptly since Congress would be providing for its own more comfortable accommodations. In his report of 1851 he reminded its members of these matters, stating that "the shortest time in which the work can be well and substantially done, and the terraces and grounds completed, is *five* years from the present date." This would depend, of course, "on the necessary appropriations being made by Congress, so as to admit of its advancing as rapidly as possible, without suspension or hinderance [sic]."[22]

Work did proceed fairly rapidly following the laying of the cornerstone on 4 July 1851 in a ceremony overladen with Masonic rites, as had been true when President Washington presided over the cornerstone festivities that marked the beginning of the original building. By the end of 1852 Walter could report that all the foundations had been laid, the cellars of both wings were completed, and the arches supporting basement floors stood in place. Moreover, the congressional library in the central part of the west front of the old building—destroyed by fire on Christmas Eve, 1851—had been rebuilt.

Another two years saw further progress, with the marble-faced exterior rising to the top of the windows of the main floor and the interior walls built as high as the ceilings of the two halls of Congress. In the spring of 1855, just before their adjournment, Congress authorized a new dome of cast iron to replace the old, copper-clad wooden dome surmounting the old building. Almost immediately Sachse revised his view by adding a badly drawn version of the new dome to the image of the Capitol.[23]

Either the artist was displeased with this lithograph of 1856 or its distorted perspective of the dome caused customers to reject it. For whatever reason, Sachse rectified this feature in another large-folio print issued three years later. At the same time he shifted his viewpoint to the north, thus moving the image of the dome southward so that it now appeared between Pennsylvania Avenue and the Washington Monument.

It was this version of the city's appearance that Sachse prepared in a smaller size in 1862, a print published jointly by Casimir Bohn in Washington and Charles Magnus in New York. This view can be seen in folio 40 together with an obviously derived version that Magnus issued in 1865. As he had done more than a decade before with his version of the Smith Brothers interpretation of the Downing plan, Magnus issued his view mounted on a black support with decorative gold borders. He probably issued an uncolored lettersheet version as well.

Magnus may have been an artistic plagiarist, but in one sense he was more accurate than Sachse, from whom he borrowed so freely. Although the House of Representatives held its first meeting in their south wing in 1857 and the Senate occupied its north wing in 1859, it was not until 2 December 1863 that workmen hoisted the statue of Freedom to its place atop the dome, and only by 1865, the year Magnus published his little view, could the work on the new wings be regarded as substantially finished. The Magnus view of the city with the Capitol in the foreground may thus be the first to appear after the completion of this massive building project.

Some American journals whose correspondents had not previously been uncritical of the progress of the capital city now began to acknowledge Washington's new character and architectural status. The long extract from a much longer article in *Harper's New Monthly Magazine* in folio 40 reflects this attitude. The author called attention to the "amazing strides toward permanent grandeur" made in the last five years and chided visiting English visitors for their unjustified criticisms.

Calling for enlarging and improving the Capital grounds, the author broadened the argument to advocate expenditures for other embellishments of the city as only fitting "the national dignity" to the end "that Washington should be . . . a great centre of whatever is noble and beautiful in architecture and the fine arts." The author maintained that "this is what people expect to find when they visit Washington, and they never fail to complain when they are in any respect disappointed."

Persons in other places whose only knowledge of Washington came from the Sachse views published during the process of enlarging the Capitol might well have expected to find a completed building when visiting Capitol Hill. As is evident from his views, Sachse drew everything as if tidy and complete. In reality, scaffolding obscured much of the structure, building materials lay scattered about, and workmen in rough clothes mingled with well-clad legislators, lobbyists, and political spectators passing among the throngs of people in front of the Capitol entrances.

The final view in folio 40, a large wood engraving published by the *Illustrated London News* in the spring of 1861, provides a more accurate idea of how the building appeared during construction, in this case as it neared completion. At the left, work is still in progress on the east portico of the House wing. Slabs of marble litter the ground below. In the center, only the drum and the first portion of the dome have been completed, and cranes extend from the timber tower with a mast attached for the U.S. flag.[24]

22. Ibid., 5.
23. Sachse's clumsy perspective made his lop-sided dome appear to be circled by a spiral ramp.

24. The source of the image used for the *Illustrated London News* wood engraving is unknown. Although it is signed by G. H. Andrews, he was probably the wood engraver in London and not the artist who drew the Capitol in Washington. George-Henry Andrews (1816–1898) was born in London, studied engineering, but adopted art as his career. He was well known for his watercolors and marine paintings and exhibited frequently at the Royal Academy. Andrews also did many of the illustrations for such English publications as the *Illustrated News* and the *Graphic*.

A year later a correspondent for other English journals visited the Capitol to report on its condition. His dispatch confirms the accuracy of the *Illustrated London News* illustration. Noting that all work on "completion of the edifice is suspended for the present, because funds are short," he described the building as having "an untidy, unfinished, almost tumble-down appearance." He found that "the immense iron dome . . . is still a bare framework of beams and girders, surmounted by a crane," and that "blocks of unhewn marble lie on every side, scattered about the pleasant grounds which lead from the Capitol to the foot of the steep hill on which it stands."[25]

This London wood engraving and nearly all the other views of this period, beginning with Smith's depiction of 1850 through the several drawn and printed from 1852 onward by Sachse, look westward toward the portion of Washington containing the most important public buildings, the shopping center, and the bulk of the residences. Only the rare, large lithograph in folio 41 presents the city as seen when viewed in the opposite direction.

Casimir Bohn, the Washington publisher whose name appears in that capacity on earlier Sachse lithographs, issued this view by Sachse in 1857. Despite its handsome depiction of the imposing west front of the Capitol, this print probably proved a commercial failure. Because it looked beyond the Capitol to the unfashionable easterly portions of the city where few, if any, members of society lived, it would not have appealed to the usual purchasers of such decorative and historic images.

The only public buildings of significance appear at the far right, where the smokestack marks the cluster of structures comprising the Navy Yard. To the right of center, one can just make out the hospital standing alone at the eastern boundary of the city. Although Bohn evidently failed to sell many copies, the lithograph is of great historic value since it is the only high-level view showing the appearance of this quarter of Washington. It discloses how backward in development these neighborhoods remained compared with those north of Pennsylvania Avenue between the Capitol and the White House.

In looking at this lithograph it is easy to understand how Edward Dicey and George Sala, the two critical English journalists whose work appears in folio 41, may have reached their unfavorable conclusions about Washington's appearance and character. To such sophisticated and worldly eyes as theirs the differences between the English and the American capital cities must have been all the more striking. Both lacked historical perspective, however, for neither understood how much the city had changed in the previous two decades.

Folio 42 presents several excerpts from an American writer's more balanced observations on Washington published a year earlier in the *Atlantic Monthly* for January 1861. Referring to the national capital as a "paradise of paradoxes," the author concludes several pages of criticism with the admission that "Washington is progressing rapidly" and "is fast becoming a large city." The map of the city reproduced with these passages provides the best documentation of the city's physical development as it entered the 1860s.

Albert Boschke drew this remarkably detailed map. A surveyor of German extraction working for the U.S. Coast Survey, he organized a team of surveyors at his own expense to prepare detailed maps of Washington and the District of Columbia. He began this project in 1856, and it soon required so much of his attention that his superiors insisted that he resign his government job. In 1857 he published his map of the city after having it lithographed in New York by Julius Bien, a well-known lithographic printer.

Sometime after completing the surveys of the remainder of the district and producing a finished manuscript of this new map, Boschke sold his interest in it to David McClelland, a Washington engraver, and Hugh B. Sweeny and Thomas Blagden. McClelland engraved the map and printed proof copies identifying him and Blanchard & Mohun as publishers. The engraving lists them—together with Sweeny and Blagden—as copyright claimants in 1861. Perhaps they published a few copies of the map, but at the outbreak of the Civil War the secretary of war sought to obtain control of the two copper plates McClelland had used.

The publishers asked $20,000; the government offered $500. After some time the publishers reduced their request to $4,000 provided the plates and the copyright would be returned to them after hostilities ended. The government declined to accept this proposal, and after the two parties failed to agree on a price, Secretary of War Stanton ordered an officer and a detachment of soldiers to seize the plates for the government. During the war the matter came before the Committee on War Claims, and the owners decided to accept a recommended settlement of $8,500.[26]

These circumstances explain why few impressions of the Boschke map can be found today, although it or portions of it, like that in folio 42, have been reproduced in several books or articles on the city's history from one of the surviving copies. It is one of several Washington maps and surveys used in this volume to show the extent of building development and, by doing so, to facilitate the reader's interpretation and understanding of what appears in the numerous city views presented in the folios.

One important feature of the city that Boschke's map portrays clearly is the line and station of the Baltimore and Ohio Railroad (B&O). The first train of this company to reach Washington arrived in the summer of 1835, using a temporary terminal at Second Street and Pennsylvania Avenue, as Tanner's 1836 map of the city in folio 25 shows. That fall a local newspaper informed its readers that they

---

25. Dicey, *Six Months in the Federal States*, 1:101.

26. For these and a few other details about this map, see Baker, "Surveys and Maps," 156–58.

soon could enjoy more comfortable facilities at this location: "Passengers from this city to Baltimore, by the Rail Road cars, will be pleased to learn that the railway . . . nearest the depot is to be immediately enclosed within capacious sheds, that will afford protection to their baggage, and constant shelter from the inclemency of the weather."[27]

Although this may have led most persons to expect the construction of a spacious and comfortable station, the reality surely proved disappointing. A former mayor of the city recalled the character of this building when he moved to Washington in 1839: "The Washington Branch of the Baltimore & Ohio Railroad . . . depot . . . was formed of a dwelling house which had been utilized for that purpose by removing the interior up to the second story. . . . This depot was located on the north side of Pennsylvania Avenue, about 150 feet from what was then called the Tiber."[28]

As the population of the city increased and travelers became more accustomed to this new form of transportation, the little station soon became inadequate, and in 1850 the Baltimore and Ohio agreed to remove its tracks west of New Jersey Avenue and build a new passenger station and terminal on the east side of that avenue between C and D streets. The following February the Washington *Intelligencer* reported rapid progress:

> It is worth a walk from any part of this city to the new Railroad Depot. . . . No one can view the buildings already erected and in progress, without being struck . . . with their capacity and the substantial and excellent workmanship. . . .
>
> It is expected the car house will be ready to receive the trains in the course of next month. In six or eight months all the buildings and works at this new and handsome depot will be completed.[29]

Although difficult to see on the map, a railroad also extends southward toward Alexandria from the Virginia side of Long Bridge. This was the Alexandria and Washington Railroad, chartered by Virginia in 1854. With congressional approval and subject to a proviso that no tracks be placed on Pennsylvania Avenue, the Washington municipal government authorized the line to lay its tracks along Maryland Avenue and then north on First Street to the B&O station.

The company proceeded to lay tracks that summer, but Congress, returning in December 1855, refused to let them be used, maintaining that tracks crossing Pennsylvania Avenue were the same as tracks on the avenue. During the prolonged controversy that ensued, the company defaulted on its bonds, thus putting

the issue to rest. However, the rails remained despite congressional authorization for the commissioners of public buildings to pull them up. During the Civil War their existence made it possible to run supply and troop trains from the north across the Potomac and on to Alexandria.[30]

Boschke's map also provides an unsurpassed record of the city's dispersed character. Only in an irregular band of development for several blocks north of Pennsylvania Avenue could one find concentrated development. Many of the streets beyond this built-up core existed solely on paper or as little better than wilderness trails. Certainly the neat geometry shown in this and other maps of Washington would not have been at all evident to persons attempting to traverse much of the outer city.

This detailed survey records conditions on the Mall as well. One can see that officials had carried out little of the Downing plan for this land. Only the grounds of the White House and those of the Smithsonian Institution followed his design, and all else lay unkempt and forgotten. One other structure occupied a tiny part of the Mall. This was the Columbia Armory, a building erected in 1855 to house the district militia. This stood on the south side of the Mall, slightly west of Sixth Street.

In tracing the development of the separate neighborhoods of Washington it is helpful to compare Boschke's detailed survey to the map of 1850 in folio 37 by James Keily, Tanner's map of 1836 in folio 25, and the map published in 1802 by Mathew Carey reproduced in folio 16. The only neighborhood not to have undergone substantial change in its general configuration is Georgetown.

The lithograph reproduced in folio 43 shows the appearance of this old and established section of the city as seen by an artist looking northwest across the valley of Rock Creek. In 1855 Edward Sachse published this print, an excellent example of the multistone, color lithography for which his Baltimore press became known. Sachse may also have been the artist, although that has not yet been determined. Whoever drew it did not need to add imaginary structures or finish with his lithographic crayon any incomplete buildings, because although Georgetown lacked any of the new buildings of the government, it had its own distinctive character of quiet dignity.

Many others before the artist had yielded to Georgetown's charms as they encountered them from the earliest days of Washington's existence. A few examples of such reactions by visitors well before and somewhat after the date of Sachse's lithograph can be found accompanying the view in this folio. Many other persons recording their opinions about the place commented approvingly on what is now Georgetown University, the oldest Catholic institution of higher learning in the United States, whose building Sachse's view shows on the skyline

27. Washington *Mirror*, 19 September 1835, as quoted in Topham, "First Railroad," 206.

28. Berret, "Address," 207.

29. Washington *Intelligencer*, 12 February 1851, as quoted in Topham, "First Railroad," 217–18. Topham reproduces two wood engravings and a photograph of the new station opposite pp. 180, 230, and 242. For another photograph of the station, long since demolished, see Reiff, *Washington Architecture*, 136 fig. 214.

30. Green, *Washington: Village and Capital*, 195–97.

above the warehouses and the commercial structures clustered along the river.[31]

Spanning the river at the left is the aqueduct bridge built in 1843 to provide a canal connection to Alexandria from the Chesapeake and Ohio Canal that Georgetown and Washington promoters planned to link the capital with the Midwest. Begun in 1828, it took more than two decades to reach its destination of Cumberland, Maryland, but the Baltimore and Ohio Railroad beat it to Cumberland by eight years. Although the C&O Canal carried a substantial amount of coal and other bulky freight, the Potomac route to the nation's interior could not survive competition with other cheaper and more direct means of transportation.[32]

Toward the right of the view one can see a cluster of brick buildings slanting up the hill to the left. They mark the alignment of the series of locks connecting the Washington Canal via the lower portion of Rock Creek with the channel of the C&O Canal, a segment of the system completed by September 1831. The Georgetown portion of the Boschke map in folio 42 shows this link. Boschke's map also shows that while nearly all earlier maps of Washington depict the Washington Canal as having two branches connecting to the Anacostia, at the time of his survey only the shorter one nearer the Navy Yard existed.

Although omitted from the portion of the map reproduced in folio 42, the Boschke map also included Alexandria, occupying the southern corner of the original boundaries of the District of Columbia as proclaimed by President Washington. By 1846, however, this town was no longer under federal jurisdiction. As one of the excerpts in folio 44 reveals, roughly one-third of the District of Columbia, including Alexandria, was retroceded to Virginia.[33]

Like Georgetown, Alexandria also existed before the establishment of Washington. Folio 17 presents its first printed town plan and descriptions by early visitors. Folio 44 continues with an impression recorded by a visitor in 1816 and a note on the town from a Virginia guide and history published in 1845. There is also an excerpt from Anthony Trollope's impressions of Alexandria on the eve of the Civil War as "melancholy and miserable" as well as the observations by a correspondent for the London *Times* near the end of the century, who found it a "finished American city" that had fallen into decay with dilapidated wharves and broken-windowed warehouses.

The first view of Alexandria that accompanies these passages of text suggests none of these problems that would befall the city. It is another of the unrivaled series of views that Edward Sachse of Baltimore produced of Washington and its surroundings. Indeed, this lithograph's imprint tells us that Sachse himself drew the scene and also put it on stone and printed it. However, accounts in Alexandria newspapers in 1853 and 1854 unmistakably identify one J. T. Palmatary as having drawn it—the same Palmatary that the print itself calls the publisher, a role that Sachse almost surely played!

Whatever the reason for this apparently innocent deception, the view itself is an interesting although not overwhelmingly attractive addition to Washington urban iconography. It, too, is exceedingly rare, known only by a unique impression in the Alexandria Public Library, one that the reproduction makes obvious is not in the best state of preservation.[34]

In drawing the city, Palmatary decided to look northeast from the outskirts of Alexandria toward the harbor along the Potomac River. In doing so, he may have saved himself a good deal of labor because the bulk of the city's buildings could be found there lining closely built-up streets. He was thus able to suggest their presence without the necessity of providing any details of their appearance. However, for the spectator the scene is neither particularly attractive nor does it tell us much about Alexandria except to furnish evidence that the houses facing the streets leading into town from the lower right were substantial in size and attractive in appearance.

More helpful in conveying the character of the city is the second view in the folio, a print issued when Alexandria figured importantly in the Civil War. The Virginia legislature passed an ordinance of secession from the Union just five days after the bombardment of Fort Sumter in Charleston harbor, and on 23 May, Virginians went to the polls to approve this action. That evening Federal soldiers set out for Alexandria, crossing the Potomac in steamers and landing early in the morning of 24 May just above the town beyond the wharves shown at the lower right of the view. Confederate forces withdrew without firing, and the town's capture took place with only one casualty.[35]

Charles Magnus published this lithograph in 1863, an image that he may actually have drawn himself rather than, as in so many other cases, depending on

31. The early development of the university from its founding in 1789 is traced in Daley, *Georgetown University*.

32. Limited service began on the canal in 1830 and did not officially close to commercial traffic until 1923. Today the canal serves as a tourist and recreational facility at the Chesapeake and Ohio Canal National Park.

33. For the events leading up to the retrocession in 1846, see Green, *Washington: Village and Capital*, 173–74.

34. The two vertical stains were caused by nitrous oxides in illuminating gas and other pollutants that entered the back of the print through cracks in the wide, flat boards often used by nineteenth-century framers. However, these stains and some general age toning cannot obscure completely what must have been the original clear colors of the print that came from the inks applied by Sachse to the surfaces of the several stones used to create this image.

35. Col. Elmer Ellsworth, commander of the New York Fire Zouaves, was shot by the owner of the Marshall House after the colonel pulled down the Confederate flag flying from the tavern's rooftop. Ellsworth thus apparently became the first soldier to fall for the Union in a military action. See Green, *Washington: Village and Capital*, 242–43; Somerville, *Washington Walked Here*, 179–84 (with a reproduction of a Currier and Ives lithograph recording Ellsworth's death); and Templeman, "In the Beginning . . . ," where on p. 44 there appears another contemporary illustration of the event by a Philadelphia publisher.

another artist to do his work or provide a view that he could pirate. His print presents Alexandria as it appeared while occupied by Federal troops. Like most Magnus lithographs, it was not particularly well printed, and its faint legend identifying places of military significance is almost impossible to read. It looks down on the harbor of Alexandria as the artist imagined its appearance from a vantage point looking southwest from the Potomac River.[36]

King Street leads inland at the center. A detachment of soldiers is marching toward the waterfront, and elsewhere one can see other evidence of the military occupation. Alexandria played an important role as a port of embarkation for Union forces and as a source of supplies for troops engaged in the Virginia peninsular campaign that began with Gen. George B. McClellan's departure from Alexandria in March 1862. Magnus's depiction of the crowded harbor suggests how busy this part of the city must have been. It was a level of maritime activity that declined abruptly with the end of hostilities and was never to resume.

It is this part of the modern city that contains most of the splendid colonial and early federal structures saved, restored, or reconstructed in what is surely one of America's most attractive centers of historic architecture. Particularly noteworthy are the two blocks on Prince Street (on the view, one block to the left of King Street) leading inland from the Potomac. There one finds handsome two- and three-story houses of great dignity and restrained beauty, each differing slightly from one another yet together comprising a unified streetscape unexcelled anywhere in the United States for true urban character.

This illustration of Alexandria is but one of the many views of Washington and its surroundings that artists produced during the Civil War. As in other periods of the city's history, they continued to record the face of Washington in printed views of all kinds. Their lithographs and wood engravings and the word pictures of journalists and other writers combine to present vivid images of a city in the chaos of wartime and during the turbulent era of Reconstruction that followed.

36. Because Magnus redrew and published as his own work about this time a view of similar style showing Annapolis, Maryland, that Edward Sachse had created a few years earlier, it is possible that there was also a Sachse view of Alexandria later than the one drawn by James Palmatary in 1854. None has been found, however, and this suggestion must be regarded as mere conjecture based on a knowledge of how Magnus operated.

Folio 36. Joseph Varnum in 1848 Emphasizes the Importance of the Mall, and an Old Resident Tells How It Appeared at the Time

*Varnum first points out the importance
of the city as a symbol of national unity.*

Notwithstanding the number who annually visit Washington on business or pleasure, there are few who rightly understand the relation in which that city stands to the general government, or appreciate its importance as the only spot where it is practically seen that, for national purposes, we are but one people. . . . It is only at Washington that one sees a whole district of country laid out expressly as a common centre of the nation, and a city planned solely with a view to the gratification of national pride, and for national convenience.

Everything that beautifies or adorns it, or in any manner affects its prosperity, should interest, to almost as great a degree, the citizen of the most distant State as the resident on the spot; for there are few who do not, in the course of their lives, expect to reside there for a longer or shorter period.

Varnum calls attention to the intended use of the Mall.

Every one who has gazed upon the landscape to be seen from the Western front of the capitol, must have observed the large tract of waste ground, between Pennsylvania and Maryland Avenues, extending from the front of the capitol to the Potomac, and terminating at a point opposite to the president's house. It is not generally known, even to the members of Congress, that this is the national mall—the very same ground which was to have formed the "grand avenue bordered with gardens, to lead to the monument of Washington, and connect the Congress garden with the president's park," by a suitable ornamental bridge, to be thrown over the Tiber, at its mouth.

He calls for the improvement of this part of the city.

Until this is improved, the two sections of the city, on different sides of the canal, will never look well, for the want of any appropriate connection; and not only this, but the capitol grounds must look half finished. Indeed, it is palpably absurd that, while thousands of dollars have been expended on the comparatively small space within the iron railing of the capitol, all beyond, comprising a fine view of the Potomac, and facilities for forming a serpentine river out of the Tiber, each has been left a mere cow-pasture; when a very small outlay in planting trees, and laying out walks and drives, would make it a second Champs-Elysees.

*He points out that similar conditions
can be found at the White House.*

At the president's house, the same kind of half-finished work is to be seen; the grounds, immediately under the windows of the mansion, being tastefully disposed, while the whole view in the distance is marred by the unsightly appearance of the low meadows, which extend to the river.

The writer advocates immediate action.

We have been thus particular in dwelling upon this part of the plan, and the necessity for improving, because no one can go there without noticing the mall; but comparatively few, even of the members of Congress, are aware that it belongs to the government, or what the design of the architect was; and we consider it important to urge the necessity of at once taking some action with regard to its completion, as the only thing, at present, wanting to give a finish to the capitol grounds, and connect the villages forming the city. (Varnum, *The Seat of Government*, I, 24–25)

Byron Sunderland describes how the Mall looked in 1852.

The Mall and the White Lot, lying much as they do today—disfigured then by no railroad tracks, but much more so by the nauseous canal—was then, as since, the scene of many a gathering and parade and pleasant drive, covered in many parts by stately forest trees and various undergrowths with intervening lawns and meadow lands with footpaths and carriage-ways running from the botanical gardens and conservatories down to the government pools by the river's brink. As I remember it in 1852–5 only three structures had been reared upon it: The government armory, where it stands to-day; the Smithsonian Institution, then recently completed . . . , and the Washington Monument then simply a huge stone stump about two hundred feet high and surrounded by piles of memorial stones intended for its walls, the gifts of individuals, societies, companies, states and foreign powers. (Byron Sunderland, "Washington as I First Knew It," 198–99)

Robert Smith Portrays the Capital City
at Mid-Century

No Washington view has more charm than this depiction of the city in 1850 when the Capitol still consisted of the original two wings and the connecting rotunda. The Mall lay empty—as it would for many years—except for the new Smithsonian Institution, where work began in the spring of the previous year, and the lower part of what would eventually become the Washington Monument. Smith decided to show both structures as he thought they would appear when finished.

At the right, midway between the Senate wing of the Capitol and the right-hand edge of the print, Smith drew the station of the Baltimore and Ohio Railroad. This line first established its station at the northwest corner of Second Street and Pennsylvania Avenue in 1835. Smith's view shows the new station at New Jersey Avenue and C Street, the point of arrival and departure for an increasing number of travelers as train travel ceased to be an adventure and came to be regarded as commonplace.

We look down on the Capitol with its handsome main entrance on the east, facing what most people expected would be the heavily populated part of the city. Because much of the land here fell into the hands of speculators who either held it off the market in the hope of spectacular profits or fell into bankruptcy and could not deliver clear title to their lots, growth took place west of the Capitol. The view shows most of the built-up area as it then existed.

Near the left side of the view, just visible to the left of the plume of smoke rising in front of the image of the Potomac River, is what appears to be an enormous electric fan four to five stories in height. This is the artist's version of a windmill located a short distance east of Sixth Street between F and G streets southwest.

View of Washington. Drawn by Robert P. Smith. Copyright by Robert P. Smith, 1850. 19 × 29¼ in. (48.4 × 74.6 cm.). Prints and Photographs, Library of Congress.

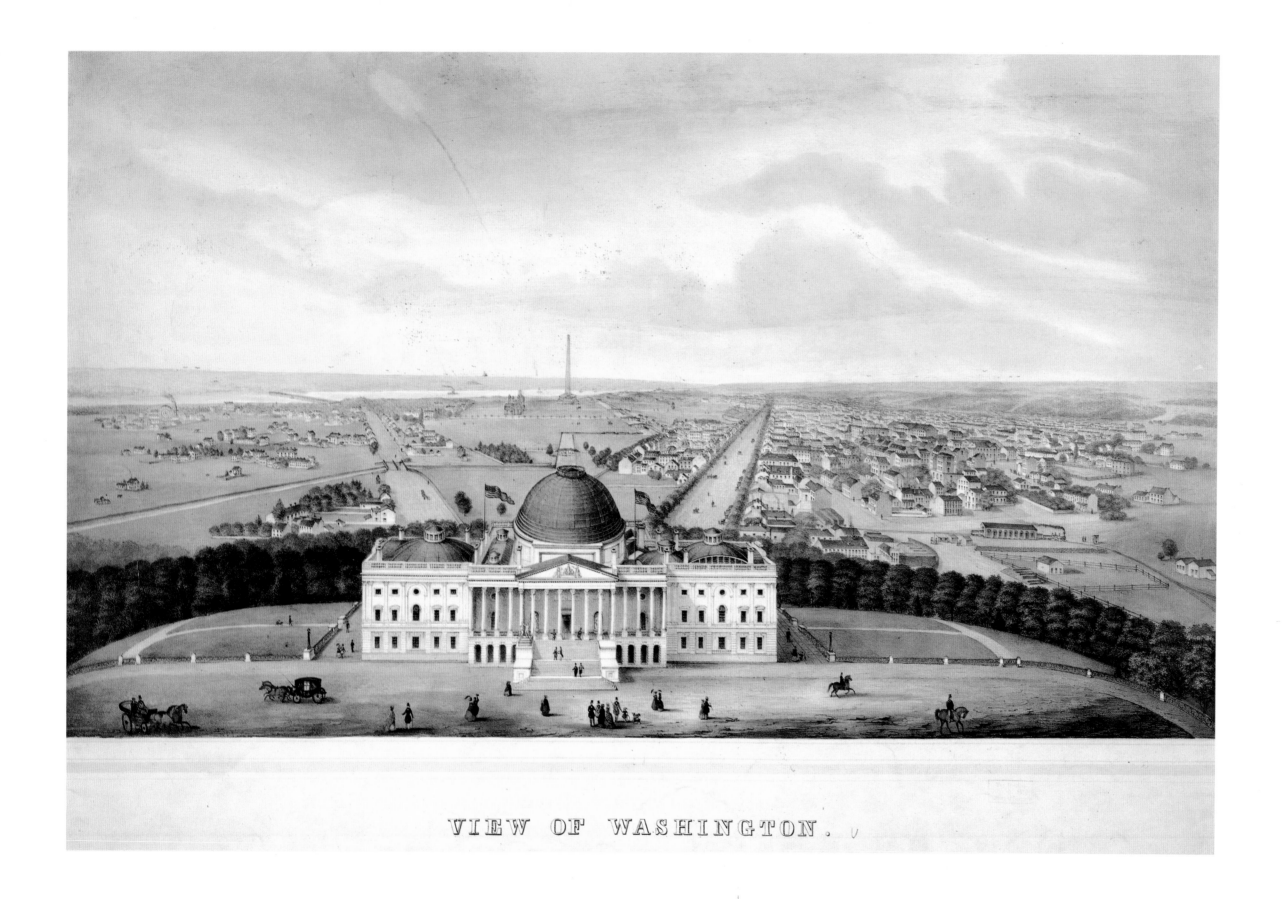

VIEW OF WASHINGTON.

Folio 37. An Old Resident of Washington Recalls Features of the City during 1852–55

Byron Sunderland tells how the city looked when he first saw it.

At that time it seemed like an overgrown, tattered village which some late hurricane had scattered along the river's edge. . . .

The plan of the city . . . had been chiefly laid out and the city proper lay within the limits of . . . Florida Avenue, Rock Creek, the Potomac and its Eastern Branch.

Within the city limits . . . scarcely one third of the space had been built up. At the Navy Yard stood the Marine Barracks and a cluster of village buildings. . . . And beyond these toward the east was the city workhouse and the "Congressional Cemetery." But the commerce with Bladensburg, which had been so lively on the Eastern Branch . . . had wholly ceased and the center of interest at the Navy Yard was the manufacture and trial of the Dahlgren guns, under the supervision of the Admiral himself. Between the Navy Yard and the east front of the Capitol large open spaces intervened, with here and there a clump of houses, or single structures with specific objects, such as the Marine Hospital.

The author remembers the importance of boarding houses.

Many of the buildings were private residences, or boarding houses, an industry . . . actively pursued . . . for at that time hardly a prominent man connected with the general government had a house of his own in the city. So on First Street east—now the Library grounds—stood a block of buildings for residences called the "Duff Green Row," and just to the north of them on the corner of A Street stood an ample structure of brick where Congress held its first sessions and which was afterwards made the prison of captured Confederates.

He describes conditions west of the Navy Yard.

From the Navy Yard westward along the Eastern Branch to Greenleaf's Point (so called from the man who owned it once) was a wild and broken stretch of land with here and there a hovel or a house—and the stouring of brick kilns—as in those days the chief industry there was brick-making—while that part of the city south of the Capitol and east of Four-and-a-half Street had scarcely yet been developed with equal pace to that of other parts.

At Greenleaf's Point the government buildings and general appearance were about the same as they are today—the Peni-

tentiary, the Arsenal, the officers' houses, the artillerymen's quarters, the grounds shaded by patriarchal trees and thickly set with cannon and cannon bases. This place was subsequently made memorable as the scene of the trial and execution of the conspirators for the murder of President Lincoln.

He provides details about the appearance of Southwest Washington and the canal.

For a considerable distance to the north of . . . [Greenleaf's] point and spreading along the Mall were the houses and structures of southwest Washington, then known as the "Island." It was made so by the construction of the Washington Canal formed in the days of Jefferson to connect the Eastern Branch with the Chesapeake and Ohio Canal at its terminus near the foot of Seventeenth Street, N.W. This was a stone-walled ditch varying in depth from ten to fifteen feet and in width from forty-five to one hundred and fifty feet. Starting from a point near the Navy Yard it met the Tiber in the Mall a little south of Pennsylvania Avenue and followed the course of that stream to its mouth at the foot of Seventeenth Street on the Potomac. Where it cut the streets, it was spanned by high, iron bridges. . . . But in 1853 it had ceased to be regarded as anything more than a huge sewer for the reception of the offal of the city.

He recalls the development north of the Mall.

Along the north side of the Mall, from Sixth to Fourteenth Streets, were numerous lumber yards, sawmills, planing mills, brass and iron foundries and coal yards, and between these and the avenue extending from Seventh to Ninth Streets the Center Market. . . . From this point outward to the northern limit the river-side sections of the city were sparsely covered with buildings. Rock Creek . . . spanned by one or two modest bridges, divided the municipalities of Washington and Georgetown as distinctly as if they had been located hundreds of miles apart. House-building had been chiefly pursued from Rock Creek on towards the Capitol and between Pennsylvania Avenue and M Streets, and, with the exception of here and there a single structure or tenement or a small cluster or clump of buildings, the entire space between M Street and the boundary was an open field. (Byron Sunderland, "Washington as I First Knew It," 195–98)

James Keily Maps the City in 1851

This survey of Washington locates major public buildings and reveals the extent of development in the city of the early 1850s as described by Byron Sunderland in the account accompanying this illustration. As earlier maps also recorded, built-up neighborhoods occupied only a small part of the vast geometric pattern of streets planned by L'Enfant sixty years earlier. Keily mapped the clusters of dwellings around the Navy Yard and the nearby marine barracks, at the river end of Maryland Avenue where it meets the Long Bridge from Virginia, in the vicinity of the White House and—the only area of real concentration—along Pennsylvania Avenue and extending northward several blocks beyond the Patent Office and Judiciary Square, the latter occupied by the City Hall, hospital, and jail.

Although this survey shows the Smithsonian Institution and the Washington Monument as the sole occupants of the Mall, neither was complete at the time. The Smithsonian was not finished until 1855, and the monument remained a stone stub until work resumed many years later. The Patent Office and the Post Office, too, had not been finished, and, as can be seen from the portion showing the vicinity of the White House, the west facade of the Treasury had not been built.

Southwest of the White House on grounds opening to the Potomac stood the Naval Observatory, built in 1844 and described two years later in Watterston's guide to Washington as on an elevation "about ninety feet above tide-water" and whose enclosed grounds were "to be laid out into walks, and ornamented with trees and shrubs, thus affording a beautiful promenade." Keily placed a small image of the observatory's elevation in the middle of the left-hand margin of his map. Other border and insert vignettes depict the other great public structures. These did not include the two occupying Greenleaf's Point: the government arsenal where the two rivers met and—a few hundred feet to the north—the penitentiary.

Map of the City of Washington D.C. Surveyed by James Keily. Published by Lloyd Van Derveer, Camden N. Jersey, 1851. Lithograph, 30 × 42 in. (76.2 × 106.5 cm.). Geography and Maps, Library of Congress.

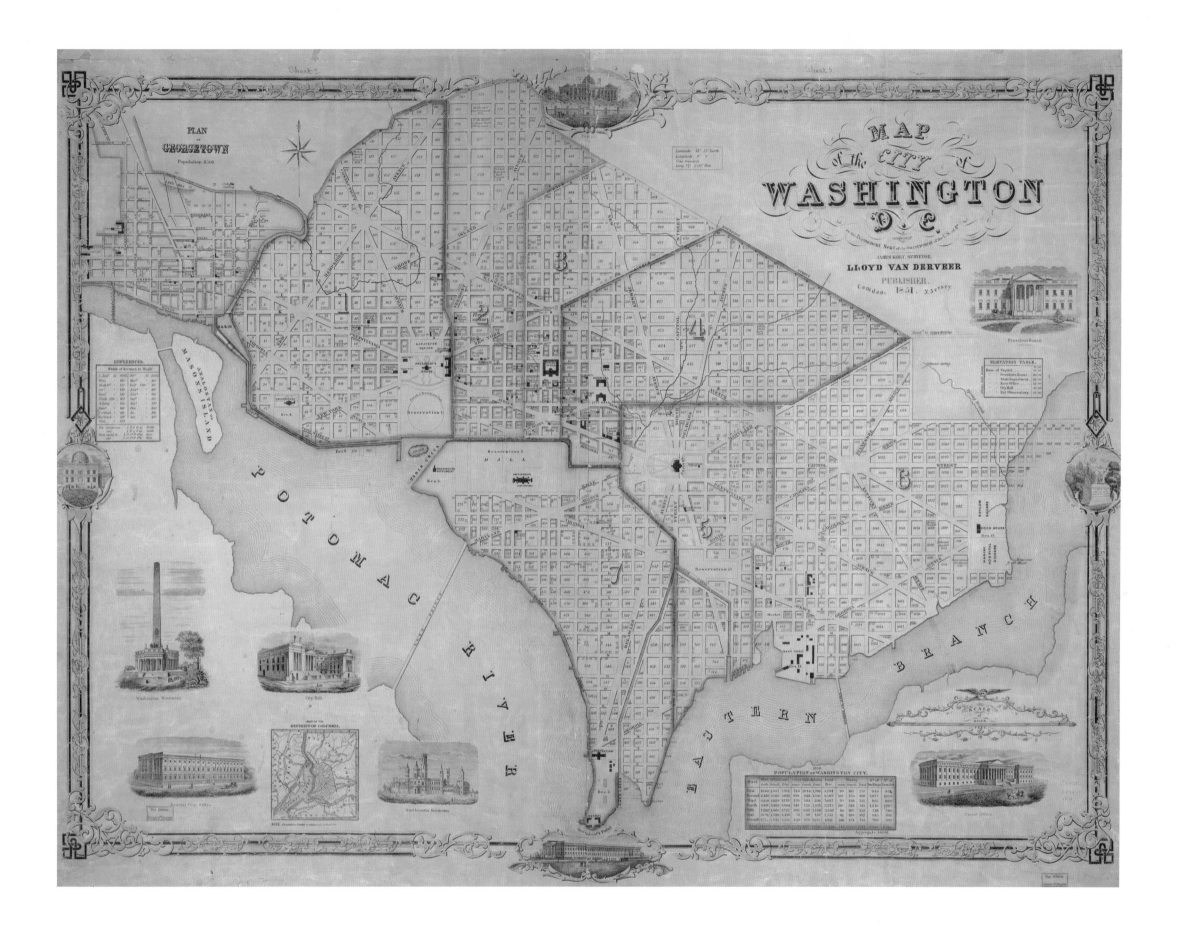

PLAN of GEORGETOWN
Population 8,500

MAP of the CITY of WASHINGTON D.C.

JAMES KEILY, SURVEYOR.
LLOYD VAN DERVEER
PUBLISHER.
Camden, 1851. N. Jersey.

President House.

REFERENCES.

ELEVATION TABLE.

POTOMAC RIVER

EASTERN BRANCH

MASONS ISLAND

Washington Monument.

City Hall.

General Post Office.

MAP OF THE DISTRICT OF COLUMBIA.

Smithsonian Institution.

POPULATION OF WASHINGTON CITY.

Patent Office.

Andrew Jackson Downing summarizes his objectives.

My object in this Plan has been three-fold: 1st To form a national Park, which should be an ornament to the Capital of the United States: 2nd To give an example of the natural style of Landscape Gardening which may have an influence on the general taste of the Country: 3rd To form a collection of all the trees that will grow in the climate of Washington, and by having these trees plainly labelled with their popular and scientific names, to form a public museum of living trees and shrubs where every person visiting Washington could become familiar with the habits and growth of all the hardy trees.

He begins his description of the design at the White House grounds.

The open Ground directly south of the president's House . . . I propose to keep . . . open, as a place for parade or military reviews, as well as public festivities or celebrations. A circular carriage-drive, 40 feet wide, and nearly a mile long, shaded by an avenue of Elms, surrounds the Parade, while a series of footpaths, 10 feet wide, winding through thickets of trees and shrubs, forms the boundary to this park, and would make an agreeable shaded promenade for pedestrians.

I propose to . . . place at the end of Pennsylvania Avenue a large and handsome Archway of marble . . . , which shall not only form the main entrance from the city to the whole of the proposed New Grounds, but shall also be one of the principal Architectural ornaments of the city.

He plans changes for the Washington Monument grounds.

I propose to cross the canal by a wire suspension bridge, sufficiently strong for carriages, which would permit vessels of moderate size to pass under it, and would be an ornamental feature in the grounds. I propose to plant Monument Park wholly with *American* trees, of large growth, disposed in open groups, so as to allow fine vistas of the Potomac River.

The designer describes the adjacent portion of the Mall.

We next come to what I term the Evergreen Garden. . . . I propose to collect here all the evergreens, both foreign and native, that will thrive in the climate of Washington. . . . It would be a particularly valuable feature in Washington, where the Winter and early Spring months, are those in which the City has its largest population.

The Fountain Park adjoins the Smithsonian grounds.

This park would be chiefly remarkable for its water features. The Fountain would be supplied from a basin in the Capitol. The pond or lake might either be formed from the overflow of this fountain, or from a filtering drain from the Canal. The earth that would be excavated to form this pond is needed to fill up low places now existing in this portion of the grounds.

Downing completes his design at the Botanic Garden.

This is the spot already selected for this purpose and containing three green-houses. It will probably at some future time, be filled with a collection of hardy plants. I have only shown how the carriage-drive should pass through it . . . and making the exit by a large gateway opposite the middle gate of the Capitol Grounds.

He points out some additional features of his design.

If this plan . . . is adopted, it would afford some of the most beautifully varied carriage-drives in the world.—These drives . . . , commencing at the Arch at the end of Pennsylvania Avenue and ending at the gate at the foot of the Capitol grounds— would cover an extent of between 4 and 5 miles in circuit. The foot paths . . . would give additional interest by showing the grounds more in detail.

The pleasing natural undulations of surface, where they occur, I propose to retain, instead of spending money in reducing them to a level. The surface of the Parks, generally, should be kept in grass or lawn, and mown by the *mowing machine* used in England.

Downing claims his plan would improve public taste.

A national Park like this, laid out and planted in a thorough manner, would exercise as much influence in the public taste as Mount Auburn Cemetary [*sic*] near Boston, has done. Though only twenty years have elapsed since that spot was laid out, the lesson there taught has been so largely influential that at the present moment the United States, while they have no public parks, are acknowledged to possess the finest rural cemeteries in the world. (A. J. Downing, "Explanatory Notes")

The Nation's Leading Landscape Designer Plans a Naturalistic Park for the Mall and the White House Grounds

In the spring of 1851 Andrew Jackson Downing submitted a plan for the Mall and the White House grounds as requested by President Millard Fillmore the previous year. Downing proposed to treat this huge open space in the middle of L'Enfant's great baroque city very much like the numerous private estates he had laid out in isolated, rural settings along the Hudson Valley.

Sinuous, curving drives and paths, informally arranged groups of trees and shrubs enclosing irregularly shaped expanses of grass, a great circular lawn south of the White House, and a more formal garden between the Smithsonian and the Washington Monument grounds combined to create a unified concept in place of the chaos that existed.

Downing regarded this as an opportunity to create a great, centrally located park within the bounds of a major city, a development he had vigorously advocated in the pages of his influential journal, the *Horticulturist.* He saw in the public grounds of Washington the opportunity to begin what he hoped would become a nationwide movement. He also believed that such a park would provide an educational experience for its visitors and that it would help to persuade others that the naturalistic style he favored in landscape design should be universally adopted.

However, Downing's tragic death in a steamboat fire on the Hudson brought his influence to an end, and only portions of the public grounds were landscaped in something like the style he had proposed.

Plan Showing Proposed Method of Laying Out the Public Grounds at Washington. Unsigned manuscript copy made for General N. Michler in 1867 of Andrew Jackson Downing's drawing of February 1851. Record Group 77, Civil Works File F116–1. Drawing, 36⅝ × 66 in. (93 × 167.9 cm.). Cartographic and Architectural Branch, National Archives.

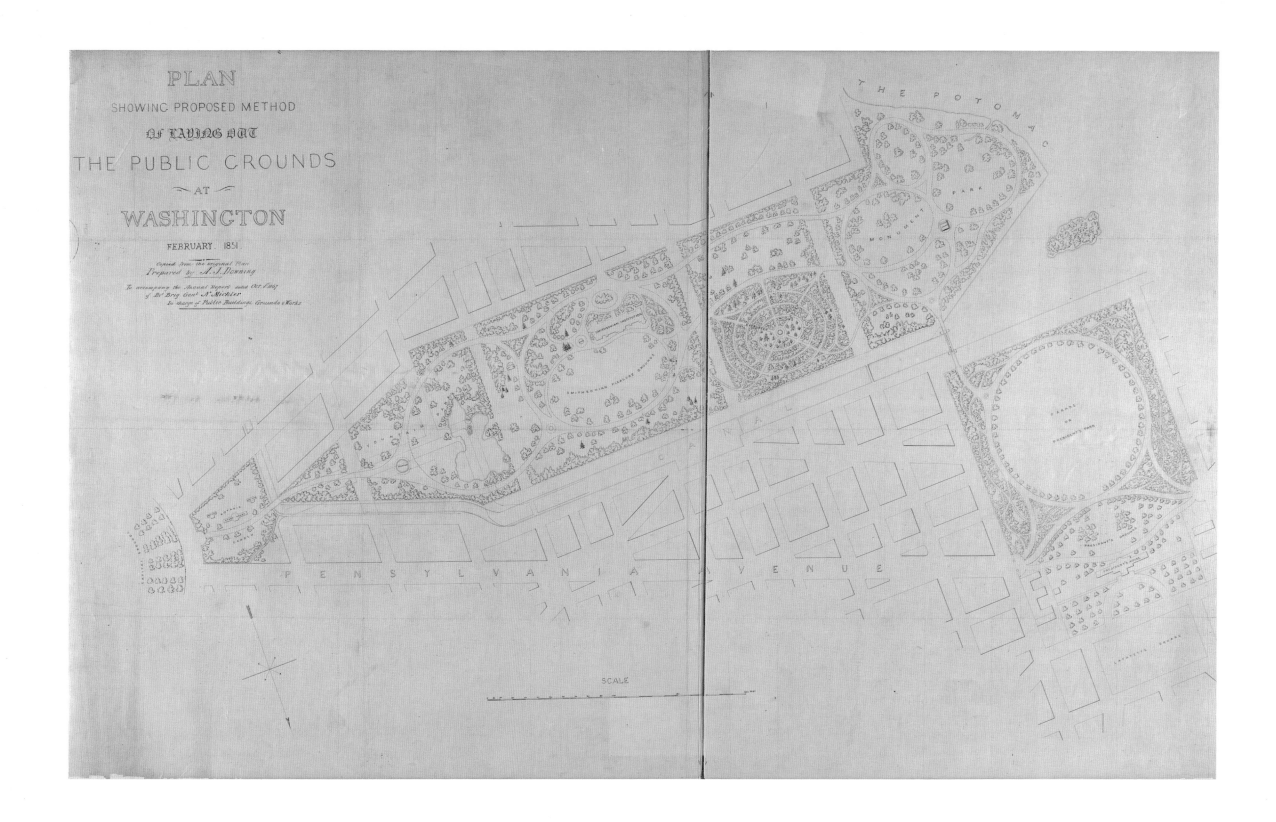

PLAN

SHOWING PROPOSED METHOD

OF LAYING OUT

THE PUBLIC GROUNDS

AT

WASHINGTON

FEBRUARY. 1851.

Copied from the original Plan
Prepared by. A.J.Downing

To accompany the Annual Report dated Oct. 1867
of Bt Brig Gen. N. Michler
In charge of Public Buildings, Grounds & Works

THE POTOMAC

SCALE

PENSYLVANIA AVENUE

127

A correspondent for Harper's New Monthly Magazine *in 1852 tells of new plans for the Mall.*

The open waste . . . between the Capitol, the president's house, and the Potomac, is about to be converted into a National Park, upon a plan proposed by Mr. Downing, to whom we already owe such a national debt of gratitude for the taste and elegance he has introduced into the architecture of country residences . . . , and the country can have no better guarantee of the excellency of the plan than to know that he conceived and is to execute it. The area contains about one hundred and fifty acres, and the principal entrance is to be through a superb marble gateway in the form of a triumphal arch, which is to stand at the western side of Pennsylvania Avenue, and which will form one of the most striking features that meets the eye of a stranger on entering the city. From this entrance a series of carriage drives, forty feet wide, crossing the canal by a suspension bridge, will lead, in graceful curved lines, beneath lofty shade trees, through the whole park to the gate at the other extremity. The carriage drive, going and returning, will give a circuit of between five and six miles. The park will include within its area both the Washington Monument and the Smithsonian Institution, which, with its fountains, pavilion, and summer-houses, will give it an architectural and picturesque interest, apart from its silvan and rural beauties.

He describes the designer's proposal for an arboretum.

Besides the most effective groupings of trees and shrubs, besides the smooth lawns, embowered walks, and artificial lakes, Mr. Downing proposes to introduce another and higher feature in the National Park; this is an *arboretum,* or scientific collection of trees, forming a kind of boundary plantation to the whole area, where will be assembled at least one specimen of all the trees and shrubs that will grow in the climate of Washington. It is especially his intention to plant specimens of every American tree that belongs to our widely extended silva; and each, marked with its popular and scientific name, and the part of the country from which it has been obtained, will thus be made to convey instruction in a form as novel as it is agreeable. To enliven the winter landscape the park will be largely planted with evergreens.

The project is to require several years for completion.

The transformation of this marshy and desolate waste into a National Park, has been already begun, but it will probably not be completed for four or five years to come—even with all the aid that the advanced science of the day affords for preparing the soil, and transplanting nearly full grown trees. (Lynch, "A Sketch of Washington City," 5–6)

A correspondent for the same journal seven years later reports that little has been accomplished.

In the article [published in 1852] the hope is expressed that in five or six years what is known as the Mall would be improved so as to furnish a park worthy of the capital of the great republic; but, alas! . . . in the melancholy death of Downing, America lost a man who had the wide vision to perceive and the genius to execute, a work such as would have done honor to the nation. Since his decease but little has been done toward beautifying the space between the Capitol and the Potomac which is set apart for the people's park. ("Washington in 1859," 8)

The artist of a view showing how Washington would look with the Downing plan realized writes to the architect of the Washington Monument.

I have almost finished the [view] of Washington and from present appearances it will be a very fine picture. When finished I shall send it on to Washington for a few days . . . and will let you know so that you may be able to see it. I have taken some liberties with the Monument which I was obliged to do in order to make it correspond with the rest of the picture. I think it will be the best drawing of the Monument (the best to display the architecture . . .) yet made. (Smith to Mills, 23 April 1852, in Smith, Letters)

A week later the artist writes a second letter.

My drawing of Washington will be finished by the middle of next week. I shall send it to Washington immediately so it will be there by the end of the week. I should like to have you see it. There may be something to alter about the Monument. The front of the National Theatre also shows very conspicuously in it. You can see the size and the alterations. I should be happy to receive also any other suggestions you might be pleased to make. (Smith to Mills, 30 April 1852, in Smith, Letters)

Benjamin Franklin Smith Carries out Downing's Plan for the Mall—on Paper

The first view in this folio and the three others derived from it allow one to see how the Mall would have looked if Downing's plan had been carried out. The artist was Benjamin Franklin Smith, Jr., one of four Smith brothers who published more than forty very large views of American cities in the decade ending in 1855. A year after issuing this sizable print, Smith drew a smaller version of the same scene. This extremely rare print resembles an etching more than a lithograph and is quite different in style and size than any other example of the firm's work. At about the same time, a rival publisher in New York, Charles Magnus, produced the two views illustrated on the last page of the folio. Magnus used images in many ways, and the first of the reproductions shows one of his most effective techniques. He printed the image on paper having wide black margins, colored the view, and enclosed it within gold borders. When framed it would have resembled an expensive glass-mounted print. The second version is the same but left uncolored and used on an illustrated lettersheet.

Washington, D.C. with Projected Improvements. Drawn and lithographed by B[enjamin] F[ranklin] Smith, Jr. Printed by F[rancis] Michelin, New York. Published by Smith and Jenkins, New York, 1852. Lithograph, 24⅝ × 42¹⁵⁄₁₆ in. (62.6 × 109.2 cm.). Prints and Photographs, Library of Congress.

Washington, D.C. Drawn by B[enjamin] F[ranklin] S[mith], Jr. Published by Smith & Jenkins, Lithographers and Engravers, Ocean Bank Building, 218 Fulton St., New York, 1853. Lithograph, 14¼ × 18¼ in. (36.2 × 46.3 cm.). Machen Collection, Historical Society of Washington, D.C.

Unsigned, untitled, and undated lithograph, probably by Charles Magnus. Mounted on black and with gold border. 4⅜ × 7½ in. (11.1 × 19 cm.). Kiplinger Collection.

Washington. D.C. Lettersheet view published by Charles Magnus & Cie. 12 Frankfort Street, N. York. Lithograph, 5 × 7½ in. (12.7 × 19 cm.). John W. Reps.

WASHINGTON, D.C.

Respectfully dedicated to the President and Citizens of the United States, by the publishers. Smith & Jenkins N.Y.

129

A journalist in 1859 for Harper's New Monthly Magazine *calls attention to Washington's new character and scolds English critics.*

During the last five years Washington has made amazing strides toward permanent grandeur; and already the "City of Magnificent Distances" has become more remarkable for its magnificence than for its distances. No longer are our legislators compelled to wade through a morass in order to pass from the Capitol to the White House. . . .

For a long period Washington expectancy was a laughingstock for every wandering Englishman, who chose to dish up our national peculiarities in a hash of guide-books, private journals, Munchausen stories collected in cars and stage-coaches, and confused recollections of three months devoted to diligent examination into the properties of sherry-cobblers, large oysters, and Catawba wine.

The writer describes the splendid view from the Capitol.

In the city, right under the spectator's gaze, are the Smithsonian Institution, the Washington Monument, the Patent-Office, the Observatory, the Treasury Department, and various beautiful edifices, while in Pennsylvania Avenue, from the Capitol to the White House, he sees the panorama of life reduced to a mimic scale.

He provides details of the Capitol's expansion.

The rotunda is 96 feet in diameter, and was surmounted by a dome . . . now demolished to make way for the noble construction which is to replace it. The new dome will rise 241 feet above the building, which is itself 69 feet in height, making 310 feet above the level of the ground. . . .

The extensions are connected with the old building by very fine corridors, each 44 feet in length, and 26 feet wide, with outside colonnades, consisting of four columns, making a total width of 56 feet. The new wings, which constitute the extension, are each 324 feet in length from east to west, and 152 feet wide from north to south, making the total length of the new building, comprising the old edifice, the corridors, and the width of the extension, 745 feet 8 inches. The corner stone of the south wing was laid with very imposing ceremonies by President Fillmore, on the 4th of July, 1851, and the occasion was made memorable by the delivery of an eloquent oration by Daniel Webster.

The author advocates enlarging the capital grounds as well.

The present inclosure around the Capitol contains only thirty-five acres, a space quite too contracted to permit the construction of the ornamental grounds necessary to do justice to a building which itself covers 62,000 square feet. The necessity for purchasing several squares of land adjoining the present grounds is so manifest, and has been so frequently admitted by the successive administrations, that persons owning the property necessary for the enlargement have from year to year delayed the erection of buildings, so that at this time the houses immediately surrounding the Capitol are of the commonest sort, with a few exceptions. During the thirty-fifth Congress an attempt was made to bring the negotiations to a close, but although well advanced when the adjournment occurred, the all-absorbing Kansas discussion occupied so much time that this important matter was again deferred. It is to be hoped that the new Congress about to assemble may determine to purchase the required land.

The writer believes Washington should serve as an example of great architecture and civic art.

It is due to the national dignity that Washington should be, if not a great city, a great centre of whatever is noble and beautiful in architecture and the fine arts. The president could live in a log cabin, and Congress might meet under a tent, in good weather, or perhaps your rigid economist would grant a large square brick building, such as is used for cotton factories. But the public intelligence and taste demand that the halls of legislation and the departments of Government shall be noble in construction and of the best materials; combining the greatest degree of comfort with the highest style of beauty. Any thing short of this would be derogatory to the national character, and for that reason we might almost say unconstitutional! Hence, the Capitol, the president's House, and the Departments must be marble palaces, adorned with statuary and painting, and surrounded by parks, and trees, and flowers, and fountains. There should be libraries, and picture-galleries, and museums, and whatever illustrates civilization in its highest walks. This is what people expect to find when they visit Washington, and they never fail to complain when they are in any respect disappointed. ("Washington in 1859," 1–2, 5, 7, 15)

Edward Sachse Records (and Anticipates) the Evolution of the Capitol

In 1852, Baltimore artist, printer, and publisher Edward Sachse issued the first of his several large lithographic views of Washington. It looked northwest with Pennsylvania Avenue and the Mall stretching off in the distance. Sachse accurately depicted many of the major public buildings, but he portrayed the Washington Monument as if the Robert Mills design had been followed and completed. He also used his imagination for the Capitol, drawing it as if the two huge new wings authorized in 1851 had been completed. The next two illustrations are smaller versions of Sachse's view. The earlier scene represents a collaboration of Sachse, Bohn, and Magnus, and the other one, issued by Magnus, was probably used for both a lettersheet version and one intended for framing. Both show the great cast-iron dome that marked the completion of the Capitol in its new and much enlarged form. The last illustration of the folio provides a more accurate representation of the Capitol at this time. It appeared in the leading English illustrated periodical in May 1861.

View of Washington. Drawn, lithographed, printed, and published by E. Sachse & Company, 3 North Liberty St., Baltimore. Lithograph, 20 × 27⅜ in. (50.8 × 69.7 cm.). Prints and Photographs, Library of Congress.

View of Washington City, D.C. Printed by E. Sachse & Co. 104 S. Charles St., Baltimore. Published by C[asimir] Bohn, 268 Penn. Ave., Washington, D.C., and Charles Magnus, 12 Frankfort St., N.Y., 1862. Lithograph, 9 × 16¼ in. (22.8 × 41.2 cm.). Kiplinger Collection.

View of the City of Washington with Capitol in Foreground. Printed by Charles Magnus, [N.Y.], 1865. Lithograph, 4¼ × 7½ in. (10.8 × 19 cm.). Kiplinger Collection.

Birdseye View of the City of Washington with Capitol in Foreground. Drawn or engraved by G[eorge] H[enry] Andrews. From *The Illustrated London News*, 25 May 1861. Wood engraving, 13¹¹/₁₆ × 19⅞ in. (34.8 × 50.5 cm.). Kiplinger Collection.

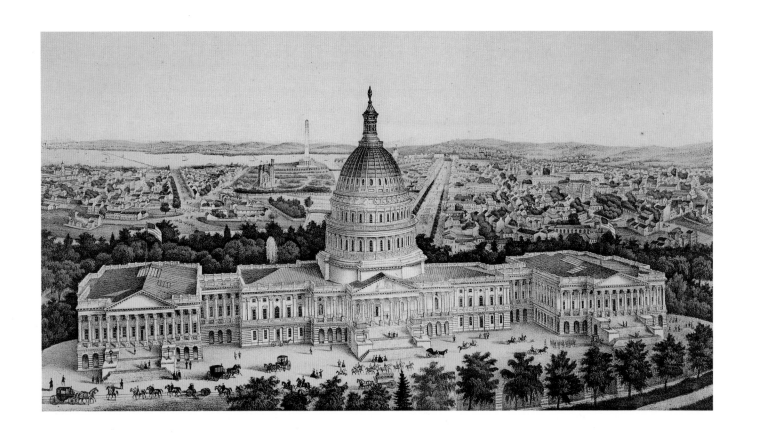

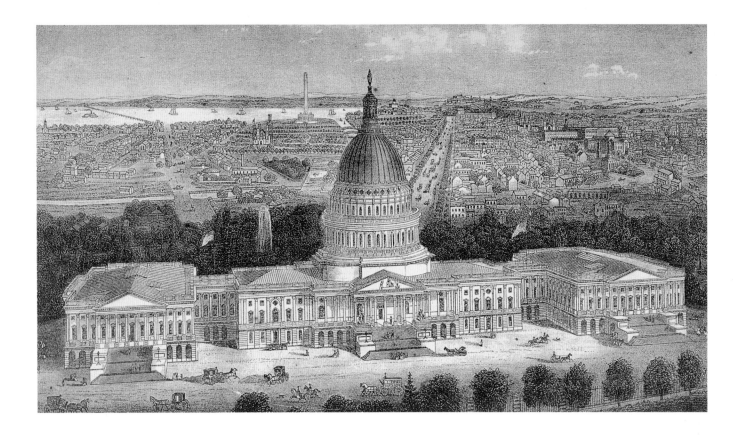

134

A correspondent for the Spectator *and* Macmillan's Magazine *tells of his reactions to Washington in 1862.*

To a stranger, Washington must be a quaint residence, even in ordinary days. Had it progressed at the rate of ordinary Northern cities, it would have been by this time one of the finest capitals of the world; as it is, it was built for a city of the future, and the future has not yet been realized. It is still, as it was once called, the city of magnificent distances. On two low hills, a couple of miles apart, stand the white marble palaces of the Houses of Congress and the Government Offices. At their feet stretches the grand Potomac, just too far off to be visible as a feature in the town; and across the low, broken, marshy valley between them runs the long, broad, irregular Pennsylvania Avenue, a second-hand Broadway out at elbows. On either side hosts of smaller streets branch out for short distances, ending abruptly in brick-fields or in the open country; and that is all. If the plan of the city had ever been carried out, the Capitol would have been the centre of a vast polygon, with streets branching out from it in every direction. But . . . the city sprawled out on one side only of the intended polygon, and left the Capitol stranded, so to speak, at the extremity of the town. So Washington has not the one merit of American architecture—symmetry. The whole place looks run up in a night, like the cardboard cities which Potemkin erected to gratify the eyes of his imperial mistress on her tour through Russia; and it is impossible to remove the impression that, when Congress is over, the whole place is taken down, and packed up again till wanted. . . . There are no commercial or manufacturing interests to induce merchants or capitalists to settle here. . . . There is nothing attractive about the place to make any one, not brought there by business, fix on it as a place of residence. With the exception of a few landowners who have estates in the neighbourhood, a score of lawyers connected with the Supreme Court, and a host of petty tradesmen and lodging-house keepers, there is nobody who looks on Washington as his home.

He compares Washington to an overgrown watering-place and calls it a detestable place to live.

The city, in fact, is an overgrown watering-place. The roads appear to have been marked out and then left uncompleted, and the pigs you see grubbing in the main thoroughfares seem in keeping with the place. . . . The private houses, handsome enough in themselves, are apparently stuck up anywhere the owner liked to build them, just as a travelling-van is perched on the first convenient spot that can be found for a night's lodging.

. . . When it rains, the streets are sloughs of liquid mud; and, by some miraculous peculiarity I could never get accounted for, even in the paved streets, the stones sink into the ground, and the mud oozes up between them. . . . I had many friends in Washington, and my recollection of the weeks I spent there is a very pleasant one; but, as a place of sojourn, Washington seems to me simply detestable. (Dicey, *Six Month in the Federal States*, 2:92–99)

Another writer for the London Telegraph *shares his English colleague's feelings.*

I have been endeavouring for a long time and at many different intervals, but with indifferent success, to determine in my mind what Washington is like. That it resembles in any way the metropolis of a great, powerful, and wealthy commonwealth can at once, without much fear of contradiction, be denied. It contains, certainly, some noble public buildings, but they are scattered far and wide, with all kinds of incongruous environments, producing upon the stranger a perplexed impression that the British Museum has suddenly migrated to the centre of an exhausted brickfield . . . or that St. Paul's Cathedral, washed quite white, and stuck upon stone stilts, has been transferred to the centre of the Libyan Desert, and called a Capitol.

The author looks on the city as an architectural conundrum and a practical joke.

Washington . . . is an architectural conundrum which nobody can guess, and in which I candidly believe there is no meaning. The Vitruviuses and Palladios of America have perpetrated a vast practical joke, and called it Washington. There is no beginning, no centre, and no end to Washington. It is the most "bogus" of towns—a shin-plaster in bricks and mortar, and with a delusive frontispiece of marble. . . . Washington will be, when completed, the most magnificent city on this side the Atlantic; and some of its edifices, as for instance the Post-Office, the Patent-Office, and the Treasury Buildings are really magnificent in proportions and design; but it is not quite begun yet. We are still at the soup and fish, and have not got to the first *entrée*. . . . Washington will be, I have no doubt, some day uproariously splendid; but at present it isn't anything. It is in the District of Columbia and the State of the Future. (Sala, *My Diary in America*, 2:68–70)

Edward Sachse Provides a Rare Glimpse of Washington East of the Capitol

In 1857 Edward Sachse drew and printed this view of Washington that Casimir Bohn published. Bohn had published other Sachse views before this, beginning in 1850. These handsome lithographs depicted Baltimore, Maryland, and Richmond, Norfolk, Charlottesville, and Lexington, Virginia. Bohn's name also appears as publisher on a single impression of Sachse's view of Washington in 1852.

One presumes that these joint efforts proved financially rewarding, but it seems unlikely that this view of Washington in 1857 would have appealed to many purchasers. It portrayed those neighborhoods where society did not live and where—apart from the Capitol—the only buildings of significance were those at the Navy Yard, whose images can be seen at the extreme right-hand side of the print, and the Alms House, also on the Anacostia but much farther east. Known in only a very few impressions, this view doubtless proved a financial failure.

It has some artistic shortcomings as well. Bulfinch's two small domes over the old House and Senate chambers have disappeared. Sachse shows the great cast-iron dome that replaced Bulfinch's copper-clad wooden structure as if complete, when in reality that event lay seven years in the future. Nevertheless, the lithograph displays with reasonable accuracy the appearance of the new House and Senate wings as occupied in December 1857 and January 1859, respectively, although work on their exteriors continued. Sachse's lithograph also shows the terrace with its great staircases leading down the slope toward the Mall.

Panoramic View of Washington City from the Dome of the Capitol, Looking East. Drawn and printed by E. Sachse & Co., Sun Iron Building, Baltimore, Md., Published by Casimir Bohn, Washington, D.C., 1857. Lithograph, 20¹/₁₆ × 32⁵/₁₆ in. (51 × 82.3 cm.). Prints and Photographs, Library of Congress.

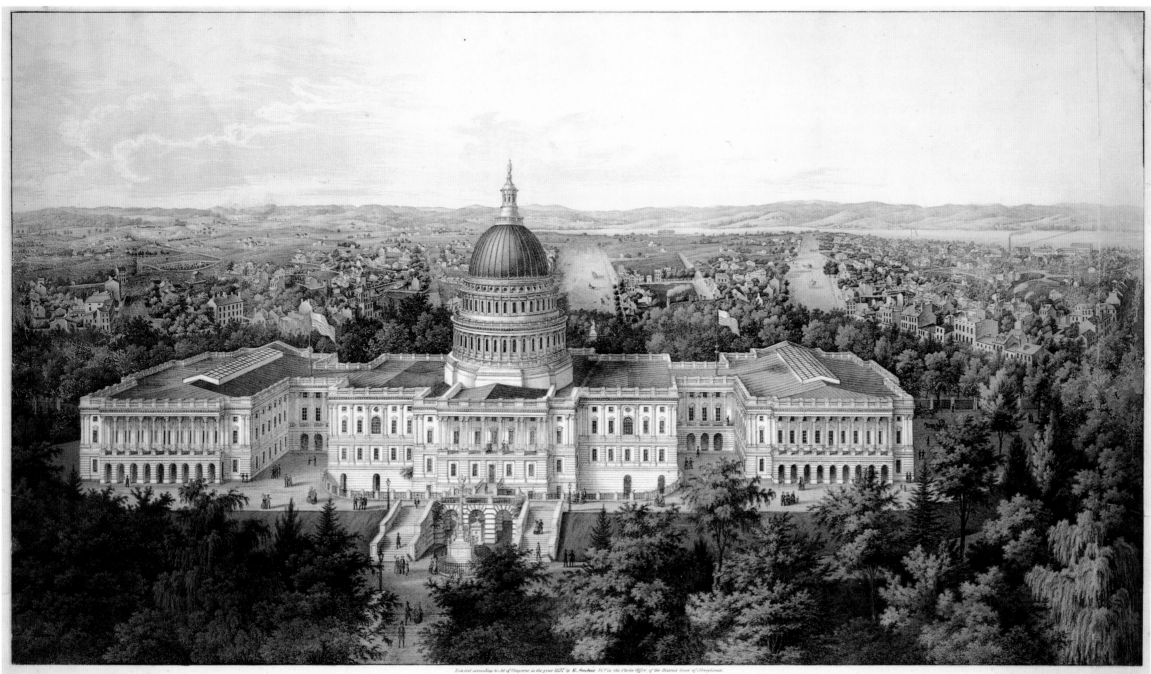

DRAWN FROM NATURE & PRINT. IN COLORS BY E.SACHSE & CO.

Entered according to Act of Congress in the year 1857 by E. Sachse & Co in the Clerks Office of the District Court of Maryland.

SUN IRON BUILDING BALTIMORE, MD.

PANORAMIC VIEW OF WASHINGTON CITY

FROM THE NEW DOME OF THE CAPITOL, LOOKING EAST.

Published by Casimir Bohn, Washington D.C.

The Atlantic Monthly *correspondent
examines a paradoxical city.*

Washington is the paradise of paradoxes,—a city of magnif-icent distances, but of still more magnificent discrepancies. Anything may be affirmed of it, every thing denied. What it seems to be it is not; and although it is getting to be what it never was, it must always remain what it now is. It might be called a city, if it were not alternately populous and uninhab-ited; and it would be a wide-spread village, if it were not a collection of hospitals for decayed or callow politicians. It is the hybernating-place of fashion, of intelligence, of vice,—a resort without the attractions of waters either mineral or salt, where there is no bathing and no springs, but drinking in abundance and gambling in any quantity. Defenceless, as regards walls, redoubts, moats, or other fortifications, it is nevertheless the Sevastopol of the Republic, against which the allied army of Contractors and Claim-Agents incessantly lay siege. It is a great, little, splendid, mean, extravagant, poverty-stricken bar-rack for soldiers of fortune and votaries of folly.

*The journal criticizes the plan with its numerous
radial streets and acute-angled intersections.*

Scattered helter-skelter over an immense surface, cut up into scalene triangles, the oddity of its plan makes Washington a succession of surprises which never fail to vex and astonish the stranger, be he ever so highly endowed as to the phrenological bump of locality. Depending upon the hap-hazard start the ignoramus may chance to make, any particular house or street is either nearer at hand or farther off than the ordinary human mind finds it agreeable to believe. The first duty of the new-comer is to teach his nether extremities to avoid instinctively the hypothenuse [*sic*] of the street-triangulation, and the last lesson the resident fails to learn is which of the shortcuts from point to point is the least lengthy. Beyond a doubt, the corners of the streets were constructed upon a cold and brutal calcula-tion of the greatest possible amount of oral sin which disap-pointed haste and irritated anxiety are capable of committing; nor is any relief to the tendency to profanity thus engendered afforded by the inexcusable nomenclature of the streets and avenues,—a nomenclature in which the resources of the alpha-bet, the arithmetic, the names of all the States of the Union, and the presidents as well, are exhausted with the most unsys-tematic profligacy.

The article points out some difficulties in finding one's way.

A man not gifted with supernatural acuteness, in striving to get from Brown's Hotel to the General Post-Office, turns a corner and suddenly finds himself nowhere, simply because he is everywhere,—being at the instant upon three separate streets and two distinct avenues. And, as a further consequence of the scalene arrangement of things, it happens that the stranger in Washington, however civic his birth and education may have been, is always unconsciously performing those military evolu-tions styled marching to the right or left oblique,—acquiring thereby, it is said, that obliquity of the moral vision which soon-er or later afflicts every human being who inhabits this strange, lop-sided city-village.

*The writer lists some of the paradoxes in which
the city is said to abound.*

Its public buildings are splendid, its private dwellings gener-ally squalid. The houses are low, the rents high; the streets are broad, the crossings narrow; the hacks are black, the horses white; the squares are triangles, except that of the Capitol, which is oval; and the water is so soft that it is hard to drink it, even with the admixture of alcohol. It has a Monument that will never be finished, a Capitol that is to have a dome, a Scien-tific Institute which does nothing but report the rise and fall of the thermometer, and two pieces of Equestrian Statuary which it would be a waste of time to criticize. It boasts a streamlet dignified with the name of the river Tiber. . . . It rains, hails, snows, blows, freezes, and melts in Washington, all in the space of twenty-four hours. After a fortnight of steady rain, the sun shines out, and in half an hour the streets are filled with clouds of dust.

*The author sees the future of the city
depending on the future of the nation.*

Notwithstanding all these impediments and disadvantages, Washington is progressing rapidly. It is fast becoming a large city, but it must always remain a deserted village in the sum-mer. Its destiny is that of the Union. It will be the greatest capital the world ever saw, or it will be "a parched place in the wilderness, a salt land and not inhabited," and "every one that passeth thereby shall be astonished and wag his head." ("Wash-ington City," 1–8)

Albert Boschke Surveys the District
of Columbia for a Map Published in 1861

By far the most detailed and accurate surveys of Washington were carried out in 1856–59 by Albert Boschke, a German working for the Coast Survey. Two maps resulted from his painstaking work: one of the city that Boschke published himself in 1857 and a mar-velously detailed engraving of the entire District of Columbia, dated 1861, whose plates the War Depart-ment seized, evidently for security reasons, after a few proof impressions had been made. It is the urban por-tion of that map that is reproduced here. No other source so clearly reveals the exact extent of building development that existed immediately before the Civil War changed forever the character of Washington from a collection of almost separate Southern villages to a far more physically cohesive and socially cosmopolitan political metropolis.

The number of totally undeveloped blocks and the amount of vacant land in others with fewer than a half-dozen structures strikes one immediately. Beyond a narrow fringe of buildings to the north and east of the capital and north of Rhode Island Avenue lay huge portions of the city that seemed to have been over-looked or forgotten. It is safe to conclude that the streets Boschke shows with such geometric precision in these areas did not exist except as surveyed lines on maps such as this. No wonder this half-built, dusty, sprawl-ing, and discontinuous place seemed strange, confus-ing, oppressively geometric, and paradoxical to the author of the accompanying article in the *Atlantic Month-ly*, a journal edited and published in Boston. To a cor-respondent from that city's closely built central neigh-borhoods and elegant townhouses, with its combination of meandering streets and rational grids and its self-image as the intellectual capital of America, nothing could have seemed more foreign than this raw, new center of American political power and authority.

Topographical Map of the District of Columbia, Surveyed in the Years 1856–59. Detail. Drawn by A[lbert] Boschke. Engraved by D[avid] McClelland, Washington, D.C. Published by D. McClelland, Blanchard & Mohn, Washington, D.C. 1861. Engraving, 40 × 40 in. (101.5 × 101.5 cm.). Geography and Maps, Library of Con-gress.

James Kent found the view from Georgetown attractive in 1793.

George-Town . . . is a pleasant Village situated on the waving Hills on the N. side of the Potomack & about 1 mile W. of the president's House in the City. . . . This Town has a fine view of the Potomack . . . & the Hills on the back of the Town . . . command a noble View of the Town, of the City of Washington & of the Potomack quite down to Alexandria. Mason's Island in front of the E. End of the Town adds much to the Beauty of the view. (Junior League of Washington, *City of Washington*, 37)

Georgetown favorably impresses John Melish in 1806.

I entered the town, which I found regularly laid out, and compactly built. It stands on the side of a hill, having a considerable descent to the river, of which it has a fine view. It contains about 300 houses, and 4500 inhabitants. Most of the houses are built of brick, and some of them are elegant. The public buildings are five places for public worship, an academy, and a bank. It is a place of considerable trade, which, in consequence of the rapid settlement of the back country, is yearly increasing. (Melish, *Travels*, 1:197)

Anne Royall liked Georgetown when she visited there in 1826.

Georgetown is . . . separated from Washington by a large creek, called Rock Creek, over which are thrown three bridges. Georgetown has a romantic appearance, being built mostly on hills. It rises up from the water's edge and spreads out in all directions. The streets, which are few and narrow, are paved with stone.

On the top of the hill, at the extremity of the town, stands the Georgetown College, two stately buildings of brick. It has a handsome square in front, planted with trees, and commands an extensive view of the Potomac, Washington, and the surrounding country. . . .

Besides the college, they have an academy, and a seminary for young ladies. . . . All denominations send their children to this seminary, which is much celebrated for its salutary regulations. ([Royall], *Sketches of History*, 179)

Frances Trollope in 1830 compliments the town on its appearance.

George Town . . . is a very pretty town, commanding a lovely view, of which the noble Potomac and the almost nobler

capitol, are the great features. The country rises into a beautiful line of hills behind Washington, which form a sort of undulating terrace on to George Town; this terrace is almost entirely occupied by a succession of gentlemen's seats. (Frances Trollope, *Domestic Manners of the Americans*, 2:16–17)

Charles Dickens writes in 1842 of Georgetown's attractions.

The heights of this neighbourhood, above the Potomac River, are very picturesque; and are free, I should conceive, from some of the insalubrities of Washington. The air, at that elevation, was quite cool and refreshing, when in the city it was burning hot. (Dickens, *American Notes*, 123)

In 1861 J. G. Kohl admired the view to and from Georgetown.

The skirts of the wooded range of Georgetown, in the distance enclosing Washington, which lies in the heart of a plain, are adorned by a number of very pretty country-houses and gardens, in which we spent many a pleasant hour. With most pleasure, however, I visited the Jesuit college enthroned on those heights. . . .

The prospect from the towers of the building is as fine as that enjoyed from the terrace of the Capitol. You can overlook thence the city, with its wholly or half-finished palaces and monuments extending at its feet, and in the background the green skirt of the woods forming a semicircle to the north. (Kohl, "The Federal City of Washington," 392–93)

In 1872 an observer finds Georgetown picturesque but unimportant commercially.

Its former commercial bustle has departed from it [but] it is . . . a more picturesque place than Washington; built mostly on hills which rise above the Potomac, affording really beautiful views of the river and its umbrageous shores. The town has many of those substantial old red-brick mansions where long ago dwelt the political and social aristocracy, and which are to be found in all Virginia and Maryland towns of a century's age, surrounded often with high brick walls, approached by winding and shaded avenues, sometimes with high-pillared porticos, and having, over the doors and windows, some attempt at modest sculptured ornamentation. (Towle, "Washington and its Vicinity," 570–71)

Edward Sachse Displays the Beauty of Georgetown

In 1855 Edward Sachse, the Baltimore artist, lithographer, printer, and publisher, issued one of the most appealing city views of the many he produced during his quarter-century career in America. Looking toward Georgetown from a point southeast of the mouth of Rock Creek, the artist—perhaps Sachse himself—drew the attractive scene reproduced here.

At his Baltimore printing plant on Liberty Street, Sachse skillfully used several lithographic stones, each inked with the appropriate color, to reproduce the colors of early fall in the wooded slopes of the town. Few American printers matched Sachse's skills in color lithography. He doubtless learned these as an apprentice and then as a small-scale publisher of views in his native Silesian town of Görlitz, which he left to come to America, probably in 1848.

A reporter for the first issue of the New York *Illustrated News* described the little city of Georgetown for the journal's readers on 8 January 1853 after seeing the town from a vantage point that must have been similar or identical to that used by the artist of Sachse's attractively colored lithograph: "The range of hills well termed 'Georgetown Heights,' overhang the town of that name, which is built, as it were, upon ranges of small precipices, increasing in height until they find shelter under the towering hills behind them. The noble aqueduct of the Chesapeake and Ohio canal, with its many massive piers, terminates the river view on that side. Still further to the right, perched high among the 'heights' of Georgetown, is seen the venerable college of the Jesuits, where the Superior of the order in the United States has resided almost since the organization of the government."

View of Georgetown D.C. Unsigned view lithographed, printed, and published by E. Sachse & Co., N[umber] 3 N. Liberty St., Baltimore, [1855]. Lithograph, 18⁹⁄₁₆ × 26³⁄₄ in. (47.2 × 68 cm.). Prints and Photographs, Library of Congress.

Folio 44. Alexandria and the Rest of the Capital Territory West of the Potomac Leave the District of Columbia

*David Warden describes Alexandria
as a prosperous town when he saw it in 1816.*

The town . . . is pleasantly situated on the Virginia, or west side of the river Potomac, at the distance of six miles, in a southern direction, from Washington. . . . The houses are of a neat construction. Those erected at the expence of the public are an Episcopal church, an academy, court-house, bank, and jail. . . . The warehouses and wharfs are very commodious. Vessels of 500 tons . . . have sailed from this port with 1200 hogsheads of tobacco on board. (Warden, *Account of the United States*, 3:215)

Anne Royall describes the city's houses in 1826.

The houses in Alexandria are built of brick mostly, three stories high, they are comfortable and convenient, but not very splendid. Instead of [a] wooden cornice, the top of the house walls are ornamented with from one to three rows of point brick, (in the form of a wedge;) these brick[s] project beyond the wall, and gives it a handsome appearance; most of the houses are covered with slate and tile. ([Royall], *Sketches of History*, 108)

A Virginia history and guide of 1845 praises the site.

The town is situated in the bottom of a valley, which to the eye of an observer is terminated in every direction by lofty and verdant hills. To the north he sees the city of Washington.—the capitol with its beautiful columns, white walls, and towering dome, forming a most conspicuous object. (Henry Howe, *Historical Collections of Virginia*, 513)

A journalist tells of the retrocession to Virginia.

In the year 1846, in the Presidency of Mr. Polk, the people of Alexandria, who were then sanguine as to their trade, railroads, security of slaves, and superior navigation, voted by more than two-thirds majority to leave the District of Columbia. . . . Already there are symptoms of regret for a secession which in fifteen years was imitated by every thing south of the Potomac, and the Northern man can see in that impetuous little city the grass growing in the streets—the first civic grass between the North Star and Mount Vernon. (Townsend, "New Washington," 307)

Anthony Trollope sees Alexandria in the winter of 1861–62.

We landed . . . at Alexandria, and saw as melancholy and miserable a town as the mind of man can conceive. Its ordinary male population, counting by the voters, is 1500, and of these 700 were in the southern army. The place had been made a hospital for northern soldiers, and no doubt the site for that purpose had been well chosen. . . . The people were all secessionists, but the town was held by the northern party. Through the lines, into Virginia, they could not go at all. Up to Washington they could not go without a military pass, not to be obtained without some cause given. All trade was at an end. In no town at that time was trade very flourishing; but here it was killed altogether,—except that absolutely necessary trade of bread. Who would buy boots or coats, or want new saddles, or waste money on books, in such days as these, in such a town as Alexandria? (Anthony Trollope, *North America*, 322)

The correspondent for the London Times
views Alexandria in 1887.

The old town of Alexandria . . . , formerly a place of considerable commercial importance . . . is sleepy and falling into decay—a "finished American city" of about 10,000 people, who cherish many memories of Washington, who came into town frequently on business and attended church there. The wharves seem to be declining into dilapidation, the storehouses have broken windows, and negroes loll idly on the docks, where little goes on. A propeller, a ferry-boat, a couple of tugs, and a half-dozen smaller craft represented the active commerce of Alexandria. Its people, who live in rows of comfortable-looking brick houses, built on the gently ascending slope from the river, have a pretty view over the water at the greater city, stretching all across the scene, with the Washington Monument and the Capitol dome rising high above, these being the landmarks for all the country round. Back in the town is seen the modest little steeple of Christ Church, where Washington was a member of the Parish vestry, while nearer the river is the "Carey House," with its yellow walls and dormer windows, where Washington, in 1755 received his first commission as aide to the British General Braddock with the rank of Major. (*A Visit to the States*, 223–24)

*James Palmatary in 1854 and Charles Magnus
in 1863 Draw Views of Alexandria*

Late in the summer of 1853 the *Alexandria Gazette and Virginia Advertiser* informed its readers that "Mr. J. T. Palmatary, a professor in drawing, is now on a visit to our city, with the intention of getting up a view of it." On 2 January 1854 the newspaper announced that Alexandrians could find the "View of Alexandria taken lately by J. Palmatary, for sale at Richards' Fancy Store." Although these newspaper accounts tell us that Palmatary was the artist, the imprint on the lithograph identifies him as the publisher. Almost certainly the real publisher (and printer) was the Baltimore company headed by Edward Sachse, confusingly identified on the lithograph as artist as well as printer. The artist looked south to the Potomac from a point several blocks inland at what must have been the edge of the developed portion of the little city. It shows a solidly built community composed mainly of brick structures. They stood at or near the lines of the grid streets, whose boundaries were marked by white picket fences. Rear gardens and street trees softened the hard lines of streets and structures to produce a townscape of grace and charm.

Charles Magnus displays Alexandria as seen from the opposite direction. His view looks up King Street leading from the busy waterfront through the center of town. His scene suggests the importance of this port for Union forces during the Civil War. Supplies and troops moved to and from the city throughout the conflict, but after the war, shipping declined, and Alexandria resumed its role as a retail and residential community. Many of its fine eighteenth- and early nineteenth-century houses shown on this view still survive.

View of Alexandria Va. Drawn from nature & Printed in colors by E. Sachse & Co., Baltimore Md., Published by J. T. Palmatary, [1854]. Lithograph, 20 × 30⅝ in. (50.8 × 77.9 cm.). Public Library, Alexandria, Virginia.

Birds Eye View of Alexandria, Va. Published by Chas. Magnus, 12 Frankfort St., New York, & 520 7th St., Washington, D.C., 1863. Lithograph, 14³⁄₁₆ × 23³⁄₁₆ in. (36.1 × 59 cm.). Prints and Photographs, Library of Congress.

6 Washington at War and in the Early Years of Reconstruction

ON the eve of the Civil War, Washington lay virtually defenseless, little changed in this respect since the city's capture by the British in the War of 1812. The occupation of Alexandria in May 1861, described in the previous chapter, was part of a military operation designed to discourage a Virginia-based attack. Two other Union detachments crossed the Potomac by the Long Bridge and the Aqueduct Bridge and began to fortify Arlington Heights on the Virginia side of the river.

After their stunning defeat of the Union army on 21 July at the battle of Bull Run, Confederate forces—had they seized the opportunity—could have marched into Washington almost without opposition. As a result, the army built several forts to guard the approaches to the city, and in the fall of 1862 Secretary of War Edwin Stanton appointed a commission to plan a coordinated system of forts extending around the city and its immediate surroundings. It is this defensive system of sixty-eight forts and batteries in a thirty-seven-mile ring that the map in folio 45 displays and the passages of text describe.[1]

Only once did the Confederates attack this ring of forts. In a surprise raid in July 1864 Gen. Jubal A. Early led his Confederate troops to within five miles of the Capitol and was stopped only by the timely arrival at Fort Stevens of troops sent by Gen. U. S. Grant from Petersburg. It was here that President Lincoln watched the battle, part of the time standing unprotected on the top of a parapet to the dismay and against the advice of the commanding officer, Gen. Horatio G. Wright. Wright finally and hesitantly ordered the commander-in-chief to climb down from a spot so dangerous that a medical officer standing near him had been wounded by a rifle shot.[2]

Throughout the war, artists and illustrators produced a large number of views showing the city from a variety of perspectives. Three of these appear in folio 46, the first being a very large and rare lithograph drawn and published by John Bachmann in 1862. Bachmann was an experienced urban viewmaker, probably from Germany, who began drawing and publishing city views in America at mid-century. Among his several beautifully drawn and skillfully printed bird's-eye lithographs were those of such major cities as New York, Boston, and New Orleans.[3]

In this highly detailed view of Washington, Bachmann looked down on the city from the north, a viewpoint used by few other artists of the capital. Bachmann followed Sachse's practice of "completing" the Washington Monument. He even added a dome to City Hall, a long-abandoned feature of its original plan four decades earlier. As so embellished, the building appears prominently in the left foreground of the print. In the center foreground Bachmann shows the Patent Office as it would look with its final wing completed five years after Bachmann published his view.

Beyond, one can see northern wing of the Post Office. Here, too, Bachmann anticipated the future, for the structure was not completed until 1866. For some reason the artist did not follow this same practice in depicting the Treasury. Here Bachmann correctly rendered the still incomplete building abutting the old State Department at its north end. His portrayal of the White House is curious: the portico on the north side of the White House looks like an entire wing of the building, and the semicircular projection on the south facade seems much larger than reality.

Nevertheless, these exaggerations can be overlooked because of the view's other merits. It provides a glimpse of the buildings on the south side of Pennsylvania Avenue and the congested conditions in the triangular area to the south. It displays the domestic character of those substantial portions of the city between the concentrations of public buildings. One can also see clearly the sparsely developed character of the area south of the Capitol and the vast expanses of open land on the Virginia side of the Potomac.

The other two illustrations in folio 46 also show the city from high-level viewpoints. The first displays the familiar elements and major public buildings of

1. This map was printed by one of the towering figures in American lithography, Julius Bien, who came to the United States from Germany at mid-century and established his shop in New York City. It was there that he prepared the lithographic version of John James Audubon's *The Birds of America*, a project begun in 1858 but never completed, possibly because of the Civil War. Bien also printed many maps and a variety of other subjects in his shop that at one time employed as many as 200 persons. See Marzio, *Mr. Audubon and Mr. Bien*, and Marzio, *The Democratic Art*.

2. For the establishment of the fortification system, illustrations of a few of the forts, and accounts of their only real use in combat, see Cox, "Defenses of Washington," and Cooling, "Defending Washington." See also a description by the engineering officer in charge of the forts: Barnard, "Defenses of Washington." The definitive study of the subject is Cooling and Owen, *Mr. Lincoln's Forts*.

3. Such biographical information about Bachmann as I have been able to find is summarized in my note about him in Reps, *Views and Viewmakers*, 160–61.

Washington that the previous chapters have discussed. The second encompasses an area far larger than the city, its horizon extending south and west many miles beyond Washington to show the Virginia and Maryland terrain over which troops would move to and from some of the major battles of the war.

Both illustrations were done in the medium of wood engraving and appeared in *Harper's Weekly*, one of the American illustrated periodicals that had recently begun publication and that were widely read throughout the country. Their editors soon realized that artists were as important as journalists and that wood engravings made from their sketches made their publications far more attractive to general readers. A brief description of this process of reproductive image making can be found in appendix B.

Although the Civil War caused no dramatic changes in the plan of Washington or added to the stock of public buildings, the city acquired an entirely new character, a metamorphosis alluded to in one of the passages of folio 46 written by Noah Brooks, who, among many other journalists and along with diplomats, public officials, military personnel, and residents, provided accounts of Washington during the Civil War. None offered their readers more perceptive impressions than Brooks, a special correspondent for the *Sacramento Daily Union*.

Beginning in December 1862, this energetic and perceptive observer sent more than 250 dispatches to his paper during the two and one-half years he spent in the city. Although Brooks concentrated on congressional activities, decisions of the Supreme Court, and military campaigns, he also included notes about physical conditions in the capital. His early training in Boston as a landscape artist sharpened his eye in noting details about the urban environment, and his long experience as a journalist provided the ability to convey what he observed in succinct and vivid prose.[4]

In a dispatch to his paper written on 9 October 1863, Brooks reported that Washington was enjoying a building boom despite very high prices for materials. He explained that "the incentive to build is certainly very great, for . . . the demand for room is truly unprecedented." As a result he predicted that "the 'magnificent distances' of the national village will be pretty well filled up if the demand for houses continues much longer."

Throughout the city he found "that every street has its piles of brick, stone, marble, and iron encumbering the ground and stopping the way preparatory to the erection of dwellings." Brooks claimed that everywhere he heard "the sound of the hammer, the ringing of the trowel, and calls for 'more mort'" resounding "in every direction."

Brooks noted that "heretofore Washington people have not been willing to risk much money in building," explaining that "before the war dwellings and hotels were vacant half of the year." Nor did much building take place in the first year of the war because many owners feared a Confederate victory, or as Brooks put it: "Real estate owners have hesitated to build houses which Jeb Stuart might burn or Jeff Davis confiscate."

By the end of 1863, however, "that feeling has vanished before the moral certainty that the end of the rebellion and the safety of the capital are secure." Brooks foresaw what might then occur:

> Before another year shall have passed buildings for rent will be plentiful enough in Washington. Whether there will not be a great collapse in business in this now bustling city when the war shall be over is not doubtful. The trades and avocations which an expensive war has called into existence and centered here will find their occupations gone. The hosts of interests which now depend upon the army for support will vanish from Washington, and all of those who now supply with the necessaries of life the increased civil and military forces here will go with them.

New houses were not the only buildings under construction. The New York banking company of Jay Cooke had a large office under way on Fifteenth Street, and across the street, work still proceeded on the Treasury extension. Brooks also reported that renovations had been made in the Capitol, ornaments were being installed on the cast-iron dome, the portico for the Senate wing was nearing completion, and the sculptural composition for its pediment by Thomas Crawford had already been put in place. His description of this work is both informative and amusing.[5]

Brooks, along with countless others, attended the ceremony on 2 December 1863 when the statue of Freedom was at last hoisted into place at the top of the Capitol dome:

> Precisely at noon the last section of the bronze statue, consisting of the head and shoulders of the incomplete goddess, left the mass of material at the foot of the dome, and, drawn upward by a slender wire cable and serenely smiling upon the crowd below, the majestic face rose slowly toward the scaffolding around the statue. It passed into the timbered chaos above and soon emerged therefrom, swung lightly over the gleaming torso below it, then calmly settled into its place.[6]

Readers of the *Sacramento Daily Union* learned about other real or proposed

---

4. My knowledge of Brooks comes from the editor's introduction, pp. 7–20, in Staudenraus, *Mr. Lincoln's Washington*.

5. "The statuary . . . is said to be illustrative of the progress of America. In the center is the Genius of America, a nice young woman stroking the head of a rampant eagle and gazing intently on the top of an immense sycamore tree which is just in front of the portico. On her left is a lusty backwoodsman chopping down a tree. Next, an Indian boy with spoils of the chase. Beyond him is a meditative Indian . . . , while a sorrowful squaw and an infant Pah Utah sitting at the head of an Indian grave complete that side of the pedimental procession. On the right of the central figure is a militia general 'a-drawin' of his sword,' a Boston-looking wholesale dry goods dealer sitting on a cotton bale, a pedagogue fingering a terrestrial globe and teaching the young, two young ideas coming up to be taught to shoot, and a very clean-looking blacksmith . . . with a sheaf of wheat and an anchor (a portion of the harvest of the sea, I suppose) at his feet. Which way America is supposed to progress in this extraordinary collection of statuary does not appear." The text of this dispatch of 9 October 1863 is found in ibid., 238–43.

6. Ibid., 265. See also Brooks's dispatch of 25

events affecting the physical fabric of Washington life. On 5 April 1864 Brooks told them that since the White House was "in an unhealthy location, is inadequate and inconvenient for its purpose, and is now crowded into an undesirable portion of the city by the growth of the adjacent neighborhood," the Senate Committee on Public Buildings and Grounds was considering a proposal to build "a new establishment, handsome, spacious and modern in its appurtenances" for presidential use. For this purpose a site was to be selected in "an airy and quiet suburb of the city."[7]

Brooks also described for his California readers the fire that on 24 January 1865 destroyed much of the Smithsonian Institution. At first a "dense cloud of smoke" enveloped the building, and then flames "burst from all of the upper portions of the towers," causing a roaring noise "like the blasts of a great furnace." His dispatch blamed the incompetence of the Washington Fire Department for the extent of the disaster, complaining that "the miserably inefficient fire department of the national capital [was] unusually conspicuous for its valuelessness."[8]

The views in folio 47 all were published before that unhappy event, and the image of the Smithsonian appears unaltered. The first is yet another lithograph of Washington from the firm of Edward Sachse. At the top Sachse placed four segments of a novel 360-degree panorama of Washington, each looking toward one of the cardinal points of the compass. In thirty-one additional vignettes Sachse presented views of important buildings, interior spaces, and monuments of the city as well as a view of Mount Vernon and George Washington's tomb.

At the top of the two pages to follow is the unusual colored panorama of Washington by Lewis N. Rosenthal, founder of one of Philadelphia's most important lithographic printing firms. A legend identifies the many features of the Washington skyline that the artist portrayed in this long, narrow view whose scope extends from Georgetown on the left to the arsenal at Greenleaf's Point on the right. This splendid addition to Washington iconography appeared in 1862 and probably enjoyed a substantial sale among soldiers passing through the city and eager to find some souvenir of their visit.[9]

Folio 47 also presents a quite different kind of print published by Charles Magnus a year later. It records the busy scene that could be observed at the foot of Sixth Street where supplies for Union forces arrived to be transported further by land or shipped down the Potomac for use in military campaigns farther south. Another small view by Sachse, a more placid scene of the Mall as seen from the balustrade of the Capitol, adds to the numerous images of Washington that this prolific Baltimore lithographer produced.[10]

The Rosenthal, Magnus, and Sachse lithographs accompany descriptions of Washington during this period by J. G. Kohl, a German visitor; Edward Dicey, an English newspaper reporter; and John Ellis, an American author of a popular book on Washington. The passage by Ellis is particularly useful in connection with the Rosenthal view since he describes the city as a visitor would have seen it coming up the river from Alexandria—a real-life panorama of Washington very much like the image created by Rosenthal a few years earlier.[11]

The four illustrations in folio 48 and the text that accompanies them provide additional information about the appearance of and conditions in the capital during the Civil War. The first image represents another collaboration between Casimir Bohn, the Washington publisher, and Baltimore artist, lithographer, and printer Edward Sachse. To create this panoramic map with its pictorial representations of Washington and Alexandria, the artist imagined himself high over the Potomac River looking north to Baltimore (on the Chesapeake Bay at the right) and the upper reaches of the Potomac at the left.

Three other views that came from the Sachse press show Washington in more detail. The two that appear together look at the city from the north ("View from the Military Asylum") and the south ("View from the Lunatic Asylum"). Both of these attractive prints are quite small, each measuring a little more than four inches by about seven inches. Sachse may have drawn and published them himself, but neither lithograph offers any clues on this matter. Possibly Bohn commissioned and published them as he had done with other prints that Sachse created.

The last view in the folio is another Sachse-Bohn collaboration, using an image drawn by Frederick Dielman. The artist looked down from Georgetown

November 1864 on pp. 390–91 describing how "from the chaos of paint buckets, carpenter's trash, and whitewash, the noble pile [the Capitol] is emerging in pristine beauty."

7. Ibid., 312. According to Brooks, the old White House was to become the office of the State Department, "which is in a narrow, old-fashioned building now being absorbed into the growing Treasury building."

8. He described the appalling loss, pointing out that while a "fireproof floor saved the museum hall on the lower floor . . . , the upper halls . . . were all destroyed." These included a gallery of the paintings of John Mix Stanley whose "work

of a lifetime was thus swept away immediately." Fortunately, the "library of the Institution and many valuable records were saved," and "the walls of the building stand intact." Altogether, Brooks concluded, it was "a sad sight to the lover of science and art." This is one item in a long dispatch dated 2 February 1865. The portion quoted can be found in ibid., 412.

9. Lewis N. Rosenthal was one of five brothers born in Poland. He was sent to London with his brother Simon to learn lithographic printing and later, about 1849, came to the United States and settled in Philadelphia. Shortly thereafter he

formed a partnership with his brother Max, who had worked briefly for Napoleon Sarony. It was probably Max who drew the Washington panorama, since according to Max's son, Lewis confined his activities to printing and publishing. The Rosenthal firm produced a large number of prints of the Civil War, as well as scenes of Philadelphia, and other lithographs. There is a long note about their work in Peters, *America on Stone*, 343–46. See also listings or reproductions of Rosenthal lithographs in Wainwright, *Philadelphia in the Romantic Age of Lithography*.

10. Magnus, doing business in New York,

probably sold many copies of his Washington area views to customers in the Northeast seeking some kind of visual record of the war more impressive than the newspaper and magazine wood engravings used so frequently in the illustrated journals published in New York. Like Sachse and Rosenthal, he doubtless also distributed his several views through agents or retail outlets in Washington.

11. Ellis's book published in 1869, *The Sights and Secrets of the National Capital*, also described at length what a visitor could see from the outer gallery of the newly completed Capitol dome. Portions of his text also appear in folio 49.

on the Chesapeake and Ohio Canal and the Aqueduct Bridge, a structure converted to a vehicular bridge by the army during the war. At the left one can see some of the Georgetown warehouses and above them the observatory. A flag flies from the top of the incomplete Washington Monument, and in the distance the low Long Bridge connects Washington with Arlington on the right bank of the Potomac.

In addition to its value in documenting the appearance of Washington as seen from Georgetown, this image is of interest because of its artist, Frederick Dielman, then a young man of seventeen. Born in Germany in 1847, he came to Baltimore as a child and studied at Calvert College. Edward Sachse apparently then employed him, for Dielman drew several other views that Sachse printed and Bohn published. From 1866 to 1872 Dielman worked in Virginia as a topographical artist for the U.S. engineers, leaving to study art in Munich. Soon after establishing a New York studio in 1876, he became an important figure in the American art world and was a founding member of the American Society of Artists.[12]

The descriptions of Washington in folio 48 by the English novelist Anthony Trollope clash harshly with the appealingly peaceful scenes of the preceding three views. Trollope's devastatingly sarcastic comments about Washington recall the similar criticisms written twenty years before by his fellow countryman Charles Dickens. By contrast, Walt Whitman presents a dreamily poetic impression of the White House in perhaps the loveliest tribute ever composed to the beauty of that building.

But Whitman offers us as well a dreadful glimpse of another side to Washington in describing a typical military hospital, one of twenty or more that had to be improvised to care for the thousands of wounded men brought back from the battles that were being fought nearby. These could be found in almost every portion of the city. Sachse's lithographic press in Baltimore printed several views of these hospitals, but one wonders how many surviving occupants ever purchased such reminders of the terrible conflict in which they participated.[13]

With the war over, viewmakers returned to a more familiar way of depicting the city. Sachse made some minor changes in his earlier lithographs showing Washington from the east with the Capitol in the foreground. He changed the dates in the imprint, and reissued them in 1867, 1869, and 1870, an apparent indication that he found a ready market for them among the many new residents and visitors in what had become a much more populous city.

However, it was John Bachmann who produced the first of the postwar views of Washington when he drew the first print illustrated in folio 49. This high-level perspective published in 1865 captures the image of a city still in transition to peacetime activities. As attractive at first glance as his earlier lithograph of 1862 (illustrated in folio 46), this later and smaller version retains the errors of the previous work while introducing many new distortions.

The most obvious is the way the artist rotated the image of the Capitol, probably so that he could show more of its west facade. He also drew the Mall so that it appears to have a sharp bend, thus obscuring its axial relationship with the Capitol. It is possible that Bachmann himself was not responsible for these additional exaggerations and distortions. Instead, the printers and publishers, Kimmel & Forster of New York, may have borrowed his earlier image and had it redrawn by a less skilled artist to commemorate an important event in the city's history whose occurrence the lithograph records in hundreds of tiny images.

A careful examination of the print reveals columns of troops crossing the Long Bridge from Arlington, marching up Maryland Avenue, circling the south, east, and north flanks of the Capitol, leading northwest along Pennsylvania Avenue, turning north on Fifteenth Street by the Treasury, and then passing in front of the White House. This re-creates on paper the stirring parades of late May 1865 when on two successive days seemingly unending units of the victorious Union army marched in review by civil and military dignitaries before being mustered out of service and passing into history.[14]

Only a month earlier Abraham Lincoln's funeral cortege followed the same path in reverse from the White House to the Capitol as it brought the martyred president's body to the Capitol rotunda to lie in state. Artists present at both these occasions drew the scene for illustrated magazines, creating wood engravings that are moving reminders of these events but useful as well for their depictions of the appearance of Pennsylvania Avenue.

Perhaps the most elaborate of these is the second illustration in folio 49, a large wood engraving used in the 10 June 1865 issue of *Frank Leslie's Illustrated Newspaper*, the rival of *Harper's Weekly* and a publication also noted for the excellence and timeliness of its illustrations. The caption of this illustration suggests that an anonymous artist or wood engraver in the New York offices of *Leslie's*

12. Among other positions, Dielman served as president of the National Academy of Design from 1889 to 1909, professor of art at the City College of New York in 1903–18, and as art director of Cooper Union from 1905 to 1931. In addition to genre paintings, he designed many mosaics, including those representing Law and History in the Library of Congress and one in the building of the Washington *Star*. His name appears on at least four other lithographs that Bohn published and Sachse lithographed—two of Richmond in 1865 and those of Petersburg and City Point, Virginia, in 1866.

13. Some of the views published at the time showing the temporary hospitals in Washington are reproduced in Kimmel, *Mr. Lincoln's Wash-*

ington. See the view on p. 123 of Mount Pleasant Hospital located at Fourteenth Street NW, north of Florida Avenue, and on p. 169 of Campbell Hospital at Florida Avenue between Fifth and Sixth streets NW. Kimmel's book is a rich source of images of Washington during the Civil War. Unfortunately, although the author identifies the library, museum, or archive in which he found the images he reproduces, he fails to provide the dates or other information about the sources in which they originally appeared (in the case of printed illustrations) or, for photographs, the photographer who captured the image with a camera. Alas, Kimmel's otherwise very helpful work is not unique in this respect among the several pictorial

studies of Washington—or, indeed, of most other American cities.

14. In 1873 the publisher of *Behind the Scenes in*

Washington, written by James McCabe, used a much smaller version of the same image but did not bother to inform his readers of its source.

created the final composition, using, as the caption states, sketches by W. T. Crane and photographs provided by the studio of Mathew Brady.[15]

Crane, like such artists for *Harper's* as Theodore Davis, contributed many Civil War scenes to *Leslie's*. Mathew Brady was, of course, the well-known photographer from New York who had also set up a studio in Washington. He became particularly noted for the Civil War photographs he and his assistants took in the field. Before the development of a feasible method of reproducing photographs on the printed page, their images had to be transformed into wood engravings like this to reach a mass audience.

For the view in folio 49, Brady or one of his many assistants mounted his camera on a platform near the south portico of the Treasury and looked southeast along Pennsylvania Avenue to the Capitol. Presumably Crane spent some time here as well, sketching details that the camera might miss. These would include anything in motion, because the fairly long exposures needed to capture images on the emulsion-coated glass plates used in cameras of the time would cause them to blur.

Thus it was probably Crane who recorded the appearance of the spectators in the foreground cheering and waving approval as the marching troops execute a column half-right in turning from the avenue to continue north along Fifteenth Street. Doubtless the wood engraver relied on Brady's photographs for architectural information. The view is generally accurate in its portrayal of the buildings at the Treasury end of Pennsylvania Avenue, although the engraver simplified some of their architectural details. The most prominent—the Willard Hotel with its rooftop flag—occupied the northwest corner of Pennsylvania Avenue and Fourteenth Street.[16]

Few other buildings along Pennsylvania Avenue approached its size and commanding appearance. In the engraving, trees mercifully obscure the mediocre facades of all but the nearest structures facing Pennsylvania Avenue. For although many new buildings now stood where there had been only vacant lots, the avenue's unimpressive appearance recorded by the artists of the views in folio 33 still characterized it three decades later even though by that time few sites lay vacant.

Occupying the area south of the avenue and the Mall in the area now known as the Federal Triangle were the worst slums of Washington. In 1867 the head of the police force described the deplorable conditions in "Murder Bay," the familiar name for the western part of the triangle:

> Whole families are crowded into mere apologies for shanties, which are without light or ventilation. During the storms of rain or snow their roofs afford but slight protection; while beneath a few rough boards the miasmatic effluvia from the most filthy stagnant water renders the atmosphere within these hovels stifling and sickening in the extreme. Their rooms are usually not more than six or eight feet square, and not a window or even an opening . . . for the admission of light.[17]

The extraordinary view by Theodore Davis presented in folio 50 looks east toward this portion of the city where so many former slaves from Virginia and other Southern states had settled. The only high-level depiction of the city from such a viewpoint, this wood engraving provides an excellent guide to postwar Washington. *Harper's Weekly* published the results of Davis's work in its issue for 13 March 1869, slightly more than a week after President Grant's inauguration. The magazine devoted two of its folio-size pages to the view, and it is an illustration that repays careful study.[18]

Although Pennsylvania Avenue appears only in the distance, it is obvious that the thoroughfare had failed to develop as intended and remained indistinguishable from any of several others in the city. The view thus confirms what nearly every articulate visitor to Washington had to say. Closer at hand, Davis meticulously delineated that portion of Washington clustered around the White House and in the vicinity. Perhaps realizing that the inauguration ceremony on 4 March 1869 would focus the attention of their readers on the presidency, the editors of *Harper's* may have asked Davis to select a viewpoint that would display the Grant White House with special prominence.

Davis gives us by far the best drawing of the historic old War and Navy Department buildings occupying sites west of the White House and that were among the oldest public structures in Washington. Davis shows them as enlarged

---

15. Mary Cable, in her *Avenue of the Presidents*, reproduces on p. 138 a photograph of the victory parade taken from the Treasury that may be the source of the *Leslie's* illustration used in folio 49. She identifies the source only as Brown Brothers, New York City. Cable traces the history of Pennsylvania Avenue from its origin through the 1960s, including many fine, old photographs of the avenue and its buildings. A more recent book on Pennsylvania Avenue is the beautifully illustrated and informative *Pennsylvania Avenue: America's Main Street*, by Carol Highsmith and Ted Landphair. In one of the several books on Brady, *Mr. Lincoln's Camera Man*, Roy Meredith reproduces as plate 119 two Brady Studio photographs of the parade, one taken along Pennsylvania Avenue at a spot other than the Treasury. The other shows the reviewing stand in front of the White House.

16. For a history of the hotel, excluding its renovations in the last decade, see Eskew, *Willard's of Washington*.

17. W. W. Moore, "Contraband Suffrage," *Journal of the 64th Council of Washington*, 6 June 1867, as quoted in Whyte, *The Uncivil War*, 32. For the history of the triangle in which Murder Bay was located, see Press, "South of the Avenue." According to Press, Moore presented his report on the area before a U.S. Senate committee.

18. Theodore Russell Davis (1840–1894) was born in Boston but spent his boyhood in Washington where he graduated from Rittenhouse Academy. He received some training as an artist and wood engraver in Brooklyn and at the age of twenty-one became a staff member of *Harper's Illustrated*. He was one of the magazine's chief artists for years, beginning with his 252 illustrations of the Civil War drawn on the spot as he followed the armies into battle. Two gunshot wounds testify to his presence during engagements. In 1867 the magazine noted that Davis "witnessed the capture of Port Royal; the battle between the *Monitor* and *Merrimac*; the conflict at Shiloh; the capture of Corinth; the first bombardment of Vicksburg . . . ; the battle of Antietam; the surrender of Vicksburg; the seizure of Morris Island; the battle of Chickamauga; the siege and battle of Chattanooga; the Atlanta campaign and the Grand March to the sea." See "Theodore Russell Davis," in Kelly, *The South on Paper*, 33. Davis continued to draw for *Harper's* after the war, his assignments including a trip across the plains to the West in 1865–66. Robert Taft, *Artists and Illustrators*, 62–71, describes this phase of his career.

by the construction of new stories and—in the case of the Navy Building—by a new wing added on the south. Both would soon be gone, replaced by a single and vastly larger structure on quite a different scale.

Facing them across the street to the west and shown by Davis in the center foreground stood the Winder Building on the west side of Seventeenth Street. This large, L-shaped structure with entrances also on F Street had been completed twenty years earlier. Its warren of offices housed the many military activities that long ago had outgrown their modest departmental lodgings across the street and had spilled over into other accommodations elsewhere. To the south, on the other corner of Seventeenth and F streets, a private residence served as General Grant's headquarters until he moved into the White House.[19]

Another private building of more lasting importance can be seen above the lower left corner of the view. Here at the intersection of Seventeenth Street and Pennsylvania Avenue stood the art museum begun ten years earlier by Washington banker William Wilson Corcoran to display his collection. The army appropriated it for military use during the Civil War. Not until 1874 could the public be admitted to the finally completed building, but its Second Empire facade that James Renwick designed had already attracted admirers and made it an architectural landmark.[20]

The Davis view shows two important structures, among others, built after the war, with mansard roofs and other architectural features that departed from the prevailing classical style of the major public buildings. One is the Franklin School on the southeastern corner of K and Thirteenth streets, built in 1868 from plans by Adolph Cluss. This is the prominent structure rendered in darker tones appearing above the image of Lafayette Square opposite the White House. Recently restored, it now serves as a community and cultural center and stands as proud reminder of Adolph Cluss's talents as an architectural designer.[21]

The building was evidently widely admired. Writing not quite thirty years after its completion, a historian of the Washington school system described the impression it made:

> The Franklin school, in its elevated and prominent location, grand proportions, and architectural characteristics, became at once one of the sights of the capital city. General Francis A. Walker said that whenever he passed that noble American public school-house he turned to look and

felt like lifting his hat in token of respect; and even today, more than a quarter of a century after its dedication, the intelligent guide in making the rounds of the capital city to show to tourists its chief attractions . . . halts and points with pride to the Franklin school.[22]

Cluss also designed the second building worth noting. Its image can be seen halfway between the Washington Monument and the Smithsonian Institution. Here the Department of Agriculture in 1868 occupied its new quarters, finished only six years after the creation of the department. Those responsible for locating this building selected a site well into the south side of the Mall on the axis of Thirteenth Street.

Its north facade was set back from the center line of the Mall like the Smithsonian Institution but without a projection similar to the Smithsonian's porte cochère. Soon its grounds were laid out in the same style as its neighbor, but these two sections of the Mall stood side by side as separate parklike enclosures and lacked any unifying design.[23]

On the Davis wood engraving a legend at the bottom identifies all these buildings and several other places of importance. The magazine also provided its readers with a long description of additional features of the city shown in the view. The caption to the illustration in folio 50 transcribes a portion of this passage. Finally, one should note that Davis shows us a city that, although far from fully built up, at last begins to look like something more than a collection of related villages and neighborhoods.

Nevertheless, many visitors continued to criticize what they saw. The two authors represented in the passages of text in folio 50 certainly felt no constraints in pointing out shortcomings they perceived. Rufus Phineas Stebbins, a Unitarian pastor from New England who served as president of the American Unitarian Association during the Civil War, complained about the poor locations chosen for the public buildings, stating bluntly that "the Capitol is the only one whose situation is not worse than a blunder."

Stebbins also criticized what he regarded as the enormous distances separating these centers of governmental activity, declaring "that one needs to live as long as the antediluvians, and have the power of endurance of a prize-fighter, to do any business with the different departments." Although he saw "no possible way now to remedy this unpardonable blunder," he told his readers how the city should have been designed: "The whole of Capitol Hill should have been re-

19. Shipley, "The Historic Winder Building," and Topham, "The Winder Building."

20. For the Corcoran Gallery, see Reiff, *Washington Architecture*, 105–10, and McKenna, "James Renwick, Jr." The army appropriated the still unfinished building for military use during the Civil War and did not return it to Mr. Corcoran until the year Davis drew his view. Although this building did not introduce the mansard roof to Washington, it made it both fashionable and popular.

After the completion in 1897 of the new Corcoran Gallery not far away on Seventeenth Street, the old building served a number of functions before finally being returned to its original purpose under the name of the Renwick Gallery.

21. For the life and work of this architect, see Beauchamp, "Adolph Cluss."

22. Wilson, "Eighty Years of Public Schools," 26.

23. This lack of coordination can be seen on a map of the city drawn in 1870 by William Forsyth. The central portion of this is reproduced in Reps, *Monumental Washington*, 57 fig. 32. See also fig. 35, p. 63, for a view of the building and grounds from the north published about the same time. Another view of the building and a second showing the extensive greenhouses can be found in Keim, *Keim's Illustrated Hand-Book*, 157, 161. On p. 158 Keim describes the building as "of the *renaissance* style, 170 ft. long by 61 ft. deep, with a finished basement, three full stories and Mansard roof. It was erected by contract, under the superintencence [sic] of the architect, is constructed of pressed brick, with brown-stone bases, belts, cornices, and trimmings, and cost, including apparatus for laboratory, $140,420. The front presents a centre building with main entrances, and is flanked by two wings."

served for [the public buildings] arranged around a square . . . three or four miles in circumference." Such an arrangement, Stebbins claimed "would have made a display second to none in the world."[24]

It would have been more helpful if Stebbins had directed his attention to problems capable of solution. National legislators confronted one of them daily as they entered or left the Capitol from the west. One of the illustrations in folio 51 shows what greeted them: the tracks and rolling stock of a railroad running along First Street just outside the gates to the Capitol grounds.

This almost unthinkable intrusion was a legacy of the Civil War, when without any formal permission but with the approval of both civil and military authorities, the railroad between Alexandria and Washington was allowed to extend its tracks northward to the station of the Baltimore and Ohio Railroad at C Street and New Jersey Avenue. This made it possible to link Alexandria directly with Northern supply points via the rail route across Long Bridge.

The railroad successfully resisted the halfhearted attempts to remove the tracks after hostilities ended, and they remained in place until their eventual removal in the early 1870s, an event described in the next chapter. In the meantime, the smoke and noise of the passing locomotives continued to disrupt the vistas to and from the Capitol as well as vehicular and pedestrian traffic in the vicinity. The lively wood engraving that *Harper's* published depicts the result.[25]

Stebbins might also have complained justifiably about the slow progress in completing the Treasury, a building so long in the making. The second illustration in the folio records the curious appearance of the north end of the building until 1866 when workmen finally pulled down the old State Department to make way for the last part of the Treasury. Its completion required another three years, however, and it was not until 1869 that the north end of the building facing Pennsylvania Avenue could be occupied.

Washington offered other targets for criticism. An important document prepared in 1867 mentions a number of these. This was the report of Maj. Nathaniel Michler, the officer from the Corps of Engineers placed in charge of public buildings, grounds, and works when Congress transferred this responsibility from the commissioner of public buildings. Most of the reservations, parks, and other sites in federal ownership thus came under his direction, including all but the Smithso-

nian portion of the Mall. He was also made responsible for all the avenues of the city, some of the streets, and the Washington aqueduct, a water supply project then still under construction.[26]

Michler responded to the challenge of this assignment with a remarkable statement of the problems and what needed to be done. Not since L'Enfant had anyone examined the physical city as broadly and with as much care as Michler. Further, since his report appeared as a congressional document, presumably at least some members of that body read his words and may have been influenced by them. Private citizens, too, surely found his recommendations persuasive, although they were unable to take steps to see that they were carried out.

Michler, his immediate successor, Maj. Orville Babcock, and the others who followed after them continued to survey the needs of and opportunities for the development of the city, not always limiting their observations and recommendations to those matters under federal control. These annual reports by the officer in charge of public buildings, grounds, and works drew attention to important issues in the city's development even if they did not always produce sufficient appropriations to implement their recommendations. The contribution to Washington of these farsighted engineering officers deserves more general recognition than it has so far been accorded.[27]

It is appropriate, therefore, to give extended consideration to this first report that set the tone for many others to follow. In it Michler bluntly called attention to the appalling sanitary conditions bordering the old canal that ran along the north side of the Mall. He first mentioned the topic indirectly after reporting on the construction of a culvert under the botanical garden at the foot of Capitol Hill. This project, he said, converted "the exposed bed of . . . Tiber creek into an extensive sewer." He used this example to make his point:

> This work will not only remove a disagreeable feature from the sight of the many visitors . . . but will also aid in improving the sanitary conditions of a section so nearly contiguous to the grounds surrounding the very Capitol of the nation. It would be well if the same system could be adopted in covering from sight and smell that pestiferous ditch of water styled the "Washington City canal," into which the Tiber empties.

Later in the report he returned to this matter in language that could leave no doubt in the reader's mind about the seriousness of the problem:

> The Washington canal . . . is nothing more than an open sewer, constantly generating noxious gases, which are most deleterious to those not only residing immediately along its banks, but to the inhabitants of the entire city. Many plans have been proposed for cleaning it; the most

24. Stebbins served as a Unitarian pastor in Leominister, Massachusetts, after graduating from Harvard Divinity School in 1837. Moving to Meadville, Pennsylvania, in 1844, he became president of the Meadville Theological School, a position he held until 1856. From 1857 until 1863 he was the Unitarian pastor in Woburn, Massachusetts, and it was in his last year there that he served as president of the American Unitarian Association. He is next recorded as a Unitarian pastor in Ithaca, New York, during the years 1871–77. He re- turned to New England in 1877 to become the pastor at Newton Center, Massachusetts, until he died in 1885. He evidently visited Washington during the war years, and he is mentioned as being a minister at the Unitarian church located at Sixth and D streets NW, a building designed by Charles Bulfinch. See Scudder, "Historical Sketch," 177.

25. This wood engraving is the work of Frederick Dielman, the artist of the view of the city from Georgetown reproduced in folio 48.

26. Michler, *Report*.

27. I completely overlooked the Corps of Engineers' contributions in my *Monumental Washington*, one of several oversights, misinterpretations, and outright errors that the present work may set right. There is an excellent summary of the work of the engineers in Washington in Gutheim, *Worthy of the Nation*, 78–98. See also Duryee, *Historical Summary*.

impracticable and expensive having generally been adopted. . . . It is the main artery of the sewerage of the largest part of the city, it being the receptacle not only of the excrement and sediment of the sewers, but also of the surface drainage. . . . No one can appreciate the large amount of deposits thus formed unless by actual examination.

Conditions at and near the city's markets also distressed Michler. He pointed out that one of these occupied half of Mount Vernon Place, one of the largest and best located of Washington's civic spaces. There, New York and Massachusetts avenues crossed at K Street, and Eighth Street provided access from the north and south along one of the intended major axes in the L'Enfant plan. Calling the market building "unsightly," Michler asserted that it created "an intolerable nuisance." To make certain that his readers understood why, he stated exactly what he found so objectionable:

On market days the most offensive matter accumulates in the adjoining streets, greatly detrimental to the health of the residents. . . . The refuse vegetable matter thrown from the wagons of the hucksters, and the offal from the stall of the butcher, mingle with the filth created by the many animals which are brought and allowed to stand around the place, causing a most disagreeable stench, especially in summer, and thereby engendering sickness.

Michler noted that similar conditions prevailed at "the dilapidated and unsightly buildings on Pennsylvania avenue known as the 'Centre Market.'" Here a sprawling, ramshackle frame building housed market stalls located on the public reservation that L'Enfant provided to carry out President Washington's promise to the landowners in 1791 that a market and exchange would be placed somewhere between the Capitol and the White House. In 1857 the federal government transferred control over this site to the city on condition that by 1862 the municipality build a new market structure.

The Civil War prevented this from being done, and when Michler wrote in 1867, another ten years of deterioration and dilapidation had made the situation far more objectionable. After referring to the market as a nuisance that "should be abated," he continued with a bill of particulars:

It is not only a reflection upon the good taste of the community that such an old and objectionable structure should meet the gaze upon the principal avenue of the capital, but it is a disgrace to see this main artery, connecting the Capitol with most of the public buildings, obstructed by such a diversified and by no means pleasing collection of commodities as are usually offered for sale on every market day.

The major advocated finding "a more suitable locality" and "one equally convenient of access" for a new structure to replace the unsightly building. If the market was relocated, as he wished, he wanted it to be "ornamental as well as

. . . commodious . . . [and one] which will be a credit to the city." He recommended that if the municipality did not act to do so, "the government should resume control of the reservation for the purpose of improvement," pointing out that "it is still a matter of controversy whether the government has yielded its claim to it, and whether the corporation holds it by any other title or authority than that of actual possession."

Conditions like these could not be overlooked forever, for they provided additional ammunition in the battle begun by those who sought to move the seat of government to a more central location. At the time many thoughtful persons confidently expected that the city would soon cease to be the national capital. The long extract from Albert Richardson's impressions of the city in folio 51 includes a passage in which this astute observer of political affairs flatly predicted in 1867 that "the National Capital will be removed beyond the Mississippi River."

Several Western states—Indiana, Illinois, Iowa, and Missouri—submitted petitions to Congress urging removal of the seat of government. A convention held in St. Louis in 1869 considered how this might be achieved. The proposal naturally attracted support from the cities considered the most likely candidates—St. Louis, Cincinnati, and Chicago—but prominent Easterners like Horace Greeley, the influential owner and editor of the *New York Tribune*, also favored moving the capital.[28]

Of course there were many who thought otherwise, and they could point to significant advantages in and improvements to Washington that had gradually made it a far more pleasant place in which to live and conduct the affairs of government than before the Civil War. Indeed, Major Michler's report of 1867 placed as much emphasis on the advantages of Washington as it did on several pressing problems. In doing so, however, Michler bracketed his comments about the positive features of the city with suggestions about how they could be made even better.

Among Washington's outstanding attractions, Michler stated, were its "many public places . . . consisting of circles, triangles, and squares . . . set apart as reservations for the benefit of citizens." He noted that "many of these have already been beautified" and had added "so much to the appearance of the city [and] at the same time largely contribute to the health, pleasure, and recreation of its inhabitants." He singled out Lafayette Square as "one of the most charming places for recreation," but he pointed out that its subsurface drainage needed to be improved.

Michler also provided examples of how odd-shaped parcels of land along some streets had been treated and advocated that this program should be extended:

28. Proposals of this sort were nothing new, but except for the beginning of the nineteenth century, at no time had they become so numerous or attracted so much support. Constance Green, in her *Washington: Village and Capital*, refers to these efforts in several places, but it is pp. 328–32 that deal with the post–Civil War events mentioned here.

Most of the triangular places along the main avenues have been enclosed, and some of them very prettily ornamented with trees and shrubbery: a great deal more in the way of similar improvements should be attended to as soon as practicable, as they not only very much enhance the value of property, but afford for both rich and poor the means of enjoyment. Particular attention is called to Lincoln square, which has been simply enclosed by a paling fence; the beds and paths have still to be laid out, trees and shrubbery planted, and other important changes to be made.[29]

In other portions of this document Michler reported on some limited street improvements that he had been able to carry out or bring to completion since assuming his duties, but he made it clear that far more needed to be done and stated bluntly that the federal government had failed to meet its obligations in this respect. He emphasized particularly the importance of Pennsylvania Avenue to Washington and that "some most marked improvements should be inaugurated to render it as great and beautiful in appearance as it has proved to be necessary and accessible."

At the same time he noted that the limited funds at his disposal had made possible "only such repairs as were most needed." Some parts of Pennsylvania Avenue, Michler claimed, "had become almost impassable, either from the effects of the weather, or from having been cut up by the immense amounts of travel over them." Although he maintained that he had done his best with the money appropriated by Congress, he remained far from satisfied and characterized the surface of the avenue as "now only in tolerable order."

It was not only Pennsylvania Avenue that needed attention, but virtually all thoroughfares throughout the city. Michler stated that "there is scarcely a street or avenue in the city over which one can drive with ease and comfort." He identified one of the causes as the lack of storm drainage, noting that "the numerous deep gutters, which cross the streets of Washington in every block, cause constant wear and tear to both horse and vehicle." "Why," he asked, "is not more attention paid to paving and ornamenting" the streets "in which all citizens are more or less interested?"

Michler's report at this point quotes from a letter received from Gen. Montgomery Meigs, the wartime quartermaster general. Then touring Europe to regain his health, Meigs described and sent a sketch of Unter-den-Linden, Berlin's most elegant and fashionable thoroughfare. Meigs expressed his hope that Pennsylvania Avenue could be developed in similar fashion with rows of trees down its

length providing shade and separating carriageways and walkways, and Michler enthusiastically endorsed this idea.[30]

Michler forcefully called for devising and then carrying out promptly a comprehensive plan for the Mall, noting that "the extent of this reservation is greater than any other within the city limits, and is centrally located for the establishment of a limited park for a large part of the city." Unfortunately "only one portion of it has been tastefully laid out in accordance with the plan proposed by Mr. Downing in 1851." He referred, of course, to the grounds of the Smithsonian Institution.

He recognized the problem created by the four streets—Sixth, Seventh, Twelfth, and Fourteenth—that traversed from north to south this long expanse of open space with its east-west orientation. Michler considered making the streets "subterranean by tunnelling" but rejected this as impracticable because the land was too level. Instead, he proposed the following approach:

Let the whole extent of the reservation be laid out in carriage ways, paths for equestrians, and walks for pedestrians, as if the different parts formed a unit; gates with their lodges could be placed where the different walks would pass from one section to another, the crossing of the streets between them being handsomely paved with flagging. The keepers of these gates . . . could, by some mechanical arrangement, manoeuvre . . . the gates, opening or closing them for the passer by.[31]

Michler's report contained many other recommendations, including two that L'Enfant would have applauded and that one might not have expected from a military engineer. He advocated on both "ornamental, as well as sanitary" grounds, "the free introduction of water, as jets d'eau, fountains, miniature lakes, into each and all" of the public grounds of Washington. Further, Michler proposed that "groups of statuary should be artistically arranged throughout the grounds as another evidence of enlightened taste."[32]

Almost certainly this remarkable document would have been carefully studied by a person whose accomplishments and impact on Washington will be followed in the next chapter. This was young Alexander Shepherd, a rising civic leader who would shortly run successfully as a city alderman and then—in 1873—would assume a position where his extraordinary energies could be directed toward implementing a massive program of public works. These projects transformed Washington from a backwater town to a modern city with street surfaces, a water system, and sewerage works second to none in the country. Shepherd's contributions to Washington will be reviewed in the next chapter.

29. Michler, *Report*, 523.

30. His report concludes this section with this question: "Is it not possible, in view of any contemplated improvement of Pennsylvania avenue, to adopt some of the plans proposed for ornamenting this prominent thoroughfare, and relieving it from its present unfinished appearance?"

31. The gatekeepers would be "selected from the many dependent and worthy soldiers who have been disabled during the war by loss of an arm or leg." Michler's report refers to an "accompanying sketch" illustrating his ideas for developing the Mall according to this recommendations. This was not published in the printed version.

32. In these recommendations Michler's report refers to the "public grounds of the Capitol," but the wording suggests that he meant the entire city and that the word should have been *Capital*.

Folio 45. Army Engineers Construct a Ring of Forts and Batteries to Protect a Defenseless City

The former inspector-general of the District of Columbia describes the forces available for defense in early 1861.

The only regular troops near the capital of the country were three . . . or four hundred marines at the marine barracks, and perhaps a hundred enlisted men of ordnance at the Washington arsenal. The old militia system had been abandoned (without being legally abolished), and Congress had passed no law establishing a new one. The only armed volunteer organizations in the District of Columbia were: One company of riflemen at Georgetown . . . , one company of riflemen in Washington . . . , a skeleton battalion of infantry . . . of about one hundred and sixty men, and another small organization called the National Guard Battalion. (Stone, "Washington on the Eve of the War," 458–59)

An officer of engineers who helped plan Washington's system of forts recalls some of its early features.

After the disaster of Bull Run . . . the necessity of the thorough fortifying of Washington ceased to be doubtful. . . . The *first* exigency was to fortify the position on the heights of Arlington, the most obvious manner of doing which was to connect Forts Corcoran and Albany by intermediate works . . . covering at the same time the bridges and the heights. . . . Forts Craig, Tillinghast, Cass, Woodbury, and De Kalb (subsequently called Fort Strong), were speedily laid out and begun.

He mentions some of the forts south of the Anacostia.

The first . . . works . . . were to fortify the debouches from the bridges and the heights overlooking the Navy Yard. With that object Fort Stanton was begun early in September. . . . Forts Greble and Carroll were begun in the latter part of September and Fort Mahan near Bennings' Bridge, about the same time. . . . Fort Meigs, occupying the extreme point of the ridge from which artillery fire might be brought to bear upon the Capitol or Navy Yard, was begun somewhat later in the season, as were also Forts Dupont, Davis, Baker, Wagner, Ricketts, and Snyder.

After major construction efforts in 1862 and later years, the system is complete.

Thus, from a few isolated works covering bridges or commanding a few especially important points, was developed a connected system of fortification by which every prominent point, at intervals of 800 to 1,000 yards, was occupied by an inclosed field-fort, every important approach or depression of ground, unseen from the forts, swept by a battery for field-guns and the whole connected by rifle-trenches which were in fact lines of infantry parapet, furnishing emplacement for two ranks of men and affording covered communication along the line, while roads were opened wherever necessary, so that troops and artillery could be moved rapidly from one point of the immense periphery to another, or under cover, from point to point along the line. (Barnard, "Defenses of Washington," 27, 33, 41)

A young Union volunteer tells of building a fort on Arlington Heights in Virginia.

The New Jersey brigade were [working] on the ridge just beyond us. The road and railroad to Alexandria follow the general course of the river southward along the level. This ridge to be fortified is at the point where the highway bends from west to south. The works were intended to serve as an advanced *tête du pont*,—a bridge-head with a very long neck connecting it with the bridge. That fine old Fabius, General Scott, had no idea of flinging an army out broadcast into Virginia, and in the insupposable case that it turned tail, leaving it no defended passage to run away by.

This was my first view of a field-work in construction,—also, my first hand as a laborer at a field-work. I knew glacis and counterscarp on paper; also, on paper, superior slope, banquette, and the other dirty parts of a redoubt. Here they were, not on paper. A slight wooden scaffolding determined the shape of the simple work; and when I arrived a thousand Jerseymen were working . . . with picks, spades, and shovels, cutting into Virginia, digging into Virginia, shovelling up Virginia, for Virginia's protection against pseudo-Virginians.

I swarmed in for a little while with our Paymaster, picked a little, spaded a little, shovelled a little, took a hand to my great satisfaction at earth-works, and for my efforts I venture to suggest that Jersey City owes me its freedom in a box, and Jersey State a basket of its finest Clicquot. (Winthrop, "Washington as a Camp," 116)

By the End of the Civil War Sixty-eight Forts Ring the City to Protect It from Enemy Attack

This War Department map locates the scores of new forts that had to be hastily erected around Washington to prevent Confederate forces from occupying the Union capital. More than once during the conflict this appeared to be almost inevitable, but the enemy approached no closer than five miles. That occurred late in the war when Gen. Jubal Early mounted a surprise attack on Washington that almost succeeded. At the last moment Union reinforcements arrived to turn back the attack at Fort Stevens, the most northerly of these outposts.

Gen. J. G. Barnard, who helped plan the system and served as chief engineer for the defenses of Washington, described the completed system as consisting "of 68 inclosed forts and batteries having an aggregate perimeter of 22,800 yards (13 miles) and emplacements for 1,120 guns, 807 of which and 98 mortars were actually mounted; of 93 unarmed batteries for field-guns having 401 emplacements; and of 35,711 yards (20 miles) of rifle trenches, and 3 block houses. Thirty-two miles of military roads, besides the existing roads of the District and the avenues of Washington, served as the means of communication from the interior to the defensive lines, and from point to point thereof. The entire circuit, including the distance across the Potomac from Fort Greble to Fort Lyon (four miles), was thirty-seven miles."

This map also identifies many other places in and around Washington, making it useful in charting the expansion of the city. It also indicates that except for the tiny settlement of Uniontown south of the Anacostia no suburban communities existed in the District of Columbia.

Defenses of Washington. Extract of Military Map of N. E. Virginia, Showing Forts and Roads. Engineer Bureau, War Department, 1865. Printed by Julius Bien & Co, Lith. N.Y. [From U.S. War Department, *Atlas to Accompany the Official Records of the Union and Confederate Armies.* Compiled by Capt. Calvin D. Cowles (Washington, D.C.: Government Printing Office, 1891–95), plate 89.] Lithograph, 16¼ × 13 in. (41.2 × 33 cm.). John W. Reps.

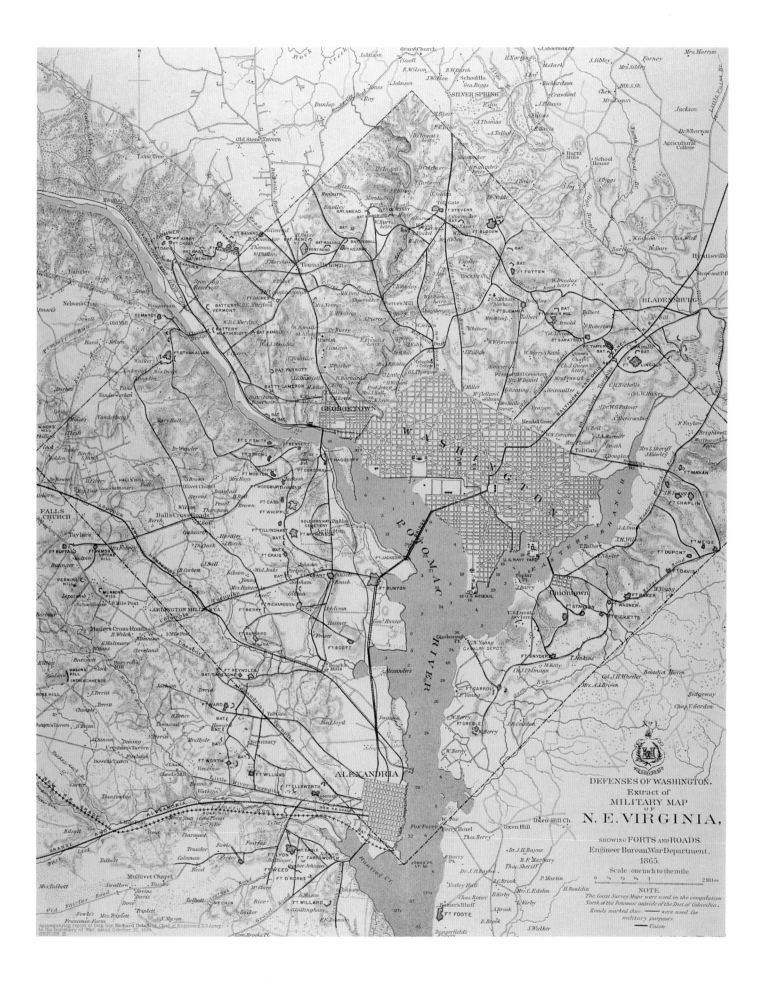

DEFENSES OF WASHINGTON.
Extract of
MILITARY MAP
OF
N. E. VIRGINIA,
SHOWING FORTS AND ROADS.
Engineer Bureau War Department,
1865.
Scale : one inch to the mile.

NOTE.
The Coast Survey Maps were used in the compilation
North of the Potomac outside of the Dist of Columbia.
Roads marked thus ▬ were used for
military purposes
▬ Union

Brooks recalls the city when he arrived in December 1862.

Washington was then a military camp, a city of barracks and hospitals. The first thing that impressed the newly arrived stranger . . . was the martial aspect of the capital. Long lines of army wagons and artillery were continually rumbling through the streets; at all hours of the day and night the air was troubled by the clatter of galloping squads of cavalry; and the clank of sabers, and the measured beat of marching infantry, were ever present to the ear.

He tells his readers of the many temporary hospitals needed to care for the wounded.

At the height of the war there were twenty-one hospitals in and about Washington. Some were in churches, public halls, the Patent Office, and other public buildings; but many were temporary wooden structures built for this special purpose. One of the representative hospitals was that of Harewood, erected by the government on the private grounds of W. W. Corcoran, in the outskirts of the city. There was a highly ornamented barn filled with hospital stores, clothing, and sanitary goods. A long row of cattle-sheds was boarded in and transformed into a hospital bakery. The temporary buildings constructed by the government were one story high, arranged in the form of a hollow square, row within row.

Brooks describes how the city changed because of the Civil War.

Before the war the city was as drowsy and as grass-grown as any old New England town. Squalid negro quarters hung on the flanks of fine old mansions, and although in the centers of this "city of magnificent distances" there were handsome public buildings, with here and there a statue or some other work of art, the general aspect of things was truly rural. The war changed all that in a very few weeks. The streets were crowded by night and day, and the continual passage of heavily loaded quartermasters' trains, artillery, and vehicles of kinds before unknown in Washington, churned the unpaved streets into muddy thoroughfares in winter, or cut them deep with impalpable dust in summer.

The author recalls the condition of two major public structures.

Over the flats of the Potomac rose the then unfinished white obelisk of the Washington monument, a truncated cone; and in the weather-beaten sheds around its base were stored the carved and ornamented blocks that had been contributed to the structure by foreign governments, princes, potentates, and political and social organizations. On its hill rose the unfinished dome of the Capitol, whose bare ribs were darkly limned against the sky. It was a feeling of pride, or perhaps of some tenderer sentiment, that induced the government to insist that work on the Capitol should go on in the midst of the stress and strain of civil war. (Brooks, *Washington in Lincoln's Time,* 2–4, 8)

Brooks criticizes the state of the city's streets.

At this writing the city of Washington . . . is probably the dirtiest and most ill-kept borough in the United States. It is impossible to describe the truly fearful condition of the streets. They are seas or canals of liquid mud, varying in depth from one to three feet, and possessing as geographical features conglomerations of garbage, refuse, and trash, the odors whereof rival those of the city of Cologne which Coleridge declared to be "seventy separate and distinct stinks." (Dispatch to the *Sacramento Daily Union,* 28 February 1863, in Staudenraus, *Mr. Lincoln's Washington,* 116)

Brooks also recorded the lack of adequate public sanitation.

Washington is notoriously a dirty and sickly city, but just now it is more dirty and sickly than ever before. . . . A hospital is an undesirable adjunct to a crowded and dirty city; but just now we have more than twenty of these institutions in the neighborhood, and to their freight of woe is superadded the filth, offal, refuse, and impurities, which must flow therefrom. The city sanitary regulations are very bad; little or no attempt is made to clean the streets which spend most of their filth in the air; and one section of the city—the Island, upon which the Smithsonian Institution and other buildings stands—is bounded on two sides by a stagnant canal of ooze, open to the sun's hot rays, the receptacle of all of the imperfect system of drainage. So ill-kept, noisome, and stinking is the national capital that one might well believe that the man in the moon would hold his nose in going over it. (Dispatch to the *Sacramento Daily Union,* 27 June 1864, in Staudenraus, *Mr. Lincoln's Washington,* 345)

John Bachmann and American Illustrated Periodicals Depict Washington in Wartime

John Bachmann drew many city views, almost all of them showing his subjects from an elevation high enough to reveal street patterns and full-length facades of buildings. The large view of Washington is by far the most detailed of those depicting the city from the north. This rare lithograph provides a wealth of architectural information on such matters as the appearance of buildings facing Pennsylvania Avenue, the elegant townhouses fronting G Street in the immediate foreground, and the public buildings of Washington as they existed then or were soon to be completed.

Throughout the war years artists and illustrators for American and foreign magazines and newspapers provided their readers with many views of Washington, two of which appear on the pages overleaf. The first looks down on the Capitol from the northeast. It is carelessly drawn, with the City Hall turned at an angle, the Post Office nearly as large as the Patent Office, and most of the nonpublic structures depicted in an arbitrary and stylized manner. The other provides realistic details of conditions in the vicinity of the city as far south as Fredericksburg, Virginia, and to the southwest toward Bull Run and Manassas Junction. It suggests how vulnerable Washington was to enemy attack, bordered as it was by the Confederate state of Virginia and by Maryland, where proslavery sentiments remained strong.

Bird's Eye View of the City of Washington, D.C. and the Seat of War in Virginia. John Bachmann, Publisher, New York, 1862. Drawn from nature and lith by John Bachmann. Lithograph, 25½ × 33½ in. (64.7 × 85.1 cm.). Machen Collection, Historical Society of Washington, D.C.

Balloon View of Washington, D.C. Drawn or engraved by [J?] Wells, from *Harper's Weekly,* July 27, 1861. Wood engraving, 9¼ × 13⅞ in. (23.5 × 35.3 cm.). Kiplinger Collection.

General Bird's-Eye View of Washington and Vicinity. Unsigned view from *Harper's Weekly,* 4 January 1862. Wood engraving, 14½ × 20¼ in. (36.8 × 51.5 cm.). John W. Reps.

J. G. Kohl finds the capital scattered and strung out along the Potomac on the eve of war.

The federal capital necessarily bears the character of all the other seats of government in the country, which resemble straggling villages set down in the midst of a pleasant landscape, though some here and there have assumed urban elements. Washington extends along the water-side for more than five miles, and covers nearly as much ground as London, with its population of two and a half millions. But only fifty thousand souls are scattered over this wide field, and hence we can imagine what an unfinished aspect it offers. The streets are miles in length and superfluously broad. . . . Only in the centre is there a more compact body.

Kohl tells his readers about conditions on Pennsylvania Avenue.

Pennsylvania Avenue . . . was for a long time the only paved street in Washington, and indeed, the majority of the streets are still without that useful article. During rainy weather, consequently, the city is a swamp, and in the dry season constantly full of dust clouds. Along Pennsylvania Avenue are the principal shops, and hence it is the favourite, almost sole promenade, of the fair sex. The public processions march along this avenue, and it is to a certain extent the Via Sacra of this American New Rome. The president, after being installed at the Capitol, also drives triumphantly along Pennsylvania Avenue to the White House. As this road runs from one hill to the top of another, with the Capitol and the White House in the distance, it might have become a splendid street had the other public buildings been erected along its line. But that is not the case; on the contrary, the different large governmental buildings have . . . been scattered over distant parts of the city. Concealed among clumps of small private houses, with which they do not harmonise, their splendour is thrown away, while, had they been arranged along the above avenue, they would have formed a magnificent colonnade, and produced a very imposing effect. (Kohl, "The Federal City of Washington," 381–82)

Edward Dicey describes the unfinished Capitol in 1862 after work on its enlargement was suspended.

The grand, half-finished front facade is turned away from the city, owing to the fact that the building was planned before the town was built. So, as a matter of fact, nobody enters, or

ever will enter, by the front entrance except to see the facade; and all persons on business approach the Capitol by the back door. The completion of the edifice is suspended for the present, because funds are short and the architect is away at the war. The whole building has still an untidy, unfinished, almost tumble-down appearance. The immense iron dome, which will vie in magnitude with that of St. Peter's, and which like the Roman cupola, you can see for miles and miles away . . . is still a bare framework of beams and girders, surmounted by a crane. . . . Blocks of unhewn marble lie on every side, scattered about the pleasant grounds which lead from the Capitol to the foot of the steep hill on which it stands. The niches are still without their statues . . . while, in many parts, the staring red-brick walls are still without their marble facings. (Dicey, *Six Months in the Federal States*, 1:100–101)

John Ellis guides those entering the city by boat shortly after the Civil War.

The . . . boat passes nearly all the points on the lower Potomac made famous during the late war, and also affords a view of Mount Vernon and Fort Washington. After passing Mount Vernon, and sweeping around a graceful bend in the stream, the cities of Alexandria and Washington come in sight at the same moment—the one in plain view, and the other surrounded by a faint haze. The boat touches at Alexandria for a moment, and then speeds on.

Washington is now in full view. The gigantic Capitol looms gradually up against the sky, with the sunlight glittering on the glorious embodiment of Freedom which surmounts it. Below the Capitol, and clinging along the river-shore, are the Navy Yard, the Arsenal, and the Penitentiary. To the left the city rises gradually from the river to the high grounds in the rear, and the eye can easily distinguish the stately outlines of the Government buildings. The unfinished monument to Washington attracts but a momentary gaze, and few think of their remissness in allowing it to remain in this condition. Georgetown is seen in the distance, beyond the Long Bridge, and Arlington Heights rise boldly on the left. An excellent view of the city is gained from the deck of the steamer, and it is a pleasure which should not be missed. (Ellis, *The Sights and Secrets of the National Capital*, 25–26)

Edward Sachse, Charles Magnus, and L. N. Rosenthal Produce Wartime Views of the Capital City

For the unusual lithograph reproduced on the opposite page, Edward Sachse used views of individual buildings in Washington with a 360-degree panorama of the city on the four top panels. Certainly it would have been a suitable souvenir for any soldier who had passed through or been stationed in the city. At the top of the pages overleaf is the unusual panorama of Washington as seen from the south. L. N. Rosenthal, whose brother Max may have drawn it, published it in 1862. A legend identifies all major buildings in easily readable lettering below their images, this making the view largely self-explanatory. Although exaggerating the size of the public buildings, it otherwise provides an accurate delineation of how Washington would have appeared to someone arriving in the city by boat.

Below the Rosenthal view are two additional images of the city. The one at lower left is by Charles Magnus showing the center of shipping on the Potomac where Sixth Street ended at the river between N and O streets. Sachse printed the small view of Washington at the bottom of the next page, one of many from this source.

Illustrated Album of Washington City and Vicinity. Lithographed and printed by E. Sachse & Co., 5 N. Liberty St., Baltimore, [1861–65?] Lithograph, 16 × 20¼ in. (40.6 × 51.4 cm.). Machen Collection, Historical Society of Washington, D.C.

[Untitled view of Washington, D.C.]. Unsigned. Copyright by L[ewis] N. Rosenthal. [Philadelphia], 1862. Lithograph, 4⅛ × 38⅜ in. (10.6 × 96.9 cm.). Prints and Photographs, Library of Congress.

Bird's Eye View of Sixth Street Wharf, Washington D.C. Unsigned view published by Charles Magnus, 12 Frankfort Street, New York, and 520 7th St., Washington, D.C., 1863. Lithograph, 10⅝ × 16⅜ in. (26.9 × 41.6 cm.). Kiplinger Collection.

Washington. View from the Balustrade of the Capitol. [Printed by E. Sachse, Baltimore, 1861–65?]. Lithograph, 4⅝ × 7⁹⁄₁₆ in. (11.8 × 19.2 cm.). John W. Reps.

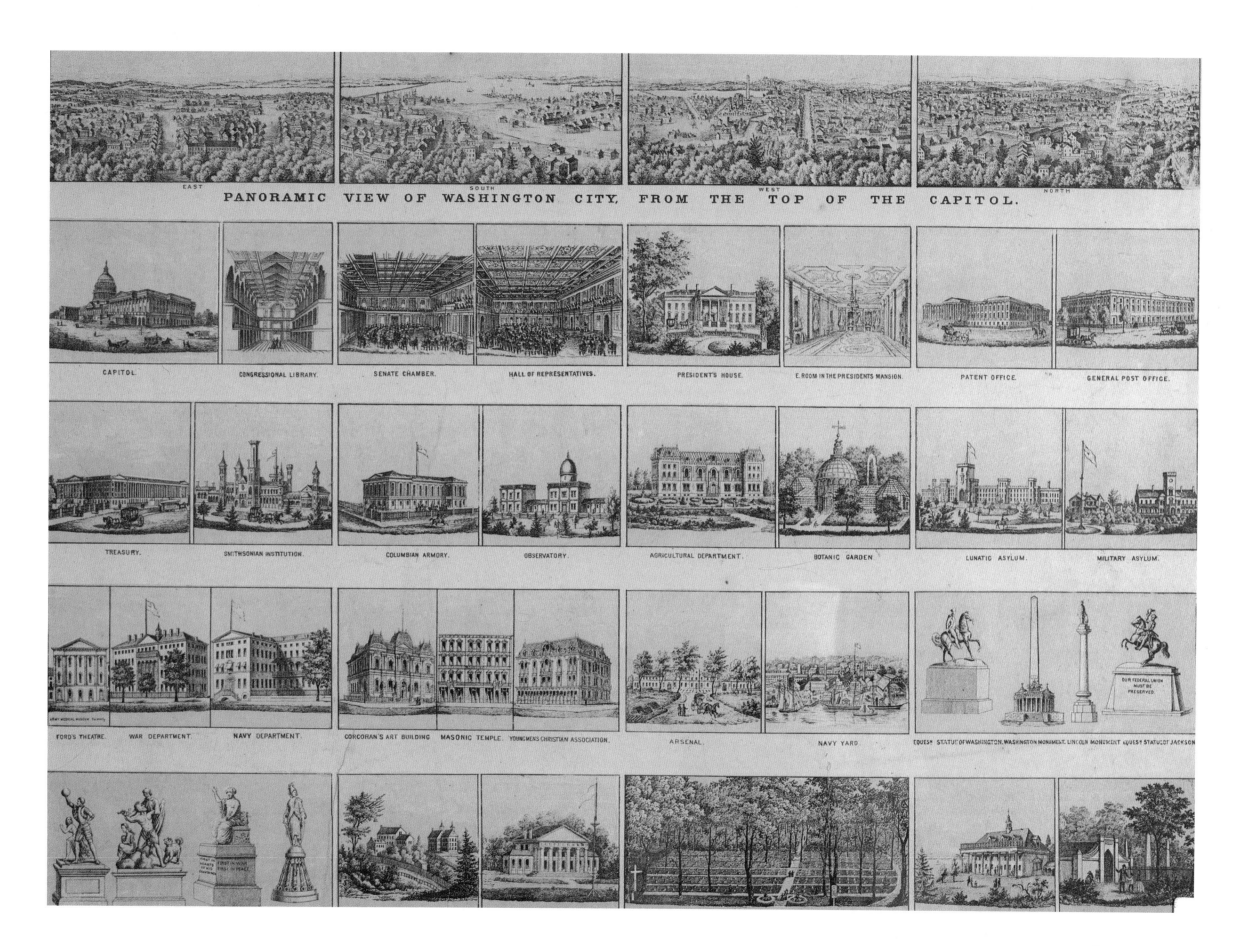

EAST   SOUTH   WEST   NORTH

PANORAMIC VIEW OF WASHINGTON CITY, FROM THE TOP OF THE CAPITOL.

CAPITOL.   CONGRESSIONAL LIBRARY.   SENATE CHAMBER.   HALL OF REPRESENTATIVES.   PRESIDENT'S HOUSE.   E. ROOM IN THE PRESIDENTS MANSION.   PATENT OFFICE.   GENERAL POST OFFICE.

TREASURY.   SMITHSONIAN INSTITUTION.   COLUMBIAN ARMORY.   OBSERVATORY.   AGRICULTURAL DEPARTMENT.   BOTANIC GARDEN   LUNATIC ASYLUM.   MILITARY ASYLUM.

FORD'S THEATRE.   WAR DEPARTMENT.   NAVY DEPARTMENT.   CORCORAN'S ART BUILDING   MASONIC TEMPLE.   YOUNGMENS CHRISTIAN ASSOCIATION.   ARSENAL.   NAVY YARD.   EQUESN STATUE OF WASHINGTON. WASHINGTON MONUMENT. LINCOLN MONUMENT EQUESN STATUE OF JACKSON

161

Penn.Avenue Bridge.   Observatory   National Gallery   War Department. White House.   Treasury Department.   Patent Office.   Post Offi

ton Mon.ᵗ Enᵗ.ᶜᵉ to Long Brᵈˢ City Hall.　　Smithsonian Institute. Armory.　　　　　U. S. Capitol.　　　　　　　　　　　　　　　　Navy Yard.　　　　Arsenal.　　Insane Asylum.

Anthony Trollope sees little to admire in the winter of 1861–62.

Washington is but a ragged, unfinished collection of unbuilt broad streets, as to the completion of which there can now, I imagine, be but little hope.

Of all places that I know it is the most ungainly and most unsatisfactory:—I fear I must also say the most presumptuous in its pretensions. There is a map of Washington accurately laid down; and taking that map with him in his journeyings a man may lose himself in the streets, not as one loses oneself in London between Shoreditch and Russell Square, but as one does so in the deserts of the Holy Land, between Emmaus and Arimathea. In the first place no one knows where the places are, or is sure of their existence, and then between their presumed localities the country is wild, trackless, unbridged, uninhabited, and desolate.

Trollope finds that Massachusetts Avenue exists only on paper.

Massachusetts Avenue runs the whole length of the city, and is inserted on the maps as a full-blown street, about four miles in length. Go there, and you will find yourself not only out of town, away among the fields, but you will find yourself beyond the fields, in an uncultivated, undrained wilderness. Tucking your trousers up to your knees you will wade through the bogs, you will lose yourself among rude hillocks, you will be out of the reach of humanity.

The author likens the city to a frontier wilderness.

The unfinished dome of the Capitol will loom before you in the distance, and you will think that you approach the ruins of some western Palmyra. If you are a sportsman, you will desire to shoot snipe within sight of the president's house. There is much unsettled land within the States of America, but I think none so desolate in its state of nature as three-fourths of the ground on which is supposed to stand the city of Washington. (Anthony Trollope, *North America*, 305)

The American poet Walt Whitman views the White House by moonlight in February 1862.

I wander about a good deal, sometimes at night under the moon. To-night took a long look at the president's house. The white portico—the palace-like, tall, round columns, spotless as snow—the walls also—the tender and soft moonlight, flooding the pale marble, and making peculiar faint languishing shades, not shadows—everywhere a soft transparent hazy, thin, blue moon-lace, hanging in the air—the brilliant and extra-plentiful clusters of gas, on and around the façade, columns, portico, &c.—everything so white, so marbly pure and dazzling, yet soft—the White House of future poems, and of dreams and dramas, there in the soft and copious moon—the gorgeous front, in the trees, under the lustrous flooding moon, full of reality, full of illusion—the forms of the trees, leafless, silent, in trunk and myriad-angles of branches under the stars and sky— the White House of the land, and of beauty and night.

He describes the appearance of one of many military hospitals created to care for injured soldiers.

Fancy to yourself a space of three to twenty acres of ground, on which are group'd ten or twelve very large wooden barracks, with, perhaps, a dozen or twenty, and sometimes more than that number, small buildings, capable altogether of accommodating from five hundred to a thousand or fifteen hundred persons. . . . They make altogether a huge cluster, with the additional tents, extra wards for contagious diseases, guardhouses, sutler's stores, chaplain's house; in the middle will probably be an edifice devoted to the offices of the surgeon in charge and the ward surgeons, principal attaches, clerks, &c. . . . Here in Washington, when these army hospitals are all fill'd (as they have been already several times,) they contain a population more numerous in itself than the whole of the Washington of ten or fifteen years ago. Within sight of the capitol, as I write [October 1863], are some thirty or forty such collections, at times holding from fifty to seventy thousand men. Looking from any eminence and studying the topography in my rambles, I use them as landmarks. Through the rich August verdure of the trees, see that white group of buildings off yonder in the outskirts; then another cluster half a mile to the left of the first; then another a mile to the right, and another a mile beyond, and still another between us and the first. Indeed, we can hardly look in any direction but these clusters are dotting the landscape and environs. That little town, as you might suppose it, off there on the brow of a hill, is indeed a town, but of wounds, sickness, and death. (Whitman, *Specimen Days*, 718, 737)

Edward Sachse Portrays the Capital in Wartime

Among the many fine lithographs printed by Edward Sachse is the pictorial map of Washington and vicinity reproduced on the opposite page. It looks north to Washington, Annapolis, Baltimore, and Harpers Ferry. A legend identifies the encampments of Union troops then stationed in and near the city. The following page presents two much smaller prints, probably published in 1861. They show Washington from opposite points of view. For one, the artist looked north from the lunatic asylum, an immense Gothic structure on the left bank of the Potomac, south of the Anacostia.

The other Sachse view of this rare pair shows the city from an uncommon viewpoint, the soldiers' home or, as it was then known, the military asylum. From this elevated location about three miles north of the Capitol, the artist had a fine outlook over the city. The third lithograph provides a fine view of the Chesapeake and Ohio Canal, the Aqueduct Bridge, and—on the left— some of the canalside buildings of Georgetown. Beyond lies Washington with the flag flying from the stump of the still unfinished Washington Monument.

District of Columbia and the Seat of War on the Potomac. Lithographed and Printed by E. Sachse & Co., 104 S. Charles-st., Baltimore, Md. Published by C. Bohn, 568 Pennsylvania Avenue, Washington, D.C., [1861– 65?]. Lithograph, 9¹³/₁₆ × 14¹³/₁₆ in. (24.9 × 37.6 cm.). Geography and Maps, Library of Congress.

Washington. View from the Lunatic Asylum. Lith. by E. Sachse & Co., Baltimore, Md., ca. 1861. Lithograph, 4³/₁₆ × 7¹/₁₆ in. (10.6 × 17.9 cm.). Kiplinger Collection.

Washington. View from the Military Asylum. Lith. by E. Sachse & Co., Baltimore, Md., ca. 1861. Lithograph, 4³/₁₆ × 7 in. (10.6 × 17.8 cm.). Kiplinger Collection.

Aqueduct of Potomac, Georgetown D.C. Drawn by F[rederick] Dielman. Lith by E. Sachse & Co., Baltimore. Published by C. Bohn, 568 Pennsylvania Av., Washington, D.C., 1865. Lithograph, 4³/₄ × 7⁵/₁₆ in. (12 × 18.5 cm.). Prints and Photographs, Library of Congress.

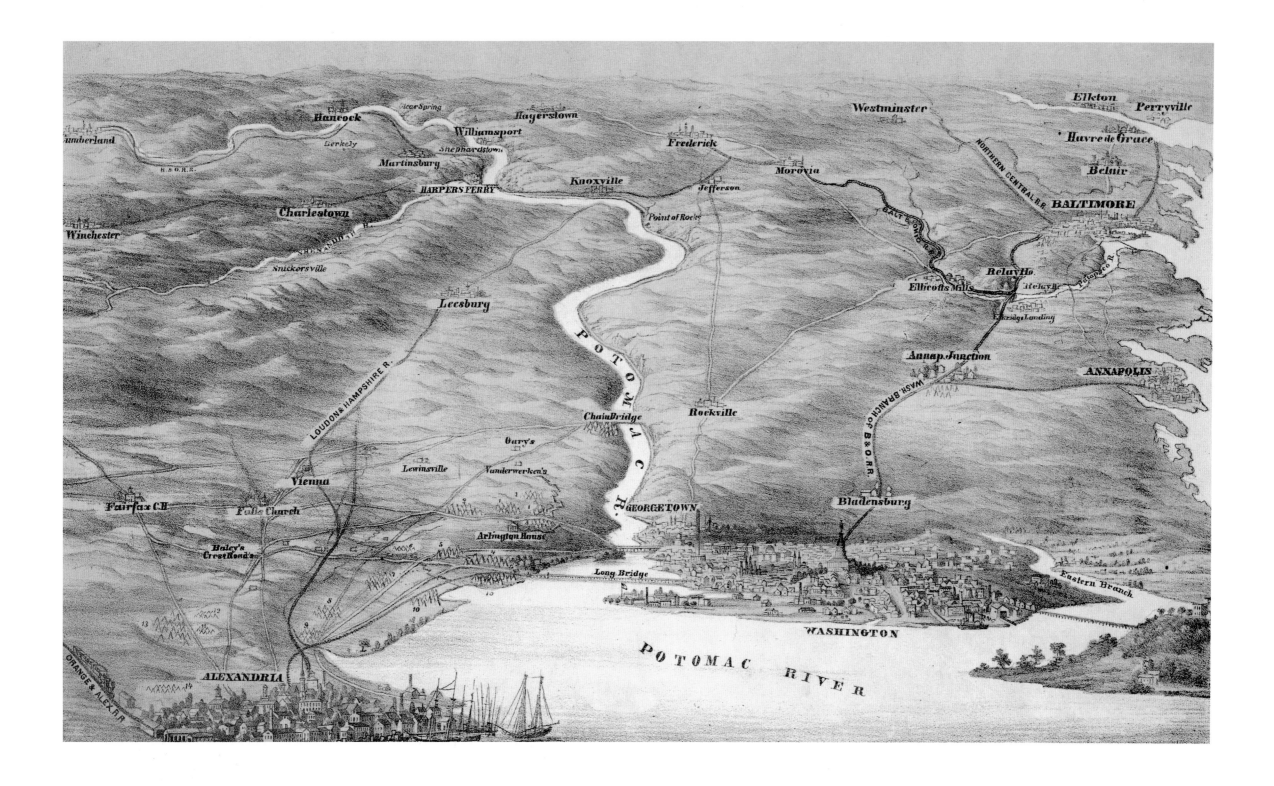

WASHINGTON.

VIEW FROM THE MILITARY ASYLUM.

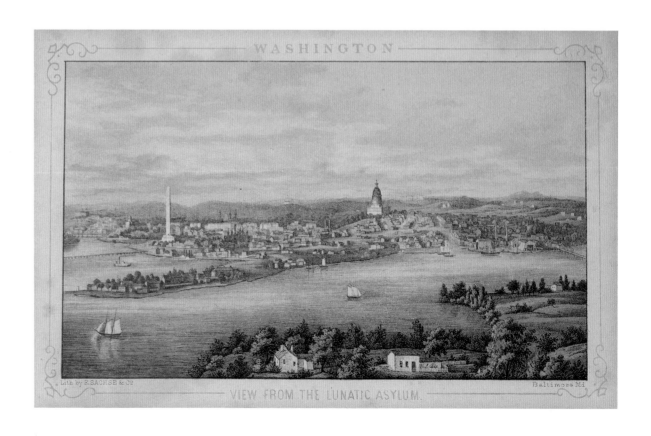

WASHINGTON

VIEW FROM THE LUNATIC ASYLUM.

*A guide published in 1864 tells its readers
about the new dome on the Capitol.*

The old dome was, to some extent, a copy of the Roman Pantheon; but in the construction of the new one . . . more modern styles were combined in the design, thus creating a light structure, decorated with pilasters, columns, rich cornices, and entablatures. The interior of the dome is 96 feet in diameter, and the interior height from the floor of the Rotunda to the ceiling is 220 feet. The dome rises 241 feet above the top of the building, and 396 feet 4 inches above the western grounds, and 300 feet above the eastern grounds. (*Morrison's Stranger's Guide* [1864], 16–17)

The author of a more detailed guide to and history of the city leads a touring party to the top of the Capitol in 1869.

A stairway leads from the gallery . . . to the base of the lantern, beyond which visitors are forbidden to ascend. A door admits us to the highest outer gallery of the dome. It requires a fatiguing journey to reach it, but the magnificent view to be obtained from it fully repays us for all our trouble. The air blows keen as we pass out upon the narrow balcony, for we are nearly three hundred feet above the ground.

He describes the view.

The view is magnificent. The whole city is at our feet, with its long lines of streets, its splendid public buildings, its parks and gardens and beyond is a panorama of unsurpassed beauty.

To the northwest the high hills in Virginia and beyond Georgetown stretch back to the horizon. The river, breaking from them, sweeps away to the southeast, and is crossed by the canal bridge at Georgetown and the Long Bridge at the foot of Maryland Avenue.

The guide directs attention to Virginia.

On the Virginia side the heights are bold and picturesque. Arlington, once the home of the Rebel General Robert E. Lee, and now a Freedmen's village and National Cemetery, stands near the Virginia end of the Long Bridge. The heights here are crowned with massive earthworks, which were erected for the protection of the Capital during the war. They are very distinct

to the eye, and with a good glass every detail of construction can be made out. Pennsylvania Avenue stretches out grandly before us, and at our feet, that portion extending from the Capitol to the president's House being handsomely built up. The various objects in the city can be distinctly made out, for the whole town is splendidly mapped out below us. To the westward the eye ranges over a vast tract of country in Virginia, and to the southwest the city of Alexandria, eight miles distant, is in full view. The Potomac, here over a mile wide, sweeps majestically by the city, and disappears amidst the southwestern woods which shut in the view.

The guide tells us to look to the south and then north.

To the south are the Eastern Branch, the Navy Yard, the Insane Asylum, and beyond, the hills crowned with the red earthworks. To the north, the Baltimore Railroad is seen emerging from the woods and descending a steep grade towards the city. On all sides, long lines of fortifications greet the eye, each telling its mute but eloquent story. (Ellis, *The Sights and Secrets of the National Capital*, 75–76)

*A longtime Washington editor and journalist
recalls the Union armies at their last review.*

On the 23d of May the "Army of the Potomac," and on the 24th the "Division of the Mississippi," swept through the metropolis for hours, the successive waves of humanity crested with gleaming sabres and burnished bayonets, while hundreds of bands made the air ring with patriotic music. . . .

The reviewing stand, erected on the sidewalk in front of the White House, was a long pavilion . . . decorated with flags and bearing the names of the principal victories won. . . . President Johnson occupied the central chair in a projection from the centre of the front, with Lieutenant-General Grant, Major-General Sherman, and the members of the Cabinet at his right and left hand. . . .

The Army of the Potomac was six hours in passing the reviewing stand. As each brigade commander saluted, President Johnson would rise and lift his hat. General Grant sat during the whole time immovable, except that he would occasionally make some commendatory comment as a gallant officer or brave regiment passed. (Poore, *Perley's Reminiscences*, 2:186, 189)

Bachmann's View Is Modified, and Brady's Camera Records a Historic Event at War's End

In 1865 the New York firm of Kimmel & Forster published the first view of Washington shown here. John Bachmann's name appears as the artist, but it is possible that P. K. Kimmel simply had someone in his shop redraw Bachmann's large view of Washington in 1862 that is reproduced in folio 46. Whether by Bachmann or someone else, the view is a clumsy and misleading depiction of Washington. The artist rotated the image of the Capitol to show more of its western front and, for some reason, gave the the Mall a pronounced bend that obscures the importance of its axial relationship with the Capitol. Kimmel & Forster were better engravers than lithographers, and in 1873 they prepared a much reduced version of the view for the steel engraving frontispiece of James Dabney McCabe's book, *Behind the Scenes in Washington*.

In both versions the artist brought the print up to date in one respect by adding figures of Union troops marching across the Long Bridge, around the Capitol, up Pennsylvania Avenue, and past the White House in a final review on 13 and 14 May 1865. That last triumphal parade is celebrated in the wood engraving reproduced at the bottom of the page, an image drawn from photographs taken by one of Mathew Brady's cameramen and from sketches on the spot by W. T. Crane, an artist for *Frank Leslie's Illustrated Newspaper* who had done many Civil War battles and other scenes for this periodical. In addition to this moving event, this view records the appearance of the buildings lining Pennsylvania Avenue in the blocks nearest the Treasury.

Bird's-Eye View of Washington D.C. and Environs, 1865. Drawn by J[ohn] Bachmann. Printed and published by Kimmel & Forster, 254 & 256 Canal Street, N.Y. Lithograph, 11½ × 17½ in. (29.3 × 44.5 cm.). Kiplinger Collection.

Home from the Wars—Grand Review of the Returned Armies of the United States. Drawn from photographs by [Mathew] Brady and sketches by W. T. Crane. *Frank Leslie's Illustrated Newspaper,* 10 June 1865. Wood engraving, 14¼ × 20⅝ in. (36.2 × 52.3 cm.). John W. Reps.

HOME FROM THE WARS—GRAND REVIEW OF THE RETURNED ARMIES OF THE UNITED STATES AT WASHINGTON, MAY 23.—VIEW FROM THE TREASURY BUILDING, SHOWING TROOPS MARCHING UP PENNSYLVANIA AVENUE ON THEIR WAY TO THE GRAND REVIEWING STAND.—From Photographs by Brady, &c.
SKETCHED BY OUR SPECIAL ARTIST, W. T. CRANE.

R. P. Stebbins complains about the sites chosen for the major federal buildings he observed during his visit.

With few exceptions, the public buildings are the only ones which attract attention; and of these, the Capitol is the only one whose situation is not worse than a blunder. Possibly the 'White House' may be excepted; but covered as that is from sight, as the stranger passes down the avenue, by the half-seen front of the Treasury Building, it can hardly be excepted from the general criticism. The Patent Office, the Post Office, the Treasury Building, are covered up by surrounding city dwellings and stores and hotels, so that one must hunt them up with a good deal of trouble; and when they are found, there is no place in the street where one can get a good view of them.

He criticizes the great distances separating these structures.

There seems to have been utter blindness on the part of the original locators of the public buildings; and, having commenced wrong, they have gone on from bad to worse. The Smithsonian is away half a mile or more in one direction, on the island, and the new Agricultural Building half a mile from that in another part of the island. It is a mile and a half from the steps of the Capitol to those of the White House. Half way between, and a third of a mile from the avenue, are the Post Office and Patent Office, occupying two squares. Near the White House is the Treasury Building, and beyond it the War and Navy Offices. The State Department is a mile in another direction; so that one needs to live as long as the antediluvians, and have the power of endurance of a prize-fighter, to do any business with the different department of the Governments. . . . There is no possible way now to remedy this unpardonable blunder in locating the public buildings.

Stebbins states what he believes should have been the policy of siting public buildings.

The whole of Capitol Hill should have been reserved for them; and there they should have been arranged around a square, or parallelogram of three or four miles in circumference. They would then have made a display second to none in the world. But now they are entirely obscured, save the Capitol.

He singles out the Treasury for special condemnation.

The Treasury is a noble building, but its situation is execrable. It looks as if it had been borne up the valley on the wave of some preadamic flood, and plunged into the hill, from which it had been dug out,—thirty feet of it being now below the level of the surface of the ground, on the upper side.

Stebbins finds fault with the Capitol as well.

The Capitol is noble for situation as well as for structure. It is worthy the nation. . . . The height of the dome is nearly three hundred feet. Crawford's statue of Liberty, which crowns it, is twenty feet high, and weighs over seven tons. It was a sad mistake, the suggestion, or rather command, of Jefferson Davis, then Secretary of War, that the liberty cap was exchanged for a part of an eagle perched on the head of Liberty. From many points of view in the city, it looks precisely as if she was carrying a sun-umbrella; from other points it does not look like anything, which is far better; and not one person in a thousand can guess what it is, standing on the ground, and not using a glass. The first thing done by the committee on public buildings should be to take the deformity off the head of Liberty, and leave her in her native glory, without an umbrella over her head. (Stebbins, "Six Months in Washington," 183–86)

A correspondent for the Overland Monthly *in 1869 joins in the criticism.*

The intention of the founders that Washington should not be a commercial capital, seems to have been carried out better than any other of their magnificent plans. But that so sleepy a place should be the political heart of so sprightly a body is just a little surprising. . . . The city of magnificent space belongs to the whole nation, and, as individuals, we have, or at least take, the right to abuse it as much as we like. . . .

Washington is, after all, a fair representative of Americanism . . . unlike any other political capital of the world—and so it should be, to represent the indefinable American spirit. The public buildings are in themselves ponderous Americanisms—as large and costly as any in the world, and yet set up in the very worst places with respect to one another and to the effect of all. (Keeler, "A View of the National Capital," 402)

Theodore Davis Sketches Washington
for *Harper's Weekly* in 1869

The 13 March 1869 issue of *Harper's Weekly* included this double-folio wood engraving by one of the magazine's most experienced artists. An accompanying passage of text provided the magazine's readers a guide to what would have been seen by an observer looking east from an elevated position two blocks west of the White House, the perspective point that Davis assumed:

"The view . . . shows in the immediate foreground many of the most interesting edifices of the city. The modest brick building at the right of the picture has been for some time the headquarters of General Grant. Across the street, at the left, is the Winder building, occupied by the numerous offices of clerks of the different departments, which . . . could not be located in their proper edifices. . . . At the extreme left of the picture is seen the building erected by the wealthy banker W. C. Corcoran, and by him dedicated to art. . . . Directly beyond this, and in the same block, is the 'Blair Home.' Vice-President Colfax has his present home also in this block, fronting upon [Lafayette] square. Across Pennsylvania Avenue, to the right, is the War Department; still further to the right stands the Navy Department, and above and beyond is the White House with its conservatory . . . ; beyond this lies the Treasury Department, from which looking down the Avenue is seen the Capitol with its extensive grounds. Beyond the Treasury, nearly half a mile distant, are the Patent and General Post offices. The large building located at some distance to the left of these, and somewhat nearer the foreground, is the Franklin School, a large edifice located at the west of a fine square of the same name. A distant view of the Potomac is given on the right, where, too, may be seen the Navy-yard with its various ship-houses and machine-shops. Across the eastern branch of the Potomac, upon which the Navy-yard is located, is seen the Insane Asylum, probably the finest in the country. Altogether our illustration presents the most comprehensive and faithful view of the Capital that has ever been presented."

Washington City, D.C. Drawn by Theo[dore] R. Davis. *Harper's Weekly*, 13 March 1869. Wood engraving, $14\frac{1}{2} \times 20\frac{3}{8}$ in. (36.8 × 51.7 cm.). Kiplinger Collection.

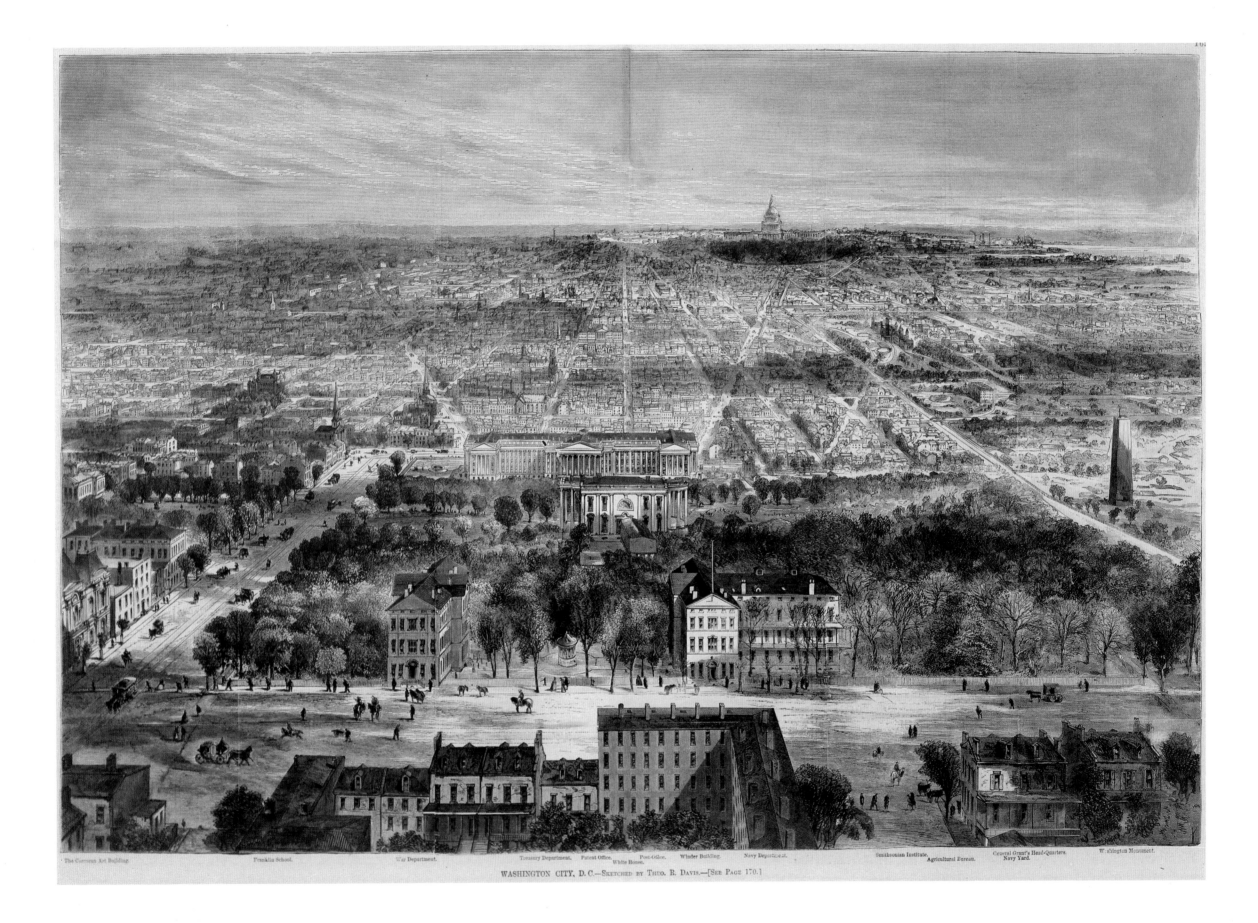

The Corcoran Art Building.   Franklin School.   War Department.   Treasury Department.   Patent Office.   Post-Office.   Winder Building.   Navy Department.   Smithsonian Institute.   General Grant's Head-Quarters.   Washington Monument.

White House.   Agricultural Bureau.   Navy Yard.

WASHINGTON CITY, D. C.—SKETCHED BY THEO. R. DAVIS.—[SEE PAGE 170.]

171

Albert Richardson supplies one more title for the city.

Washington is no longer the city of magnificent distances. Horse-railroads have abolished all that. Instead, it should be called the City of Arrested Development. Everywhere, you see workmen leisurely chipping away at unfinished blocks of stone, or polishing fluted columns, in the manner characteristic of artisans employed on the public works. There are always broken pillars lying round loose.

He confidently forecasts the movement of the seat of government to another location.

Up to the time when the seat of Government is moved west, there will still be no lack of unfinished public buildings. . . .

I fancy, however, it will not be many generations, before the National Capital will be removed beyond the Mississippi River. For a time, the jealousy of the rival cities of St. Louis, Chicago, and Cincinnati may defer the change, and the fact that we have already expended twenty-five millions in public buildings, may make our thrifty tax-payers hold out a vigorous opposition; but, for all that, it is sure to come one day.

Richardson takes his readers to Capitol Hill.

With all new-comers the first thing to be visited is the New Capitol. . . .

In 1850, the extension was authorized by the Government. Of course it is not yet completed—I suppose it never will be. . . .

Its noble site is well adapted to show off the edifice. The land slopes down from the high hill which it crowns, on every side except the east. Seen from below, miles away on the south, north and west, over the tops of the grand old trees that shade its beautiful grounds, it is imposing and handsome.

But this is because the whole of it can not be seen. On the level frontage to the east where the eye takes in its whole front, it looks squat, sprawling, incongruous.

He criticizes the appearance of the new wings on the Capitol.

The attempt to make the new wings comport with the old, is a miserable failure. The honest old homespun, pieced out with French broadcloth, looks unhappy and inharmonious. It has exactly the same effect as in the interior, where one suddenly finds the plaster and brick of the old passages changed to tessellated marble, and gorgeous fresco for the new corridors. The building will always be a disappointment till the old part is torn away and rebuilt, and the execrable half-windows of the upper story are reformed altogether.

The view from the summit of the great dome is fine beyond description.

He describes the Treasury, under construction since 1836 but still not complete.

The first Treasury here—a little brick building—was burned by the British in 1814. . . .

A new building, erected at once, was occupied until 1833, when it caught fire and burned to the ground. Then the present edifice was designed by Robert Mills. Official science exhausted itself to find a building material which could endure. . . . So the blocks were quarried out, and piled up here in an imposing structure shaped like a capital T.

The *savans* were mistaken. . . . Now, some of the exposed mouldings and little columns would break of their own weight, but for the paint which holds them together.

The extensions completed on the south end, and now building on the north, have converted the original T into an elongated H. The old stem of the T is now the middle cross-stroke of the H, which has also an additional cross-stroke at each end. Thus the double building, surrounding two square, open courts, has two long wings and three short ones.

Richardson notes how the south wing of the Treasury blocked the view to and from the White House.

On the west, the Treasury fronts upon the fountain, the elms, poplars, walnuts, and cool, green grass of the White House grounds. The south end overlooks a sickly, unshaded garden, inclosed with iron fence; beyond, the unfinished, abortive Washington Monument; and then the bright mirror-like Potomac. From the east corner of this portico, which cuts off the great Washington thoroughfare from its original intent of extending to the White House, points broad Pennsylvania avenue for a mile and a half, straight up to the sprawling, squat, top-heavy National Capitol.

Off the coast of Maine an island of sold rock rises sheer from the sea. . . . Of this beautiful Dix Island granite the enlarged Treasury is built. It stretches afar on each side from the sandstone of the primeval T, like new silk facing out old cambric. The south portico columns are five feet in diameter by thirty-two in length; yet shafts have been taken out long enough to cut into two columns and a half. (Richardson, *Garnered Sheaves,* 158–61, 188–90)

Illustrators Provide Fascinating Glimpses of Life in the Capital

In the accompanying description of the view from the Capitol, Albert Richardson does not mention the presence of the railroad at the foot of Capitol Hill. This was the Alexandria and Washington Railroad that crossed the Potomac on the Long Bridge and built its tracks up Maryland Avenue after business interests in Washington succeeded in getting approval for it to enter the city in 1854. During the Civil War the company extended its tracks to lead northward on First Street at the foot of Capitol Hill to connect with the Baltimore and Ohio line, whose station occupied a site at C Street and New Jersey Avenue.

Frederick Dielman, the artist for *Harper's Weekly* in 1866, depicts one of the locomotives crossing the Pennsylvania Avenue entrance to the Capitol just as crowds of spectators are leaving the halls of Congress after the daily adjournment. On the right the artist also shows one of the horse-pulled street railway cars that began service in 1862. After the Civil War ended and Washington began a period of postwar expansion, these routes multiplied rapidly to serve all parts of the city.

Richardson severely criticizes some aspects of the Treasury, a building long under construction but finally nearing completion when he wrote. Earlier it presented the curious appearance depicted in the second illustration reproduced here. Although its southern portico had been finished, its northern end adjoined the old State Department building that was not demolished until 1866 to allow the north facade of the Treasury to be completed.

Scene at the Pennsylvania Avenue Entrance to the Capitol Grounds at Washington on the Daily Adjournment of Congress. Drawn by F. Dielman. From *Harper's Weekly,* 28 April 1866. Wood engraving, 9³/₈ × 13¹³/₁₆ in. (23.8 × 35 cm.). Kiplinger Collection.

The State Department at Washington. Unsigned view from a photograph by A. Gardner. From *Harper's Weekly,* 15 December 1866. Wood engraving, 6¹/₁₆ × 9¹/₈ in. (5.4 × 23.2 cm.). Kiplinger Collection.

7 Washington Transformed: The Board of Public Works Modernizes the Capital, and the Government Constructs More Buildings

ALTHOUGH Major Michler's comprehensive report clearly and convincingly identified what needed to be done in Washington, he never received adequate funds to carry out major projects. It was unfortunate that the assignment of this farsighted engineer ended in 1871, the year when another energetic and imaginative person—acting with unprecedented speed and ample money—undertook many of the projects Michler had recommended.

Before we consider how this occurred and its dramatic effect on Washington, it is appropriate to look at the city as artists depicted it on the eve of what proved to be a period of radical change. Written impressions by its visitors and residents also help to recall the city's character at the beginning of the 1870s. The first of the two views in folio 52 also provides an opportunity to appreciate how the city looked in a simpler period when it was little more than a disconnected cluster of straggling villages.

The artist of this little lithograph stood on the left bank of the Anacostia and looked north from its mouth to sketch the profile of Washington. The compiler of a popular guidebook to the city published it at the end of the 1840s along with other illustrations of individual buildings. Most visitors at that time would have used this book and looked at this illustration either while in the city, preparing for their trip, or as a reminder of what they had seen while there.

For the second view the artist sketched the scene from the heights above Arlington as he looked east to the Capitol. His image of what had become an enormous building dominates the skyline, almost to the exclusion of any other elements of the townscape. Tens of thousands of Americans saw this steel engraving, for it appeared in *Picturesque America*, an immensely popular work celebrating America's cities and natural beauties that D. Appleton and Company first published in 1872 and reissued several times over the next two decades. It must have been this image that a great many Americans called to mind at the mention of the national capital.[1]

William Ludlow Sheppard doubtless drew this view at least a year before Appleton published its first edition. Unfortunately, unlike some of the other wood and steel engravings of urban scenes in *Picturesque America*, Robert Hinshelwood's engraved interpretation of Sheppard's drawing presents little more than a symbol of the city rather than a portrait. From the vantage point that Sheppard selected and within the limited size of the plates used in the book, perhaps little more could be expected. Both Sheppard and Hinshelwood were accomplished illustrators and quite capable of producing more revealing urban portraits than this uninformative if charming print.[2]

A much more detailed and attractive portrait of Washington at the beginning of the 1870s came from Edward Sachse's lithographic establishment in Baltimore. Folio 53 reproduces this typically well executed example of multistone color lithography for which Sachse had become so well known. However, despite its obvious visual appeal and appearance of realism, the view turns out to be merely an incompletely updated version of a previous lithograph Sachse issued nine years earlier: the view of Washington in 1862 reproduced in folio 40.

This was to be Sachse's last depiction of Washington prior to his death two years later, and it is disappointing to find that, except for additions of the Department of Agriculture building (just visible beyond the Smithsonian), the botanical garden (to the left of the drum of the Capitol dome), and a train crossing Long Bridge, Sachse did not modify his view of 1862 except to enlarge it substantially, eliminate its legend, and provide a new title and copyright date.

However, Sachse at last managed to draw the enlarged Capitol accurately.

1. The Library of Congress has an undated version of the book in separate parts to which it has assigned a date of 1872. The first bound edition in two volumes appeared in 1872–73. There were other Appleton editions in 1874, 1892, and 1894. The book was also published in London in four volumes, undated but presumed to be 1881–85, and again in 1894–97.

2. William Ludlow Sheppard (1833–1912) was a native of Richmond, Virginia. A sculptor and illustrator, he drew pictures for many books as well as some for *Appleton's Journal*, *Harper's Bazaar*, and other illustrated periodicals. A long list of some of the books where his work appears can be found in Hamilton, *Early American Book Illustrators*, 1:205–7 and 2:133–34. Robert Hinshelwood (or Hinshelwood) was born in 1812 in Edinburgh, where he studied drawing before coming to the U.S. ca. 1835. He worked for several publishers, including the *Harper's* firm in New York and the Cincinnati publication, *The Ladies Repository*, an illustrated periodical with high-quality steel engravings. Most of his later work seems to be for a New York City bank note company. He died sometime after 1875. Hinshelwood married a sister of James Smilie (1807–1885), another native of Edinburgh who settled in America and became one of the best known and most successful steel engravers in the country. See the note on him in David Schuyler, "Green-Wood Cemetery," 3.

Correcting his past mistakes, he rendered its east facade, the central dome, the older low domes over the original House and Senate chambers, and the elongated skylights atop the new wings with substantial fidelity to the building as it had been completed. Nevertheless, Sachse still clung to the notion that the Washington Monument would look like Mills designed it well over three decades earlier.

Perhaps he believed that just as time had justified his earlier premature depictions of the Capitol's new House and Senate wings, so, too, would the monument ultimately come to resemble the version of it he persistently used on all his views of the city. In this, of course, he would be mistaken, although five years after his last view appeared, Congress did decide to use federal funds to complete its shaft as we know it today.

Although other and more reliable illustrations of Washington for this period are not available, a number of helpful descriptions give one a sense of how the city appeared and what changes visitors noticed. The accounts excerpted in both folios 52 and 53 can be read in this context as well as suggesting how the ambitious improvement program carried out or begun between the middle of 1871 and the end of 1873 changed the character of Washington forever.

That remarkable episode had its origins, at least in part, in changes in the population composition resulting from the Civil War. Washington entered the 1870s with a population of nearly 109,000, an increase of 48,000 persons during the previous decade. These new residents alone substantially exceeded the number of people residing in the city only twenty years earlier. Another 22,500 lived in Georgetown and in unincorporated areas, bringing the total in the District of Columbia to 131,500.

A great many of the new arrivals came from the South—former slaves who found their way there during the Civil War and decided to stay, as well as other blacks who moved to Washington after the war. The more than 35,000 blacks living in Washington in 1870 represented 32 percent of the population, up from 18 percent in 1860. While the white population had increased by 41 percent, the black population jumped by 222 percent during the decade.

The complex political and social changes caused by this are beyond the scope of this book, but one aspect requires further examination: the early enfranchisement of blacks in the district as the first step by Northern Republicans in carrying out their policies of Reconstruction throughout the South. This occurred early in January 1867—a year and a half before ratification of the Fourteenth Amendment—when the Republican-controlled Congress overrode President Johnson's veto of a bill granting male blacks the right to vote in the district.[3]

Although opponents of the measure predicted violence at the polls, the first election in which blacks participated passed uneventfully in Georgetown in 1867.

Nevertheless, even some supporters of black voting rights may have been alarmed when tabulations of registration figures for Washington that March revealed that almost as many blacks had registered to vote as whites. The ensuing election resulted in an overwhelming victory for Republican candidates for alderman and the board of common council, all of whom had strong black support.[4]

In June 1868 with vigorous black endorsement, a longtime supporter of civil rights, Sayles J. Bowen, became mayor. To the older and wealthier residents of Washington, many of them former slaveowners, Democrats, and—in many instances—Confederate sympathizers, Bowen and his black followers and Republican white supporters posed a clear threat to their power and influence.[5]

Although Bowen embarked on a much-needed program of public improvements, he soon learned that without a tax increase the municipality could afford only a limited number of projects. Bowen also had difficulty finding funds to pay municipal officials. Grant's inauguration in March 1869 offered hope that the new Republican administration would provide financial aid to the district. When this failed to materialize, Bowen had to push through an enormous increase of 40 percent in the property tax.

Even Bowen's white support dwindled rapidly, an aldermanic investigation of charges against him of irregularities in arranging for a contract payment further eroded public confidence, and what was left vanished altogether in January 1870. It was then that a local firm, failing to obtain payment on a bill for goods sold to the district asylum, obtained a court judgment authorizing the seizure of furniture from the mayor's office to satisfy the claim.[6]

Nine days later a group of business and professional leaders met to discuss changing the system of local government. Alexander Shepherd, a prominent young businessman, real estate speculator, and ambitious politician, prepared a draft bill for a territorial form of administration that would replace the separate jurisdictions of Washington, Georgetown, and the county. It would have a governor appointed by the president, an elected legislature, and a delegate to sit in the House of Representatives.

3. For an extended treatment of this episode in Washington's history, see Whyte, *The Uncivil War*, 27–58. See also Green, *Washington: Village and Capital*, 296–312.

4. Whyte, *Uncivil War*, 61–62, states that there were 9,792 white and 8,212 registrants, adding that "only 14,049 . . . actually voted, and it would appear that many of the white voters registered could not bring themselves to go to the polls under the new conditions."

5. Bowen came to Washington in 1844, found a position as clerk in the Treasury Department, opened an office as a claims agent, and received appointments from President Lincoln to the board of the metropolitan police and, in 1863, as postmaster of Washington.

6. Many white residents had another reason to oppose Bowen. Republicans captured virtually every office in the Washington election in 1869, including some won by blacks. They succeeded in passing a law prohibiting theater owners from designating separate seating sections for blacks. Another law made it illegal for hotels, taverns, restaurants, and saloons to refuse service to anyone on account of race or color. Some attempts were also made to integrate the schools, but after two or three unpleasant incidents, this did not proceed further. For this and other aspects of Bowen's mayoralty, see Whyte, *Uncivil War*, 59–89.

This proposal attracted support from many quarters. Nearly everyone agreed that this might produce substantial federal support for badly needed public improvements. Further, if Washington could be thus modernized, the effort to move the seat of government to the Midwest could be ended. It also appealed to the new group of rising young businessmen and professionals as a way of establishing more local control over district affairs. Those who feared the growing influence of black voters saw a territorial form of government as a way to retain white power and authority.[7]

Protests over the rising city debt and a parallel increase in the tax rate, general local dissatisfaction with the conduct of municipal affairs, and a movement in Congress supporting a greater federal presence in the affairs of the district all helped in obtaining passage of the statute that became law in February 1871. Section 37 of the statute, providing for a board of public works, proved to be of greatest consequence.

It authorized the president to appoint its five members and specified that the board was to "have entire control of and make all regulations which they deem necessary for keeping in repair the streets, avenues, alleys and sewers of the city and all other works which may be entrusted to their charge." While the statute also established the office of governor and provided for school, police, public health, and other municipal services, it was the board of public works that dominated affairs of the new government.

Certainly Alexander Shepherd, appointed a member of the board and elected its de facto chief executive, made that clear at an early date when in late June 1871 he presented to the new local legislative body, the house of delegates, a $6.25 million plan for street grading and paving, sewer construction, tree planting, and related projects. This was an enormous sum, especially for a successor government to one deeply in debt and that had just completed the most ambitious public works enterprise of its history: paving Pennsylvania Avenue from the Capitol to the Treasury with a smooth and silent surface composed of wooden blocks.

The amount requested by the board represented more than two-thirds of the aggregate expenditures for public works since the municipality received its first charter in 1802. In less than two years, that amount soared to nearly $16 million in a cost overrun that might even excite admiration in today's Pentagon. Recalling the scope of the program, the former chief clerk of the board, Franklin T. Howe, described the ambitious plan as contemplating "improvements in every portion of the District" and involving "almost every street and avenue . . . as well as all the roads in the county."[8]

The board concentrated most of its projects in the more closely developed part of the city west of the Capitol. Here, according to Howe, the plan provided "for the improvement of the streets . . . by lessening the width of the carriageways and paving and sewering them." The most important sanitary measures would also be located here. These included "building of a main sewer from Eighth street northwest to Rock Creek [and] the sewerage of the Valley of the Tiber."

The needed funds were to come from a $4 million bond issue and $2 million raised through assessments on benefited property. The approval of this program by a distinguished advisory committee added weight to the board's proposals and helped reduce the opposition from those warning that the new territory could not afford such expenditures. The committee does not seem to have been very active, and Howe admitted that it was created "in order to guard against any criticism that might be made."[9]

A lawsuit delayed things for a time, but the board shortly began hiring crews and letting contracts. Hundreds of laborers and others with more specialized skills set to work throughout the developed portion of the city on construction jobs that soon disturbed quiet neighborhoods, interfered with the movement of traffic, made much of the city resemble a battlefield, nearly buried some buildings while leaving others atop steep slopes, and infuriated almost everyone except those who benefited from construction contracts.

Perhaps the most controversial aspect of the board's work resulted from the establishment of new street grades. This affected virtually the entire city, for until then street profiles dipped and rose throughout their length in response to the peculiarities of the terrain, much as it had existed since L'Enfant planned the city. The board determined to remedy this long-standing defect, and for each thoroughfare, their engineers surveyed smooth profiles before installing sewers, paving streets, and planting trees.

This involved grading hills and lesser elevations and filling hollows and depressions. Buildings fronting these places had of course been built in conformity with existing street levels, and Howe describes some of the consequences:

> It was not pleasant for a man who owned a house to find his street cut all the way from five to twenty feet down, and his dwelling left up in the air, as it were. On the other hand, the man who owned a house upon a street which was filled for several feet found himself way below the grade, so that possibly he could have stepped from his second-story window to

7. The events leading to the new form of government are traced in Green, *Washington: Village and Capital*, 325–38.

8. According to the *New York Times* for 2 March 1874, p. 1, the amount spent from 1802 to the beginning of 1871 came to $9,190,432. That information came from material submitted to Congress by Shepherd, but it seems to be accurate.

9. Franklin Howe, "The Board of Public Works," 261–62. Howe identified the members as "Maj. Gen. A. A. Humphreys, Chief of Engineers, U.S.A.; Gen. O. E. Babcock, Commissioners of Public Buildings and Grounds; Gen. M. C. Meigs, Quartermaster General, U.S.A.; Gen. J. K. Barnes, Surgeon General, U.S.A., and Frederick Law Olmstead [*sic*], Chief Engineer of the Improvement of Central Park, New York. To these gentlemen were submitted the plans for improvement in the District as had been formulated by the Board, and these plans received their approval, or at least the approval of a majority" (263).

the pavement. These hardships, however, could not be avoided, for the Board considered the general good and not the effect its work would have upon individual property-holders.[10]

At the end of 1872 the Board of Public Works reported to Congress what it had accomplished since its formal organization in June of the previous year. Since the voters did not approve the necessary bond issue until November 1871, the report thus apparently describes projects officially carried out in only a twelve-month period. However, planning and, in many cases, preliminary work had been undertaken earlier, some of it without benefit of legal sanction. In any event, the board could boast of impressive results.

The first map in folio 54 locates the board's street improvement projects for the years 1872 and 1873. It shows the locations of the 76 miles of newly paved streets and avenues that had been completed by 1872 and the additional 42 miles built the following year. For many of the streets the board used wooden blocks—then regarded as a desirable type of pavement but which in Washington turned out to be wholly unsatisfactory. Ultimately, these block pavements had to be replaced, but when first installed, they appeared to be smooth and durable.

For the other pavements, the board used a variety of surfaces, including concrete, cobblestone, or granite blocks. In addition, the board resurfaced in gravel 39 miles of roads outside the boundaries of the old city. Workmen also finished 90 miles of brick sidewalks and 3 of concrete by the end of 1872, and by the end of the next year more than 200 miles of sidewalks had been completed. They might have accomplished even more but for a shortage of bricks that caused the board to import them from Baltimore.[11]

The second map in folio 54 records the locations of new and improved sewers. By the end of 1872 the board had begun three large intercepter sewers. The largest and most important followed the course of Tiber Creek, another paralleled the old Washington Canal, and the third (the Slash Run sewer) generally followed a drainage channel extending from the northwestern boundary of the city to Rock Creek. In addition, the board built eight miles of brick main sewers and had finished or had in the course of installation seventy miles of smaller tile sewers.[12]

In its first year of operation the board also built thirty-one miles of water mains. Although many of these lines represented extensions into portions of the city not previously served, some of the work consisted of relocating water mains that did not conform to the newly established street grades or in the replacement of worn or inadequately sized pipes. The report also mentioned that the privately owned Washington Gas-light Company "laid and altered" gas mains whose ag-

gregate length came to forty-two miles.[13] Water and gas mains do not show on city views, and the extent and nature of the board's achievements in this respect can best be appreciated by examining the maps reproduced in folio 55.

The report also explained the board's policy for dealing with the many very wide avenues and streets of Washington, thoroughfares that were "of greater width than those of any other city in the world, and, with the alleys, comprise an area equal to about one-half of that contained within the entire city limits." Paving or otherwise improving them from property line to property line would have meant "bankrupting the people."[14]

Instead, the board adopted a suggestion that Mayor Bowen put forward in his annual message of 1869. The board's report summarized their version of this approach:

> The most feasible plan suggested was so to narrow the carriageways as to render the use of improved pavements practicable. This would place the surplus width inside the footwalks, where it could be parked and otherwise beautified at slight expense to the public, and, in many instances, at the expense of the property bordering upon it, the owners of which, for the privilege of the use of the ground, would gladly beautify and adorn it.[15]

Nor was this all the board had accomplished in making the city more beautiful. The report explained how "the waste places formed by the intersection of our board streets and avenues" had "been laid off in small parks, with fountains, and by this means an agreeable effect has been produced." The report acknowledged the "cordial co-operation" of Col. O. E. Babcock, then the engineering officer in charge of public grounds, who energetically continued and extended the improvement program for the public grounds begun so ably by Major Michler and described in the previous chapter.[16]

10. Ibid., 267.

11. District of Columbia, Board of Public Works, *Report, 1872*, 6–8, and *Report, 1873*, 4. In reporting on street distances improved, the board converted its figures on square yards of each type of surfacing constructed to miles on the assumption that all carriageways improved had a width of thirty-two feet.

12. District of Columbia, Board of Public Works, *Report, 1872*, 5–6.

13. Ibid., 6. This seems to have been an exaggeration. The map of gas mains used in the board's report for 1873 claims only thirty-nine miles of new gas mains laid since 1871.

14. The board included figures for Washington and six other cities showing the percentage of land in each place devoted to streets: Washington, 54.5; Vienna, 35.8; New York, 35.3; Philadelphia, 29.8; Boston, 26.7; Berlin, 26.4; Paris, 25.8 (ibid., 4).

15. Ibid. This portion of the report continued with this claim: "That which was a barren and unsightly waste has been made a beautiful feature in the contour of the streets and avenues." The board stated that they had adopted this system for all the streets they had improved and that this "has met with general approval." Costs had thereby been reduced, but "the capacity of the streets" had "not been in the least abridged."

Bowen did not originate this idea, since, as a recent historian of the board's work states, "There had been a plan afoot in Washington for years to narrow the streets through a system of parking." See Maury, *Alexander "Boss" Shepherd*, 30, and n. 23. For a detailed treatment of the subject, see Tindall, "Origins of the Parking System."

16. District of Columbia, Board of Public Works, *Report, 1872*, 8–9. For example, in his report covering the year ending 30 June 1873, Colonel Babcock listed many improvements made under his supervision. They included landscaping the grounds of the Washington Monument and Armory Square; improving the subsurface drainage of Lafayette Square; planting trees, shrubs, and lawns and providing fountains and other features at Rawlins and Farragut squares; constructing public toilets and a watchman's lodge at Frank-

Babcock joined with the board in planting and otherwise improving the appearance of several squares and other parks at street intersections. Among them was Scott Square, now Scott Circle. This occupied a highly visible and frequently traversed spot on the axis of the White House where Rhode Island and Massachusetts avenues cross at Sixteenth Street. Farragut Square, three blocks northwest of the White House, and Mount Vernon Place at the intersection of Massachusetts and New York avenues and Eighth and K streets also benefited from this coordinated approach.[17]

The report mentioned other accomplishments: demolition of old market buildings and construction of new ones; the planting of hundreds of shade trees, using different varieties for each street "to avoid monotony in appearance"; and replacement of obsolete bridges. The board reported that it had been "compelled to remove the track" of the Washington and Alexandria Railroad on First Street and Maryland Avenue, an action that was no doubt deliberately underemphasized and placed rather misleadingly under the heading of "Street Railroads."[18]

Shepherd orchestrated this event carefully. He first notified railroad officials that their tracks did not conform to the newly established street grade. Receiving no response, he determined to take care of this matter himself. At dusk on a mid-November day in 1872, he ordered a crew of 200 men to work through the night tearing up the tracks and regrading the portion of the two streets. The angry president of the railroad demanded a meeting with Shepherd, but took no other action.[19]

Under the best of circumstances, such a volume of public works would have cost a great deal of money. In this case, however, the board rushed into projects without much if any planning except for the sketchiest outline of what was intended and expected. Moreover, since so many projects were undertaken all at once, careless and casual review—if any—replaced adequate supervision of both their engineering and financial aspects.

Although two congressional investigations failed to produce evidence that Shepherd himself had benefited financially through favoritism, graft, or corruption, it is quite clear that many of his friends and associates did. If any of them missed out on contracts awarded during that first, furiously busy year of construction, they had ample opportunities in 1872 and 1873 when the pace of improvement projects continued unabated. Apparently confident that Congress would make up the difference, Shepherd far overstepped the limits of an already generous budget and incurred debts of unprecedented size for the district.[20]

Some of the wealthier property owners in the city had opposed the new government from the start as representing the Radical Republican approach to Reconstruction that they found repugnant. The obvious waste and inefficiencies in carrying out such a hastily devised program outraged these businessmen, and many of them found themselves personally inconvenienced by street or sewer construction jobs that often required them to pay substantial sums to have their property regraded and planted. In addition, they knew that inevitably local taxpayers would bear most of the costs and that as large landowners they could anticipate heavy assessments.

The financial panic that affected the entire nation in 1873 made the Washingtonians and national legislators even more sensitive to charges of waste, extravagance, and corruption. Of greater consequence to the board, banking failures made it impossible for it to raise money to finance its operations. The previous year a group of disgruntled residents had submitted their complaints to Congress only to have the House Committee on the District of Columbia conclude that Shepherd and the board had not overstepped their authority. Their second effort, however, resulted in new and extensive hearings before a joint committee of the House and Senate.

In responding to the charge that he and the board had incurred debts far beyond the authorized limit, Shepherd argued that the cost of all improvements would be met when property owners paid their assessments and—more importantly—when the federal government advanced the sum due the district for work done directly or indirectly benefiting the national government. At this time and in the board's annual report for 1873, Shepherd went beyond this to point out how inequitable had been the past allocation of costs between local and national governments for public works within the District of Columbia.

In a long article appearing in the *New York Times* early in March 1874, that paper—one of Shepherd's strongest supporters—provided its readers a summary of this argument, turning their attention first to the value of the land made available to the federal government through the board's activities:

lin Square; and a variety of maintenance and modernization projects for the Capitol grounds, the White House and its grounds (including a new copper roof for the executive mansion), the congressional cemetery, and elsewhere. See "Annual Report of Colonel O. E. Babcock, Corps of Engineers, for the Fiscal Year Ending June 30, 1873," Appendix AA., *Report of the Chief of Engineers*, H. Ex. Doc. 1, pt. 2, 43d Cong., 1st sess., 2:1151–69.

17. District of Columbia, Board of Public Works, *Report, 1872*, 8–9.

18. Ibid., 9–11. The board justified this action, which the railroad vigorously protested, with this explanation: "The grades of First street west and Maryland avenue having been changed, the company controlling the Washington and Alexandria Railroad were requested to conform their track thereto, and ample time was afforded for that purpose." The report stated that it acted only after the company paid "no attention . . . to this notification."

19. According to Maury, *Alexander "Boss" Shepherd*, 41–42, John Garrett, the president of the line, offered to make Shepherd vice-president of the company because of his reluctant admiration for Shepherd's decisive action in the matter.

20. Ben Perley Poore, a journalist of long experience in Washington and an observer of the turbulent Shepherd years, mentions how some newspaper reporters evidently benefited from Shepherd's policies, obviously a method for ensuring favorable reporting on the activities of the board: "Governor Shepherd . . . undoubtedly was disposed to give profitable contracts to his friends, and to the henchmen of those members of Congress whose votes secured him liberal appropriations. Newspaper correspondents received in several instances contracts for paving, which they disposed of to those engaged in that business, and realized handsome sums." See Poore, *Perley's Reminiscences*, 2:263.

The streets and avenues are held in fee simple by the General Government. . . . The United States have in one case gained 397,280 square feet by inclosing streets in the vicinity of the Capitol, which are worth, according to the appraisement of adjoining property, $576,056. The General Government has also retained the ground reclaimed by filling up the canal, worth, at the valuation of the adjoining property, $2,500,000.

The *Times* then noted the disparity between the amounts spent by the municipality over the years for citywide improvements and the much smaller expenditures by the federal government:

From 1802 to 1871 when the new Government went into operation . . . $9,190,432 had been expended by the citizens . . . for public improvements. The expenditures of the Board . . . since . . . have been on streets and avenues, $15,562,685. Total expenditures by citizens since 1802, $24,762,117. The amount expended by the United States the same period on streets and avenues, $4,476,706, showing an excess of expenditures by citizens over the Government . . . of $20,285,411.[21]

The hearings before Congress took many weeks, and the report of the joint committee filled three massive volumes. Earlier, Shepherd's admirers defended his actions. Early in 1873 in the pages of the respected *Lippincott's Magazine*, Chauncey Hickox admitted that the board had "made some mistakes" and "wrought hardships." Nevertheless, he believed that "such were the difficulties before it at the outset that it might have made greater mistakes and still been forgiven." It was not so easy to overlook the gross dishonesty and numerous irregularities brought out in the hearings before the joint committee, and in the end even Shepherd's supporters in the House and Senate conceded his defeat.[22]

Shepherd's brief but decisive part in the transformation of Washington thus came to an end, leaving unfinished projects for others to complete—albeit at a far less hectic pace than under his administration. The information uncovered during the hearings persuaded Congress to replace the territorial form of government with first a temporary and then a permanent system of government that placed authority for affairs of the district in the hands of three commissioners appointed by the president.[23]

Shepherd's haste and extravagance may have displeased Congress and angered many local taxpayers, but most visitors found the "new" Washington impressively attractive and up to date. The reports on Shepherd's vast improvement program transcribed in folios 54 and 55 indicate that major American publications regarded his efforts as highly significant. The text in folio 56 by a well-known woman journalist, Mary Clemmer Ames, reflects the general feelings of pride and satisfaction that persons living in or visiting Washington began to feel and express as they enjoyed the modernized city.

More and more visitors came to Washington, many attracted by the descriptions and admiring comments they read about in books, magazines, and newspapers telling of improved thoroughfares, beautiful parks, and modern utilities. The resident population also expanded substantially during the 1870s. The census of 1880 reported the District of Columbia's population as 177,624, a better than one-third increase for the decade over the enumeration of about 131,500 in 1870.

A guidebook to Washington stated that a census in the summer of 1878 counted 160,000 persons, a figure that, if accurate, suggests that population growth in the last two years of the decade averaged almost 9,000 persons annually. That same guide included the line drawing of the city that folio 56 reproduces. Although this scene closely resembles the Sachse views in several respects, its artist, George A. Morrison, used a slightly different perspective, added some new buildings, and showed several features of the city clearly that can be perceived only with difficulty on the Sachse lithographs.[24]

Morrison seems to have prepared his first version of the view in 1872, a copyright date that appears on the impression illustrated in the folio. Probably that date can be found on later issues as well. There are other versions with the copyright date changed to 1876, and perhaps still more editions exist of this often-republished depiction of the city. It is usually found folded inside the back cover of *Morrison's Stranger's Guide for Washington City*, published by W. H. and O. H. Morrison of Washington.[25]

21. *New York Times*, 2 March 1874, p. 1. The article also pointed out "that the real estate held by the United States in the District of Columbia fully equals, if it does not exceed in value, that owned by citizens." The writer argued that all that was needed to service the debt incurred by the board was for the federal government to contribute annually a sum matching the amount raised in the district through property taxes.

22. Some 3,000 pages of text record the hearings, submissions, and deliberations of the committee. See U.S. Congress, Joint Select Committee, *Report*. For Hickox's views on Shepherd's activities, see Hickox, "New Washington," 306-7. Hickox added his hope that the board "will have enemies enough to watch it closely, criticise it sharply and hold it to strict accountability." He concluded, however, that should there be enough criticism "to really interfere with its present course," it would be one more addition "and a great one, to the list of Washington's calamities."

23. The best account of the charges against the board brought by its opponents, the hearings of the committee, the testimony submitted to it, and the reactions of the press and public opinion can be found in Whyte, *The Uncivil War*, 143-77, 203-36.

24. The 1880 *Morrison's Stranger's Guide for Washington City*, 4, cited a census taken in the summer of 1878 as its source for using 160,000 as the population. The National Union Catalog lists a great many editions of the *Guide*. W. H. and O. H. Morrison are the authors of eleven editions from 1862 through 1881. W. H. Morrison is the author of the editions of 1883, 1884, and 1885, and William H. Morrison the editions of 1888 (said to be the fortieth) and 1889. There is an 1891 edition written by Francis H. Goodall and published by W. H. Morrison. These were all preceded by the guidebook to the city published in 1842, 1844, 1852, and 1855 by W. M. Morrison. The catalog also lists catalogs issued by W. H. and O. H. Morrison in their capacity of "law publishers and book sellers."

25. According to advertisements on the back of their guides, their "Book and Stationery Store" stood at 475 Pennsylvania Avenue and sold "Stereoscopic and Photographic Views, Russia Goods, including Pocket Books, Card Cases, Dressing Cases, Cigar and Cigarette Cases, Cabinet and Card Frames, Work Baskets, Photograph and Autograph Albums, &c.; Glass Inkstands, Gold Pens and Holders, Gold Pencils, Children's Games, Fancy Stationery—in Boxes, Paper and Envelopes and Correspondence Cards; Books of Fic-

The publishers obviously did not want or expect a work of art to embellish their guide. Instead, they commissioned and got a utilitarian image of the city that must have been used by tens of thousands of visitors and new residents over the years as they found their way about the national capital with the help of the illustration and its legend. It is a safe conclusion that in the nineteenth century, no view of Washington was seen by more persons while in the city than this enduring, homely, line lithograph.

The view shows several new buildings built or begun during this period that substantially altered the appearance of Washington. Perhaps the most important can be seen drawn somewhat out of place at the far end of Pennsylvania Avenue just below the horizon and near the center. This huge structure housing the State, War, and Navy departments replaced the two old executive office buildings west of the White House.

Congress authorized this project in 1871 to the enormous relief of Washingtonians who rightly felt that this further massive investment in government facilities would thwart even the most determined effort to move the seat of government. Alfred B. Mullett, supervising architect of the Treasury, designed the building on a ground plan that closely resembled the Treasury on the other side of the White House. Apparently many congressmen as well as others in and out of government expected that the new structure would also conform generally to the Treasury's classical, colonnaded appearance.[26]

Instead, Mullett took French Second Empire buildings as his models and fashioned an elaborate facade capped by a tall mansard roof. Although the south wing was ready for the State Department in 1875, and other portions of it were occupied in 1879 and 1882, the building was not completed until 1888. The total cost came to somewhat over $10 million. For that sum the government bought a 553-room building with two miles of corridors providing access to a warren of handsome and spacious offices.[27]

In a book published in 1884 generally extolling everything in Washington—buildings, parks, business and professional leaders, and even Congress—the author praised the still unfinished State, War, and Navy Building as "a grand edifice" and "a magnificent illustration of the advanced views held by architects." Here, he wrote, one could find "all modern ideas as to strength of construction, adaptability of arrangement; [and] heating and ventilation."[28]

Not everyone agreed. A writer in an influential architectural periodical, after calling Mullett "the enterprising head of the Government plan-factory," criticized him for his failure to repeat "as nearly as possible, the Treasury facade on the other side of the White House." This writer dismissed the building as "a costly concoction of stone, sheet-iron and slate, ugly, inconvenient, and expensive to keep in repair." Henry Adams, who lived nearby on Lafayette Square, referred to it as "the architectural infant asylum next to the White House."[29]

Although fondly regarded today by most persons and extravagantly admired by some enthusiasts, the building achieved this status only in recent times. Writing in 1900 in an important Midwestern architectural periodical, F. W. Fitzpatrick probably spoke for most of the profession when he referred to it as "a cross between an Indian pagoda and a seaside cottage done in splendidly wrought granite." He conceded only that "it is so big, so clean, and the work so well done that it satisfies the uninitiated."[30]

The immense size of the new building and how it seemed to dominate the White House and even the great mass of the Treasury not far away can best be appreciated by examining the view of Washington in 1880 in folio 57. Although small and unimportant buildings appear only in stylized form, the many details this lithograph provides of the major structures and open spaces of Washington make it one of the most important of the city's printed images. Drawn by Charles R. Parsons and published by the famous New York firm of Currier and Ives, it looks down on the city from the southwest with the Potomac River in the foreground.

tion, Science, Art, and Law, handsomely bound; Small Views of Public Buildings, Decorating Japanese Goods in large variety, White Wood Goods with Views of Public Buildings upon them." I do not know the relationship between W. H. and O. H. Morrison, nor what relation George Morrison, the artist of the view, was to them.

26. Alfred B. Mullett, born in England in 1834, came to America in 1845. In 1857 he went to work for Isaiah Rogers, a Cincinnati architect. After Rogers moved to Washington in 1861 to become supervising architect of the Treasury, Mullett entered the army. In 1863 he became a clerk in the Bureau of Construction of the Treasury Department but soon was appointed assistant supervising architect. In 1866, a year after Rogers's resignation, Mullett became supervising architect at

the age of thirty-two. He designed seven very large courthouse and post office buildings for Boston, New York, Chicago, St. Louis, Hartford, Philadelphia, and Cincinnati, and it was doubtless this experience that led to his selection as the architect for the State, War, and Navy Building, although this project was not one for which the Treasury had responsibility.

27. The history of the building, with many photographs of its predecessors, earlier European and American buildings in the same style, original designs, progress of construction, and exterior and interior details, is presented in Dolkart, Old Executive Office Building. See also Lehman, "The State, War, and Navy Building," and Wodehouse, "Alfred B. Mullett." For a description of the interior of the State Department section of the

building in 1878, see Lamb, "State and Society."

28. Historical and Commercial Sketches, 48.

29. American Architect and Building News 30 (1 November 1890): 61. The journal also referred to the facade as "a huge fussy, bulging carpenter's creation of little straddling porches, pavilions, dormers, domes, roofs, pediments, chimneys and trimmings of all shapes and sizes. Such a building would be offensive enough anywhere, but as a balance to the beautiful and quiet Treasury it is revolting." In an earlier issue (23 [21 April 1888]: 188) the journal described the building as "a poor treatment of French Renaissance. When viewed from the avenue (the principal point of view) it is down in a hollow and looks low. It is one mass of

small windows, and small porticos, each designed apparently to accentuate its smallness, making the building appear a pile of small details conspicuously obtruded." The quotation from Henry Adams is from his Education of Henry Adams, 253.

30. Fitzpatrick, "Beautifying the Nation's Capital," 10. Two modern studies of the building are full of praise. See General Services Administration, Public Buildings Service, Executive Office Building; and Dolkart, Old Executive Office Building. The foreword to the latter states that the building deserves "a place in the front rank of American historical monuments" and that it is "an architectural masterpiece." See also Allen, "Greatest Monstrosity in America."

Beginning in 1873 the artist, either alone or in association with Lyman W. Atwater, drew similar large views of several other American cities: Boston, New York, Chicago, San Francisco, and St. Louis. The Washington lithograph reached the public in the same year that Currier and Ives published another of Parsons's views, one showing Baltimore. With a great deal of experience thus behind him and with a substantially smaller city to portray, Parsons was able to draw with greater care and show with more detail a higher proportion of buildings than in his other views.[31]

One can note that many of the previously lightly built-up parts of the city have now become much more fully developed. South of the Mall, buildings now cover most of the lots. This is true only to a slightly lesser extent for the eastern portion of the city, which had long languished. In 1872 alone more that 1,200 new buildings were erected, and although the depression that began in 1873 reduced the volume of construction, Washington had clearly become a true city, whose neighborhoods no longer stood in isolation surrounded by acres of undeveloped land.

Parsons also records a significant event in this view. He drew the newly erected cranes on the top of the unfinished Washington Monument, where work resumed after Congress—finally realizing that the continued existence of the unsightly unfinished shaft on the Mall was a national embarrassment—appropriated funds for its completion. The 1880 edition of the most widely sold guidebook to Washington informed visitors to the city that year that although they might see few signs of progress, the project was indeed under way.[32]

Parsons shows two buildings near the base of the monument. The one to the east is the Agriculture Department, erected not long after the Civil War and mentioned in the previous chapter. The other to the south, with a tower and smokestack, is the Bureau of Printing and Engraving, occupying a site that the government acquired in 1878 at Fourteenth and B streets. For this prominent location so visible from many directions, James G. Hill designed a building reflecting the taste of the times for brick construction, banks of windows with rounded arches, and, in this case, a square, rather slender tower projecting well above an attic roof.[33]

Skillful architectural treatment of the building's exterior could not entirely conceal its industrial character. A correspondent for *Century Magazine* in 1884 recognized this in noting that "it is like any other four-story factory." Soon it had to be enlarged, and in 1891, 1895, and 1900 additions swelled the already substantial bulk of the original structure. This enormous printing plant could easily have been located on some other, less visible spot and its site used for another purpose more compatible with such a prominent position.[34]

The one English and two American journalists whose highly favorable impressions of the city folio 57 presents did not complain about such matters. Nor did they express surprise or disapproval over the sprawling bulk of Centre Market between the Mall and Pennsylvania Avenue on the south axis of the Patent Office, a site now occupied by the National Archives. That building came into existence after the old and rickety collection of sheds, stalls, and shelters of the old market burned in 1870. The Washington Market Company then obtained a congressional charter allowing it to build a new structure extending more than 400 feet east and west.

Although the Currier and Ives view shows Centre Market, it can be seen far more clearly on the wood engraving reproduced in folio 58—another of the revealing depictions of the city by Theodore Davis. For this portrait of the capital, Davis imagined what he would see looking directly north from a point in the air south of the Smithsonian Institution. In order to include both the Capitol and the Washington Monument and still show in considerable detail the buildings in the field of vision between these two structures, Davis drastically compressed the east-west extent of the Mall.[35]

Although the view is thus distorted, it does portray accurately the immense size of the market, a building that was widely hailed when it was built as a great improvement and that for many years served a useful function as the main food distribution center for the city. Nevertheless, eventually it came to be regarded with somewhat less admiration because of its interference with the free movement of traffic along Pennsylvania Avenue and what became Constitution Avenue bordering it on its south. This new thoroughfare, which Davis shows so clearly, came

31. Not much is known of Parsons. In Reps, *Views and Viewmakers*, 196–98, there is a biographical note that sets down such sketchy material about his life and work as I have been able to locate.

32. Beginning with a brief historical sketch about the origins of the monument, the author continued: "For many years the Monument had stood in an unfinished condition, not a Monument to the memory of Washington, but one to the indifference of the American people and to them a disgrace; but in the summer of the Centennial Anniversary and Exposition, Congress passed an act . . . creating a commission for the purpose of completing the Monument. . . . The work of construction has been resumed, but so far has been confined to the strengthening of the base, which had been pronounced defective by a Board of Engineers" (*Morrison's Stranger's Guide* [1880], 39–40).

33. Interesting views of the currency printing presses and cutting and trimming machines in the bureau's old location in the attic of the Treasury appear opposite pp. 319 and 322 in Ames, *Ten Years in Washington*. Ames describes those crowded accommodations and what took place within them at some length on pp. 309–25.

34. The quotation is from "The New Washington," 658. Tindall, *History of Washington*, 440, mentions the additions. A photograph of the building can be found in Reiff, *Washington Architecture*, 139 fig. 227. In 1911 the government began a new building for the bureau south of the old structure, completing it in 1914 from plans prepared by W. B. Olmstead under the supervision of the architect of the Treasury. An early color photograph of this building conforming to the classical models of earlier federal structures can be found in William Howard Taft, "Washington," 253.

35. This explains why what in reality was a long and fairly narrow open space appears in this illustration as a fat rectangle. For some reason that is not readily apparent, Davis also drew the Renwick building of the Smithsonian Institution and the Agriculture Department to its left as if they stood only a short distance from the street in the foreground. In reality, of course, both buildings occupied sites well into the Mall, with extensive grounds between the street and their entrances.

into existence as North B Street after Shepherd filled the old canal and built a street over its former bed.

The article in *Century Magazine* where the long extracts in folio 58 appeared in 1884 did not mention Centre Market, nor did its author or other visitors of the time who wrote of their impressions of the city comment on the building diagonally across the street from it to the southeast. Here stood the depot of the Baltimore and Potomac Railway on the north side of the Mall at Sixth Street. In a burst of misplaced generosity, Congress in 1872 authorized this affiliate of the Pennsylvania Railroad to lay its tracks across the Mall from Maryland Avenue, build a depot on the west side of Sixth Street, and use adjacent portions of the Mall for the station, railroad yards, and train shed.

Today this action seems almost unthinkable—a shortsighted blunder that no one would be idiot or bold enough to propose. At the time, however, most Washingtonians hailed the opening of the depot in 1873, apparently regarding this as an example of progressive community development that would provide Washington with improved transportation links and competitive passenger fares and freight rates. Journalists like George Alfred Townsend in *Harper's* also applauded the decision to build a new station, referring to it in his highly laudatory article as "a grand depôt worthy of the capital."

De Benneville Randolph Keim, compiler and author of a Washington guidebook that went through many editions, described J. M. Wilson's design for the passenger station as "a beautiful gothic edifice . . . built of brick, with courses of Ohio sandstone, the whole resting on a granite base. The taller tower is 134 feet high to the finial. The main building is 90 × 120 feet, and the iron passenger shed 110 × 510 feet. The interior is beautifully finished in native woods."[36]

Evidently in their admiration of its red, towered Gothic facade—an architectural echo of the Smithsonian Institution across the Mall—and enjoying its comfortable passenger accommodations, few if any Washingtonians at the time pointed out that the station, yards, and tracks drastically changed the Mall's character. The railroad so shattered the Mall's peace and quiet and interfered with the vistas to and from the Capitol as to make impossible the Mall's intended development as a single great landscape composition.

In allowing the Smithsonian Institution and the Department of Agriculture to build on the Mall, Congress at least kept open for future use a wide and unbroken shaft of space extending to the Washington Monument. However, by authorizing a railroad yard and a roofed passenger shed to cut the Mall in two, Congress appeared to have forever precluded any appropriate development as a unified landscape composition of this vital element in the city plan.

One other building new to the Washington urban scene appears in the Davis view. This is the National Museum, the largest of the structures depicted in the foreground. It occupied a site immediately east of the Renwick Building of the Smithsonian Institution and was built to house articles exhibited at Philadelphia in 1876 at the Centennial Exhibition. Congress approved construction plans in 1879, and the building was completed early in 1881, just in time to provide a setting for President Garfield's inaugural ball that March.[37]

The National Museum walls enclosed a square 327 feet on each side and thus provided exhibit, office, service, and storage space of nearly two and one-half acres. Its exterior reflected the architectural taste and the current total rejection of classical models for buildings of monumental size. The museum turned out to be something of an exhibit of building materials, with its red brick walls decoratively trimmed with buff and blue bricks—all set in black mortar—a granite basecourse and freestone sills, and its thirty-seven roofs covered with blue, red, and green slate.

At the far left Davis shows how work had progressed on the Washington Monument, a structure finally completed and dedicated on a bitterly cold 21 February 1885. Folio 59 includes extracts from dispatches prepared in Washington during the first half of the 1880s by correspondents for the London *Times*. One of them describes ascending the monument, whose windows at its top offered a splendid new view of the city for those hardy enough to mount this 555-foot shaft by foot or brave enough to trust their lives to the elevator.[38]

The folio also presents descriptions and impressions of some of the major new buildings. The images of these and others appear in the accompanying illustrations. All could be found in souvenir booklets of Washington containing views of the city and its buildings. Like those from other cities, the Washington booklets came from printing firms specializing in the production of these fanfolded illustrations printed on heavy, coated paper in sepia ink. These booklets became popular in the 1880s, and visitors to most major cities and many smaller ones

---

36. Keim, *Keim's Illustrated Hand-Book* (22d ed., 1886), ix.

37. Franklin Cluss, architect for the Franklin School and the Agriculture Department, among other Washington structures, and Paul Schulz served as architects for the building but followed generally a design first prepared by Montgomery Cunningham Meigs. There will be more to say about Meigs and his architectural achievements in the next chapter. Known first as the National Museum, it later became the Arts and Industries Museum.

38. Not everyone liked the appearance of the unadorned stone shaft, but the English editor of Baedeker's guide to the United States who first saw it in 1890 thought it admirable, as these words from his own book of impressions of America indicate: "There are those who consider this a meaningless pile of masonry; but the writer sympathises rather with the critics who find it, in its massive and heavy-reaching simplicity, a fit counterpart to the Capitol and one of the noblest monuments ever raised to mortal man. When gleaming in the westering sun, like a slender, tapering, sky-pointing finger of gold, no finer index can be imagined to direct the gazer to the record of a glorious history" (Muirhead, *Land of Contrasts*, 223–24).

found them helpful pictorial guides while on their travels and attractive souvenirs when they returned home.[39]

As more and more tourists visited Washington, these souvenir booklets must have had a particularly wide sale. Doubtless, too, residents purchased copies to keep or send to friends elsewhere. The images displayed in these booklets must therefore have been seen by many persons and were surely influential in strengthening the image of the capital as a place where monumental buildings could be seen in beautiful and impressive surroundings.

Certainly the booklets offered those who looked at them a fascinating variety of architectural styles. Buildings constructed during the decade and a half incorporating the Shepherd era and its aftermath had substantially altered the prevailing style of the prewar days. Where before only the Smithsonian Institution and the Corcoran Gallery represented marked departures from the earlier public buildings of classical inspiration, a new generation of architects had provided Washington with examples of buildings inspired by different traditions. Indeed, the city at this time had become a kind of museum of applied archaeology and architectural history.

Those souvenir images selected for folio 59 begin with a pair of general views of Washington. The one at the top shows the city as seen from the terrace of the Capitol, a viewpoint similar to several earlier illustrations reproduced in other folios. The most revealing comparison is with the lithograph in folio 35, a depiction of the city from approximately the same spot published thirty-five years earlier.

The bottom view presents a different prospect—the portion of the city visible from the Mall entrance to the Department of Agriculture Building looking north along the axis of Thirteenth Street. This records the carefully landscaped grounds of the building and how they contrasted strongly with the melange of structures then forming the north side of the Mall and extending onto Pennsylvania Avenue.

Other images in the folio show four of the new buildings discussed in this chapter: the National Museum, the Bureau of Printing and Engraving, the Department of State, War, and Navy, and the railroad depot. The last illustration is of the long delayed but finally finished Washington Monument, with a few details of this great memorial shaft whose completion provided the city its highest and most visible and readily recognizable symbol. On the eve of the centennial of its planning, the city was at last beginning to resemble the vision of its planner.

39. The first scholarly study of souvenir booklets is Brodherson, "Souvenir Books in Stone." Most of these booklets seem to have been printed by lithography, although a few printers used the collotype process, a method by which an image on a photographic negative was transferred to a glass plate coated with photosensitive gelatin. The image that resulted could then be inked and used for printing. There is a summary of how this printing process came to the United States and its use in the late nineteenth century in Helena E. Wright, "Partners in Art." Wright's more recent work, *Imperishable Beauty*, provides additional material on the collotype process and its American practitioners.

A New York Times writer tells of conditions that prevailed.

For fifty years a spirit of helplessness seemed to brood over the District of Columbia; ostensibly divided into three municipalities, it was still the creature of Congress, which did nothing for its advancement, except take very indifferent care of its own property, or provide from time to time for the absolute necessities of the public service in the matter of public buildings. But the general aspect of the city was left untouched; not a street was paved; not a sewer was laid; and even the water supply, owing to the increased public uses of the same, became reduced to an utter deprivation in some quarters of the city.

He mentions the poor state of the city's thoroughfares.

Long streets and wide avenues in the heart of Washington were alternately seas of mud or beds of dust, and there was not a drive about the District—which abounds in sightly situations and exquisite scenery—that was fit for a pleasure carriage, except in the most favorable weather.

He gives his version of how changes came about.

Shaking off the lethargy of years of inertia, and waking up the dry boards of "the oldest inhabitants," a few active, enterprising gentlemen, under the lead of Gov. Cooke and Alex. R. Shepherd, took the subject in hand, and secured, as a necessary preliminary, a change in the form of government. (*New York Times*, 4 December 1872)

A veteran Washington reporter gives President Grant credit for the change.

General Grant, soon after his election to the presidential chair, turned his attention to the improvement of the National Capital, which was then unworthy of the American people. The streets generally were wagon tracks, muddy in the winter and dusty in the summer, while the numerous public reservations were commons overgrown with weeds.

He blames "old fogies" for the lack of progress.

The growth of the city had been slow and labored, the real estate being generally in the hands of a few old fogies who manifested no disposition to improve or to sell. For many years the metropolis had been petted and spoiled by the general Government, which had doled out small annual appropriations, and the residents had been exempted from any of the ordinary burdens of municipal government and local improvement.

The author identifies the person Grant selected to modernize the city.

General Grant, with his great knowledge of men, found the right person to place at the head of the regeneration of the city. It was Alexander R. Shepherd, a native of Washington, born poor and without friends, who went from the public schools into the shop of a gas-fitter and plumber, where he learned the trade, and became, in a short time, by honesty, industry, and ability, a leading business man. (Poore, *Perley's Reminiscences,* 2:261–62)

Lippincott's Magazine *provides information on the origins of the new form of government.*

The change of local government in 1871, when Congress gave the District of Columbia a legislature and a representative, was the particular event from which may be dated such innovations as make necessary a revision of the popular opinion. . . . All will understand that it was the first gun at Charleston, startling the stagnant pool here, which set in motion the successive waves that carried the city up to this departure. A few active men, who saw that the old order of things could be endured no longer, met quietly in 1870 at the house of an honored citizen on K street to see what further they could see. They continued to meet [and] drew into their circle many influential Congressmen, and converted them to the new idea that there was something in Washington besides the national service. The result was, that the city government was abolished; a legislative assembly was created; a governor was appointed by the president of the United States; and a delegate was sent to Congress, instead of a crowd of lobbyists, to represent the District. This delegate is always to be a member of the committee on the District, Congress has the constitutional right of exclusive legislation, and the Assembly cannot impose taxes of any consequence without especial authority from the people. (Hickox, "New Washington," 305–6)

Artists in 1848 and 1872 Depict Washington from the Virginia Side of the Potomac

The first of the two views presented here is a tiny, two-stone lithograph from George Watterston's guidebook to Washington. The anonymous artist stood near the western shore of the Potomac River and looked northeast to sketch the long, low, and discontinuous profile of the then scattered city. The dome of the Capitol in the center is the most easily recognized feature. Near the right-hand side one can see the covered repair dock of the Navy Yard. The row of buildings below and to the left of the Capitol must be the arsenal at the long point of land extending southward at the mouth of the Anacostia. The small tower to the right of the mast of the single-sailed vessel on the left probably represents the building of what is now Georgetown University.

The second view, published in 1872, looks almost directly east across the Potomac from the elevated vantage point of Arlington Heights. The elaborately illustrated work on America where it appeared described the scene: "The Capitol, white and majestic, looms high above the metropolis, the rest of which seems a confused mass of houses and spires." Earlier in the text the author referred to the second most prominent object in the view as "the unfinished shaft of the Washington Monument, a square marble torso of desolate appearance." This illustration was drawn by William Ludlow Sheppard, a native of Richmond, Virginia, and engraved by Robert Hinshelwood, a Scot who came to America about 1835. Their skillful work typified the quality of the illustrations in the elaborate publication in which this engraving appeared.

Washington, from the Virginia Side. Unsigned and undated [1847–48] view from George Watterston, *New Guide to Washington.* Lithograph, 3⅛ × 5 in. (7.9 × 12.7 cm.). John W. Reps.

Washington from Arlington Heights. Drawn by W[illiam Ludlow] Sheppard. Engraved by R[obert] Hinshelwood. Published by D. Appleton & Co. 1872. From William Cullen Bryant (ed.), *Picturesque America; or, the Land We Live in: A Delineation by Pen and Pencil* (New York: D. Appleton & Co., [1872]), vol. 2. Steel engraving, 5½ × 8¾ in. (14 × 22.2 cm.). Kiplinger Collection.

In a major book on America in 1872,
G. M. Towle praises the new Washington.

Washington has not, until within comparatively recent years, been celebrated for its beauty. Formerly it was an unattractive place, composed in large part of low and mostly wooden buildings, with streets ill-paved and little cared for. Now the national metropolis, thanks to liberal expenditures and a newly-born pride in the government that its seat should be worthy of its distinction, presents an aspect not only of prosperity, but of sights agreeable to the eye and mostly in good taste.

He admires the Capitol above all.

The most striking object at Washington is undoubtedly the magnificent white-marble Capitol. . . . It rises majestically far above all surrounding objects, amid a nest of thick and darkly verdant foliage, on the brow of the hill to which it gives its name; its very lofty dome, with its tiers of columns, its rich ornamentation, and its summit surmounted by the colossal statue of Liberty, presents a noble appearance, and may be seen for many miles around; while its broad, white wings, low in proportion to the dome, give an idea of spaciousness which no palace of European potentate surpasses. (Towle, "Washington and its Vicinity," 565–66)

A correspondent for the London Daily News *comes away unimpressed by what he saw of Washington in the mid-1870s.*

By the time that the city of Washington shall be a century old, the dream of its founder may be as far from realization as it is at present. . . . The city is still surpassed by many capitals in Europe, not in magnitude only, but also in all those attractions which make cities famous. . . . A visitor to the United States could spend many months most profitably in New York, Boston, and Philadelphia, in the older cities of the South, or the younger cities of the West; but he could learn little if he were to pass the same time in Washington. After he had visited the Capitol, the public offices, the Corcoran Gallery of Art, the Smithsonian Institution, he would have beheld nearly everything worth seeing.

He regards the Capitol as very large but not beautiful.

Regarded as a mere architectural pile it is grandiose; but it wants that symmetry of form and magic of design which make

St. Peter's a thing of beauty. No architect will ever gaze upon it in order to gain inspiration and qualify himself to become a master of his profession. . . . The result is a huge dome crowning a structure which might have been planned by an intelligent bricklayer. . . . But the citizens of the United States are pleased with their Capitol, they say that it is one of the most magnificent public buildings in the world; other persons have not, perhaps, any right to complain. (Rae, *Columbia and Canada*, 151–53)

A Scottish member of Parliament disagrees
with Rae's assessment of Washington.

It seemed to me that Washington is the pleasantest and best of American cities. Mr. [Anthony] Trollope describes it in very horrible terms, but it has certainly been very much improved since those days, and appeared to me to be a charming place. . . .

The entrance to Washington [from Baltimore] is through a poor part of the town. The Capitol is very conspicuous; from a distance it looks like St. Peter's at Rome. . . . Very fine, wide avenues have been laid out, radiating from central points; and there are some fine streets. . . . Washington . . . had great ideas of the future, and a sort of mania for broad streets and magnificent designs. . . . [He] meant the principal part of the city to be on the side where it is not now, but land speculators took up the land and ran up the prices so high that people built on what he meant to be the back part of the town; that is now the City of Washington, with the Capitol, as it were, looking away from it. Some modern Americans grumble about the width of the Washington streets, and say that the vastness of the place dwarfs the buildings. I must say that I think Washington was quite right. In this climate, where trees grow easily, broad avenues are very effective and pleasing; and although the City of Washington was for upwards of half a century a complete failure, and until a few years ago was not at all successful, it has made immense strides of late years. . . . It is not only well laid out, handsome, and clean, but it has that which is altogether wanting in all other places in America that I have seen, viz., good pavement. All the principal avenues and streets are laid down with excellent asphalte [*sic*] pavement; so that instead of being the worst it is the best-paved town in the world that I know. (Campbell, *White and Black*, 33, 270–71)

Sachse Takes a Final Look at Washington in 1871

Two years before his death in 1873 Sachse printed and published what proved to be his last view of the capital city. In it he or some anonymous artist employed by Sachse finally rendered the Capitol correctly, showing the new dome over the rotunda, the two low domes atop the old Senate and House wings, and the elongated skylights on the two new legislative wings. In the distance beyond the Smithsonian Institution the view also adds the image of the new Agriculture Building, authorized by Congress in 1868 for a site on the Mall. However, Sachse persisted in depicting the original design for the Washington Monument as it would have looked if completed according to the plans drawn many years earlier by Robert Mills.

In a major book on America published in 1872, the author of the section on Washington, G. M. Towle, described what he saw from the terrace of the Capitol as he looked from right to left. His words nicely compliment Sachse's view:

"From this lookout you may discern every part of the metropolis; in the midst of the mass of houses rise the white-marble Post-Office Department and the yet handsomer Patent-Office just beside it. Some distance farther on is to be descried the long colonnade of the Treasury, and the top of the White House, just beyond, peeps from among the crests of flourishing groups of trees; more to the left are seen the picturesque, castle-like, red-sandstone towers and turrets of the Smithsonian Institution, standing solitary on a broad plain already sprouting with young foliage. Between the Smithsonian and the creek the unfinished shaft of the Washington Monument, a square marble torso of desolate appearance, meets the view; while the eye, spanning the Potomac, may catch sight, in the distance, of that lordly old manor-house of Arlington, identified, in very different ways, with the earlier and later history of the country. Georgetown Heights form the far background in the west."

View of Washington City. Unsigned view printed and copyrighted by E. Sachse & Co., No. 5 N. Liberty St., Balto., 1871. Lithograph, 19 × 26¾ in. (48.4 × 68.1 cm.). Prints and Photographs, Library of Congress.

VIEW OF WASHINGTON CITY.

Folio 54. Alexander Shepherd Transforms Washington by Building Modern Streets, Sewers, and Other Improvements

A writer for a leading New York newspaper at the end of 1872 expresses amazement at how much has been done.

The transformation which has been effected in the nation's capital within the past year is the first thing to excite the admiration and surprise of the stranger and visitor who returns to the city at the opening of another political and social season. It seems incomprehensible to many that such an enormous amount of work, and such complete and admirable effects should have been produced within so short a time.

He calls Shepherd's program the first successful effort toward beautification.

It has always been known that the plan upon which the capital was originally laid out, would, if carried out to its perfection, make of Washington the most beautiful city of the world, which was the undoubted intention of its founders. But not until within the past eighteen months has there ever been anything like a successful effort to do anything toward the improvement and beautification of the city and environs (*New York Times*, 4 December 1872, p. 2)

A journalist for Harper's Monthly *in 1875 describes conditions before modernization.*

Not one street was paved for any great consecutive distance; there was not a street car in the city. . . . The water supply was wholly afforded by pumps and springs. Gas had been in partial use for several years, but little else was lighted except Pennsylvania Avenue and the public buildings. . . . Nearly one-half of the city was cut off from the rest by a ditch, and called the Island, while an intervening strip of mall and park was patrolled by outlaws and outcasts, with only a bridge here and there for outlet. The river-side was a mass of earthen bluffs pierced by two streets, and scarcely attainable for mire and obstructions.

The writer records the extensive program of street paving.

The result has been to lay in Washington 28½ miles of concrete pavement and 58½ of wood pavement, making 87 miles of what is certainly the most agreeable roadway in the world, out of a total of 180 new miles in the city, the rest being cobble, macadam, gravel, and Belgian block. . . .

If you remember that from the Treasury gate to the gate of the Capitol is about one mile, and then multiply the distance by 180, you will begin to perceive the difference between old and new Washington.

The article mentions sidewalk and parkway improvements and summarizes the results.

Lining the above streets are nearly 208 miles of new sidewalks, of which seven miles are flag and concrete, and the rest brick, and 154 miles of new curb-stone has been set. . . . The architect . . . lighted upon the idea of reducing the width of the portions of the streets necessary to be paved by advancing the curb-stones toward the centre, and at the same time reducing the cost of the sidewalks by sodding between them and the houses. It was next suggested to devise some kind of railing, characteristic and pretty, to inclose the sodded portions, that every house might seem to have its own front yard. Afterward the renovators resolved to plant the streets with trees. . . .

Not only were the streets of the capital covered with the most noiseless and perfect pavements in the world, and embowered in the greenest borders of grass-plots, inclosed with panels of post and chain or graceful paling, and planted with trees, but at all the points of junction new squares and circles appeared, their verdure relieved with flashing fountains, or bits of statuary . . . while old gulfs and commons . . . were embanked, leveled, and brought into the common civilization of the city. . . . The public grounds, swept of their cemetery-like palings and wholly rejuvenated, lay open to equestrian and urchin. Where the old creek yawned through the heart of the commercial city, a noble mall, grand market, and depots were revealed. . . . Between the president's House and Capitol Hill a green park with graveled drives rolled away like a carpet of velvet. The river-side, with its bluffs tamed down to easy quays and paved with granite block, was at every point attainable.

This writer sees a transformed Washington.

Thus Washington . . . has clothed itself anew, thrown away its staff, and achieved a transformation bewildering to its old residents, but very grateful to the patriotic sense which had so long felt the stigma of a neglected and forlorn capital apparently without a destiny. (Townsend, "New Washington," 313–22)

Municipal Engineering Makes Washington a Modern City

In 1871 Congress established a territorial government for the District of Columbia to replace the cities of Washington and Georgetown and the county that governed the remaining, largely rural portion of the district through a body known as the Levy Court. Alexander Shepherd, a young, forceful, and wealthy alderman in the old municipality became head of the Board of Public Works and immediately began a program of thoroughfare and utility improvements unprecedented in scope anywhere in the country.

Shepherd's comprehensive plan called for street grading and paving, sewer and water main construction, and the development of planted verges or median strips along the wide avenues. It also involved filling the Washington Canal and replacing it with a main sewer, and dredging the harbors of both Georgetown and Washington.

These maps from the board's 1873 report show the two major segments of this vast program that graded and paved the city's streets and built a sewerage system as modern as any in the world. It was an astounding accomplishment, especially in a city with such a history of excessively slow public construction.

Exhibit Chart Showing Streets & Avenues of the Cities of Washington and Georgetown, Improved Under the Board of Public Works. D.C. Nov. 1st 1873. Pavements. Printed by J. F. Cedney Engraver Printer Lithographer Penn. Avenue 466 Washington D.C. From Board of Public Works of the District of Columbia, *Report*, 1 November 1873 (Washington, D.C.: Chronicle Publishing Company, 1873). Lithograph, 16⅞ × 20⅞ in. (42.9 × 53 cm.). New York State Library.

Exhibit Chart Showing Streets & Avenues of the Cities of Washington and Georgetown, Improved Under the Board of Public Works. D.C. Nov. 1st 1873. Sewers. Printed by J. F. Cedney Engraver Printer Lithographer Penn. Avenue 466 Washington D.C. From Board of Public Works of the District of Columbia, *Report*, 1 November 1873 (Washington, D.C.: Chronicle Publishing Company, 1873). Lithograph, 16⅞ × 20⅞ in. (42.9 × 53 cm.). New York State Library.

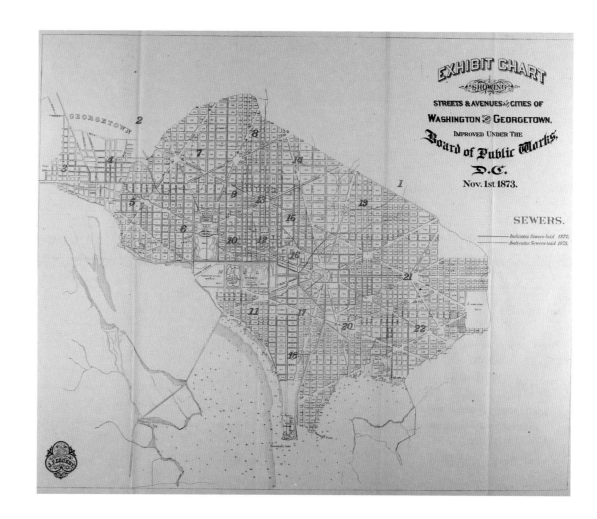

189

A reporter for the New York Times *in December 1872 contrasts old and new sanitary conditions.*

If you will conceive a city, substantially without a decent sewer, its sewage carried off through the gutters by infrequent rains, and natural water-courses depended upon for similar service, you will have an idea of what Washington was substantially less than two years ago. Today there are seventy miles of sewerage in the ground, eight of which belong to the main system, and consist of brick sewers of from four to thirty feet in the span.

He tells his readers that the canal has now been filled.

The great Tiber sewer, which drains the northeastern portion of the city, is 2,473 feet long and thirty feet span; the Slash-Run sewer, which drains the north-western portion of the city, is 2,200 feet long, and wide enough to drive a horse and buggy through, while the great B-street intercepting sewer, which drains the central portion of the city, and takes the place of the old canal, is twelve feet wide and one mile long. The old canal, so long the standing disgrace of the city is no longer in existence. Its banks are full of good solid earth, and the ground reclaimed by it is worth half a million of dollars, which is coolly appropriated by the General Government because Congress appropriated $68,000 toward filling up the ditch. A pretty good speculation. The two first-named sewers are not yet complete, and will be extended to about twice their present length. (*New York Times,* 4 December 1872, p. 2)

A Harper's *correspondent in 1875 describes the new sewerage system.*

The mouth of the Tiber was filled up, and a new mouth given it down stream; the whole stream and its three branches were arched over with brick, and the former outlet also sewered. This central system of main sewerage, of which 16,500 feet had been completed in 1873, is nowhere less than nine feet span, and for much of the distance thirty feet. A buggy can be driven through it all, a space of three miles. It empties into a broad canal, which the tide cleanses twice a day. . . . Thus a pestiferous gutter, occasionally a torrent, which . . . received annually 300,000 cubic feet of vileness, was a vast fermenting vat without a current, useless for navigation, and deadly, became an arborescent and monumental system of sewerage,

covered with grass, paved streets, and files of houses; while another sewer, tapping the Tiber as it emerged from the heights back of the city, led the natural brook and its deluges off by the rear to the Eastern Branch. The third creek, which underlies the West End, or new fashionable part of Washington, has been incased in a sewer of ten feet span, so that there are no longer puddles or ponds or open sinks in any part of Washington. At the same time Georgetown was given a great main sewer, and these four systems comprise, with their arteries of Scotch pipe and iron sewerage, 123 miles of under-ground work, hidden away so that one must seek it out, and yet a formidable expense to a population mainly clerical. There are no such sewers in extent or dimensions on the Western continent.

New and replaced water mains are installed.

In two years the city laid thirty miles of water mains . . . so that the city has at present 133 miles of water pipe. Washington has the greatest supply of water per head of any modern municipality—127 gallons *per diem.* The distributing system is fed through an infinite number of hydrants, drinking fountains, fire plugs, and ornamental fountains. . . .

The Gas-light Company was incited to equal exertion in extending its mains below the surface, and the former city, which was wrapped in comparative darkness, showed in 1873 above three thousand public lamps, partly lighted by electricity. (Townsend, "New Washington," 316–17)

A correspondent for Lippincott's Magazine *appraises the work of the board early in 1873.*

The Baron Haussmann here is the Board of Public Works. It is grading, filling, paving, planting, fencing, parking, and making the thoroughfares what they would never have become by ordinary means. At last we see what Washingtonians never saw before—vast public operations having a consistent and tangible shape; obeying a purpose that can be understood, defined and executed; beginning somewhere and ending in something. Within its sphere this Board has despotic power: it would be worthless with any less. It dares to strike without fear or favor, and hit whoever stands in the way; the way would never be cleared if it did not. It makes bitter enemies by its inexorable exactions; the public cannot be served except at the expense of the individual. (Hickox, "New Washington," 306–7)

The Board of Public Works Maps Its Progress in Extending Water and Gas Services

During the years from 1871 to 1873 construction crews could be seen everywhere in the city as the Board of Public Works carried out its projects. Regrading of streets left some structures far above new pavement levels while the owners of others constructed in modest declivities found themselves facing many feet of newly filled street embankment. Excavations for utilities disrupted traffic, and extensive street paving projects further interfered with established travel patterns and access to buildings.

The size of this program, the speed with which Shepherd carried it out, some careless planning, and illegal payments all combined to raise costs so far above original estimates that two congressional investigations resulted. The second in 1874 led to Shepherd's downfall and the replacement of the territorial government with one more closely controlled by Congress. The federal government assumed a large share of the extra costs, and most of the projects under way were completed.

The two maps reproduced here from the board's 1873 report show the locations of existing and newly constructed water mains and gas mains. These extended utility service lines complemented the board's many other improvements.

Exhibit Chart Showing Streets & Avenues of the Cities of Washington and Georgetown, Improved Under the Board of Public Works. D.C. Nov. 1st 1873. Water Mains. Printed by J. F. Cedney Engraver Printer Lithographer Penn. Avenue 466 Washington D.C. From Board of Public Works of the District of Columbia, *Report,* 1 November 1873 (Washington, D.C.: Chronicle Publishing Company, 1873). Lithograph, 16⅞ × 20⅞ in. (42.9 × 53 cm.). New York State Library.

Exhibit Chart Showing Streets & Avenues of the Cities of Washington and Georgetown, Improved Under the Board of Public Works. D.C. Nov. 1st 1873. Gas Mains. Printed by J. F. Cedney Engraver Printer Lithographer Penn. Avenue 466 Washington D.C. From Board of Public Works of the District of Columbia, *Report,* 1 November 1873 (Washington, D.C.: Chronicle Publishing Company, 1873). Lithograph, 16⅞ × 20⅞ in. (42.9 × 53 cm.). New York State Library.

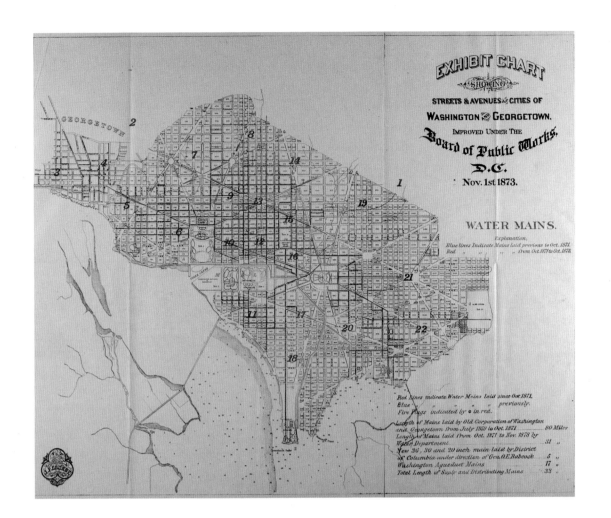

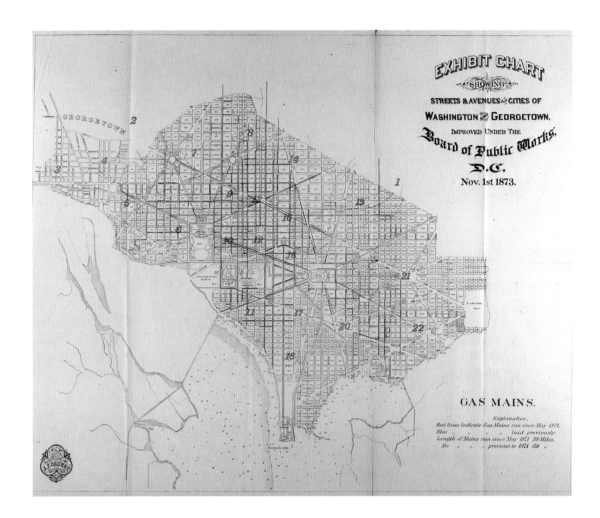

*Mary Clemmer Ames acclaims the new
Washington of the Reconstruction period.*

The citizen of the year of our Lord 1873 sees the dawn of that perfect day of which the founders of the Capital so fondly and fruitlessly dreamed. The old provincial Southern city is no more. From its foundations has risen another city, neither Southern nor Northern, but national, cosmopolitan.

She lauds the new street pavements.

Where the "Slough of Despond" spread its waxen mud across the acres of the West End, where pedestrians were "slumped," and horses "stalled," and discomfort and disgust prevailed, we now see broad carriage drives, level as floors, over which grand equipages and pony phaetons glide with a smoothness that is a luxury, and an ease of motion which is rest. Where ravines and holes made the highway dangerous, now the concrete . . . pavements stretch over miles on miles of inviting road.

She tells of new parks replacing old deserts.

Where streets and avenues crossed and re-crossed their long vistas of shadeless dust, now plat on plat of restful grass "park" the city from end to end. Double rows of young trees line these parks far as the sight can reach.

Old Washington was full of small Saharas. Where the great avenues intersected acres of white sand were caught up and carried through the air by counter winds. It blistered at white heat beneath your feet, it flickered like a fiery veil before your eyes, it penetrated your lungs and begrimed your clothes. Now where streets and avenues cross, emerald "circles" with central fountains, pervading the air with cooling spray, with belts of flowers and troops of children, and restful seats for the old or the weary take the place of the old Saharas. In every direction tiny parks are blooming with verdurous life.

She praises the sewerage system.

The green pools which used to distill malaria beneath your windows are now all sucked into the great sewers, planted at last in the foundations of the city. The entire city has been drained. Every street has been newly graded. The Tiber, inglorious stream, arched and covered forever from sight, creeps in darkness to its final gulf in the river. The canal, drained and filled up, no longer breeds pestilence.

She writes of avenues that have now become showplaces.

Pennsylvania avenue has outlived its mud and its poplars, to be all and more than Jefferson dreamed it would be,—the most magnificent street on the continent. Its lining palaces are not yet built, but more than one superb building . . . soars high above the lowly shops of the past, a forerunner of the architectural splendor of the buildings of the future. Cars running every five minutes have taken the place of the solitary stage, plodding its slow way between Georgetown and the Capital. . . . At the West End . . . solid blocks of city houses are rising in every direction. . . . Vermont, Massachusetts and Connecticut avenues are already lined with splendid mansions, the permanent winter homes of Senators and other high official and military officers. The French, Spanish, English and other foreign governments have bought on and near these avenues for the purpose of building on them handsome houses for their separate legations.

She describes improvements in the public grounds.

Capitol Hill, which had been retrograding for more than forty years, has taken on the look of a suddenly growing city. Its dusty ways and empty spaces are beginning to fill with handsome blocks of metropolitan houses. . . . The same transformation is going on in the Capitol grounds. Blocks of old houses have been torn down and demolished to make room for a park fit to encircle the Capitol. . . . No scaffolding and pulleys now deface the snowy surfaces of the Capitol. Unimpeded the dome soars into mid-air, till the goddess of liberty on its top seems caught into the embrace of the clouds.

*The author summarizes important improvements
adjoining the White House.*

The grounds of the Executive Mansion are being enlarged, extending to the Potomac with a carriage drive encircling, running along the shore of the river, extending through the Agricultural, Smithsonian and Botanical garden grounds, thus fulfilling the original intent of connecting the White House with the Capitol by a splendid drive. . . . The beautiful Treasury building is completed, and a block further on, the click of ceaseless hammers and the rising buttresses of solid stone tell of the new war and navy departments which are swiftly growing beside the historic walls of the old. (Ames, *Ten Years in Washington*, 72–75)

George Morrison Draws Washington for a
Guidebook Using Sachse's Favorite Viewpoint

W. H. and O. H. Morrison published a guidebook to Washington that went through many editions. It must have been one of the most widely used guides in the country, and all of its owners would have seen the folded line perspective of the city that is reproduced here. It was the work of George Morrison, no doubt a relative of the publishers. Probably he used one of the Sachse lithographs as a model, altered the angle of the perspective slightly, and added a few details of his own.

The legend at the bottom locates what the Morrisons felt were the most important places travelers should know about: the U.S. Capitol, Arlington, the Agriculture Department, the Smithsonian Institution (here called the "Institute"), the Washington Monument, the stations of the Baltimore and Potomac and the Baltimore and Ohio railroads, the botanical gardens, Centre Market, the State Department, the Treasury, Georgetown College, the Post Office Department, the Patent and Land Office Department, Howard University, and the Government Printing Office.

Unlike most of the other published views of Washington, this simple depiction of the city makes no claim to be decorative, and surely few if any persons ever considered using it as a wall decoration. However, its merits as a functional and easy-to-understand guide to the national capital made it attractive as a practical guide to the many features of Washington that brought increasing numbers of visitors to the city.

Bird's-Eye View of Washington City, D.C. Drawn by Geo A. Morrison, published by W. H. & O. H. Morrison, Washington, 1872. Lithograph, 14¼ × 20 in. (36.1 × 50.8 cm.). Olin Library, Cornell University.

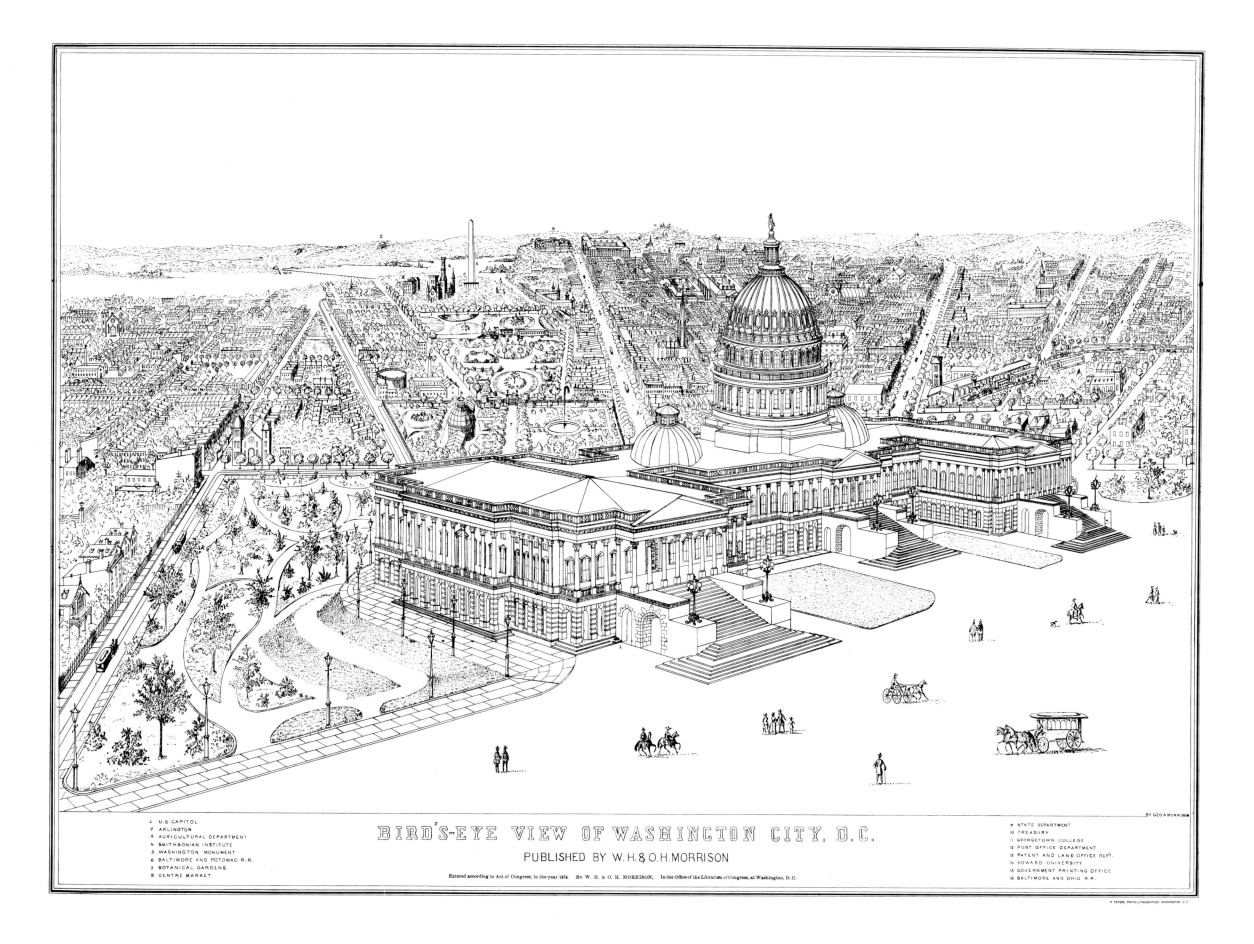

BY GEO. A. MORRISON

BIRD'S-EYE VIEW OF WASHINGTON CITY, D.C.

PUBLISHED BY W.H. & O.H. MORRISON

Entered according to Act of Congress, in the year 1874, By W. H. & O. H. MORRISON, In the Office of the Librarian of Congress, at Washington, D.C.

1 U.S. CAPITOL
2 ARLINGTON
3 AGRICULTURAL DEPARTMENT
4 SMITHSONIAN INSTITUTE
5 WASHINGTON MONUMENT
6 BALTIMORE AND POTOMAC R.R.
7 BOTANICAL GARDENS
8 CENTRE MARKET

9   STATE DEPARTMENT
10 TREASURY
11 GEORGETOWN COLLEGE
12 POST OFFICE DEPARTMENT
13 PATENT AND LAND OFFICE DEPT.
14 HOWARD UNIVERSITY
15 GOVERNMENT PRINTING OFFICE
16 BALTIMORE AND OHIO R.R.

R. PETERS, PHOTO-LITHOGRAPHER, WASHINGTON, D.C.

193

A Harper's Magazine *writer*
in 1878 hails the new Washington.

The prophecy that Washington would eventually become one of the handsomest cities in the world, which was ridiculed as wild and chimerical by many a statesman adverse to liberal expenditure in the early period, seems in a fair way to be fulfilled. The signs of promise are vividly apparent in the broad streets and broader divergent and grand transverse avenues, lined with double rows of trees, which cross each other with geometrical precision, forming upon every corner the most charming triangles, circles, and squares, filled with choice shade trees, shrubbery, statuary, fountains, and flowers; and in the elegant and costly private dwellings, surrounded by highly cultivated and spacious grounds, which have sprung up in every direction (Lamb, "State and Society," 481.)

In 1881 Harper's Magazine *once again appraises Washington for its readers.*

Washington to-day is so cosmopolitan that the proud citizen who goes thither for the first time has to stop and reflect a little before he can fully comprehend that it all belongs to him. Twenty years ago . . . it was a skeleton structure, a scattered, unhealthful village, double dwarfed by its huge public buildings. Now it is a city clean and fair, and the public buildings are connected by a living tissue of populous streets. . . . A city without a commerce and without suburbs—drive a mile or two in any direction and you find yourself in the midst of woods set but sparsely with houses or cabins, and with only the great pillard dome, like a shining cloud in the air, to remind you of the human mass so near.

The author admires the extensive use of street trees.

The broad airy streets . . . have a continental width and extent, making it impossible to crowd them except on rare occasions, and in the more retired ones children glide peacefully along the asphalt on roller-skates. . . . Many of the houses in the new northwest end are well set off by trees and lawns; some stand on terraces decked with vines and shrubbery; and the avenues are lined with more than a hundred thousand trees judiciously planted—elm and tulip, buttonwood and cottonwood, the ash, the negundo, the maple. ("A Nation in a Nutshell," 541-43)

William Edwin Adams praises the city he visited in 1882.

The Capital of the Republic is not unworthy of the great and prosperous country in which it occupies the first place. . . . Large ideas pervaded the founders of the city. They provided for a development commensurate with the development of the nation. Hence they placed the Public Departments so far away from each other that Washington was happily designated the City of Magnificent Distances. The distances are still magnificent; but the intervening spaces have now almost all been filled up with handsome residences.

Adams delights in the trees along streets and avenues.

The streets and avenues are all broad, all planted with trees, and nearly all asphalted. It is said that the average width is double that of the streets and avenues of Paris and Berlin. Pennsylvania Avenue seemed to me even finer than the Champs Elysées. The management of the thoroughfares is placed in the hands of a . . . Commission, which has done its work so well that upwards of 67,000 trees have been planted under its direction. . . . The result of the Parking Commission's operations is that one hundred and thirty miles of shaded walks are provided for the use and enjoyment of the citizens of Washington.

He admires the public buildings and their vistas.

Many of the public buildings are splendid specimens of architecture. The Capitol, however, overshadows them all. Situated on an elevation in the centre of the city, it commands a clear and unobstructed view on every side. Nothing can be finer than the prospect from the Capitol—the city, embosomed in trees, lying below; the broad waters of the Potomac beyond; and beyond the Potomac again the Heights of Arlington. . . . From the Potomac, too, the city has a charming appearance, crowned as it is by the dome of the Capitol, which shines in the sun like a globe of polished silver.

Adams equates Washington to the capitals of Europe.

I have seen many of the capitals of Europe. I have seen London, Edinburgh, and Dublin; I have seen Paris, Berlin, and Brussels; I have seen Copenhagen, Christiana, Dresden, and the Hague. But I have seen none that surpassed for effect the City of Magnificent Distances. (W. E. Adams, *Our American Cousins,* 31-33)

Currier and Ives Publishes
a View of Washington

Beginning in 1873 the famous New York firm of Currier and Ives issued a series of very large folio views of American cities drawn by Charles R. Parsons. In 1880 the firm added the Washington lithograph shown here. Work had then finally resumed on the Washington Monument, and Parsons drew the cranes extending from the top of its stone shaft. Its newly reinforced base stood close to the tidal flats of the river and two fish ponds that helped to replenish the city's supply of mosquitoes. Parsons finished on paper the huge building of the State, War, and Navy departments west of the White House, although another eight years would be required to complete the northern portion of this structure. Across Pennsylvania Avenue stood the Corcoran Gallery of Art in the building built in 1874 through the generosity of William Wilson Corcoran, a prominent Washington banker. Parsons erroneously drew it on a site one block too far east.

His depiction of the Mall is more useful. At the foot of Capitol Hill one can see the congressional greenhouse and—a few blocks to the west—the tracks and the train shed of the Baltimore and Potomac Railroad that further interrupted the continuity of the Mall. The enormous central market occupied a site diagonally across the street from the station to the northwest. Along the south side of the Mall the new arts and industries building of the Smithsonian was nearing completion next to Renwick's older building to the west. Between them and the Washington Monument the Agriculture Department looked across its own landscaped grounds to the closely packed jumble of structures between the Mall and Pennsylvania Avenue. On a choice spot facing the Washington Monument, one better suited for a more impressive structure, stood the factorylike Bureau of Printing and Engraving, its tall chimney providing a rare symbol of industrial activity in this city built on the growing bureaucracy of the federal government.

The City of Washington. Bird's-Eye View from the Potomac—Looking North. Drawn by C[harles] R. Parsons. Published by Currier & Ives, New York, 1880. Lithograph, 20½ × 33⅛ in. (52.2 × 84.3 cm.). Prints and Photographs, Library of Congress.

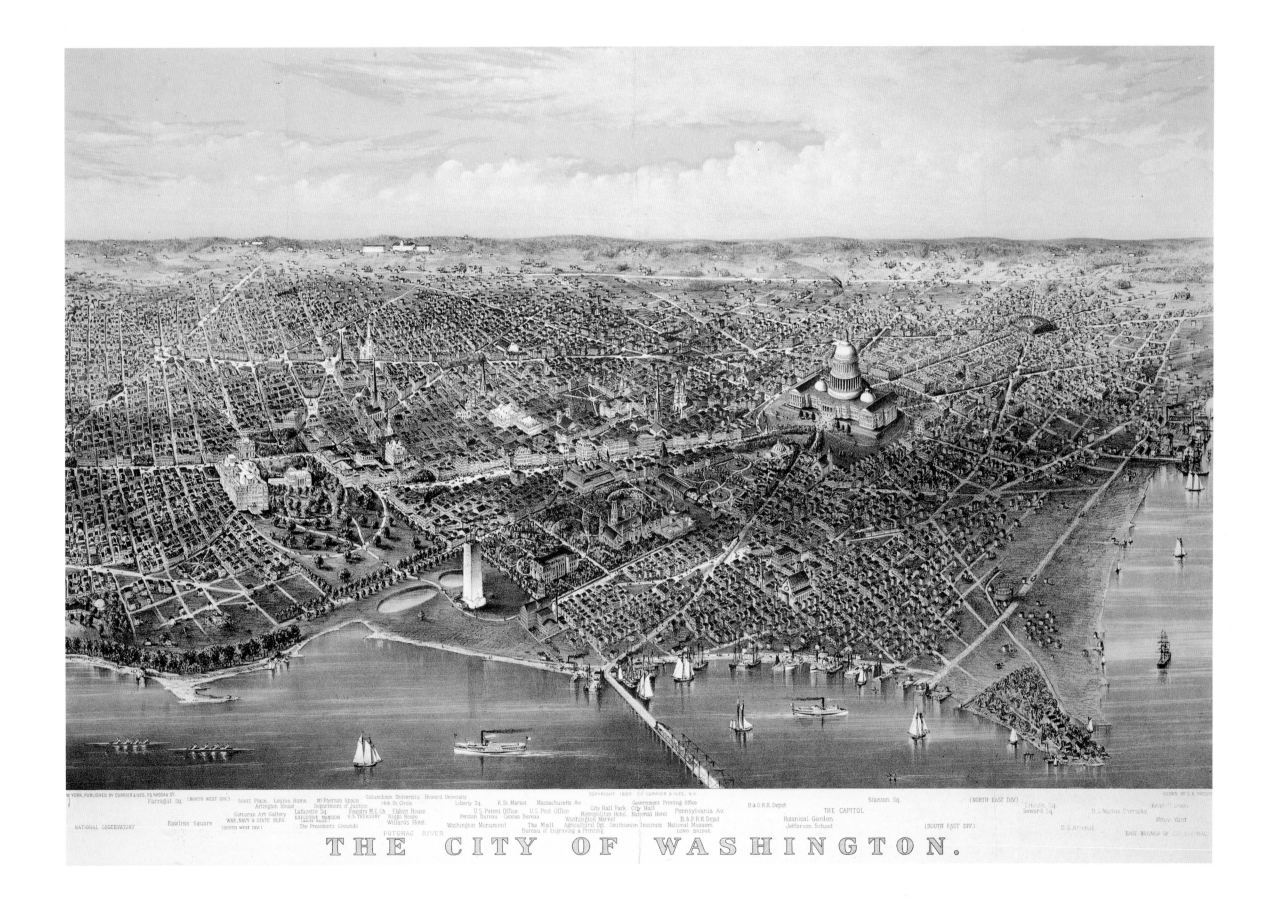

Farragut Sq.   (NORTH WEST DIV.)   Scott Place   Louise Home   McPherson Square   Columbian University   Howard University   Liberty Sq.   K St Market   Massachusetts Av.   Government Printing Office   B.&O.R.R. Depot   Stanton Sq.   (NORTH EAST DIV.)   Lincoln Sq.   Kendall Green

Arlington House   Department of Justice   14th St. Circle

Corcoran Art Gallery   Lafayette Sq.   Foundry M.E.Ch.   Ebbitt House   U.S. Patent Office   U.S. Post Office   City Hall Park   City Hall   Pennsylvania Av.   THE CAPITOL   Seward Sq.   U.S. Marine Barracks

WAR, NAVY & STATE BLDG.   EXECUTIVE MANSION   U.S. TREASURY   Riggs House   Pension Bureau   Census Bureau   Metropolitan Hotel   National Hotel   B.& P.R.R.Depot   Botanical Garden   Navy Yard

NATIONAL OBSERVATORY   Rawlins' Square   (SOUTH WEST DIV.)   (White House)   The Presidents Grounds   Willard's Hotel   Washington Monument   The Mall   Agricultural Dpt.   Smithsonian Institute   National Museum   Jefferson School   (SOUTH EAST DIV.)   U.S. Arsenal

POTOMAC RIVER   Bureau of Engraving & Printing   Washington Market   LONG BRIDGE   EAST BRANCH OF THE POTOMAC

THE CITY OF WASHINGTON.

The author points out Washington's unique character.

Within the past ten years Washington has ceased to be a village. Whether it has yet become a city depends on "the point of view." It has no elevated railroads, no palace hotels, no mammoth elevators, no great commercial establishments; it has no opera and but indifferent theaters, and for a park it borrows the grounds of the old soldiers of the army. In short, it has none of those evidences of commercial prosperity which are proudly shown to the traveler in every thriving town, all the way from New York to San Francisco. On the other hand, it has large public buildings and monuments and numerous statues; it has a mild climate, clean, well-paved streets, and no "local politics"; its chief inhabitants are those persons who guide the action and control the interests of fifty millions of people—so far as they are guided or controlled at all in a nation which so largely governs itself. Washington is thus a place quite out of the ordinary run; whether city or no, it is certainly unlike other cities. . . . Other cities have originated in the necessities of trade, and have grown in proportion as that trade increased. Washington, on the contrary, was made to order on a map; and . . . its population has not yet grown up to the limits which were originally laid out.

The article describes the city plan, including its immense size.

Everything was on a scale of large proportions, the avenues being grand boulevards of one hundred and fifty to one hundred and sixty feet in width, and even unimportant streets being ninety or one hundred feet wide. The proportion of streets and open squares, which in most cities is about one-fourth, was thus laid out in this capital city at more than one-half of the whole surface. It was to be the capital of a mighty nation, and no one was to be pinched for space in it.

The writer mentions some of the problems of development.

The plan was thus drawn on paper, and nothing remained but to fill up the uninhabited fields through which the imaginary streets ran. This was not so easy. The Government came there in 1800, and great expectations were formed, but they were not realized. For more than half a century the place remained a straggling Southern village, giving rise to much ridicule as a "city of magnificent distances." The diaries and chronicles of the first third of the century give curious accounts of the uncomfortable and dreary life in such an uninviting place.

At the time of the Civil War, conditions had scarcely changed for the better.

It had attained a population of only sixty thousand inhabitants, who were scattered over a territory of several miles; its streets were so filthy and ill-kept that they were a by-word of contempt; none of its citizens were rich, and there were no handsome dwellings or other indications of private wealth.

The article describes the improvements of the 1870s.

It began to be realized that it was a disgrace to have such a city for a capital, and that the General Government and the citizens must all unite in efforts to improve it. The result was the formation, in 1871, of a territorial government, with a Governor and Legislature and a Board of Public Works. The master-spirit of this government was Alexander Shepherd. . . . The results of his government are too recent and too well known to call for fresh comments. Vast plans were again matured, founded as in the past century, not on the actual necessities of the moment, but on the requirements of a generation hence. Costly improvements were undertaken and prosecuted far beyond the limits of habitation. Miles upon miles of expensive pavements and other works were laid across swamps and streams, and through waste places where nothing but frame shanties and government stables of the war period had as yet penetrated. In less than three years Shepherd plunged the city into a debt which, for the numbers and wealth of the population has no rival in all the world.

The author weighs the results of the Shepherd era.

The change wrought in the appearance of the city by the Shepherd government and its successors was fundamental and revolutionary. It might have been done more cheaply, but it was better to have it done extravagantly than not at all. Possibly, it never could have been done at all but by some man of Shepherd's intolerant energy, which sacrificed individual rights for the future benefit of the whole community. Had it been attempted prudently and cautiously, these individual rights would have defeated the whole scheme, for the community was not wealthy enough to compensate the injury done to them. ("The New Washington," 643–49)

Theodore Davis Draws the City
in 1882 for *Harper's Weekly.*

For *Harper's Weekly* in 1882 Theodore Davis produced this large wood engraving whose perspective is somewhat misleading. The artist artificially shortened the distance between the Capitol and the Washington Monument and moved the Smithsonian Institution—one of the three buildings in the foreground—to the south. Davis thus placed it on what is now Independence Avenue, neatly lined up with its neighbors, the Agriculture Department and the National Museum, a new structure completed in 1879.

Directly across the Mall from the National Museum, the Centre Market occupied an extensive site between Pennsylvania Avenue and what had once been the canal. After Shepherd converted the canal into a huge enclosed sewer, what we know as Constitution Avenue replaced the canal as the northern boundary of the Mall. Centre Market was built in 1871 to replace a structure destroyed by fire. It and earlier market buildings blocked what L'Enfant had intended as a major axis of the city leading southward from his proposed National Church. The splendid Patent Office that had been built on that site instead was thus cut off from what could have been an impressive approach from the south.

Diagonally across from the market stood the railroad station of the Baltimore and Potomac line. Congress in 1872 allowed the railway to lay its tracks across the Mall at Sixth Street from Maryland Avenue, a blunder that defaced the Mall and caused endless difficulties before the station and tracks could be moved early in the present century. North of the still incomplete Washington Monument and beyond the White House on its western flank rose the enormous bulk of the new building that on its completion in 1888 housed the Departments of State, War, and Navy. The view makes clear that despite earlier proposals, the grounds of the White House, monument, Agriculture Department, Smithsonian, and Capitol lacked any coordinated plan or sense of unified organization.

Our National Capitol, Viewed from the South. Drawn by Theo[dore] R. Davis. From *Harper's Weekly*, 20 May 1882. Wood engraving, 14¼ × 19⅞ in. (36.2 × 50.5 cm.). John W. Reps.

The correspondent for the London Times
sees the city from the west front of the Capitol.

From the terrace on the western front of the Capitol there is a fine outlook over the city of Washington, spread upon the lower ground. Diagonally to the south-west and north-west extend two grand avenues as far as eye can see—Maryland-avenue to the left, leading down to the Potomac, and carrying the Pennsylvania railway to the river-bank to cross over into Virginia; and Pennsylvania-avenue to the right, the chief street of the city, stretching far away to the distant Treasury building and the park south of the Executive mansion.

He visits the Washington Monument.

Rising almost at the bank of the Potomac and in front of the Executive mansion, is the Washington Monument, the pointed apex being elevated 555 ft. above the river. This is a square and gradually tapering shaft, the lower portion being built of stones contributed by all kinds of public organizations and corporate bodies, and some by States and foreign nations, each bearing suitable inscriptions in memory of Washington.

He climbs to the top of the monument and describes the view.

A dark and difficult climb elevates the visitor to the top, where through the little square windows a grand view is had over the surrounding country. To the north-west, afar off, is seen the long, hazy wall of the Blue Ridge mountain range, its prominent peak, called the Sugar-loaf mountain, being 40 miles distant. To the south-east the broad Potomac passes away from the foot of the Monument, and winds between its forest-clad shores far below Alexandria, while across the river are the heights of Arlington, looking like diminutive bluffs, and the cemeteries that now cover a large portion of the former home of General Lee. To the eastward, and a mile away, is the Capitol, with its surmounting dome, while all around the City of Washington is spread, like a toy town, its streets crossing as on a chessboard, and cut into gores and triangles by the broad diagonal avenues, the houses interspersed by many spaces covered with foliage. Carriages and people move about, and Pennsylvania-avenue gives a hum of busy traffic. From this elevated perch can be got an excellent idea of the town and its peculiarities; of the vast space taken up by the plan; the great, and in most cases unnecessary, width of streets and avenues, and the long stretches from one place to another. It is thus shown quite plainly why the Yankee nation, in their practical view of most matters, have popularly designated their national capital as the "City of Magnificent Distances."

The writer admires the State, War, and Navy Building.

Upon the western side of the White House is the most splendid of all the Washington department buildings—the structure, not yet entirely completed, for the State, War, and Navy departments. It is built of granite in the Roman Doric style, four stories high, with Mansard and pavilion roofs and porticoes. This grand edifice covers a surface of 567 feet by 342 feet, and will have cost a million and a half sterling when finished. . . .
Beyond this magnificent structure . . . Pennsylvania-avenue resumes its course north-west, and finally goes across Rock-creek, which flows through a deep ravine that divides Washington from the older city of Georgetown. (*A Visit to the States*, 201–2, 204–5, 215)

Keim's guidebook takes visitors to the National Museum.

This attractive structure, of the modernized Romanesque style . . . stands 50 feet E of the Smithsonian Institution. . . . The building was designed by Adolph Cluss and Paul Schulze, of Washington, from plans suggested by Prof Baird, Gen. Sherman and Peter Parker, after a careful examination of the most approved structures of the kind in the Old and New World. . . . There are 4 entrances: one in the centre of each facade between 2 lofty towers 86 feet high, acting as buttresses for the naves. The approach to the principal entrance is from the north by 4 granite steps 37 feet wide, with moulded side-blocks, to a richly-tiled platform with granite base-blocks, surmounted by two stately candelabra.

Keim describes Centre Market.

Strangers would find the markets a most interesting place for a visit. The largest is the *Centre Market*, erected by the Washington Market Company in 1870, comprising three commodious brick structures—a central building and two wings—length from E. to W., 410 ft., and which occupy the S. half of the square between 7th and 9th sts. W., on the S. side of Pennsylvania av. (Keim, *Keim's Illustrated Hand-Book* [22d ed., 1886], 183, 209)

Souvenir View Booklet Publisher Captures
Images of Washington in the Mid-1880s

In America during the 1880s several publishers specialized in souvenir view booklets, among them Adolph Wittemann who published under his name and also supplied local distributors like J. F. Jarvis of Washington. Typically, these booklets consisted of connected, fanfolded, postcard-sized sheets of heavy paper printed in tan and sepia ink. Some were larger, such as one of Washington measuring about 6½ × 9½ inches published by Jarvis. Decorative, embossed covers of red, green, or blue fabric protected the views when folded.

The views resemble photographs. It is no wonder, since most of them were line drawings in India ink made over photographs, with the photographic image then removed through bleaching. The remaining drawing could then be used for making a lithographic plate and as a guide for other plates that added sky and shadow details, some of which were apparently printed from collotypes. Wittemann probably used this method to prepare his two views of Washington looking west from the Capitol and north from the Agriculture Building as well as the other images of individual structures reproduced on the two following pages of the folio. An artist may have added some details, but this process essentially reproduced photographic images in the only inexpensive way possible for the mass market until the perfection of the halftone process that by the turn of the century had virtually eliminated hand-drawn view-making in America.

Panorama, From the Capitol. Washington, North from the Agricultural Dep't. Lithograph and collotype, 5½ × 8⅜ in. (14 × 21.2 cm.). From *Washington Album*, published by Adolph Wittemann Park Place, New York, 1885. Olin Library, Cornell University.

Bureau of Engraving & Printing. National Museum. Lithographs and collotypes, each 2⅝ × 4 (6.7 × 10.1 cm.); *State, War and Navy Departments.* Lithograph and collotype, 5⅜ × 8⅛ in. (13.6 × 20.6 cm.); *Baltimore & Potomac R.R. Depot.* Lithograph and collotype, 3⅝ × 2¾ in. (9.2 × 7 cm.); *Washington Monument.* Lithograph and collotype, 5½ × 8¼ in. (14 × 20.9 cm.). All from *Washington Album*, published by J. F. Jarvis, Washington, D.C., 1891. John W. Reps.

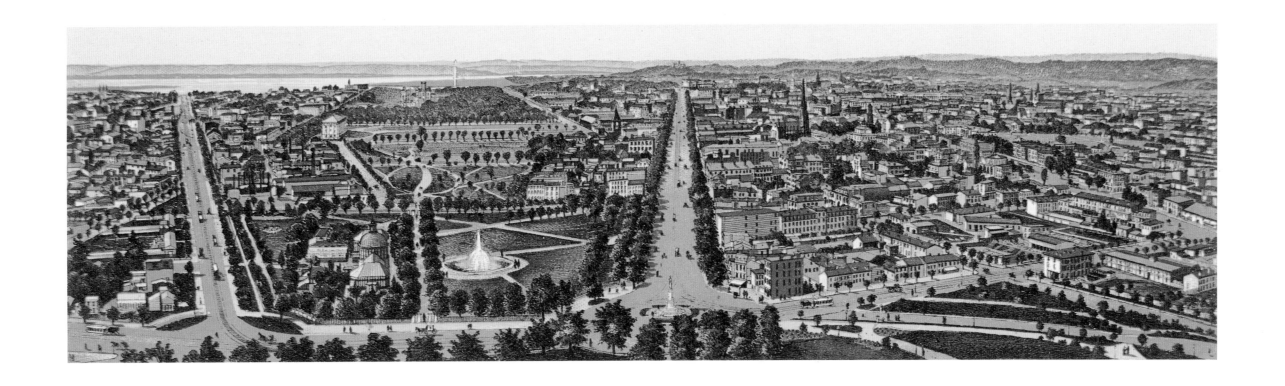

BUREAU OF ENGRAVING & PRINTING.

NATIONAL MUSEUM.

DIPLOMATIC RECEPTION ROOM.

STATE, WAR AND NAVY DEPARTMENTS.

BALTIMORE & POTOMAC R.R. DEPOT.

SETTING THE CAP STONE.

IN THE ELEVATOR.

CAPSTONE OF THE MONUMENT, SHOWING THE ALUMINIUM TIP.

HEIGHT 555 FEET.
WEIGHT 81,120 TONS.
COST # 1,187,710.

WASHINGTON MONUMENT.

CORNER STONE LAID JULY 4TH 1848.
CAP STONE SET DECEMBER 6TH 1884.
INAUGURATED FEBRUARY 22° 1885.

ENTRANCE TO THE MONUMENT.

8 Washington Comes of Age

IN the last half of the 1880s and during the decade to follow, Washington continued to grow, change, and—increasingly—win the admiration of new generations of residents and visitors from home and abroad. Where once many observers dismissed the national capital as little more than a sleepy and dusty Southern town, now both foreign and domestic travelers enjoyed its cosmopolitan atmosphere. And, as always, many others journeyed to Washington to observe the legislative sessions, to lobby congressmen, or to seek political or economic favors from some government department or bureau.

The number of permanent residents grew substantially. Although the *rate* of population increase declined between 1880 and 1890 to just under 30 percent from nearly 35 percent in the the previous ten years, and again in the following decade to 21 percent, this still represented very rapid growth. In each of the last two decades of the century, population increased more in absolute numbers than between 1870 and 1880. Then, the increment was only 46,000 persons, compared with increases of 52,800 between 1880 and 1890 and 48,000 over the next ten years.

The pace of home building followed the surging population. Observers of Washington during the Shepherd era in the 1870s frequently commented on how the city's neighborhoods were filling up and expanding into what had previously been open land at the outskirts. Writing in the spring of 1873, Chauncey Hickox pointed out that "the recent building in Washington has been mostly that of dwellings, which the ordinary visitor, following the old routes between the Capitol and West End, will hardly notice." Nevertheless, he noted, "they have covered many acres within the past four years."[1]

Styles in domestic architecture also changed. One writer observed that "the old square barrack houses of brick have in many cases been pulled down and rebuilded in lighter forms." The new houses had "Mansard-roofs, crotcheted pinnacles, airy verandas, and such a plentitude of bay-windows in all forms as to show the geniality of a climate and people and open air habits." The author commented on the influence of L'Enfant's radial avenues and the irregularities of the site on house design:

The oblique course of the great avenues toward the building lots as surveyed required such ingenuity in the architects that many of the façades are wholly novel, the houses overlapping each other, and decorated in such a way as often to appear fanciful and grotesque. Terraces adapted to the changed grades start up in all parts of Washington, and this again has led to a variety of stairs, balustrades, and vase and fountain ornaments charming to the eye.[2]

In his informative and attractively illustrated book, *Picturesque Washington*, published in 1887, Joseph West Moore emphasized how conditions had changed in the city since the early 1870s. Where before one found streets with only "rude specimens of architecture," now many of them contained "very handsome structures, varied and ornate." Moore called attention particularly to the extensive development in the northwest part of Washington where "there have been erected during the past ten years large numbers of very costly and magnificent houses."

He described the newest and most fashionable neighborhood in this district as the "West End." This consisted of "about five miles of territory" having "Connecticut Avenue, with a roadway one hundred and thirty feet in width" as its principal thoroughfare. Massachusetts, Rhode Island, New Hampshire, and Vermont avenues also provided access to this neighborhood whose development could not have taken place without the extensive grading and drainage works carried out by the Board of Public Works.[3]

Before, this had been "a dreary, unhealthy part of the city, covered with swamps," where the army built barracks during the Civil War. Real estate speculators bought land here after the board's improvements revealed how attractive it might be for housing, and later embellishment of the "squares and circles with parks and statues" made it even more inviting. Moore maintained that building sites here were "considered to be the most valuable in Washington" in 1887. By then, according to the author, the West End contained

---

1. Hickox, "New Washington," 309.

2. Townsend, "New Washington," 320.

3. For the development and existing conditions of the neighborhoods in Washington, see the contributions by many authors in the collection of informative essays, maps, and photographs in Kathryn Schneider Smith, *Washington at Home*. Also helpful is James M. Goode, *Best Addresses*, a study of the most fashionable apartment houses of the city.

palatial mansions, the pride and boast of the capital . . . the residences of the wealthiest citizens, and those of the millionaires from different sections of the United States who make Washington their winter home. Here are . . . most of the high government officials, and the leading officers of the army and navy. Here are the foreign legation buildings. . . . On every side is a dazzling spectacle of luxury and grandeur, and one can obtain by a stroll through the avenues and streets, a realization of the enormous wealth that is centering in Washington at the present time.[4]

The many circles at the multiple intersections of avenues and streets had long been neglected, but thanks to the attention of the Corps of Engineers they now became beauty spots with flowers, fountains, and statues. Massachusetts Avenue passed through three of these newly landscaped circles. Where Fourteenth Street and Vermont Avenue crossed Massachusetts, Thomas Circle honored Civil War hero Maj. Gen. George H. Thomas with a statue erected in 1879.

Another equestrian statue of 1874 stood at Scott Circle to recall the exploits of Gen. Winfield Scott in the Mexican War. Visible from either direction along Massachusetts Avenue, it also stood on the axes of both Sixteenth and N streets as well as Rhode Island Avenue. At Nineteenth and P streets where Connecticut and New Hampshire avenues also cross Massachusetts Avenue, Pacific Circle was renamed Dupont Circle in 1884 when a statue of Adm. Samuel F. Dupont was placed at its center.[5]

Many persons of wealth erected their mansions facing or near these attractive focal points. Senator William Morris Stewart, a silver baron from Nevada, built his octagonal Stewart Castle on Dupont Circle in 1873 as the first of what would become a colony of palatial dwellings. The construction nearby of the British legation in 1875 provided an added impetus to growth in what soon became one of the most fashionable addresses in Washington.[6]

James G. Blaine, Speaker of the House, later secretary of state in the Benjamin Harrison administration, and presidential aspirant, built his mansion on Scott Circle, as did William Windom, secretary of the Treasury under Garfield. As other circles developed in similar fashion, the intervening sites along the streets and avenues filled as well. Thus, time ultimately vindicated, although in quite a different manner than he had recommended, L'Enfant's proposed but unimplemented strategy of using fifteen of the squares as nodes of growth to speed development throughout the city.[7]

Folio 60 provides an admirable window through which we can peer down on this Washington of more than a century ago. Through the illustrations and the accompanying descriptions, one can examine the new neighborhoods to the northwest as well as many other features of the capital city. It is an extraordinarily informative graphic record of Washington, the final view of the city on which the name of Sachse appears. Its publisher, Adolph Sachse, was probably Edward's nephew. He was in charge of the Sachse firm in Baltimore in 1884, the date of this print's publication.

It is the largest of all the Washington views, measuring nearly three and one-half by more than five and one-half feet. As as example of lithographic craftsmanship this huge view does not approach the best work of Edward Sachse, and its advertisements detract from its decorative appeal. Nevertheless, this extremely rare print—known only through a single impression in the Library of Congress—provides far more detail about the appearance of the entire city in the last years of the nineteenth century than any other. The folio reproduces the complete lithograph on the page opposite the caption and displays details of three quite different neighborhoods on the pages following.[8]

The large detail includes the still developing neighborhoods in Northwest Washington. Pennsylvania Avenue leads diagonally from the southeast at the lower right corner, and the Mall runs east and west in the foreground. Thomas, Scott, and Dupont circles can be seen where Vermont, Rhode Island, and New Hampshire cross Massachusetts Avenue in a southwest-northeast direction. Residential Washington is clearly on the march to the northwest, and not long after Sachse published this view, builders advanced into the open land beyond this new district to meet the demand for additional houses.

The smaller details show two other sections of Washington. That at upper left looks at the old neighborhood of Georgetown that began its existence in the middle of the eighteenth century and which Sachse shows as now enlarged somewhat around the edges but retaining much of its original character. The detail at lower right reveals conditions in the area east of the Capitol, a part of the city that early in Washington's existence speculators found attractive but that proved unpopular with persons seeking places to build.

4. Joseph West Moore, *Picturesque Washington*, 239–40.

5. In 1921 a large fountain replaced the statue.

6. Stewart was a supporter of Shepherd during the congressional investigation of Shepherd's activities. That he may have benefited personally from Shepherd's projects is suggested by his re-jection by his colleagues as the chairman of the joint committee. See Whyte, *The Uncivil War*, 207–8.

7. The owners and dates of construction of many of the houses and other notable buildings along Massachusetts and Connecticut avenues are provided in U.S. Federal Writers' Project, *Washington*, 676–703. In Joseph West Moore, *Picturesque Washington*, there are wood engravings of the British legation building (301), the Blaine Mansion (241), and the Windom mansion (257). A drawing of Stewart Castle with some shacks in the foreground is reproduced in Junior League of Washington, *City of Washington*, 250. There is also an engraved view of the British legation on p. 248 and an early photograph of Thomas Circle on p. 251.

8. This size exceeded the single-sheet capacity of the Sachse press, and the lithograph was printed on four sheets. The illustration used in this folio from the Library of Congress impression, which had once been mounted as one, was later sectioned into three parts that could be folded to fit in the largest file drawers then available in what is now the Division of Geography and Maps. Adolph Sachse was probably the son of Theodore Sachse, Edward's brother, who joined the firm in the mid-1850s. Theodore's name appears as lithographer of several views issued by the firm, two of them showing Baltimore as recent as 1880.

The Sachse view of this area depicts it shortly before a modest boom in building filled most of its vacant lots. This occurred in the late 1880s when the pace of residential construction in the fashionable northwest apparently slackened in favor of the eastern part of the city. In the neighborhoods between Capitol Hill and the Anacostia, builders concentrated on erecting houses smaller than the great mansions of Connecticut Avenue. In reporting on this shift in housing demand, the *American Architect and Building News* in January 1890 noted that

> there were more six, seven, eight and nine room houses built last year, than at any time in the history of the city. The largest number of these houses have been built in Northeast and Southeast Washington. In this section the ground has been cheap, compared with ground in the Northwest, so people with limited means and investors who believe in small houses have been turning their attention in that direction for the last few years.[9]

Two large government buildings not previously mentioned appear on this detail. North of the Capitol at H Street and North Capitol Street stood the Government Printing Office in a district where the Bureau of Printing and Engraving would also have been appropriate, instead of at its conspicuous location near the Washington Monument. Additions to the printing office in 1865, 1871, and 1879 vastly enlarged the first building erected for this purpose in 1861, and the Sachse view shows its appearance after yet another addition in 1881.

The other building on this detail is depicted correctly as still under construction. This appears as a series of columns without walls or roof located at the north end of Judiciary Square. There within a few years the Pension Office would begin operations. This building, whose novel design and appearance stimulated much comment, will be discussed at greater length later in this chapter.[10]

On the entire view reproduced on the second page of the folio the other slow-to-develop part of the city—the southeast—appears in the center foreground. Here, too, vacant lots and blocks existed at the time Sachse or his artist drew the view. However, by the end of the decade most of them west of Delaware Avenue

(the thoroughfare extending from the Capitol to Greenleaf's Point) were occupied by houses. Even so, Southeast Washington remained one of the least desirable parts of town for residential purposes, with its poor drainage and worse reputation.

Along with changes in the patterns and locations of residential neighborhoods, the 1880s also saw the construction in Washington of types of buildings new to the city. Large office blocks began to change the skyline. A writer for a national architectural periodical informed his readers early in 1889 that "three years ago there was nothing . . . that could be classed as an office-building in Washington City. To-day we have several that claim attention." He listed the Kellow Building on F Street "as the first of its kind devoted entirely to office purposes." He then mentioned three more recent buildings in this category:

> The Pacific finished about two years ago and The Atlantic completed last fall, both of which are situated on F Street, are alike excellent in their arrangement, size and grouping of the rooms. . . .
> The *Sun* Building, erected by the Baltimore *Sun* on F Street, is decidedly the most costly and pretentious office-building in the city. It has been completed in the last year.[11]

Until the beginning of the 1880s, Washington also lacked apartment buildings. A writer for the *American Architect and Building News* in the summer of 1889 informed his readers that in this respect, too, Washington had changed. He recalled that "some eight or nine years ago" the city's first apartment, "The Portland" made its appearance. He mentioned three newer buildings of this type:

> "The Richmond Flats," corner 17th and H Streets, were built five or six years later. . . .
> "The Maltby" . . . was completed in the early part of this year. It is finely situated at the intersection of New Jersey Avenue and B Street, N.E. . . .
> Decidedly the most pretentious apartment-building in the city is "The Morton Flats" now in process of erection on H Street and 15th.[12]

Although home, office, and apartment buildings thus proceeded apace, few new hotel rooms existed to accommodate the increasing number of visitors. The writer stated that "Washington is very much in need of a first-class hotel" and complained that the hotels, with one exception, "are all old buildings, built years before the War, or a combination of old hotel, old dwelling-houses, new additions and alterations." He listed some of the most famous of Washington's stopping

9. *American Architect and Building News* 27 (18 January 1890): 44. This report also noted, "Of course, improvements in the way of houses also bring improvements in the way of sidewalks, and all the improvements are making the Hill, or East Washington take on a new aspect. . . . The real-estate market seems to hold its own, as prices are firm. . . . Suburban property acts as a check upon city property, and property in the Northeast keeps down extravagant prices in the Northwest. High prices on Capitol Hill drove investors Northwest some years ago, now high prices Northwest seem to be having the opposite tendency." For the residential development of Capitol Hill, see Myers,

"Capitol Hill." Myers indicates that in 1889 the district was populated by the middle class and that few wealthy persons, professionals, or members of Congress still lived there.

10. The compiler of one of Washington's many guidebooks recognized that this structure would surely become one of the sights of Washington and added a new section to his book. Its highly technical wording could have been of interest only to art historians. Perhaps the architect, Montgomery C. Meigs or someone else associated with the building provided the text. See Keim, *Keim's Illustrated Hand-Book* (22d ed., 1886), 143–44.

11. *American Architect and Building News* 25 (19 January 1889): 34.

12. Ibid. (22 June 1889): 294–95. The writer also mentioned the Woodmont on Iowa Circle, located at the intersection of Rhode Island and Vermont

avenues a short distance northeast of Thomas Circle where the Portland stood. The other apartments mentioned were built much closer to either the White House or the Capitol. See James M. Goode, *Best Addresses*.

places in this category: " 'Willard's,' 'The Ebbitt,' 'The Arlington,' and others have this history."[13]

Some features of the new face that Washington began to present to the world at this time can be seen in the illustrations in folio 61. Accompanying them are additional passages from Joseph West Moore's entertaining and informative book. The illustrations all come from contemporaneous souvenir view booklets whose help in documenting the appearance of and changes in the cityscape of America has not yet been fully appreciated or exploited.[14]

The first view repeats the now familiar outlook on Washington from a point southeast of the Capitol, with the Mall and Pennsylvania Avenue stretching off in the distance to the west. In fact, it is simply an altered version of the line drawing reproduced in folio 56, the view used by the Morrisons in so many editions of their guidebook to Washington. Without altering its content but by adding some stipple and collotype tone effects with a second plate, the publisher of the souvenir booklet transformed it enough to make it look like a new portrait of the city.[15]

More helpful in understanding how the city looked near the end of the century are the other views in the folio. They offer images of several of the streets and civic spaces described by Moore as well as some of the leading hotels in the city mentioned in the article quoted above from the *American Architect and Building News*. This folio also includes an illustration of one of the national capital's most controversial structures, the Pension Office, a building completed in 1885 after only three years of construction.[16]

Few persons admired the Pension Building that Gen. Montgomery Meigs, its designer, modeled after the Palazio Farnese in Rome. Benjamin Perley Poore referred to it contemptuously as "that hideous architectural monstrosity." A correspondent for the London *Times* in 1887 called it "a large-barn-like structure" that "has been put up cheaply." According to a more recent historian of Wash-

ington, a French commentator thought that the building resembled " 'Ze Ufizzi palace, wiz a r-r-rail-r-r-road depot on top o' dat, and' a g-r-ain elevator on top o' dat!"[17]

In her book on Washington published in 1901, Mrs. John A. Logan, a senator's wife who came to the city first in 1858 and lived there for more than thirty years, devoted only a paragraph to the structure's appearance. Stating firmly that "the building is not a work of art," she did find one feature of the exterior worth a further comment: "There is one distinctively artistic thing about it, . . . the ornamental terra-cotta frieze over the first-story windows, portraying a spirited procession of soldiers, infantry, cavalry, and artillery; and many a veteran feels his pulse quicken as he beholds the details of the frieze, reviving never-to-be-forgotten scenes in the great Civil War."[18]

Although private landowners erected several new buildings along Pennsylvania Avenue at this time, the small view of the thoroughfare in folio 61 suggests that they had done little to improve its appearance. The three more detailed illustrations in folio 62 bear out this conclusion. Although the passage quoted in the text of the folio from James Dabney McCabe's book on Washington praises the thoroughfare as "handsomely built up" and lined by "many buildings which would do credit to any city," the writer in *Century Magazine* a decade later noted more accurately that it "possessed . . . every requisite for a famous boulevard—except buildings."

That observer maintained that except for "a dozen large structures" he found "all the rest are dilapidated and wretched little houses of ancient date, which look singularly out of sympathy with their surroundings." The correspondent for the London *Times* whose report is also transcribed in the folio agreed with this judgment. Writing in 1887, he stated that although he found some recent buildings "quite imposing," most of those facing Pennsylvania Avenue were "usually commonplace." He did, however, refer to this thoroughfare as a "magnificent highway . . . wide and as smooth as a floor."

13. *American Architect and Building News* 25 (22 June 1889): 294–95.

14. J. F. Jarvis, the publisher in 1901 of three of the souvenir view booklet images in folios 61 and 62, advertised that he had established his business in 1875. He styled himself as "Photographer and Publisher of Views" and "Importer and Dealer in Souvenirs of Washington." His place of business was then 135 Pennsylvania Avenue, "One Block from Capitol." Under an engraved image of what appears to be a sizable store, Jarvis stated, "Visitors to Washington should not fail to visit this old established and extensive wholesale and retail SOUVENIR EMPORIUM. Here they will find the most complete assortment of PHOTOGRAPHS, VIEWS, and SOUVENIRS of all descriptions" (Rand, McNally & Co., *Pictorial Guide*, xxx). This is a full-page advertisement inside the rear cover

of this 200-page guide. Jarvis probably had his souvenir booklets printed by Adolph Wittemann in New York. Wittemann's own albums of Washington contain some of the same views. For the work of the Wittemann firm, see Brodherson, "Souvenir Books in Stone."

15. Since few large, new buildings had been constructed in the area shown in the view, it served its purpose well enough. The only large government buildings that do not seem to be shown are the Pension Office and the Post Office building on Pennsylvania Avenue.

16. One of the images in folio 61 shows Thomas Circle with the Portland Flats. For another early view of the circle from the opposite direction showing this early apartment building designed by Adolph Cluss and completed in 1880, see Junior League of Washington, *City of Washington*, 272.

17. Poore, *Perley's Reminiscences*, 471; *A Visit to the States*, 204–5; and, for the unidentified French observer, Nicolay, *Our Capital on the Potomac*, 503–4.

18. Mrs. Logan told the story of General Sheridan's tour of the building and his response to the guide's observation that the "structure was perfectly fire proof." Sheridan responded: " 'What a Pity!' " Logan, *Thirty Years in Washington*, 367. The remark attributed to Sheridan, reworded to "It's too bad the damn thing is fireproof," is, according to Maddox, *Historic Buildings*, 127, "sometimes credited to William Tecumseh Sherman." A writer in the *American Architect and Building News* 23 (23 June 1888): 292–93 used more specific language

but seemed to come to the same conclusion as Sheridan/Sherman: "The design of the Pension Building is a slavish copy of the Farnese Palace with just enough variation in proportion and detail to destroy its beauty." He then added a sarcastic comment about the unusual exterior decorations. "The ornaments on the frieze are original; they consist of a bursting bomb and a cannon 'standant,' alternating, instead of the beautiful Greek acanthus and fleur-de-lis which alternate on the original." Maddox states that the building was familiarly known as "Meigs' Old Red Barn." For an opinion by a current architectural critic, see Goldberger, "The Pension Building."

The four views in the folio show the ceremonial portion of Pennsylvania Avenue between the White House and the Treasury from both directions but at different times during this period. The anonymous artist of the first one probably relied on a photograph for his architectural details. He looks down from the dome of the Capitol on the occasion of President Garfield's inaugural parade. *Frank Leslie's Illustrated Newspaper* used this wood engraving in its 19 March 1881 issue.[19]

Three other views in the folio picture Pennsylvania Avenue from the opposite direction in 1886, 1889, and (supposedly) 1891. The earliest is a steel engraving book illustration made from a photograph and is a faithful rendering in print of the image captured by the lens of the photographer. The caption on the long wood engraving from *Frank Leslie's Illustrated Newspaper* on the same page states that it, too, was done from photographs, and the caption on the other—an identical perspective—from a Jarvis souvenir album dated 1891 identifies the location of the camera as the State Department.[20]

Obviously both the wood engraving and the lithograph come from the same source. Either both publishers used the same photograph or, more likely, the artist of the Jarvis album appropriated the image from the issue of *Leslie's Illustrated* in which it appeared. The increasing use of photographs as sources for printed views illustrates the utility of this new method of catching images of persons, places, and objects. Soon, with the advent of the halftone method of printing photographs from screened plates, older methods of preparing topographic views would almost entirely disappear.

A curious and now rare lithograph printed in 1888 shows the city at this time. Reproduced in folio 63, this view depicts Washington as it would have appeared to an observer looking northeast from a point above the Potomac River. In the foreground one can see the proposed sites for a projected Exposition of the Three Americas that was to open in time to help commemorate in 1889 the centennial of the U.S. Constitution. In 1892 other buildings were to be constructed as part of a world's fair to celebrate the four-hundredth anniversary of the landing of Columbus in the New World.

Anticipating the completion of the Potomac tidal flats reclamation project (a subject this chapter will take up shortly), a Senate resolution introduced in April 1886 called for the reservation of space near the Washington Monument for the needed buildings, provided they would not obstruct the view to and from the monument and the White House and Capitol. The *American Architect and Building News* reported that the exhibition buildings would cover "the space extending from the Capitol westward to Fourteenth Street."

Although the editor of this journal found the concept "bewildering" and noted that "the Potomac flats . . . must be reclaimed before they can become serviceable for this interesting occasion," he added: "If the long-talked of and deferred reclamation of these flats, comprising about one thousand acres . . . can be in this way brought about, the good citizens of the capital will have enough to rejoice over."[21]

Three years later in the same journal Glenn Brown, a Washington architect, wrote an impassioned article that championed Washington as the logical spot for what became the World's Columbia Exposition held in Chicago. In his statement, Brown pointed out that the Smithsonian Institution, the Corcoran Gallery, the projected new Library of Congress, the Treasury, the Patent Office, and other government buildings with exhibitions of one kind or another all provided impressive scientific and cultural resources.[22]

Additional exposition buildings stretching from the Capitol to the new bank of the Potomac would cover "an area of about one thousand three hundred acres," of which seven hundred acres represented reclaimed land. Brown pointed out that not all of these structures would be temporary: "The intention of the Board [of Promotion] is to have, at least, a part of the exhibition retained as a permanent one, displaying the products of the different States and nations, adding to the long series of interesting collections which already occupy the mall as enumerated above. This would be of permanent advantage and interest to our country."[23]

It was to publicize this proposal that the Board of Promotion evidently issued the view in folio 63. Although Chicago triumphed over Washington and New York in the battle to secure congressional approval as site of the world's fair, and the exposition of the three Americas never materialized, this view of Washington is more than a mere reminder of a failed effort. It provides a valuable image of the capital as it entered a new period of change, showing several features of Washington that do not appear as clearly in other graphic records, if at all.[24]

19. The monument in the foreground at the Capitol end of Pennsylvania Avenue is the Peace or Naval Monument, dedicated in 1877 to commemorate sailors, marines, and officers of the United States Navy who died in the Civil War. Franklin Simmons was the sculptor of the statue depicting America weeping upon the shoulder of History. Adm. Davis Porter designed the memorial, for which Edward Clark served as architect. There is a photograph of the memorial in Caemmerer, *Washington, the National Capital*, 627. For a photograph of Washington that exactly duplicates the perspective of the 1881 wood engraving, see Cable, *The Avenue of the Presidents*, 175, where it is dated ca. 1890; and Chalmers Roberts, *Washington,*

Past and Present, 133, where the author states that it was taken about 1885. It may be earlier. In 1881 the artist of the wood engraving almost certainly relied on this or a similar photograph, adding only the images of parading figures. He also depicted in the foreground a group of spectators atop the Capitol, a feature that has been cropped in the illustration reproduced in the folio.

20. For a copy of the photograph of 1885 evidently used by William Wellstood, Jr., the engraver of the 1886 view, see Roberts, *Washington, Past and Present*, 133. Wellstood's father and uncle, both born in Scotland and brought to New York by their parents when young, were well-regarded engravers.

21. *American Architect and Building News* 19 (12 June 1886): 277.

22. Brown was then emerging as one of the leaders for a better Washington. He later would become secretary of the American Institute of Architects, publish a two-volume history of the Capitol, and be among the leaders at the turn of the century who established new goals and direc-

tions for the national capital. His memoirs make interesting reading. See Brown, *Memories*.

23. *American Architect and Building News* 26 (24 August 1889): 83–84.

24. The view was expertly printed by the Baltimore firm of A. Hoen & Co. August and Ernest Hoen were nephews of Edward Weber, and on his death in 1848 they carried on the business. See

It is one of the first views or maps to show how the Potomac flats might be used when the project for their reclamation—discussed for years but at last under way—was finally complete. The view also offers perhaps the best impression of the appearance of buildings on the south side of the Mall and how strongly the red stone and brick exteriors of the two Smithsonian structures and the Bureau of Printing and Engraving contrasted with the Capitol at the far end of the Mall to the east and the White House and Treasury to the north.

Apparently this is also the first Washington city view to show the Pension Building as it looked when completed. One can understand why those who disliked the building's design—possibly a majority of those with opinions on such matters—objected to it so strongly. On its central location at the elevation where L'Enfant placed Judiciary Square, Meigs's lofty, red structure seemed to dominate the skyline and rival the Capitol itself as the most prominent building of the city.

Finally, this large lithograph also records the condition of the Mall itself. One can see how, from the monument to the Capitol, it was divided into discrete sections, each set off by trees planted along the streets crossing it from north to south. The view also shows clearly the Department of Agriculture greenhouses occupying the western part of the department's grounds. Midway to the Capitol the long train shed of the railroad depot extends halfway across the Mall, threatening any hopes of planning the Mall according to L'Enfant's recommendations or—indeed—for any design calling for unified treatment of this vital element in the city plan.[25]

The railroad on the Mall is only one of the many subjects considered by Theodore Noyes in his remarkably farsighted statement quoted at length in the folio. Noyes, then only thirty, looked forward to a future Washington when the railroad would be banished from the Mall, which then—enlarged by land reclaimed from the Potomac—could be replanned as "a magnificent park," with drives "winding through trees, flowers and well-kept turf, and passing buildings of great public interest, historic monuments and statues."

Noyes did not originate this idea of ridding the Mall of the railroad. The notion received official approval when the first permanent board of district commissioners under the new government issued its initial report in 1878. At that time the board suggested that the Baltimore and Potomac move its depot to a location south of the Mall. Nothing came of this, however, and to most Washingtonians the tracks, yards, and train shed on the Mall must have seemed a permanent fixture.[26]

None of these views presented so far showed the new city Post Office, the first government building built on Pennsylvania Avenue. Like the Smithsonian Institution, the National Museum, the Railroad Station, and the central market, this new structure also departed from the earlier major edifices of Washington that had followed classical models. In this case, the architect recommended and the government accepted a Romanesque design.[27]

The site selected extended 300 feet north from C Street to Pennsylvania Avenue and occupied the entire 200-foot block between Eleventh and Twelfth streets. Willoughby J. Edbrooke, the supervising architect of the Treasury Department, designed for this site a massive building of granite over whose triple-arched entry facing Pennsylvania Avenue a square clock tower extended 300 feet above the sidewalk. Turrets at the cornice corners of protruding wings and framed dormer windows relieved the severity of the facade.[28]

Perhaps the first depiction of this building on a Washington view is the tiny image appearing on the unusual combined map and view reproduced in folio 64. Submitted for copyright by James T. DuBois in 1892, the year construction began on the Post Office, this helpful graphic record of Washington and its major buildings was probably drawn by DuBois as well, although nothing seems to be known about him. Whoever was the artist, he or she relied on architectural drawings for the building's appearance, for this project encountered many delays, and it was not until 1899 that the Post Office was finally completed.[29]

McCauley, *A. Hoen on Stone*. See also the notes to the several Hoen lithographs in McCauley, *Maryland Historical Prints*.

25. The aerial photograph of the Mall from the west reproduced on p. 119 of Gutheim, *Worthy of*

the Nation, reveals the large area occupied by the greenhouses on their site west of the Department of Agriculture building.

26. The commissioners report in 1878 also recommended that both branches of the Baltimore

and Ohio Railroad entering Washington from the north be consolidated and terminate at "a station somewhere north of Massachusetts Avenue," a location that was eventually agreed to by the Pennsylvania Railroad a quarter of a century later. Tindall, *History of Washington*, 289, summarizes the commissioners' recommendations and quotes from their report.

27. The *American Architect and Building News* in its issue of 1 November 1890, p. 61, informed its readers of the decision to build the Post Office on Pennsylvania Avenue "on one of the most conspicuous sites in Washington." In another of its frequent verbal jabs at the office of the supervising architect of the treasury, where government buildings were designed, the journal added: "It does not seem as if it would be asking too much to beg, in the name of the community, not alone of architects and artists, but of all people of ordinary taste and education, that the intended structure may not be a 'polychromatic' object, with red and yellow stripes; that, if adorned with familiar classical features, these may be designed by some person who has seen and studied good examples of them, and not by people who don't know how they ought to look, and don't care."

28. The author of an article in an architectural journal told his readers that on the interior above the second story "an open light-well about 100 by 200 feet . . . roofed over with ornamental iron trusses and covered with glass skylight" would provide access to offices by way of corridors "extending around the entire court." A colonnade "relieved by ornamental wrought-iron work" would support the corridors. The effect was in many ways similar to the Meigs design for the Pension Building, with its great central court giving access to offices by way of continuous galleries on each level. See *American Architect and Building News* 35 (12 March 1892): 174. For the history of this building, with photographs of exterior and interior, see Kassan, "The Old Post Office Building."

29. The building's awkward orientation to Pennsylvania Avenue is difficult to explain. Instead of its north facade being parallel to this important thoroughfare, it runs perpendicular to the streets on either side that, of course, do not intersect the avenue at right angles. This feature is all the more jarring today because of the contrast in this respect with the neighboring government buildings in the Federal Triangle whose facades parallel the lines of Pennsylvania Avenue.

This is not the only example of anticipatory detail to be found on the lithograph. For the large site east of the Capitol bounded by East Capitol Street, B Street, and First and Second streets, the artist drew the image of the new Library of Congress. After years of procrastination, Congress finally decided on this site that had to be purchased from private owners in favor of one on Judiciary Square where no acquisition would be required. Although finally authorized in 1886, this building did not open until eleven years later.[30]

Its history is much longer than that, since it was in 1873 that its architects, John L. Smithmeyer and Paul J. Pelz of Washington, won a competition for its design. Then followed a protracted period of design changes at the requests of congressional committees when the architects prepared drawings for a building in a variety of styles: 1875, Gothic; 1877, French Renaissance; 1879, German Renaissance; 1880, Italian Renaissance; 1882, Gothic; 1886, Italian Renaissance.

If nothing else, the architects must have had their knowledge of architectural history continually refreshed before the original Italian Renaissance facade eventually won final approval in 1886 and construction began. It was unfortunate that Congress paid more attention to the appearance of the facade than to the building's location, for it blocks the view to the Capitol along Pennsylvania Avenue from the southeast, just as many years earlier the decision to place the Treasury on its present location spoiled the views along that section of the avenue to and from the White House.[31]

The dome of the new structure also clashes with that of the Capitol. Sophia Antoinette Walker, art critic for the *Independent*, pointed this out immediately, noting that "the old primacy of the Capitol dome is disputed by a gilded dome rising from a vast white granite building." She added that the new dome was "so near . . . that perspective lends undue prominence" to it. The dome is objectionable for another reason: from the Mall it seems to be sitting atop the House wing of the Capitol and gives the building a decidedly asymmetrical appearance.

The DuBois "Altograph," as the publisher called his plan-view, also shows many other features of Washington that are of interest. In addition to those improvements so proudly described by Theodore Noyes in his statements extracted for the text of the folio, the expanded metropolis could boast of two new educational institutions of national importance. Just beyond Florida Avenue in north-

eastern Washington, DuBois drew the image of what is now Gallaudet College, founded before the Civil War as an institution for the deaf, mute, and blind. Its campus, designed by Frederick Law Olmsted, provided superb sites for the High Victorian buildings designed by Frederick Clarke Withers.[32]

Not so easily seen on the lithograph is the artist's drawing of Howard University. It appears near the top of the lithograph beyond the north end of Sixth Street. Located about two miles north of the Capitol on a fine, elevated site, Howard received its charter from the Federal Government in 1867 as a biracial educational institution, although black students have always been in the majority. While its original student body came mainly from the Washington region, it has since become a far more cosmopolitan place with students and faculty from many countries and all regions of the United States.

The DuBois view also provides an excellent record of Washington's street railway network. Although few lines served the city's northeastern and southeastern sections, many routes led through the more prosperous northwest. Two extended to Georgetown, one following Pennsylvania Avenue to Rock Creek and continuing west on M Street, the other leading west on P Street from Dupont Circle. Noyes, writing in the same year the view appeared, proudly referred to the district's more than one hundred miles of streetcar lines that he felt would soon "furnish . . . a model local rapid transit system to the capital."

Finally, one can note the artist's version of how the reclaimed Potomac flats might be laid out with winding pleasure drives that would vastly extend the open space provided by the Mall as it then existed. Reclaiming the marshy land and mud flats along the Potomac had long been a dream of Washingtonians. Not only was this dismal stretch of the river unsightly and unhealthy, but floods in years of peak runoff and severe storms brought waters lapping at the edge of Pennsylvania Avenue.[33]

Just such a flood occurred in 1881 when parts of the Mall, the botanical garden at the foot of Capitol Hill, and a section of Pennsylvania Avenue were inundated in February. At last Congress acted, appropriating $400,000 the following year for a project to dredge the Potomac, deepen its channel, and use the material removed from the river to fill the adjoining marshes, tidal flats, and low-lying land. During the years it took to finish this work, the Corps of Engineers produced several plans showing how this new part of the city could be laid out as a vast extension of the Mall.[34]

The text and illustration from *Scientific American* reproduced in folio 65 show and tell what was done and how. Under the direction of Maj. Peter C. Hains, the

30. The *American Architect and Building News* followed "progress" on the building with many articles or notices. The story of the library's design, the controversy and lawsuit that arose when the architect was dismissed from supervising construction, and many other aspects of the project are fascinating but too complicated to recount here. The following issues can be consulted by anyone concerned with the details: 9 (22 January 1881): 37; 9 (5 March 1881): 108; 11 (21 January 1882): 25; 11 (8 April 1882): 157; 11 (17 June 1882): 277; 29 (19 July 1890): 33. Easier to find and to follow is the material in the October 1972 issue (vol. 29) of the *Quarterly Journal of the Library of Congress*. Most of the issue is devoted to a history of the library's design and construction.

31. Their renderings of the building's facade for these designs are reproduced in Cole, "Smithmeyer & Pelz."

32. Kowsky, "Gallaudet College."

33. When a site for the Pension Building was originally considered on Pennsylvania Avenue, its architect, Montgomery Meigs, insisted that it be changed to one where flooding would not be a hazard.

34. For a reproduction of one of these designs dated 1887, see Gutheim and Washburn, *The Federal City*, 25. The design resembles in general character but differs in many details from the pattern used by DuBois on the altograph in folio 64.

engineers undertook to raise the reclaimed land six feet above water level and to provide subsurface drainage with a system of pipes. Almost immediately, property owners of adjacent land or those with real or supposed title to the adjoining flats began legal action to obtain compensation or the right to use the land. Finally settled in 1896, this case resulted in payments of more than $26,500,000 to claimants, but it firmly established federal ownership to the reclaimed land.35

The next year Congress formally declared the 621 acres of land and 118 acres of the tidal reservoirs in what was then named Potomac Park to be "forever held and used as a park for the recreation and pleasure of the people." Early in 1890, Congress—at last seemingly aware of its obligation to add to the capital's recreational opportunities—also provided $200,000 to acquire land for the National Zoological Park located a mile north of the city limits. Less than two years later a further appropriation made it possible to buy more than 1,600 acres of land for what became Rock Creek Park, a beautiful and varied tract extending along both side of Rock Creek north of the zoological park.36

These important measures to beautify the city were followed by many proposals in the last decade of the century for further improvements. Perhaps the most ambitious came from Franklin Webster Smith in 1891 when he issued a profusely illustrated prospectus of more than 100 pages describing his proposal and James Renwick's design for an enormous complex of buildings to be called the National Gallery of History and Art. Smith suggested an appropriately huge site stretching westward from Seventeenth Street to the Potomac River and running five blocks south of F Street to what was later to become Constitution Avenue.37

Smith also included plans for two new avenues—National Avenue and Union Avenue—to lead westward on diagonal alignments from the base of Capitol Hill through the triangular space formed by the Mall and Pennsylvania Avenue. He advocated condemnation of all the land between the Mall and Pennsylvania Avenue and property one or two blocks north of the avenue. He also wanted the Treasury to take a strip one block wide between F and G streets along the northern edge of the proposed museum. Any land not needed for new streets or the museum could then be sold for what the author confidently claimed would be greatly enhanced prices.38

Shortly thereafter the postmaster general, John Wanamaker, the Philadelphia department store tycoon, proposed the creation of a body responsible for planning the location of future public buildings. For this task he recommended the establishment of "a commission of citizens, engineers, members of Congress, and perhaps Cabinet officers," with the duty to "suggest how some wise, economical and far-seeing plan for the erection of needed public buildings might be accomplished according to a definite, artistic, business-like plan." This approach, he felt, would save money and also eliminate what he called an "architectural hodge-podge." The secretary of war recommended a similar body.39

An unofficial voice spoke on these matters even more comprehensively and convincingly. It belonged to the Reverend Frank Sewall, a graduate of Bowdoin College in 1858 who studied in Tübingen and Berlin and who later attended lectures at the Sorbonne. Returning to America, he served sixteen years as president of Urbana University in Ohio before coming to Washington in 1890 as pastor of the Swedenborgian congregation, a position he retained for more than twenty-six years.

Two years after his arrival in Washington, he contributed a remarkable article to *American Architect and Building News*, one that began by citing the statement of the postmaster general quoted above. A second article followed in 1893, portions of which appear in folio 66. In both, the author put forward closely reasoned arguments for creating what he first called a national art commission and a year later a bureau of public building. He defined its responsibilities to include the preparation of a plan for governmental buildings looking ahead many years and anticipating needs that would materialize in the future.

35. Gutheim, *Worthy of the Nation*, 94.

36. "The Parks and Proposed Parks of Washington City," 72, describes this new acquisition in glowing words: "In this tract of land . . . is every variety of landscape: Precipices, rugged and bare, or covered with clinging plants and vines; woodland, of old and new growth; foliage, which makes the scene rich with the many hues of nature, varying from the tender green of early spring to the dark evergreens of the pine and cedar, the white of the dogwood, the pink of the laurel; the varied autumn hues of green, yellow, red, brown, with their hundreds of variations and combinations, always changing, always beautiful." Probably written by Glenn Brown, this article noted that the district commissioners in 1894 had requested $5,000 to retain a landscape architect to prepare "a scheme for laying-out this park, but Congress . . . cut the item from the bill." The size of the park was soon increased, and other additions have been made over the years.

37. According to Smith, "In April, 1890, Mr. Renwick Senior listened to the substance of [the proposal] with a responsive interest. . . . The firm then offered to illustrate my conception of the buildings gratuitously." Smith claimed this took six months, utilized "the best talent of their office," and cost the firm more than $1,500. See Franklin W. Smith, *Design and Prospectus*, 10. The imprint of the illustration following the title page states that it was designed by Smith and James Renwick, that the architects were Renwick, Aspinwall, and Russell, and that it was drawn by B. G. Goodhue. Bertram G. Goodhue, then a young man, went on to a distinguished career in architecture, designing, among many other important structures, the Nebraska State Capitol in Lincoln.

38. Smith's museum site and street plan of 1890 are reproduced in Reps, *Monumental Washington*, 71 fig. 40. His revised plan is mentioned in the next chapter. For a well-illustrated account of Smith's museums in Saratoga Springs, New York, and in Washington, see Dahl, "Mr. Smith's American Acropolis."

39. Quoted from Sewall, "Washington's Architectural Need," 107. In 1895 the *Washington Evening Star* reported that the secretary of war "voices a wide public sentiment when he pleads in his annual report for the creation of a permanent Commission to pass upon all questions of art involved in the erection of monuments and statues." In endorsing this proposal the paper noted that "the city will soon receive many additions to its already munificent store of monuments, and the creation of this permanent Commission should not be postponed until all the best sites along [Pennsylvania Avenue] have been occupied." As quoted in *American Architect and Building News* 50 (28 December 1895): 148.

It is clear as well that he thought of this agency as one that would pay close attention to architectural appearance and the broader considerations of urban design, not one that would simply concern itself with providing enough space for government employees and activities when and where needed. Sewall cited the example of the supervising architect who had been quoted in a newspaper as stating that when considering the design of the Post Office "it had not entered into his mind to consider the relation the style of the new building would bear to that of adjoining sections of the avenue."[40]

This, Sewall asserted, illustrates an attitude that called for "precautionary action" by a "government art commission in determining . . . what sort of buildings shall and what shall not be allowed henceforth to be built on the nation's most conspicuous avenue." He cited Munich as a relevant example of what government "can do in the architectural control of a city." Munich, he pointed out, had a population about that of the District of Columbia, and its growth had taken place during the same period as Washington's.[41]

Maintaining that the government soon would need to double the space then occupied by its employees, Sewall concluded that "now, at the beginning [of] a new architectural era in our city" plans should be prepared both to save unnecessary expense and to take advantage of "the unparalleled opportunity for the artistic embellishment of the national capital that the erection of these buildings will afford." Sewall believed that what was needed was "a government commission . . . to agree in general under the wisest architectural engineering and artistic counsel" on a plan for "building up of the avenue on . . . a scale of grandeur, dignity and beauty."[42]

In the same year that Sewall wrote his first appeal for firm federal measures to guide Washington's growth, the New York firm of Currier and Ives published the view in folio 66. Outdated as it is in failing to include such structures as the Pension Building, the new terrace at the Capitol, the Post Office, and—most obvious of all—the reclaimed land of the tidal flats, the lithograph did at least convey an image of a city that had grown steadily not only in size but in beauty and dignity. It was to speed and guide this movement in the proper channels that Sewall and others advanced their proposals.[43]

Although his recommendations and those of the secretary of war and the postmaster general produced no immediate results, officials had already started planning another and not entirely unrelated element of the city. The portion of a topographic map showing Washington and vicinity in 1886 reproduced in folio 67 illustrates the problem they began to address: the subdivision of land for new neighborhoods beyond the boundaries of the original city as defined in the L'Enfant and Ellicott plans.

In 1888 Congress passed an act requiring all new subdivision plats in the county to conform to Washington's street plan, but in the absence of any official plan for this area the District commissioners found this difficult to enforce. A second act passed five years later remedied this defect. It directed the commissioners to retain a landscape architect to draw up a preliminary plan for new streets, maps the commissioners could use in preparing detailed plans for each suburban section of the county.

After approval by a highway commission composed of the secretaries of war and the interior and the chief of engineers, these sectional plans would constitute the official map of public streets to be followed by all private owners when subdividing their holdings. In 1895 the *American Architect and Building News* reported that Frederick Law Olmsted had been engaged for this purpose and had finished a plan for four-fifths of the first section lying between North Capitol Street and Rock Creek Park.[44]

It took until 1900 to overcome the last objections of property owners in the county and to secure final approval by the highway commission for the official plan of future streets and parks. Although a later generation of planners would

40. In his second article Sewall criticized the design of the Post Office in these words: "The building itself is wholly without ornament or grace, we might almost say devoid of style of any kind. Without condemning it in the least as a building suited for commercial or manufacturing purposes in a crowded business thoroughfare, one can hardly help feeling that here an opportunity has been lost for gracing our broad national avenue with a building of distinguished beauty, in harmony with the other Government buildings, and capable of lending itself to a comprehensive architectural scheme for the adornment of the entire avenue" (Sewall, "A Government Bureau of Public Building," 87).

41. As a model of what Pennsylvania Avenue might become, he singled out Munich's Ludwig's Strasse, calling it "a magnificent avenue leading from the royal palaces out to the Arch of Triumph and the Art Academy, and bordered on either side by a continuous line of government buildings, churches, public libraries, academies and

the University, all harmonious in style, and exhibiting a unit of design in all the several structures." Sewall saw nothing less imposing as within Washington's grasp if proper steps were taken promptly: "With such a commission in charge, we might look hopefully forward to seeing not many years hence the avenue graced on either side with beautiful colonnades and arcades lining the front of our new . . . buildings . . . and possibly the government's own national university. . . . Let the government begin now a symmetrical and intelligent architectural development of Washington according to a wise, liberal and far-seeing plan worthy in dimensions and artistic idea, of the seat of government of a nation that calls itself a leader in the civilization of the world" (Sewall, "Washington's Architectural Need," 108).

42. Ibid. Sewall was minister of the Swedenborgian church in Washington in 1901 and 1902 when Daniel Burnham—also a Swedenborgian—visited the city frequently in connection with his duties as chairman of the Senate Park Commis-

sion. One wonders if the two men met and discussed their common interests in matters of civic art, beautification, and planning. Or perhaps Burnham saw Sewall's statements in the *American Architect and Building News* earlier and got in touch with him.

43. As most persons will recognize, this lithograph is a later version of the view in folio 57, and one only slightly revised since the previous edition appeared in 1880. Aside from a new sky, the most substantial change is the completion of the

Washington Monument, a modification made by reworking the original lithographic stone or plate—or by revising an impression from it on transfer paper. For the evidence that this is so, one need only look at the reflection of the monument: it shows only the stub that appeared in the earlier version!

44. Green, *Washington: Capital City*, 48; "The Parks and Proposed Parks of Washington City," 73. This was Frederick Law Olmsted, Jr.

complain that it was too rigid and not well adapted to the terrain, at least it provided some measure of guidance for Washington's growth during the period of rapid suburban expansion that lay ahead.[45]

A year earlier, regulations limiting the height of buildings in the district gave the city additional controls over private development. The concern exhibited by Congress over these matters suggested that a bright future lay ahead. It was just such a vision of Washington that Theodore Noyes looked forward to in the metaphorical statement quoted in folio 67—a shining city emerging like a lovely piece of sculpture from what had once been only a rough block of stone.

At the end of its first century as the nation's capital, Washington in 1900 had become a city unlike any other in the world. If it did not yet rival in beauty and architectural harmony the monumental portions of such cities as Paris and Vienna, Washington exhibited a character of its own as well as a number of individual buildings of handsome appearance. Moreover, although some unfortunate changes had been made in the city plan, nearly all of the features designed by Pierre L'Enfant and subsequently modified by Ellicott and Jefferson remained substantially intact.

Nevertheless, in the city's physical development and growth serious problems existed, and many issues remained unresolved. Perhaps the most pressing was how the Mall should be treated. The tourist guidebook map reproduced in folio 68 records its condition at the turn of the century. The presence of the railroad on the Mall was an admitted disaster and one that seemed to be permanent. On the other hand, no other blunder of that type had as yet been made, and most of the Mall still lay vacant awaiting future decisions about how it should be developed.

Further, the existence now of the vast expanse of reclaimed land beyond the monument offered completely new opportunities. Called Potomac Park but consisting of nothing more than a level, muddy plain, it offered a clean slate to an imaginative designer. North of the Mall to Pennsylvania Avenue lay a motley collection of buildings of which only one—the new Post Office—represented a step by the national government to make the avenue a stately and impressive vehicular and ceremonial connector between Capitol and White House.

The folio text that accompanies this map provides a suitable appraisal of the city as seen at this time by an English visitor, William Archer. A drama critic by profession, Archer's remarks also reflect a remarkable sensitivity to urban design. He recognized that Washington was "not yet the city it is manifestly destined to become" and that "its splendid potentialities do some wrong to its eminently spacious and seemly actuality." Washington, crossing the mark between centuries, needed to consider carefully how those "splendid potentialities" of its physical fabric could be realized. The opportunity to do so soon materialized with results to be considered in the final chapter.

45. The Washington plan was criticized in 1928 by a distinguished member of the National Capital Park and Planning Commission, J. C. Nichols of Kansas City, then (and still) regarded by many as the country's foremost developer of high-quality suburban neighborhoods. See Gutheim, *Worthy of the Nation*, 187–88, who also reproduces a plate showing old and new street layouts for a neighborhood off the northwestern extension of Massachusetts Avenue.

A correspondent for Harper's New Monthly Magazine
in 1881 mentions improvements in the public grounds.

From the park east of the Capitol to the president's House and Lafayette Square there is a long stretch of government land, within which stand the Capitol itself and the Congressional Greenhouse . . . , the Smithsonian Institution and new National Museum, the Department of Agriculture, the Washington Monument, the Departments of State, War, and Navy, the Treasury and White House, and the superb building dedicated to official printing and engraving, together with a large but still unfinished parade-ground by the Potomac. This territory, several miles long, and from a half-mile to a mile wide, has been hitherto short-sightedly broken up by fences and walls, and a railroad even yet scars it with a cindery track; but it has nevertheless almost taken shape as the continuous public park it is intended to be. One President gets this fence taken down, and another President demolishes that wall; and so the process goes on of making the tract a noble pleasure-ground, containing the central offices of a great nation's popular government. A carriage and pair can thus be driven through our political system from one end to the other without disturbing it in the least. ("A Nation in a Nutshell," 544)

A writer for Century Magazine *in 1884
notes the effect of the city plan on house design.*

In a city laid out like New York and most other cities, in monotonous parallelograms, all the lots are of the same pattern. What can an architect do with the unvarying 25 × 100 feet? He may double it, and make it 50 × 100, and he may expend vast sums upon it, but it is still the same. The streets of Washington, however, with its various intersecting avenues, afforded building lots of every conceivable variety of houses,— square houses and round houses, houses with no two walls parallel, with fantastic roofs and towers and buttresses and bay windows and nameless projections. Some of them were good and some bad, but hardly any two were alike. Even after making all deductions for the mistakes and failures, the result of this variety is certainly pleasing. . . . As the eye wanders along the street, it constantly finds some new shape, some odd design, some strange combination in color. Many of these alleged "Queen Anne" houses with their rooms cut up into all sorts of angles, are reputed to be most uncomfortable places to live in; but they serve an admirable purpose in street decoration.

*The writer finds Washington neighborhoods
still only partly developed.*

With streets, however, laid out for more than double the actual population, one has a wide range in which to choose a lot. This option has been freely availed of, and there are, consequently, three vacant lots to one which is built upon. The new buildings have clustered about the Scott Square and Dupont Circle, and the other little squares and circles, forming small settlements, separated from each other by long distances of vacant fields, unbroken except by the asphalt roads and the lines of trees. This scattering of the new building forces has given a very incongruous and ludicrous appearance to some of the most handsome avenues. ("The New Washington," 650–51)

A London Times *reporter in 1887 describes the city's suburbs.*

The American capital has attractive suburbs, particularly to the north and west. From the White House as a centre, various fine streets and avenues lead into the north-western section, which contains most of the newer and more elaborate residences. The prices of land in this favourite quarter have risen to high figures, for it is the location of the homes of most of the leading public men, and there are many costly dwellings bordering the attractive streets. . . . It is in this prized quarter that the broad brick building with brownstone facings has been built by England which is the home of Her Majesty's Minister and the office of the Legation, on Connecticut-avenue. When built . . . it was thought to be almost out of town, while now the city has reached and passed it for a long distance.

*The writer notes that the city has expanded into formerly
open land and that there are signs of overdevelopment.*

The town goes beyond, and gradually fades into the rural region, where vacant lots are numerous. Here, and in fact in most parts of Washington, away from the business and fashionable residential sections, one is struck by the indication that most of the land and houses are for sale. Huge signboards announcing this are seen all about the suburbs, and there would be little difficulty in buying eligible lots in these remote parts if enough money were offered. It is quite evident that in some localities the building of new houses has been pushed beyond the immediate necessities of the increased population, for almost the whole region appears to be offered to let or for sale. (*A Visit to the States*, 220–22)

The Largest of All Washington Views
Documents the Appearance of the Enlarged City

Included in this folio are three details from the last view of Washington to come from the Sachse firm in Baltimore. Edward, the artist, printer, and publisher of so many images of the capital city, died a decade before this view appeared. It bears an imprint stating that it was "sketched from nature by Adolph Sachse 1883–84." Adolph, probably Edward's nephew, inherited the business but not the artistic talent of his uncle. However, his immense, multisheet view reveals many details that no other provides, and it allows one to examine the newly built-up, fashionable neighborhoods along and beyond Massachusetts Avenue where construction was finally catching up with L'Enfant's vision of nearly a century earlier.

The entire view is also reproduced here, with an enlargement of the descriptive text panel that Adolph Sachse printed along the top half of the left margin. The new owner of the firm obviously did not depend entirely on sales of the view to recover his costs, for the many advertisements at the lower left and right of the lithograph must have yielded substantial revenues. Not a single public building is among the vignettes at the bottom of the view; instead, Adolph Sachse obviously sold the space to owners of various enterprises willing to buy this form of publicity for their businesses.

The three details offer glimpses into three quite different sections of Washington. The larger view shows the fast-developing and fashionable northwestern neighborhoods. The smaller sections depict the older community of Georgetown, once a separate municipality but now part of the district government; and a detail of Capitol Hill, a neighborhood that had been slow to develop but that finally had begun to attract builders and new residents.

The National Capital Washington City D.C. Drawn by Adolph Sachse. Lithographed and printed by A. Sachse & Co. Balto., Md., [1884?]. Lithograph, 39⅝ × 67⅞ in. (100.8 × 172.7 cm.). Geography and Maps, Library of Congress.

213

WASHINGTON CITY.

Washington, the seat of Government of the United States, is situated upon the Potomac, at the head of tide water and of navigation, at the confluence of the Anacostia. The Potomac is the broadest river in the Union, and one of the most beautiful. At its mouth it is 7½ miles wide; at Washington its width is 1½; while the Anacostia at its mouth is about as wide as the main stream. A great natural amphitheatre is formed by a chain of low wooded hills encircling the city on the east, north, and south, the sides and tops of which afford commanding views.

The site is one of the most beautiful in the Union, and admirably adapted to manufacturing and commerce. But owing to the immediate vicinity of Baltimore and Alexandria, and the official gifts of the Government, the attention of the inhabitants has never turned toward the great natural advantages of the position for business enterprises. The city is contemporaneous with the Capitol.

Thousands visit Washington every year for pleasure. Some for a short trip, and others for a brief residence. Tens of thousands come to Washington having business with the Departments, the Courts, or Congress. Of the pleasure seekers, the many who make but brief visits, see everything. And there is no city in this country where a week of sight seeing is more satisfactory. The visitor from any of the other cities of the Union is surprised and delighted when he strolls through the broad avenues lined with living green, rests his eyes on the parks and circles, and observes the high culture and artistic arrangement of the parks and gardens.

The park south of the Avenue is larger, more varied, better cultivated, and more beautiful and interesting, than any park in the country. There are the Propagating, Agricultural, and Botanical gardens, with a wonderful variety of trees and plants to attract the eye and interest the mind. Beside these are the Lafayette, Lincoln, Mount Vernon, and Franklin squares, the numerous circles, cultivated and kept with a taste and care absolutely unknown outside of Washington. In climate it is a midway city. It is equally attractive to the people of the South and North, and being near the ocean makes it attractive to Western people. The winters are milder, the spring earlier, and the summer months cooler than in New York City. The streets and avenues, being wider and the houses mostly separated from each other, afford an opening for every breeze. There are over 120 miles of shade trees in the streets, and the streets mostly laid in concrete pavement. Washington affords a delightful residence for at least ten months in the year, and no place can excel its charming spring or fall months.

For persons fond of society or intellectual amusements or pursuits, it affords a pleasant home. The session of Congress, the residence here for a large part of the year of all the Supreme Court Judges, the Foreign Diplomats, the Heads of Departments, all necessarily highly educated and able men, the Army and Naval officers, the scientific officers of different departments, the retired officers, all make up an attractive society. Information from every part of the country and of the world is at hand. The libraries are complete. Social enjoyment is the aim of all. Every one who is himself companionable can enter society freely.

STREET DIRECTORY.

The streets running east and west are named A, B, C, D, &c., both north and south of East and West Capitol streets; north to W, omitting J and south to P, omitting F east of South Capitol street.

The streets running north and south, both east and west of North and South Capitol streets, are numbered First, Second, Third, west, including 27th, and east including 25th street.

One hundred numbers are allowed for each square, without regard to avenues, which run diagonally; thus, for instance, 125 C street would be between 1st and 2d, 809 G street between 8th and 9th, &c., on numbered streets 222 2d street would be between B and C, 809 14th street between H and I, &c.

Going in any direction from the Capitol the odd numbers are on the right hand side of any street.

Numbers corresponding with lettered streets:

1	2	3	4	5	6	7	8	9
A	B	C	D	E	F	G	H	I
10	11	12	13	14	15	16
K	L	M	N	O	F	Q
17	18	19	20	21	22
R	S	T	U	V	W

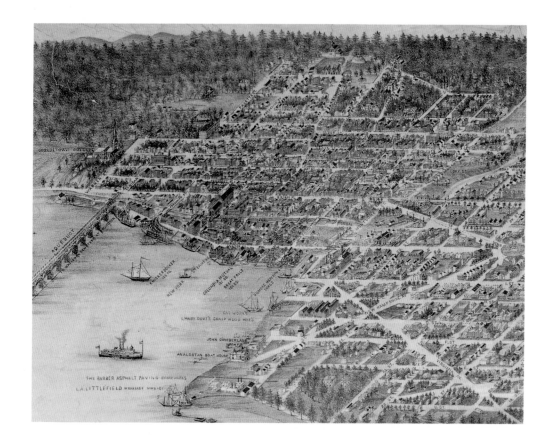

Joseph West Moore recalls conditions in 1870.

The project to remove the national capital to St. Louis, vigorously started by a Western man of rare energy and persistency, gave Washington at this time a great fright. The proposition of removal received the hearty indorsement of the West, and a large delegation in Congress was pledged to its advocacy. Prominent newspapers in New York and elsewhere favored it, and the scheme began to grow rapidly in public estimation. St. Louis was ready to expend millions to obtain the splendid prize, and the other large Western cities came forward with offers of their influence and money, enthusiastic over the plan to have the capital city located in "the great golden harvest land," as the West is glowingly described.

At this juncture a strong man came into leadership, and turned aside the current that was flowing perilously against the city. . . . This man was Alexander R. Shepherd.

He tells about the city plan and its streets.

Washington, in its general plan, has been called a combination of ancient Babylon and modern Philadelphia, with much of the grace and beauty of Versailles. L'Enfant's design has been closely followed, and the result is a broad, spacious city, pleasing in all its parts. Within its boundary are 6,111 acres, and of this amount 3,095 acres are used for public purposes. . . . The streets and avenues in general are of greater width than those of any other city in the world. They are mostly paved with concrete or asphalt, and are very smooth and well kept. Carriage-riding through the centre of the city and on the principal streets of residences is delightful. . . .

The wide avenues, with their concrete pavement, the principal ones extending in an almost straight line for several miles, are among the prominent attractions of Washington. On pleasant days they are full of gay equipages, and present a very brilliant appearance. They command extensive prospects, and on many of them the view is unbroken as far as the eye can reach.

He describes the principal thoroughfares.

Pennsylvania Avenue is one of the longest in the city, and the most prominent. It is four and one-half miles in length, but its continuity is twice broken, once by the White House and Treasury, and again by the Capitol. . . . Many of the leading business establishments, several prominent hotels, the Center Market, and the newspaper offices are located on it, and the theatres are adjacent to it. It is the fashionable thoroughfare, and during most hours of the day it is bright and lively with thousands of pedestrians and carriages. A number of parks are situated on "the avenue," and its broad walks are lined with trees.

He mentions other important avenues and streets.

The longest unbroken avenue is Massachusetts Avenue. . . . On its course through the northwest quarter of the city are many elegant residences, and several squares and circles. . . . New York, Connecticut, New Hampshire, Vermont, and Rhode Island avenues also traverse the northwest quarter. . . .

In addition to the fashionable avenues there are numerous streets extensively built up with costly dwellings of brick and stone, and comparing favorably in elegance with the avenues. Seventh, Ninth, and F streets are thriving business sections, filled with fine buildings. On both sides of Seventh Street, above Pennsylvania Avenue, are continuous blocks of business establishments for over a mile, and there is an enormous daily traffic in this quarter.

*Moore provides information on many parks
and civic spaces, including Farragut Square.*

Farragut Square is on Connecticut Avenue, between I, K, and Seventeenth Streets. It covers a little more than an acre, and contains a small park in which is a colossal bronze statue of Admiral David Glasgow Farragut. . . . The figure is ten feet high, and the granite pedestal on which it stands is twenty feet, and has an ornamental base holding several mortars. Farragut is portrayed in naval uniform, standing with one foot resting on a block, telescope in hand, watching the enemy's movements.

*The writer notes that a new building for the
Library of Congress has been authorized.*

An appropriation act has been passed to construct a large building adjacent to the Capitol, to cost about $3,000,000, for the use of this inestimable National Library. This new library edifice will be located at the junction of East Capitol and First streets, directly opposite the House of Representatives, and fronting the Eastern Capitol Park. It will measure 460 feet front by 310 feet in depth, and will cover about three and a half acres, being designed to store about three million volumes. (Joseph West Moore, *Picturesque Washington*, 49–50, 56–60)

Souvenir View Booklets Capture the
Appearance of Washington near the End
of the Nineteenth Century

Among the views of Washington and its buildings appearing in the souvenir albums of Adolph Wittemann of New York and J. F. Jarvis of Washington are several images in this folio. For the general view of Washington, the artist simply "borrowed" the line drawing used earlier in several editions of a popular guidebook to Washington and reproduced in folio 56. By adding sky, shadows, and tone, the artist made the image look like an entirely new depiction.

Subsequent illustrations evidently come from photographs made on the spot. The first provides glimpses along some of Washington's major commercial and residential streets. It includes a view of fashionable Connecticut Avenue and the imposing British legation that helped to establish the character of this thoroughfare. The final collection includes smaller images of major hotels, a view of Thomas Circle on Massachusetts Avenue, and a new government building, the U.S. Pension Office on Judiciary Square.

Panoramic View of Washington. From *Washington Album*, published & Copyrighted, 1891 by J. F. Jarvis, Washington, D.C. Lithograph and collotype, 5½ × 8 in. (14 × 20.3 cm.). John W. Reps.

Principal Streets. From *Washington Album*, published and copyrighted by Adolph Wittemann, 25 Park Place, New York, ca. 1892. Lithograph and collotype, 6 × 9¼ in. (15.2 × 23.5 cm.). John W. Reps.

Riggs House. Metropolitan Hotel. The Arlington. St. James Hotel. Willard's Hotel. The Ebbitt House. From *Washington Album*, published and copyrighted by Adolph Wittemann, 25 Park Place, New York, ca. 1892. Lithographs, each ca. 1⅝ × 2½ in. (4.1 × 6.4 cm.). John W. Reps.

Thomas' Circle from the Portland Flats, Looking N.W. U. S. Pension Bureau. From *Washington Album*, published & copyrighted, 1891 by J. F. Jarvis, Washington, D.C. Lithographs, each 2⁹⁄₁₆ × 3⅞ in. (6.5 × 9.8 cm.). John W. Reps.

BRITISH LEGATION. CONNECTICUT AVENUE. FARRAGUT SQUARE.

TENTH AND G STREETS. PENNSYLVANIA AVE, FROM THE STEPS OF THE TREASUPY. SEVENTH STREET.

METROPOLITAN
HOTEL, PENNSYLVANIA AVE.

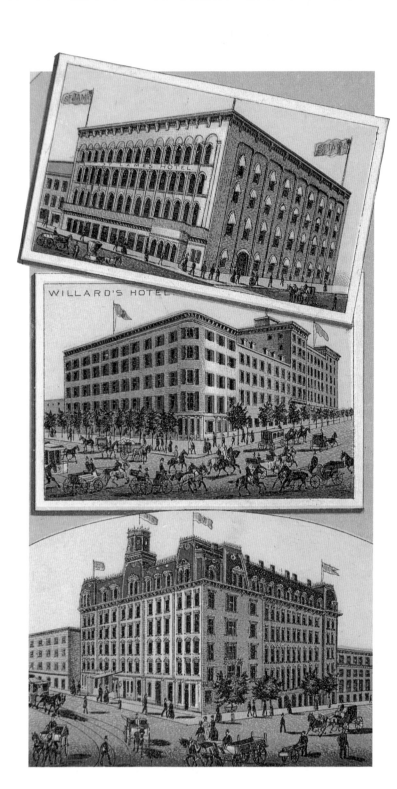

WILLARD'S HOTEL

THOMAS' CIRCLE FROM THE PORTLAND FLATS, LOOKING N.W.

U. S. PENSION BUREAU.

219

*James Dabney McCabe in 1873 recalls
the history of Pennsylvania Avenue.*

The Principal thoroughfare is Pennsylvania Avenue, a noble street, one hundred and sixty feet in width. It traverses the entire length of the city, from Rock Creek, which separates Georgetown from Washington, to the Eastern Branch. It was originally a swampy thicket. The bushes were cut away to the desired width soon after the laying out of the city, but very few persons cared to settle in the swamp. Through the exertions of President Jefferson, the avenue was subsequently planted with four rows of Lombardy poplars—one on each side and two in the middle—with the hope of making it equal to the famous *Unter den Linden* in Berlin. The poplars did not thrive, however, and when the avenue was paved, in 1832 and 1833, by order of Congress they were cut down.

McCabe tells how the street appears to him.

The street is now well paved and lighted. It is handsomely built up, and contains many buildings which would do credit to any city. The principal hotels and stores are situated in this avenue, which always presents a busy and enlivening appearance. The public processions and other festivities take place here, the broad avenue affording ample room for such displays. The distance from the Capitol to the president's house is one mile and a half. The best point of view is from the grounds of the Treasury Building. Standing on the steps of the Treasury and looking down the avenue, one sees a broad, noble street stretching away until it enters the thick green shade of the trees in the Capitol Square, and above these trees rises the glorious Capitol, flashing and glittering in the sunlight. (Martin, *Behind the Scenes in Washington*, 52–53)

A writer in Century Magazine *describes
the paradox of Pennsylvania Avenue in 1884.*

Pennsylvania Avenue . . . is of unrivaled width, beautifully paved both for vehicles and pedestrians, flanked at either end by the magnificent Capitol and Treasury buildings, and possessed of every requisite for a famous boulevard—except buildings. There are, perhaps, a dozen large structures in its length of more than a mile, which tower high in the air, and are suited to the character of the thoroughfare. All the rest are dilapidated and wretched little houses of ancient date, which look singularly out of sympathy with their surroundings. ("The New Washington," 651)

A correspondent for the London Times *in 1887
tells his readers about Pennsylvania Avenue.*

There is a fine view from the western front of the Capitol . . . for a great distance along Pennsylvania-avenue. This magnificent highway, 160ft. wide and as smooth as a floor, leads straight to the Treasury Building, its southern portico being seen afar off with the president's gardens behind. This is the chief street of Washington and is the route taken by every new President after his inauguration, when he is escorted from the Capitol, where he takes the oath, to his home at the . . . White House. . . .

The broad avenue has a double line of tram cars in the centre, and on either hand a smooth, wide carriage-way, Washington having the most cleanly kept and best-paved streets of all the American cities. The spacious sidewalks are generally shaded by trees, and are bordered by buildings usually commonplace, though some of recent construction are quite imposing. A large portion of the houses on Pennsylvania-avenue are lodging-places and restaurants, interspersed with many shops, for the numerous visitors have to be cared for. Many hotels are among these buildings, the chief ones being near the Treasury. The avenue crosses all the streets diagonally, thus cutting the lots into triangles, with various open spaces at the intersections that are availed of for little parks.

*He identifies some of the other important
thoroughfares in central Washington.*

Seventh-street crosses the avenue about mid-way between the Capitol and the Treasury, and has many business establishments. At this intersection is the large Centre-market which supplies the city with food. . . . Proceeding further westward along the avenue, beyond Seventh-street, we come among the theatres, and finally get into the region of the newspapers. Fourteenth-street north of Pennsylvania-avenue is known as "Newspaper-row," and the offices also overflow into adjacent streets. . . .

At Fifteenth-street the magnificent Ionic colonnade of the Treasury building interrupts the progress of Pennsylvania-avenue. The eastern front of this fine structure stretches nearly 500 ft. along Fifteenth-street, and its grand colonnade, modelled from that of the Athenian Temple of Minerva, is 350 ft. long. (*A Visit to the States*, 206–10)

Pennsylvania Avenue Remains an Architectural
Hodgepodge in the 1880s

Pennsylvania Avenue resisted all attempts to make it a great monumental thoroughfare. In the 1880s it existed as a kind of architectural ragout: a mixture of buildings lacking unity of height, size, style, or materials. Each property owner—unfettered by building regulations—followed his own inclinations and built without regard for anything but profit. These views show the avenue from both directions and at the beginning and the end of the 1880s. The first looks from the top of the Capitol during the inaugural parade for President Garfield. From this perspective and distance the mishmash of lackluster buildings becomes less obvious, and the avenue's potential as a rival to any of the great boulevards of Paris can be appreciated. The subsequent illustrations all depict the avenue from the Treasury, with the Capitol in the distance. The two high-level views obviously come from the same source—photographs taken no later than 1889 at the time Harrison became president. The other brings us to ground level to examine more minutely the wide variety of cornice lines, facade details, and architectural styles.

Washington, D.C.—The Inauguration of President Garfield. From *Frank Leslie's Illustrated Newspaper*, 19 March 1881. Wood engraving, 14 × 20 in. (35.5 × 50.8 cm.). Machen Collection, Historical Society of Washington, D.C.

Washington from the White House to the Capitol. Engraved by W. Wellstood, Jr., from a photograph. From Ben Perley Poore, *Perley's Reminiscences*. Steel engraving, 4½ × 6⁷⁄₁₆ in. (11.4 × 16.3 cm.). Machen Collection, Historical Society of Washington, D.C.

Washington, D.C.—The Inauguration of President Harrison. From photos by C. M. Bell, Dillon, Gutekunst, Graeff and Black. From *Frank Leslie's Illustrated Newspaper*, 9 March 1889. Wood engraving, 5⅞ × 13⁷⁄₈ in. (14.9 × 35.2 cm.). John W. Reps.

Washington from the State Department. From *Washington Album*, published & copyrighted 1891 by J. F. Jarvis, Washington, D.C. Lithograph and collotype, 5⅜ × 8¼ in. (13.7 × 20.9 cm.). John W. Reps.

THE NATIONAL LIBRARY.

CITY HALL & LINCOLN COLUMN.

WASHINGTON, FROM THE STATE DEPARTMENT.

Theodore Noyes projects a glorious future for the city.

The Washington of a not remote future will be still more distinctively a city of magnificent distances than at present. Though limited only by the boundaries of the District, it will be compactly knit together by a uniform system of streets and avenues, and by cable or electric railways, which shall utilize additional bridges across intervening waterways, such as Eastern Branch and Rock Creek. . . .

The surface of the city will retain and develop present charms, and be freed from present defects. Overhead poles will go, and overhead wires will be buried. A comprehensive system of underground conduits will accommodate . . . not only telegraph and telephone wires, but also an adequate supply of electric-light wires for Washington's broad streets are to be brilliantly illuminated at night. . . .

The city of asphalt pavements will be the paradise of bicyclists, carriage users and equestrians, and sidewalks fit to be trod, showing the same mercy to man that concrete pavements show to beasts, will replace the present mud-bespattering aggregations of loose bricks. . . . Thousands of additional trees will contribute to the city's health and beauty. Attractive residences, with the same pleasing variety of architecture that distinguishes those which now adorn Washington, will ornament every eligible site in the expanded capital. New public buildings will delight the eye at every turn. They . . . will not be planted upon the reservations to clog the city's lungs with brick and mortar, to disfigure the capital's grand design, and to torture the spirit of poor L'Enfant, already too much vexed.

Among improvements in the park system,
Noyes foresees an improved Mall.

In the southern part of the city the Mall, cleared of railroad tracks, and enlarged by the addition of several hundred acres of reclaimed flats, will make a magnificent park, and furnish a famous driveway by which the visitor, having swiftly traversed historic Pennsylvania avenue from the president's House to the Capitol, may return to his starting point by way of the Botanical Gardens, Armory Lot, Smithsonian Grounds, Agricultural Grounds, Monument Lot and White House Grounds, winding through trees, flowers and well-kept turf, and passing buildings of great public interest, historic monuments and statues. To the other end of the city Rock Creek Park will furnish a breathing place, with its thousand acres of surface, its beautiful, winding stream, and its wild and diversified scenery.

Noyes turns his attention to the Potomac River.

In the future Washington the Potomac River will be utilized to its full capacity for the benefit of the trade, health, and pleasure of the city. The present impediment to easy access to the river front, the impassable barrier of a belt of surface railroad tracks, illegally occupied by standing cars, will be sent to join the obstacles of the past—a pestiferous canal, a criminal-infested Mall, and high bluffs which needed to be pierced. The local rapid transit system will bring the Potomac within easy reach. . . . Handsome and substantial bridges—perhaps a memorial bridge connecting with a broad avenue leading to Mount Vernon—will furnish communication with Virginia, and the Long Bridge, that shabby, flood-threatening nuisance of the present, will be only a disagreeable reminiscence.

The author looks at the prospects for business.

The city will not be pre-eminent in wholesale trade, . . . nor will the great manufacturing centers of the country find in Washington a dangerous competitor. . . . Modelling after Paris rather than Pittsburg, it will doubtless develop the various branches of light and clean manufacturing, which, with the departmental workshops, will give employment to many and make profitable returns, without interfering by noises or smells, with the capital's attractions as a residence city. In the latter capacity, Washington will distance every competitor. To live at Washington, not to die at Paris, will become the American aspiration.

Noyes envisions Washington as a center
of education and science.

Nowhere else on the continent will the student of science or of law find in museums and libraries such treasures for his enjoyment. With the institution upon which Mr. Corcoran lavished a million and a half dollars in his life, and $100,000 at his death, as a foundation, a thorough and admirable system of art instruction will be developed and become a notable feature of the educational facilities furnished by the capital. The vast national library, conveniently arranged and easy of access in the immense structure to be erected for its accommodation . . . will materially aid Washington to become . . . the home not only of the nation's students but of its authors. (Theodore W. Noyes, "The Good Time Coming," *Washington Evening Star*, 17 March 1888)

Washington Plans for (but Does Not Get)
the World's Columbian Exposition

As the four-hundredth anniversary of Columbus's first voyage of discovery and exploration approached, several cities vied for the honor and financial rewards of host community. Before Congress selected Chicago to receive federal sponsorship and funding, leaders in Washington began a campaign to capture the fair for the national capital, coupling it with a proposed permanent Exposition of the Three Americas. The large and attractive lithograph shown here resulted from that unsuccessful campaign. Reclaimed lands of the former tidal flats of the Potomac were to provide the sites for several buildings placed near the waters of four ponds near the Washington Monument. The anonymous artist added an elaborate bridge across the Potomac to continue the line of New York Avenue into Virginia, a project that would be much talked about but never realized.

This view also provides a useful record of central Washington's character and appearance at the end of the 1880s. The Washington Monument—done, at long last—provided an inspiring landmark that served as the perfect foil for the great dome of the Capitol. The Pension Building also furnished the Washington skyline with a distinctive profile, its massive facade of red brick and terra cotta looming even larger than the huge Centre Market facing the Mall. These structures and those on the south side of the Mall contrasted with other monumental buildings in the city, almost all of which had been built of white limestone or marble. The lithograph also reveals how the Mall had been divided into separate rectangles of green, each defined by trees along the cross streets and by individual landscape treatment of the institutions responsible for their own grounds. The view provides a good look at the extensive greenhouses of the Department of Agriculture between that building and the factorylike Bureau of Printing and Engraving.

Birdseye View of the National Capital Including the Site of the Proposed World's Exposition of 1892 and Permanent Exposition of the Three Americas. Printed by A. Hoen & Co. Baltimore. Copyrighted by E. Kurtz Johnson, Treasurer, Bd. of Promotion, 1888. Lithograph and collotype, 23⅝ × 34⅝ in. (60 × 87.9 cm.). Wisconsin Historical Society.

*Theodore Noyes summarizes changes in Washington
from the beginning of the Civil War to 1888.*

From the time when the capital was a camp and hospital . . . its development as a city has been continuous. The greater part of this magical transformation has been wrought within the last eighteen years. In place of a straggling country village, with zig-zag grades, no sewerage, unimproved reservations, second-rate dwellings, streets of mud and mire, and wretched sidewalks, the modern Washington has arisen a political, scientific, and literary center, with a population trebled since 1860; a city sustained, improved and adorned by an annual expenditure of more than four million dollars; with surface remodeled; with an elaborate and costly system of sewers and water mains; with about 150 miles of improved streets, nearly one-half of which are paved with concrete; with convenient transportation by 33 miles of street railway; with numerous churches and schools, as well as government buildings of architectural pretensions; with broad streets shaded for a distance of 280 miles by more than 60,000 trees, destined to make Washington a forest city; with attractive suburban drives; with reservations and parkings given a picturesque beauty by shrubbery and rich foliage, statuary, fountains and flowers, and with costly private dwellings, rivaling palaces in size and splendor of interior adornment springing up in rapid succession where Trollope sank knee-deep in mud. (Theodore W. Noyes, *Washington Evening Star*, 25 February 1888)

*In welcoming veterans of the Grand Army of the Republic
to Washington in 1892 he calls for metropolitan planning.*

The capital . . . has not only built up its ragged collection of unfinished streets, and the bogs and swamps and commons that dotted and surrounded them, but has spread settlement over the . . . heights on the northwest and northeast and the duty and responsibility of planning and developing a new Washington, more extensive in area than the original city, which shall not be inharmonious and discreditable when compared with the work of the forefathers, is imposed upon the legislators of to-day.

*Noyes contrasts Washington streets of the Civil War years
with those in the contemporary city.*

The streets of depthless mud and blinding dust are now in large measure concreted and fringed with thousands of shade trees. In the matter of smooth streets the capital is foremost among the cities of the world. Broad Pennsylvania avenue, with its rough cobblestones of the [Civil War] times, has been converted through the skillful use of asphalt into the finest parade street that any capital can boast, . . . and when the work of erecting public buildings along it in accordance with the original plan, already revived and initiated, shall be fully accomplished, and its surroundings thus acquire suitable dignity and impressiveness, this historic avenue will rival in all respects the famous streets of the capitals of the old world, whether the boulevards of Paris, Unter den Linden in Berlin, the Ring Strasse of Vienna or Andrassy street in Buda-Pesth. Massachusetts avenue . . . displays to-day as a specimen residence street of the modern Washington buildings of the most varied and attractive architecture.

*He points to other improvements in transportation,
utilities, parks, and civic art.*

Without a street car at the outbreak of the [Civil War] the District now has over a hundred miles of street railway, which promise soon to furnish . . . a model local rapid transit system to the capital. Then pumps and springs supplied the city with water; now through the great aqueduct . . . the waters of the upper Potomac are lavished upon Washington. The then unfinished public buildings have been completed, and, with additional structures which have been erected, adorn the city. The stub which represented the Washington monument has become the towering, impressive shaft of to-day. . . . The reservations and parking, then neglected and unkempt, the browsing place of the cow and the wallowing place of the hog, have been improved and adorned, and now in a number of them the statues of men who were then struggling to save the Union and the capital . . . stand out in marble or bronze in a picturesque setting of flowers and rich foliage.

*He ends by emphasizing again the need
to plan the expanding suburbs.*

There is no act of the forefathers which gives more convincing evidence of wise forethought than the creation and general design of the national city. What they planned the men of to-day are to fully carry out. There is in addition the new Washington that has sprung up outside of the original boundaries which needs its George Washington, its Jefferson, its L'Enfant. (Theodore W. Noyes, *Washington Evening Star*, 19 September 1892)

James T. DuBois Creates a Unique Pictorial
Map of the Federal Capital

In seventeenth-century Europe many cartographers created so-called plan-views—city maps showing streets in the conventional way, but with the addition of all of the buildings or selected major structures drawn in perspective and properly located. These have now become commonplace for tourist maps, but few such maps had come from the hands of American cartographers before the appearance of the one reproduced here. The publisher (who may have been the artist) could not even find a familiar name for this type of cartographic representation. His use of *Altograph* in the title may be the first (and probably the last) occurrence of this word.

If the word did not catch on, perhaps the map did not either, for few collections can boast of having one. Nevertheless, it is a particularly good depiction of Washington in the last decade of the nineteenth century. Many features are worth noting: the reclaimed land along the Potomac (shown inaccurately as if laid out in winding park drives and paths); the railroad tunnel just north of the Navy Yard; the two railroad stations, one on the Mall and the other north of the Capitol; the size of Centre Market bounded by Seventh and Ninth streets, Pennsylvania Avenue, and the Mall; the many trolley and interurban lines; two institutions on the Mall east of the National Museum, the National Medical Museum and the Fish Commission; and the Panorama, occupying a circular building east of the circle on the White House lawn.

DuBois also shows several new government buildings. They include the massive State, War, and Navy Department west of the White House, the Pension Building north of the City Hall, and the Library of Congress, then still under construction but "finished" five years early by the obliging Mr. DuBois. The artist also shows the new Post Office building on Pennsylvania Avenue although construction on that Romanesque building did not begin until the year the altograph was published.

The Altograph of Washington City, or, Strangers' Guide. Copyright by James T. DuBois, 1892. Lithograph, 25 × 35 in. (63.5 × 88.8 cm.). Geography and Maps, Library of Congress.

THE ALTOGRAPH
OF
WASHINGTON CITY,
OR,
STRANGERS' GUIDE.

An ISOMETRIC VIEW of the NATIONAL CAPITAL, showing the PUBLIC BUILDINGS, PARKS,
PRINCIPAL CHURCHES, HOTELS, BRIDGES, STATUES, STEAMBOAT LINES, STREET RAIL-
WAY ROUTES, &c.; also, indicating the location of all places of public interest immediately
adjoining the City.

Scientific American *explains the problem of the flats to its readers in 1891.*

The improvement of the river front of the city of Washington, D.C., popularly known as the Potomac Flats Improvement, was intended to accomplish two objects. First, to improve navigation, for which annually the government has for years been expending a large sum of money; and second, to fill up a large area of marsh land, which was overgrown with a dense growth of grass. The marshes were what are known as the Flats. There were many acres of these marshes bordering on the river bank, which were exposed at low and covered at high tide. One of the largest sewers of the city discharged its contents on these flats, and being exposed daily to the rays of the sun, when the tide was low, rendered a large section of the city almost uninhabitable. The Executive Mansion itself was only about 2,500 feet from the flats, which became such a public nuisance that what had been one of the most desirable sections of the city became the most undesirable for residence.

The journal describes the nature of the project.

In 1881 the Senate appointed a committee to investigate the case. The direct result of this investigation was an appropriation by Congress of $400,000 to begin the work of improvement. Since then successive appropriations have been made at intervals of two years, and the amount expended up to the present time has been $1,624,798. The estimated cost of the entire work was $2,716,365, and notwithstanding the unbusinesslike methods of Congress in appropriating insufficient sums to prosecute the work vigorously, and the damage it has consequently sustained from freshets, the work has been brought to that advanced state that it could yet be completed within the estimates. Considering the magnitude of the work, and the fact that the estimates were regarded as low, this is justly regarded as a satisfactory exhibit.

The total area of land reclaimed is in round numbers 621 acres. The material with which the fill was made was taken from the river channels, and thus accomplished the double purpose of improving the navigation and reclamation of the flats.

The article explains how sewage will be handled.

The filling of the flats converted the old Washington Channel into an arm of the river, closed at the upper end, into which

some sewage would necessarily go. To purify this, a tidal reservoir of about 110 acres was constructed just above Long Bridge, from which about 250,000,000 gallons of water would be discharged daily into the head of the Washington Channel. The water is taken into the reservoir from the Virginia Channel on the flood tide and discharged into the Washington Channel on the ebb. To control this operation it was necessary to construct, near Long Bridge, the reservoir outlet, which is provided with gates that work automatically, closing on the flood and opening on the ebb tide.

The writer refers to illustrations accompanying the article.

One of the views shows the condition of the flats at low tide, as given by a photograph taken from the top of the unfinished Washington monument in October, 1883, when the monument had reached a height of 384 feet. Another view represents the improvement as it appears to-day, and was taken from the top of the present Washington monument. The diagram, drawn to a scale, gives the relative size and positions of different parts of the work, all of which has been done under the direction of Col. Peter C. Hains, U.S.A. in charge of various public works in the immediate vicinity of Washington, and to whom we are indebted for the details given.

The readers learn the results of this project.

The total cost of the entire work this far, including everything, has been $1,624,798. The value of the land reclaimed, in its present condition, is estimated at not less than about $3,000,000, so that viewed as a commercial enterprise, it has been a profitable undertaking for the government.

From the Capitol to the Virginia Channel is now one large park, marred only by the unsightly tracks of the Baltimore and Potomac Railroad. Embraced in this area are the Botanical Gardens, Medical Museum, Smithsonian, Agricultural Department, Bureau of Engraving and Printing, and the Washington monument. This park is a favorite drive for the thousands of visitors to the capital, and the grounds of the White House border it on the northwest. ("Improvement of Potomac Flats, Washington," 180–81)

Engineers Fill the Potomac Tidal Flats

Early efforts by the Army Corps of Engineers to obtain adequate funding to improve navigation by dredging the Potomac River failed to attract the support of Congress. A proposal in 1879 to couple this project with filling and reclaiming the tidal flats that extended almost to the White House met a similar fate. The unsightly and unhealthy marsh and mud flats so near the executive mansion prompted many proposals to build a new residence and offices for the president at a more favorable and attractive site in the city.

A disastrous flood in 1881 when waters overflowed the Mall and parts of Pennsylvania Avenue prompted Congress to appropriate $400,000 that began a program requiring many years to complete. It improved navigation, reduced a serious hazard to public health, and created more than 600 acres of filled land that nearly doubled the length of the Mall and added a new peninsula separated from the southwestern part of the city by the Washington Channel.

This illustration from *Scientific American* in 1891 and the accompanying description of the work being carried on provides the best account of this multipurpose project. The lower illustration on the page records what had already been accomplished in the area south of the Washington Monument. The large body of water in the foreground is the tidal basin whose waters, impounded at high tide, can be released at low tide to provide a current that flushes the Washington Channel. The illustration shows this narrow body of water between the original shore on the left and the new curving peninsula extending south to the mouth of the Anacostia. The land extending west from the Washington Monument ultimately provided the site for the Lincoln Memorial, the reflecting pool, and the more recently created Constitution Gardens. In 1897, however, Congress designated the entire 739 acres occupied by the reservoirs and reclaimed flats as Potomac Park, a portion of the city "to be forever held and used as a park for the recreation and pleasure of the people."

Improvement of the Potomac Flats, Washington D.C. From *Scientific American*, 19 September 1891, p. 175. Wood engraving, 15 × 9⁹⁄₁₆ in. (38 × 24.3 cm.). Olin Library, Cornell University.

Folio 66. An English Travel Writer Points to Washington's Beauty, While a New Resident Warns of Difficulties Ahead

The editor of Baedeker's handbook to the United States describes Washington in 1893.

The city is beautifully laid out . . . , the rectangular arrangement of the streets having superimposed on it a system of radiating avenues, lined with trees and named for the different States of the Union. . . . The sobriquet of "City of Magnificent Distances," applied to Washington when its framework seemed unnecessarily large for its growth, is still deserved, perhaps, for the width of its streets and the spaciousness of its parks and squares. The floating white dome of the Capitol dominates the entire city, and almost every street-vista ends in an imposing public building, a mass of luxuriant greenery, or at the least a memorial statue. The little wooden houses . . . that used to alternate freely with the statelier mansions of officialdom are now rapidly disappearing; and some, perhaps, will regret the obliteration of the element of picturesqueness suggested in the quaint contrast. The absence of the wealth-suggesting but artistically somewhat sordid accompaniments of a busy industrialism also contributes to Washington's position as one of the most singularly handsome cities on the globe. (Muirhead, *Land of Contrasts*, 223–24)

The Reverend Frank Sewall explains why the city needs to plan its future.

One has but to imagine what the city might now have become without Washington's plan, and left to the chances of speculation and trade, and the conclusion is clear as to what risk the city now incurs in its coming architectural development should the Government now omit to exercise a similar foresight in projecting the future building of the city so far, at least, as concerns the location and style of the public buildings and the general architectural and ornamental aspect of our great public thoroughfares and spaces. Unless some such wise forethought is exercised by Congress now . . . the result will be . . . the loss for long years to come of all that prestige and dignity which Washington might have claimed among the cities of our country in the beauty and fitness of its architecture.

He proposes the creation of a permanent agency for this purpose.

The United States Government needs . . . a Bureau of Public Buildings, attached, it may be, to the Department of the Interior, but as complete in its establishment as the other Bureaus of that Department. . . . It would constitute a means of bringing out the best architectural ability of the nation through competitive designs for public buildings, of exercising a careful and skilful supervision over all the work being carried on by the Government and of preventing unworthy structures being erected and the wasting of the money of a generous people in the purchasing of bogus works of art. Finally such a Bureau could be made the instrument by Congress of securing the architectural development of the City of Washington upon a plan of broad magnificence, dignity and symmetry such as cannot be secured by any amount of random legislation at odd intervals, giving license to the ambitious ventures of any single Government employe or to spasmodic exhibitions of "economy" by some Congress bidding for votes.

Sewall looks ahead to future requirements of the government.

The question will arise, if not for the present, then for some Congress soon to follow, of providing buildings for the now temporarily and poorly housed Census, Education, Indian, Railroads, Geological, Labor and other Bureaus. Why should not the design for these buildings enter now into some comprehensive scheme whose realization is wholly feasible and economical. . . .

A series of building of the dimensions of the Patent Office alone, would, if arranged continuously in a single façade instead of being built into a quadrangle, occupy the front of four entire squares on Pennsylvania Avenue. . . . Let the reader imagine the imposing effect that might be produced under competent architectural direction by such a continuous line of buildings. How many decades will pass by before the increased demands for office-room and for great national institutions, such as schools and conservatories, museums, galleries and libraries, will require a similar occupation of the squares on the north side of the avenue? Should not these be included in the prospective design for the avenue's architectural completion? Not hidden from view by the narrowness and darkness that characterize the chief thoroughfares of the cities of the Old World, the magnificent breadth of the avenue would bring out and display a noble range of palatial buildings such as few cities, ancient or modern, could rival. (Sewall, "A Government Bureau of Public Building," 86–87)

Currier and Ives Slightly Update an Old View but Neglect to Change an Important Detail

The accompanying excerpts from Muirhead's book reflect his impressions of Washington while he prepared the first Baedeker guide to the United States of 1893. That publication proved more reliable that this lithograph that Currier and Ives issued a year earlier. Although far from accurate, it does offer an instructive example of an all-too-frequent failing of American print publishers: the continued use of images of cities long after they ceased to reflect the true appearance of their subjects. Because the print shows the Washington Monument as it looked after its completion in 1884, the portrayal of the city seems reasonably up-to-date at first glance.

Closer scrutiny, however, quickly reveals that aside from the monument, this view omits many features that had been changed or added during the previous decade. The bank of the Potomac still reaches almost to the base of the monument as if the labors of the Corps of Engineers had been fruitless. The fish ponds still provide a mosquito breeding-place that presidents and their wives had complained about in vain for many years. The huge Pension Building north of the old City Hall is nowhere to be found, nor is there any sign of construction of the Library of Congress on Capitol Hill.

Twelve years after Charles Parsons drew Washington for the firm in 1880, Currier and Ives simply had a lithographic artist add the top of the Washington Monument to the stone stump of the older view and substitute the firm's 1892 copyright claim for Parsons's name at the lower right corner of the print. They forgot one little-noticed but fascinating and telltale feature: the reflection of the monument in the waters of the Potomac is still that of the incomplete structure and not the full shaft that rises proudly from its base at the end of the Mall.

The City of Washington. Birds-Eye View from the Potomac— Looking North. [Drawn by Charles Parsons]. Published by Currier & Ives, 115 Nassau St., New York, 1892. Lithograph, 22¾ × 33 in. (57.9 × 83.9 cm.). Prints and Photographs, Library of Congress.

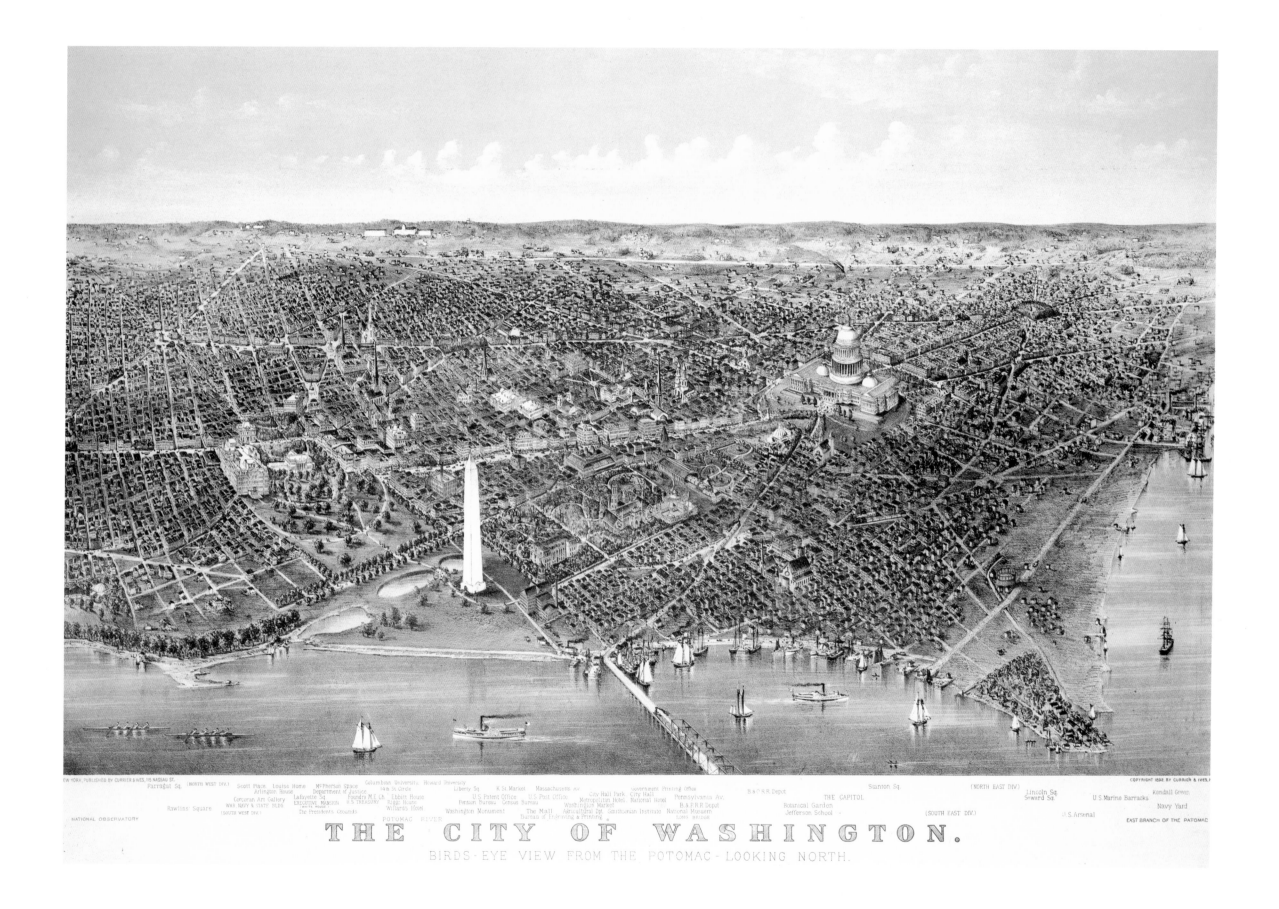

Farragut Sq.   (NORTH WEST DIV.)   Scott Place   Louise Home   Mc.Pherson Space   Columbian University.   Howard University   Liberty Sq.   K St Market   Massachusetts av   City Hall Park   City Hall   Government Printing Office   B & O R.R. Depot   Stanton Sq.   (NORTH EAST DIV.)   Lincoln Sq.   Kendall Green.

Arlington House   Department of Justice   14th St. Circle   U.S Patent Office   U.S Post Office.   Metropolitan Hotel   National Hotel   Pennsylvania Av.   THE CAPITOL.   Seward Sq.   U.S Marine Barracks

Corcoran Art Gallery   Lafayette Sq.   Foundry M.E. Ch.   Libbit House   Pension Bureau   Census Bureau   Washington Market   B.& P.R.R Depot   Botanical Garden   Navy Yard

Rowlins Square   WAR, NAVY & STATE BLDG   EXECUTIVE MANSION   U.S TREASURY   Riggs House   Willards Hotel

(SOUTH WEST DIV.)   The Presidents Grounds   Washington Monument   The Mall   Agricultural Dpt   Smithsonian Institute   National Museum   Jefferson School   (SOUTH EAST DIV.)   U.S Arsenal

NATIONAL OBSERVATORY   POTOMAC RIVER   Bureau of Engraving & Printing   LONG BRIDGE   EAST BRANCH OF THE POTOMAC

THE CITY OF WASHINGTON.

BIRDS-EYE VIEW FROM THE POTOMAC-LOOKING NORTH.

The author of the entry on Washington in a geography introduces the city with a summary of its history.

The city of *Washington*, which contains nearly all the inhabitants of the district, no longer deserves its former title of the "City of Magnificent Distances," where interminable shady avenues, mostly destitute of houses, intersected each other at all angles. On the contrary, it has kept pace with the portentous growth of the Union itself, and is now really a great city, with a permanent population of nearly 250,000, increased during the sessions of Congress by many tens of thousands attracted to the spot by the endless interests associated with public administration.

The text tells of the construction of a new Library of Congress.

Students are impatiently awaiting the completion of the new building now in progress in the immediate neighbourhood, where ample room will be provided, not only for the treasures of the present library, but for its future expansion to the extent of about three and a half million volumes altogether.

The author recounts efforts to make the city healthier.

Washington had long the reputation of being an unhealthy city . . . , but the low-lying lands have been drained, and transformed to a public park. The flow of the river has been regulated and a muddy estuary changed to a convenient harbour. . . . An abundance of pure water is obtained from the great falls of the Potomac, some 18 miles higher up, by an aqueduct carried through eleven tunnels and six bridges.

The health of the city has also been improved by extensive plantations of over 60,000 trees of 37 different species lining 120 miles of streets. In the north there are some extensive pleasure-grounds, such as the fine parks surrounding the Soldiers' Home, for disabled soldiers of the regular army, and the Howard University, a non-sectarian school of higher instruction, founded immediately after the Civil War for young negroes of both sexes. (Reclus, *The Earth and Its Inhabitants*, 171–74)

A writer in an influential journal of architecture recalls the recent convention of architects in the city of Washington.

Every architect at the late convention must have been more than ever convinced of the unrivalled architectural magnificence of Washington in its present state, as well as of the seriousness of the danger which threatens its artistic splendor through the unhappy system which now controls the erection of public buildings. Even without the terraces now being completed . . . which add immensely to the effect of the building, the Capitol is, it seems to us, the noblest architectural object in the world.

He admires the Treasury and the White House.

At the other end of Pennsylvania Avenue we find, in the Treasury, a building little inferior to the Capitol in simplicity and beautiful proportion, and at least equal to anything else of the kind in the world. . . . The White House . . . agrees with it in scale and style, and is a building of which we have at least no reason to be ashamed. (*American Architect and Building News*, 1 November 1890, p. 61)

A Washington journalist toasts the city at a Board of Trade banquet in 1891.

One hundred years ago a great mind conceived the idea of a statue of perfect symmetry and beauty. This idea was impressed upon the snowy whiteness of the heart of a huge block of marble and the statue's outlines lay hid beneath the stone's rough and discolored surface. For a century at intervals men have worked with drill and blast, with pick and chisel, to reach the heart of this rocky mass and to expose to sunlight and the eyes of men the perfect statue. Stroke by stroke the statue is uncovered. Inch by inch it rises in dazzling and perfect loveliness from all that is coarse and rude and ugly in the stone and earth of its surroundings, as the goddess of beauty rose in days of old from the rough gray surface of the ocean. The century-old ideal of Washington is fast becoming real, tangible, visible. It is for us of the republic's second century to give the finishing touches to the work designed one hundred years ago. Let no blundering chisel mar the delicate outlines of the developing statue whose beauty, half concealed, half exposed, assures to America and the world a perfect embodiment of the ideal capital. (Noyes, *The National Capital*, 59–60)

The Government Maps the Topography of Washington and Vicinity

In 1885–86 the U.S. Coast and Geodetic Survey completed its first topographic map of the capital and its environs, a document that became available in published form in 1891. Although by today's standards its scale of one inch to one mile and contour interval of 20 feet would be regarded as inadequate, this map provided accurate information on the shape of the land and what had been placed on it. Among many other features, it shows with particular clarity the location, shape, and size of the large area reclaimed from the Potomac tidal flats by the Corps of Engineers.

The survey also clarifies some of the decisions made by L'Enfant a century earlier. The contour lines emphasize the importance of Capitol Hill and why L'Enfant almost immediately selected it for the purpose it has served so long. A little less obvious is a ridge line extending almost from the foot of Capitol Hill to the White House. He laid out Pennsylvania Avenue to parallel the ridge.

One can also see why L'Enfant brought six of the diagonal avenues together at Lincoln Square, a civic space given further emphasis by being on the axis of East Capitol Street. It was at this place, one mile east of the Capitol, that L'Enfant proposed an itinerary column from which all distances were to be measured. The contours show that he placed this square at the brow of a slope leading on its south and east flanks to the Anacostia River.

This map also reveals the extent to which little patches of suburban development had begun to occupy land once only sparsely built on or completely given over to woods and fields. No plan then existed for streets and avenues beyond the limits of the city of Washington, and each property owner proceeded to subdivide the land with no regard for how it should be related to topography or to neighboring property.

Maryland–District of Columbia–Virginia Washington Sheet. U. S. Geological Survey, U. S. Coast and Geodetic Survey of 1885–86. [Washington], 1891. Lithograph, 18½ × 27⁵⁄₁₆ in. (47 × 69.3 cm.). Olin Library, Cornell University.

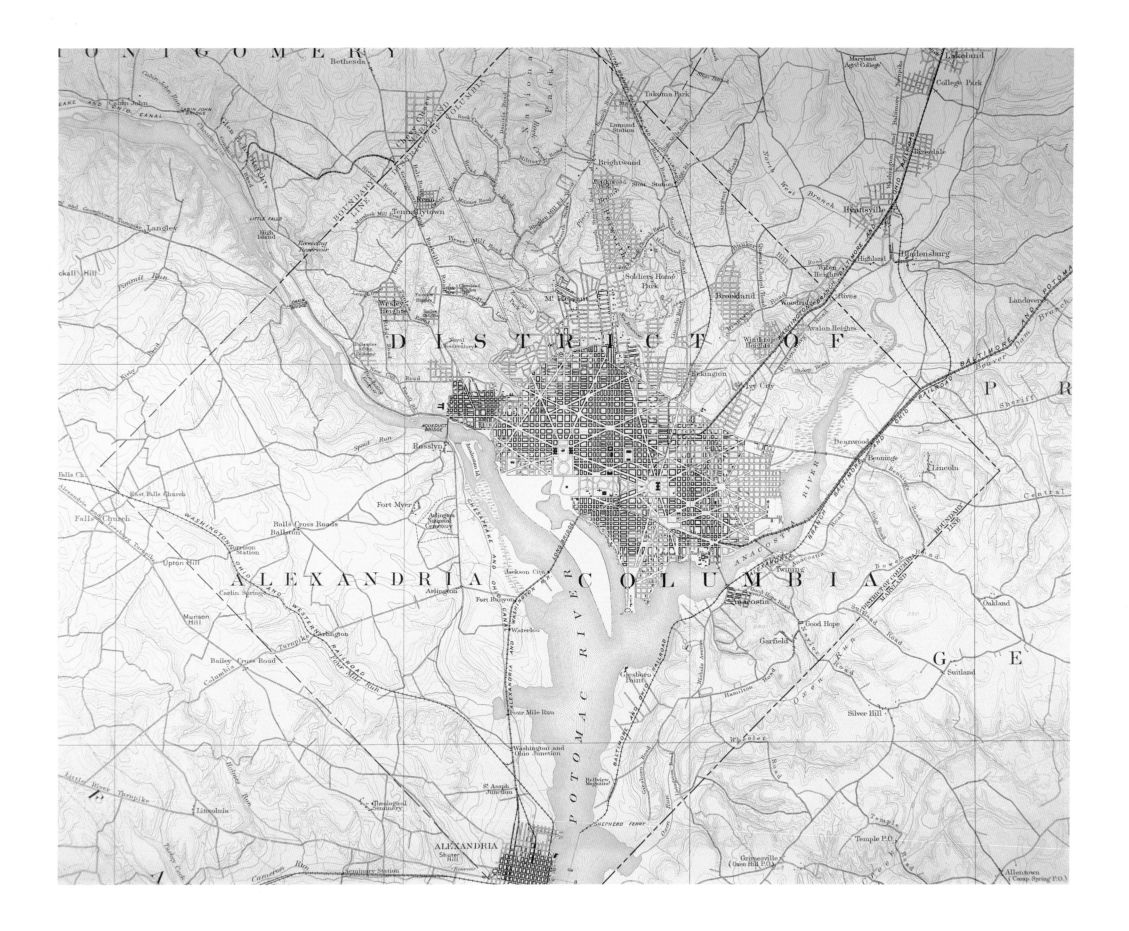

233

Folio 68. An English Drama Critic Views Washington As a Still Unfinished Production with Other Acts Yet to Be Staged

*William Archer visits the city in April 1899
before the arrival of spring foliage.*

I have chanced upon [Washington] without her make-up, and seen the real face of the city divested of its wig of leafage and rouge of blossoms. Here, for the first time, at any rate, I am impressed by that sense of rawness and incompleteness which is said to be characteristic of America. Washington will one day be a magnificent city, of that there is no doubt; but for the present it is distinctly unfinished. The very breadth of its avenues, contrasted with the comparative lowness of the buildings which line them, gives it the air rather of a magnified and glorified frontier township than of a great capital on the European scale. Here, for the first time, I am really conscious of the newness of things.

Archer comments on the city's streetscape and the difficulties encountered by strangers.

Here . . . one instinctively craves for something of that uniformity which one instinctively deprecates as an idea for New York. The buildings on the main streets are too haphazard, like the books on an ill-arranged shelf: folios, quartos, and duodecimos huddled pell-mell together. But when some approach to a definite style is achieved, how noble will be the radiating vistas of this spacious city! The plan of the avenues and streets, as has been aptly said, suggests a car-wheel superimposed upon a gridiron—an arrangement, by the way, which may be studied on a small scale in Carlsruhe. The result is dire bewilderment to the traveller; my bump of locality, usually not ill-developed, seems to shrink into a positive indentation before the problems presented in such formulas as "K Street, corner of 13th Street, N.E." But from the Capitol, whence most of the avenues spread fanwise, the views they offer are superb.

*He envisages the Pennsylvania Avenue of the future
but criticizes the new Post Office.*

Pennsylvania Avenue, leading to the Government offices and the White House, will one day, undoubtedly, be one of the great streets of the world. For the present its beauty is not heightened by the new Postal Department, a massive but somewhat forbidding structure in grey granite, which dominates and frowns upon the whole street. From certain points of view, it seems almost to dwarf the Washington Obelisk, the loftiest stone structure in the world.

He admires the recently completed Library of Congress.

This new Library of Congress is certainly the crown and glory of the Washington of today. It is an edifice and an institution of which any nation might justly boast. It is simple in design, rich in material, elaborate, and for the most part beautiful, in decoration. The general effect of the entrance hall and galleries is at first garish, and some details of the decoration will scarcely bear looking into. Yet the building is, on the whole, in fresco, mosaic, and sculpture, a veritable treasure-house of contemporary American art.

Archer concludes by balancing criticism with compliments.

Let me not be understood, I beg, to make light of the National Capital. I merely say that to the outward eye it is not yet the city it is manifestly destined to become. Its splendid potentialities do some wrong to its eminently spacious and seemly actuality. But to the mind's eye, to the ideal sense, it has the imperishable beauty of absolute fitness. . . . Since Alfred the Great, the Anglo-Saxon race has produced no loftier or purer personality than George Washington, and his country could not blazon on her shield a more inspiring name. . . . And if the city is named with exquisite fitness, so are its radiating avenues. Each of them takes its name from one of the States of the Union—names which, as Stevenson long ago pointed out, form an unrivalled array of "sweet and sonorous vocables."

The author sees the capital as a symbol of the entire nation.

In its whole conception, Washington is an ideal capital for the United States—not least typical, perhaps, in its factiousness, since this Republic is not so much a product of natural development as a deliberate creation of will and intelligence. It represents the struggle of an Idea against the crude forces of nature and human nature. The Capitol, with its clear and logical design, is as aptly symbolic of its history and function as are our Houses of Parliament, with their bewildering but grandiose agglomeration of shafts and turrets, spires and pinnacles; and the two buildings should rank side by side in the esteem of the English-speaking peoples, as the twin foci of our civilisation. (Archer, *America To-Day*, 69–77)

**Rand, McNally & Company
Map the City in 1901**

Although bearing a copyright date of 1895, this map shows conditions in the city in 1901, the date of a guidebook to Washington in which it appeared folded inside the back cover. Its date of depiction is also indicated by its location of the Carnegie Library in Mount Vernon Park, north of the Patent Office. Congress did not appropriate funds for this building until 1898; Andrew Carnegie matched this the following year, and by 1902 the building opened for use by the public. In addition to all of the major older buildings of federal Washington, the map shows the new Post Office. Although always referred to as located on Pennsylvania Avenue, the map shows how it really stood on D Street west of its intersection with Pennsylvania Avenue. It set a poor example by its awkward orientation, sitting uncomfortably on its massive foundations as if it did not know which way to face. Widely regarded as an architectural mistake, today it has been restored as an historic attraction and is generally admired.

On Capitol Hill the map records the footprint of the Library of Congress, the first of what would eventually become a frame of monumental structures of suitable scale to complement the Capitol. Unfortunately, the library blocks the view to the Capitol from Pennsylvania Avenue SE. This blunder thus duplicates the earlier mistake made in siting the Treasury to block the axis to the White House. One can note how the axis of the Capitol slices through the north face of the botanical garden and that the Washington Monument had to be located far east of the White House axis. The map also shows the huge area reclaimed from the Potomac River. The western portion of this later became the site of the Lincoln Memorial and the reflecting basin. Note the channel between the lower end of the reclaimed area and the steamboat docks to the east. The tidal reservoir at its upper end was designed to retain water at high tide that, when released at low tide, would flush the channel clear of refuse.

Washington, D.C. Published by Rand, McNally & Co., [Chicago]. From *Rand, McNally & Co's Pictorial Guide to Washington and Environs.* Lithograph, 18¹⁵⁄₁₆ × 19⁷⁄₈ in. (48 × 50.5 cm.). Olin Library, Cornell University.

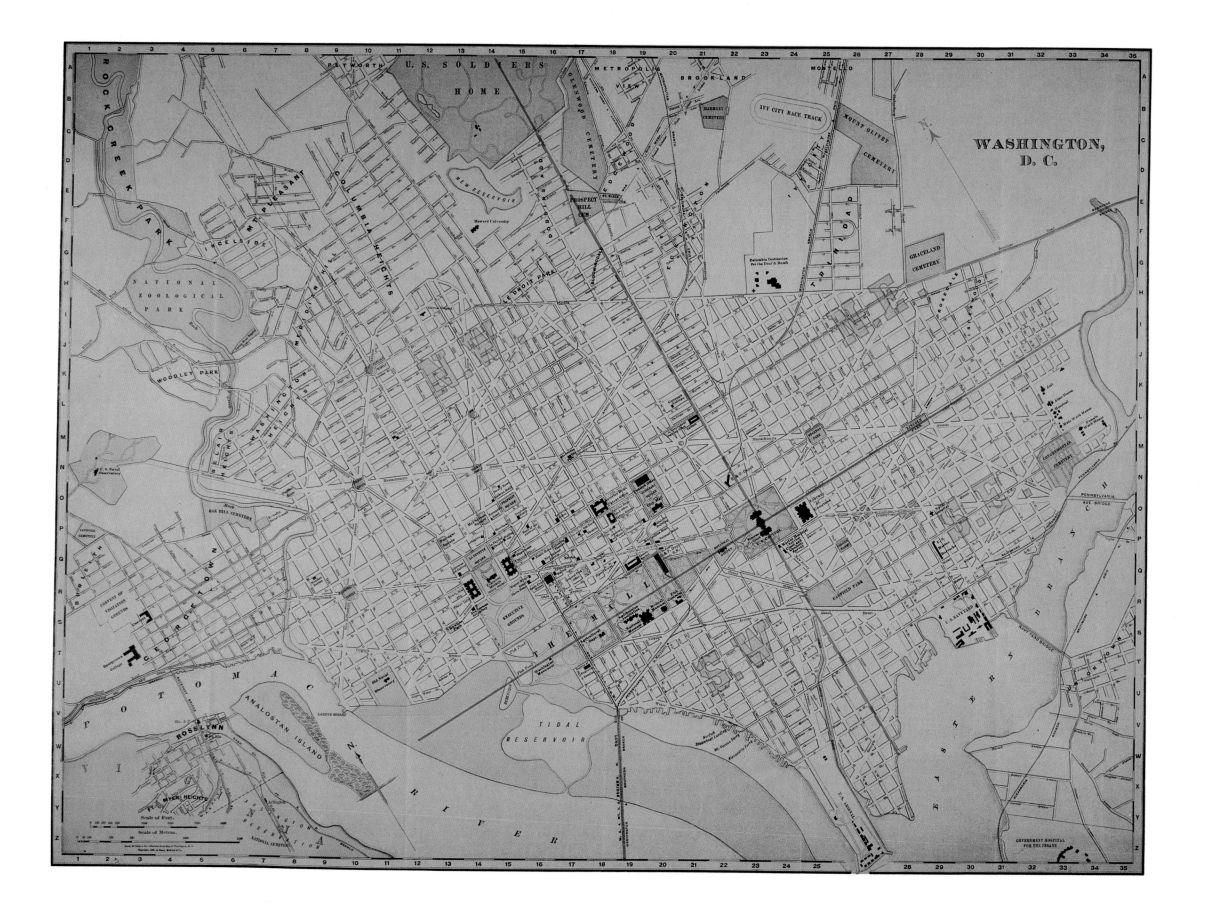

WASHINGTON,
D. C.

235

9 Washington Replanned: The Nation Takes a New View of Its Capital

WELL before 1900—the date marking the centenary of Washington as the seat of national government—civic leaders, members of Congress, and federal officials began considering how this anniversary might be appropriately observed. Many hoped for something more than banquets, speeches, and souvenir programs. At a public meeting in the fall of 1898, a committee of nine distinguished citizens representing the Washington community met with President McKinley to recommend the construction of some permanent monument, memorial, or other project to commemorate the event.[1]

The president endorsed the idea in his message to Congress that December when he recommended the appointment of a joint committee of its members to work with other groups. The president himself created the National Committee composed of the forty-nine governors of states and territories. Together with the Citizens Committee from the district, the governors and the congressional representatives constituted a joint committee to plan a suitable centennial celebration.

Other persons or groups interested in promoting improvements in the capital hastened to link their favored projects with the event or used it to focus attention on their efforts. Franklin Smith revised his plan for central Washington described in the previous chapter, presenting a new version in 1899 and yet another in 1900. Congress took Smith's proposals seriously enough to print his museum designs and his several plans for the Mall as a four-part public document totaling 449 pages.[2]

Smith's Mall plan of 1900 shows a squiggly drive waving its serpentine way down the center of the Mall to the Washington Monument and on to a new bridge over the Potomac. He added a south entrance to his proposed museum as well. On this map, reproduced in folio 69, Smith also designated the very large areas he proposed to clear of buildings to add park lands to the Mall and, between it and Pennsylvania Avenue, to provide sites for public buildings.

Other projects jostled with Smith's for public attention, popular approval, and political support. The March 1900 issue of the *Inland Architect and News Record*, a Chicago-based, professional journal, contained an article on a design for central Washington by Henry Ives Cobb, a well-known architect from Chicago. His plan, dated 15 February 1900, is also reproduced in folio 69.

F. W. Fitzpatrick, the article's author, explained Cobb's concept for "a great avenue . . . on a line from the Capitol dome at the east, straight to the end of New York Avenue at the river." According to Fitzpatrick, Cobb "would have the railways build a magnificent union depot just south of the present antique station, giving them in consideration the remainder of the block back of it for trackage, approaches, etc."[3]

Cobb's proposal for a new and expanded railroad station did not originate with him. Instead, it resulted from an agreement between railroad officials and congressional leaders on a plan to eliminate the numerous grade crossings in Washington where each year some thirty persons were killed or injured. Discussions during the previous three years between Senator James McMillan, chairman of the Senate Committee on the District of Columbia, and representatives of the two railways serving the city culminated in an agreed course of action.

This agreement would have virtually destroyed the Mall if it had been im-

---

1. The report of the committee to the president concluded with a statement that its members "are unanimously of the opinion that so important an event could well be marked by the erection of a type of architecture which will in itself inspire patriotism; and a broader love of country, such as a memorial hall, a bridge connecting the District of Columbia with the sacred ground of Arlington, or some other permanent structure." The text is provided in Cox, *Celebration*, 20–21.

2. The earlier, dated 1899 shows a 200-foot-wide "Centennial Avenue" leading west on the axis of the Capitol, passing to the north of the Washington Monument, and leading across the reclaimed flats to a new bridge across the Potomac. Smith also proposed to construct a new White House directly south of the original and fronting the Mall. His plan shows this as a building substantially larger in dimensions than the Treasury. See Franklin W. Smith, *Petition*, pt. 3, 55. Smith seems to have changed his mind about this location and later to have favored one north of the old city boundary at the end of Sixteenth Street. His map of this location is on pp. 56–57. On p. 41 there is a rendering of the proposed building by Paul J. Pelz, one of the architects of the Library of Congress.

3. Fitzpatrick explained that Cobb proposed to use the site of the market for the City Hall, a building that would face Pennsylvania Avenue and be connected to the new avenue by broad streets on both sides. Cobb's plan called for "sites for other important departmental or other federal buildings flanking" the City Hall. Cobb provided, facing the new avenue on its north side, "ample grounds upon what was the Mall for as many buildings as the Government is liable to require for years to come." Six additional buildings could be erected south of the White House "without cutting off the view from the Executive Mansion." Fitzpatrick, "Beautifying the Nation's Capital," 13–14.

plemented, for in return for eliminating many grade crossings the Pennsylvania Railroad—owner of the Baltimore and Potomac—would be allowed to build a much larger depot for that line on the north side of the Mall. Even worse, the existing tracks were to be elevated so as to run across the Mall on a massive aqueductlike structure. The only passage along the axis of the Mall would be through its arches.[4]

When the joint committee of civic leaders, state governors, and congressmen first met on 21 February 1900, the citizens' committee from Washington recommended that among other events to mark the centennial that December, the cornerstone of a major structure should be laid. The committee proposed that this project be a bridge across the Potomac to Arlington—a subject that had been under consideration for some time and for which Congress had already appropriated funds for preliminary surveys and plans.[5]

After hearing this report, the joint committee referred it to a committee of five, chaired by Senator James McMillan, "for consideration and report." That afternoon the joint committee assembled to learn that McMillan and his colleagues had agreed unanimously on a substantially different proposal. The McMillan committee recommended two projects. One called for "an enlargement of the Executive Mansion," because "everyone recognizes that [it] is not adequate for the purposes for which it is used."

The second must have come as a complete surprise to nearly everyone. McMillan and his fellow committee members endorsed Cobb's plan for a new avenue running obliquely across the Mall. The senator, misleadingly stating that this was L'Enfant's original intention, was able to secure the unanimous approval of this proposal by the joint committee.[6]

Perhaps the proposed Centennial Avenue was part of Senator McMillan's accommodation with the Pennsylvania Railway, for it led directly past the entrance of the intended new and enlarged depot. Or, possibly, Cobb and McMillan saw it as a way of achieving some kind of monumental, building-lined thoroughfare as a substitute for the Mall that the elevated tracks of the railroad would so disfigure. These reasons did not persuade many others outside the joint committee to support the proposal. Instead, it aroused strong opposition from many quarters.[7]

The most influential official voice of the opposition belonged to Col. Theodore Bingham, head of the Office of Public Buildings and Grounds of the army engineers. Bingham had already bluntly attacked McMillan's bill to allow elevated tracks and a new railroad station on the Mall. Less that two weeks after the joint committee approved the McMillan-Cobb proposal, Bingham submitted his own plan for the Mall to President McKinley.

It located the station on the Mall's south side and showed a boulevard leading to the Washington Monument from the bottom of Capitol Hill. A month later Bingham revised this plan to include the triangular area between Pennsylvania Avenue and the Mall. He proposed this site as the appropriate location of future government buildings.[8]

The architects also opposed McMillan's plan. Glenn Brown, Washington architect and author of an exhaustive, two-volume history of the Capitol, led this group as secretary of the American Institute of Architects, an office he assumed in 1898 shortly after that organization moved its office to Washington. No other architect had a deeper interest in and knowledge of Washington affairs; he had studied the L'Enfant plan thoroughly, and he was personally acquainted with many members of Congress, including Senator McMillan and his able personal secretary, Charles Moore.[9]

4. Green, *Washington: Capital City*, 52–55. By far the most complete analysis of the events leading up to the creation of the Senate Park Commission and the preparation of its influential plan is Peterson, "Hidden Origins." Peterson goes well beyond my treatment of the same events in Reps, *Monumental Washington*, and for his research and writing I freely and gratefully acknowledge my debt.

5. The Citizens Committee report also listed many other suggested improvement projects: "The erection of a municipal building . . . ; a memorial arch at the head of Sixteen street; a series of statues of American worthies; a new Executive Mansion; the reclamation of the flats of Anacostia River . . . ; the enlarging of the Capitol grounds . . . ; the policy of erecting all future Government buildings on the south side of Pennsylvania avenue . . . ; a new building for the Supreme Court of the United States, to be erected on a site corresponding to that of the Congressional Library building." The proceedings

of this meeting and much other material on the centennial appear in a large volume written and compiled by the secretary of the joint committee: Cox, *Celebration*. The quotation is on p. 34.

6. McMillan told the assembly that "strange to say, upon looking at the maps which the committee had before it" they saw "that the original plan of Washington, as prepared by Major L'Enfant, provided for just such an avenue, public buildings to be erected on either side of the same." The record does not indicate if the senator exhibited a map of his proposals at that time, and those voting may have believed they merely endorsed some version of L'Enfant's Grand Avenue leading westward along the axis of the Capitol. A diagram of the proposed Centennial Avenue appeared in the *Washington Post* on 26 February, and there were early news stories about the joint committee's recommendations in the *Washington Evening Star* on 22 February and in the *Post* on 23 February.

7. Peterson, in his "Hidden Origins," mentions many other concerned parties who joined in the controversy: merchants and property owners on Pennsylvania Avenue who feared the new avenue would siphon away trade, financial conservatives who favored the plan because no private land would need to be acquired, those supporting an expanded park and parkway system who worried about the effect of the railroad on the Mall as the most visible element of such a system, and civic boosters in and out of the Board of Trade, favoring any and all improvements. The *Washington Evening Star* ran no fewer than seven editorials from late February to early May criticizing the idea. Its first statement on 22 February expressed the objections many persons found in the plan. The editorial called it "in effect a new scheme unverified by official surveys, virtually unheralded

and unknown, and of, as yet doubtful propriety." The writer pointed out that the proposed Centennial Avenue was not what L'Enfant had planned and that "the effect would be to make Pennsylvania avenue virtually a back street."

8. Bingham included both versions in his annual report published in 1901. They are dated 1 March and 1 April 1900. Both are reproduced on pp. 77–78, figs. 43 and 44, in Reps, *Monumental Washington*.

9. Brown's two-volume study of the Capitol made him the unquestioned authority on that building. Brown had lived in Washington since 1880, "was the grandson of a U.S. Senator, and a habitué of the Capitol building, [and] the guiding spirit and lobbyist of the Public Art League since its inception in 1895 to agitate for the creation of a national fine arts commission" (Peterson, "Hidden Origins," 8).

To counter the joint committee endorsement of the McMillan-Cobb plan, Brown secured approval from the president of the institute to adopt as a theme for its annual meeting in Washington the unified and artistic development of the city. Brown also began to draft his own plan for the Mall and adjoining portions of the city, a design that the *Architectural Review* published with the author's explanation of it in its August issue. That plan is reproduced as the third illustration in folio 69.[10]

Almost certainly Brown conferred with McMillan at this time, perhaps showing the senator his design for a ceremonial avenue down the center of the Mall that would bridge the depressed tracks of the railroad and lead directly to the Washington Monument. Brown also proposed to clear the triangle south of Pennsylvania Avenue and to line it and the sides of the Mall with government buildings and other large structures. In his article Brown vigorously criticized the Cobb plan for an oblique avenue.[11]

Others who for various reasons opposed the oblique orientation of the proposed avenue or the construction of a new railroad station doubtless let McMillan know their views. By late spring he either changed his mind on the matter or decided to remove himself from the center of political pressure. On 14 May he introduced a measure in the Senate to authorize the president to appoint a board of experts in architecture, landscape architecture, and sculpture to plan the Mall and its environs, the enlargement of the executive mansion, and a connection between the Mall and the zoological park.[12]

Although the Senate approved, the House did not, and the compromise measure that passed placed responsibility for preparing the plan with the chief of engineers, who was authorized to "employ a landscape architect of conspicuous ability in his profession." The resulting design for the Mall came from Samuel Parsons, who on 14 November 1900 submitted to Bingham his design for a system of drives laid out in a pattern of interlocking ovals. The Parsons plan failed to attract any significant support when it was made public, and it was soon forgotten altogether in the events that followed the convention of the American Institute of Architects in mid-December.[13]

At that meeting the members assembled at an evening session on 13 December to hear and discuss four papers on the design of the center of Washington. C. Howard Walker of Boston spoke on the general principles that should govern the grouping of public buildings. H. K. Bush-Brown presented his thoughts on sculpture and its place in the capital city. Frederick Law Olmsted, Jr., delivered a thoughtful talk on landscape design that must have seemed surprising coming from the son and professional heir of the landscape architect who so ardently championed the informal or romantic style of design.

Pointing out that the character of the buildings in a city must influence landscape design, Olmsted offered this principle to be followed: "Great public edifices must be strongly formal, whether they are perfectly symmetrical or not, and this formal quality ought to be recognized in the plan of their surroundings if the total effect is to be consistent."

Without identifying them by name, Olmsted criticized the plans put forward by Smith, Parsons, and Bingham when he observed that "the axis of the Capitol should neither be ignored by the use of a wiggling road and confused informal planning, nor should it be marked by a mere commonplace boulevard." Instead, Olmsted proposed to treat the Mall as "a sort of compound 'boulevard', marked by several parallel rows of trees with several pavements and turf strips."[14]

Edgar V. Seeler, a prominent architect from Philadelphia titled his paper "The Grouping of Public Buildings in a Great City." Cass Gilbert, Paul Pelz, and George Totten, Jr., apparently used the discussion period to reveal their own designs for the central part of the city. Folio 70 reproduces the four plans they presented as well as excerpts from the explanations each architect prepared for the occasion.[15]

At the beginning of the session the following morning the institute passed a resolution submitted by William A. Boring. This called upon Congress to create a commission to plan "the location and grouping of public buildings, the ordering of landscape and statuary, and the extension of the park system in the District of Columbia." These matters, the resolution stated, were "of national concern," and any improvements "should be made in accordance with a comprehensive artistic scheme."[16]

10. For Brown's role in organizing the institute meeting, see Reps, *Monumental Washington*, 84, and Peterson, "Hidden Origins," 8.

11. Brown, "A suggestion for Grouping Government Buildings."

12. The three appointive members—an architect, a landscape architect, and a sculptor—were "to be associated with the Chief of Engineers of the United States Army" in this venture. The bill directed them to report to Congress on the first Monday in December, the precise centennial of the first meeting of Congress in Washington. The full text of McMillan's proposal, an amendment to an appropriations bill, can be found in Cox,

Celebration, 200–201. The composition of this group strongly suggests that Brown and other architects had convinced McMillan not to permit Bingham to dominate the field of battle.

13. Parsons relocated the railroad station on the south side of the Mall, placing it squarely in the path of Maryland Avenue. The text of Parsons's report and his several drawings, with letters of transmittal from Bingham and the chief of engineers, are reprinted in Cox, *Celebration*, 319–28. His plan is reproduced in Reps, *Monumental Washington*, 81 fig. 46. The official publication is Samuel Parsons, "Report of Mr. Samuel Parsons, Jr., Landscape Architect."

14. Frederick Law Olmsted, Jr., "Landscape in Washington," 25, 30.

15. The plans and text of all four can be found in Brown, *Papers*. Of the four, only Totten proposed to relocate the railroad station. The others, like Brown, accepted the site on the north side of the Mall, although Gilbert and Seeler, as well as Brown, assumed that the tracks could be depressed so that a central Mall avenue could pass over them without obstruction. Seeler did state that the best solution would be to relocate the sta-

tion south of the Mall, but his plan does not incorporate this feature. Peterson explains that the architects and McMillan had apparently come to an agreement that if the architects would drop their opposition to the depot location, the senator would support their proposal for a commission of designers to plan the city. See Peterson, "Hidden Origins," 9.

16. The institute further directed its president to appoint a committee to draft appropriate legislation to this end and to "present the same to Con-

A few days later an institute committee met with the Senate Committee on the District of Columbia, and on 17 December Senator McMillan introduced a resolution to create such a commission. In reporting to the Senate a month later on what became Senate Resolution 139, McMillan's Senate committee argued that Washington had now arrived at the stage of development when "a well-matured scheme of development for its parks and boulevards, the location of its new public buildings, and the treatment of its bridges and monuments must be adopted."[17]

Although opposition in the House prevented its passage, Senator McMillan kept the issue alive by a last-minute maneuver. At an executive session of the Senate, he obtained approval of a resolution directing his committee to "report . . . plans for the development and improvements of the entire park system of the District of Columbia." The Senate authorized the committee to "secure the services of such experts as may be necessary for a proper consideration of the subject," their expenses to be "paid from the contingent fund of the Senate."[18]

It was in this last-minute and irregular manner that the Senate Park Commission came into being. Other than L'Enfant's, no proposals would have such far-reaching and enduring results in the shaping of the city as those put forward by the commission. Its members were all eminent professionals headed by Senator McMillan's choice, Daniel Burnham. A well-known architect from Chicago, Burnham gained national prominence as the designer who coordinated the architects, engineers, and landscape architects who created the celebrated Chicago World's Fair in 1893.[19]

The commission's other members were Charles McKim, another leading architect and partner in the renowned New York firm of McKim, Mead, and White; Augustus St. Gaudens, the country's most highly regarded sculptor; and Frederick Law Olmsted, Jr., the successor with his half-brother to their father's practice of landscape architecture and already achieving his own reputation as a teacher and consultant.[20]

McMillan's selection of Burnham could not have been more fortunate. Not only did he possess great persuasive powers and the ability to coordinate and reconcile conflicting opinions, but—like L'Enfant—he understood as few other American planners have that great urban designs must ignore the limitations of the present and concentrate on the long future. Because Burnham was being considered as the architect for the new railroad station, his appointment to the commission turned out to be fortunate in another respect, as will be explained shortly.[21]

At the first meeting of the commission early in April 1901, Burnham surprised his colleagues by announcing they would visit Europe "to see and discuss *together* parks in their relation to public buildings—that is our problem here in Washington and we must have weeks when we are thinking of nothing else." Before departing, Burnham on 20 May traveled to Philadelphia to meet with President Alexander J. Cassatt and other executives of the Pennsylvania Railroad, which controlled both the Baltimore and Ohio and the Baltimore and Potomac lines serving Washington.[22]

Cassatt and his colleagues understood the purpose of the meeting was to interview Burnham as a possible architect of the new Baltimore and Potomac station on the Mall. Burnham came with quite different ideas. He and McKim

gress on behalf of the Institute." The proceedings of the meeting were reported in "Thirty-Fourth Annual Convention of the American Institute of Architects," with the text of the resolution to be found on p. 47.

17. The committee stated that the Board of Trade and the Business Men's Association of Washington endorsed the legislation, as did the American Institute of Architects. The text of the report and an appended statement by Glenn Brown appeared in a Chicago architectural periodical. See "Commission to Consider Improvements in the United States Capital." In his "Hidden Origins," Peterson argues at some length that in later discussions with the members of the Senate Park Commission, McMillan and his committee colleagues favored preparing a plan limited only to parks and parkways. According to Peterson, it was the members of the Senate Park Commission who pressed successfully for the inclusion of public buildings in the plan. The wording of this committee report suggests otherwise, as does the text of the resolution itself calling for a

presidentially appointed commission, "to consist of two architects and one landscape architect eminent in their professions, who shall consider the subject of the location and grouping of public buildings and monuments to be erected in the District of Columbia and the development and improvement of the entire park system."

18. Congress had already adjourned, but the Senate held an executive session on 8 March. The text of this resolution is in U. S. Senate Committee on the District of Columbia, *Report*, 7.

19. Burnham's place in American architecture and planning has been the subject of many studies. The two-volume work by Charles Moore, *Daniel H. Burnham*, is indispensable, but the more recent study by Hines, *Burnham of Chicago*, is more balanced and relates Burnham's work to more recent developments. See also Cynthia Field, "The City Planning of Daniel Hudson Burnham." My own summary of Burnham's work before he produced his Chicago plan of 1909 is Reps, "Burnham before Chicago."

20. Surely McMillan would not have asked Burnham to head the commission or approved the selection of McKim by Burnham and Olmsted if he expected, as Peterson maintains, a report to be limited to the park system of the District of Columbia. What seems much more likely is that the senator, aware that other committees of the Senate had primary jurisdiction over public buildings and related public works, masked his real intentions under the phrase in his resolution, "development and improvement of the entire park system of the District of Columbia." It also seems to be the general understanding that public building locations were an important element in the commission's work. On 23 March 1901 the *Washington Post* reported that McMillan, Burnham, and Olmsted drove through Rock Creek Park "for the purpose of acquainting the park commissioners with the work which has already been accomplished." The paper then added that the

commissioners "will also have authority to suggest a general plan for continuing the erection of public buildings in Washington, the idea being to avoid, as far as possible, incongruities in architecture, and also the construction of buildings without surrounding ground."

21. William Boring, the chairman of the AIA committee that met with McMillan, had recommended Burnham, although the senator had already asked Burnham to come to Washington. Olmsted's name came up in the same way, but McMillan had anticipated this as well. When McMillan served as a Detroit park commissioner, he had met the senior Olmsted, who designed Belle Isle Park in that city. Burnham and Olmsted were free to select the third member, and, after some discussion, they decided on McKim.

22. As quoted in Charles Moore, *Burnham*, 1:142.

had conferred earlier and had agreed that another site must be found for the railroad—one that would remove it altogether from the Mall. They did so despite Senator McMillan's instructions that the commission was to regard the station location as fixed.[23]

Burnham reported to McKim that President Cassatt and his engineers had been much more receptive to this idea than could have been expected and had agreed to suspend land acquisition for the site on the north side of the Mall until Burnham could prepare a more detailed presentation for a station location south of the Mall, the place he then had in mind. Shortly before the group's European trip Burnham also suggested to Cassatt the possibility of building a union station north of the Mall on the site the railroad legislation had provided for the Baltimore and Ohio depot.[24]

It was there that the matter rested when the commission left for Europe on 13 June. On board the steamship *Deutschland* outbound from New York in June, the group met daily. Olmsted brought with him detailed maps of the city, and they spread these on tables in one of the lounges and discussed how the city might be replanned. In Europe they visited, photographed, sketched, studied, and discussed great urban projects in Paris, Rome, Venice, Vienna, Budapest, Paris again, Versailles, and London in a busy and highly productive tour.[25]

In their absence McMillan made his own approach to Cassatt. At a meeting at the senator's summer home in New Hampshire the two reached an understanding that was later formalized by legislation. They agreed that the Pennsylvania Railroad would abandon its rights to the station on the Mall and construct a union terminal north of the Capitol for the newly merged Baltimore and Potomac and Baltimore and Ohio lines if the government would pay the cost of a railroad tunnel under Capitol Hill.[26]

Burnham did not learn of this until he met President Cassatt in London on 18 July near the end of the group's European tour. He and his companions received this news with enormous relief, for elevated tracks crossing the Mall would have

made it impossible to plan this great central feature of the city in ways that would rival or exceed in beauty the famous landscape and urban design compositions they had examined during their trip.[27]

It is clear from the diary of one of the participants that by the time they sailed for America on 26 July they had agreed on the broad outlines of their plan. The removal of the railroad from the Mall meant that this general concept could now be adopted, refined, and made more precise. On their return to America the commission members began to work out its details. A drafting room in Washington, a studio in New York in the building where McKim had his office, and another in Boston where Olmsted worked, provided three centers of activity.

Charles Moore had accompanied the group to Europe, and he and Senator McMillan arranged for an exhibit of the commission's plan in the new Corcoran Gallery, a building completed in 1897 facing the State, War, and Navy Department from the corner of Seventeenth Street and New York Avenue. The exhibit—designed by McKim and the first in America on city planning—opened 15 January 1902 with President and Mrs. Theodore Roosevelt, members of the cabinet, legislators, and other dignitaries in attendance. The following day the exhibition was opened to the general public.[28]

Visitors looked down from a viewing platform on two huge models, one showing existing conditions in the governmental core of Washington, the other that part of the city as it would appear if the recommendations of the commission were carried out. They then descended for a more detailed inspection. McKim mounted the models at eye level so that one had realistic views down the streets of the models. On the walls of the museum galleries McKim hung large and handsome color renderings illustrating individual features of the plan.[29]

23. By this time the legislation authorizing the new railroad station had been passed by Congress and signed by the president. In return for its rights to build and operate a station "of ornamental or monumental character," the railroad was required to "construct, and maintain beneath its tracks and structures on the line of West Capitol street . . . a substantial arch or arches not less than two hundred feet in width, as a public passageway for vehicular and pedestrian traffic." The station was to cost "not less than one million five hundred thousand dollars" and was to be "designed, as far as practicable, so as not to impair the appearance of the Mall." The text is given in Charles Moore, *Park Improvement Papers*, 89 n. 1.

24. Peterson, "Hidden Origins," 11, citing letters from Burnham to McKim and Burnham to Cassatt.

25. St. Gaudens did not accompany the group to Europe.

26. The story of this meeting in New Hampshire comes from what Charles Moore told William T. Partridge many years after the fact. In 1901 Partridge assisted McKim in New York when the park commission plan was taking form in a studio on the floor above the McKim, Mead, and White office. See William T. Partridge, "McMillan Commission: Personal Recollections," pp. 3, 15, Partridge Papers, Library of Congress, as cited in Peterson, "Hidden Origins," 17 n. 80.

27. Although there were certain economic benefits to a union station, the railroad surrendered an immensely valuable site on the Mall. Cassatt may have been moved by other considerations. He had spent much of his youth in Europe, attending schools in Paris, Heidelberg, and Darmstadt. He traveled throughout Europe as a member of a wealthy family that moved frequently. His sister was Mary Cassatt, the prominent American painter, and although at first he discouraged her from studying art abroad, he later came to appreciate her artistic talents and may well have shared some of them. Before entering Rensselaer Polytechnic Institute, from which he received a degree in civil engineering in 1859, he was more at home with French and German than English. At the time of his discussions with Burnham in May 1900, Cassatt had been president of the Pennsylvania Railroad for less than a year but had already proved to be an aggressive executive who had brought many changes to the company. With this background, Cassatt would have been receptive to the kinds of arguments that Burnham must have used in describing what the Senate Park Commission hoped to accomplish. Cassatt's full role in this matter has yet to be fully investigated. It is not discussed in the otherwise useful biography by Patricia T. Davis, *End of the Line*.

28. That morning Senator McMillan presented to the Senate a brief report of his committee and the long report of the commission. The printed and profusely illustrated version of the report apparently did not become available until later in the year.

29. Olmsted supervised a Boston model-maker who built the two huge models of the city. When they arrived in Washington, they had not yet been finished, and evidently some damage had occurred in shipping. The only photograph of the exhibit itself is one showing workmen finishing and

These views illustrating the recommendations of the commission first appeared in the commission's published report and in several contemporary periodicals. In 1915 the *National Geographic Magazine* reproduced a few of the renderings in color, apparently their first appearance in that form. Two illustrations in folio 71 are the original renderings exhibited in Washington, and two others are from the plates printed in 1915.[30]

A large rendered plan and a beautiful perspective of the city as it would look in the future are the first illustrations in folio 71. The plan makes clear the commission's intention to establish the monumental core of the city between Maryland Avenue on the south and Pennsylvania Avenue and the blocks fronting the White House and Lafayette park to the north. From east to west the plan began at the tier of blocks facing the Capitol and included the reclaimed flats of the Potomac River. Also included were recommendations for parks, parkways, and bridges extending well beyond these limits of the central urban composition.

The general visitor doubtless found the perspective by F. L. V. Hoppin more attractive and easier to understand. Hoppin imagined how the future city would appear from a point 4,000 feet above Arlington looking northeast to Washington. His perspective demonstrates how the commission brought together, modified, and refined many earlier suggestions while adding features of their own.[31]

The extracts from the commission's report in folio 71 present important elements of the plan and make unnecessary more than a brief summary here. The commission proposed to ring Capitol Square with monumental buildings of the same scale as the existing Library of Congress. These would provide offices for members of the Senate and House of Representatives and would create a suitable frame to enclose and unify the space occupied by the Capitol and its grounds. They planned another group of equally imposing buildings for "scientific pur-

poses and . . . museums" to line both sides of the Mall between the Capitol and the Washington Monument.

At the foot of Capitol Hill the commission designed a formal square that would "compare favorably, in both extent and treatment, with the Place de la Concorde in Paris." An illustration in folio 71 shows how this would appear if seen from above the Senate wing of the Capitol. This also shows how the commission proposed to treat the Mall with a broad expanse of lawn flanked on each side by four rows of elms. Shaded drives and walks laid out parallel to this central carpet of green would extend westward to the Washington Monument.

North of the Mall the plan set aside the extensive triangular space extending to Pennsylvania Avenue for buildings of the District of Columbia. The central market was to be moved as part of a policy to improve the appearance of and reduce traffic congestion on the avenue. For the vicinity of the White House the commission recommended a frame of buildings housing executive offices, thus creating an effect similar to those surrounding the Capitol. Buildings fronting Lafayette Square were to be demolished to make way for these new structures.

For the Washington Monument the commission planned a formal terrace with flower beds, fountains, and pieces of sculpture. On the west side a broad stairway led to a sunken garden with a round pool to mark the intersection of the axis of the White House and the center line of the Mall. The last illustration in folio 71 displays these features in a view looking east to the Capitol with the monument and its gardens in the foreground.

To terminate the White House axis the commission proposed a complex of buildings slightly more than a mile to the south of the presidential residence. Here a future generation could decide to erect a memorial to some single national hero or could develop a pantheon commemorating several illustrious citizens. It is on this location that the Jefferson Memorial was ultimately placed.

Beyond the monument and sunken garden the commission extended the Mall west over reclaimed land. Here they planned a long, narrow reflecting basin with wooded areas on each side cut through by radial paths. The character of this design closely resembled that of Versailles, which the commission members visited and admired on their trip to Europe. At the western end of this area the commission placed a templelike memorial to Abraham Lincoln, noting that Lincoln was "that one man in our history as a nation who is worthy to be named with George Washington."

The Lincoln Memorial occupied the center of a large circular drive. From it vehicles could cross the Potomac River on a new bridge leading to the national cemetery at Arlington or could gain access to a parkway following the left bank of the Potomac River. This linked the great central landscaped Mall to Rock Creek Park and to a proposed parkway system that would encircle Washington and connect both existing recreational facilities and a number of new areas that the commission identified for future acquisition and development.

repairing the model of the proposals. One can see in the background a few of the many renderings and photographs. This photograph is reproduced in Reps, *Monumental Washington*, 106 fig. 54. See also pp. 100–107 for additional material on the exhibit. McKim argued that the average person found perspective drawings and photographs far easier to understand than plans and maps. McMillan agreed and even offered to pay the extra cost of the artists' fees from his own funds if necessary. See Charles Moore, *Burnham*, 1:159 n. 4.

30. The National Geographic Society republished the Washington material from its March 1915 issue of the *National Geographic Magazine* (vol. 27) as a separate book: William Howard Taft and James Bryce, *Washington: The Nation's Capital*. Several periodicals used illustrations in reviewing the recommendations of the commission, and these

may have appeared before the Government Printing Office issued the commission's report. The commission also prepared at least one special line drawing of the plan that could easily be reproduced in periodicals. For the suggestions of Elihu Root, secretary of war, concerning publicity for the recommendations, see Reps, *Monumental Washington*, 104.

31. Thousands of persons saw this perspective reproduced in black and white in the articles published about the commission's work in the months following the exhibit. In 1915 the *National Geographic Magazine* published a redrawn version of it in color as a foldout illustration for an issue featuring the commission's plan and how it had been followed during the subsequent thirteen years. See Taft and Bryce, *Washington* for the separately published version of the journal articles.

Detailed stories about the commission's proposals first appeared in Washington newspapers. They were uniformly enthusiastic, as the excerpts in folio 72 demonstrate. Almost immediately newspapers throughout the country joined in acclaiming the work of the commission and urging Congress to carry out its recommendations. Charles Moore wrote an article about the plan in *Century Magazine*, which published the first part in its February 1902 issue. In that influential journal Moore used the line drawing reproduced in folio 72, one specially prepared by the commission for this purpose.[32]

Other thoughtful and informed articles by other authors soon appeared elsewhere. Professional periodicals reported at length on what the commission had recommended. All this favorable publicity encouraged citizens and public officials in many cities to expand the efforts to improve their own communities, programs that had begun with the park and municipal art movements and that the Chicago World's Fair had done much to stimulate.

The Washington plan of 1902 thus provided an inspiring example of how these civic design principles developed for a temporary exposition could be applied in a real city. More than any single event, the Senate Park Commission plan for Washington created the environment in which modern American city planning took root and began to grow.[33]

Washington became the exemplar of good planning because almost immediately officials with responsibility for deciding on the location of public buildings in Washington began to follow the Senate Park Commission recommendations. Some did so willingly and enthusiastically; others agreed to conform to its proposals only reluctantly. This book, concentrating on the physical city and limited to an examination only of its youth and coming of age, cannot examine this aspect of Washington's subsequent growth in any detail.[34]

Instead, as a kind of epilogue, the balance of this chapter will examine conditions in Washington at several stages of its development as the artists of the few drawn views of the city produced in the twentieth century recorded its changed appearance. Urban images of this type had largely gone out of fashion by the time the Senate Park Commission report appeared, and aerial photographs began to take their place not long after the Wright brothers made the airplane a

reality in 1903. Hoppin's wonderfully inspiring vision of the future city from 4,000 feet above Arlington, reproduced in folio 71, was thus one of the last of its kind.

Another quite extraordinary view of the city was discovered only in 1989. It depicts Washington as it existed in 1901 and therefore is a fitting companion to Hoppin's contemporary vision of the city as it might look sometime in the future. Folio 73 includes this heretofore unknown bird's-eye view that looks almost directly north. The work of John L. Trout, listed in the Washington city directory for 1901 as a lithographer, its copyright inscription at the bottom indicates the artist intended to publish it. No such printed view is known, however, and it is likely that for some reason—perhaps Trout's death—this project had to be abandoned.[35]

Trout was clearly a skilled artist whose work ranks with the best of his many predecessors who produced their own versions of the city's appearance. One almost gets the impression of looking at the city itself rather than at its picture. Further, it is an unrivaled historic record of conditions in the capital on the eve of the gradual metamorphosis of its central area into the urban design composition that we know today, one that in its broad outlines and in many of its details follows closely what the Senate Park Commission proposed.

No comparable drawn view of Washington shows the results of the first decade that followed the completion of the plan, and for a graphic record of changes during that period we must use a rendered map of the central part of the city published in 1915 by the National Geographic Society. This illustration in folio 73 identifies in dark red the buildings that existed in 1902 or those erected since that date that conformed to the Senate Park Commission plan. The text by ex-president William Howard Taft that accompanied the map originally and that is abstracted in the folio mentions most of the changes that had occurred.

Two new buildings now stood on sites facing the Mall and at the recommended 400-foot distance from its center line: the Museum of Natural History on the north side and the two wings of the new building for the Department of Agriculture on the south. On Capitol Hill, new House and Senate office buildings joined the existing Library of Congress to begin the architectural frame for the Capitol. At the far end of the Mall the Lincoln Memorial (not yet completed) occupied the commanding site selected for it by the Senate Park Commission.

Pennsylvania Avenue remained almost unchanged. The only near neighbor to the Post Office was the new District of Columbia building a block from the Treasury. This map also shows three buildings south of the new Corcoran Gallery. These faced the White House grounds south of the intersection of New York

32. Moore obviously sent the illustration and the manuscript to the editor well before the exhibit opened so that the article could appear in the same month. See Charles Moore, "The Improvement of Washington City."

33. Burnham and Olmsted played significant roles in establishing city planning as a permanent function in civic affairs. By far the best study of Olmsted is Susan L. Klaus, "'Intelligent and Comprehensive Planning.'"

34. I have written about the immediate events that followed the plan's publication and, in less detail, of developments up to 1965 in chaps. 6 and 7 of my *Monumental Washington*. In the final chapter of that volume I attempt to answer the question of why so many of the Washington plan's recommendations were carried out as compared to plans prepared for other American cities. For this material, see pp. 139–98.

35. This view was brought to my attention in November 1989 by James and Judith Blakely, owners of The Old Print Gallery in Washington, who acquired the view shortly before. The Blakelys have been generous in sharing with me what little information they have been able to find on the artist. Trout's name does not appear in any of the Washington directories after 1901, but whether this indicates that he died or merely moved away from the city cannot as yet be determined.

Avenue and Seventeenth Street. They housed the American Red Cross, the Daughters of the American Revolution, and the Pan-American Union—all conforming in their style, size, and location to the proposals put forward in 1902.[36]

Although not depicted on the rendered map whose scope does not extend that far north, two other important additions to the Washington scene were illustrated in the same publication. Folio 73 shows their appearance: the impressive Union Station that Daniel Burnham designed on Massachusetts Avenue and the large, new city Post Office, also by Burnham, adjoining the station to the northwest.

The Fine Arts Commission that Congress authorized in 1910 and whose members President Taft appointed became the watchdog over the Senate Park Commission plan. Subsequent executive orders widened the Fine Arts Commission's jurisdiction to give it approval power over the design of federal buildings, parks, monuments, statues, and fountains. This body patiently and skillfully promoted the plan and successfully blocked nearly every proposed building that did not conform to it.[37]

Its report for 1921, portions of which can be found in folio 74, noted that work had begun on landscaping the Mall, that the Lincoln Memorial no longer appeared isolated from the rest of the monumental center of Washington, and that a beginning had been made on buildings that were to face the north side of the Mall at its western end. The commission pointed out, however, that much remained to be done and that the many temporary buildings erected during World War I on the Mall and elsewhere in Washington must be removed.

These appear near the upper left of the splendidly clear and complete bird's-eye view of the city at that time drawn by William Olsen. These buildings persisted through the next two decades, saw a second round of military service during World War II, and were not finally demolished until the 1960s. Other temporary structures occupied the land that had been cleared between the Capitol and Union Station. The view shows the railroad terminal with admirable clarity, and its size demonstrates what a catastrophe it would have been to have located a new and enlarged railroad station on the Mall.

To the left and somewhat above the center of the view one can see the buildings of Washington's central business district. Olsen labeled a great many of the stores, offices, and hotels with signs that are too small in the reproduction to be read but that are quite legible on the original print that measured an impressive 29 and 44 inches. Olsen also identifies in similar fashion the public buildings, diplomatic missions, headquarters of national organizations, and other places of interest in the capital.

These include the House and Senate office buildings in the center foreground. To their right one can see the great bulk of Union Station facing the plaza, and the park between the station and the Capitol. During the war, temporary buildings occupied much of this generous expanse of open land. Adjoining Union Station to the northwest is the new city Post Office.

On the Mall the new National Museum on the north and the two wings of the new Agriculture Building can be seen, the beginning of the ranks of institutions envisaged by the Senate Park Commission. Beyond the Washington Monument and the temporary buildings stands the Lincoln Memorial, a structure that would not be dedicated until the following year. When Olsen drew the view only a small portion of the reflecting basin had been completed, but this 2,000-foot sheet of water would soon enhance the approaches to the memorial structure.[38]

The other illustrations in folio 74 represent a selection from the pages of one of the many souvenir booklets available to visitors and residents of Washington seeking pictorial records of the city's major buildings. Particularly noteworthy are the four structures erected on sites along Seventeenth Street and facing the White House grounds and the adjoining ellipse to the south. Although built by four different sponsors, together they comprise an even more effective street composition than the Senate Park Commission had proposed for this location.

With folio 75 we see Washington two and one-half decades later and read impressions of the city written in the 1930s and 1940s. The first passages of text come from the bulky guidebook compiled by the Federal Writers' Project of the Works Progress Administration. As in the more than one hundred other guides in this remarkable series, the identity of the writers remains unknown. In this case the person or persons assigned to comment on the architecture of the city reflected the newer attitude toward buildings not designed in "contemporary" or "modern" style that would prevail for decades.

A few years later an English journalist who later served in Washington during World War II as a member of the British mission left his impressions of a city whose climate he hated but whose beauty he admired. In the passage selected for the folio he describes one of Washington's notable new buildings, the great National Art Gallery presented to the nation by Andrew Mellon. This visitor, while finding its architecture "disappointing," admired its interior spaces in words that most others have echoed.

The National Gallery's strategic location facing the Mall between the older National Museum and the Capitol can be seen on the colorful plan-view in the folio. As in the altograph in folio 64 published more than half a century earlier, the artist shows in perspective only the major buildings and landscape features against a street map of the city. This technique makes it easier to grasp how many

36. Like the Post Office, the district building half turned away from the avenue, for its entrance facade, too, followed an exact east-west orientation instead of being parallel with the potentially great thoroughfare on which it faced.

37. Taft issued executive orders on 10 October 1910 and 2 February 1912, Woodrow Wilson on 28 November 1913, and Warren Harding on 18 July 1921.

38. I have been unable to find any information about Olsen, the artist of this view.

new buildings had been constructed and how at long last the Mall had become the great central axis of the city that L'Enfant had envisaged, although in somewhat different form.

The map records the appearance of what everyone now refers to as the Federal Triangle—the large site bounded by Pennsylvania Avenue, the White House grounds, and Constitution Avenue. Congress in 1928 authorized the acquisition of this area, and by the mid-1930s the classical facades of a half-dozen departments and agencies provided uniform cornice and belt lines along Constitution Avenue and—except for the Post Office and District of Columbia Building—on Pennsylvania Avenue as well.[39]

The artist of this depiction of Washington, an architect from New York named Oliver Whitwell Wilson, shows us other changes in the city whose growth had been so stimulated by the expansion of federal employment in the Great Depression and during World War II. The Federal Triangle, large as it was, could not accommodate the government's needs. West of the White House grounds between Eighteenth and Nineteenth streets, a two-block site held the Department of the Interior, whose immense building was completed in 1937. Beyond that at Twenty-first Street one can see the first part of the State Department, a building that nearly quadrupled in size within two decades.

The map also shows the huge addition to the Department of Agriculture, immediately south of the building, begun on the Mall in 1902. To the southwest, directly on the axis of the White House, stands the Jefferson Memorial near the site proposed by the Senate Park Commission to commemorate one or many national heroes. This, too, came in classical garb in a form similar to the Rotunda at the University of Virginia, whose first buildings Jefferson had designed.[40]

The artist depicts several bridges crossing the Potomac, including the handsome Arlington Memorial Bridge dedicated in 1932 to connect the Lincoln Memorial to Arlington Cemetery in Virginia. On that side of the river the artist portrays the huge Pentagon surrounded by the looping ramps of the first expressways in what would eventually become a far more extensive system. This culminated in the Washington Beltway, designed to circle the sprawling metropolis but which now has itself been overtaken by further suburban growth beyond its circumference.

In 1975 Austin and Knight Kiplinger, second and third generation journalist-observers of the city, noted that while in 1950 "the population of the whole Washington metropolitan area was about 1.5 million," by the mid 1970s it had more than doubled to become the eighth largest such urban complex in the nation. The Kiplingers pointed out that although the District of Columbia had lost population, suburbs of the metropolis in only twenty years had "tripled their population from 705,000 in 1950 to 2.1 million in 1970."[41]

The first of the accounts of Washington by five distinguished commentators presented in folio 76 reflects this new aspect of the city. Tom Wicker's observation, written in the 1960s, reminds us that in addition to its role as the nation's capital, Washington now faced all the problems of other metropolitan centers, of which traffic congestion is but one of many.

The folio also contains a perceptive passage on the Federal Triangle by the author-painter and then chairman of the Fine Arts Commission, William Walton. Bitterly criticized two decades earlier by modern architects, the buildings of the Federal Triangle can now be appreciated as examples of fine workmanship and as a civic composition providing a dignified unity for strategic stretches of two of Washington's most visible and heavily traveled thoroughfares.

The longer excerpts by Robert Smith and Eric Severeid and by the nation's leading architectural critic, Ada Louise Huxtable, express the prevailing attitudes toward Washington by most American observers. A century earlier few American journalists could find much to praise in the raw, widely dispersed, and only partly built-up community. Now these writers celebrate Washington as a triumph of urban planning and development.

Their opinions reflect the changed character of Washington as depicted in the view reproduced in folio 76, a record not only of the city as those observers saw it in the 1960s but also of the expected future. The artist, Snejinka Stefanoff, included many buildings and other features that existed only on paper, including such proposals as the Pennsylvania Avenue plan that the president's Council on Pennsylvania Avenue issued in 1964.

Their plan called for redevelopment of the north side of the avenue and the creation of civic plazas at the Treasury end and at the southern end of the axis connecting the old Patent Office and the National Archives. New buildings on the north side of the avenue were to be set back from the street to permit rows of trees to be planted along its length, and stepped curbs were to provide better views for spectators during parades and celebrations.[42]

39. One part of the Federal Triangle remained unfinished, a large L-shaped section on the east side of Fourteenth Street and extending to Pennsylvania Avenue on the eastern side of the District of Columbia Building. The Pennsylvania Avenue Development Corporation in 1989 invited proposals for a new building to complete the governmental complex and chose one submitted by the firm of Pei Cobb Freed & Partners. This building will be constructed by a consortium led by the Zeckendorf Company. The International Cultural and Trade Center will occupy much of the space, which the government will lease for thirty years, becoming the building's owner at the end of that time. See Goldberger, "After 60 Years."

40. The proliferation of public buildings during the administrations of President Franklin Roosevelt and his active role in determining their location and design is the subject of Rhoads, "Franklin D. Roosevelt and Washington Architecture."

41. Kiplinger, *Washington Now*, 91. The authors point out some of the changes this has meant: "Once merely tack-ons to the District, the Washington suburbs are now nearly self-sufficient in shopping, office buildings, and night life. These days, more than half of the area's labor force goes to work each morning in the suburbs rather than the District. And the District itself has a population of only 720,000 out of the more than 3 million people in the whole metropolitan area" (91–92).

42. For a summary of progress to the beginning of 1989 in reshaping Pennsylvania Avenue,

The most sweeping changes appear in Southwest Washington, the portion of the city bounded on the north by the Mall and extending from the Washington Channel to South Capitol Street. In the northern section of this area lying between Independence Avenue and the Southwest Freeway, more than a dozen federal departmental and agency buildings had been erected to create an office complex larger than the Federal Triangle, far more diverse in architectural character, and lacking the coherent site plan of that earlier complex of public buildings.

Across Independence Avenue between Fourth and Seventh Streets one can see the National Air and Space Museum, planned at the time this view was published but not opened until 1976. Its huge bulk dwarfs the other major addition to the Mall museums during this era, the National Museum of American History, opened in 1964 as the National Museum of History and Technology, on the Mall across from the Agriculture Department.

South of the freeway below the new cluster of federal offices are the many buildings of the southwest redevelopment area that replaced the acres of blighted and slum dwellings once occupying the site. A general plan for the more than 400 acres of this neighborhood was adopted in 1956, and work began shortly thereafter on individual projects, each designed by different architects. This approach produced an attractive variety of designs that avoided the stereotyped appearance of so many other projects of this scale in other cities.

Near the lower left of the view the artist has included two other developments that have changed the face of Washington. The large rectangle west of the enlarged State Department in Foggy Bottom marks the location of the Kennedy Center, completed in 1971 to house a theater, concert hall, opera house, and other facilities for the performing arts. Adjoining it to the northwest are the curving facades of the Watergate complex of apartments, hotel, restaurants, and shops.[43]

As had been true in Washington's youth and middle age, visitors differed in their reactions to the maturing city of these later years. A foreign-born but longtime resident of the country, Rom Landau, looked at Washington with a sculptor's eye when he observed that the city "contains a larger number of Greek temples than the whole of Attica under Pericles could boast." Indeed, he asserted, "practically every building of importance—Government Department, Museum, Bank, Library, School, Club, and so on—is fashioned as a Greek temple."

Landau stated that "since the material used is whitish-grey stone or white marble, the general impression tends to be one of unredeemed monotony." Although he believed that "there is nothing more beautiful than one or two Greek

temples placed by themselves in sacred seclusion," this critic concluded that "Greek temples by the score, squashed among other buildings, easily look cold and flat."[44]

The American writer Roger Angell looked at Washington with different eyes. He visited the city in the spring and called it "perhaps the most beautiful springtime city I have ever seen." He tells of coming out of his hotel early one morning, turning into "one of the great avenues," and having his "heart . . . lifted by Washington's great white distances, by the subtlety and sweep of the genius of L'Enfant, the city's designer."

When he walked to the base of the Washington Monument and looked in both directions to the Lincoln Memorial and the Capitol, he found them "both more lovely, for all their familiarity, than the heart had remembered. Here, enjoying this carefully contrived, classical and sentimental landscape, I realized . . . how much of Washington is a cliché—and what a beautiful cliché it is, retaining always its capacity to stir you and to arouse the expected feelings of quiet pride and proprietary excitement."

Angell adds that he welcomed the companionship of his fellow sightseers, "for I suddenly realized that I would be worried about a country whose citizens had become so sophisticated and so bored with the obvious and the patriotic that it could not muster a long line of tourists around the foot of a national shrine on a fine Easter Sunday morning."[45]

Folio 77 provides another leap forward in time of two decades in this summary of Washington's development in the twentieth century. Although most of what is

44. Landau, *Among the Americans*, 60–61. This foreign policy expert who was also an artist added this comment: "The man who stands overawed and ennobled in front of the profoundly moving Lincoln Memorial, views it in the same spirit of reverence that might flood his being as he contemplates a sunrise or a magnificently rolling sea. It is right that he should feel dwarfed and insignificant. But is it reasonable to expect him to measure up to an equally monumental architecture while adding up figures, filling in Income Tax returns, or crossing the corridor to visit the W.C.? No man or woman should have to exist *all* the time on the plane of the heroic, and his mundane voice should not be reduced to a whisper by the rhetoric of great columns." Landau amusingly points out that along Massachusetts Avenue the visitor to Washington could find some relief from the prevailing white classical buildings filling the monumental core of the city: "Florentine Cinquecento *palazzos* rub shoulders with Tudor oak and Gothic fantasies in stone; a flamboyant French Renaissance château flanks a reticent Queen Anne mansion in rose-brick; the painted wood of a Swiss chalet follows upon the iron grills of an Andalusian-Moorish house, and American Colonial upon aluminium-functional; the red-brick and yellow tiles of a Victorian monstrosity are framed by columned Georgian on the one side, and Monte-Carlo-Edwardian stucco on the other."

45. Angell, "Washington, D.C.," 259–64. Angell, however, found the Jefferson Memorial a disappointment: "I liked the challenging, dangerous words on the walls ('. . . laws and institutions must go hand in hand with the progress of the human mind. As that becomes more developed, more enlightened, as new discoveries are made, new truths discovered and manners and opinions changed, with the change of circumstances, institutions must advance also to keep pace with the times . . .'). . . . But I could not help thinking that Jefferson, the architect and patrician, the man of Monticello, would have preferred a statue six feet high instead of nineteen feet, and would have voted for his beloved Virginia brick instead of for glaring white marble."

see Goldberger, "Ebb and Flow." A much longer account can be found in Highsmith and Landphair, *Pennsylvania Avenue*, 115–56. In addition to many photographs of proposals and executed work, a double-page map on pp. 148–49 reveals the substantial scope of these improvements already carried out as well as those now under way or approved.

43. Ralph Becker's *Miracle on the Potomac* tells the history of the Kennedy Center.

written now about the city concerns urban problems such as crime, drugs, law enforcement, welfare, and education or Washington as the scene of executive, legislative, or judicial activities of the federal government, guidebooks continue to remind residents and visitors of the importance and attractions of the physical city. The folio includes excerpts from several guides that carry on the long tradition of such works published in or for the national capital.

They accompany the most recent of Washington's perspective views, the creation of David A. Fox, a Philadelphia artist who has produced similar depictions of other American cities. It shows few changes of any importance from the one reproduced in the previous folio. Perhaps the most significant addition is the east wing of the National Gallery. Fox also shows, as the previous view did not, all of the buildings around Capitol Square, including the newly completed James Madison Building of the Library of Congress.[46]

This view and that in folio 76 otherwise resemble each other so closely partly because the earlier view included many proposals that were carried out in the intervening period. Another reason is that the central core of Washington portrayed in Fox's view of 1984 had already reached a mature stage of development in which major structures occupied almost all of the available sites. Although the future will surely see further changes in the monumental core of Washington,

they are unlikely to do more than refine and elaborate on the pattern that now exists.

The photograph reproduced in folio 77 records the appearance of Washington as one can see it today from the air. It should be compared to the reproduction in folio 71 of the aerial perspective displayed by the Senate Park Commission in 1902 and with Trout's depiction of the city in folio 72 showing Washington as it then existed. The photograph provides convincing graphic evidence of the enormous accomplishment in urban planning that Washington represents.[47]

No city is ever "complete," but two hundred years after L'Enfant first conceived of his design, that part of his plan for which he held the highest hopes and regarded as of greatest importance and which the Senate Park Commission designed in more detail has finally achieved what is likely to be its ultimate scale and character. Altered from L'Enfant's original concept, as almost every city plan in history must ever be, harmed in some respects, improved and augmented in others, that design is now firmly and irrevocably fixed on the land as a part of the heritage of every American.

46. David Fox is a practicing architect in Philadelphia. He has worked as a Peace Corps volunteer teaching English in Ethiopia for two years, as an artist of Philadelphia scenes painted in acrylics, as an illustrator of the children's book *A Little Miracle*, and—beginning in 1976—as the artist of axonometric views of Philadelphia, Boston, Chicago, New Orleans, and Washington. More recently he has prepared aerial views of lower Manhattan, St. Louis, and the financial district of Boston.

47. Alex S. Maclean (1947–   ), the photographer of this view, graduated from Harvard in 1969 and from that institution's Graduate School of Design in 1973 with a master's degree in architecture. Shortly thereafter he founded Landslides, a Boston firm specializing in photographing the earth from the air and serving the needs of environmentalists, publishers, planners, architects, and others. Maclean flies fixed-wing aircraft while photographing in color with gyro-stabilized 35mm and medium-format cameras. His photographs are represented in a large number of individual and corporate collections, and his images have appeared in many one-person and group exhibits. Among his current projects is a collaborative study with the author matching and comparing modern aerial images with nineteenth-century bird's-eye lithographs of cities on the Mississippi River from New Orleans to St. Cloud, Minnesota.

*An architectural journal describes
Franklin Smith's plan for a huge museum.*

Mr. Franklin W. Smith, of Boston, who has made himself somewhat famous by his Pompeiian villa at Saratoga, his Moorish one at St. Augustine, and his scheme, which has not yet been carried out, for a Roman palace at the same place, is . . . now in Washington, with a plan more extensive than any of the previous ones. He proposes now . . . to erect . . . a building which, with its terraces, triumphal arches and so on, is to cover an area of one hundred and fifty acres. The idea, we are told, was suggested by an old plate representing a restoration of the Roman Forum, but a Greek flavor is to be imparted to it by making the central motive a reproduction of the Parthenon, while on either side, as well as in front, extend ranges of galleries, divided by a sort of Via Sacra, which crosses a bridge, lined with statues, in front of the group, and extends in a straight line to the centre of the Parthenon portico, passing under two triumphal arches on the way, while semicircular colonnades, like those in front of St. Peter's at Rome, are arranged on each side, to diversify the perspective. This decidedly ambitious structure, or rather, group of structures, is intended to serve as a national art museum. (*American Architect and Building News*, 10 January 1891, p. 18)

*An article in another architectural journal
explains a plan by Henry Ives Cobb.*

Mr. Cobb's idea is to cut a great avenue, not *through* the Mall, but off its northern edge, and on a line from the Capitol dome at the east, straight to the end of New York avenue at the river, to the west. It is now planned to build the Memorial Bridge across the river to Arlington at that point, and on a line with New York avenue. Mr. Cobb would build that bridge at the same place, but upon the axis of this new avenue. That avenue, "Centennial," "National" or "Washington," would be an almost perfectly level stretch, and, with the bridge, nearly three miles long. Imagine the vista from the Arlington end of the bridge with the Capitol as its vanishing point! To the south of the avenue, he would redeem and turn into a beautiful river park that great area of marshy land west of the Monument. . . . The rest of the Mall to the south he would leave untouched . . . excepting that he would have the railways build a magnificent union depot just south of the present antique station, giving them in consideration the remainder of the block back of it for trackage, approaches, etc. . . . The impression that would

be made upon one in stepping out of this station would not soon be forgotten, and something certainly worth remembering. Just to the west of that station, Mr. Cobb would leave a great open space or plaza. Then upon the space now occupied by the Market he would build the City Hall, facing upon Pennsylvania avenue and the new avenue, and with broad streets either side of it connecting the two. Flanking this building, he plans for sites for other important departmental or other federal buildings. (Fitzpatrick, "Beautifying the Nation's Capital," 13–14)

Glenn Brown produces a plan for central Washington.

The plan contemplates the purchase of the property between the Mall and Pennsylvania avenue on the north of the park, and the purchase of the squares facing the park on the south. On this purchased property buildings could be erected facing the Mall on the north and south and facing Pennsylvania avenue on the south. Then a boulevard could run through the Mall from the Capitol grounds to the Monument, with the Capitol as the vista on the east and the Washington Monument as the western vista. . . .

At the foot of the Capitol grounds, first are proposed two groups of monumental fountains, then two squares are devoted to statuary and monuments within formal gardens. The boulevard is intended to have a gradual rise and pass over the railroad tracks on Sixth street. . . . Over Sixth street and the adjoining park I would propose a colonnade of detached columns, together with thick planting, so as to screen the railroad and traffic. . . .

I would propose a grand circular colonnade 800 feet in diameter, surrounding the Monument, but detached therefrom, leaving a plaza between the colonnade and monument of more than 700 feet in diameter. . . . In this plaza formal parades, presentations, Presidential reviews, games, and other spectacular events could be viewed by the populace. . . .

After passing the monument the scheme proposes to continue the boulevard with its statuary on either side to a point near the Potomac River, where another circular plaza surrounded by groups of statuary would form the entrance to the memorial bridge which it is contemplated will be built across the river to Arlington.

Adjoining the Mall on the south and on a line with the Monument the Government has acquired, by reclaiming marsh land, a park area of about 700 acres. From the Mall roadways would pass directly into this riverside park. (Brown, "A Suggestion for Grouping Government Buildings," 91–94)

*A Museum Owner and Two Designers Suggest
How Washington Should Be Planned*

The centennial of Washington as the seat of government inspired many persons to propose improvement projects. One plan came from Franklin Smith, promoter of a proposed museum of civilization. In 1900 he revised an earlier design, substituting a roadway snaking through the Mall in a series of linked curves. Public buildings would be placed in the space between the Mall and Pennsylvania Avenue, and a gigantic museum of civilization would occupy the land west of the White House.

Architect Henry Ives Cobbs offered a plan that called for an avenue passing by the north side of the proposed new railroad station and providing sites on the avenue's north side for public buildings. A new bridge would cross the Potomac as a continuation of the avenue's axis.

Glenn Brown's plan proposed an avenue through the center of the Mall on the Capitol axis, bridging the railroad whose tracks would be concealed by colonnades and landscaping. The avenue would continue to the Washington Monument and a new Potomac bridge. Brown suggested acquiring all the land between the Mall and Pennsylvania Avenue and using the triangular space for public buildings.

Final Plan Showing Condemnations. From Franklin Webster Smith, *Designs, Plans, and Suggestions for the Aggrandizement of Washington*, pt. 3, p. 117, in Smith, *Petition.* Photoengraving, 4 × 7⅝ in. (10.1 × 19.3 cm). Olin Library, Cornell University.

Suggestions for Locating Future Government Buildings in the District of Columbia. Drawn by Henry Ives Cobb, 15 February 1900. From *Inland Architect and News Record*, March 1900. Photoengraving, 4¾ × 12¹/₁₆ in. (12.1 × 30.7 cm). Ryerson and Burnham Libraries, The Art Institute of Chicago.

Scheme for Grouping Government Buildings Landscape and Statuary on the Mall and Pennsylvania Ave. Washington D.C. Drawn by Glenn Brown. From Glenn Brown, *Papers Relating to The Improvement of the City of Washington.* Photoengraving, 12¼ × 7½ in. (31 × 19 cm). Fine Arts Library, Cornell University.

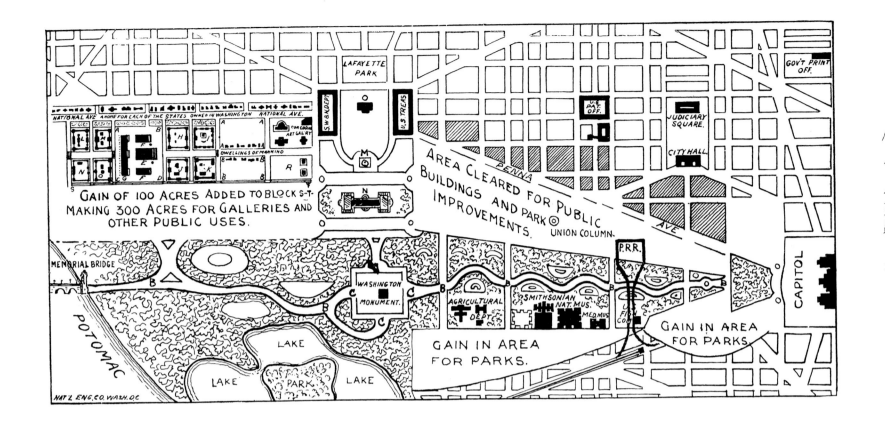

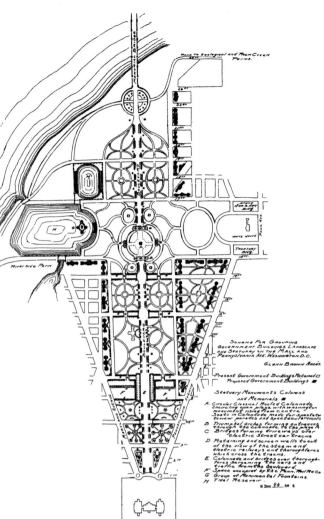

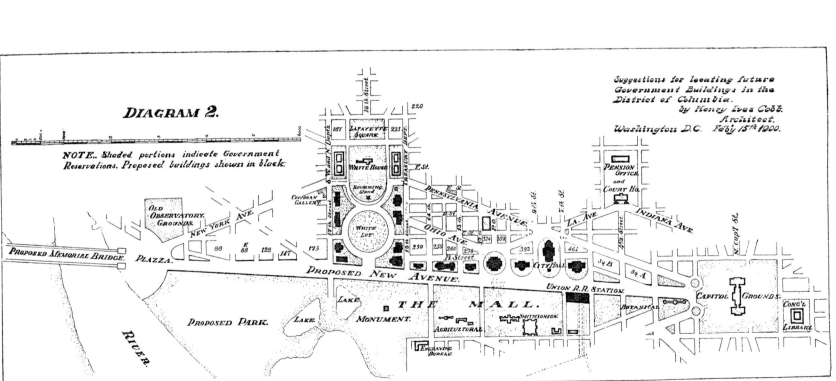

249

Cass Gilbert describes his plan.

I would construct a great boulevard extending from the Capitol to the Monument . . . so that the Monument would be central on this axis, and it would not be noticeable that the boulevard did not approach the Capitol at an exact right angle. . . .

I would frankly accept the fact that the Monument is off axis with the White House, and would place at an equal distance from its axis a low but very large important monument, richly adorned with sculpture of grandiose scale and acting as a foil for the Monument itself. . . . I would then terminate the vista from the White House by a group of buildings to be used as military, naval, and historical museums. . . .

Assuming the old White House to remain as the center of the executive business of the Government and to be used as the office of the president, I should locate the departmental buildings near it. . . . Placing the executive branches of the Government on the east side of Fifteenth street and thence down to the Mall, I would form a great group of such buildings around a grand square at the west end of the Mall. . . .

On the west side of Seventeenth street I should form a special group of buildings for the scientific and educational departments of the Government. (Gilbert, "Grouping of Public Buildings and Development of Washington," 80–81)

A Washington architect offers his thoughts on the subject.

I would like to see the Mall extended in its full width to meet the lines of the Capitol grounds by extending B street . . . and by converting the blocks from Third to First streets into approaches and parks. . . .

The Capitol and the Library are already in close relationship; a balance building will soon be built to form a trine of principal structures. As the Capitoline hill falls rapidly to the north and southward from the two C streets, an acropolis effect would indeed be had by the creation of such a group of seven or nine buildings. . . .

In a strictly utilitarian sense nothing could be better for the General Government than the acquisition of all the blocks south of Pennsylvania avenue and between the Treasury Department and the Capitol for public building sites. . . . Aesthetically, Pennsylvania avenue would by this measure become a park avenue second to none of the great streets of European capitals. (Pelz, "The Grouping of Public Buildings in Washington," 88–89, 91)

Edgar V. Seeler explains his design for the city.

The development of the Mall into a monumental boulevard, if it is undertaken, must not be all gardening, as some have proposed, nor can sculpture do much of itself, whether isolated or grouped; it would be even worse if nothing but architecture were contemplated. It must be a judicious combination of all these essentials. . . .

There is a unique condition . . . in the possibility of continuing such a boulevard by a monumental bridge. . . . In [one] solution, the axis . . . passes through the center of the Washington Monument. . . . Groups of fountains, statuary, and monuments, rows of free-standing columns and formal gardens lead from the foot of the Capitol, by bridges, across the steam railroad tracks and the streets where trolley cars run, to a grand circular colonnade surrounding the Monument. . . .

The trolley roads which cross the Mall can all be depressed without difficulty, and the boulevard carried across them by bridges, as the ground now rises to what would be the line of the boulevard. But the Pennsylvania Railroad tracks are a more serious problem. The desirable thing to do would be to move the station to the south side of B street South, thus doing away with the tracks altogether across the Mall. . . .

It would seem . . . that the Mall in its present extent is wide enough to admit of the placing of buildings on its outer edge without materially reducing its function as a park, and the buildings thus disposed would be . . . easy . . . of access one to another. (Seeler, "The Monumental Grouping of Government Buildings in Washington," 53–55)

George Totten applies design principles of exposition architecture to Washington.

The grouping of government buildings would . . . follow the same natural laws as in the grouping of exposition buildings; the more important ones would be made the more monumental and dignified and given the most prominent locations—vista terminations where possible; lesser ones arranged along avenues somewhat according to their needs and uses, leading up to the former or to other monuments of special interest. (Totten, "Exposition Architecture in its Relation to the Grouping of Government Buildings," 84)

Four Unofficial Proposals for Replanning Washington Influence Public Policy

Glenn Brown, secretary of the American Institute of Architects, organized its national convention of 1900 so that its first session focused on how public buildings in Washington should be located and grouped and how its parks and other open spaces should be designed. Four participants prepared drawings illustrating their proposals. Each contained ideas that in one way or another were adopted or modified by the Senate Park Commission. That body came into being when Senator McMillan, chairman of the Senate Committee on the District of Columbia, abandoned his own proposal for a boulevard cutting diagonally across the northern part of the Mall and accepted the notion of having a board of expert designers prepare a comprehensive plan for the area.

None of the designs illustrated here dealt adequately with the vexing problem of the railroad tracks crossing the Mall to the station on its northern side. Gilbert and Seeler simply led their central avenues on bridges over the tracks. Pelz frankly accepted the railroad's presence as fixed and final. Totten shows a station south of the Mall, a solution that Seeler suggested in his text but did not dare show in his design.

Study for Grouping of Buildings, City of Washington, D.C. by Cass Gilbert. Lithograph, 7³/₁₆ × 8³/₁₆ in. (18.2 × 20.8 cm.).

Study for the Grouping of Public Buildings in the City of Washington, D.C. by Paul J. Pelz. Drawn by J. M. Stewart, printed by Norris Peters Photo-Litho, Washington, D.C. Lithograph, 7⁵/₈ × 11¹³/₁₆ in. (19.3 × 30 cm.).

Sketch Plan of Proposed Boulevard [by Edgar Seeler]. Printed by Norris Peters Co., Photo-Litho, Washington, D.C. Lithograph, 7¹/₄ × 15³/₄ in. (18.4 × 40.1 cm.).

Suggestion for Grouping Government Buildings upon the Mall by G. O. Totten, Jr. Lithograph, 7³/₁₆ × 10⁵/₁₆ in. (18.2 × 26.1 cm.).

From Glenn Brown, *Papers Relating to the Improvement of the City of Washington, District of Columbia.* Fine Arts Library, Cornell University.

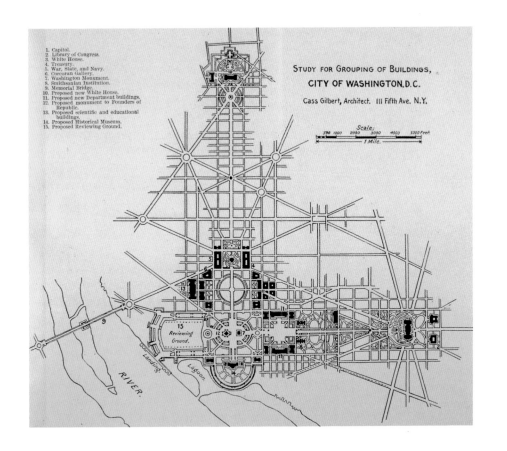

1. Capitol.
2. Library of Congress.
3. White House.
4. Treasury.
5. War, State, and Navy.
6. Corcoran Gallery.
7. Washington Monument.
8. Smithsonian Institution.
9. Memorial Bridge.
10. Proposed new White House.
11. Proposed new Department buildings.
12. Proposed monument to Founders of Republic.
13. Proposed scientific and educational buildings.
14. Proposed Historical Museum.
15. Proposed Reviewing Ground.

STUDY FOR GROUPING OF BUILDINGS,
CITY OF WASHINGTON, D.C.

Cass Gilbert, Architect. 111 Fifth Ave. N.Y.

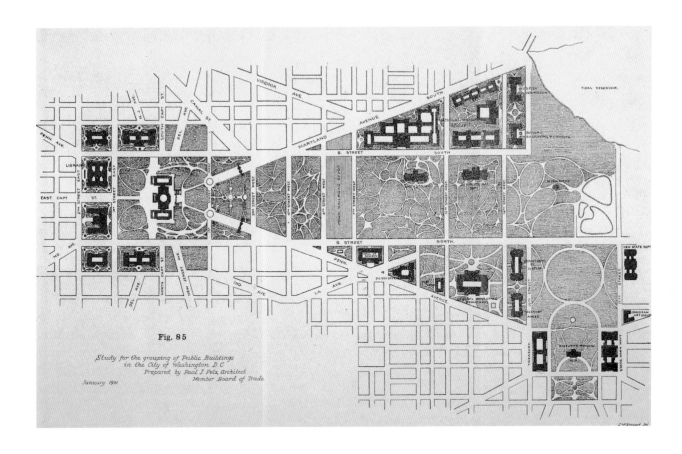

Fig. 85

Study for the grouping of Public Buildings
in the City of Washington D.C.
Prepared by Paul J. Pelz, Architect
Member Board of Trade.

January 1901

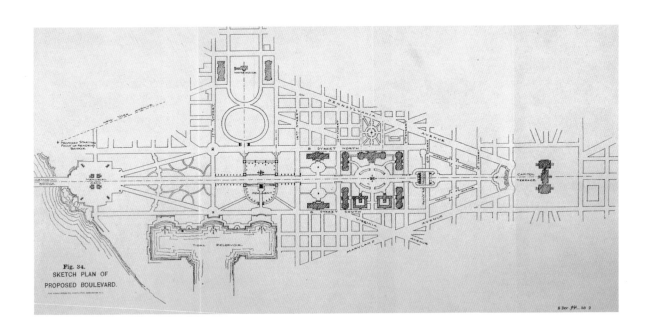

Fig. 34.
SKETCH PLAN OF
PROPOSED BOULEVARD.

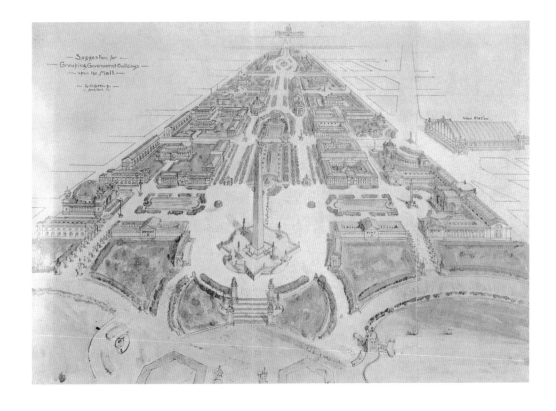

Suggestion for
Grouping Government Buildings
upon the Mall

The commission proposes a frame of monumental buildings around Capitol Square.

Facing the Capitol grounds on the east stands the Congressional Library; and it is contemplated that at no distant day the Supreme Court of the United States shall be accommodated in a building constructed for the exclusive use of that tribunal, on the square directly north of the Library; and that the Senate and the House of Representatives will have constructed for the uses of their members buildings respectively on the north and on the south of the grounds of the Capitol. . . .

The report calls for a square at the base of Capital Hill.

On the western side of the Capitol grounds . . . it is proposed to treat the space now occupied by the Botanic Garden as a broad thoroughfare, so enriched with parterres of green as to form an organic connection between the Capitol and the Mall. . . .
Brilliantly illuminated, embellished with fountains, and commanded by terraces, this square would compare favorably, in both extent and treatment, with the Place de la Concorde in Paris.

The report describes the proposed treatment of the Mall.

The axis of the Capitol and Monument is clearly defined by an expanse of undulating green a mile and a half long and three hundred feet broad, walled on either side by elms, planted in formal procession four abreast. Bordering this green carpet, roads, park-like in character, stretch between Capitol and Monument, while beneath the elms one may walk or drive, protected from the sun.

A terrace and stairway are to provide a suitable setting for the Washington Monument.

Axial relations between the White House and the Monument are created by the construction of a sunken garden on the western side of the great shaft, the true line passing through the center of a great round pool, to which marble steps three hundred feet in width lead down forty feet from the Monument platform. Surrounded by terraces bearing elms, laid out with formal paths lined by hedges and adorned with small trees, enriched by fountains and temple-like structures, this garden becomes the gem of the Mall system.

The commission proposes a memorial group on the axis of the White House.

Where the axis of the White House intersects the axis of Maryland avenue a site is found for a great memorial. Whether this memorial shall take the form of a Pantheon, in which shall be grouped the statues of the illustrious men of the nation, or whether the memory of some individual shall be honored by a monument of the first rank may be left to the future; at least the site will be ready.

Executive departments are to be grouped at Lafayette Square.

There is a present and pressing need for new buildings for existing Departments. . . . For the sake of convenience these Departments should be accessible to the White House, which is their common center. The proper solution of the problem of the grouping of the Executive Departments undoubtedly is to be found in the construction of a series of edifices facing Lafayette Square, thus repeating for those Departments the group of buildings for the Legislative and Judicial Departments planned to the Capitol grounds.

The triangle north of the Mall is to be redeveloped.

The area between Pennsylvania avenue and the Mall should be reclaimed from its present uses by locating within that section important public buildings. . . . The upbuilding of Pennsylvania avenue, therefore, must of necessity have consideration in any comprehensive plan for the treatment of Washington.

A reflecting basin is to stretch westward from the base of the Washington Monument.

From the Monument garden westward a canal three thousand six hundred feet long and two hundred feet wide, with central arms and bordered by stretches of green walled with trees, leads to a concourse raised to the height of the Monument platform.
At the head of the canal, at the eastern approach to the memorial, it is proposed to place a statue of Abraham Lincoln, while surrounding the memorial and framing it are linden trees, planted four rows deep, to form a peristyle of green, from which radiate various avenues centering upon the memorial itself. (U.S. Senate Committee on the District of Columbia, *Report*, 38–39, 41–42, 44–45, 47, 50–52, 64, 69)

Artists Depict the Proposals of the Senate Park Commission in Attractive Renderings

In February 1902 the Senate Park Commission revealed its plans for Washington at an exhibition held at the Corcoran Gallery. Large rendered views and two huge models of the city depicted the commission's proposals. The two paintings reproduced on the opposite page are among the few that have survived. The renderings also exist of the two details reproduced in printed versions on the following pages. The first pair shows Washington as it could be developed in the future. The two others overleaf provide details of the formal square planned below the Capitol and the elaborate terrace and sunken garden that was to provide a setting for the Washington Monument. The particularly striking high-level view depicting the future city from the air 4,000 feet above Arlington became one of the most frequently reproduced images of the commission's report as magazines throughout the country reported on the plans for the national capital.

Unsigned view by Francis L. V. Hoppin, first published in 1902 with the title, *Bird's-eye View of General Plan, from Point Taken 4,000 Feet above Arlington*. Rendering, 34 × 71½ in. (86.3 × 181.6 cm.). U.S. Commission of Fine Arts.

Unsigned rendering, first published in 1902 with the title, *General Plan of the Mall System*. Rendering, 45½ × 110 in. (115.7 × 279.7 cm.). U.S. Commission of Fine Arts.

View Showing the Proposed Treatment of Union Square, at the Head of the Mall, [by Charles Graham], from William Howard Taft and James Bryce, *Washington: The Nation's Capital*. Color halftone, 4¾ × 8 in. (12 × 20.3 cm.). John W. Reps.

The Washington of the Artist's Dream, by C[harles] Graham, from Taft and Bryce, *Washington: The Nation's Capital*. Color halftone, 4½ × 8 in. (11.4 × 20.3 cm.). John W. Reps.

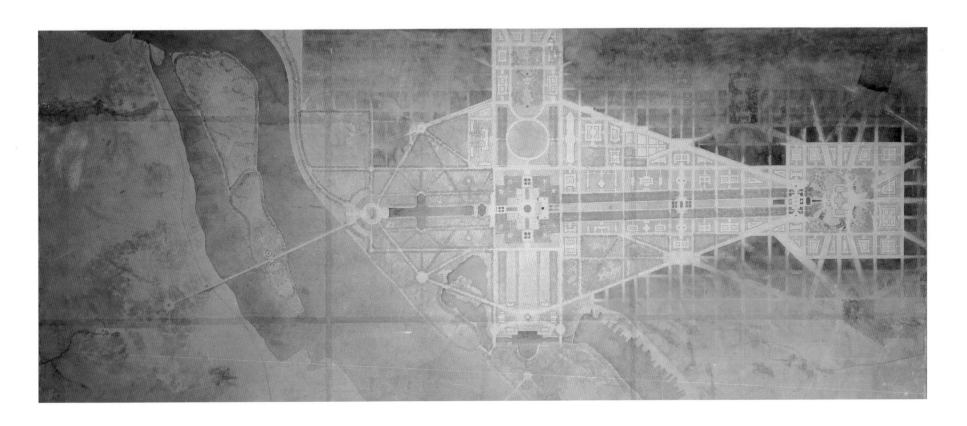

The Washington Evening Star *praises the plan.*

Now that the commission has finished its task and its report has been laid before the Senate with the warm approval of the committee itself there is no longer reason to fear that the old haphazard, hit-or-miss methods of capital making will be followed. These reports, though not yet adopted by Congress, or given form in legislation even in part, may be regarded as the new foundation stones of the Washington that is to become the world's most beautiful city. . . .

The new plan, modernizing and supplementing the original project of L'Enfant, will become the guide to all future improvements. By adopting this scheme now, leaving its components to be worked out in detail as necessities and opportunities arise, Congress will demonstrate its foresight and its wisdom as well as its intelligent pride in the national capital. (*Washington Evening Star*, 15 January 1902)

The Washington Post *supports the commission's proposals.*

The exhibition in the Corcoran Gallery of Art of the plans, or maps, prepared by the Senate's special commission on the improvement of the parks and reservations and general beautifying of the Capital City will add to the interest with which this long-neglected work has been regarded since its inception. . . . The press of the entire country has watched the progress of the commission and shown a lively appreciation of its purpose as well as of its capacity. The American people are proud of their Capital, and they will applaud the determination of Congress to make it what it ought to be and what its founders intended it should be. (*Washington Post*, 16 January 1902)

The New York Times *calls attention to the national importance of Washington.*

Whatever concerns the capital concerns the Nation. And the exhibition which was to-day opened to the public in the Corcoran Art Gallery, of the plans for what modestly calls itself "the improvement of the park system in the District of Columbia," is of National importance and should be even of international interest. ("The Nation's New Capital," 4)

A leading architectural periodical backs the plan.

The new Commission for the improvement of the city of Washington has placed on view, as promised, its preliminary plans and models for the scheme which it proposes. They are, certainly, sufficiently radical to suit the most ardent lover of reform, but it can hardly be said that they are too much so, in view of the end which it is desired to accomplish, and which can be accomplished more easily and cheaply now than in the future. . . .

The whole is a masterly presentation of the most important work of artistic significance very projected in the United States. It marks an epoch in our national progress. It educates. It calls aloud for realization. It crowns gloriously the labors of this Commission and should effect their retention as a permanent board to inaugurate the plan they have conceived and to direct what the nation should do in the arts which they so honorably represent before the country. (*American Architect and Building News*, 1 February 1902, pp. 33, 36)

The American Institute of Architects urges action.

According to the suggestions of the American Institute of Architects, the proposed improvements of Washington have been, through the broad capacity of Senator McMillan, started on practical lines. Every member of the Institute, every person of culture, every one interested in the United States should be zealous in their efforts to foster and urge upon their representative body, the Congress of the United States, that the capital city should be made the artistic achievement of the century, the pride of all Americans and an attraction to all foreigners. ("The Park Commission and the Improvement of Washington City," 5)

A noted architectural critic adds his endorsement.

The authors can scarcely hope to see even the first and most important of their intended effects realized in the growth to maturity of the four live colonnades of elms that are to border the Grand Avenue from the Capitol to the White House. It is not necessary, though of course it is very desirable, that the execution should be begun at once. But it is necessary to the beauty and worthiness of the capital that the plan should be adopted at once and that the Congress should commit itself to the plan, and determine that all future improvements shall be made in accordance with it. (Montgomery Schuyler, "The Art of City Making," 19–22)

Charles Moore Explains the Proposals to the Readers of *Century Magazine*

Senator McMillan's secretary, Charles Moore, had been a journalist, and he understood both the importance of favorable publicity for the commission's work and how to achieve it. He provided advance copies of maps and photographs of the plan's features to editors of newspapers, magazines, and professional journals. He also obviously supplied details of the proposals to several publications so that their February issues could include informed articles concerning the recommendations.

Moore also wrote a two-part article on Washington and the commission's design for the city that appeared in the February and March issues of *Century Magazine*, an influential journal of opinion. Among the twelve illustrations was this line drawing showing most of the features of the plan for central Washington although omitting the proposed buildings around the Capitol as well as those suggested for Lafayette Square. In his article Moore summarized the scope of the plan as involving "not only the improvement of the Mall and the monument grounds, but also driveways, boulevards, and park connections, the reclaiming for park purpose of the Anacostia Flats, the acquisition of additional park areas in those portions of the District now ill provided with breathing-spaces, and the development of areas already possessed and awaiting improvement."

He described how the Mall would appear: "Let one imagine himself standing on the western terrace of the Capitol on a summer afternoon. . . . From the foot of the Capitol hill to and up the monument slope, a mile and a half distant, two lines of stately elms march majestically in column of fours, one column on each side of a carpet of greensward three hundred feet wide. Buildings of white marble gleam behind the rows of elms." At the opposite end "nearly a mile away, where the axis meets the Potomac, is a great *rond-point* surmounted by a Doric portico commemorating the one man in our national history who is worthy to stand with Washington—Abraham Lincoln."

The Mall. Unsigned plan from *Century Magazine*, February 1902, p. 624. Photoengraving, 5 × 8⁹⁄₁₆ in. (12.7 × 21.1 cm.). Olin Library, Cornell University.

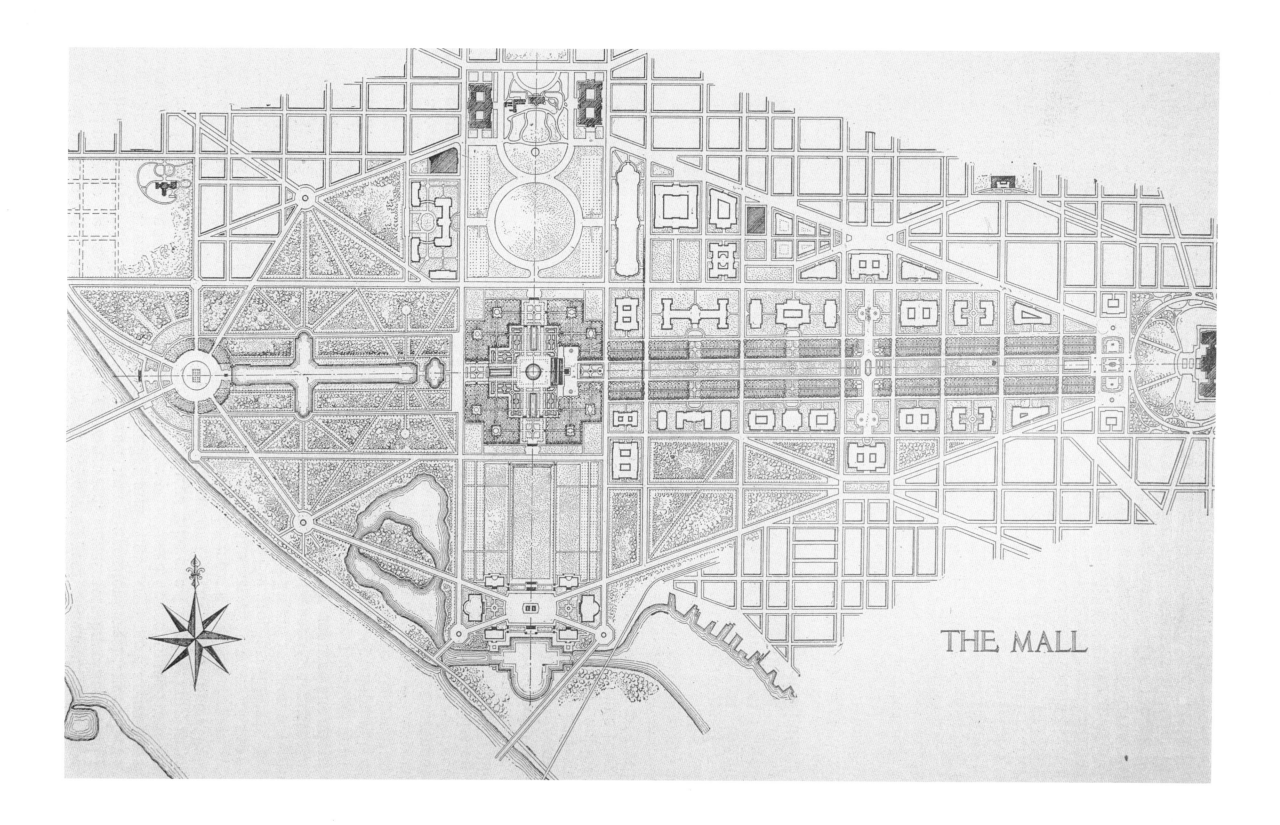

THE MALL

257

Former president Taft traces progress up to 1915.

Since the revival of interest in the capital . . . in 1902, many steps have been taken of a substantial character that make for the proper growth of Washington along the original plans. The movement for the clearing of obstructions in the Mall and the erection of that great monumental entrance to Washington, the Union Station, were the result of coöperation between Senator McMillan, James Cassatt, President of the Pennsylvania Railroad, and Daniel F. Burnham. The erection of the Columbus statue and fountain in the plaza before the Union Station and the appropriation of the land between the station and the Senate Building and the Capitol, so as to make that all an open park, is an accomplishment the difficulties of which are rapidly being forgotten, but which at the time seemed well-nigh insurmountable. The House and Senate Office buildings fill important links in the plans for Capitol Hill; the removal of the Botanical Gardens and the consequent improvement of the lower end of the Mall has been provided for; the National Museum and the Department of Agriculture buildings have been located in accordance with the Park Commission's recommendations; the Bureau of Engraving and Printing has been fitted into the general scheme; Potomac Island and Potomac Park are coming to be dreams realized; the Lincoln Memorial is now taking physical shape; the buildings on the west side of Seventeenth street, facing the White Lot, have all been erected but one, and that one is under construction; the ground on the east side of Fifteenth street, facing the same park, has been acquired.

And so it happens that, except for a few departures, which will stand as object lessons to prevent others, there has been a consistent adherence to the well-considered recommendations of the Park Commission.

Taft reports on progress with the Lincoln Memorial.

Upon the recommendation of the Fine Arts Commission, Henry Bacon was selected as the architect of the memorial, and the site upon the axis of the Mall, near the bank of the Potomac River, was selected. This was in exact accord with the recommendations made a decade before by the Park Commission. . . .

The work upon the memorial has gone on with great speed, the foundations are completed, and the work upon the superstructure is begun. Daniel C. French, the greatest of living American sculptors, has been selected to design and execute the statue of Lincoln . . . and I think we may reasonably expect that in two years' time the memorial will be complete. . . .

Thus we shall have the great axis of the Mall beginning with the Capitol Dome, running through the Grant Monument at the foot of Capitol Hill, and the Washington Monument two-thirds of the distance to the Potomac and ending in the Lincoln Memorial on the banks of the Potomac, high above the river, where it will suitably crown a memorial bridge uniting the North and South, and leading to Arlington, the valhalla of the nation's patriotic dead.

Taft calls for progress on the park recommendations in the plan.

The great addition to the L'Enfant plan made by the Park Commission was the development of the park system of Washington outside of its original limits. . . . They thought that the high ridges and hills all about the city had not been sufficiently improved as places of summer resort. They sought to impress upon Congress the necessity for the acquisition of these tracts for park purposes now, when the land could be bought at a comparatively cheap price. They wished to secure a circular zone . . . from the hills overlooking the upper Potomac . . . and following a line of abandoned, but picturesque and historically interesting, fortifications erected during the Civil War . . . extending southeastwardly clear around to the hills above Anacostia and reaching down to the Potomac below the Eastern Branch. . . .

I am very hopeful that some executive agency will be given power to act and to acquire this park zone bordering the perimeter of the District. . . . The connection between Rock Creek Park and the Soldiers' Home and the grounds of the Capitol and the Mall is, of course, of the highest importance.

The former president looks on Washington
as a model city that can elevate those who see it.

The people of the United States love Washington. They are proud of the city. When they visit the city they walk upon her streets with a consciousness that she belongs to them, and that her dignity and beauty and the grandeur of her buildings are an expression of her sovereignty and her greatness.

The educational effect that the architectural development of Washington along proper lines will have upon our people will be most elevating. It will show itself in the plans for the improvement of other cities and it will cultivate a love of the beautiful that will make for the happiness of all. (William Howard Taft, "Washington," 278–83)

An Unknown Artist and an Influential Journal Turn Their Attention to the City of Washington

In 1901 John L. Trout, then living in Washington, painted a meticulously rendered view of Washington, an image of the city as seen from the south that is reproduced on the opposite page. Although inscribed "copyright 1901," no published version has been found, and until this painting came into the hands of Washington's leading print dealers in 1989 its existence was unknown. Clearly, Trout knew the city thoroughly, and he painted it with skill and assurance. No other view of Washington surpasses it in interest and beauty, and its discovery represents a major addition to the rich iconographic history of the city.

The other illustrations present examples of the many color plates from the March 1915 issue of the *National Geographic Magazine* containing a profusely illustrated article on the development of Washington. It reproduced in color several of the Senate Park Commission renderings, and the map on the page overleaf and the facing illustration of the new Union Station and Post Office buildings were among the other illustrations.

The buildings in red on the map are those that conform to the Senate Park Commission plan. Several existed before 1902: the Capitol, the Library of Congress, the city Post Office, the White House, the new Corcoran Gallery, and the two buildings for the Treasury and State, War, and Navy departments. New buildings include the National Museum on the Mall and three buildings on the west side of the "White Lot" extending south of the White House—the American Red Cross, the Pan American Union, and the Continental Hall of the D.A.R., among others.

Untitled painted view of Washington, D.C. in 1901 by John L. Trout. 21⅞ × 47⅝ in. (55.6 × 120.9 cm.). Old Print Gallery, Washington, D.C.

The Mall Washington. D.C. Plan Showing Building Development to 1915 in Accordance with the Recommendations of the Park Commission of 1901. From *National Geographic Magazine*, March 1915. Four-color halftone engraving, 8⅝ × 17 in. (21.8 × 43.1 cm.). John W. Reps.

The Union Station (right) and the Washington Post Office (left). From *National Geographic Magazine*, March 1915. Four-color halftone engraving, 4¹⁵⁄₁₆ × 8 in. (12.6 × 20.3 cm.). John W. Reps.

259

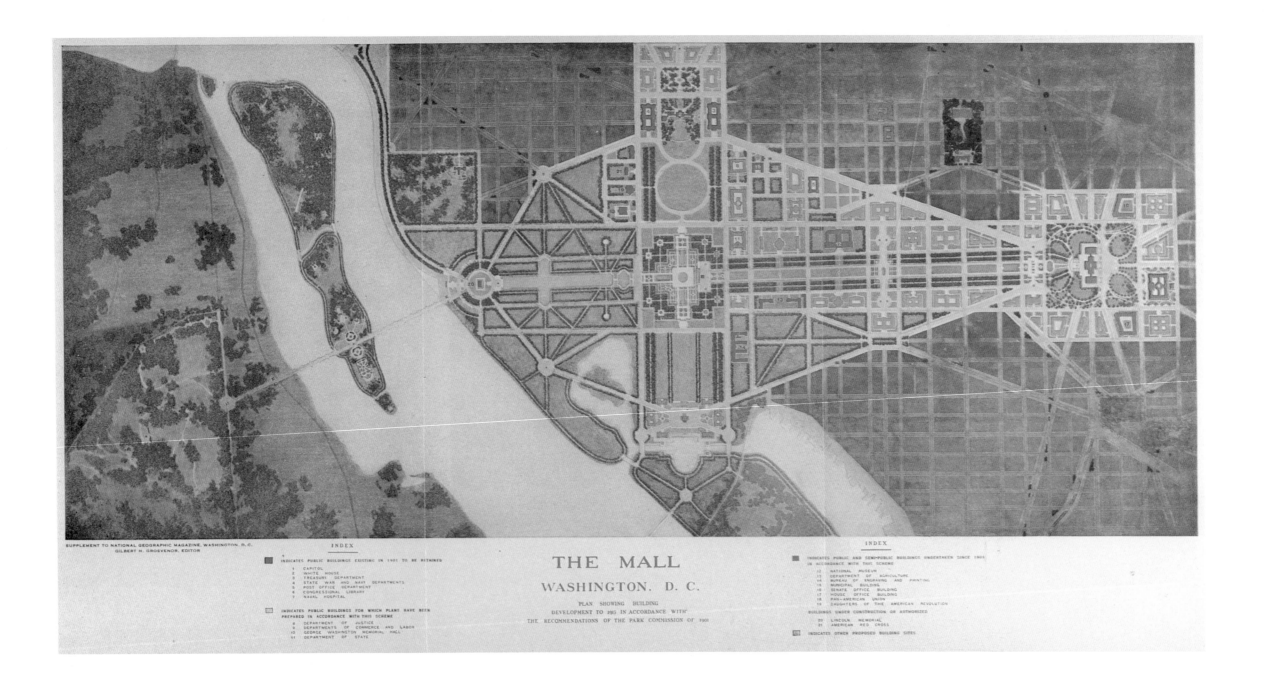

INDEX

INDICATES PUBLIC BUILDINGS EXISTING IN 1901 TO BE RETAINED

1   CAPITOL
2   WHITE HOUSE
3   TREASURY DEPARTMENT
4   STATE WAR AND NAVY DEPARTMENTS
5   POST OFFICE DEPARTMENT
6   CONGRESSIONAL LIBRARY
7   NAVAL HOSPITAL

INDICATES PUBLIC BUILDINGS FOR WHICH PLANS HAVE BEEN
PREPARED IN ACCORDANCE WITH THIS SCHEME

8   DEPARTMENT OF JUSTICE
9   DEPARTMENTS OF COMMERCE AND LABOR
10 GEORGE WASHINGTON MEMORIAL HALL
11 DEPARTMENT OF STATE

THE MALL

WASHINGTON, D. C.

PLAN SHOWING BUILDING
DEVELOPMENT TO 1915 IN ACCORDANCE WITH
THE RECOMMENDATIONS OF THE PARK COMMISSION OF 1901

INDEX

INDICATES PUBLIC AND SEMI-PUBLIC BUILDINGS UNDERTAKEN SINCE 1901
IN ACCORDANCE WITH THIS SCHEME

12 NATIONAL MUSEUM
13 DEPARTMENT OF AGRICULTURE
14 BUREAU OF ENGRAVING AND PRINTING
15 MUNICIPAL BUILDING
16 SENATE OFFICE BUILDING
17 HOUSE OFFICE BUILDING
18 PAN-AMERICAN UNION
19 DAUGHTERS OF THE AMERICAN REVOLUTION

BUILDINGS UNDER CONSTRUCTION OR AUTHORIZED

20 LINCOLN MEMORIAL
21 AMERICAN RED CROSS

INDICATES OTHER PROPOSED BUILDING SITES

260

Union Station is seen as a vital improvement.

In its architecture, its landscape setting, and in its subordinate but vital relation to the buildings on Capitol Hill the Union Station is unsurpassed among the railroad terminals of the world. If the plan of 1901 had produced only the one result of removing the railroads from the Mall and the creation of the Union Station with its plaza, the Senate commission would have justified its creation.

The commission discusses Capitol Hill.

The . . . office buildings for the Members of the Senate and the House of Representatives . . . have been designed and constructed in such manner as to make them an integral part of the Capitol group. Simple, elegant, dignified, the Senate and House Office Buildings carry on the great tradition established by Washington and Jefferson in the selection of the Thornton design for [the] original building.

Work begins on landscaping the Mall.

That section of the Mall between Third and Four-and-a-half Streets has been laid out and planted with elms in accordance with the plan of 1901, and Congress have provided for putting in the roadways. The temporary war buildings in the Mall were so located that upon removal the roadways will be in accordance with the Mall plan, and as fast as the buildings are razed the planting of trees can be made.

Museums promise development of the Mall according to the plan.

The space between Seventh and Ninth (extended) Streets, now occupied by temporary buildings, is reserved for the site of a building to hold the National Gallery of Art. . . . The new National Museum building was the first structure to be located and erected according to the plan of 1901, having been aligned in conformity to the new Mall axis. On the south side of the Mall the new Freer Gallery . . . conforms to the revised axis.

The Lincoln Memorial no longer appears isolated.

It is both interesting and instructive to note that the chief objection raised to the present location of the Lincoln Memorial was that the flats were so remote. . . . Yet by the time the memorial was begun the new driveways around the site had made the location so popular that the object now is to secure by proper planting a needed degree of isolation.

The lesson is that no space within the District of Columbia is now so remote as to be beyond the reach of the people, provided only that means of access are provided.

The commission reports on buildings near the White House.

The line of semipublic buildings along Seventeenth Street has been completed by the erection of the Bureau of American Republics, with its beautiful gardens, and by the building of the American Red Cross. The corresponding area along Fifteenth Street has been purchased by the Government for departmental buildings.

Building begins on the north side of the western end of the Mall.

The completion of the Lincoln Memorial calls for the continuation along B Street of semipublic buildings architecturally in harmony with the Memorial, which shall serve as a frame for that structure. One such building has been provided in the headquarters of the National Academy of Sciences, designed by Bertram G. Goodhue, to occupy the square between Twenty-first and Twenty-second Streets.

The Fine Arts Commission hopes to see all temporary buildings removed.

These temporary buildings are so factorylike in design and they so invade, encroach upon and disfigure Potomac Park that the American people will not suffer them permanently to overawe and dwarf one of their greatest memorials. Sooner or later the Lincoln Memorial will drive the intrusive structures to destruction. They represent to-day one of the hideous consequences of the Great War.

The report summarizes the record of the past twenty years.

In comparing the projects for the improvement of the park system . . . as presented in the report of the Senate Park Commission with the actual accomplishment during two decades one must be struck with the largeness of the actual accomplishment. . . . It is a tribute to the inherent worth of the plan that, while so little has been done contrary to it, so much has been achieved in accordance with it. (U.S. Commission of Fine Arts, *Annual Report*, 11, 13–14, 16–17, 20, 25–26)

William Olsen and an Anonymous Photographer Depict the City at the Beginning of the 1920s

For this very large and comprehensive view, the artist, William Olsen, selected an extremely high elevation that allowed him to embrace almost all of the city except for the southeast and a portion of the northeast. It is a revealing portrait of Washington at the beginning of the post–World War I period. Olsen included not only the several new permanent buildings proudly mentioned in the report of the Fine Arts Commission but the graceless temporary structures erected on the Mall to overcome the wartime shortage of office space. Olsen labeled dozens of buildings with their titles or the names of the businesses or other activities each housed. They make clear that Washington by that time had become a city of diversified retail and office occupations while retaining its nonindustrial character.

Also included here are eight photographs from an attractive souvenir booklet containing twenty-two color photographs of buildings in Washington, each described in a paragraph of text on the opposite page. The first three of these illustrations show buildings associated with the Mall. The fourth presents the structure housing the district offices that faced Pennsylvania Avenue. The final four buildings provided an appropriate enclosing frame for the west side of the White House grounds and their extension south to the Mall.

Washington the Beautiful Capital of the Nation. Compiled and copyrighted by William Olsen. Printed or published by A. B. Graham Co., Washington(?), 1921. Lithograph, 29¼ × 44 in. (74.4 × 111.9 cm.). Geography and Map Division, Library of Congress.

The Lincoln Memorial. New Bureau of Engraving and Printing. The New National Museum. The Municipal Building. The Corcoran Art Gallery. The Continental Memorial Hall. The Red Cross Memorial Building. International Union of American Republics. From *Washington: The City Beautiful.* Published by W. B. Garrison, Inc., Washington, D.C. [ca. 1921]. Lithographs, each 4¾ × 6⅝ in. (12 × 16.8 cm). John W. Reps.

WASHINGTON

THE BEAUTIFUL CAPITAL OF THE NATION

263

The Lincoln Memorial

New Bureau of Engraving and Printing

The New National Museum

The Municipal Building

The Corcoran Art Gallery

The Continental Memorial Hall

The Red Cross Memorial Building

International Union of American Republics

An architectural critic for the federal writers' guide dislikes Washington's new scale in 1937.

It was perhaps inevitable that the chances for "aggrandizement and embellishment" so lavishly provided for in L'Enfant's plan of Washington should have led to an increasing desire for magnitude in its architecture. The trend is unmistakable, and the city gives every promise to sustaining its course toward grandeur and magnificence. Already many of its more recent buildings surpass in sheer monumentality any possible interpretation of the commodious and agreeable L'Enfant spoke of. Their scale . . . relentlessly dwarfs the dignified simplicity of an earlier period. They are the pride and the glory of Washington; yet they seem somehow arid and self-conscious.

The guide condemns the Federal Triangle.

The buildings of the Triangle . . . were conceived as a single unit, a great composition of monumental orders, behind which one discovers six-story buildings struggling vainly for expression. Every device of classic and Renaissance architecture was employed to disguise this signal difficulty. The result is an imposing array of classic detail; of admirable colonnades, Renaissance pavilions, beautifully proportioned porticoes, and impressive pediments. The six stories remain; and no end of balustrades, Roman capitals and monumental sculpture can redeem the fundamental disparity. Only an extreme romanticism concerning the nature of the activity behind these fronts could find any reasonableness in their architecture. Functionally weak in plan, the buildings are too imposing to be real; too grand to be impressive; and one comes at length to doubt whether they are inhabited. (U.S. Federal Writers' Project, *Washington*, 108, 119)

Cecil Roberts complains about Washington's climate in 1947.

The site proved to be a lamentable choice. . . . Washington is stuck in a northeast corner of the vast American territory. It is built on a swamp. In summer it is fiercely hot and steamy, in winter it is damp and bitterly cold. . . . It is generally agreed that Washington has one of the worst climates in the United States.

Roberts finds Washington beautiful but confusing.

Nature having done her worst for Washington, man has done his best. It is a beautiful city, a place of magnificent vistas, tree-bordered, yet for me it has always been the most exasperating place in the world. The renowned L'Enfant, who planned it, ruined it. With its intersecting boulevards, its crisscross of acute-angled streets, its circles, squares, triangles and tangents, and its elaborate system of alphabetical partition, it is a bewildering and infuriating place that would defeat Theseus himself. . . . The utmost logic has resulted in the utmost confusion, since the centre of this carefully designed plan, the Capitol, is down on one side of the city. The official Washington, of the White House, State Department, Treasury, etc., seems to be slipping into the basin of the Potomac only three feet above sea level.

The author visits one of the newest of Washington's monumental buildings.

The . . . great National Art Gallery . . . was the gift of Andrew Mellon at a cost of fifteen million dollars. It occupies a site on a magnificent quadrilateral of buildings along the Mall. But I found it to be, Architecturally, disappointing, for all its grandeur and wonder efficiency as an art gallery. Since all lighting comes from the roof, its exterior façade has no windows, and except for a central colonnade it presents a long blank wall to the eye, resembling a furniture repository more than an art gallery. Broken only by a shallow pediment and dome, the roof has a tedious horizontal line. It is built of a rose-white Tennessee marble, a glaring mass as yet untoned by the patina of age. The twin colonnaded courts within are pleasant, but the chef-d'oeuvre is the central rotunda. Twenty-four Ionic columns over thirty-six feet high support an entablature sixteen feet high.

Roberts tells about the building's construction, its architect, and its donor.

The gallery itself, the largest marble building "in the world" (one must use that term again) was built on an old swamp. The friction with earth of 6,800 deeply driven concrete piles supports the vast weight of masonry and steel. Palladio and other Venetian architects who built "the most beautiful city in the world" by driving wood piles into the Adriatic mud would be impressed. The planner of all this, John Russell Pope, died in 1937, before it was complete, and the donor died three years and three months before the Gallery was opened. (Roberts, *And So to America*, 394–96, 406)

A New York Architect Produces an Attractive Plan-View of Washington Three Years after World War II

The style of this appealing and colorful record of conditions in Washington in 1948 resembles the Altograph published nearly sixty years earlier that folio 64 reproduces. Comparisons with this and the Olsen view in folio 74 help one appreciate how the city had changed. The artist, New York architect Oliver Whitwell Wilson, here shows us a Capitol Hill with a new Supreme Court Building and a second office structure for the House of Representatives as part of the frame of buildings that the Senate Park Commission had proposed. On the Mall the National Gallery of Art helps to define the central axis of the city as does the completed Department of Agriculture Building near the monument. A much larger departmental office building had been erected to the south.

At the far end of the Mall the reflecting basin leading to Lincoln Memorial is now complete. A new bridge to Arlington crosses the Potomac beyond the circle containing the memorial. Along the north side of the Mall between the Washington Monument and the Lincoln Memorial now stand several buildings housing scientific and professional organizations. On the axis of the White House and at the edge of the tidal basin the artist shows the new memorial honoring Thomas Jefferson. Almost directly across the Potomac one can see the enormous bulk of the Pentagon set in a labyrinth of highway interchanges.

Most changed is the triangular district between Pennsylvania Avenue and the Mall. Here the artist depicts the several major federal buildings housing several departments and agencies as well as the structure for the National Archives that took the place of the old Centre Market. This made the south side of Pennsylvania Avenue more impressive; buildings on the north side of this thoroughfare displayed such a variety of facades and uses that the artist omitted them from his urban portrait altogether.

Washington, District of Columbia, Our Nation's Capital. Drawn by Oliver Whitwell Wilson, Architect, N.Y., with the aid of Fairchild Air Views. Published by Lintner Maps Inc., 941 Highland St., Arlington, Va., 1948. Lithograph, 22 × 34½ in. (55.8 × 87.6 cm.). John W. Reps.

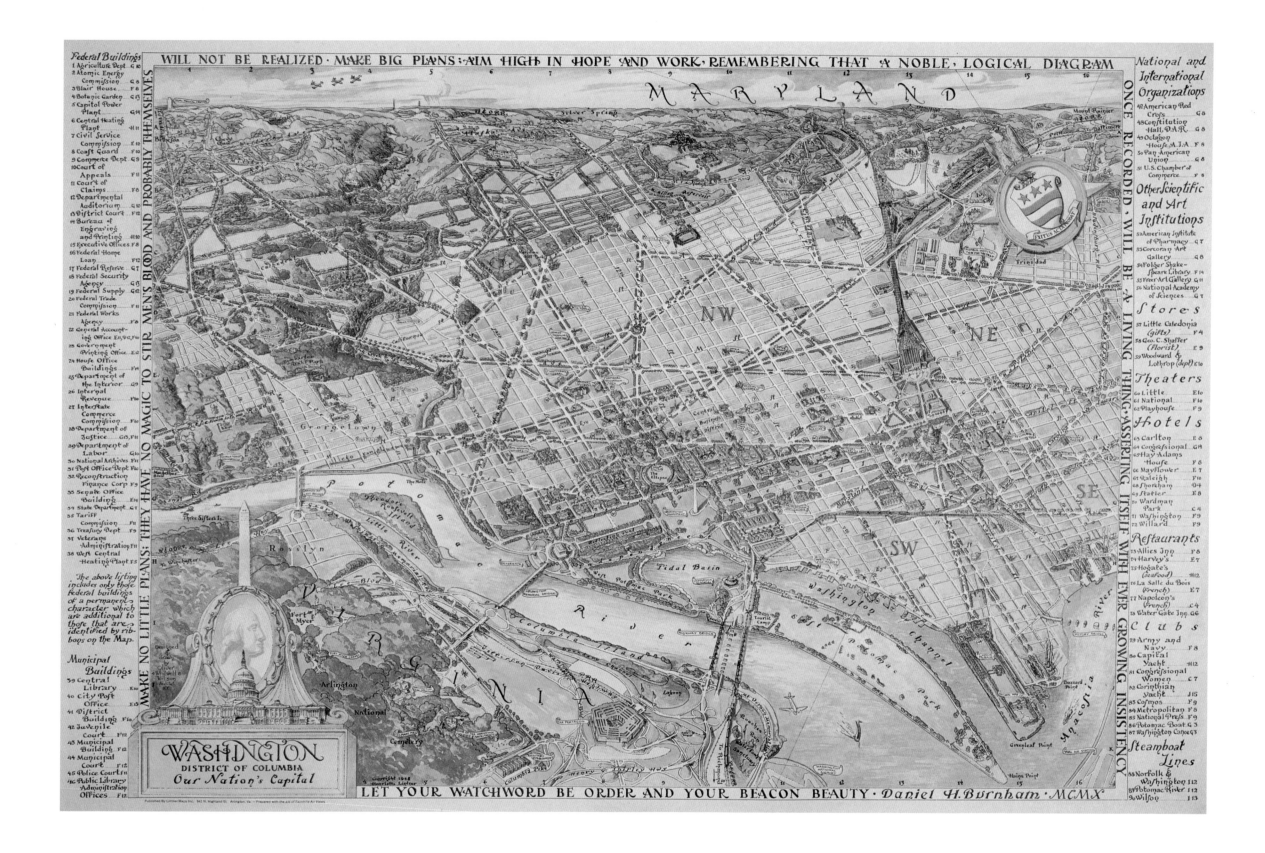

A well-known New York Times *columnist decries the sprawl of greater Washington.*

Far into the Virginia and Maryland countryside sprawl the suburbs, some tight and lovely like Kenwood with its cherry trees, most flung down by a builder's careless hand on treeless plains that were formerly forests, some waiting hideously to become officially slums. The freeway builders, frantically flinging as much traffic as possible into Washington's already strangling thoroughfares, are at once behind in their work and agitating for the privilege of pouring concrete over everything. (Wicker, "Introduction," 7)

William Walton reflects on the Federal Triangle.

The dozen designers of the Federal Triangle . . . managed to supress themselves. In the architectural profession this is a rarity, especially when one receives a commission for a prominent public spot. Then most architects are prone to write their egos across the landscape, even at the cost of an inharmonious building. A supervisory committee directed development of the Triangle, imposing regulations, such as a common cornice line, which kept the various buildings closely related to scale. The committee also saw to it that designs, though all in a similar Roman idiom, varied enough to prevent the facades from becoming nine long blocks of monotony. In the process, some truly beautiful areas developed. . . . One other quality shines forth—the superb workmanship that American architecture had at hand. Limestone and granite are cut with tremendous skill; the detailing is beautiful. After three decades the buildings look even better than when they were completed. (William Walton, *The Evidence of Washington*, 43–44)

Robert Smith and Eric Sevareid record the look of the "new" Washington.

A new city, reflecting the spirit and appetites of a world capital, is swiftly emerging along the river Potomac. George Washington would be dazzled by the city's commercial success. . . . L'Enfant would be gratified that it is taking on fresh aspects of his original plan for a capital of sweeping vistas, public gardens, broad boulevards, fountains, squares, and parks.

The new Washington hugs its monumental core. It includes new museums along the great Mall, plans for landscaping the Mall itself, the creative accommodation of the new and old around Lafayette Square, the beginnings of Pennsylvania Avenue as the grand axis of the nation, the magnificent John F. Kennedy Center for the Performing Arts rising in redeveloped Foggy Bottom, the restoration of Capitol Hill, and the utter transformation of Southwest Washington from the city's worst slums to America's largest venture in urban renewal. (A. Robert Smith and Eric Sevareid, *Washington*, 149)

The architectural critic for the New York Times *emphasizes the importance of the plan.*

At its formal best . . . Washington has a solemn, full-blown beauty. It is a sybaritic city in correct academic dress. Spring is a romantic overstatement. Summer is a sultry surrealist nightmare as the cool temples shimmer and dissolve in steamy heat. Winter buries the proper palaces in snowdrifts, while the sun hints warmly and regeneratively of spring. There is an hour before twilight, with the glow of the sun still illuminating the horizon, when serene white buildings stand luminous against a clear sky, set stagily amidst the flowers or foliage of a warm spring evening or the bare branches of a crisp winter day. Then the city is touched with its own magic. In the Venetian light the art of politics recedes into the art of architecture. The eye rejoices and the soul expands. The experience is more than the pleasurable recognition of an impressive vista or a successful dialogue between structures and spaces. It is an act of love between citizen and stone, and Washington has many lovers, in the tradition of all great cities that have captured the hearts of men. . . .

Typically, in the American scheme of things, the Washington ideal developed somewhat haphazardly. But unlike most American cities, this one was not just an urban happening. It started with a vision of the ideal in the concrete terms of the ambitious L'Enfant plan.

Washington succeeds as a city because of that plan. It is the glue that holds its urban achievements and fumbles together with visible pattern and style. It is this grandiose, extravagant, aspiring, Baroque system of grids, diagonals, Versailles-inspired vistas, 150-foot-wide avenues and monumental settings for monumental buildings covering 16 per cent of the District of Columbia, given by L'Enfant to the American commissioners in 1791, ignored by 19th-century builders, rescued and enlarged by the McMillan Commission of 1901, that unifies and binds the city with singular grace, character and charm. (Huxtable, "Architecture," 198–99)

The National Geographic Magazine *Displays Present and Future Washington in a Fine Plan-View*

For this attractive and easy-to-read depiction of central Washington, the artist, Snejinka Stefanoff, combined a plan of the streets and landscape and water elements with isometric representations of every structure. The legend at the bottom identifies nearly two hundred buildings, monuments, bridges, and other features of the national capital. The result is a striking example of urban cartography combining detail and clarity.

This city portrait includes many buildings that did not then and still do not exist, such as the several similar structures shown on the north side of Pennsylvania Avenue, the bridge over the Washington Channel, and the Franklin Roosevelt Memorial in West Potomac Park. It also shows the north side of the Mall along the Lincoln Memorial reflecting pool laid out in rectilinear form. This and such other features as the National Square at the Treasury end of Pennsylvania Avenue had then been proposed either by the Pennsylvania Avenue Commission or by other agencies or groups concerned with improvements in the city. The legend carefully identifies these projects, classifying thirty-eight as "planned or under construction" and another forty-eight as "proposed."

This map records the locations and provides a good sense of the shape and appearance of many new buildings. They include the Kennedy Center and the nearby Watergate complex at the left, the huge warren of offices for the State Department in Foggy Bottom between Twenty-first and Twenty-third streets, the National Air and Space Museum on the south side of the Mall, the Rayburn and Cannon buildings for the House of Representatives flanking the original House office building, the precinct of large federal departmental buildings south of Independence Avenue, and the vast redevelopment area of Southwest Washington beyond the freeway.

Future Washington. Drawn by Snejinka Stefanoff. Research by Dorothy A. Nicholson, Geographic Art Division. Published by the National Geographic Society, Washington, 1967. Lithograph, 17^{15}/$_{16}$ × 28^{15}/$_{16}$ in. (45.5 × 73.5 cm.). Olin Library, Cornell University.

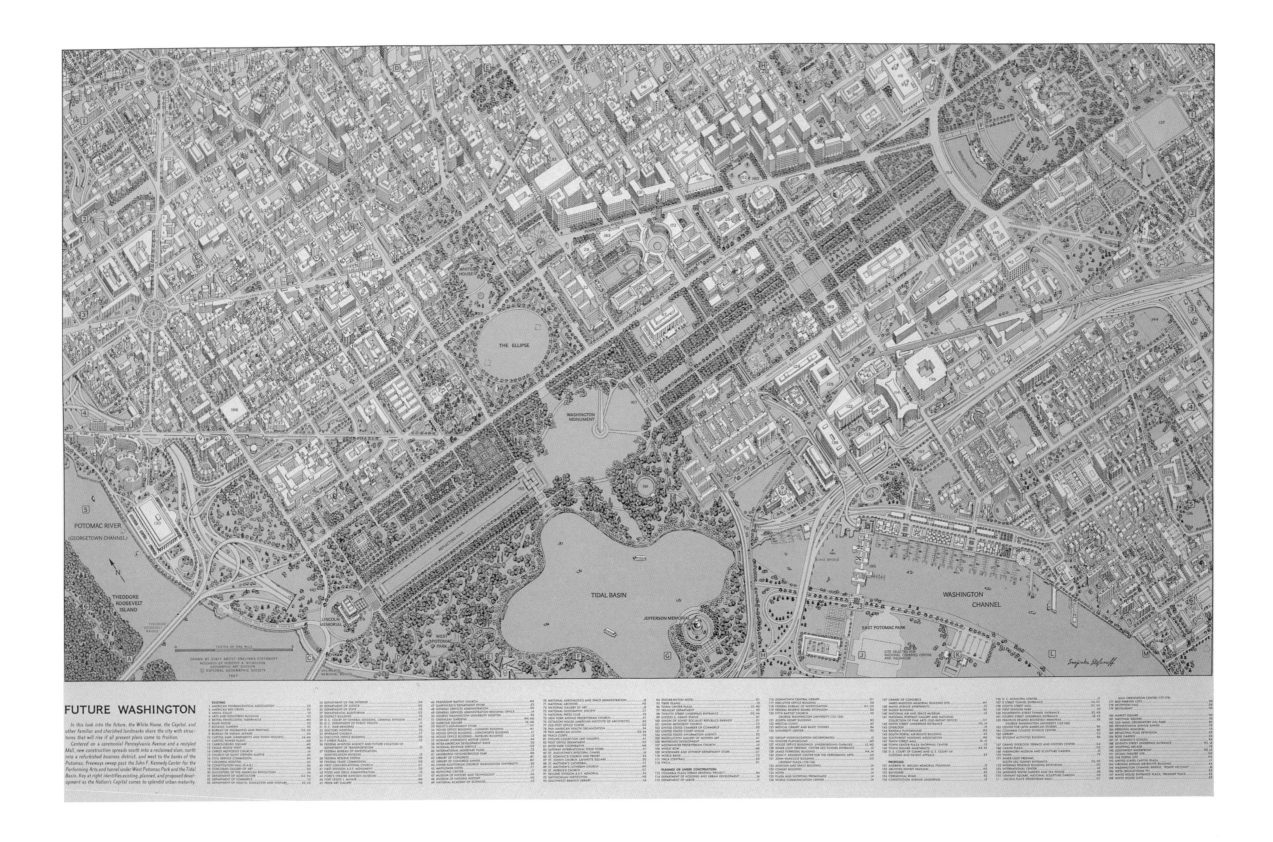

FUTURE WASHINGTON

In this look into the future, the White House, the Capitol, and other familiar and cherished landmarks share the city with structures that will rise if all present plans come to fruition.

Centered on a ceremonial Pennsylvania Avenue and a restyled Mall, new construction spreads south into a reclaimed slum, north into a refurbished business district, and west to the banks of the Potomac. Freeways sweep past the John F. Kennedy Center for the Performing Arts and tunnel under West Potomac Park and the Tidal Basin. Key at right identifies existing, planned, and proposed development as the Nation's Capital comes to splendid urban maturity.

*A guide written in 1983 by city planners
reviews the city's change in character.*

Long regarded as a city of monuments, monumental buildings, and government workers, but otherwise reminiscent of a small town, Washington has emerged in recent years as a more cosmopolitan, fast-paced, and vibrant city. This change has been accomplished without transforming the city into a monolithic and overwhelming metropolis. Overall, the human scale has been retained.

The authors credit the Kennedy Center for its contribution.

Washington now rivals in entertainment and cultural offerings cities whose reputations in this regard are well established. This change can be partly attributed to the opening of the Kennedy Center for the Performing Arts in 1971. The facilities of this imposing structure on the banks of the Potomac attract a variety of outstanding talent.

*The guide mentions recent additions
to the Smithsonian Institution museums.*

The Smithsonian Institution's contribution to Washington's culture is unsurpassed. It has one of the most impressive (and still expanding) arrays of museums in the world, a high-quality education program, and a unique performing-arts program, all available to the public. The most notable of the Smithsonian's newer museums are the National Air and Space Museum, the East Wing of the National Gallery, and the Hirshhorn Museum and Sculpture Garden.

Visitors learn about downtown Washington.

For over 150 years, Downtown Washington was the commercial center of the city and of the surrounding region. Although this role was challenged somewhat during the 1950s and 1960s, Downtown still offers the greatest variety of goods and services to be found anywhere in the Washington metropolitan area. During the past two decades, a number of plans and programs were initiated to revitalize Downtown. Some were very successful, while others languished. Much of the development in Downtown today resulted from ideas formed during the last decades. Metrorail, the newly opened Convention Center, and the refurbishing of Pennsylvania Avenue are notable examples. (Protopappas and Brown, *Washington on Foot*, 7–9)

*The United States Capitol Historical Society
guide of 1983 lists new buildings.*

New construction in the city has included the Rayburn House Office Building, the Hoover FBI building, the James Madison building of the Library of Congress, and the Hart Senate Office Building. The recently completed Master Plan for the United States Capitol, charting growth for the next 50 to 75 years, identifies potential sites for new congressional office buildings and also provides for the closing of selected streets to traffic, extensive landscaping, and the construction of underground parking.

*The author contrasts the city of the past
and the Washington of today.*

Although much remains to be done to make Washington the model city it should be, the contrast between the city today and that of just a century ago could not be greater. The Mall area, the Capitol, the White House, and the monuments—the areas tourists most wish to see—reflect the foresight of the city's founders. But Washington has become more than a collection of marble monuments to the past; it has become a dynamic city with a character and a charm all its own. (Kennon, "Washington Past," 51)

Another guidebook extols the many museums of Washington.

Slowly, almost imperceptibly, during the past forty years, Washington has been evolving into a world-class city. With its greater sophistication—in terms of theater, entertainment, restaurants, and art galleries—has come an increasing number of museums, historic houses, and special places open to the public.

Few cities in this country have as rich a treasure trove of museums as Washington. And more are on the horizon. Consider, for example, the new Arthur M. Sackler Gallery, the National Museum of African Art, and the National Museum of Women in the Arts.

In addition to world-class museums, Washington has a host of specialized institutions, such as Dumbarton Oaks, the Textile Museum, the Freer Gallery of Art, the Folger Shakespeare Library, and the Museum of Modern Art of Latin America—to name just a few.

The 1980s are the Golden Age of Museums, and Washington is now a museum capital as well as the capital of the nation. (Betty Ross, *A Museum Guide to Washington, D.C.*, 2)

The Bird's-Eye View Finds a New Champion in David A. Fox, Who Depicts Washington in 1985

David Fox chose Washington as one of the American cities to depict in his series of urban bird's-eye views. He thus recalls the traditions of the nineteenth-century viewmakers of the city who produced so many notable images of the capital. His work provides a useful guide to the unique combination of streets, parks, and buildings that make up the intricate pattern of modern Washington.

His view includes a number of new buildings not on earlier prints of Washington. Among them are the east wing of the National Gallery, a second office building for the Senate and the James Madison Building of the Library of Congress filling the northeast and southeast corners of Capitol Square, the new central public library named for Dr. Martin Luther King diagonally to the northwest of the old Patent Office (now housing the National Museum of American Art and the National Portrait Gallery), and—north of the library—the great bulk of the Washington Civic Center. Fox's view records the circular shape of the Hirshhorn Museum across the Mall from the National Archives. It also shows Constitution Gardens on the north side of the reflecting pool and the Vietnam Veterans Memorial at its western end not far from the Lincoln Memorial.

The most recent image of Washington comes from the camera of Alex Maclean, a Boston photographer specializing in depicting the appearance of American urban and rural buildings and landscapes from the air. Maclean's view captures the city from a viewpoint similar to that adopted by Francis Hoppin for his splendid rendering of Washington in 1902 reproduced in folio 71. It is a revealing record of the national capital at the end of its second century of change and growth.

Washington, D.C. [Drawn and published by David A. Fox]. Copyright 1985 by David A. Fox, P.O. Box 780, Narberth, PA 19072. Lithograph, 21½ × 33⅞ in. (54.6 × 86 cm.). Olin Library, Cornell University.

Untitled air photograph of Washington, D.C., taken by Alex Maclean on 27 October 1990. Landslides, Boston, Massachusetts.

WASHINGTON D.C.

271

272

Appendix A

Biographical Notes on Folio Text Authors

ADAMS, WILLIAM EDWIN (?–?). After visiting the United States in 1882 Adams published a book about his experiences. It consisted of a collection of letters that originally appeared in the Newcastle, England, *Weekly Chronicle*.

AMES, MARY CLEMMER (1839–1884). Born in Utica, New York, Mary Clemmer moved to Westfield, Massachusetts, where she received her education at the Westfield Academy. At the age of sixteen she married the Reverend Daniel Ames, but the union ended in divorce in 1874. The two lived in several places, but in 1862 Mrs. Ames was in Harpers Ferry when the Confederate troops arrived, and she was held prisoner by them for a short time. She began to write when still young and was the author of several novels. For the New York *Independent*, beginning in 1866, she contributed a series of dispatches under the title "A Woman's Letters from Washington," and these provided the basis for her book, *Ten Years in Washington*, that appeared in 1874.

ARCHER, WILLIAM (1856–1924). A graduate of Edinburgh University, Archer traveled extensively, studied law, and began a career as drama critic for the London *Figaro* in 1879. During his career he contributed to many journals, among them the *World*, the *Nation*, the *Manchester Guardian*, and the *Tribune*. Archer translated and edited dramas by Ibsen and wrote many books on the theater and several plays. His book *America Today* is based on his observations during his U.S. travels in 1899, but he had made an earlier trip in 1877 and returned in 1910, the latter trip resulting in his *Through Afro-America*.

BAILY, FRANCIS (1774–1844). Although he became an eminent astronomer, it is as a youthful traveler in America in 1796 and 1797 that this English author is important for the present study. Baily's book was not published until 1856, twelve years after the author's death. It is fortunate that there was then enough interest to warrant its appearance, for it provides an excellent impression of what Washington was like midway through its first decade.

BARNARD, JOHN GROSS (1815–1882). In 1833 Barnard graduated from West Point, second in a class of forty-three. Assigned to the engineers, he eventually was put in charge of fortifying coastal installations. He served in the Mexican War, as superintendent of West Point, and as officer in charge of the fortifications of Washington during the Civil War. He was a prolific writer on engineering matters, science, and on the campaigns of the Civil War in which he took part.

BIRKBECK, MORRIS (1764–1825). A prosperous English farmer in Surrey, Birkbeck emigrated to the United States to lead a group of English agricultural colonists who settled in Illinois. His book, *Notes on a Journey in America*, published in 1817, proved immensely popular, being printed in eleven English editions within two years as well as in a German version in 1819. Many persons of the period, American as well as foreign, must have gained at least some of their knowledge and opinions about Washington from Birkbeck's book.

BLODGET, SAMUEL (1757–1814). The son of a Massachusetts merchant, Blodget made his fortune in the East India trade. Although untrained as an architect, he designed the first Bank of the United States in Philadelphia, a city to which he had moved in 1789. Blodget was among the first purchasers of property in Washington and became an active promoter of the city's development. Among the speculations that led to his financial downfall was a lottery, the first prize of which was to be a hotel costing $50,000. Although Blodget's Hotel was never finished, it was among the earliest large buildings built in the new capital.

BROOKS, NOAH (1830–1903). Brooks attended schools in Castine, Maine, until, at the age of eighteen, he went to Boston to study landscape painting. He proved to be better at words than at graphic art, and within three years saw his essays and stories published in magazines and newspapers. Moving to Illinois, Kansas, and then to California, Brooks joined with a friend in publishing the *Marysville Daily Appeal*. He also regularly contributed to the *Overland Monthly*, then under the editorship of Bret Harte. After selling his interest in the Marysville newspaper, he came to wartime Washington as correspondent for the *Sacramento Union*. There he resumed his friendship with Abraham Lincoln and frequently visited the White House. In later life he settled in New York as, among other positions, an editor for the *New York Times* and the editor of the *Newark Daily Advertiser*. He wrote fifteen books, among which is *Washington in Lincoln's Time*, based on his wartime dispatches to Sacramento.

BROWN, GLENN (1854–1932). Brown studied at Washington and Lee University, worked for two years in an architect's office, and completed his academic training at the Massachusetts Institute of Technology in 1876. After working for a time in New England, in 1880 Brown established an office in Washington where he practiced his profession until 1921. During 1899–1913 Brown also served as secretary of the American Institute of Architects. In addition to articles in professional journals, Brown wrote a massive, two-volume study published in 1901–3, *History of the United States Capitol*. Brown participated actively in many civic affairs and was among the most effective supporters of and publicists for the proposals of the Senate Park Commission and the Commission of Fine Arts.

BROWN, LIN (?–). Joint author with John Protopappas of a popular guide to Washington, *Washington on Foot*.

BUCKINGHAM, JAMES SILK (1786–1865). Buckingham produced many travel books during his long and active life. His five-volume description of his journeys in North America contain some of the clearest and most detailed passages on the appearance of and conditions in American cities. Buckingham went to sea at the age of ten, captained a large ship when only twenty-one, established a newspaper in Calcutta in 1818, founded three short-lived journals in London, and served from 1832 to 1837 as an M.P. from Sheffield. He wrote voluminously, but he also derived much of his income from lecturing. In 1851 he was awarded a pension "in consideration of his literary works and useful travels in various countries."

CAMPBELL, SIR GEORGE (1824–1892). Campbell was a Liberal member of Parliament from Scotland. Formerly he served as a colonial official in India.

CANDLER, ISAAC (?–?). Author of an important early book on America published in 1822, *A Summary View of America*.

COMBE, GEORGE (1788–1858). Combe had an unhappy childhood and an indifferent education, although he attended classes at Edinburgh University from 1802 to 1804. In 1815 he heard a lecture on phrenology, studied it for three years, and began to write and lecture on the subject. Soon he was accepted as a leading authority on phrenology. In 1838 he toured the United States and Canada as a lecturer, and the experiences of that trip supplied the material for his book, *Notes on the United States . . . during a Phrenological Visit in 1838–40*, a three-volume work published in 1841.

DE ROOS, FREDERICK FITZGERALD (1804–1861). De Roos was born in Surrey and entered the Navy at the age of fourteen. It was evidently while assigned to North America that he wrote his *Narrative of Travels in the United States and Canada* in 1827. In 1834 he was promoted to the rank of captain.

DICEY, EDWARD (1832–1911). Dicey graduated from Cambridge University in 1854. Pursuing a career in journalism, he contributed to a number of journals of the time: *Fortnightly Review, St. Paul's,* and *Macmillan's Magazine,* among several others. He also wrote for the London *Daily Telegraph* as a special correspondent during his travels on the continent. He came to America during the Civil War as a war correspondent for two British publications: the *Spectator* and *Macmillan's Magazine.* Historians regard his reports on the Civil War as among their most useful sources concerning the conduct of the war. In 1870 Dicey became editor of the London *Observer.*

DICKENS, CHARLES (1812–1870). Although Dickens was still a young man at the time of his American trip, he had already achieved world renown with such novels as *Pickwick Papers, Nicholas Nickleby,* and *The Old Curiosity Shop.* Like Frances Trollope before him, Dickens found little to admire in America. Washington offered a tempting target for his scorn, and his notoriously derogatory comments about the city in his book *American Notes* lingered in the memory of Washingtonians long after the book's publication in 1842.

DOWNING, ANDREW JACKSON (1815–1852). Downing began work early in the nursery that his father had established at Newburgh, New York. He became friends with a cultivated Austrian who had a summer home on the Hudson, and there he met travelers and writers from abroad, including Charles Augustus Murray, whose book contained observations on Washington. Downing's early writings remained unpublished, but in 1841 his *A Treatise on the Theory and Practice of Landscape Gardening* made him famous and went through many editions. Other books followed, and in 1846 he also became editor of the *Horticulturist and Journal of Rural Art and Rural Taste.* In its pages Downing advanced his ideas of naturalistic landscape treatment of estate grounds, heralded the design of rural cemeteries, and led the fight to establish large public parks in American cities. Retained in 1851 to design the Washington Mall, he had scarcely completed the basic design before his tragic death in a Hudson River steamboat fire.

DWIGHT, THEODORE (1796–1866). After graduating from Yale in 1814, Dwight traveled abroad for several years. Returning to New York, he taught school, wrote for his father's newspaper, the *Daily Advertiser,* translated books into Spanish, engaged in a variety of educational, religious, and charitable activities, and wrote extensively. Among his books are many volumes on travel in the United States and Europe.

ELLIOT, JONATHAN (1784–1830). Elliot was born in England, came to New England and at the age of eighteen, and moved to New York to take a job in a printing office. He volunteered as a freedom fighter under General Bolívar in 1810, and he saw military service again for the United States in the War of 1812. Settling in Washington in 1814, a year later he became editor and publisher of the *City of Washington Gazette,* a position he held until 1826. Elliot wrote and compiled several books on diplomacy, political history, and public finance, but his 1830 publication, *Historical Sketches of the Ten Miles Square Forming the District of Columbia,* bears most directly on the history and development of the city of Washington.

ELLIS, JOHN B. (?–?). In his *Sights and Secrets of the National Capital,* published in 1866, Ellis presented a highly readable account of the city and its society up to the end of the Civil War.

FARKAS, SÁNDOR B. (1795–?). Born in Transylvania, Farkas was a member of a noble but impoverished Hungarian family. He studied at the Unitarian College in what is now Cluj, Rumania, and as a Protestant in a country attempting sternly to bring all its residents into Catholicism, Farkas began to think about ways that government might be reformed. As a young man he translated foreign books in his spare time while earning a living as a bureaucrat. In 1831 he came to America to observe what he felt was a system of government that could serve as a model for his own country, and it is from his book based on that trip that the excerpt about Washington in this volume is taken.

FITZPATRICK, F. W. (1863–?). By 1896 Fitzpatrick had begun to write on a variety of subjects for several American periodicals. These included *Arena, Cosmopolitan Magazine, Outlook, Open Court, Littell's Living Age, Spectator,* and *Midland Monthly.* He also wrote at least four articles on architecture for *American Architect and Building News.* Folio 69 contains a portion of one of those dealing with the plan for central Washington by the Chicago architect Henry Ives Cobb. Fitzpatrick may have lived in Chicago, for he prepared the instruction paper in 1911 and the text in 1913 on building codes used by the American School of Correspondence in that city. He is also the author of *A Chat with the Ladies about House Building.*

GALLATIN, ABRAHAM ALFONSE ALBERT (1761–1849). Born into a prominent Swiss family in Geneva, Gallatin was orphaned at eleven and put under the care of a relative who saw to it that he received a fine education. Gallatin found himself attracted to the radical wing of students at the academy, refused a commission at high rank in Hessian troops being recruited to fight under the English in America, and decided to emigrate to the New World. Gallatin was not involved in the Revolution except as a merchant, and after the war he settled in what was then the wilderness of western Pennsylvania to pursue the ideas of Rousseau. He was elected to the state legislature in 1790. That body sent him to the U.S. Senate in 1793, but he was forced to step aside when challenged that he had not been a U.S. citizen for nine years. He then won election to the House of Representatives, serving from 1795 to 1801. He became recognized as an expert in public finance, and in May 1801 Jefferson appointed him secretary of the Treasury, a position he held until February 1814.

GILBERT, CASS (1858–1934). Gilbert's early career included an apprenticeship in St. Paul, a special course at the Massachusetts Institute of Technology, European travel, and a two-year period in the office of the New York architectural firm of McKim, Mead, and White. Shortly after he established an office in St. Paul, he won the competition for the design of the Minnesota capitol. His election at the age of thirty-one as a Fellow of the American Institute of Architects followed. During his distinguished career he served as president of that body as well as the American Academy of Arts and Letters, the Architectural League, and the National Academy of Design.

GRATTAN, THOMAS COLLEY (1792–1864). Grattan was born in Dublin and studied law for a time before joining the militia for service in several places in England. In 1818 on his way to South America, he met and married Eliza O'Donnel and decided to settle in Bordeaux. There he began to write and shortly thereafter moved to Paris to continue his literary career. He translated French poetry, contributed articles to several English reviews, and began a journal of his own. In 1828 Grattan moved to Brussels, Antwerp, The Hague, and Heidelberg before returning to Brussels, where he continued to write for a variety of publications. In 1839 he was appointed British consul in Massachusetts, a position he held until 1846. His comments about Washington are evidently based on observations made there while negotiating the boundary issues between the United States and Britain, leading to the treaty of April 1842.

HALL, LT. FRANCIS (?–1833). An officer in the Fourteenth Light Dragoons, Lieutenant Hall toured portions of eastern Canada and the United States from March 1816 to February 1817. Of the book that recounted his impressions, *Travels in Canada and the United*

States, a reviewer in the *North American Review* noted that "he has good sense enough to think that a country is not to be judged by its tavern-keepers and hostlers, and too much good-humour to rail at a whole people because he meets with occasional instances of fraud and churlishness." Hall also wrote a book on his travels in France and, after serving as a hydrographer in Colombia, wrote a book about his experiences in that South American country as well.

HICKOX, CHAUNCEY (?–?). Nothing seems to be known about this author who between 1868 and 1882 wrote at least ten feature articles for two American journals, *Galaxy* and *Lippincott's Magazine of Popular Literature and Science*. It was for the latter that Hickox prepared his informative summary of Alexander Shepherd's public works programs in the early 1870s.

HOWE, HENRY (1816–1893). Born and brought up in New Haven, Connecticut, where his father published books and ran a well-patronized bookstore, Howe decided to become a historian of towns and cities. He joined with the older John Warner Barber in gathering material for their *Historical Collections of the State of New York*, a volume patterned after Barber's similar work on Connecticut that strongly influenced Howe when he read it in 1846. The two produced a companion volume for New Jersey, and Howe alone compiled the volumes for Virginia and Ohio. While working on the latter, Howe settled in Cincinnati, where he lived for thirty years. The *Historical Collections of Virginia* contains the description of Washington used in the present study. All of these books make extensive use of illustrations, many of which are the earliest graphic records extant of street scenes and buildings in smaller towns and villages.

HUXTABLE, ADA LOUISE (1921–). Huxtable was educated at Hunter College and the Institute of Fine Arts at New York University. For five years she was assistant curator of architecture and design at the Museum of Modern Art. A Fulbright fellowship in 1950 made it possible for her to study architecture and design in Italy, following which she began her career in journalism as a free-lance writer and contributing editor to *Progressive Architecture* and *Art in America*. From 1963 to 1982 she was architectural critic for the *New York Times*, resigning to begin her tenure through 1986 as MacArthur Prize Fellow. Huxtable has lectured at universities and elsewhere throughout the United States and has received honorary degrees from nearly thirty educational institutions. She was awarded the first Pulitzer Prize for distinguished criticism in 1970. She is the author of many books on architecture, the most recent in 1986 titled *Architecture Anyone?*

JANSON, CHARLES (?–?). Janson apparently studied law in Britain, but in 1793 was living in Rhode Island, where he evidently made his home until 1806. His book, *The Stranger in America*, that appeared in 1807 was widely reviewed, usually unfavorably for its harsh comments about America. However, the descriptions and observations in it on Washington are long and detailed and indicate a thorough familiarity with the city. The title page illustration of the White House is one of the earliest printed depictions of the building.

KEELER, RALPH (1840–1873). Sent to live with an uncle in Buffalo when orphaned at the age of eight, Keeler ran away after three years to take a job as a cabin boy on a Great Lakes steamer. He learned to dance and play the banjo, joined a minstrel troop and became a child star, and attended a Jesuit school in Missouri for a year and a half and Kenyon College in Ohio for another two years. Leaving in 1861 without a degree, Keeler then traveled to Germany for further studies, finally settling in San Francisco to teach English as a foreign language and to write for several California newspapers. At various times he wrote for the *Atlantic Monthly*, *Old and New*, and *Every Saturday*, the latter being a large-format weekly with excellent illustrations. While on a boat between Havana and Santiago in Cuba, where he had gone in 1873 as a newspaper correspondent, he drowned after falling or being thrown into the water.

KEIM, DE BENNEVILLE RANDOLPH (1841–1914). Keim was a prolific author. His several Washington guidebooks of the 1880s went through dozens of editions and were obviously successful business ventures. He edited a massive memorial volume dedicated to General Sherman, and he wrote other books on General Sheridan, Alexander Hamilton, and Alaska. Keim's handbook on Washington diplomatic protocol and customs of society evidently filled a need for visitors and foreign officials assigned to the national capital. Keim also wrote at least two five-act dramas, one based on the life of Frederick the Great and the other on General Lafayette. A later one-act play was set in the time of the American Revolution. At one time he was U.S. agent for examination of the accounts of business practices of American consulates abroad and submitted reports on his various missions. He also served as a Washington correspondent in the 1880s. He was a friend of President Grant and was particularly successful in obtaining frequent interviews with him that became the basis for published accounts of the president's opinions.

KENNON, DONALD R. (1948–). Kennon received his B.A., M.A., and Ph.D. degrees from the University of Maryland. Since 1981 he has been associated with the United States Capitol Historical Society. In 1985–86 he was visiting assistant professor of history at the University of New Mexico, Albuquerque. With Richard Striner, he is the author of *Washington Past and Present: A Guide to the Nation's Capital*.

KENT, JAMES (1763–1847). A graduate of Yale College in 1777, Kent was profoundly influenced by his reading of *Blackstone's Commentaries*, an experience that made him chose law as his profession and eventually to become a professor of law at Columbia College, a judge of the New York supreme court, and chancellor of the New York court of chancery. His *Commentaries on American Law* became one of the fundamental works on American law.

KLINKOWSTRÖM, BARON AXEL LEONHARD (1775–1837). The baron lived and traveled in the United States during 1818–20 when this aristocrat was an official emissary of Sweden. He wrote copiously about what he saw, and his letters were published in his country in 1824. He also sketched several views that appeared as aquatints in an atlas accompanying his book on the United States, *Bref em de Förenta Staterne*.

KNIGHT, HENRY COGSWELL (1789–1835). Knight was a writer and Episcopal minister who attended Phillips Andover Academy and Harvard College before graduating from Brown University in 1812. He had begun to write poetry while still in school, and in 1814 he began an extended tour of the South that provided the basis for his book, *Letters from the South and West*, published in 1824 under the pseudonym of Arthur Singleton, Esq. He spent most of his life in or near Boston, publishing some of his lectures and sermons in addition to volumes of verse.

KOHL, JOHANN GEORG (1808–1878). Kohl was born in Bremen and spent much of his life traveling in Europe and North America and writing works of geography. He also held the post of librarian of the Bremen city library. When he came to America in 1854, he brought with him copies he had made of scores of printed and manuscript maps illustrating the discovery and exploration of the New World, drawings that constitute the Kohl Collection in the Division of Geography and Maps of the Library of Congress. In addition to several studies of American cartography, he wrote *Travels in Canada* (1855) and *Travels in the Northwestern Parts of the United States* (1857). His several other books dealt with European countries and regions.

LAMB, MARTHA JOANNA READE NASH (1829–1893). Martha Nash grew up and received her education in Plainfield, Massachusetts. Her first published writing was a letter to a newspaper in Northampton. She married Charles Lamb in 1852, and the two lived in Chicago. After the Civil War she moved to New York, where she wrote several children's books, but her most impressive achievement was a two-volume history of New York City. She also became editor of the *Magazine of American History*. For these and other contributions to knowledge and culture, the New York *World* called her "one of the most advanced women of the century." For

Harper's Monthly Magazine she wrote the perceptive article about Washington that is used in the present study.

LANDAU, ROM (1899–1974). Landau came to this country as professor of Islamic and North African Studies at the University of the Pacific. He wrote many books, being best known perhaps for his several studies of Morocco, a country on which he was recognized as a world authority. Landau was also known as a sculptor.

LA ROCHEFOUCAULD-LIANCOURT, DUC DE (1747–1827). After serving in the French army, this nobleman studied agricultural conditions in England before returning to France to establish a model farm and a technical school for sons of soldiers. A member of the Constituent Assembly, he fled France for several years of travel in the United States. His book on this country is considered one of the best descriptive works of the period and was translated into English for a London edition of 1799, with the title *Travels through the United States of North America &c in the Years 1795, 1796, and 1797.*

LATROBE, BENJAMIN (1764–1820). Born in England and educated in Germany, Latrobe studied architecture and engineering under two English authorities in these fields. In 1796 he emigrated to America, settling first in Virginia where, among other buildings, he designed the state penitentiary at Richmond. Shortly after his first visit to Philadelphia in 1798 he decided to move there, and in that city he designed several important structures as well as the city's first modern water pumping and reservoir system. In 1803 President Jefferson appointed him surveyor of public buildings, and for the following fourteen years he contributed to the development of the new capital city in many ways until his retirement from public service in 1817.

LATROBE, JOHN HAZELHURST BONEVAL (1803–1891). A lawyer and inventor as well as a public official, John H. B. Latrobe exhibited some of the versatility of his illustrious father. His familiarity with Washington began when he attended Georgetown College before continuing his education at St. Mary's College in Baltimore and at West Point. In later life he practiced law, serving as counsel for the Baltimore & Ohio Railroad. He also write both prose and poetry, invented a new and more efficient stove, designed several buildings, and was active in public and philanthropic affairs.

LEAR, TOBIAS (1762–1816). A native of New Hampshire and a graduate of Harvard College in 1783, Lear also traveled and studied in Europe. George Washington engaged him as his private secretary in 1785, a position Lear held for seven years. While living at Mount Vernon, he published his *Observations on the River Potomack, the Country Adjacent, and the City of Washington*, a tract de-

signed to encourage settlement in the city and the region. Jefferson appointed him to diplomatic posts, his longest service being as consul general in Algiers where he remained until 1812.

LYNCH, ANNE CHARLOTTE (1815–1891). Lynch graduated from the Albany Female Academy in 1834, taught there for a time and—after moving to Providence, Rhode Island—gave private lessons to young women. In 1845 she accepted a teaching position at the Brooklyn Academy for Women, and her home became a gathering place for many writers, including William Cullen Bryant, Horace Greeley, Edgar Allan Poe, Margaret Fuller, and Bayard Taylor. She spent the social season of 1851 in Washington, and it was this experience that provided the basis for her perceptive article about the city in *Harper's New Monthly Magazine*. Married to Professor Vincenzo Botta in 1855, Lynch continued to write, including the highly regarded *Handbook of Universal Literature* published in 1860.

MCCABE, JAMES DABNEY (1842–1883). McCabe wrote under the pseudonym Edward Winslow Martin. Born the son of a clergyman and educated at the Virginia Military Institute, McCabe chose a literary career. His early works focused on the events of the Civil War, and during 1863–64 he edited the *Magnolia Weekly*. His extensive literary output in a relatively short life consisted of several hundred titles including stories, plays, poetry, history, and biography. Among those in the latter category were studies of Gen. Thomas J. Jackson, Gen. Albert S. Johnston, and Gen. Robert E. Lee. His observations on Washington come from his book published in 1873, *Behind the Scenes in Washington*.

MACKAY, ALEXANDER (1808–1852). Mackay, a Scot, came to Canada where he operated a newspaper in Toronto. He returned to Britain to write for the London *Morning Chronicle*. For that newspaper he visited the United States to cover congressional debates on the Oregon question. While writing for the paper, he apparently began the study of law and was called to the bar in 1847. Resigning from his newspaper, he represented the chambers of commerce of Manchester, Liverpool, Blackburn, and Glasgow on a fact-finding trip to cotton-producing regions of India. Although little known, his three-volume study of what he saw during his American travels, *The Western World, or, Travels in the United States in 1846–47*, is one of the most informative and entertaining of all such works.

MARRYAT, FREDERICK (1792–1848). Navy captain and novelist, Marryat traveled extensively throughout the world as a naval officer from 1806 to 1830. While in service he had begun to write, his first novel being published in 1829. In the next sixteen years he produced thirteen more novels, most of them well received and financially rewarding. He spent 1837 and 1838 in Canada and the United States, his experiences and impressions appearing as *A*

Diary in America. Toward the end of his life he turned to writing books for children, regaining through them a fortune that had been lost by bad investments in the West Indies.

MARTINEAU, HARRIET (1802–1876). Martineau endured a sickly childhood, saw her fiancé die, lost her money in a business failure, and was denied a teaching career because of her deafness. Rising above these hardships, she became a successful and highly respected author of works on political economy. Martineau came to America in 1834 for a two-year visit. On her return to England she produced two books on the United States, of which her *Retrospect of Western Travel* records in three volumes her impressions of people, places, and customs of the country.

MAXWELL, ARCHIBALD MONTGOMERY (?–?). Lieutenant Colonel Maxwell saw his two-volume book, *A Run through the United States during the Autumn of 1840*, published in 1841. An English reviewer in *Blackwood's Magazine* had this to say about Montgomery's feelings toward the country he visited: "He sees every thing in the broadest sunshine, and every mile of his road is strewed with flowers. All the men are full of intelligence, and all the women unrivalled for beauty. . . . He has, at all events, made a very pretty book; and, if Jonathan is not pleased, he must be a sour fellow indeed."

MELISH, JOHN (1771–1822). In 1806 Melish left his home in Glasgow to come to Savannah, Georgia, where he established a mercantile business. From there he traveled widely throughout the country, and in 1811, after returning briefly to Scotland and living for a time in New York, he moved to Philadelphia. The next year saw the publication of his *Travels through the United States*, one of several books by him on the geography of his adopted country. Melish was also an excellent cartographer, and with Samuel Harrison he developed an engraving and map publishing business in Philadelphia. He wrote several books of travel and geography during his lifetime, works that as one contemporary reviewer put it were "without any material errors; with no palpable falsehoods; no malignant abuse of individuals; no paltry calumnies on the institutions of the U.S."

MOORE, JOSEPH WEST (?–?). Moore's book, *Picturesque Washington*, appeared in 1887. Although ignored by modern students of the city, Moore's book is a useful source of information about the capital as the nineteenth century neared its close. It also contains many fine illustrations of buildings in the capital.

MUIRHEAD, JAMES FULLARTON (1853–1934). Muirhead was a Scot, educated at the University of Edinburgh and the University of Leipzig. For twenty-five years Muirhead was in charge of the English edition of the guidebooks produced by the Leipzig publisher Karl Baedeker. Muirhead edited Baedeker's guide to the U.S. published in 1893, and for that work he traveled extensively throughout the country in the period 1890–93. An earlier trip in 1888 had introduced him to America. One authority calls his book *The Land of Contrasts* "the best single-volume travel study of the United States." The public must have shared this opinion, for a third edition was issued in 1902 of this volume that first appeared in 1898.

MURRAY, CHARLES AUGUSTUS (1806–1895). Murray was the second son of the fifth Earl of Dunmore. He received his education at Eton and at Oriel College, Oxford, where he graduated in 1827. After serving in the royal household, he obtained a series of consular appointments in Italy, Egypt, Switzerland, Persia, Saxony, Denmark, and Portugal. His *Travels in North America*, one of several travel books by him, appeared in 1854. He was also an essayist and novelist. His *The Prairie Bird* was set in America and dealt with Indian life.

NOYES, THEODORE (1858–1946). Noyes became one of Washington's most distinguished and effective civic leaders. Noyes was born in Washington and spent most of his life there. His father edited the *Washington Evening Star*, and the younger Noyes also became a journalist after earning undergraduate and graduate degrees at Columbia University. He worked for the *Star* for several years, then studied law and for health reasons moved to Dakota Territory in 1883. He practiced law in Sioux Falls until 1887 when he returned to the *Star*. After his father's death in 1908 he assumed the editorship of the paper, a position he held until his death. Throughout his career Noyes championed political representation for the district in both Congress and the electoral college, improvements in the park and school system, and numerous other civic causes. He led the campaign for a tax-supported public library in Washington and became the first president of its board of trustees. He served as a member or chairman of countless other boards and was the recipient of many honors and awards. These included an honorary LL.D. degree from George Washington University in 1917.

PELZ, PAUL J. (1841–1918). As a youth Pelz studied in Germany, coming to the United States to serve his apprenticeship with a firm of architects in New York City. He moved to Washington to accept a position with the U.S. Lighthouse Board as architect and engineer. In 1873 he and John L. Smithmeyer formed an architectural partnership and won the competition for the design of the Library of Congress.

POORE, BENJAMIN PERLEY (1820–1887). Poore came to Washington as a boy of seven. His well-to-do parents took him to Europe and sent him to Dummer Academy in Massachusetts to study for entrance to West Point. Poore had other ideas and left school to become a printer's apprentice. In 1841 Poore became an attache at the American legation in Belgium. In 1844 Massachusetts retained him to obtain in Paris copies of French documents and manuscripts related to American history. On his return to America he held several editorial positions with Boston and Philadelphia newspapers, finally being designated Washington correspondent for the *Boston Morning Journal* and other papers. He remained in this position for thirty years. He wrote eight books, including the informative and delightful two-volume *Perley's Reminiscences of Sixty Years in the National Metropolis*, published in 1886.

PROTOPAPPAS, JOHN (?–?). Holder of a doctorate in Chinese literature, Protopappas edited a popular walking-tour guide to Washington whose third edition was published in 1984. He has also lectured in design studio courses in Washington universities.

RAE, WILLIAM FRASER (1835–1905). Fraser was called to the bar at Lincoln's Inn in 1861, but it was journalism that he practiced as a special correspondent for several English newspapers. As a correspondent for the London *Daily News*, Rae traveled by rail from New York to San Francisco in 1869 as one of the first to cross the country on the newly completed Union Pacific line. The *Saturday Review* said of his book, *Westward by Rail*, that "Mr. Rae unites the powers of a keen and thoughtful observer with the tact and skill of a graphic delineator."

RECLUS, JEAN JACQUES ELISÉE (1830–1905). Although French by birth, Reclus studied geography under Karl Ritter at the University of Berlin. For six years from 1852 to 1857 he toured the British Isles, the United States, Central America, and portions of South America. After returning to Paris he began to write for the *Revue des Deux Mondes* and *Tour du Monde*, among other journals. His early books included the two-volume *La Terre*, but this was eclipsed by his great nineteen-volume world geography that appeared during 1875–94, *La Nouvelle Geographie Universelle, la Terre et les Hommes*.

RICHARDSON, ALBERT (1833–1869). At the age of eighteen Richardson left his Massachusetts home and moved west. For a few years he taught school, wrote and acted in plays, and worked on a newspaper in Pittsburgh before leaving for Cincinnati in 1852. He lived there for five years, writing for several newspapers. In 1857 he moved to Kansas, where he wrote for the *Boston Journal*. In Kansas and on trips farther west he gathered material for his extremely popular book, *Beyond the Mississippi*, a volume that also incorporated his travels to California in 1865. From 1859 until his death at the hands of his fiancée's ex-husband, he wrote for the *New York Daily Tribune* and was the paper's chief Civil War correspondent.

ROBERTS, CECIL (1892–1974). Roberts served as literary editor of the *Liverpool Daily Post* from 1915 to 1918, during which time he also was a correspondent with the navy and the army during World War I. After the war he became editor of the *Nottingham Journal* and, after 1925, devoted himself to a career as playwright, poet, novelist, and lecturer. He was the author of more than fifty plays, books of poetry and travel, and an autobiography. During the years between the two world wars, he made six lecture tours to the United States and Canada. From 1940 to 1946 he was a member of the wartime British mission to the United States. The following year his book *And So to America* was published.

ROSS, BETTY (1925–). A native of Hartford, Connecticut, and a graduate in 1946 of Smith College, Ross's early career was in radio in Washington, D.C. She also worked as a free-lance writer and from 1962 to 1971 was public relations director for the Shoreham Hotel. She served as press secretary to Alfred Kahn when he was a White House adviser to President Carter on inflation. The author of *A Museum Guide to Washington, D.C.*, Ross was also area editor of *Fodor's Guide to Washington, D.C.* from 1984 to 1988. She is a contributor to several travel magazines as well as other periodicals and is the owner and publisher of Americana Press.

ROYALL, ANNE (1769–1854). Her marriage to a much older Revolutionary War veteran ending in his death, Anne Royall turned to writing as a means of support. In five years she wrote and published eleven volumes of books on local history and lore, including an anonymous first effort in 1826 called *Sketches of History, Life, and Manners in the United States*. In 1831 she began a Washington weekly journal, *Paul Pry*, that contained, according to one who knew her, "a curious mixture of politics, personalities, anti-church screeds, and slang." This was succeeded by *The Huntress* in 1836, a newspaper she continued to publish and do most of the writing for until three months before she died in 1854.

SALA, GEORGE AUGUSTUS (1828–1895). Sala recorded his impressions of America in the Civil War, drawing on his diary and his dispatches to the London *Daily Telegraph*. The resulting two-volume book, *My Diary in America in the Midst of War*, was published in 1865 and contains his comments on Washington. He revised and supplemented his views on the United States after a second visit in 1880. This appeared as *America Revisited*. Still later he wrote *The Life and Adventures of George Augustus Sala*, published in New York in 1895.

• SARMIENTO, DOMINGO FAUSTINO (1811–1888). Sarmiento was born in Argentina a year after it declared its independence. His education was limited to elementary school and what books he could find to read. His liberal political views led to his banishment to Chile where he distinguished himself as an educator. In the 1840s he visited Europe and the United States, and his long letters from America during a two-month visit were collected and published in 1847. In 1865, after a distinguished career in Chile and Argentina, Sarmiento returned to America in 1865 for a three-year assignment as ambassador to the United States, and in 1868 he was inaugurated as president of Argentina.

SCHUYLER, MONTGOMERY (1843–1914). Schuyler studied at Hobart College and eventually found his way to New York and a position on the staff of the New York *World*, moving to the *New York Times* in 1883. He also served as managing editor of *Harper's Weekly* from 1885 to 1887. Schuyler contributed articles to many journals, including the *Architectural Record*, which he helped to found in 1891. Although he wrote on a variety of topics, it is his architectural criticism that endures, for although without formal training in the subject, he became recognized as the nation's foremost critic on the topic. A number of his essays were published in his book of 1892, *American Architecture: Studies*.

SEELER, EDGAR V. (1867–1929). After Seeler graduated from the Massachusetts Institute of Technology, he continued his studies in architecture at the Ecole des Beaux Arts in Paris. In Philadelphia he taught for three years at the University of Pennsylvania before opening an office in Philadelphia.

SEVAREID, ARNOLD ERIC (1912–). Sevareid is a native of North Dakota who graduated from the University of Minnesota in 1935 and studied at the London School of Economics in 1937 and at the Alliance Française in 1938. He began his life of reporting and commenting on the news with the *Minneapolis Journal* and the Paris edition of the *New York Herald Tribune*. He joined the Columbia Broadcasting System in 1939 as a member of the team reporting on the war in Europe and in 1943 was in China. For CBS after the war he filled many positions as reporter, interviewer, and commentator on radio and television. His autobiography, *Not So Wild a Dream*, describes his early life and his initial years as a reporter and broadcaster. He is the author of many books on American politics and culture, including the volume with A. Robert Smith, *Washington: Magnificent Capital*, published in 1965.

SEWALL, REV. FRANK (1837–1915). Following his graduation from Bowdoin College in 1858, Sewall traveled in Italy and studied at Tübingen in Germany under an important Swedenborgian scholar. After taking an A.M. degree at Bowdoin, Sewall was ordained a minister of the General Convention of the New Jerusalem in the United States of America. After pastorates in Ohio and Glasgow, Scotland, Sewall came to Washington where he lived from 1889 to 1915. He wrote more than a dozen books on religion and Swedenborgian philosophy, but he also found time to contribute the thoughtful essay on the city of Washington that is excerpted in this volume.

SMITH, A. ROBERT (1925–). After service in the navy and graduation from Juniata College, Smith began a career in journalism that took him to newspapers in Huntingdon, Pennsylvania; Washington, D.C.; and Bremerton, Washington. In 1976 he became Washington bureau chief for the King Broadcasting Co. Among other works, he is the author of a biography of Senator Wayne Morse of Oregon, *The Tiger in the Senate*. Smith has also taught courses in journalism at the University of Maryland.

SMITH, BENJAMIN FRANKLIN, JR. (1830–1927). Born in Maine, Smith and his three brothers published many large and attractive lithographic views of American cities in 1848–55. Benjamin Smith's first effort at viewmaking came when he was only sixteen—a small engraving of Albany, New York, in 1846 used as the frontispiece of a book on the history of the city. Benjamin Smith drew and put on stone the Smith Brothers view of Washington showing how the city would look if the Washington Monument were completed according to the design of Robert Mills and if the Mall and White House grounds were landscaped according to Andrew Jackson Downing's design.

SMITH, WILLIAM LOUGHTON (1758–1812). Born into an old and prosperous South Carolina family, Smith came to London at the age of twelve to study. He began the study of law in 1774 in London and in Geneva, but in 1782 he returned to America. The following year he was admitted to the Charleston bar and also won election to the legislature. A member of the first Congress, Smith strongly supported Hamilton's plan for the assumption of state debts, an issue that came to be associated with the location of the national capital. He won election to Congress five times but was not among the vanguard of legislators who assembled in December 1800 for the first session in the new capital city. He left that body by resignation in 1797 to become minister to Portugal.

STEBBINS, R. P. (1810–1885). After graduation from Amherst College in 1834 and three years at the Harvard Divinity School, Stebbins was ordained a minister of the Congregational church in Leominster, Massachusetts. Seven years later he accepted the presidency of the Theological School at Meadville, Pennsylvania, a post he held until 1856. During the Civil War he served as president of the American Unitarian Association, and it was doubtless his duties in that organization that brought him for a time to Washington. Following the war, he ministered to Unitarian congregations in Ithaca, New York, and Newton Center, Massachusetts.

STONE, CHARLES P. (1824–1887). Stone graduated from West Point in 1845, saw duty in the Mexican War and, after a short period as a civilian, was reappointed a colonel in the regular army in 1861 and made a brigadier general of volunteers. After being blamed unfairly for a defeat in an engagement commanded by

another officer, Stone's military career came under a cloud, and he resigned from the army in 1864.

SUNDERLAND, BYRON (1819–1901). Sunderland was pastor of the First Presbyterian Church of Washington for more than fifty years, and he also served as chaplain of the Senate. An ardent supporter of the Unionist cause during the Civil War, he was characterized by one of his colleagues as "a little man physically, but a big man mentally and morally; an impulsive and fiery speaker . . . and very courageous and outspoken in announcing and defending his convictions."

TAFT, WILLIAM HOWARD (1857–1930). The twenty-sixth president of the United States held a variety of judicial and administrative posts in local and federal government before being named secretary of war. Elected president in 1908, he was defeated at the next election and taught at the Yale Law School. In 1921 he became chief justice of the U.S. Supreme Court, serving until his retirement in 1930 because of ill health. It was during his presidency that the Fine Arts Commission was created, and throughout his career in public life Taft consistently supported programs for the development of Washington.

TOTTEN, GEORGE OAKLEY, JR. (1865–1939). Totten began his studies of architecture at Columbia University, and after his graduation he continued them in Paris at the Ecole des Beaux Arts. He came to Washington to work in the office of the U.S. supervising architect. After two years he resigned to go into private practice. He is best known in Washington as the designer of many embassy buildings. They include those for France, Spain, and Poland.

TOWLE, GEORGE MAKEPEACE (1841–1893). Towle was a native of Washington, although he moved to Boston when a child. He graduated from Yale in 1861 and from Harvard Law School in 1863. He practiced law in Boston for only two years before becoming associate editor of the *Boston Post*. In 1866 he saw the appearance of the first of his more than twenty books, and in that same year he accepted an appointment as U.S. consul at Nantes, France. From there he was moved to England where in 1870 he published his two-volume work, *American Society*. On his return to Boston in 1870 he began to contribute to many English and American periodicals, and he also held high editorial positions with the Boston *Commercial Bulletin* and the *Boston Post*. In 1890 he was elected to the Massachusetts senate.

TOWNSEND, GEORGE ALFRED (1841–1914). After a high school education in Philadelphia, Townsend worked first for two Philadelphia newspapers, the *Philadelphia Inquirer* and the *Philadelphia Press*, before joining the staff of the *New York Herald* in 1861. His dispatches as a war correspondent for this paper and later the New

York *World* made his name well known, and the *World* sent him to Europe to cover the Austro-Prussian War. In 1867 he moved to Washington where, except for the period 1880 to 1892 when he lived in New York, he spent the next forty years writing books of prose and poetry and contributing to nearly 100 newspapers and magazines.

TROLLOPE, ANTHONY (1815–1882). One of two sons of Francis Trollope, Anthony had already achieved a full measure of fame as the author of such novels as *Barchester Towers* before he came to America in 1859 and again in 1861. On those trips he gathered material for his massive, three-volume work, *North America*. Although critics regard this as overly long and poorly organized, it is also recognized as being full of useful descriptions of and insights into America and American society of the time. The extensive treatment of Washington in his book provides one more view of the city by a foreign observer at a period when it was attracting increasing attention.

TROLLOPE, FRANCES (1780–1863). Frances Trollope is best remembered in America for her first book, *Domestic Manners of the Americans*, whose publication in 1832 caused an uproar in the United States because of her highly critical judgments about the country and its people. Only rarely in this volume did she voice approval of anything American, the public buildings in Washington comprising one of these exceptions.

TWAIN, MARK (pseudonym of Samuel Langhorne Clemens) (1835–1910). Twain's novel *The Gilded Age*, written with his friend and Hartford, Connecticut, neighbor, Charles Dudley Warner, came before his more famous books, *Tom Sawyer*, *Life on the Mississippi*, and *The Adventures of Huckleberry Finn*. The passage quoted in this book on the Washington Monument is the humorist at his sardonic best. He had first visited the city in February 1854, when he wrote a not very original report on his impressions for a Midwestern newspaper, probably the Muscatine, Iowa, *Journal*, edited by his brother, Orion.

TWINING, THOMAS (1776?–1861). Twining went to India from England at the age of sixteen in 1792 and spent the next decade and a half in that country as a colonial administrator. He visited America in 1796 on his way back to England between two terms of service. In 1805 he left India for good, living for a short time in Northamptonshire before making his home on the continent for twenty years. He returned to England in 1837 to settle in Twickenham, where he died in 1861.

VARNUM, JOSEPH BRADLEY, JR. (1818–1874). Varnum was a native of Washington and the grandson of Gen. Joseph B. Varnum, a Revolutionary War officer who served in the House of Representatives and the Senate for more than twenty years. After two years at the Yale Law School, Varnum entered the Baltimore office of Chief Justice Taney and practiced law in that city for a few years after gaining admission to the bar. Moving to New York, he entered politics and was elected a member of the state assembly, becoming its Speaker in 1851. He was highly regarded in New York society as a founder of both the Union League and Century clubs and as a member of the New-York Historical Society and the American Geographical Society, among other institutions. In addition to *The Seat of Government of the United States*, he wrote *The Washington Sketch Book* as well as several contributions to newspapers and magazines.

WALTON, WILLIAM (1909–). Walton graduated from the University of Wisconsin in 1931. Until 1949 he wrote for newspapers and magazines, serving as a war correspondent for *Time* and *Life* magazines in Europe from 1942 to 1945. He turned to painting, and his works have been exhibited in several one-person shows. President Kennedy appointed him a member of the Council on Pennsylvania Avenue in 1962 and to the Commission of Fine Arts in 1963. His book, *The Evidence of Washington*, was published in 1966.

WANSEY, HENRY (1752?–1827). Wansey lived in Wiltshire, England, where he operated a clothing business. Retiring from business in midlife, he spent his time in travel, writing, and historical research. In 1789 the Society of Antiquaries elected him a fellow. He journeyed to the United States in 1794, publishing his account of his travels two years later as *An Excursion to the United States of America*. It apparently enjoyed considerable popularity, for a second edition appeared in 1798.

WARBURTON, GEORGE DROUGHT (1816–1857). Warburton studied at the Royal Military College in Woodwich and served until 1833 in the royal artillery. After being posted to Spain, where he was wounded, he left for North America in 1844. Warburton spent most of his time in Canada, but he visited Washington and a few other places in the United States. His two-volume book describing his impressions was published anonymously in 1846 as *Hochelaga; or England in the New World*. Warburton wrote well, and this publication went through five editions through 1854. Returning to England, he retired as a major in 1854, three years later gaining a seat in the House of Commons, which he held only briefly until his suicide in the fall of 1857.

WARDEN, DAVID BAILLIE (1772–1845). Warden, of Scottish descent, was born in Ireland but received his university degree from Glasgow in 1797. Arrested as a member of an Irish paramilitary organization, he accepted banishment from Britain instead of standing trial and came to America in 1799. He was principal of academies at Kinderhook and Kingston, New York, acquired citizenship in 1804, and went to Paris as private secretary to the American minister, later being appointed consul. After leaving office in 1814, Warden elected to remain in France where he wrote and saw his several books published, among them *A Statistical, Political, and Historical Account of the United States of North America* that appeared in 1819. Its three volumes provided a wealth of information about industry, business, transportation, education, publishing, health, agriculture, and other topics for each state then comprising the nation. Warden was a member of both the American Philosophical Society and the Lyceum of Natural History of New York.

WARNER, CHARLES DUDLEY (1829–1900). This popular author graduated from Hamilton College where as an undergraduate he contributed to the *Knickerbocker Magazine*, and he turned his commencement oration into his first book in 1851. He is listed here as a collaborator with Mark Twain in their novel, *The Gilded Age*, although the passage quoted must surely have come from Twain's pen.

WATTERSTON, GEORGE (1783–1854). At the age of eight Watterston was brought to Washington, and after his school years he began the practice of law in Hagerstown, Maryland. In 1808 he published his first novel, followed by a comedy, a second novel, and some poetry. He became editor of the *Washington City Weekly Gazette* in 1813, but in 1815 he began a fourteen-year tenure as librarian of Congress, followed in 1830 by his appointment as editor of the Washington *Daily National Journal*. Over the ensuing fifteen years he produced a guidebook series, textbooks, lectures, sketches of eminent personages, and other writings. He led the movement to build the Washington Monument and was the first secretary of the Washington National Monument Society, a post he retained until his death. Few people equaled his knowledge of the city.

WELD, ISAAC (1774–1856). Isaac Weld was born in Dublin and was educated in England. In 1795 he set off for America where he traveled for more than two years, reaching some places not normally visited by those with less time at their disposal. His book about his observations met with instant success. There were two English editions of *Travels through the States of North America and the Provinces of Upper and Lower Canada during the Years 1795, 1796, and 1797*, one in French, two in German, and another in Dutch. Weld never returned to America, but he wrote works on Irish topography that, like his American study, were illustrated with his own drawings.

WHITMAN, WALT (1819–1892). Whitman came to Washington during the Civil War as a volunteer nurse after an early life as a printer, carpenter, and writer and editor for a number of newspapers. In 1855 the first edition of his *Leaves of Grass* appeared, although it then consisted of only twelve poems. His moving passages of prose descriptions of the wartime city seem to be little known, but they are among the most perceptive and touching words ever to be written about Washington.

WICKER, THOMAS GREY (1926–). Born in Hamlet, North Carolina, Wicker graduated from the University of North Carolina in 1948 with a degree in journalism. He began his career as the executive director of the Southern Pines, North Carolina, Chamber of Commerce before serving as reporter or editor of newspapers in Aberdeen, Lumberton, and Winston-Salem, North Carolina, and Nashville, Tennessee. He joined the Washington Bureau of the *New York Times* in 1960 and was its chief in 1964–68. From 1968 to 1985 he was associate editor of the *Times*, and since then he has been a columnist for that paper. Wicker held a Nieman fellowship at Harvard in 1957–58. He is a novelist as well, having written eight under his own name and as Paul Connolly. He is also the author of several books on American politics as well as many articles and book chapters.

WILLIS, NATHANIEL PARKER (1806–1867). This journalist, poet, editor, and playwright had become known as a writer even before he received a degree from Yale in 1827. Two years later he founded the short-lived but influential *American Monthly Magazine* in Boston, then moved to New York as a writer for the *New York Mirror*. That newspaper sent him abroad as a foreign correspondent at the age of twenty-five, and his dispatches made him famous. In England he wrote for several periodicals, then he returned to America in 1836 to write plays and travel accounts and within a short time to begin research and writing for the massive two-volume work, *American Scenery*, in which the extract appearing in this study originally appeared.

WINTHROP, THEODORE (1828–1861). At thirty-three this Union volunteer lost his life in the Civil War. Earlier he had traveled in Europe for more than a year after earning his degree at Yale. From 1851 to 1857 he worked in New York, traveled in the U.S. and abroad, studied law, engaged in a political campaign, and began and abandoned a law practice in St. Louis before deciding to make writing his career. His several novels appeared posthumously, and during his life his major works were limited to a book about his friend, the artist Frederick E. Church, and two shorter pieces published in the summer of 1861 by the *Atlantic Monthly*.

WOLCOTT, OLIVER (1760–1833). Wolcott received an excellent education at the grammar school in Litchfield, Connecticut, Yale College, and private study of law under Tapping Reeve. After serving in several Connecticut public offices, he accepted in 1789 a post as auditor of the new Department of the Treasury. When Alexander Hamilton resigned as secretary of the department in 1795, President Washington appointed Wolcott to succeed him. Wolcott thus joined other federal officials who in December 1800 began to administer national affairs in the new city of Washington. He left office two months later for Connecticut. In his later life he filled banking positions in New York, and in 1817 he was elected governor of Connecticut and served for ten years.

Appendix B
Notes on Printmaking

All nineteenth-century prints were produced by applying a sheet of paper to an inked metal, stone, or wooden printing medium or other surface containing the artist's image. The pressure from the press transferred the ink from the printing surface to the paper. Three general categories of prints can be distinguished: *intaglio*, *relief*, and *planographic*. The first includes etchings, engravings, aquatints, and mezzotints. The second refers to woodcuts and wood engravings. The third categorizes lithographs and collotypes.

This classification is based on how the printmaker creates the features of the image on the metal plate, wooden surface, or stone used to transfer ink to paper. Printmakers could proceed in one of three ways: making what are known as intaglio prints by incising the printing surface mechanically or chemically to form indentations to hold ink, creating relief prints by cutting away portions of the surface to leave as raised parts only the design elements that would be inked and printed, or producing prints by the planographic process by drawing a design on a treated stone or metal surface with materials that attract printing ink only to the design and not to the surrounding areas.

Printmakers also frequently employed more than one technique in creating prints of each category. For example, etching or engraving was normally used in connection with the aquatint process, and a few lithographs seem to combine lithography with elements of collotype. Each of the three major categories of prints requires its own kinds of tools and instruments, demands special skills on the part of the printmaker, needs a different kind of press, produces distinctive results, and possesses characteristic advantages and drawbacks.

Because the book's illustrations have been printed as halftones on a modern offset lithographic press, their appearance differs somewhat from the originals. Although these illustrations provide a close approximation of the corresponding print photographed for this purpose, the true character of the original and its distinctive features can be fully appreciated only by firsthand examination.

AQUATINT. To produce an aquatint the printmaker first coats a copper plate with finely ground rosin that is fixed on the plate by heating it from the reverse. This creates an irregular, reticulated, and porous ground that, after being treated with acid, inked, and printed, would produce a rectangle of grey. Instead, by "stopping out" portions on the plate with wax and by altering the duration and number of acid treatments, the printmaker creates a plate capable of printing an extensive range of tones. Nearly all eighteenth- and nineteenth-century aquatints were hand colored before sale, and the combination of the varied tonal character of the printed surface and skillfully applied transparent watercolors produced prints of exceptional beauty.

COLLOTYPE. Collotypes begin with a glass plate coated with a thin layer of light-sensitive gelatin. As it dries, the film of gelatin becomes a surface composed of extremely fine, irregularly spaced, reticulated, and curving cracks. This provides a grained surface resembling an aquatint plate. The printmaker places a negative of the image to be printed on the collotype plate and uses light to transfer the lines or tones of the image to the sensitive gelatin. Those portions receiving the most light harden while those protected by darker portions of the negative remain soft and receptive to water. The hardened portions that are to print can be made receptive to greasy ink, and the remaining areas made receptive to water. When a greasy printing ink is applied to the plate, it clings only to the lines or areas of hardened gelatin. The inked plate can then be passed through a press to transfer the printing ink to a sheet of paper, or the image can be printed on transfer paper that can in turn transfer the image to a lithographic stone or lithographic zinc plate. The stone or plate with the second generation image is then available for inking and printing in the normal lithographic manner. The Washington prints using collotype come from souvenir booklets of the late nineteenth century. They appear to have combined this process and lithography—the collotype part providing only the tonal portions of the sky or other background elements.

ENGRAVING. An engraving is printed from a metal plate, usually copper or steel, into whose surface the engraver incises grooved lines, dots, or other indentations that make up the image. The features of the design are thus created as the engraver removes part of the surface of the copper or steel plate using a variety of sharpened instruments. The burin or graver is the most common—a pointed tool that gouges a sliver of metal as it is pushed along the lines of the design. These grooves receive the ink that will print as lines. Heavier or lighter pressure on the burin creates lines of greater or lesser depth and width depending on the desired appearance of the finished print. The tiny burrs that are thrown up are removed by scraping and burnishing, and changes or corrections can be made by hammering from the reverse and burnishing the front to flatten a portion of the plate so that new lines can be made. Most engravings include hatching, cross-hatching, or stippling to create a print simulating shades or tones, although some—like maps—consist only of lines. In printing, the plate is inked and then wiped to remove any ink from the surface. Only the ink that has been worked into the incised lines or indentations remains. The paper to be used in printing is slightly dampened and placed over the plate. Plate and paper are then passed between two rollers that exert great pressure, compressing the paper slightly into the indentations of the plate and causing the ink to adhere to the paper, which can then be removed from the plate and hung to dry. Like other prints, engravings may be published as printed with a single color ink (usually black), or images may be hand colored after the inked lines are dry.

ETCHING. Beginning with a copper plate covered with wax, the etcher uses a sharp needle to draw the design that is to be printed. This exposes the copper surface below the wax. When the plate is treated with an acid solution, a minute portion of the exposed part is eaten away and thus becomes an indentation in the plate. Other parts of the design can then be drawn and the plate treated with acid a second time. The lines first drawn become deeper and capable of holding more ink, or they can be "stopped out" by a coating of wax or varnish to prevent the acid from making selected lines deeper. The etcher can thus vary the intensity of lines in the final print by the number and length of times the plate is exposed to acid and by selective protection of parts of the plate. Although no purely etched views of Washington appear in this book, etching was commonly used to place the outlines of a design on a copper or steel plate as a guide for an engraver. Many engravings also exhibit faint lines or hatching that were created by the etching process and never strengthened by burin work. Etched lines also are important components of aquatints.

HALFTONE LITHOGRAPHY. The search for a practical method of reproducing continuous-tone photographs or other artwork with continuous tones culminated in the halftone process that came into commercial use in the late 1880s. The original image is photographed through a very fine screen that divides the image into a myriad of dots. The dots are largest where the original image is darkest and smallest where the image is light. The resulting negative can be used to make a relief block or—almost universally now—a lithographic plate. In the image printed from this plate, the dots are so small and closely spaced that the normal human eye cannot distinguish them and registers the image as one consisting of continually varying tones. In four-color process lithography the colored original is photographed successively through filters that allow light from only one primary color at a time to reach individual negatives. Plates are made from each negative in addition to one used for black, inked with the appropriate color, and applied to the paper. The superimposition of dots of varying sizes and colors reproduces the elements of the visible color spectrum and creates on paper an image that resembles the colored original. In contemporary color printing, like this book, the several negatives needed are produced from photographic color transparencies that are electronically scanned.

LITHOGRAPH. Lithography is based on the antipathy of water and grease and not on the lowering or raising of the inked printing surface. Lithographs are drawn with greasy ink, pencil, or crayon on the grained surface of a slab of limestone slate or a treated and textured zinc plate. The surface is then washed with a solution of dilute nitric acid and gum arabic. This makes the undrawn portions more receptive to water without affecting the previously drawn design. The lithographer then wipes the surface with water, which the pores of the stone or zinc absorb except where inked. A greasy printing ink is then rolled over the surface where it is repelled by the dampened portions and adheres only to the elements of the drawn design. Paper is then placed over the stone or plate, covered with a protective mat, and passed under the scraper bar of the press that exerts the pressure needed to transfer the ink from stone to paper. The first lithographs were printed in black ink only, some of them being hand colored. Others used a second stone to add a tone for sky and shadow effects. Color lithographs, sometimes referred to as chromolithographs, require a separate stone for each color added to the paper, although some colors seen by the eye are the result of two colors printed over one another. The character of the print can be varied enormously depending on the grain of the stone, how it has been polished, whether the design is drawn with a fine pen or blunt crayon, the skill of the lithographic artist in using these variables to achieve a desired effect, and the number of tint or tone stones used in addition to the one carrying the basic design. The development of transfer paper made it possible to move an entire design or parts of it from one stone or plate to another. Or, an engraving could be transferred to transfer paper and the resulting image printed as a lithograph. Artists drawing directly on transfer paper did not need to reverse their design and lettering, as was required for all other nineteenth-century prints except those involving photography.

MEZZOTINT. A copper mezzotint plate is first prepared by roughening its surface so as to cover it with tiny burrs. Although many other devices are used, the most common tool employed for this is the rocker, a knifelike instrument with curved serrated edges and a long handle extending at right angles whose end rests on a raised support. When rocked back and forth in different positions and at many angles to the axis of the plate, the rocker throws up minute burrs throughout the surface of the plate. The design is then created by differential scraping and smoothing of those portions of the plate to print in lighter tones and burnishing those parts to be left as highlights. Burins and other engraving tools and drypoint needles are often used to add small details or to create precise lines or boundaries to toned areas of the print. When inked, the burrs hold ink and create on the paper print a rich, velvety character unmatched by any other technique. Because of the fragility of the burrs, mezzotint plates can produce only a limited number of good impressions, perhaps fifty to a hundred at the most. Although in theory the technique could be used for any kind of scene, in practice it was limited almost entirely to portraits. In this book only one mezzotint appears, the portrait of Washington holding the plan of the city in his hand.

STEEL ENGRAVING. Many of the same techniques used in engraving copper plates are employed in steel engraving, whose development in England dates from about 1820. By mid-century in America it was in common use, generally for illustrations in books where large press runs made a harder material than copper needed to avoid excessive wear in printing. Steel engraving also gave rise to the development of various kinds of mechanical devices to make working on this material easier and faster. Chief among them were ruling machines that allowed the printmaker to add closely spaced, precisely parallel lines that added tonal effects to the print. The great majority of steel engravings are no larger than book-size. Although some of them may have been hand colored before being issued, and others colored by individual owners at the time, nearly all colored versions found today are the result of modern coloring by print dealers.

STEREOTYPE AND ELECTROTYPE. Both techniques were used in America as extensions of wood engraving as well as for other types of prints or set type. Stereotypes required a mold of the wood engraving from plaster of Paris, clay, or papier-mâché to use in casting a metal plate. Although satisfactory for duplicating set type, this did not work as well on wood engravings with very fine lines. Electrotype plates were made by an electrochemical process that deposited a film of copper on a wax molding of the wood engraving. Backing metal composed of tin, antimony, and lead strengthen and thicken the copper plate which can then be used for printing. In the United States the first electrotypes from woodcuts were made experimentally in 1839, and the first such illustration appeared two years later. By the 1850s the process was in general use by printers in major cities. These techniques protected the original image, since it was possible to use the engraved wood blocks only to make the stereotype or electrotype metal plate needed for printing. These metal plates did not wear nearly as rapidly as wood, and—in case of accident—a new plate could always be made from the original wood engraving.

WOOD ENGRAVING. In creating the surface used for printing a wood engraving, the printmaker uses some of the same tools employed to incise lines for copper or steel engravings but applies them instead to create lines in relief on a wood surface. The engraver does this by cutting away all of the surface from a smooth wooden block except the portions to be printed. A single line thus requires two cuts to remove material from both sides of the line. For large illustrations several smaller pieces of end-grain wood are bolted together from the underside to increase the dimensions of the printing surface. The fine grain of the wood—preferably boxwood—and the gravers or burins and thin-bladed tint-tools of the engraver's trade made it possible to achieve very fine detail and also to simulate various shades of grey through variations in the spacing of lines used in hatching and cross-hatching. Wood engraving appealed particularly to publishers of illustrated newspapers and magazines because a wood engraving (like set type) is in relief, with the portion of a plate or block to be printed raised above its supporting base. Illustrations done in this medium thus can be printed on the same page and at the same time as accompanying text. Further, the development of methods of duplicating the illustration by stereotyping or electrotyping made it possible to use multiple presses if necessary.

Bibliography

Adams, Henry. *The Education of Henry Adams*. Boston: Massachusetts Historical Society, 1907.

Adams, W[illiam] E[dwin]. *Our American Cousins: Being Personal Impressions of the People and Institutions of the United States*. London: Walter Scott, 1883.

Alexander, Sally Kennedy. "A Sketch of the Life of Major Andrew Ellicott." Columbia Historical Society, *Records* 2 (1899): 158–202.

Allen, Marie B. "The Greatest Monstrosity in America: A Brief History of the Old Executive Office Building." *Prologue* 17 (1985): 247–58.

American Institute of Architects, Committee on Town Planning. *City Planning Progress in the United States 1917*. Washington, D.C.: Journal of the American Institute of Architects, 1917.

Ames, Mary Clemmer. *Ten Years in Washington: Life and Scenes in the National Capital, as a Woman Sees Them*. Hartford: A. D. Worthington & Co., 1875.

Andrews, Wayne. "The Baroness Was Never Bored: The Baroness Hyde de Neuville's Sketches of American Life 1807–1822." *New-York Historical Society Quarterly* 38 (April 1954): 105–17.

Angell, Roger. "Washington, D.C." In *American Panorama East of the Mississippi*, by the editors of *Holiday* magazine, 259–74. Garden City, N.Y.: Doubleday & Co., 1960.

Archer, William. *America To-Day: Observations and Reflections*. New York: Charles Scribner's Sons, 1899.

Babcock, Col. O. E. *Annual Report of Colonel O. E. Babcock, Corps of Engineers, for the Fiscal Year Ending June 30, 1873*. H. Ex. Doc. 1, Pt. 2, 43d Cong., 1st sess., 2:1151–69.

Baily, Francis, F. R. S. *Journal of a Tour in Unsettled Parts of North America in 1796 & 1797*. Edited by Jack D. L. Holmes. Foreword by John Francis McDermott. Carbondale, Ill.: Southern Illinois University Press, 1969.

Baker, Marcus. "Surveys and Maps of the District of Columbia." *National Geographic Magazine* 6 (1 November 1894): 149–66.

Baldwin, Elbert F. "Washington Fifty Years Hence." *The Outlook* 14 (5 April 1902): 817–29.

Barnard, John Gross. "The Defenses of Washington." In *Washington during War Time*, edited by Marcus Benjamin, 27–43. Washington, D.C.: National Tribune Co., [1902].

Beale, J. H. *Picturesque Sketches of American Progress. Comprising Official Descriptions of Great American Cities Prepared under the Supervision of the Authorities of the Respective Cities, Showing their Origin, Development, Present Condition, Commerce and Manufacture*. New York: The Empire Co-Operative Association, 1889.

Beauchamp, Tanya Edwards. "Adolph Cluss: An Architect in Washington during the Civil War and Reconstruction." Columbia Historical Society, *Records* (1971–72): 338–58.

"The Beautifying of Washington." *Harper's Weekly* 46 (1 February 1902): 144–46.

"Beautifying Washington." *Washington Post*, 16 January 1902.

Becker, Ralph E. *Miracle on the Potomac: The Kennedy Center from the Beginning*. Silver Spring, Md.: Bartley Press, 1990.

Benjamin, Marcus, ed. *Washington during War Time*. Washington, D.C.: National Tribune Co., [1902].

Berret, James G. "Address of Ex-Mayor James G. Berret." Columbia Historical Society, *Records* 2 (1899): 206–18.

Birkbeck, Morris. *Notes on a Journey in America from the Coast of Virginia to the Territory of Illinois*. 3d ed. London: J. Ridgeway, 1818.

Bowling, Kenneth R. " 'A Place to Which Tribute is Brought': The Contest for the Federal Capital in 1783." *Prologue* 8 (Fall 1976): 129–39.

————. *Creating the Federal City, 1744–1800: Potomac Fever*. Washington, D.C.: American Institute of Architects Press, 1988.

Boyd, Julian P. "Fixing the Seat of Government." In *The Papers of Thomas Jefferson*, edited by Julian P. Boyd, 20:3–72. Princeton: Princeton University Press, 1982.

Bradford, T[homas] G[amaliel]. *A Comprehensive Atlas Geographical, Historical & Commercial*. Boston: William D. Ticknor; New York: Wiley & Long; Philadelphia: T. T. Ash, 1835.

Brodherson, David. "Souvenir Books in Stone: Lithographic Miniatures for the Masses." *Imprint* 12 (Autumn 1987): 21–28.

Brooks, Noah. *Washington in Lincoln's Time*. New York: The Century Co., 1895. (*See also:* Staudenraus, P. J.)

Brown, Glenn. *History of the United States Capitol*. 2 vols. Washington, D.C.: Government Printing Office, 1900.

————. *Memories*. Washington, D.C.: W. F. Roberts Co., 1931.

————. "The Plan of the City and Its Expected Growth." Columbia Historical Society, *Records* 7 (1904): 114–17.

————. "A Suggestion for Grouping Government Buildings; Landscape, Monuments, and Statuary." *Architectural Review* 7 (August 1900): 89–94.

Brown, Glenn, comp. *Papers Relating to the Improvement of the City of Washington, District of Columbia*. S. Doc. 94, 56th Cong., 2d sess., 1901.

Bryan, John M., ed. *Robert Mills, Architect*. Washington, D.C.: American Institute of Architects Press, 1989.

Bryan, Wilhelmus Bogart. "The Central Section of the City." Columbia Historical Society, *Records* 7 (1904): 135–45.

————. *A History of the National Capital from its Foundation Through the Period of the Adoption of the Organic Act*. 2 vols. New York: Macmillan Co., 1914–16.

————. "Hotels of Washington Prior to 1814." Columbia Historical Society, *Records* 7 (1904): 71–106.

————. "Something about L'Enfant and his Personal Affairs." Columbia Historical Society, *Records* 2 (1899): 111–17.

Buckingham, J[ames] S[ilk]. *America, Historical, Statistic, and Descriptive*. 3 vols. London: Fisher, Son, & Co., [1841].

Bugbee, Mary F. "The Early Planning of Sites for Federal and Local Use in Washington, D.C." Columbia Historical Society, *Records* 51–52 (1955): 19–31.

Burnham, Daniel. "White City and Capital City." *Century Magazine* 63 (February 1902): 619–20.

Burr, Nelson. "The Federal City Depicted, 1612–1801." *Quarterly Journal of the Library of Congress* 8 (November 1950): 64–77. Reprinted in *A la Carte: Selected Papers on Maps and Atlases*, compiled by Walter W. Ristow, 126–43. Washington, D.C.: Library of Congress, 1972.

Butler, Jeanne F. *Competition 1792: Designing a Nation's Capitol*. Special Issue, *Capitol Studies* 4 (1976). Washington, D.C.: United States Capitol Historical Society, 1976.

Cable, Mary. *The Avenue of the Presidents*. Boston: Houghton Mifflin Co., 1969.

Caemmerer, H. Paul. *The Life of Pierre Charles L'Enfant*. Washington, D.C.: National Republic Publishing Co., 1950.

————. *A Manual on the Origin and Development of Washington*. Washington, D.C.: Government Printing Office, 1939.

———. *Washington, the National Capital.* S. Doc. 332, 71st Cong., 3d sess., 1932.

Campbell, George. *White and Black: The Outcome of a Visit to the United States.* London: Chatto & Windus, 1879.

[Candler, Isaac]. *A Summary View of America: Comprising a Description of the Face of the Country, and of Several of the Principal Cities; and Remarks on the Social, Moral and Political Character of the People: Being the Result of Observations and A Complete Historical, Chronological, and Geographical American Atlas.* Philadelphia: H.C. Carey & I. Lea, 1822.

Carey, John Thomas. "The American Lithograph from Its Inception to 1865 with Biographical Considerations of Twenty Lithographers and a Check List of their Works." Ph.D. diss., Ohio State University, 1954.

Carter, Edward C. II. "Benjamin Henry Latrobe and the Growth and Development of Washington, 1798–1818." Columbia Historical Society, *Records* 48 (1971–72): 128–49.

Ceremonies and Oration at Laying the Cornerstone of the City Hall of the City of Washington. Washington, D.C.: Jacob Gideon, Jr., 1820.

"The City of Washington." *Harper's Weekly* 26 (20 May 1882): 314.

Clark, Allen C[ulling]. "Development of the Eastern Section and the Policy of the Land Owners." Columbia Historical Society, *Records* 7 (1904): 118–34.

———. "Doctor and Mrs. William Thornton." Columbia Historical Society *Records* 18 (1915): 144–208.

———. *Greenleaf and Law in the Federal City.* Washington, D.C.: W. F. Roberts, 1901.

Clemens, Samuel Langhorne, and Charles Dudley Warner. *The Gilded Age: A Tale of To-day.* Hartford: American Publishing Co., 1873.

Cobb, Josephine. "The Washington Art Association: An Exhibition Record, 1856–1860." Columbia Historical Society, *Records* 63–65, (1963–65): 122–37.

Cole, John Y. "Smithmeyer & Pelz: Embattled Architects of the Library of Congress." *Quarterly Journal of the Library of Congress* 29 (October 1972): 282–307.

Combe, George. *Notes on the United States of North America during a Phrenological Visit in 1838-9-40.* 2 vols. Philadelphia: Carey & Hart, 1841.

"Commission to Consider Improvements in the United States Capital." *Inland Architect and News Record* 37 (February 1901): 7.

Cooke, Henry. "Notes of a Loiterer in Philadelphia, Baltimore, and Washington." *Bentley's Miscellany* 17 (1845): 99–104.

Cooling, Benjamin Franklin. "Defending Washington during the Civil War." Columbia Historical Society, *Records* (1971–72): 314–37.

Cooling, Benjamin Franklin, and Walton H. Owen II. *Mr. Lincoln's Forts: A Guide to the Civil War Defenses of Washington.* Shippensburg, Pa.: White Mane Publishing Co., 1988.

Cosentino, Andrew J., and Henry H. Glassie. *The Capital Image: Painters in Washington, 1800–1915.* Washington, D.C.: Smithsonian Institution Press, 1983.

Cowdrey, Bartlett. "William Henry Bartlett and the American Scene." *New York History* 22 (October 1941): 388–400.

Cox, William V., comp. *Celebration of the One Hundredth Anniversary of the Establishment of the Seat of Government in the District of Columbia.* Washington, D.C.: Government Printing Office, 1901.

———. "The Defenses of Washington—General Early's Advance on the Capital and the Battle of Fort Stevens, July 11 and 12, 1864." Columbia Historical Society, *Records* 4 (1901): 135–65.

Craig, Alexander. *America and the Americans: A Narrative of a Tour in the United States and Canada with Chapters on American Home Life.* Paisley and London, 1892.

Crompton, Robert D. "James Thackara, Engraver, of Philadelphia and Lancaster, Pa." *Journal of the Lancaster County Historical Society* 62 (April 1958): 65–95.

Crowe, Eyre. *With Thackeray in America.* New York: C. Scribner's Sons, 1893.

Dahl, Curtis. "Mr. Smith's American Acropolis." *American Heritage* 7 (June 1956): 38–43, 104–5.

Daley, John M. *Georgetown University: Origin and Early Years.* Washington, D.C.: Georgetown University Press, 1957.

Davis, Madison. *A History of the Washington City Post Office.* Lancaster, Pa.: New Era Publishing Co., 1903.

Davis, Patricia T. *End of the Line.* New York: Neale Watson Academic Publications, 1978.

Davis, Richard Beale. *The Abbé Correa in America, 1812–1820.* American Philosophical Society, *Transactions,* New Series, vol. 45, pt. 2 (1955).

Deák, Gloria-Gilda. *American Views: Prospects and Vistas.* New York: Viking Press and The New York Public Library, 1976.

———. *Picturing America 1497–1899: Prints, Maps, and Drawings Bearing on the New World Discoveries and on the Development of the Territory That Is Now the United States.* 2 vols. Princeton: Princeton University Press, 1988.

Dearborn, Nathaniel. *Dearborn's Guide through Mount Auburn.* Boston: n.p., 1851.

De Roos, Fred Fitzgerald. *Personal Narrative of Travels in the United States and Canada in 1826 . . . with Remarks on the Present State of the American Navy.* London: William Harrison Ainsworth, 1827.

"A Description of the Situation and Plan of the City of Washington, in the District of Columbia, in North America, now Building for the Metropolis of the United States." *Universal Magazine of Knowledge & Pleasure* 93 (July 1793): 41–43.

Dicey, Edward. *Six Months in the Federal States.* 2 vols. London and Cambridge: Macmillan and Co., 1863.

Dickens, Charles. *American Notes.* 1842. Reprint. New York: Fromm International Publishing Co., 1985.

———. *The Letters of Charles Dickens.* 2 vols. London: Chapman and Hall, 1880.

The District in the XVIIIth Century: History, Site-Strategy, Real Estate Market, Landscape, &c. as Described by the Earliest Travellers: Henry Wansey, Francis Baily, Isaac Weld, Duke of La Rochefoucauld-Liancourt, John Davis of Salisbury. [A. J. Morrison?], 1909.

District of Columbia. Board of Public Works. *Report of the Board of Public Works of the District of Columbia, from its Organization until November 1, 1872.* H. Ex. Doc. 1, pt. 3, 42d Cong., 3d sess., 1872, ser. 1562.

Dolkart, Andrew. *The Old Executive Office Building: A Victorian Masterpiece.* Washington, D.C.: Government Printing Office, 1984.

Dougherty, J. P. "Baroque and Picturesque Motifs in L'Enfant's Design for the Federal Capital." *American Quarterly* 26 (March 1974): 23–36.

Downing, A. J. "Explanatory Notes to Accompany the Plan for Improving the Public Grounds at Washington," 3 March 1851. Manuscript, National Archives, Record Group 42, LR, vol. 32, no. 1358 ½.

Duncan, John M. *Travels Through Part of the United States and Canada in 1818 and 1819.* Glasgow: Hurst, Robinson & Co., 1823.

Duryee, Sacket L. *A Historical Summary of the Work of the Corps of Engineers in Washington, D.C. and Vicinity, 1852–1952.* Washington, D.C.: n.p., 1952.

[Dwight, Theodore]. *Things As They Are: or, Notes of a Traveller.* New York: Harper & Brothers, 1834.

"Edward Savage (1761–1817)." Philadelphia Museum of Art, *Philadelphia: Three Centuries of American Art.* Philadelphia: Philadelphia Museum of Art, 1976.

Ehrenberg, Ralph E. "Mapping the Nation's Capital: The Surveyor's Office, 1791–1818." *Quarterly Journal of the Library of Congress* 36 (Summer 1979): 279–319.

Elliot, Jonathan. *Historical Sketches of the Ten Miles Square Forming the District of Columbia; with a Picture of Washington. . . .* Washington, D.C.: J. Elliot, Jr., 1830.

Ellis, John B. *The Sights and Secrets of the National Capital: A Work Descriptive of Washington City in all its Various Phases.* New York: United States Publishing Co., 1869.

Enquiries During a Journey in the United States. By an Englishman. London: T. Cadell, 1824.

Eskew, Garnett Laidlaw, assisted by B. P. Adams. *Willard's of Washington: The Epic of a Capital Caravansary.* New York: Coward-McCann, 1954.

Evans, George W. "The Birth and Growth of the Patent Office." Columbia Historical Society, *Records* 22 (1919): 105–24.

An Excursion through the United States and Canada during the Years

1822–23 by an English Gentlemen. 1824. Reprint. New York: Negro Universities Press, 1969.

Farkas, Sándor Bölöni. *Journey in North America, 1831*. Translated by Arpad A. Kadarkay. Santa Barbara, Calif.: American Bibliographical Center Press, 1978.

Ferguson, William. *America by River and Rail: or, Notes by the Way on the New World and its People*. London: James Nisbet & Co., 1856.

Fergusson, Charles Bruce. "George Isham Parkyns." *Journal of Education* [Halifax, Nova Scotia] 19 (March 1970): 9–12.

Field, Cynthia. "The City Planning of Daniel Hudson Burnham." Ph.D. diss., Columbia University, 1974.

Fielding, Mantle. "Edward Savage's Portraits of George Washington." *Pennsylvania Magazine of History and Biography* 48 (July 1924): 193–200.

Fitzpatrick, F. W. "Beautifying the Nation's Capital." *Inland Architect and News Record* 35 (March 1900): 10–14.

Forbes-Lindsay, C. H. *Washington: The City and the Seat of Government*. Philadelphia: John C. Winston Co., 1908.

Formwalt, Lee. "A Conversation between Two Rivers: A Debate on the Location of the Capital in Maryland." *Maryland Historical Magazine* 71 (Fall 1976): 310–21.

Fowble, E. McSherry. *Two Centuries of Prints in America, 1680–1880: A Selective Catalogue of the Winterthur Museum Collection*. Charlottesville: University Press of Virginia, 1987.

Freeman, Robert Belmont, Jr. "Design Proposals for the Washington National Monument." *Columbia Historical Society, Records* (1973–74): 151–86.

French, Stanley. "The Cemetery as Cultural Institution: The Establishment of Mount Auburn and the 'Rural' Cemetery Movement," *American Quarterly* 26 (March 1974): 37–59.

Furer, Howard B., ed. *Washington: A Chronological and Documentary History, 1790–1970*. Dobbs Ferry, N.Y.: Oceana Publications, 1975.

Gallagher, H[elen] M[ar] Pierce. *Robert Mills, Architect of the Washington Monument, 1781–1855*. New York: Columbia University Press, 1935.

Gambee, Budd Leslie. *Frank Leslie and His Illustrated Newspaper, 1855–1860*. Ann Arbor: University of Michigan Department of Library Science, 1964.

General Services Administration, Public Building Service. *Executive Office Building 17th Street and Pennsylvania Avenue, NW*. Historical Study No. 3. Washington, D.C.: Government Printing Office, 1964.

Gibbs, James, *A Book of Architecture, Containing Designs of Buildings and Ornaments*. London: n.p., 1728.

Gibbs, George, ed. *Memoirs of the Administrations of Washington and John Adams, Edited from the Papers of Oliver Wolcott, Secretary of the Treasury*. 2 vols. New York: n.p., 1846.

Gilbert, Cass. "Grouping of Public Buildings and Development of Washington." In *Papers Relating to the Improvement of the City of Washington, District of Columbia*, compiled by Glenn Brown, 78–82. S. Doc. 94, 56th Cong., 2d sess., 1901.

Gilchrist, Agnes Addison. *William Strickland: Architect and Engineer, 1788–1854*. New York: Da Capo Press, 1969.

Glazier, Willard. "Washington." In *Peculiarities of American Cities*, by Willard Glazier, 528–58. Philadelphia: Hubbard Brothers, 1886.

Goff, Frederick R. "Early Printing in Georgetown (Potomak), 1789–1800 and the Engraving of L'Enfant's Plan of Washington, 1792." Columbia Historical Society, *Records* 51–52 (1955): 103–19.

———. "The Federal City in 1793." In *A la Carte: Selected Papers on Maps and Atlases*, compiled by Walter Ristow, 144–51. Washington, D.C.: Library of Congress, 1972.

Goldberger, Paul. "After 60 Years, a Triangle is Rounded Off." *New York Times*, 11 February 1990, Arts & Leisure, sec. 2, pp. 37, 43.

———. "Ebb and Flow of Time and Tastes Reshape Kennedy's Grand Vision." *New York Times*, 19 January 1989, B12.

———. "The Pension Building, Home of the National Building Museum." *Antiques* 128 (October 1985): 724–31.

Goode, George Brown, ed. *The Smithsonian Institution 1846–1896, the History of its First Half Century*. Washington, D.C.: [Smithsonian Institution], 1897.

Goode, James M. *Best Addresses: A Century of Washington's Distinguished Apartment Houses*. Washington, D.C.: Smithsonian Institution Press, 1988.

"The Grander Washington Plan." *Washington Evening Star*, 15 January 1902.

Grant, Robert W. *The Handbook of Civil War Patriotic Envelopes and Postal History*. Hanover, Mass.: Grant, 1977.

Grattan, Thomas Colley. *Civilized America*. 2 vols. 2d ed. London: Bradbury & Evans, 1859.

Green, Constance. *Washington: Capital City 1879–1950*. Princeton: Princeton University Press, 1963.

———. *Washington: Village and Capital 1800–1878*. Princeton: Princeton University Press, 1962.

Gutheim, Frederick. *Worthy of the Nation: The History of Planning for the National Capital*. Washington, D.C.: Smithsonian Institution Press, 1977.

Gutheim, Frederick, and Wilcomb E. Washburn. *The Federal City: Plans & Realities*. Washington, D.C.: Smithsonian Institution Press, 1976.

Hall, Basil. *Travels in North America in the Years 1827 and 1828*. 3 vols. Edinburgh: Cadell & Co., 1829.

Hall, Francis. *Travels in Canada, and the United States, in 1816 and 1817*. London: Longman, Hurst, Rees, Orme, & Brown, 1818.

Hall, Louise. "The Design of the Old Patent Office." *Journal of the Society of Architectural Historians* 15 (March 1956): 27–30.

Hamilton, Alexander. *The Papers of Alexander Hamilton*. Edited by Harold C. Syrett. 27 vols. New York: Columbia University Press, 1961–1987.

Hamilton, Sinclair. *Early American Book Illustrators and Wood Engravers, 1670–1870*. Princeton: Princeton University Press, 1958.

Haugen, Eva L. "The Story of Peder Anderson." *Norwegian-American Studies* 26 (1974): 31–48.

Hazelton, George C., Jr. *The National Capitol: Its Architecture Art and History*. New York: J. F. Taylor & Co., 1907.

Hening, William Walter, ed. *The Statutes at Large . . . of Virginia*. 13 vols. Richmond: Samuel Pleasants, 1809–23.

Hibben, Henry B. *Navy-Yard, Washington. History from Organization, 1799 to Present Date*. S. Ex. Doc. 22, 51st Cong., 1st sess., 1890.

Hickox, Chauncey. "New Washington." *Lippincott's Magazine of Popular Literature and Science* 11 (March 1873): 302–10.

Highsmith, Carol M., and Ted Landphair. *Pennsylvania Avenue: America's Main Street*. Washington, D.C.: American Institute of Architects Press, 1988.

Hines, Thomas S. *Burnham of Chicago: Architect and Planner*. New York: Oxford University Press, 1974.

Hinton, John Howard, ed. *The History and Topography of the United States*. 2 vols. London: R. Fenner, Sears & Co., and Philadelphia: T. Wardle & I. T. Hinton, 1830–32.

Historical and Commercial Sketches of Washington and Environs: Our Capital City "The Paris of America" Its Prominent Places and People. Leading Merchants, Manufacturers, Artisans and Professional Men. Its Improvements, Progress and Enterprise. Washington, D.C.: E. E. Barton, 1884.

Hooper, William R. "Our Capital." *Lippincott's Magazine* 5 (January 1870): 42–52.

Howe, Franklin. "The Board of Public Works." Columbia Historical Society, *Records* 3 (1900): 257–78.

Howe, Henry. *Historical Collections of Virginia; Containing a Collection of the Most Interesting Facts, Traditions, Biographical Sketches, Anecdotes, &c. Relating to Its History and Antiquities, Together with Geographical and Statistical Descrpitions. to which is Appended, An Historical and Descriptive Sketch of the District of Columbia*. Charleston, S.C.: Babcock & Co., 1845.

Hunsberger, George S. "The Architectural Career of George Hadfield." Columbia Historical Society, *Records* 51–52 (1955): 46–65.

Hunt, Gaillard, ed. *The First Forty Years of Washington Society. Portrayed by the Family Letters of Mrs. Samuel Harrison Smith (Margaret Bayard) from the Collection of her Grandson J. Henley Smith*. New York: Charles Scribner's Sons, 1906.

Huxtable, Ada Louise. "Architecture." In *Washington: The New York Times Guide to the Nation's Capital*, edited by Alvin Shuster, 197–216. Washington, D.C.: Robert B. Luce, 1967.

"Improvement of Potomac Flats, Washington." *Scientific American* 65 (19 September 1891): 175, 180–81.

Jackson, Donald E. "L'Enfant's Washington: An Architect's View." Columbia Historical Society, *Records* (1980): 398–420.

James, Henry. *The American Scene.* Introduction by Irving Howe. New York: Horizon Press, 1967.

Janson, Charles. *The Stranger in America, 1793–1806.* London, 1807. Reprint. New York: The Press of the Pioneers, 1935.

Jefferson, Thomas. *The Papers of Thomas Jefferson.* Edited by Julian P. Boyd. Vols. 1– . Princeton: Princeton University Press, 1950– .

———. *The Anas 1791–1806.* In *The Works of Thomas Jefferson,* edited by Paul Leicester Ford, 1:163–430. New York: G. P. Putnam's Sons, 1904.

Jennings, J. L. Sibley, Jr. "Artistry as Design: L'Enfant's Extraordinary City." *Quarterly Journal of the Library of Congress* 36 (Summer 1979): 225–78.

Jensen, Amy La Follette. *The White House and Its Thirty-Three Families.* New enl. ed. New York: McGraw-Hill Book Co., 1962.

The Junior League of Washington. *The City of Washington: An Illustrated History.* Edited by Thomas Froncek. New York: Alfred A. Knopf, 1977.

Kassan, Gail Karesh. "The Old Post Office Building in Washington, D.C.: Its Past, Present and Future." Columbia Historical Society, *Records* (1971–72): 570–95.

Keeler, Ralph. "A View of the National Capital." *The Overland Monthly* 3 (November 1869): 400–407.

Keim, De B[enneville] Randolph. *Keim's Illustrated Hand-Book of Washington and Its Environs: A Descriptive and Historical Hand-Book to the Capital of the United States of America.* 8th ed. Washington, D.C.: For the Compiler, 1876.

———. *Keim's Illustrated Hand-Book of Washington and its Environs.* . . . 22d ed. Washington, D.C.: De B. Randolph Keim, 1886.

Kelly, James C. *The South on Paper: Line, Color and Light.* Spartanburg, S.C.: Robert M. Hicklin, Jr., 1985.

Kennon, Donald R. "Washington Past: The City That History Made." In *Washington Past and Present: A Guide to the Nation's Capital,* by Donald R. Kennon and Richard Striner, 9–51. Washington, D.C.: United States Capitol Historical Society, 1983.

Kimmel, Stanley. *Mr. Lincoln's Washington.* New York: Coward-McCann, 1957.

Kipling, Rudyard. *American Notes.* New York, 1891. Boston, 1899.

Kiplinger, Austin H., with Knight A. Kiplinger. *Washington Now.* New York: Harper & Row, 1975.

Kite, Elizabeth Sarah. *L'Enfant and Washington, 1791–1792.* Baltimore: Johns Hopkins University Press, 1929.

Klaus, Susan L. " 'Intelligent and Comprehensive Planning of a Common Sense Kind.' " M.A. thesis, Graduate School of Arts and Sciences, George Washington University, 1988.

Klinkowström, Baron Axel. *America 1818–1820.* Translated and edited by Franklin D. Scott. Evanston, Ill.: Northwestern University Press, 1952.

Knight, Henry Cogswell [Arthur Singleton, pseud.]. *Letters from the South and West.* Boston: Richardson & Lord, 1824.

Knittle, Rhea Mansfield. "The Kelloggs, Hartford Lithographers." *Antiques* 10 (July 1926): 42–46.

Kohl, J. G. "The Federal City of Washington." *Bentley's Miscellaney* 50 (1861): 381–93.

Kowsky, Francis R. "Gallaudet College: A High Victorian Campus." Columbia Historical Society, *Records* (1971–72): 439–67.

Lamb, Martha J. "State and Society in Washington." *Harper's New Monthly Magazine* 56 (March 1878): 481–500.

Landau, Rom. *Among the Americans.* London: Robert Hale, 1953.

La Rochefoucauld-Liancourt, [François Alexandre Frédéric, duc de]. *Travels Through the United States of North America, the Country of the Iroquois, and Upper Canada, in the Years 1795, 1796, and 1797.* Translated by H. Neuman. 4 vols. London: R. Phillips, 1800.

Latrobe, John H. B. "Construction of the Public Buildings in Washington." *Maryland Historical Magazine* 11 (September 1909): 221–28.

[Lear, Tobias]. *Observations on the River Potomack, the Country Adjacent, and the City of Washington.* New York: Samuel Loudon & Son, 1793.

Lehman, Donald J. "The State, War, and Navy Building by Alfred B. Mullett." *Journal of the Society of Architectural Historians* 29 (October 1970): 267.

L'Enfant, Pierre Charles. "Note Relative to the Ground Lying on the Eastern Branch of the River Potowmack and Being Intended to Parallel the Several Position [*sic*] Proposed within the Limits Between the Branch and Georgetown for the Seat of the Federal City." In Columbia Historical Society, *Records* 2 (1899): 27–32.

"The L'Enfant Memorials." Columbia Historical Society, *Records* 2 (1899): 72–110.

Library of Congress. *District of Columbia Sesquicentennial of the Establishment of the Permanent Seat of the Government: An Exhibition in the Library of Congress, Washington, D.C., April 24, 1950, to April 24, 1951.* Washington, D.C.: Government Printing Office, 1950.

———. *The Grand Design: An Exhibition Tracing the Evolution of the L'Enfant Plan and Subsequent Plans for the Development of Pennsylvania Avenue and the Mall Area, Organized Jointly by the Library of Congress and the President's Temporary Commission on Pennsylvania Avenue.* Washington, D.C.: Government Printing Office, 1967.

Logan, Mrs. John A. *Thirty Years in Washington or Life and Scenes in Our National Capital.* . . . Hartford: A. D. Worthington & Co., 1901.

Looney, Robert F. "Thomas Doughty, Printmaker." In *Philadelphia Printmaking: American Prints before 1860,* edited by Robert F. Looney, 130–48. West Chester, Pa.: Tinicum Press, 1976.

Low, Sir Alfred Maurice. *America at Home.* London: G. Newnes, 1908.

Lynch, Anne C. "A Sketch of Washington City." *Harper's New Monthly Magazine* 6 (December 1852): 1–15.

McCabe, James Dabney [Edward Winslow Martin, pseud.]. *Behind the Scenes in Washington.* [Washington, D.C.?]: Continental Publishing Co. and National Publishing Co., 1873.

McCauley, Lois B. *A. Hoen on Stone: Lithographs of E. Weber & Co. and A. Hoen & Co., Baltimore, 1835–1869.* Baltimore: Maryland Historical Society, 1969.

———. *Maryland Historical Prints, 1752 to 1889: A Selection from the Robert G. Merrick Collection, Maryland Historical Society and other Maryland Collections.* Baltimore: Maryland Historical Society, 1975.

McCord Museum of McGill University. *Everyman's Canada: Paintings and Drawings from the McCord Museum of McGill University.* Text by J. Russell Harper. Ottawa: [National Gallery of Canada], 1962.

McDaniel, Joyce L. "Caspar Buberl: The Pension Building Civil War Frieze and Other Washington, D.C. Sculpture." Columbia Historical Society, *Records* (1980): 309–44.

Mackay, Alex. *The Western World; or, Travels in the United States in 1846–47: Exhibiting them in their Latest Development, Social, Political, and Industrial; Including a Chapter on California.* 2 vols. Philadelphia: Lea & Blanchard, 1849.

McKenna, R. T. "James Renwick, Jr. and the Second Empire Style in the United States." *Magazine of Art* 44 (March 1951): 97–101.

McPeck, Eleanor. "George Isham Parkyns: Artist and Landscape Architect, 1749–1820." *Quarterly Journal of the Library of Congress* 30 (July 1973): 171–82.

Maddox, Diane. *Historic Buildings of Washington, D.C.* Pittsburgh, Pa.: Ober Park Associates, 1973.

Malte-Brun, M. *A System of Universal Geography, or a Description of All the Parts of the World, on a New Plan.* . . . 3 vols. Boston: Samuel Walker, 1834.

Mann, Maybelle. "Augustus Kollner." *Imprint* 6 (Spring 1981): 19–22.

Mannix, Richard. "Albert Gallatin in Washington, 1802–1813." Columbia Historical Society, *Records* (1971–72): 60–80.

Marryat, Frederick. *A Diary in America with Remarks on its Institutions.* 1839. Reprint, edited with notes and an introduction by Sydney Jackman. New York: Alfred A. Knopf, 1962.

Marsh, Blanche. *Robert Mills: Architect in South Carolina.* Columbia, S.C.: R. L. Bryan Co., 1970.

Martin, Edward Winslow. See McCabe, James Dabney.

Martineau, Harriet. *Retrospect of Western Travel*. 2 vols. New York: Charles Lohman, 1838.

Marzio, Peter C. *The Democratic Art: Pictures for a 19th-Century America*. Boston: David R. Godine, in association with the Amon Carter Museum of Western Art, Fort Worth, 1979.

———. *Mr. Audubon and Mr. Bien: An Early Phase in the History of American Chromolithography*. Washington, D.C.: Hall of Printing and Graphic Arts, National Museum of History and Technology, Smithsonian Institution, 1975.

Mathews, Catherine Van Cortland. *Andrew Ellicott: His Life and Letters*. New York: Grafton Press, 1908.

Maury, William M. *Alexander "Boss" Shepherd and the Board of Public Works*. GW Washington Studies Number 3. Washington, D.C.: George Washington University, 1975.

———. "Alexander R. Shepherd and the Board of Public Works." Columbia Historical Society, *Records* (1971–72): 394–410.

Maxwell, A. M. *A Run Through the United States, During the Autumn of 1840*. 2 vols. London: Henry Colburn, 1841.

Mayo, Robert. *A Synopsis of the Commercial and Revenue Systems of the United States*. 2 vols. Washington, D.C.: J. & G. S. Gideon, 1847.

Mayor, A. Hyatt. "Aquatint Views of our Infant Cities." *Antiques* 88 (September 1965): 314–18.

Mearns, David C. "A View of Washington in 1863." Columbia Historical Society, *Records* 63–65 (1963–65): 210–20.

Melish, John. *Travels Through the United States of America in the Years 1806, 1807 and 1809, 1810 & 1811*. 2 vols. Philadelphia: The Author, 1812.

Meredith, Roy. *Mr. Lincoln's Camera Man: Mathew B. Brady*. 2d rev. ed. New York: Dover Publications, 1974.

Michler, N. *Report of Brevet Brigadier General N. Michler, Major of Engineers, United States Army, in Charge of Public Buildings, Grounds, Works, &c.*, 1 October 1867. H. Ex. Doc. 1, 40th Cong., 2d sess., ser. 1325, 519–31.

Mills, Robert. *The Papers of Robert Mills 1781–1885*. Edited by Pamela Scott. Scholarly Resources microfilm edition produced by the Robert Mills Papers Project. Wilmington, Del.: Scholarly Resources, 1990.

Monaghan, Frank. "The American Drawings of Baroness Hyde de Neuville." *Franco-American Review* 2 (Spring 1938): 216–20.

Moore, Charles. *Daniel H. Burnham*. 2 vols. Boston: Houghton Mifflin Co., 1921.

———. "The Improvement of Washington City." *Century Magazine* 63 (February 1902): 621–28; (March 1902): 747–57.

Moore, Charles, comp. *Park Improvement Papers. A Series of Seventeen Papers Relating to the Improvement of the Park System of the District of Columbia; Printed for the Use of the Senate Committee on the District of Columbia*. Washington, D.C.: Government Printing Office, 1902.

Moore, Joseph West. *Picturesque Washington: Pen and Pencil Sketches of its Scenery, History, Traditions, Public and Social Life, with Graphic Descriptions of the Capitol and Congress, the White House and the Government Departments, together with Artistic Views at Mount Vernon, a Map of the City of Washington, and Diagrams of the Halls of Congress*. Providence: J. A. & R. A. Reid, 1887.

Moore, S. S., and T. W. Jones. *The Traveller's Directory, or a Pocket Companion: Shewing the Course of the Main Road from Philadelphia to New York, and from Philadelphia to Washington. With Descriptions of the Places Through which it Passes, and the Intersections of the Cross Roads. Illustrated with an Account of such Remarkable Objects as are Generally Interesting to Travellers. From Actual Survey*. Philadelphia: Mathew Carey, 1802.

Moore, Thomas. *The Poetical Works of Thomas Moore*. New York: D. Appleton & Co., 1868.

Morgan, J. Dudley. "L'Enfant's Idea as to how the Capitol Building Should Face." Columbia Historical Society, *Records* 7 (1904): 107–13.

———. "Maj. Pierre Charles L'Enfant, the Unhonored and Unrewarded Engineer." Columbia Historical Society, *Records* 2 (1899): 118–57.

Morgan, James Dudley. "The Reinterment of Major Pierre Charles L'Enfant." Columbia Historical Society, *Records* 13 (1910): 119–25.

Morrison, Alfred J., comp. *The District in the XVIII Century . . . as Described by the Earliest Travellers*. Washington, D.C.: Judd & Detweiler, 1909.

Morrison, William M. *Stranger's Guide to the City of Washington*. Washington, D.C.: William M. Morrison, 1842.

Morrison's Stranger's Guide and Etiquette for Washington City and its Vicinity. Washington, D.C.: W. H. & O. H. Morrison, 1862.

Morrison's Stranger's Guide and Etiquette for Washington City and its Vicinity. [6th ed.] Washington, D.C.: W. H. & O. H. Morrison, 1864.

Morrison's Stranger's Guide for Washington City. Washington, D.C.: W. H. & O. H. Morrison, 1876.

Morrison's Stranger's Guide for Washington City. Washington, D.C.: W. H. & O. H. Morrison, 1880.

Muirhead, James Fullarton. *The Land of Contrasts: A Briton's View of his American Kin*. London: J. Lane, 1900.

Murray, Charles Augustus. *Travels in North America During the Years 1834, 1835, & 1836*. London: Richard Bentley, 1839.

Myers, Susan H. "Capitol Hill, 1870–1900: The People and Their Homes." Columbia Historical Society, *Records* (1973–74): 276–99.

Naeve, Milo M. " 'The Best likeness' of George Washington by Edward Savage." *Bulletin of the Art Institute of Chicago* 40 (July–August 1976): 13–16.

"A Nation in a Nutshell." *Harper's New Monthly Magazine* 62 (March 1881): 541–55.

"The Nation's New Capital." *New York Times* supplement, 19 January 1902, p. 4.

"New Post Office Building, Washington." *American Architect and Building News* 35 (12 March 1892): 174.

"The New Washington." *Century Magazine* 27 (March 1884): 643–59.

Nicolay, Helen. *Our Capital on the Potomac*. New York: The Century Co., 1924.

Norton, Bettina. *Edwin Whitefield: Nineteenth-Century North American Scenery*. Barre, Mass: Barre Publishing, 1977.

Noyes, Theodore W. *The National Capital: Newspaper Articles and Speeches Concerning the City of Washington*. Washington, D.C.: Byron S. Adams, 1893.

Osborne, John Ball. "The Removal of the Government to Washington." Columbia Historical Society, *Records* 3 (1900): 136–60.

Olmsted, Frederick Law, Jr. "Beautifying a City." *The Independent* 54 (7 August 1902): 1870–77.

———. "Landscape in Connection with Public Buildings in Washington." In *Papers Relating to the Improvement of the City of Washington, District of Columbia*, compiled by Glenn Brown, 22–34. S. Doc. 94, 56th Cong., 2d sess., 1901.

Owen, Robert D. *Hints on Public Architecture, Containing, Among Other Illustrations, Views and Plans of the Smithsonian Institution: Together with an Appendix Relative to Building Materials*. New York: George P. Putnam, 1849.

Padover, Saul K., ed. *Thomas Jefferson and the National Capital: Containing Notes and Correspondence Exchanged between Jefferson, Washington, L'Enfant, Ellicott, Hallett, Thornton, Latrobe, the Commissioners, and Others, Relating to the Founding, Surveying, Planning, Designing, Constructing, and Administering of the City of Washington, 1783–1818*. Washington, D.C.: Government Printing Office, 1946.

"The Park Commission and the Improvement of Washington City." *American Institute of Architects Quarterly Bulletin* 3 (April 1902): 5–16.

Parker, Alice Lee, and Milton Kaplan. *Charles Fenderich: Lithographer of American Statesmen*. Edited with a foreword by Lillian B. Miller. Chicago: University of Chicago Press, 1978.

"The Parks and Proposed Parks of Washington City." *American Architect and Building News* 47 (16 February 1895): 72–73.

Parsons, Samuel. "Report of Mr. Samuel Parsons, Jr., Landscape Architect." *Plans for Treatment of that Portion of the District of Columbia South of Pennsylvania Avenue and North of B Street, SW, and for a Connection Between Potomac and Zoological Parks*. H. Misc. Doc. 135, 56th Cong., 2d sess., 1900.

Peets, Elbert. "The Genealogy of L'Enfant's Washington." *American Institute of Architects Journal* 15 (April 1927): 115–19; (May 1927): 151–54; (June 1927): 187–91.

———. *On the Art of Designing Cities: Selected Essays of Elbert Peets*.

Edited by Paul D. Spreiregen. Cambridge, Mass.: MIT Press, 1968.

Pelz, Paul J. "The Grouping of Public Buildings in Washington." In *Papers Relating to the Improvement of the City of Washington, District of Columbia*, compiled by Glenn Brown, 87–91. S. Doc. 94, 56th Cong., 2d sess., 1901.

Peters, Harry T. *America on Stone: The Other Printmakers to the American People*. Garden City, N.Y.: Doubleday, Doran & Co., 1931.

Peterson, Jon A. "The Hidden Origins of the McMillan Plan for Washington, D.C., 1900–1902." In *Historical Perspectives on Urban Design: Washington, D.C. 1890–1910*, edited by Antoinette J. Lee. Occasional Paper No. 1. Center for Washington Area Studies, George Washington University, [1983?].

Phillips, P. Lee. *The Beginnings of Washington as Described in Books Maps and Views*. Washington, D.C.: The Author, 1917.

Phipps, Frances. "Connecticut's Printmakers: The Kelloggs of Hartford." *The Connecticus Antiquarian* 21 (June 1969): 19–26.

Poore, Ben[jamin] Perley. *Perley's Reminiscences of Sixty Years in the National Metropolis*. 2 vols. Philadelphia: Hubbard Brothers, 1886.

Power, Tyrone. *Impression of America, During the Years 1833, 1834, and 1835*. 2 vols. London: Richard Bentley, 1836.

Press, Donald. "South of the Avenue: From Murder Bay to the Federal Triangle." Columbia Historical Society, *Records* (1984): 51–70.

Proctor, John Clagett. "The Tragic Death of Andrew Jackson Downing and the Monument to His Memory." Columbia Historical Society, *Records* 27 (1925): 248–61.

Protopappas, John J., and Lin Brown, eds. *Washington on Foot: 24 Walking Tours of Washington, D.C., Old Town Alexandria, Historic Annapolis*. 3d rev. ed. Washington, D.C.: National Capital Area Chapter, American Planning Association and Smithsonian Institution Press, 1984.

Rae, W. Fraser. *Columbia and Canada: Notes on the Great Republic and the New Dominion. A Supplement to "Westward by Rail."* London: Daldy, Isbister, & Co., 1877.

Rand, McNally & Co. *Rand, McNally & Co.'s Pictorial Guide to Washington and Environs*. Chicago: Rand, McNally & Co., 1901.

Rapson, Richard L. *Britons View America: Travel Commentary, 1860–1935*. Seattle: University of Washington Press, 1971.

Reclus, Elisée. *The Earth and Its Inhabitants: The Universal Geography*. Vol. 16, *The United States*. Edited by A. H. Keane. London: J. S. Virtue & Co., ca. 1890.

Reiff, Daniel D. *Washington Architecture, 1791–1861: Problems in Development*. Washington, D.C.: U.S. Commission of Fine Arts, 1971.

Reinhardt, Richard. *Out West on the Overland Train: Across-the-Continent Excursion with Leslie's Magazine in 1877. . . .* Palo Alto, Calif.: American West Publishing Co., 1967.

Reps, John W. "Burnham before Chicago." Art Institute of Chicago. *The Art Institute of Chicago Centennial Lectures*, 191–217. Chicago: Contemporary Books, 1983.

———. *The Making of Urban America: A History of City Planning in the United States*. Princeton: Princeton University Press, 1965.

———. *Monumental Washington: The Planning and Development of the Capital Center*. Princeton: Princeton University Press, 1967.

———. "Romantic Planning in a Baroque City: Downing and the Washington Mall." *Landscape* 16 (Spring 1967): 6–11.

———. *Saint Louis Illustrated: Nineteenth Century Engravings and Lithographs of a Mississippi River Metropolis*. Columbia: University of Missouri Press, 1989.

———. *Tidewater Towns: City Planning in Colonial Virginia and Maryland*. Williamsburg: Colonial Williamsburg Foundation, 1972.

———. *Views and Viewmakers of Urban America: Lithographs of Towns and Cities in the United States and Canada, Notes on the Artists and Publishers, and a Union Catalog of their Work, 1825–1925*. Columbia: University of Missouri Press, 1984.

Rhoads, William B. "Franklin D. Roosevelt and Washington Architecture." Columbia Historical Society, *Records* (1989): 104–62.

Richardson, Albert D. *Garnered Sheaves from the Writings of Albert D. Richardson, Collected and Arranged by his Wife; to which is Added a Biographical Sketch of the Author*. Hartford: Columbia Book Co., 1871.

Ringwalt, J. Luther, ed. *American Encylopaedia of Printing*. Philadelphia: Menamin & Ringwalt and J. B. Lippincott & Co., 1871.

Ristow, Walter W. *American Maps and Mapmakers: Commercial Cartography in the Nineteenth Century*. Detroit: Wayne State University Press, 1985.

Roberts, Cecil. *And So to America*. Garden City, N.Y.: Doubleday & Co., 1947.

Roberts, Chalmers. *Washington, Past and Present: A Pictorial History of the Nation's Capital*. [Washington, D.C.]: Public Affairs Press, 1950.

Rose, George. *The Great Country; or, Impressions of America*. London: Tinsley Brothers, 1868.

Ross, Alexander M. *William Henry Bartlett: Artist, Author, and Traveller*. Toronto: University of Toronto Press, 1973.

Ross, Betty. *A Museum Guide to Washington, D.C.: Museums, Historic Houses, Art Galleries, Libraries, and Special Places Open to the Public in the Nation's Capital and Vicinity*. Washington, D.C.: Americana Press, 1986.

Rotundo, Barbara. "Mount Auburn: Fortunate Coincidences and an Ideal Solution." *Journal of Garden History*: 4 (July–September 1984): 257–67.

———. "Mount Auburn Cemetery: A Proper Boston Institution." *Harvard Library Bulletin* 22 (July 1974): 268–79.

———. "The Rural Cemetery Movement." *Essex Institute Historical Collections* 109 (July 1973): 231–40.

[Royall, Anne]. *Sketches of History, Life and Manners in the United States*. New Haven: The Author, 1826. Reprint. New York: Johnson Reprint Corp., 1970.

Roylance, Dale, and Nancy Finlay. *Pride of Place: Early American Views from the Collection of Leonard L. Milberg '53*. Princeton: Princeton University Press, 1983.

Rudolph, Marilou Alston. "George Cooke and His Paintings." *Georgia Historical Quarterly* 44 (June 1960): 117–57.

"S. St. J. Morgan Collection of Kellogg Prints." *Connecticut Historical Society Bulletin* 13 (October 1948): 25–32.

Sala, George Augustus. *My Diary in America in the Midst of War*. 2 vols. London: Tinsley Brothers, 1865.

Sarmiento, Domingo Faustino. *Sarmiento's "Travels in the United States in 1847."* Translated by Michael Aaron Rockland. Princeton: Princeton University Press, 1970.

Schurz, Carl. *The Reminiscences of Carl Schurz*. 3 vols. New York: The McClure Co., 1908.

Schuyler, David. "Green-Wood Cemetery As Image and Cultural Artifact." *Imprint* 14 (Spring 1989): 2–11.

Schuyler, Montgomery. "The Art of City Making." *The Architectural Record* 12 (May 1902): 1–26.

———. "The Nation's New Capital." *New York Times* supplement, 19 January 1902, 4–5.

———. "The New Washington." *Scribner's Magazine* 51 (February 1912): 129–48.

Scisco, Louis Dow. "A Site for the 'Federal City': The Original Proprietors and their Negotiations with Washington." Columbia Historical Society, *Records* 57–59 (1957–59): 123–47.

Scudder, Jennie W. "Historical Sketch of the Unitarian Church of Washington, D.C." Columbia Historical Society, *Records* 13 (1910): 168–87.

Seale, William. *The President's House: A History*. Washington, D.C.: National Geographic Society and White House Historical Association, 1986.

Seeler, Edgar V. "The Monumental Grouping of Government Buildings in Washington." In *Papers Relating to the Improvement of the City of Washington, District of Columbia*, compiled by Glenn Brown, 48–58. S. Doc. 94, 56th Cong., 2d sess., 1901.

Sewall, Frank. "A Government Bureau of Public Building." *American Architect and Building News* 40 (6 May 1893): 86–87.

———. "Washington's Architectural Need." *American Architect and Building News* 35 (13 February 1892): 107–8.

Shipley, Ruth B. "The Historic Winder Building." Columbia Historical Society, *Records* 50 (1948–50): 235–42.

Simon, Donald. "Green-Wood Cemetery and the American Park Movement." In *Essays in the History of New York City: A Memorial to Sidney Pomerantz*, edited by Irwin Yellowitz, 61–77. Port Washington, N.Y.: Kennikat Press, 1978.

"A Sketch of Washington City." *Harper's New Monthly Magazine* 6 (December 1852): 1–15.

Smith, A. Robert, and Eric Sevareid. *Washington: Magnificent Capital*. Garden City, N.Y.: Doubleday & Co., 1965.

Smith, B. F., Jr. Letters to Robert Mills, 23, 30 April 1852. Papers of Robert Mills, Manuscript Division, Library of Congress.

Smith, Edward S. "John Rubens Smith: An Anglo-American Artist." *Connoisseur, An Illustrated Magazine for Collectors* 85 (May 1930): 300–307.

Smith, Franklin Webster. *A Design and Prospectus for the National Gallery of History and Art at Washington*. Washington, D.C.: Gibson Bros., 1891.

———. *Petition of Franklin Webster Smith for the Site of the Old Naval Observatory for the National Galleries of History and Art. Descriptive Hand-Book of the Halls of the Ancients Constructed for Promotion of Said Galleries According to Design Annexed*. S. Doc. 209, 56th Cong., 1st sess., 1900.

Smith, Kathryn Schneider, ed. *Washington at Home: An Illustrated History of Neighborhoods in the Nation's Capital*. Northridge, Calif.: Windsor Publications, 1988.

Smith, William Loughton. *Journal of William Loughton Smith, 1790–1791*. Massachusetts Historical Society, *Proceedings* 51 (October 1917–June 1918): 20–88.

Snyder, Martin P. "William Birch: His 'Country Seats of the United States.'" *Pennsylvania Magazine of History and Biography* 81 (July 1957): 225–54.

Somerville, Mollie. *Washington Walked Here: Alexandria on the Potomac, One of America's First "New" Towns*. Washington, D.C.: Acropolis Books, 1970.

Spofford, A. R. "The Nation's Library." *Century Magazine* 53 (March 1897): 682–94.

Staudenraus, P. J., ed. *Mr. Lincoln's Washington: Selections from the Writings of Noah Brooks, Civil War Correspondent*. South Brunswick, N.J.: Thomas Yoseloff, 1967.

Stebbins, R. P. "Six Months in Washington." *The Monthly Religious Magazine* 40 (September 1868): 183–94.

Steinway, Kate. "The Kelloggs of Hartford: Connecticut's Currier & Ives." *Imprint* 13 (Spring 1988): 2–12.

Stephenson, Richard W. "The Delineation of a Grand Plan." *Quarterly Journal of the Library of Congress* 36 (Summer 1979): 207–24.

Stewart, John. "Early Maps and Surveyors of the City of Washington, D.C." Columbia Historical Society, *Records* 2 (1899): 48–71.

Stokes, I. N. Phelps, and Daniel C. Haskell. *American Historical Prints: Early Views of American Cities, etc*. New York: New York Public Library, 1933.

Stone, Charles P. "Washington on the Eve of the War." *Century Magazine* 26 (July 1883): 458–66.

Sunderland, Byron. "Washington as I First Knew It. 1852–1855." Columbia Historical Society, *Records* 5 (1902): 195–211.

Swayne, Wager. "The Site of the National Capital." *Harper's Magazine* 40 (January 1870): 181–92.

Taft, Robert. *Artists and Illustrators of the Old West, 1850–1900*. New York: Charles Scribner's Sons, 1953.

Taft, William Howard. "Washington: Its Beginning, Its Growth, and Its Future." In *Washington: The Nation's Capital*, by William Howard Taft and James Bryce. Washington, D.C.: National Geographic Society, 1915.

Tatham, David. "The Pendleton-Moore Shop—Lithographic Artists in Boston, 1825–1840." *Old-Time New England* 62 (Fall 1971): 29–46.

Templeman, Eleanor Lee. "In the Beginning. . . ." *Arlington Historical Magazine* 1 (October 1960): 43–49.

"Thirty-Fourth Annual Convention of the American Institute of Architects." *Inland Architect and News Record* 36 (January 1901): 43–48.

Thiry, Paul, ed. *Washington in Transition*. [Washington, D.C.: American Institute of Architects, 1963].

Tindall, William. *Origin and Government of the District of Columbia*. Washington, D.C.: Government Printing Office, 1908.

———. "The Origins of the Parking System of the City." Columbia Historical Society, *Records* 4 (1904): 243–56.

———. "A Sketch of Alexander Robey Shepherd." Columbia Historical Society, *Records* 14 (1911): 49–66.

———. *Standard History of the City of Washington*. Knoxville, Tenn.: H. W. Crew, 1914.

Topham, Washington. "Centre Market and Vicinity." Columbia Historical Society, *Records* 26 (1924): 1–88.

———. "First Railroad into Washington and its Three Depots." Columbia Historical Society, *Records* 27 (1925): 175–247.

———. "The Winder Building." Columbia Historical Society, *Records* 37–38 (1937): 169–72.

Totten, George Oakley, Jr. "Exposition Architecture in its Relation to the Grouping of Government Buildings." In *Papers Relating to the Improvement of the City of Washington, District of Columbia*, compiled by Glenn Brown, 83–86. S. Doc. 94, 56th Cong., 2d sess., 1901.

Towle, G. M. "Washington and its Vicinity." In *Picturesque America; or, the Land We Live in: A Delineation by Pen and Pencil*, edited by William Cullen Bryant, 2:565–76. New York: D. Appleton & Co., [1872].

Townsend, George Alfred. "New Washington." *Harper's New Monthly Magazine* 50 (February 1875): 306–22.

Trollope, Anthony. *North America*. 1862. Reprint, edited with an introduction, notes, and new materials by Donald Smalley and Bradford Allen Booth. New York: Alfred A. Knopf, 1951.

Trollope, Frances. *Domestic Manners of the Americans*. 2 vols. New York: Dodd, Mead, & Co., [1832].

Twain, Mark. See Clemens, Samuel Langhorne.

Twining, Thomas. *Travels in America 100 Years Ago*. New York: Harper & Brothers, 1894.

U.S. Commission of Fine Arts. *Annual Report*. Washington, D.C.: Government Printing Office, 1921.

U.S. Congress. Joint Select Committee of Congress Appointed to Inquire into the Affairs of the Government of the District of Columbia. *Report*. S. Rep. 453, 43d Cong., 1st sess. Parts 1, 2, and 3, 16 June 1874.

U.S. Federal Writers' Project, Works Progress Administration. *Washington: City and Capital*. Washington, D.C.: Government Printing Office, 1937.

U.S. Naval Facilities Engineering Command. Chesapeake Division. *Washington Navy Yard Master Plan*. N.p., 1979.

U.S. Senate Committee on the District of Columbia. *Report of the Senate Committee on the District of Columbia on The Improvement of the Park System of the District of Columbia*. Washington, D.C.: Government Printing Office, 1902.

Varnum, Joseph, Jr. *The Seat of Government of the United States*. New York: Press of Hunt's Merchants' Magazine, 1848.

[Varnum, Joseph, Jr.]. "The Seat of Government of the United States." *Hunt's Merchants' Magazine* 18 (January 1848): 18–31; (February 1848): 142–51; (March 1848): 270–79; (April 1848): 367–75.

Verner, Coolie. "Surveying and Mapping the New Federal City: The First Printed Maps of Washington, D.C." *Imago Mundi: A Review of Early Cartography* 23 (1969): 59–72.

A Visit to the States. A Reprint of Letters from the Special Correspondent of The Times. First Series. London: George Edward Wright, 1887.

Wainwright, Nicholas B. "Augustus Kollner, Artist." *Pennsylvania Magazine of History and Biography* 84 (July 1960): 325–51.

———. *Philadelphia in the Romantic Age of Lithography: An Illustrated History of Early Lithography in Philadelphia with a Descriptive List of Philadelphia Scenes Made by Philadelphia Lithographers before 1866*. Philadelphia: Historical Society of Pennsylvania, 1958.

Walter, Cornelia W. *Mount Auburn Illustrated*. New York: R. Martin, 1847.

Walter, Thomas U. *Report of the Architect for the Extension of the Capitol*, 23 December 1851. H. Ex. Doc. 60, 32d Cong., 1st sess., 1851, 1–9.

Walton, William. *The Evidence of Washington*. New York: Harper & Row, 1966.

Wansey, Henry. *The Journal of an Excursion to the United States of North America in the Summer of 1794*. 2d ed. London: J. Easton, 1798.

[Warburton, George Drought]. *Hochelaga; or, England in the New World*. Edited by Eliot Warburton. 2 vols. 3d rev. ed. London: Henry Colburn, 1847.

Warden, D[avid] B[aillie]. *A Chorographical and Statistical Descrip-*

tion of the District of Columbia, the Seat of the General Government of the United States. Paris: Smith, 1816.

————. Statistical, Political, and Historical Account of the United States of North America; from the Period of their First Colonization to the Present Day. 3 vols. Edinburgh: Archibald Constable & Co., 1819.

Washburn, Wilcomb E. "Vision of Life for the Mall." Journal of the American Institute of Architects 47 (March 1967): 52–59.

"Washington, D.C." Harper's Weekly 13 (March 13, 1869): 170.

Washington, George. The Writings of George Washington. 39 vols. Washington, D.C.: Government Printing Office, 1931–44.

————. "The Writings of George Washington Relating to the National Capital." Columbia Historical Society, Records 17 (1914): 3–232.

Washington: The City Beautiful. Washington, D.C.: W. G. Garrison, Inc., ca. 1921.

"Washington: The Development and Improvement of the Park-System." American Architect and Building News 75 (1 February 1902): 33, 35–36; (8 March 1902): 75–77.

"Washington City." Atlantic Monthly 7 (January 1861): 1–8.

"Washington in 1859." Harper's New Monthly Magazine 20 (December 1859): 1–17.

Watterston, George. New Guide to Washington: Containing a History and General Description of the Metropolis, its Public Buildings, Institutions, Etc., with Seventeen Beautiful Lithographed Engravings. Washington, D.C.: Robert Farnham, [1847–48].

Weld, Isaac, Jr. Travels Through the States of North America, and the Provinces of Lower Canada, During the Years 1795, 1796, and 1797. 2 vols. 3d ed. London: J. Stockdale, 1800.

Wells, H. G. The Future in America: A Search after Realities. New York: Harper & Brothers, 1906.

Whibley, Charles. American Sketches. Edinburgh: W. Blackwood & Sons, 1908.

Whitman, Walt. Specimen Days. In Complete Poetry and Collected Prose, with Notes and Chronology by Justin Kaplan, 675–926. New York: Library of America, 1982.

Whyte, James H. "The District of Columbia Territorial Government, 1871–1874." Columbia Historical Society, Records 51–52 (1955): 87–102.

————. The Uncivil War: Washington during the Reconstruction, 1865–1878. New York: Twayne Publishers, 1958.

Wick, Wendy C. "American Icon: The Eighteenth-Century Image of George Washington." Imprint 7 (Autumn 1982): 1–9.

————. George Washington an American Icon: The Eighteenth-Century Graphic Portraits. Washington, D.C.: Smithsonian Institution Traveling Exhibition Service and the National Portrait Gallery, 1982.

Wicker, Tom. "Introduction." In Washington: The New York Times Guide to the Nation's Capital, edited by Alvin Shuster, 1–11. Washington, D.C.: Robert B. Luce, 1967.

Willis, Nathaniel Parker. American Scenery; or, Land, Lake and River Illustrations of Transatlantic Nature. 2 vols. London: G. Virtue, 1840.

Wilmerding, John. Fitz Hugh Lane. New York: Praeger Publishers, 1971.

————. Fitz Hugh Lane, 1804–1865: American Marine Painter. Gloucester, Mass.: Peter Smith, 1967.

Wilson, J. Ormond. "Eighty Years of the Public Schools of Washington—1805 to 1885." Columbia Historical Society, Records 1 (1896): 1–52.

Winthrop, Theodore. "Washington as a Camp." Atlantic Monthly 8 (July 1861): 105–18.

Wodehouse, Laurence. "Alfred B. Mullett and His French Style Government Buildings." Journal of the Society of Architectural Historians 31 (March 1972): 22–37.

Wright, Carroll D. "The Embellishment of Washington." The Independent 54 (13 November 1902): 2683–87.

Wright, Edith A., and Josephine A. McDevitt. "Henry Stone, Lithographer." Antiques 34 (July 1938): 16–19.

Wright, Helena E. Imperishable Beauty: Pictures Printed in Collotype. An exhibition in the Hall of Printing and Graphic Arts, National Museum of American History, January 1988. Washington, D.C.: Smithsonian Institution, 1988.

————. "Partners in the Business of Art: Producing, Packaging, and Publishing Images of the American Landscape 1850–1900." Chap. 26 in Pioneers of Photography: Their Achievements in Science and Technology, 274–85. Springfield, Va.: SPSE—The Society for Imaging Science and Technology, 1987.

Young, James Sterling. The Washington Community, 1800–1828. New York: Columbia University Press, 1966.

Ziolkowski, John E. Classical Influence on the Public Architecture of Washington and Paris: A Comparison of Two Capital Cities. New York: Peter Lang, 1988.

Index

References to illustrations appear in italic type.

Acknowledgments

Many persons have assisted me in locating written and graphic material used in this book. As in the past, I have called on the staff of several units of the Cornell University Libraries. Robert Kibbee, Barbara Berthelsen, Marie Gast, and Judith Holiday bore the brunt of my inquiries and requests for help, but I am also grateful to all the others at Cornell who aided me less frequently.

In Washington the curators of several pictorial collections provided access to the materials under their direction, furnished information from their records, and offered suggestions that guided me to additional plans or views of the city. They include Frances Turgeon of the Kiplinger Washington Collection; Margaret Burri of the Historical Society of Washington, D.C.; Mary Ison, Helena Zinkham, and Bernard Reilly of the Division of Prints and Photographs of the Library of Congress; Patrick Dempsey, Ronald Grim, Richard Stephenson, and their colleagues at the Division of Geography and Maps of the Library of Congress; and Charles Atherton of the U.S. Commission of Fine Arts.

In addition to those mentioned above who made it possible to reproduce several maps and views from their collections, I also thank the following for similar assistance with single pictorial records: Mrs. Florian Thayn, Office of the Architect of the Capitol; Richard H. Smith, Cartographic and Architectural Branch, U.S. National Archives; Jerome Yavarkovsky, the New York State Library; Geraldine Strey, State Historical Society of Wisconsin; Lois Oglesby, the Mariners' Museum of Newport News, Virginia; Roberta Waddell, the New York Public Library; and Jeanne Plitt, the Alexandria, Virginia, Library.

For permission to quote brief passages from books published by them, I wish to thank the following: the New York Times Company; the United States Capitol Historical Society; Americana Press; the National Capital Area Chapter of the American Planning Association; Harper and Row; and Doubleday and Company. Copyright maps are reproduced by permission of the National Geographic Society and David A. Fox.

Helena Wright of the National Museum of American History read and commented on the manuscript at two stages of its development. Her knowledge of nineteenth-century printmaking saved me from errors, and I benefited from her many other suggestions for improvements in substance, style, or clarity. While thanking her for her help I wish also to absolve her from deficiencies that may persist.

Pamela Scott called my attention to an important but obscure document in the papers of Robert Mills that I would have otherwise overlooked, and in several conversations her comments on aspects of the original plan for Washington stimulated me to revised attitudes about some aspects of L'Enfant's design. Don Hawkins, also of Washington, showed me the results of his studies in reconstructing the early topography of the city and shared with me his opinions about L'Enfant's approach to his task.

I owe a special debt to Judith and James Blakely, proprietors of The Old Print Gallery in Washington, for helping me over the years in finding images of the city. They have my special thanks for allowing me to reproduce in this book an extraordinary aerial perspective of Washington painted in 1901 that was unrecorded until they acquired it in 1989.

As he has for four other books of mine, Edward King has designed this one with care, imagination, and characteristic skill and good taste. It is a pleasure to be able to express my thanks and appreciation for his contribution to the appearance of this volume. I am also grateful to those members of the editorial staff of the University of North Carolina Press who have provided such able help and assistance in guiding this book through the process of publication.

The Kiplinger Foundation has generously provided a grant to help with the cost of color reproduction, and it is a pleasure to record here my deep appreciation for that assistance to Austin and Knight Kiplinger, who opened the doors of their superb collection of Washington views and maps that graces the offices and corridors of the Pennsylvania Avenue office of the Kiplinger Washington Editors.

Finally, to my wife, Constance Peck Reps, my thanks once again for her support, confidence, encouragement, and love during a lifetime of research and writing about the American urban scene.

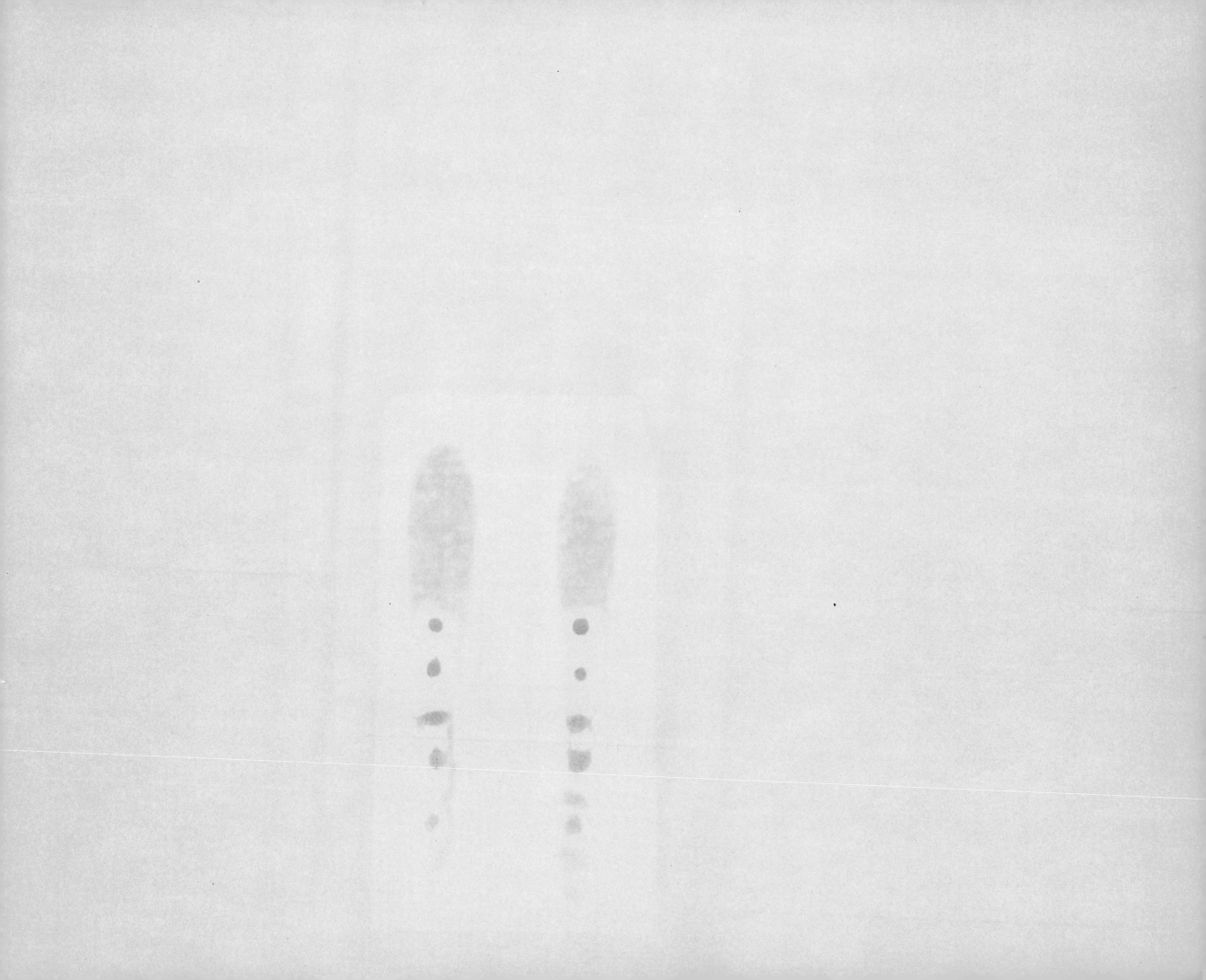